CONTENTS

ILLUSTRATIONS   vii

LIBRARY SYMBOLS   ix

Emerson's Unpublished Boyhood and Collegiate Verse   1
    Albert J. von Frank

A Conservative Transcendentalist: The Early Years (1805–1835) of
    Frederic Henry Hedge   57
    Charles Wesley Grady

Longfellow's Bowdoin Dialogue   89
    Edward L. Tucker

"That Sainted Spirit"—William Ellery Channing and the
    Unitarian Milton   101
    Kevin P. Van Anglen

Christopher Pearse Cranch's "Journal. 1839"   129
    Francis B. Dedmond

A New Checklist of the Books in Henry David Thoreau's
    Library   151
    Walter Harding

Romantic Epistemology and Romantic Style: Emerson's
    Development from *Nature* to *Essays*   187
    H. Meili Steele

"Classic Art": Emerson's Pragmatic Criticism   203
    Charles W. Mignon

An American Episode of *Martin Chuzzlewit*: The Culmination
of Dickens'Quarrel with the American Press   223
    Sydney P. Moss

Edgar Allan Poe and John G. Chapman: Their Treatment of
the Dismal Swamp and the Wissahickon   245
    Burton R. Pollin

Poe, Mrs. Osgood, and "Annabel Lee"   275
    Buford Jones and Kent Ljungquist

Contexts of Bravery in Thoreau's Revisions of "The Service"
for *A Week*   281
    Linck C. Johnson

The Bible in *Walden*: Further Additions   297
    Edward C. Jacobs

New Evidence for Melville's Use of John Harris in *Moby-Dick*   303
    John M. J. Gretchko

Mary Russell Mitford: Champion of American Literature   313
    John L. Idol, Jr.

Arranging the Sibylline Leaves: James Elliot Cabot's Work as
Emerson's Literary Executor   335
    Nancy Craig Simmons

BOOKS RECEIVED   391
    Caroline Bokinsky

CONTRIBUTORS   415

STUDIES
IN THE
AMERICAN
RENAISSANCE

1983

10

"Standing on the bare ground, — my head bathed by the blithe air, & uplifted into infinite space, — all mean egotism vanishes. I become a transparent Eyeball."

Nature. p. 13

FRONTISPIECE
Caricature based on a line from Emerson's *Nature*, in C. P. Cranch's "Journal. 1839."
Courtesy Francis B. Dedmond

STUDIES
IN THE
AMERICAN
RENAISSANCE

1983

Edited by JOEL MYERSON

THE UNIVERSITY PRESS OF VIRGINIA
CHARLOTTESVILLE

STUDIES IN THE AMERICAN RENAISSANCE

EDITOR

Joel Myerson

EDITORIAL ASSISTANTS

Robert Morace (1974-1975)
Robert E. Burkholder (1975–1979)
Stephen Garrison (1979–1981)
Caroline Bokinsky (1981–1983)

*The editor would like to thank the College of Humanities and Social Sciences
and the Department of English of the University of South Carolina,
and especially George L. Geckle, for their support.*

STUDIES IN THE AMERICAN RENAISSANCE examines the lives and works of mid-nineteenth-century American authors and the circumstances in which they wrote, published, and were received. The Editor welcomes biographical, historical, and bibliographical articles on the literature, history, philosophy, art, religion, and general culture of America during the period 1830–1860. Editorial correspondence should be addressed to Joel Myerson, Department of English, University of South Carolina, Columbia, South Carolina 29208.

STUDIES IN THE AMERICAN RENAISSANCE is indexed by *America: History and Life, American Humanities Index, American Literary Scholarship/An Annual, American Literature, Historical Abstracts*, and the MLA *International Bibliography*.

ISSN 0149-015X
ISBN 0-8139-0997-X

STUDIES IN THE AMERICAN RENAISSANCE is published annually by The University Press of Virginia, Box 3608, University Station, Charlottesville, Virginia 22903, and is available on a standing order basis.

ILLUSTRATIONS

Frontispiece: C. P. Cranch's caricature of a line from Emerson's *Nature*. ii

Plate One: The first page of text in C. P. Cranch's "Journal. 1839." 137

Plate Two: C. P. Cranch's caricature of a line from Emerson's *Nature*. 141

Plate Three: Map of the region served by the Dismal Swamp Canal. 249

Plate Four: Thomas Williamson's print of the "Half Way House." 250

Plate Five: Cypress trees in Lake Drummond. 251

Plate Six: J. G. Chapman's "The Lake of the Dismal Swamp." 254

Plate Seven: J. G. Chapman's "Ruins of James Town." 255

Plate Eight: John Sartain's "The Island of the Fay." 257

Plate Nine: W. Croome's "A Pic-Nic on the Wissahickon." 262

Plate Ten: J. G. Chapman's "Morning." 263

Plate Eleven: Granville Perkins' "Wissahickon, near Paper-Mill Bridge." 264

Plate Twelve: View of the upper Wissahickon. 265

Plate Thirteen: Winter on the Wissahickon. 266

Plate Fourteen: View of the Wissahickon. 267

Plate Fifteen: J. G. Chapman's "View of the Hudson River: The Palisades." 268

Plate Sixteen: J. G. Chapman's "The First Ship." 268

Plate Seventeen: Whaling scenes in John Harris' *Navagantium* . . . (1705). 305

Plate Eighteen: Whales with perpendicular flukes in John Harris' *Navagantium* . . . (1705). 306

LIBRARY SYMBOLS

BL	British Library
CSmH	Henry E. Huntington Library
CtY	Yale University
DLC	Library of Congress
ICarbS	Southern Illinois University
InU	Indiana University
MArFP	First Parish Unitarian Universalist Church, Arlington, Massachusetts
MCR-S	Schlesinger Library, Radcliffe College
MCo	Concord Free Public Library
MCoA	Concord Antiquarian Society
MH	Harvard University
MH-AH	Andover Harvard Theological Library
MHarF	Fruitlands Museums
MHi	Massachusetts Historical Society
MPB	Berkshire Athenaeum
MPM	Berkshire Museum
MSaE	Essex Institute
MeBa	Bangor Public Library
MeBaHi	Bangor Historical Society
MeBaUC	Bangor Unitarian Church
NCaS	Saint Lawrence University
NN	New York Public Library
NNC	Columbia University

NNPM	Pierpont Morgan Library
RPB	Brown University
TxU	University of Texas
ViU	University of Virginia
VtMiM	Middlebury College
WyU	University of Wyoming

EMERSON'S BOYHOOD AND COLLEGIATE VERSE: UNPUBLISHED AND NEW TEXTS EDITED FROM MANUSCRIPT

Albert J. von Frank

THE SHAPE OF EMERSON'S CAREER AS A POET, evident perhaps in broad outline, has always been a little obscure in its details and nuances, largely because the materials for studying it have not been readily accessible. The lack of a good text of the poetry and a dearth of information concerning dates of composition have been especially troublesome, though, happily, efforts are now under way to remedy these difficulties.[1] The present article seeks to remove a less conspicuous obstacle by making available the texts of the poems that Emerson composed between 1812, when he began to write, and his graduation from Harvard in 1821, most of which have never before been published. The typically crude but high-spirited versifying that he engaged in during these nine years resulted in nothing that Emerson himself ever wished to publish, but it constituted, nevertheless, a distinct era in his consciousness of the art of poetry, and without some knowledge of these earliest efforts, the next and subsequent periods of his development cannot be fully understood.

In *Emerson as Poet*, Hyatt Waggoner observes that as a boy Emerson's chief distinction was his knack for composing verses.[2] From at least the age of nine, when he wrote "The Sabbath," the earliest of the surviving poems, he was cultivating what seemed to him a very special talent. The attention it brought him from friends, teachers, and members of the family was gratifying not only in itself, but also as setting him off from his brothers, who chose for the most part to pursue other interests. His poems were therefore to a great extent statements of identity and independence, and yet, whether one considers the hymns, the elegies, or the convivial songs composed at college, they were also—and very consistently—affirmations of social connectedness. As expressions of identity and as vehicles of character formation, the early poems belong to the record of Emerson's growth as an individual, and, indeed, it is quite probably owing to his sense of their value in this regard that the manuscripts were preserved.

James Elliot Cabot was the first to venture the opinion that the poems of Emerson's boyhood "show some facility at rhyming, without much appearance of any other aim,"[3] and most who have bothered to look at them since have agreed. Only Waggoner has been even marginally more enthusiastic: the juvenilia, he suggests, "make it very clear that he had a high level of verbal facility and a good enough 'ear' for verse forms to be able to imitate them flawlessly."[4] From one point of view such items as "Independence," the "Poem on Eloquence," or "Apropos" seem mere gestures of youthful homage to favored British poets from Pope to Byron: in most of them the writer is all too evidently concerned to achieve a particular tone, to fit a certain form, to introduce approved figures, and to speak a conventional diction—and where he most succeeds he is inevitably most mechanical. All the juvenile poems are training exercises in one sense or another, and yet they are not what is ordinarily meant by the phrase "apprentice verse." The purpose of the distinction is to suggest that these efforts have, perhaps surprisingly, almost nothing in common with the mature poetry and are not, therefore, usefully to be regarded as in a line of continuous development with it. Emerson's nine-year first phase was, in short, an artistic dead end, as appears both from the curious fact that at eighteen he was not a significantly better poet than he had been at nine, and equally, from the transformed quality of vision and purpose detectable in the verse written immediately upon his departure from Harvard. In order, however, to understand the transformation that finally set Emerson on course, it will be helpful to establish first what sort of a history these early poems make, for if the period was a dead end artistically, it was certainly not without consequence in forming attitudes, suggesting themes, and offering influences that would bear fruit under later and far different inspirations.[5]

After the death of Emerson's father in 1811, the responsibility for Ralph's religious education was divided between his mother Ruth and the pious but eccentric Mary Moody Emerson, who is known to have written the prayers that were "read aloud morning and evening" by the older boys.[6] Part of this education, for Ralph at least, involved the writing of hymns. In 1907, almost a century afterwards, Ellen Tucker Emerson recalled what her father had told her of the sabbath-day routine of these years:

> In the afternoon [the boys] each had to learn a hymn. Sometimes instead of learning one Father wrote one, and Uncle Edward had great delight in laying it in the hymn-book, running to his Mother and asking "Wouldn't you like to have

me read you a hymn, Mamma?" Of course she said yes; he would read it and say "Isn't that a good hymn?" And poor Mamma would say "Yes, my son, excellent." Then Edward triumphant would cry "Ralph wrote it!!"[7]

Three of these compositions have survived. The fact that the third, the "Hymn Written in Concord, Sept. 1814," carries the notation "No. 13" suggests how often the young Emerson preferred composing hymns to memorizing them, a preference which incidentally lends weight to Waggoner's belief that the influence of the hymn form on Emerson's mature poetry has generally been underestimated.[8]

"The Sabbath," probably written in 1812,[9] departs from the "long measure" of the hymnals by being cast in couplets—Emerson's preferred mode throughout these years—while the customary four-line stanza is retained. The sentiments expressed in the hymn seem closer to Aunt Mary's conservative theology than to Unitarian views and suggest that Emerson may have reached the zenith of his orthodoxy before the age of ten:

> If you have sinn'd, repent and live;
> Fly to your God, and he'll forgive,
> The broken-hearted he will spare,
> And hear the contrite sinner's prayer.

The hymn "Written on Sabbath," dating from perhaps a year later, is a far less polished though more interesting performance than "The Sabbath" for having as its center an imaginative experience rather than a statement of religious duty. Its inspiration is the vision, in Revelation, of the four and twenty elders clustered about the throne of God and, more especially, the striking and exotic details of the white robes and crowns of gold. The essential connection between physical light and spiritual glory, implicit in the Bible and confirmed by Milton, was a beautiful fact for Emerson, as his writings throughout his life consistently show. Thus the "white-rob'd martyrs" are envisioned:

> Enrob'd in light they cease not day nor night
> To sing hosanna's in their raptrous flight
> They tune their harps they touch the golden strings
> And shield their faces with their glorious wings.

It is often true of Emerson's early poems that a certain isolating fascination with pictorial elements succeeds in conferring an additional importance on an image, perhaps because the context is less sharply imagined: here the evidence of fascination is the symmetry of the allusions (in the third and fourteenth line of the sixteen-line poem) to the martyrs' brilliant gear.

The "Hymn Written in Concord, Sept. 1814" is mainly interesting as the earliest indication of Emerson's feelings for his ancestral home. It was composed shortly after the family, forced by food shortages and high prices to flee the threatened city of Boston, had taken refuge with the Ripleys in Concord. They came upon the town at harvest time, and the hymn, as a response, conveys Emerson's genuine delight in having exchanged the straitened circumstances of a city under seige for the abundance of a quiet rural retreat. That the associations formed on this occasion were of lasting importance is suggested by, among other things, the way in which the central conception of the poem—that of the individual soul as the focal point of a divine providence working through the natural order—anticipates the "Commodity" chapter of *Nature*.

While it is unreasonable to hold Emerson to strict account for poems written at the age of ten or eleven, they can and perhaps should be taken seriously as documentary evidence of the style and quality of his imaginative life during these formative years. What the first two hymns especially reveal, in their emphasis on the "reward" of a glowingly portrayed if conventionally stylized afterlife, is that the Puritan contempt of the world was still, for young Emerson, a force to be reckoned with. The Concord hymn is affirmative in more characteristic ways, but that, too, as a poem of deliverance, is substantially a rejection of the writer's familiar world. A strikingly high proportion of Emerson's juvenile poems (including, significantly, two valedictories) concern departures or depict "worlds elsewhere," and if they are generally free of any profound sense of displacement, they nevertheless repeatedly enact the provincial urge, amounting almost to an imaginative requirement, to look well beyond the confines of one's present environment.

The War of 1812, which is alluded to in "The Sabbath" as an occasion for prayer and which is the not quite proximate cause of the Concord hymn, was among the most imaginatively significant events of Emerson's childhood, and very probably contributed to the enjoyment he felt at this time in reading about the wars of antiquity. In May of 1814, in a verse epistle to Sarah Alden Bradford, he said:

> I wish that Rollin in his history brought
> The wars of Troy to every reader's thought,
> The burning city, and Æneas' flight
> With great Anchises on that fatal night.[10]

Emerson had no difficulty in attributing a similar significance to the victories of American naval power in two patriotic poems, the lost verses to Captain Hull of the frigate *Constitution* (possibly as early a composition as "The Sabbath") and "Perry's Victory," written in 1814 but commemorating the triumph on Lake Erie of 10 September 1813.[11] They would seem, from what little survives, to have been entirely conventional examples of a popular form. "Perry's Victory" confidently announces the passing of military laurels from Britain to the United States, though the poem is perhaps more interesting for showing that the writer was already acquainted with or influenced by Scottish associationalism. In Emerson's view an important part of what Oliver Hazard Perry has won for America are poetic values:

> When late Columbia's patriot brave
> Sail'd forth on Eries tranquil wave
>   No hero yet had found a grave—
>   Within her watery cemetery.
> But soon that wave was stained with gore
> And soon on every concave shore
> Reechoed with the dreadful roar
>   Of thundering artillery.

Sometime in 1813, after the verses to Hull but before "Perry's Victory," Emerson wrote "The History of Fortus," a more or less whimsical attempt at an epic romance in 102 tetrameter couplets. No less a glorification of prowess in combat than the purely national poems, it was undoubtedly yet another product of the war fever, written under the influence of a deliberately cultivated, though, to be sure, universally shared admiration for military genius. The "Lines on Washington written in Concord Dec. 24th 1814"[12]— another poem of the same sort—places its central figure in a light scarcely to be distinguished from that in which the magic Fortus slays his twenty thousand in a day. Within a few years, however, Emerson would sort out these poetic motives, with the result that from this vaguely concatenated response to the war two increasingly distinct sorts of poems emerged. The romantic, European Fortus stands at the head of a series of historical or anecdotal verses including "Earl Brodin's Plea" (1821), "King Richard's Death" (1820–22), and the first work in verse that Emerson published, "William Rufus and the Jew."[13] (Emerson's later avoidance of strictly narrative poetry may have arisen in part from an early and dispassionate judgment of these efforts, though his prejudice against fiction was strongly ingrained. In any event, the impulse had died out by 1826.[14]) In the other group, elaborated from the patriotic poems, the significance of persons and of personalized history declines, while elements of moral and political idealism, present from the start, loom larger. Pointing away from Emerson's early idolatry and ambiguously toward the representative man, this development implies an increasing maturity in his sense of the heroic. The "Poetical Essay" of 1815 and the Harvard Valedictory six years later are the primary examples of this trend.

The distribution of these motives began with the announced cessation of hostilities in February 1815, when Emerson abruptly dropped his martial muse, noting that "Fair Peace triumphant blooms on golden wings / And War no more of all his victories sings."[15] With the exception of a trip to Boston for the funeral of his grandfather John Haskins, Emerson had been in Concord, and probably attending school, since September or October of the previous year. The family were now planning to return to Boston in late March, and so, with sly humor and high sententiousness, Emerson took leave of his teacher and his classmates in a brief valedictory poem, the earliest example of his writing for an audience outside the family circle:

> This morning I have come to bid adieu
> To you my schoolmates, and, Kind Sir to you;
> For six short months my lot has here been cast,
> And oft I think how pleasantly they've past,
> In conversation with companions gay,
> The time has past like one long summer's day,
> But as I now go hence to other skies,
> Where Boston's spires in goodly order rise,
> A few short lines permit me here to say,
> Whilst Sol prolongs the cheering light of day.

The poet goes on to recommend to his classmates the virtue of hard work in school and closes with several jocular references to his brothers.[16] The tone of the piece is awkwardly mixed, being at certain points addressed to his teacher and at others, in a very different voice, to his "companions gay." Unlike any of his earlier efforts, this poem is above all else a performance, influenced by oratorical conventions, and aiming at certain quite specific audience responses. The story that he delivered the valedictory from a barrel-top may be apocryphal,[17] but it captures the spirit of the address—and the stance of the poet—very aptly.

As later efforts of a similar sort show, the condescending, rather Olympian note that pervades this poem is indeed the keynote of young Emerson's conception of public poetry, insofar as he could be said at the age of eleven to have had any conception at all. It has been suggested already that as a boy he wrote to some extent to confer importance on himself, to create his own identity in the image of the poet and thereby to distinguish himself from his brothers. Few poems show these motives—unconscious as they no doubt were—more clearly than the "Valedictory Poem Spoken at Concord." Why, we may ask, does he so ungraciously congratulate himself on his return to the "goodly order" and excitement of Boston when, as he knew, his comrades would be doing farm chores all summer in and around a small provincial town? Is it quite the handsome thing to tell one's classmates to study harder? And why, finally, does he joke at the expense of his brothers? Emerson is clearly tweaking the noses of all concerned, and it is the role of the poet, as he now understands it, that creates the opportunity, the confidence, and the immunity.

The importance of all this is just that by suggesting the specific grounds for his in any case inevitable appropriation of Augustan models, we can better understand the meaning of the link in Emerson's mind between neo–classic conventions and public poetry. And to grasp that is also to understand the meaning of his later dissatisfaction with both. All the evidence suggests that at this point in his life Emerson approved of poetry for the same reasons he approved of history and chivalry and visions of white-robed martyrs—because it was different from and superior to the world he knew. His initial liking for poetry was a product on the one hand of his belief in the rhetorically privileged status of the poet, and, on the other, of his admiration for the poet's gift of fancy, that constant implication in all that is extraordinary and imposing. Demonstrably, what Emerson responded to most thoroughly in the prevailing aesthetic was its concern for grandeur and elevation, while the immediate effect of this response was a remarkable amount of posturing, a fondness for the sweep and majesty of the sounding phrase, and a feeling, in the poet himself, of power and control. The sort of poet Emerson wished to become, therefore, was a figure of individual importance (an early desire was to win Fame through poetry), but a figure also who conferred importance, who made of the dross of life something impressive. Throughout these years this transforming power seemed to Emerson an inherent aspect of the accustomed rhetoric; as he said in 1816, "even Nonsense sounds good if cloth'd in the dress of Poetry."[18] It was not until he was graduated from Harvard that he even began to liberate himself from this view and from all that it implies. The earliest hint of a different conception is contained in a journal entry of 1822: "poetical expression serves to embellish dull thoughts," he said, "but we love better to follow the poet when the muse is so ethereal and the thought so sublime that language sinks beneath it."[19]

Emerson's course of study at the Boston Latin School between 1812 and 1816 was largely a training in rhetoric that sharpened one's sense of correct expression and cultivated, in the brighter students, a taste for the well-turned phrase. William Henry Furness, Emerson's closest friend at school, recalled those times as "the era of rhetoric; we boys went into ecstasies over a happy expression or a brilliant figure of speech."[20] One such "happy expression" that caught the young Emersonian fancy depicted man as "coming into the world girt in the poison robes of hereditary depravity, and with the curses of his Maker upon his head."[21] Obviously the argument hardly mattered so long as the adolescent hunger for images was fed. It was under these conditions that Emerson first contracted his life-long habit of "reading for the lustres," a practice positively encouraged by such school texts as the *Gradus ad Parnassum*, a popular Latin phrase book.[22]

Perhaps even more important for Emerson and his versifying was the arrival of Benjamin Apthorp Gould as Master of the Latin School in May of 1814. In a letter written toward the end of his life, Emerson acknowledged that he was "always indebted to Mr. Gould for [his] kindness. He had discovered some of my foibles, as of writing rhymes at that early time, and at three successive Exhibitions gave me the task of writing a poem, which of course was as delightful to me as tedious to the audience."[23] These public Exhibitions were very elaborate affairs, advertised in printed circulars and attended by the president and certain of the professors of Harvard, as well as by the most important officials of the commonwealth government.[24] If Emerson's recollection is accurate concerning the "three successive Exhibitions," he may have made his debut in August 1814, though no record of that year's performance has been discovered.[25] At the Exhibition of 25 August 1815, however, he read his "Poetical Essay—Independence," noting that ambitious tyrants from Xerxes to Napoleon have been regularly thwarted by the idea of Independence, which mercifully raised up its champions to meet the successive crises. A few months earlier Emerson had treated this idea from a religious or providential point of view in the "Lines on Washington": "The God of Israel heard our groans and cries / And bade to life A WASHINGTON arise." In the "Poetical Essay" the formula is varied in the direction of a personified principle of compensation: when, stirred by Ambition, England

> Infring'd those rights to freemen ever dear,
> And dar'd the wrath of those unknown to fear;
> Then Independence with indignant eyes,
> Bade quick to life a Washington arise!

This reworking of old material occurs again the the "Poem on Eloquence," delivered at the Latin School Exhibtion of 21 August 1816. The portion of the poem that survives, its first fifty-six lines, is an elaboration of the brief section of "Independence" devoted to Philip of Macedon. In the earlier poem, Emerson's attention had been fixed on the proposition offered by the Athenians to the tyrant Philip, and therefore Demosthenes, though praised as the "Prince of Eloquence," is forced to assume a role subordinate to that of Phocion. In the later poem, however, he emerges as the pattern not only of eloquence, but implicitly of the sort of public poetry that Emerson now aspired to under Gould's encouragement. Eloquence, as the poem defines it, is more than the ability to persuade: in essence it is no less than the power of nature itself, which Emerson renders in an excess of sublime, volcanic images. Later on, referring to Demosthenes, he declares that Eloquence

> Gave thee the power the hearts of men to bind
> The magic springs to know that actuate the mind
> The strong in war thy strength resist in vain
> The great and brave obey thy guiding vein
> Twas with that power endued each sep'rate clause
> Drew from the listening crowd the loud
> applause.

Nothing was more encouraged in Emerson's school than eloquence: Gould, at his own expense, commissioned a number of bronze medals inscribed "Palma Eloquentiae" and awarded them to deserving students—though never, it would appear, to the most constant poet of the class.[26]

These exercises held Emerson to a monotonously lofty tone, but he showed in the elegies he wrote during the same years that he could command a quite different voice, even if it were still not his own. "On the Death of Mr. John Haskins," written toward the end of October 1814, is closely allied in imagery and religious sentiment to the hymns that Emerson may still have been writing. Rusk notes the irony of his having made "a merely conventional angel" of the proud old man whose long and adventurous life at sea had included a stint as a privateer.[27] Yet for all its conventional imagery—the gathered children, the pious farewell, the angelic wings, even, once again, the "crown of gold" and the "golden harp"—the poem is personalized, though not with respect to John Haskins. The detail of the "withered pallid hand," as the eleven-year-old fixes upon it, becomes the emotional center of the elegy, while the supposition that those familiar hands are to be renewed in immortality was probably, to the poet, a more satisfying stroke of the imagination than the more conventional and theatrical properties of crowns and harps. The revision of the ending seems an effort to bring this out more clearly.

Within a span of a few weeks in the winter of 1816, Emerson wrote two elegies, commemorating the death first of Sarah Bradford, the sister of his life-long friend Sam Bradford, and then of Mary Bliss Farnham, a Newburyport cousin.[28] In their dependence on personified abstractions these elegies show Emerson moving away from the resources of the hymnal under the influence of that more formal eighteenth-century impulse evident in the Exhibition poems. The refreshing irregularity of meter in the naive, dramatic Haskins elegy gives way in the lines on Sarah Bradford to a plodding imitation of Pope's heroic couplets. What he has thereby lost in metrical spontaneity and dramatic value he attempts to recover with a labored and coldly artificial show of feeling:

> Oh! I have seen a fair and tender frame,
> In life most lovely, and in death the same.
>
> *   *   *

> Ne'er since my own loved sister met her doom,
> Ne'er since I saw her yielded to the tomb,
> Has such a pang assailed my bleeding heart
> As when your sister felt the fatal dart.

While neither of the elegies is absolutely impressive, the "Lines on the Death of Miss M. B. Farnham" is a decided improvement. It is noteworthy as the earliest surviving instance of Emerson's writing in the genuine quatrains that he so much favored in later years. Its seven elegiac stanzas are well formed, including especially the first two, in which Emerson seems to be experimenting with devices for closing and connecting poetic units:

> Come heavenly Muse a suppliant asks thine aid,
> No common theme his feeble pen pursues,
> Where the blue grave-stone marks the silent dead,
> There would he go and there in silence muse.
>
> Here let unhallowed feet ne'er bend their way,
> Here where decaying, youth & Beauty sleeps,
> Here where cold Death holds his imperious sway,
> And fond affection clad in mourning weeps.

The conclusion of the first stanza with its repetition in a different sense of the word "muse" seems no more accidental than the play on "silent" and "silence." Just as effective is the anaphoric linking of "There" in line four and "Here" in lines five through seven, to suggest the writer's imagined movement to the grave site (not, however, a feature of all the manuscripts). Though he is still very much a captive of the predictable epithet, Emerson is beginning to pay attention to words as well as to phrases. The control of feeling, more or less of a problem throughout this period, is also better managed than in the Bradford elegy, partly because references to the deceased are more generalized, and partly because the poem is not addressed to a specific third party who has to be consoled. As with the rewriting of old material in the Exhibition poems, one senses that here again in the elegies Emerson is testing out different ways of saying the same thing.

With his graduation from the Latin School he all but ceased to write formal poetry and turned increasingly to light verse, as if to combat the awful seriousness of his impending adulthood. In September 1817, he wrote to his brother some doggerel lines on his situation:

> That is—poor Ralph must versify,
> Through College *like a thousand drums*
> But when well *through* then then o my
> The dark dull *night* of *Business* comes.[29]

Between August 1816 and the end of his freshman year at Harvard two years later, Emerson wrote *"lots* of poetry," but all that has survived, apart from the scraps of light verse in the letters, are a metrical history of Europe during the middle ages ("Egbert, bred with Charlemagne") and "Apropos," a nocturne partly imitative of Gray, but showing the newer influence of Scott and Byron as well.[30] The first may have been an aid in recalling the details of a history lesson, although the humor with which this otherwise negligible performance was kept up argues a certain delight on the writer's part with the epigrammatic compression required by the form.[31] The main significance of "Apropos" is that it is the earliest indication of a romantic influence in Emerson's poetry.

More respresentative of the college verses, however, are the lost poems that Emerson read to Samuel Lothrop, whom he tutored during the first months of his freshman year. Lothrop recalled that during their hour-long sessions together his rather unexacting teacher was

> disposed to talk with me of his own poetry and prose composition. The various pieces of poetry were not sentimental; their prevailing qualities, according to my recollection, might rather be described as sarcasm and fun. One of them, I remember, related to his minister and his father's successor, Rev. N. L. Frothingham, whose marriage had occurred about this time; another to the scenes and incidents at the Latin school, which he had recently left; and others to College and college life, upon which he had just entered. All these have very likely been forgotten or destroyed before this time; but my recollection is that they were very droll in humor, and quaint in expression.[32]

This is a fair description of the Hudibrastic "Song for the Freshman Class Supper," the first of several of Emerson's compositions to be publicly performed at college. As a drinking song it is both an instance of social recreation and a recommendation of it:

> To bless the glad year as it closes tonight
> Let Friendship with Reason and Pleasure unite,
> To its close let Philanthropy bear it along
> With the god of the vine and the spirit of song.

To almost all who remembered him at college Emerson seemed rather staid and self-controlled, "never demonstrative or boisterous," as John Boynton Hill recalled, yet one who "keenly enjoyed scenes of merriment."[33] Emerson himself often complained of his lack of sociability, and it was precisely because he was not naturally gregarious that these ventures in light verse played so important a role in his social life at college. They helped to break down the barriers that certain circumstances of his first year at Harvard had placed between him and his fellows. As the "President's freshman" he lived segregated from his class in rooms below the apartments of John Thornton Kirkland, whose messenger he was. In the friendly antagonism between students and the "Government," Emerson's position was equivocal: he knew his eighty classmates, but as often as not he met them as the president's agent. To make matters worse he was for a time self-conscious about having received financial support, and about the necessity for it.[34] As a serious student conscious of academic honors he was of course further isolated by his own advice about "Application": time not given to Lothrop or to running errands for the president was devoted to a long and unsuccessful struggle with mathematics and the *Græca Majora.* "Freshmen's evils are many," he had written at the end of his year-closing "Song,"

> yet leave them at rest,
> And remember the maxim "tis all for the best;"
> Now to Bacchus commend them, both great ones and small,
> And in one cordial bumper amnestify them all!

Emerson returned to the octosyllabic couplet in three more drinking songs, probably dating in each case to 1820—one composed for the Conventicle, another, more subdued, for the Pythologians, and the last for the Knights of the Square Table, a club to which he did not belong.[35] Clearly a demand was building for his verses, as shown also by the Song he wrote for the celebration of the Fourth of July of that year, the only occasion on which he is known to have joined in the singing of his own composition. It was "Eloquence," as he had said, that had given to Demosthenes "the power the hearts of men to bind," and he had found from the beginning a similar effect to follow from his verses. With the new strain of genial humor and the aid of some memorable Malaga wine, his poems continued into his senior year to draw "from the listening crowd the loud applause."

During these years Emerson had not altogether lost his desire to write "serious" poems, but the impulse had obviously been disciplined. Toward the end of his first year he had written a reasonably accurate summation of his prospects as a poet: "Were it my fortune to be in a situation like Lord Byron . . . I think I would cultivate Poetry & endeavour to propitiate the muses. . . . But in this country where every one is obliged to study his profession for assistance in living & where so little encouragement is given to Poets . . . it is a pretty poor trade. . . . I have not the least thought of determination to follow it."[36] But in his last two years it became clear that while he would not in the end cut an especially significant figure as a scholar, he could still secure some reputation as a poet. The three increasingly ambitious works with which he closed out his undergraduate career strongly suggest, in the way each builds on its predecessor, that he was hoping for a dramatic public triumph to punctuate this phase of his life. Ironically, the attempt to bring his conservative idea of public poetry to one final grand fruition ran directly into conflict with his own emerging preference for a very different aesthetic, one that derived mainly from his reading in Byron, the poet whose creative freedom he so much admired.

The first of his major college poems was "Improvement," written in April 1820 for the Pythologian Club. No complete manuscript of the work exists, but the sprawling rough drafts in his journal indicate that in subject and method it was safely conventional.[37] In depicting the westward course of empire as coinciding with the moral and intellectual improvement of the world, Emerson fell naturally into the chronological structure of the poems on "Eloquence" and "Independence," and again cast the verses, though not without some fretting, in heroic couplets. The fretting is significant. In the opening lines he refers to "The silver fetters of old Rhyme" as an obstacle to Improvement in poetry, a constraining artifice invented by "gowned monks with censer cross & bell" to "shackle . . . the soarings of the mind."[38] His still strong dislike of Wordsworth's blank verse seems to have prejudiced him against experimental imitations of Shakespeare or Milton: as he wrote in "Improvement," "some have sought them for their guiding star / Dreaming they raise the glory which they mar." This new interest in the problems of rhyme and poetic diction reflects a restless dissatisfaction with the old style as well, perhaps, as with the upstart reformers who were so prone to slight the dignity of the muse. Longing for emancipation from the predictable, lock-step couplets he had been turning out, he was not yet prepared for the blank verse alternative: the compromise that seemed most attractive at this time involved the spontaneous originality he had discovered and praised in Byron's rhymes. In them it was not form that spoke, but personality: "His own wild character as a man stamped the character of his poetry."[39] On the one hand he wished to stand up for the "good old-fashioned march of Milton or Pope & Dryden," which by convention was suitable for a learned poetry, while on the other hand he was increasingly drawn to a less regulated, a less stately and familiar sort of expression, represented in one of his moods by the figure of Byron and in yet another by his recorded vision of the medieval minstrels who "demonstrate[d] the congeniality of poetry to nature" in their wandering mode of living and in their "wildest tales of lawless power."[40] Emerson's commitment to iambic pentameter and an elevated diction nevertheless held fast through his three performances because these qualities remained for him the correct outward signs of his serious intent.

The second of the poems was "Indian Superstition," written for the College Exhibition of 24 April 1821. It draws together a considerable amount of research, as Kenneth Walter Cameron has shown,[41] but as a poem it is cer-

tainly very unattractive—less because the scholarship is undigested than because it proceeds from the same revolted fascination with Hindu culture that
Southey had demonstrated in *The Curse of Kehama,* Emerson's main
source. The point of the labored indictment of Indian "superstition" is simply that it allows the poet to say, toward the end, that "No Indra thunders in
Columbias sky," and that America is to be congratulated as the guardian of
the principle that may yet deliver Asia from darkness. The poem is the most
convoluted in syntax of any of the juvenile verse and was surely a difficult
and awkward piece to recite.[42]

It is not true, as Rusk has suggested, that "Indian Supersition" was Emerson's "one serious bid for fame as a college poet."[43] If, as seems likely, that
poem was not well received, he was shortly to have occasion to recover his
losses, though not, as it turned out, the occasion he most wanted. He had
hoped to be allowed to deliver a poem at the official commencement on 29
August, and was bitterly disappointed to find that he had been assigned instead to discuss the character of John Knox—in prose.[44] The office of "class
poet," however, was at the disposal of his fellow students, who, according to
Emerson's later recollection, selected him only after seven others had declined the honor.[45] In any event, on "Class Day," 17 July 1821, he delivered
much the longest and clearly the most accomplished poem he had yet written, a valedictory address of 370 lines.

While the poem has most of the stylistic faults of its didactic predecessors,
it no longer depends for effect on the oratory of conventional patriotism or
the sheer manipulation of abstract qualities. Compelled by the requirements of a valedictory, Emerson has blended a vision of his own future with a
sense of the meaning of America to produce a personalized mythology of
great interest. In the opening lines Emerson identifies the poem as in effect
a valedictory to his own childhood, and speaks of the trepidation he feels
about crossing "youth's last threshold." The theme of an innocent golden
age—"life's young holiday"—giving way to the mature necessity of climbing
"*Ambitions* rugged steep" is fortunately only half the poem's major design:
the other, complementary half involves the passing of Europe into *its* own
maturity, "when the world's days of infancy are told." The phase into which
Europe is entering is figured as a total moral eclipse and a prelude to the
Millennium: "When vanquished Virtue's reign is fully past / And stern Corruption climbs the throne at last." The phase into which Emerson and his
generation are entering is, however, less certain. Fate has located them in
the New World, an Eden when discovered (ll. 39–42), and an Eden still (ll.
69–74), "The pillared gate to Glory's narrow way."

> *Perhaps tis our's* to rend the veil away;
> To bid men see their honour, and their bliss,
> The proud connection of that world and this;

> To shew the triumphs of a loftier scene,
> Than on this humble ball hath ever been,
> Ourselves, heavens honoured instruments prepared,
> Whose little band even savage death has spared.

The last line, a reference to the slightly unusual fact that no deaths had occurred in Emerson's class, is a long-descended remnant of the Puritans' special providence, just as the whole poem is very much in the tradition of the errand into the wilderness.

In a line surprisingly prophetic in a different way, Emerson alludes to the possibility that his generation will become "The Ministers of Fate, the priests of Destiny." This, he knows, is a presumptuous expectation and much of the poem is therefore a concession to the reality of human weakness. He invokes something like the lords of life in the personified "objects of pursuit"—Fortune, Ambition, the Muses, Honour, Beauty (ll. 85–90)—that generally govern in life. These

> are the living principles, which weave
> Lifes treacherous web, to flatter and deceive;
> Through every age, they lead the lot of life,
> And grasp the Urn with human fortunes rife.

In the Valedictory, Emerson imagines a laborious life—likened to the career that young Hercules chose—crowned by a rural retirement to the "groves of peace, / Where all the turmoils of ambition cease," there to recover in Memory the Eden which, in a Miltonic image, he is now being driven from (see l. 198). The poem is, in short, a rich evocation of the mythology of American provincialism, ranging from the motif of Adamic innocence and the national exemption from history to the assumptions of millennialism and the fear of Catholic Europe.

Again, however, the poem seems not to have been well received. Cabot reports that it was "pronounced superior to the general expectation," [46] though the meaning of this frosty verdict is perhaps clearer in the response of Josiah Quincy, a classmate: "At half past ten we assembled at Keating's room, and marched from there to the President's, and escorted him, with the rest of the government, to the chapel, where Barnwell and Emerson performed our valedictory exercises before all the scholars and a number of ladies. They were rather poor and did but little honor to the class." [47]

Leaving Harvard (and so leaving his childhood) seems to have been quite as painful as the poem implied it would be, and indeed within a few months Emerson returned to the college for a visit ("my love for it was so wonderful," he explained, "passing the love of women"). [48] The valedictory poem, barely concealing a deep anxiety over the unsettled question of vocation, stands above the trauma of graduation as the biographical landmark it was meant to be. That it was not the public triumph he hoped for must have further contributed to the depressed spirits that inform some of the letters and most of the poetic fragments that he wrote over the next year and a half.[49] The valedictory mood, so to call it, remained with him while the audience he had meant to impress (but which had in fact controlled all of his choices) now vanished. With the failure of his most avowedly social poems, he was left to cultivate a new, more private voice in solitude, and the influence of Byron, now more congenial than ever, was at last allowed a freer field:

> O, when I am safe in my sylvan home,
> I tread on the pride of Greece and Rome;
> And when I am stretched beneath the pines,
> Where the evening star so holy shines,
> I laugh at the lore and the pride of man,
> At the sophist schools and the learned clan;
> For what are they all, in their high conceit,
> When man in the bush with God may meet?[50]

When, in "The Poet," Emerson feelingly advised, "Thou shalt leave the world, and know the muse only,"[51] he spoke the creative lesson he had learned in his liberating dispossession from Harvard and the eighteenth century.[52]

NOTES

1. Emerson's poetry notebooks, containing rough drafts and fair copies of almost all the verse, are currently being edited by Ralph H. Orth, Linda Allardt, David W. Hill, and the present writer, and will be published in two volumes by the University of Missouri Press. A new edition of the poems—a volume in the on-going *Collected Works*—will appear under the editorship of Thomas Wortham and Douglas Wilson.

2. *Emerson as Poet* (Princeton: Princeton University Press, 1974), p. 77.

3. *A Memoir of Ralph Waldo Emerson* (Boston: Houghton, Mifflin, 1887), 1:45; hereafter cited as *Memoir*.

4. *Emerson as Poet*, p. 75.

5. Since the following essay is intended as an introduction to a body of unpublished or incompletely published juvenile poetry, I have been only very incidentally concerned with the fragmentary verses belonging to Emerson's early letters, and with those (also mainly fragments) from the journals that Emerson kept at college.

6. Ralph L. Rusk, *The Life of Ralph Waldo Emerson* (New York: Scribners, 1949), p. 31; hereafter cited as *Life*.

7. "What I Can Remember About Father . . . 7 April 1907," p. 11, MH.

8. *Emerson as Poet*, p. 84.

9. For discussions of the date of composition of each of the poems, see below.

10. *The Letters of Ralph Waldo Emerson*, ed. Ralph L. Rusk (New York: Columbia University Press, 1939), 1:5; hereafter cited as *Letters*.

11. Rusk accounts for the late date of the poem by supposing that Emerson's immediate inspiration was a "grand naval panorama of the fight" mounted by the Columbian Museum (*Life*, pp. 34–35).

12. Given in *Letters*, 6:329.

13. Composed in the summer of 1824 (see *The Journals and Miscellaneous Notebooks of Ralph Waldo Emerson*, ed. William H. Gilman et al., 16 vols. [Cambridge: Harvard University Press, 1960–82], 2:267, hereafter cited as *JMN*) and published anonymously in *The Offering for 1829*, edited anonymously by Andrews Norton (Cambridge: Hilliard and Brown, 1828), pp. 17–18.

14. See the journal entry for 3 April 1826: "But all I wish to say is an opinion I am proud to owe to my youngest brother [Charles]. . . . Let the fictions of Chivalry alone. Fictions whether of the theorist or poet have their value as ornaments but when they intrude into the place of facts they do infinite injury inasmuch as it is only by the perception & comparison of Truth that we can perceive & enjoy the harmonies of the system of human destinies which the Deity is accomplishing from age to age" (*JMN*, 3:19).

15. Emerson's couplet, from a letter of 24 February 1815 to his brother William in *Letters*, 1:9.

16. Emerson's delight at the discomfort suffered by his brother Charles on this occasion lasted well into adulthood (see *Memoir*, 1:47).

17. *Memoir*, 1:46. Cabot seems to have imported the detail incorrectly from Edward Waldo Emerson, *Emerson in Concord* (Cambridge: Houghton, Mifflin, 1889), p. 17.

18. *Letters*, 1:25. When William Cullen Bryant was preparing his Harvard Phi Beta Kappa Poem, "The Ages," in 1821, he was told by a correspondent that "an indifferent poem, if it could be spoken in a fine manner, would achieve an undoubted success" (Park Godwin, *A Biography of William Cullen Bryant* [New York: D. Appleton, 1883], 1:171). Young Emerson's belief that the poet had to elevate his material to the realm of the poetic led him, as it led other conservatives, to dismiss Wordsworth on first inspection as a trifler and a threat. To Emerson as a sophomore, Wordsworth was "the poet of pismires" (*JMN*, 1:162). It is interesting to note that Bryant, who responded very differently to Wordsworth, was not a captive of eighteenth-century prosody: "The Ages," in Spenserian stanzas, broke a strong tradition that Phi Beta Kappa poems were to be in heroic couplets.

19. *JMN*, 1:65.

20. *Memoir*, 1:44.

21. *Memoir*, 1:44.

22. Pauline Holmes, *A Tercentenary History of the Boston Public Latin School* (Cambridge: Harvard University Press, 1935), p. 269.

23. MH (*51M–274[9]). The undated manuscript seems to be related to the notes that Emerson made for the "Speech at the Meeting of the Latin School Association," delivered on 8 November 1876. The letter contains an account of Gould's arrival, which has never been published: "In Mr. Biglow's reign the boys discovered his foible of drinking, and one day when he was giving orders to ⟨one⟩ ↑east↓ side of the house, there was a shout from the ⟨other⟩ ↑west↓ side. He turned round amazed to them, & ↑instantly↓, the boys on ⟨this⟩ ↑the east↓ side roared aloud. ↑I have never known any rebellion like this, though the Barring out of the English schools may surpass it. ↓ I think the School was instantly dismissed and ⟨in a few days⟩ I think he did not come to the School again. Certainly in a few days afterward Mr Bull-

finch, Mr Thacher, ↑ Mr Wells ↓ & the rest of the Committee came to the School & introduced ⟨to the school⟩ Mr Gould as the Master. Mr Thacher ⟨I⟩ the Chairman of the Committee ⟨made⟩ expressed the confidence in the merits of Mr Gould as a Scholar & Gentleman & congratulated the boys on his ⟨merits⟩ appointment. As soon as the Committee took their hats, & turned to the door, the boys began to ⟨give to each other⟩ ↑ buzz ↓ their opinions of the new master ↑ in low tones ↓ Mr Gould turned round to them, & lifted his finger to command silence, which was instantly obeyed, and from that moment he ruled ↑ in my class ↓ ." This and other manuscripts are quoted by permission of the Houghton Library and the Ralph Waldo Emerson Memorial Association.

24. *Life*, p. 58.

25. If he did perform in 1814, he may have read the lost poem "Solitude," though the date of this item cannot be established definitely (see *Life*, pp. 57–58).

26. *Life*, p. 57.

27. *Life*, p. 42.

28. For the Bradford elegy, see "Lines Addressed to Samuel Bradford on the Death of his Sister, January 24, 1816," in *Some Incidents in the Life of Samuel Bradford, Senior*, ed. Samuel Bradford, Jr. (Philadelphia: n.p., 1880), p. 40. For the Farnham elegy, see below.

29. *Letters*, 1:42.

30. *Letters*, 1:74. In November 1816, Emerson wrote a poem on "Thanksgiving" which has not survived (see *Letters*, 1:27).

31. Perhaps the earliest of Whittier's juvenile verses is a similar sort of catalogue, a rhymed list of the books in his father's library (see Samuel T. Pickard, *Whittier-Land: A Handbook of North Essex* [Boston: Houghton Mifflin, 1904], pp. 24–25).

32. *Some Reminiscences of the Life of Samuel Kirkland Lothrop*, ed. Thornton Kirkland Lothrop (Cambridge: John Wilson and Son, 1888), p. 62.

33. *Memoir*, 1:63.

34. Aunt Mary wrote to him during freshman year: "Some lady observed that you felt your dependent situation too much. Be humble and modest, but never like dependence. . . . Be generous and great and you will confer benefits on society, not receive them, through life" (quoted in Emerson, *Emerson in Concord*, p. 21).

35. See *JMN*, 1:244, 246–47, and Waggoner, p. 89. Possibly the anniversary poem that Emerson wrote for the "Society Without a Name" was of a similar character with these, but it has not survived (see Kenneth Walter Cameron, *Emerson the Essayist* [Hartford: Transcendental Books, 1972 (1945)], 1:451–52).

36. *Letters*, 1:63.

37. *JMN*, 1:235–42.

38. The last quoted phrase is from the notes in prose on which this section of the poem is based (*JMN*, 1:242). Shortly after graduation, Emerson was a little more temperate on the subject of rhyme (see *JMN*, 1:278). Cameron rightly observes that this section of "Improvement" is "an expansion" of the opening of Bishop Berkeley's "Verses on the Prospect of Planting Arts and Learning in America," and that, in fact, all of Emerson's didactic poems draw on the vision of history suggested by this poem (see *Indian Superstition*, ed. Kenneth Walter Cameron [Hanover, N.H.: The Friends of the Dartmouth Library, 1954], p. 26).

39. *JMN*, 1:166.

40. *JMN*, 1:165, 264.

41. "Young Emerson's Orientalism at Harvard," in *Indian Superstition*, pp. 13–14.

42. The fragment of rough draft that survives (see below) shows that Emerson's revision involved the interpolation of whole passages, a characteristic practice of later years as well in the composition of poems of more than about fifty lines. The draft further shows that Emerson had

substantially completed the poem in a version of approximately 105 lines (the stipulated limit was 100 lines: see *Indian Superstition*, p. 17).

43. *Life*, p. 83; but see *Letters*, 1:99, as an indication of Emerson's hopes for the poem.

44. *Life*, p. 86.

45. See the headnote, below, to "Valedictory Poem."

46. *Memoir*, 1:60.

47. Josiah Quincy, *Figures of the Past* (Boston: Roberts Brothers, 1883), p. 50.

48. *Letters*, 1:107.

49. The end of Emerson's college career had an equally maturing effect on his prose, as Mary Moody Emerson remarked to him; see Rusk's discussion of "the new mastery of style" in *Letters*, 1:102n.

50. "Good–Bye," in *The Complete Works of Ralph Waldo Emerson*, ed. Edward Waldo Emerson (Boston: Houghton, Mifflin, 1903–1904), vol. 9, *Poems* (1904), p. 4; see Kendall B. Taft, "The Byronic Background of Emerson's 'Good–Bye,'" *New England Quarterly*, 27 (December 1954): 525–27. Other examples one might cite from this period (1822–24) are "The Bell" (p. 379), "Thought" (p. 380), "To-day" (pp. 382–83), and "The Summons" (pp. 384–85). In the two last named, Emerson invites "an unlaurelled Muse" and describes himself as "the bantling of a country Muse."

51. *The Complete Works*, vol. 3, *Essays: Second Series* (1903), p. 41.

52. It is a pleasure to acknowledge the assistance and helpful advice I received in the course of researching this article from William H. Bond of the Houghton Library and the Ralph Waldo Emerson Memorial Association, Suzanne Currier of the Houghton Library, Jeanne M. Mills of the Pilgrim Society, Joel Myerson, Tom Wortham, Joel Porte, Allen Danforth Russell, and especially Eleanor M. Tilton, who very generously supplied me with copies of Rusk's notes in her possession.

THE POEMS

THE SABBATH

Text: The original manuscript is lost. As Rusk indicates (*Life*, p. 511, note to p. 33), a handwritten copy was made some time in the nineteenth century by Laura Dewey Russell, daughter of Emerson's friend Andrew Leach Russell of Plymouth. This copy, owned in 1948 by A. Le Baron Russell, was the source of a typescript sent to Rusk 5 August 1948, from which he printed the third stanza (*Life*, p. 33). The Laura Russell copy cannot at this time be traced, but the typescript made from it is among the Rusk papers deposited in the Columbia University Library. A second copy (or, conceivably, the original manuscript itself) appears to have been given to John Lewis Russell of Hingham and Salem, Mass., a Harvard classmate of Charles Emerson's. This copy was published in *The Book-Lover's Almanac for 1897* (New York: Duprat, [1896]), pp. 22–23, an annual publication limited to an edition of 400 numbered copies. "The Sabbath" appears there with another early poem, entitled "A Fragment" (cf. "I dreamed . . . ," *JMN*, 1:320, probably composed in 1818), and the following anonymous headnote: "We offer our readers two unpublished poems composed by Ralph Waldo Emerson when he was very young. The longer one [i.e., "The Sabbath"] is said to have been written at the age of nine, when young Emerson was obliged for some fault to stop at home and keep his room while the rest of the family had gone to church. Both poems were given to the present owner by the late Rev. John Lewis Russell, of Salem, Mass., a Unitarian minister and a botanist of considerable reputation, who knew Emerson, Thoreau, Hawthorne, Ripley, and the rest of the famous circle. . . ." Since the writer of the headnote does not explicitly claim to be presenting a text based on Emerson's holograph manuscript, the authority of this text and of Rusk's typescript must be judged equally good or faulty. The text below is that, arbitrarily, of *The Book-Lover's Almanac*; variants from the Rusk typescript are given in the notes.

Date: The typescript includes an endnote possibly supplied by Laura Russell in her manuscript copy: "(Written by Ralph Waldo Emerson at the age of nine years.)" All the available evidence, therefore, points to 1812 or 1813. This poem and the lost verses to Hull are the earliest poems by Emerson of which any record survives.

THE SABBATH.

This day the Lord of Heaven hath chose
For weary mortal to repose;
Forget and leave all earthly cares,
And offer at his house your prayers.

5   Let not the world fill up your heart,
    But learn to act the heavenly part,
    Let holy books your thought engage,
    And read with care the sacred page.

    Remember your Redeemer's love,
10 And mediate on things above.
    Forsake while you are here below,
    The path that leads to realms of woe.

    When to high heaven your prayers you give,
    And ask that grace you may receive,
15 Then let your prayers be lifted too,
    For the whole world as well as you.

    If war prevail, then ask release
    From wars and fighting, and for peace;
    If famine desolate the land,
20 Then pray for God's all plenteous hand.

    If you have sinn'd, repent and live;
    Fly to your God, and he'll forgive,
    The broken-hearted he will spare,
    And hear the contrite sinner's prayer.

25 Make resolutions on this day,
    Do what is right without delay,
    And after death you'll have reward,
    And live forever with the Lord.

Notes: The Rusk typescript has the following variants: *Title* The Sabbath   *1* heaven   *2* mortals / repose,   *3* [no comma]   *7* thoughts   *10* above,   *12* which   *13* [no comma]   *15* [no comma]   *17* prevails [no comma]   *19* desolates   *20* all-plenteous   *21* sinned,   *22* forgive;   *23* [no comma]   *25* day;

[VERSES TO HULL]

Only a single line of the poem has survived. The verses are referred to in Emerson's letter of 20 September 1838 to William Henry Furness, with whom he had attended

Rufus Webb's South Writing School in 1812: "It is the pleasure of your affections & nobleness to exaggerate always the merits of your friends—I know the trait of old from Mr. Webb's school onward. . . . Nobody but you & my brother Edward would praise the verses to the immortal Hull! nor could be induced, though I read them never so often" (*Records of a Lifelong Friendship*, ed. H[orace]. H[oward]. F[urness]. [Boston: Houghton Mifflin, 1910], p. 6; hereafter cited as *Records*). Hull is, of course, Isaac Hull, commander of the American frigate *Constitution* in its battle of 19 August 1812 with the British *Guerriere*. Ellen Tucker Emerson recalled that "One line of his poem on a naval battle was often declaimed to us with much amusement to think it once had seemed very glorious to him: 'Then the Consitution did advance'" ("What I Can Remember About Father . . . 7 April 1907," p. 11, MH).

THE HISTORY OF FORTUS

Text: The text of the manuscript (now at MH), was published by Furness in *Records*, pp. 178–85. This is a scrupulously accurate text, as collation shows, though Furness chose not to indicate Emerson's corrections or transcribe the "Notes" that Emerson added between 1813 and 1816. These are given below.

Date: The manuscript is dated "1813" on the first page. On the recto of the last leaf Emerson wrote: 'This whimsical employment of my time was begun at Bennett Str. when I was 10 years old & completed by various dates to 1816. Cambridge 1821.' It is not known just when the Emersons lived in Bennett Street, but the evidence of this manuscript suggests that the family may have relinquished the parish house earlier than has been suspected. Furness says flatly that the "completion" consisted of the addition of the editorial notes, implying, as seems reasonable, that the poem itself was wholly the product of 1813.

Notes: 39 ⟨suspended⟩ ↑ and fastened ↓ 52 p(e) ↑ u ↓ rsued 94 ⟨eager⟩ ↑ e-qual ↓ 105 Fortus, ⟨with⟩ 126 ⟨out⟩ ↑ thick ↓ 127 look'd, ⟨each with⟩ in each 128 brand, 140 ⟨escap'd⟩ ↑ survived ↓ 159 ⟨he drew his⟩ ↑ he added not a word ↓ 193 master ↑ 's voice ↓ perceives

The following notes occupy pp. 12–14 of the manuscript. They are in ink in Emerson's hand:

Editor's
N O T E S

Page 1 "Brave Fortus turned his courser straight" It would be rather a singular sight in modern days to see a horse or other animal *turned straight*, but every thing was different we suppose in the days of Chivalry.

Page 2—I grant thy wish the warrior cries
    And to his steed impatient flies
    Then ask'd her wish—

It appears by this extract that the volatility of the knight exceeded all bounds[.] With all his love he could not even wait to hear the lady's request but *flew* to his horse to prepare himself to perform it and then recollecting himself trudged back again to find out her wish.

Page 4th. And if thou take my life away
     The ring I freely give to thee
Generous proposal!! Quere. How could he help it?
Page 4.   —in a scabbard placed
     Which in a belt hung dangling at his waist
This circumstance is rather singular that the poor man should have no sword—Probably says an eminent critick on this passage it had been purloined by some sly rogue when the knight was asleep & no shop being nigh he had been compelled to trust to providence or more probably he had spent all his money at the last Grog Shop & therefore did not possess the means to obtain a new one—any how the good damsel [*one word*] supplied one
Page 6. Fortus proceeds with steady tread.
We are apt to suppose Fortus not over given to the use of *Ardent Spirits* since he was so steady having as above a "steady hand" [*here a line and a half is heavily inked over.*]
Page 7. Then arms &c
After all his battles he is just arming himself.
Page 7th Six score alone surviv'd—In these days of degeneracy it would be a tough day's work for one man to kill twenty thousand fighting men but Fortus it appears accomplished it in about half an hour.
Page 11.—He gave the ring to her he lov'd—
This is almost the first intimation of the grand plot of the Poem & in the last lines too—Oh the genius of the Poet that could at once surprise the enchanted reader so agreeably & elegantly. But their love was as sudden as it was ardent—he went though all the pains and toils of knighthood to pay the lady for the Cold Beef etc which she had given & the love which he expected in return!
     O tempora Oh mores of[?] the days of Old
                    FINIS

                    WRITTEN ON SABBATH

Text: The manuscript (at MH) is inscribed in faded ink in Emerson's neat schoolboy hand. The text occupies one side of a single sheet of white laid paper, 9.1 x 11.5 cm., evidently clipped from a notebook. The verso is covered with faint, mainly illegible pencil writing which may have comprised notes for a sermon by William Emerson. The signature is preceeded by a decorative device of intertwined lines, also in ink.
Date: The poem bears no date and internal evidence is lacking. The manuscript occurs in a folder along with the "Hymn Written in Concord Sept. 1814" (see below),

though the present poem is in a somewhat less mature handwriting. The metrical irregularities and relative crudeness of composition seem to point to a slightly earlier date.

Written on Sabbath

Begin O Muse begin the angelic song
Of white-rob'd martyrs and the heavenly throng
Enrob'd in light they cease not day nor night
To sing hosanna's in their raptrous flight
5   They tune their harps they touch the golden strings
And shield their faces with their glorious wings
While thus they cry, "O holy holy holy Lord!"
"Almighty God by heaven ador'd"
"Who wast and art and art to come"
10 "All beings hang upon thy doom."
This through Eternity their theme
They sing forever to the God supreme.
O happy spirits of the perfect made
With crowns of gold in robes of white array'd
15 On earth you serv'd the ⟨a⟩Almighty Lord
In Heaven you now receive reward.

R W Emerson.

Notes: The hymn is based on Revelation, chapter 4, especially verses 4 and 8. The popular hymn, "Holy, holy, holy," by Reginald Heber, based on the same verses, was not published until 1827.

PERRY'S VICTORY

Text: Two manuscript copies in an unknown hand were examined as recently as 1945 by Rusk, although neither can be located at present. Among Rusk's notes are transcripts of the first and last stanzas from each of the copies of this seven-stanza poem. Rusk printed the first stanza (*Life*, p. 35) from the text given below. Variants from the other copy are given in the notes.
Date: Both transcripts give the date as 1814.

When late Columbia's patriot brave
Sail'd forth on Eries tranquil wave
   No hero yet had found a grave—
     Within her watery cemetery.
5 But soon that wave was stained with gore
And soon on every concave shore
Reechoed with the dreadful roar
   Of thundering artillery.

[*Five stanzas omitted*]

Barclay thy deed of glory done
10 Thy Laurels at Trafalgar won
Shall now adorn our gallant son
   And signalize his victory.
His country shall with glory crown
His deeds of emprize and renown
15 And history shall hand them down
   To emulous posterity.

Notes: *Title* The poem celebrates the victory of Captain Oliver Hazard Perry 10 September 1813 against the British forces on Lake Erie under the comamnd of Commodore Henry Barclay, a veteran of Trafalgar. *2* Sailed / Erie's *3* [no punctuation] *4* cemetry. *6* soon did *7* Re-echo *9* deeds *10* laurels *14* Thy

HYMN WRITTEN IN CONCORD SEPT. 1814

Text: The "Hymn" is inscribed in ink on one side of a single sheet of white laid paper similar to that on which "Written on Sabbath" was copied out (MH). This, too, has been cut down (to 11.6 x 13.5 cm.) from a notebook. The verso is headed "Extract from the pleasures ↑ of ↓ Hope", followed by some lines of Campbell's poem, all in ink in the hand of William Emerson.

Date: The inscribed date of "Sept. 1814" presents some difficulties. On 20 September the family (all but Bulkeley, who was living with relatives in Maine) were still in Boston, planning their escape from the high prices and mounting war hysteria of the city (*Life*, pp. 40–41). Emerson's brother William entered Harvard on 30 September, and the letter he wrote home on 1 through 4 October—which makes no mention of the family's move—seems to have been sent to Boston rather than to

Concord (*Letters*, 1:48–49*n*). Evidence that Ralph had been in Concord for six months by late March 1815, however, is contained in the "Valedictory Poem," printed below. Either the date given in the title is in error by a month or more or Emerson preceded his mother to Concord. She arrived on or about 1 November (*Life*, p. 43).

No. 13 ↑ Hymn written in Concord Sept. 1814 ↓

Come heavenly Muse my voice inspire
Teach me to tune the poet's lyre
In feeble notes that I may sing
And ⟨bi⟩ let Religion guide the string.
5　The works of God demand a song
From spirits and the angelic throng
O then let mortals also raise
In humbler strains their songs of praise
My soul ⟨o⟩O look around and see
10　How many things are made for thee
For thee the fields are cover'd o'er,
For thee the harvest yields its store,
Speech, reason, sight, and every sense
Is given thee by Providence
15　God's praise is sung by every rill
O then let not my tongue be still
Let morn, and noon, and shady night
Hear praise to him who made the light
And to his ⟨s⟩Son who willing came
20　To save ↑ mankind ↓ from death and shame.

R W Emerson.

ON THE DEATH OF MR. JOHN HASKINS

Text: No manuscript in Emerson's hand is known to have survived. The poem was first published by David Greene Haskins in "The Maternal Ancestors of Ralph Waldo Emerson," *Literary World*, 17 (7 August 1886): 267, with the possibly unauthorial title given above. The entire essay, bearing the same title and including the poem, was reprinted in pamphlet form during the same year by Cupples, Upham & Company of Boston, and in book form (a new edition) by the same publisher in 1887. The poem appears on pp. 17–18 of the pamphlet (the same type-setting as the *Literary World* and on p. 27 of the book. The texts in all three printings are the same. Among the Emerson papers in MH, however, is a copy which seems to bear a close relation to the original manuscript and which differs from the published text. This copy carries a pencil inscription in the hand of Edward Waldo Emerson: "Copied for me by Mrs. Wier, RWE's cousin, from lines given her by her aunt in olden time / St. Paul, Jan 14. '84." This text, with Mrs. Wier's end-note, is given below.

Date: John Haskins, Emerson's maternal grandfather, died on 27 October 1814 and was buried on the 31st (*Life*, p. 43). Fanny Haskins, John's sister, asked Ruth Emerson for a copy of these verses in a letter of 16 December 1815. It is possible that Emerson revised the ending at this time.

> See the calm exit of the aged Saint,
> Without a murmur, and without complaint,
> Whil'st round him gathered his dear children stand
> And some one holds his withered pallid hand.
> 5 He bids them trust in God, nor mourn nor weep;
> He breathes Religion, and then falls asleep.
> Then on angelic wings he flies to God,
> Rejoiced to leave this earthly mortal clod.
> His head is covered with a crown of gold.
> 10 A golden harp his hands immortal hold.

> Lines written by Ralph Waldo Emerson
> on the death of his grandfather,
> at the age of ten or eleven years.

Notes: The text as printed has the following variants: *1* saint *2* murmur [no comma] / complaint; *3* While / gathered, / stand, *4* withered, *6* religion *7* soars to God *8* his earthly, mortal load; *9* gold, *10–12* His hands, renewed, a harp immortal hold; / Thus clothed with light, the tuneful spirit sings— / He sings of mercy and of Heavenly things.

VALEDICTORYE POEM SPOKEN AT CONCORD

Text: The original manuscript (now in the Lilly Library, InU) was reproduced in facsimile in *The Month at Goodspeed's*, 7 (April 1936): 262–63. The recto contains the title and first thirty-seven lines; the verso contains the final couplet and signature. Two related manuscripts are at MH: 1) a late nineteenth-century copy in an unknown hand containing several minor errors of transcription, and 2) notes on the poem in the hand of Ellen Tucker Emerson. The latter, with its misquotations, was evidently the source of the six lines given by Cabot in his *Memoir*, 1:47. Rusk quoted from the Goodspeed's text in *Life*, p. 52, but regularized the punctuation and omitted ll. 11–25. The text given here is that of the original manuscript.

Date: The inscribed date of 1815 is correct, since Emerson left Oliver Patten's school in Concord in the spring of that year. The evidence of the "Hymn Written in Concord" would suggest that a term of "six short months" would end around the time Ruth Emerson is known to have returned to Boston, about 25 March 1815 (see *Life*, pp. 52–53).

Valedictorye Poem spoken at Concord

This morning I have come to bid adieu
To you my schoolmates, and, Kind Sir to you;
For six short months my lot has here been cast,
And oft I think how pleasantly they've past,
5   In conversation with companions gay,
The time has past like one long summer's day,
But as I now go hence to other skies,
Where Boston's /*streets*/spires/ in goodly order *rise*,
A few short lines permit me here to say,
10 Whilst Sol prolongs the cheering light of day.

    'Tis Application only we shall find,
As oft we've heard, that makes the man of mind,
'Tis this alone that makes the statesman great,
And teaches him to guide the affairs of state,
15 'Tis this that makes the scholar, and the trade,
On this is Manhood's firm foundation laid,
When Riches take their wings and fly away,
And Poverty comes on in dire array,
This with Religion gives a hopeful ray;
20 If we have this the sun of hope shall dawn,
Though every other comfort else, be gone.
    Then do we not this Application need?
That straight to Manhood, & to Fame, shall lead
Join'd with Religion, through this vale of strife,
25 Up to the gates of everlasting life.

　　　　To you, Respected Sir, alone I owe
　　　　More than I now, or ever can bestow,
　　　　Such tribute only as I have, I give,
　　　　That is my thanks, that tribute, Sir, receive;
30　　A Brother too by sickness long detain'd
　　　　From study; at his loss is pain'd.
　　　　Another Brother small and younger too,
　　　　New to the school⟨s⟩, and to its studies new,
　　　　Has here imbib'd impressions of that kind,
35　　To banish all its dullness from his mind
　　　　　　And now farewel my schoolmates, happy days,
　　　　　　And Peace attend you in all virtuous ways,
　　　　　　Farewel ye walls where ⟨L⟩ Science ever shines,
　　　　　　And smiling virtue opes her golden mines.

　　　　　　　　　　　　　　　　　R. W. Emerson. 1815.

　　Notes: The following references are made:　2 As in l. 26, to Oliver Patten　*30* To
Edward Bliss Emerson　*32* To Charles Chauncy Emerson

POETICAL ESSAY—INDEPENDENCE

　　Text: The earliest surviving manuscript of this poem is an ink fair copy (MH, Autograph file) consisting of a single sheet of white laid paper folded to make four pages,
each measuring 19.1 x 31.8 cm. The text occupies the first three of the unnumbered
pages; the fourth is blank. A second or subsequent draft was published by Rusk in
Appendix I to *Letters*, 6:330–32. Rusk describes this manuscript, owned in 1948 by
James B. Thayer, as a single large sheet containing both the "Poetical Essay" and the
"Lines on Washington written at Concord Dec 24th 1814" (*Letters*, 6:329). The text
below is that of the earlier (MH) manuscript.

　　Date Rusk's conjecture (*Letters*, 6:329) that the "Poetical Essay" was the same as
the "English Poem, 'Independence'" described in the *Order of Performances at the
Latin School, August 25, 1815* as Emerson's is confirmed by the title supplied in the
present text. Whereas the Thayer manuscript carries the dateline 'Boston 1815—',
the Houghton MS is inscribed 'August 1815'.

Poetical Essay—Independence

When dread Ambition first her flag unfurl'd,
And taught her votries to subdue the world,
A God decreed in mercy to mankind,
(O thought most worthy of the Mighty Mind!)
5 That Independence should descend to earth,
Goddess divine! of high, immortal birth,
With laurel crown'd, in majesty arrayd,
From Ida's top descends the heav'nly maid;
Where e'er Ambition spread her influence round,
10 Where'eer her sons the brazen trumpet sound,
There Independence rais'd her silver Star,
And led to Peace, through Battle, blood, and War.
    If here, a Xerxes mad with lust, and power,
Collects his millions in a fatal hour,
15 And vainly thinks by numbers to enslave
The hardy Grecians warlike, fierce & brave,
Yet there, stern youths their countrys martial pride,
To die determin'd by their country's side;
Steady & close their iron front appears,
20 Nor shines with golden, but with hostile spears
Twas Independence taught them Glory's way,
And led through war to victory's brightest day.
    If here, a Philip with Ambition fir'd,
The whole extent of Græcia's fields desir'd,
25 Yet there, a Phocion fill'd with patriot blood,
His schemes of conquest, and of power withstood;
Nor he alone—another noble name
Stands high, unrivall'd, on the list of Fame;
Demosthenes, great Prince of Eloquence sublime,
30 Whose name shall triumph o'er the wreck of time.
    If here, abandon'd Catiline proceed,
And find each plan, & every crime succeed,
Yet there, with keen, and ever-watchful eye,
Stands the great Father of his Country by,
35 And nobly jealous of his Country's laws,
Before Ambition pleads her injur'd cause.
Thus through the circles of each rolling age,

The names of Heroes fill the historick page.
  In later times when Albion, Ocean's Queen,
40 Who rules supreme o'er Neptune's wide domain,
Infring'd those rights to freemen ever dear,
And dar'd the wrath of those unknown to fear;
Then Independence with indignant eyes,
Bade quick to life a Washington arise!
45 Fair Victory follow'd where the chieftain mov'd,
Him angels ⟨follow'd⟩ guarded, and his country lov'd,
Vengeance to foes beam'd from his awful eye,
Far from his arm the chiefs of Albion fly,
Then Albion sign'd with slow, reluctant, hand
50 The sovreign freedom of our happy land.
  If here, Napoleon thought to rule the world,
And in his course each prince from kingdom hurl'd,
Yet there to stop his vast, destructive force,
And brave the torrent in its headlong course,
55 The northern nations all their force combine,
And patriot millions crowd the banks of ↑ Rhine! ↓
If blood, and desolation mark'd his way,
Yet scenes more direful, dark before him lay;
Dreadful afar the low'ring storm appears,
60 The region flashes with the Russian spears,
In one firm cause his adverse foes unite,
And Alexander le⟨ads⟩d the⟨i⟩ ranks to fight;
Here, Independence hover'd oer their head,
Ambition there, witheld her wonted aid.
65   And if again by her wild power impell'd,
He rose to view oer the forsaken field,
Yet Independence rising once again,
Frown'd on his arms, destroyed his bravest men,
Inflaming patriots with a patriot fire,
70 She doom'd his armies to destruction dire.
  Thus wild Ambition ever leads astray,
And blind like Fortune throws her gifts away,
While Independence like a polar Star,
Unvarying guides her brilliant, fiery car,
75 She bids her sons to fame, & honor rise,
And speads their glory to remotest skies.

Hail Independence! richest gift of⟨f⟩ Heav'n
In kindest mercy ⟨to⟩ ↑ by ↓ immortals giv'n,
Continue thou to bless our happy shore,
80   With thee and Peace we ask no blessing more;
Continue thou to be our guide by day, ⟨our⟩
Our star by night, to ⟨guide⟩ ↑ light ↓ the darksome way!

Ralph W Emerson.
August. 1815

LINES ON THE DEATH OF MISS M. B. FARNHAM

Text: Three manuscripts of this unpublished poem survive. The earliest (at MH) consists of a single sheet of white laid paper, 17.8 x 24.9 cm., inscribed in ink on one side with the verso blank. A second manuscript (in the Barrett collection at ViU, #6248-a), is entitled "Lines on the death of Miss Mary B. Farnham." It is inscribed in ink in Emerson's mature hand on both sides of a single sheet of white laid paper, 18.5 x 22.8 cm. The third manuscript (also at MH) is an early copy in an unknown hand, entitled "Lines on the death of Miss M. B. F." The text given below is that of the first Houghton manuscript; variants from the two copies are given in the notes.

Date: Emerson's cousin, Mary Bliss Farnham, of Newburyport, was the daughter of William and Hannah Bliss (Emerson) Farnham, sister of Emerson's father William. Mary was born 1 December 1792 and died 10 February 1816 (see the *Columbian Centinel*, 14 February 1816, and *Vital Records of Newburyport, Massachusetts* [Salem: Essex Institute, 1911], 1:135, 2:626).

Lines on the death of Miss. M. B. Farnham

Come heavenly Muse a suppliant asks thine aid,
No common theme his feeble pen pursues,
Where the blue grave-stone marks the silent dead,
There would he go and there in silence muse.

5   Here let unhallowed feet ne'er bend their way,
Here where decaying, youth & Beauty sleeps,
Here where cold Death holds his imperious sway,
And fond affection clad in mourning weeps.

Lowly beneath this green and nameless sod,
10   Rests the frail body of departed worth;
Her happy soul has mounted to her GOD,
And gone forever ⟨to⟩from this narrow Earth.

Her's was the brightness of the noonday Sun
Her fancy brilliant as his golden ⟨beams⟩ rays,
15   Judgement & Reason, mounted on the throne,
And pure Religion shone in all her ways.

Long as the life blood flows within the veins,
Long as the throbbing heart persists to move,
So long shall thought of Mary lessen pains,
20   And bring to Memory all her cares, and love.

Her brilliant taste, and manners well refined,
Shone with bright splendor on this lower earth,
Her graceful form, and modesty combined,
Proclaimed her value, excellence, and worth.

25   Farewel thou dear departed! ah farewel,
Peace to thine ashes in their clay cold bed,
Till the last trump shalt burst thy narrow cell,
And bid thee leave the mansions of the dead.

Ralph W *Emerson*

Notes: The ViU manuscript has the following variants: *1* muse! / aid; *2* pursues; *4* go, *5* There / way; *6* There, where decaying youth & beauty sleep; *7* There / death *8* affections, / weep. *9* Lo⟨ve⟩wly, / & *11* God, *12* earth. *13* noon-day sun; *14* rays; *15* reason seated *16* religion *20* memory / cares & *21* polished taste, & manners well refin'd, *23* & modesty combin'd, *25* Farewell / departed; oh farewell; *signature* [also in Emerson's hand] Ralph Emerson aged 12

The second MH manuscript has the following variants: *1* Muse! *6* beauty *7* death *8* Affections / weep *11* God *12* earth *13* noon⟨d⟩ day Sun *15* and reason seated *17* life-blood *20* memory / cares and *21* polished taste and *22* splendour *23* form and / combin'd *24* Proclaim her valued excellence and worth *25* departed   ah farewell *27* shall *Signature* R.W.E. aged 12 yrs [in the same unknown hand as the text.]

POEM ON ELOQUENCE

Text: The "Poem on Eloquence" exists in a single fragmentary fair copy (MH). It is inscribed in what is for Emerson an unusually neat hand, in ink, on a single sheet folded to make four pages, where it occupies pp. 1–2. The paper is a white laid stock with the watermark 'G H 1812'. The pages measure 15.4 x 18.2 cm. At the top of the first page is a notation in pencil in the hand of Edward Waldo Emerson indicating that the manuscript had been found "Among the author's papers."

Date: The broadside *Order of Exercises at the Latin Grammar School, August 21, 1816* lists "An English Poem on 'Eloquence'" as Emerson's (see Holmes, *History of the Boston Public Latin School*, p. 63). The performance was sketchily reported in the *Columbian Centinel* on 24 August. Emerson's teacher, Benjamin Apthorp Gould, asked him to repeat the poem at a recitation on 4 January 1817 for a certain Mr. Ogilvie who was to visit the class on that day. Emerson said in a letter to his brother Edward that "when I came home I could not find any complete copy and so was obliged to make a new end in the evening to speak the next day—Miss Urania, luckily, being propitious it was finished, approved etc." (*Letters*, 1:32). Neither the first nor the second ending seems to have survived.

Poem on Eloquence by R. W. Emerson.

When oer the world the son of genius rose
And woke mankind from indolent repose
When Science first diffused her genial rays
And Learning fair enlightened elder days
5   Then Eloquence descending from above
Left the high palace of Olympian Jove
To earth's fair field she bent her airy way
Guided by Hermes from the realms of day
Thrice happy Greece her lighting footsteps bore
10 When first the Goddess on earthly shore
In thy fair realm Polymnia fix'd her throne
And raised her sacred fane,—nor there alone—
Where to bright knowledge Ignorance gave way
Where Superstition fled the dawn of day
15 There in the temple of the Muses shone
Polymnia star by radiant lustre known.

First mid the band that sought her courts for fame
Stood cloth'd in light the great Athenian name
Hail great Demosthenes! thine ardent soul
20 Could nature's arts and nature's self controul
Thy speech inspired with accents clear and loud
Flash'd like the lightning from the thunder cloud
As the fierce flame that rends the rumbling ground
With sudden blaze throws dire destruction round
25 From Etna's top with mad resistless force
In liquid fire precipitates its course
Nor shepherd's hut nor prince's stately tower
Can save the tenant from the torrent ↑ s ↓ power
Thus from thy lips the fire of Hermes flow'd
30 And from a mortal almost made a God
Gave thee the power the hearts of men to bind
The magic springs to know that actuate the mind
The strong in war thy strength resist in vain
The great and brave obey thy guiding vein
35 Twas with that power endued each sep'rate clause
Drew from the listening crowds the loud applause.
When Freedom from thy lips in thunder spoke
And all her spirit flash'd in every look.
When Phillip vainly tried each subtle art
40 To tempt ⟨with⟩ with venal gold each patriot's heart
Rous'd by their "last great man" they tried the field
But not those Greeks unknowing how to yield—
One mercy more oh! had the Gods bestow'd
Courage on him whose lips with ardour glow'd
45 Then had led their armies to the plain
And falling Greece had conquered once again
The dubious field of battle's strife been won
And set majestic had their falling sun
But time forbids that more the muse should name
50 Of Grecian orators well known to fame
Farewell to Greece of liberal arts the nurse
Turn now Oh Muse to Rome direct thy course
See where with awful majesty arise
Her mighty leaders eloquent & wise
55 See great Hortentius to a greater yield
And stript of laurels quit the long-fought field

APROPOS

Text: The poem is written in dark brown ink on one side of a sheet of light greenish-blue laid paper, torn off at the left edge, measuring 22.2 x approximately 32.5 cm. (MH). The poem follows a prose fragment which, occupying the top quarter of the page, begins in mid-sentence: 'two Stanzas so admirably express; every one will gaze with admiration on the stern indifference to mortals and to mortal things which characterises the writings of his Lordship, but there are few who can feel with him—Few are so insensible to the pleasures of Society, (without which man could ill exist) that they can sympathize with feelings of this nobleman—yet if he can in reality feel those emotions he describes with what respect, nay almost awe would the gaze of his intelligent readers be fixed upon him—but goodnight to his Lordship, to his *cogitations* his rhapsod⟨ys⟩ies and poetry; ⟨dein⟩ *denique*, I say, Good night!' The verso contains the tribute of Gamaliel Bradford to Emerson's poem "Solitude," dated "Aug 16", quoted by Rusk in *Life*, pp. 57–58. The sheet belonged at one time to a notebook: the recto is marked '6' in the upper right corner, the verso '7' in the upper left, both in ink. Emerson's numbering of the stanzas, 1 through 6 in the left margin, has been ignored, as have the broken lines separating the stanzas.

Date: The date "Aug 16" and the reference to "Solitude" probably belong to 1816 (see *Life*, p. 57). Although this inscription bears no relation to the poem on the recto of the same sheet, such a date is consistent with the evidence of the handwriting, which is similar in its ornamental peculiarities to that of the letters of 1816–17, Emerson's last year at the Latin School.

↑ Original—"Apropos". ↓

Night slowly stretches o'er the changing skies
And killing darkness shrouds the rolling Earth
Up to her well-known rock the night-owl hies
And wizard hags begin their cursed mirth.

5   A misty cloud bedims the rising moon
Few are the stars that cheer the evening sky
And dark and gloomy is the night; and soon
The light that issues from those stars will die.

This night, I deem, the moon is in her spell
10 And fiends have mutter'd incantations dire
This night in revelry, the hags of hell
Dance in deep cave, around th'infernal fire

Ah! bleakly blows the Ocean's stormy blast
Grim Water-Sprites bestride the foaming wave,
15   Woe to the hapless bark, the towering mast
The careworn sailor finds tonight his Grave!

On Ballans lonely moor what sounds were heard!
When the chill night brought on the darkness drear
And in thy lofty towers lone Villagird!
20   What startling noise came sudden on the ear.

I passed at eve the foot of Ben-lide's hill
I heard a voice as the sad breeze blew by
Starting I listened—all again was still
Nought through the mist could ⟨then my⟩ ↑ mortal ↓ sight descry.

Notes: *13–16* Cf. Scott, *The Lay of the Last Minstrel*, VI, 360–63: "The blackening wave is edged with white; / To inch and rock the sea–mews fly; / The fishers have heard the Water Sprite, / Whose screams forebode that wreck is nigh." The third of these lines was quoted by Emerson in a letter of 20–21 July 1818 to his brother William (*Letters*, 1:66).   *21* Ben-ledi, highest peak of the Trosachs near the river Teith in Perthshire, Scotland. Emerson may have encountered the name in Scott's *Lady of the Lake*, where it is mentioned several times. Neither "Ballans moor" nor "Villagird" has been identified, and are probably Emerson's invention.

EGBERT, BRED WITH CHARLEMAGNE

Text: The manuscript (at MH) of the following poem—or rather versified history lesson—consists of fourteen pages, disbound from a commercially prepared blank book, and existing now in two parts: 1) a single leaf, pp. 1–2, along with the stub of the cognate leaf, which bears no evidence of writing, and 2) a gathering of six leaves, at one time stitched together, containing pp. 3–14. The poem, in ink, occupies pp. 1–7, while pp. 8–14 are blank. The pages are of white wove paper measuring 10.4 x 16.8 cm. One board, stripped of most of its covering but evidently belonging to the original blank book, survives with the manuscript; it bears on one side drawings in ink of two heads and a reclining figure, similar to sketches found in Emerson's early journals.

Date: There is no evidence but the handwriting and the character of the poem itself to aid in establishing a date. Perhaps 1817 or 1818 is a reasonable conjecture. Richard Valpy's *Poetical Chronology of Ancient and English History* (Boston, 1816) may have inspired Emerson, though it did not become part of the Latin School curriculum until 1823.

Egbert, bred with Charlemagne ⟨⟨we⟩run⟩
The ⟨seven⟩ ↑ 3 ↓ kingdoms into one
Which by Ethelwolf was sundered
Whose realm by Danes & monks was plundered
5   And pass͜ed thence to two sons called
Ethelbert eke & Ethelb⟨er⟩ald
This was a rake & ruled the west
That rules the East & was the best
Their brother Ethelred came next
10   Whose reign like theirs by Danes was vexed
And passed to Alfred surnamed Great
Who routs the Dane & rears the state
Aideth justice eke & knowledge
Founding juries & a college.
15   The throne he so had shone upon
He leaves to Edward his brave s[on]
Whose child Athelstan did inheri[t]
His father's luck & martial merit
And leaves to Edmund crown & care
20   Which till murdered he did wear
And next to Edred it descended
Who Benedictines much befriended.
His nephew Edwy young & brave
By these same monks found early grave
25   And then to Edgar fell the crown
Who wore it well then handed down
Not without broil to Edward styled
The Martyr because early killed
For Ethelred the throne to mount
30   A sorry prince by all account
Who paid the Danes to ⟨run⟩go away
And come again another day.
Next Edmund surnamed Ironside
With Canute doth the realm divide
35   Until by his adherents slain
Leaves England wholly to the Dane
In year ⟨1017⟩
[F]ull twenty years Canute was king
[A]nd thro' his life went prospering

40 And at his death the Crown did fall
    [To] Harold whom men ⟨h⟩Harefoot call
    ⟨Who tho' his claim was men's affection⟩
    ⟨Yet found from death no sure protection⟩
    ⟨But fell in⟩
45 Two years his cruel reign extended
    Canute the Hardy then ascended
    The vacant throne and altho' hated
    Reigned till he died intoxicated.
    And now at length the Crown did grace
50 A monarch of the English race
    Edward Confessor & Saint
    Anointed is without complaint
    A clever prince & just & good
    But ruled by those who near him stood
55 And when at length he breathed his last
    The sceptre to duke Harold passed
    Who tho' his claim was men's affection
    Yet found from death no sure protection
    But fell in battle warm one day
60 With William duke of Normandy
    Who straightway doth his title fix
    In year 1066.
        Six centuries have now swept by
    Into their home, Eternity.

65 Betwixt the invasion of the Saxon
    And Conqueror William's attacks on
    This doughty island of the brave
    Which now may boast to be mistress of the wave
    Throughout the ancient time a fine would pay for killing
70 An ox was worth six sheep and a sheep was worth one shilling.
        ↑ But bear in mind that a shilling of old ↓
        ↑ Was worth more than now a hundredfold. ↓

    But to return, the Norman king
    ⟨Throughout his life⟩ ↑ With all his lords ↓ went Conquering
75 The English whom they quickly carry
    From wealth & rank to beggary

Twas now that bulls began to go forth
About investitures and so forth
From the strong & cunning hand
80   of Gregory VII Hildebrand
And Guelf & Ghibbeline arose
To interrupt the worlds repose
Doomsday Book was also done
In 1081
85   Six years thence he wills the crown
To William Rufus, second son
Who gains this summit of ambition
In spite of Robert's opposition.

Twas now that Europe took in hand
90   To win from Turk the Holy Land
And sinners tho't alas poor fools
By losing lives to save their souls
First Hermit Peter without sense
And active Walter without pence
95   Did lead thro' Hungary a mob
For daily bread who needs must rob
Which did the peasants so incense
They took their lives for recompense.
Thus perished all this rabble band
100 Nor won one inch of Holy Land.
        After these with caution due
Godfrey Stephen Raimond Hugh
Boemond & Tancred too
Robert with his Norman crew
105 And Flemish Robert also view
All marching into Asia's plain
With near 600, 000 men
The tomb & love of Christ to gain.
Whilst all these great events do move us
110 Calm as a clock sits William Rufus
⟨Bu⟩ And buys up Normandy & Maine
As also Poitou & Guienne
Builds Westminster the bridge & tower
And gains & squanders wealth & power

115 At last Sir Walter Tyrrel blundered
     And shot him dead in 1100.
        Henry hears the news with pleasure
     Hastes to Winchester for treasure
     Knowing no hand so well can hold
120 The crown as one that's filled with gold
     Next he strengthens usurpation
     By the form of coronation
     Buys Normandy & baffles Rome
     Has fame abroad & peace at home.
125 Hunting & books the Beauclerc moved
     And lampreys ah! too well he loved
     Which made this monarch cease to live
     In 1135.
        His nephew Stephen without right
130 Grasps the royal sceptre bright
     The fair Matilda's claim despite
     The broil brings wo upon the land
     And barons bold with lawless hand
     And crown & church the firebrand
135   Of civil discord throw
     Stephen is ta'en but soon set free
     With prince Henry doth agree
     That he till death shall monarch be
        And Henry heir shall go
140 But all poor Stephen's reign was o'er
     In 1154.

Notes: *1* cancellation in pencil *2* 'seven' cancelled and '3' added in pencil *16–17* Here and elsewhere text supplied in brackets indicates a torn manuscript *37* Corrected to '1117' in pencil, then cancelled in pencil.

SONG FOR FRESHMAN CLASS SUPPER AUG 17. 1818

Text: The "Song" exists in two manuscript copies, each made by a Harvard classmate of Emerson's. The first, a transcription by Josiah Quincy (now at MHi), was published with notes by Tremaine McDowell in "A Freshman Poem by Emerson," *PMLA*, 45 (March 1930): 326–29. The second was made by William Henry Furness and is now at MH. While the Quincy copy is clearly the more accurate and complete, nevertheless three of Furness's readings seem preferable: in line 2 'Let Friendship with' rather than 'Let Friendship and'; in line 31 'friend of the glass' rather than 'Friend of the Class' and in line 40 'That Senate' rather than 'The Senate'.

Date: Only the Furness copy supplies the date of the event: 17 August 1818. In a letter to his brother William dated only "Thursday Morn.g" (*Letters*, 1:69), Emerson indicates that "Next Tuesday is my Examination," and, in the postscript, that "[John R.] Adams sings my song Ex[amination]. evening." Therefore, Emerson's letter can confidently be assigned to 13 August, rather than to Rusk's conjectural "August? 6?"; the Freshman Examination would have been held on Tuesday, 18 August, despite the erroneous manuscript *Records of the College Faculty* which indicates that it was given on 8 August, a Saturday, and the Class Supper was held on the evening pre-ceeding the examination, not the evening following, as Rusk supposed (*Letters*, 1:69–70).

SONG

Text: The following song, which supplies new lyrics to Burns' popular "Scots wha hae," is written in ink on one side of a single sheet of white paper 20 x 23.3 cm. (at MH). The verso is blank. In the upper left corner of the page, Emerson has written '"Scots wha hae" &c' followed by a notation, in long and short slashes, of the scansion of one stanza.

Date: The bottom fifth of the page is inscribed in ink with the following note: 'My college class that of 1821 in Harvard College celebrated the 4th of July 1820, by a dinner in the dining room of the college Hall at which the venerable Dr John Popkin Professor of the Greek Language and Literature was present and presided, and when called upon for a toast, ⟨and when called upon for a toast⟩ gave in response that very expression one in two Greek words μηδεν αγαν nothen too much This song written by Ralph Waldo Emerson for the occasion, was sung, in the singing of which he joined voices ↑ with ↓ us. This is the original in his hand writing. I am now undoubt-edly now the only survivor of the company then present   John B Hill   March 20 1884'. Undoubtedly Hill's note was written in response to Cabot's request for in-formation regarding Emerson's undergraduate life: the occasion and the song are re-ferred to in *Memoir*, 1:63–64.

Song   Tune "Scots wha hae wi' Wallace bled."

Shout for those whose course is done,—
Bow you to their setting sun,
—Souls of patriots who won
          Noble Liberty.

5 Fell Brittania's tyrant power
 Quailed in combats fearful hour;
 Lowly did the Lion cower
   To their victory.

 Stars of Freedom's spangled banner!
10 Burst ye forth in loud hosanne,
 While the morning breezes fan her
   Passing cheerfully.

 Celebrate with song today⟨,⟩
 Feats of eras far away
15 ⟨Independence from the sway⟩
 Ruin to the British sway
   O'er Columbia

For the Fourth of July 1820

SONG FOR KNIGHTS OF SQUARE TABLE

Text: The manuscript of the "Song" (at MH) consists of two sheets of gray laid paper: the first, 18.7 x 30.2 cm., contains, on the recto, the first seven stanzas, and, on the verso, stanzas eight through ten as well as the title and author's initials, written upside down at the foot of the page. The second sheet is torn at the top and measures 18.7 x 11.7 cm. The recto contains the final two stanzas and the chorus. The verso is covered with sums in addition and the phrase 'John's move'.

Date: Evidence supplied by John Lowell Gardner in a letter to Oliver Wendell Holmes points to 1820–21 (Emerson's senior year at Harvard) as the period of composition. Gardner wrote to Holmes to give his impressions of Emerson at college and enclosed two manuscripts. The first, partially quoted in Holmes, *Ralph Waldo Emerson* (Boston: Houghton, Mifflin, 1885), p. 32, along with portions of the letter itself, was intended as advice to Gardner in preparing an Exhibition part dealing with the profession of the law. Gardner is understandably hazy about the date of this piece, but as such parts were given only to students in their last two years, it could not have been written earlier than 1819–20. Gardner continues in his letter: "The other piece The Song for the Supper of the Knights of the Square Table—must have been the work of a year later—whether it was sung or not I have no recollection—I[t] strikes me as admirable in spirit & execution—it was written at my Solicitation" (quoted from the manuscript letter, MH). This letter is now in an envelope inscribed in Cabot's hand: 'Papers ⟨to be sent to Judge Holmes⟩ / College writings of R.W.E. / and letter of John L. Gardner'. The two sheets of the manuscript "Song" had at some time become separated, and it was mainly owing to Holmes' description—"There are twelve verses of this song, with a chorus of two lines" (*Emerson*, pp. 32–33)—that they have been brought back together.

Ye Muses descend & the melody raise
Bring the Bacchanal harp hung with poesy's bays
Let the doors of Olympus be opened for all
To descend & make merry in Chavalrys hall.

5   Apollo's invited & will not refuse
Jove's dignity can't run the risk of a bruise
And we lest a *blow* peradventure should hurt us
Our watchword is '*Cassis tutissima* virtus."

Let Envy foul hag of unhappiness say
10   That the splendours of Knighthood have fallen away
We defy the dark demon to point to the place
In our brilliant Escutcheon that's dim with disgrace

Old Shakspeare, whom all must acknowledge is right,
Most fervently blesses the fair "*hood of ⟨Kn⟩Night*"
15   By which it is plain as
That he meant to bless *Knighthood* & Knighthood alone

The Knights of King Arthur of chivalrous fame
When the world echoed wide to each champion's name
Yet equalled not Harvards fraternity fair
20   But the Round Table yields to the fame of the *Square*.

Though history tell us how mighty their foes
How tremendous the ⟨giants⟩ they had to oppose
Of the giants they slaughtered in mountain or pass
Or magician mischievous in castle of brass.

25   Yet slight were their perils to those which we feel
Our tyrants are fierce & accustomed to steel
Despite all that love & affection could do
Our *Darling* they mulct a round dollar or two.

Our habits are hardy but that's all in vain
30   Our pitiless tyrants ⟨neglect⟩ ↑ regard not ↓ our *Paine*
They forget in their ⟨g⟩age the good deeds we have done
Though countless in number I'll mention but one

The Kirk was protected some ages ago
By the Knights who relieved her from many ↑ a ↓ ⟨a⟩foe
35   But the ⟨tyrants⟩ ↑ giants ↓ who now our glory withstand
Are headed by those who controul the *Kirk-land*

But Nil Desperandum's the motto for men
So toast we the order of Knighthood again
Then spirit to spirit we'll fervently join
40   And amalgamate wit with affection & wine

Song for Knights of Square Table
R. W. E

Oh circulate freely the full-flowing bowl
That logick which drives every mist from the soul
For any optician though dull as an ass
Knows Science improves by the use of *the glass*

45   And when we are lost in the trances divine
The blisses that make the true value of wine
Then tyrants & foes & misfortune & evil
With hearty good wishes we'll toss to the d---l

Chorus | So merrily join in the /echoing/bacchanal/ cry
         | That ⟨hallows⟩welcomes & hallows this festival high

Notes: Title "The 'Porcellian Club,' instituted in 1791, and the 'Order of the Knights of the Square Table,' instituted in 1809, were united into one Association in the year 1831, under the title of the 'PORCELLIAN CLUB'. For some time previous, the Members of one Club had generally been Members of the other . . ." (*Catalogue of the Honorary and Immediate Members . . . of the Porcellian Club* [Cambridge: Metcalf, Torry, and Ballou, 1834], p. [3]). John Gardner joined in 1818; Emerson is nowhere listed as a member of either club.   *7* "blow": "A drinking spree" (*A Dictionary of American English*, ed. Sir William Craigie [Chicago: University of Chicago Press, 1936]. The earliest citation (1827) is from Harvard.   *8* "Virtue is the best (safest) helmet."   *14* No such phrase occurs in Shakespeare's plays or poems.   *15* The line was left incomplete in the manuscript.   *28* Timothy Darling, of Henniker, N.H., class of 1822, joined the Knights in 1819 (*Catalogue*, p. 27).   *30* Charles Paine, of Williamstown, Vermont, class of 1821, is listed as a member of both clubs.   *33–36* The allusion is obscure, but may have to do with the completion in 1814 of a chapel in University Hall. Previously students and faculty worshipped with the congregation of the First Parish in Cambridge (see Josiah Quincy, *The History of Harvard University* [Boston: Crosby Nichols, 1860], 2:310). John Thornton Kirkland was the president of Harvard during Emerson's term.   *37* "Never despair": Horace, Odes, I, vii, 27.

[INDIAN SUPERSTITION: A FRAGMENT]

Text: The manuscript (at MH) is a single sheet of white laid paper folded to make four pages measuring 23.8 x 16.4 cm. The main sequence of the text occupies pp. 1, 3 and 4 (which Emerson has numbered 5, 6 and 7 in ink). On the verso of the first leaf is a list of rhyme words, 'viewed include conclude rude strewed', in a vertical column above the following draft lines: 'When awful Brahrma pleased with all he viewed / Abandoned his empyreal solitude / ⟨And⟩ ↑ Complacent ↓ owned his vast creation good' (see note to l. 4, below). The sequence of verses on pp. 1, 3 and 4 carries line numbers supplied by Emerson in the left margin, by fives, beginning with '70' at 'Young muses caroled . . . ' (l. 3 of the fragment as renumbered here), and concluding with '105' at 'Then, may the fiends . . . ' (l. 39 of the fragment). All the writing is in ink.

Date: The inscription 'March 1821' is consistent with the date the subject was assigned to Emerson, 7 March, and the date of its completion, 14 April (see *Indian Superstition*, pp. 17, 54).

(Insert 24 lines)

Oh once illustrious in the elder time,
Young muses caroled in thy sunny clime;

(Insert 6 lines)

5　　Fair Science pondered on thy mountain brow,
　　And sages mused where Havoc welters now.
　　The dazzling crown was thine which soothed the brave,
　　Gathered in their rich glory, to the grave.
　　Alas! thy wreath is sear, thy banners stained,
10　　Thy faith perverted, & thy shrines profaned,
　　The cormorant sits lonely on thy walls,
　　The bittern shrieks to Ruins echoing halls,
　　Robbed of its ancient pride, thy brow appears
　　Sad with the sorrows of unnumbered years.
15　　—What choral burst awakes the startled deep?
　　What visions strike Oblivion's iron sleep,
　　—Gaze on yon parting cloud's refulgent shew!
　　Revealing angel forms to men below,—
　　The maids of empire come, whose awful sway

20   The prostrate nations of the world obey,
     The cloud pavilion ⟨‖ . . . ‖⟩purples round the throng,
     Whose sweeping folds give echo to their song;—
     India, they come to see thy shackles riven,
     To throw thy thraldom to the winds of heaven:
25   The holy cherubim in heaven shall bow,
     The archangel's trump ring out its triumph now,
     Whose raptured note sounds out for aye farewell
     To Superstition & the hosts of hell.

       First in that throng, gathering her Eagles food,
30   Land of our pride! thy guardian angel stood;
     Hushed from her strife in Freedom's conquering cause
     Her hand unfolds, ⟨her sword protects the⟩ ↑ her free
                         sword-sanctioned ↓ laws
     Fair as the dayspring, clad in burnished mail,
     Queen of the East! she hastes to bid thee hail.

35   No Indra thunders in Columbian sky,
     No "man-almighty" grasps at destiny,
     Bold were the man whose rash presumption strove
     To tamper with the Power whose law we love,
     Then, may the fiends storm Heaven's eternal court,
40   Or boys with bursting thunderbolts may sport.
     ⟨This ponderous globe with all its vast array⟩
     ⟨Of clamoring nations wait Columbia's sway,⟩
     ⟨Proclaim her matchless progeny of gods⟩
     ⟨The fair inhabitant of bright abodes⟩
45   ⟨The reign of Peace commissioned to restore⟩
     ⟨And wield their blazing bolt till crime shall be no more.⟩

March 1821
R. W. Emerson.

Notes: *1* The insertion corresponds to ll. 79–102 of the finished poem (see *Indian Superstition*, pp. 49–54).   *2–3* Cf. ll. 103–104   *4* The insertion corresponds to ll. 105–10 (cf. the early draft of this passage, given in the headnote).   *5–38* Cf. ll. 111–44   *39–46* These lines do not appear in the final draft, though with l. 46, cf. l. 155.

VALEDICTORY POEM

Text: The manuscript (at MH) of Emerson's Harvard Valedictory Poem consists of three sheets of white laid paper, each folded once to make four pages (19.9 x 24.9 cm.) and hand stitched in black thread, probably by Ruth Emerson (see *Indian Superstition*, p. 7). To this was prefixed a single free leaf of the same paper containing the "Analysis" on the recto and, on the verso, the signature and college address in pencil. The poem begins on the recto of the second leaf. Beginning with the verso of the free leaf, Emerson numbered the pages in ink 2 through 11, omitting the last three pages, of which 12 and 13 are blank. Page 14 is inscribed, sideways along the right margin, "R. Waldo Emerson's Valedictory poem 1821" in an unknown hand.

Date: The poem was delivered on "Class Day"—17 July 1821 (see *Life*, p. 84). Edward Emerson first recorded the tradition that no fewer than seven students had declined the honor of serving as class poet before Emerson accepted (*Emerson in Concord*, p. 27). The poem incorporates verses written as early as 6 October 1820 (see endnote).

Analysis.

Introduction. Meeting of the *destinies*, three centuries ago, to prepare the discovery, & prophesy the greatness of America; landing of Columbus, & further introduction of Europeans into America. Song of the destinies, foretelling America to be an Asylum, after the corruption of the rest of the earth. The near fulfilment of such a prophecy, suggested, under the auspices of the rising generation. Immediate allusions to the Occasion; Personifications of the objects of pursuit, as, Honour, &c. The ancients found them in the stars, and hence, "Judicial Astrology." Our expectations in life, as Scholars; our prospects as Americans. Notices to fellow students, to Government, &c. College recollections; Conclusion.

R. Waldo Emerson
Hollis, No. 9.

Valedictory Poem.

Gambol and song and jubilee are done,
Life's motley pilgrimage must be begun;—
Another scene is crowding on the last,—
Perhaps a darkened picture of the past;
5 And we, who leave Youth's fairy vales behind,
Where Joy hath hailed us on the summer wind,
Would fain, with fond delay, prolong the hour,
Which sternly strikes at Friendship's golden power.
Then chide us not, though idly we may strew

10 Some blooming chaplets in the way we view.
    We cannot weep—while Hope is dancing nigh,—
    We may not smile at Sorrow's withering eye.
    On Youth's last threshold, while we doubtful stand,
    What crowded scenes of various hues expand,—
15 A thousand fears the fields of Time deform,
    Hope's gilded rainbows resting on the storm.

        Oh long ago, while Freedom yet was young,
    Her wreaths ungathered, and her praise unsung,
    While Europe languished in barbaric night,
20 And young Columbus kindled life and light,—
    Fate's finger pointed to the brooding cloud
    Which wrapped a new world in its ponderous shroud.
    On three full ages has the seal been set
    Since, o'er this land, Fate's awful Angels met;—
25 This land,—the scene of glory unrevealed,
    Pregnant with powers her Genius woke to wield.
    Here stood those Angels, on our mountain strand,
    And looked through Time, and waved their charmed wand,
    Hailed the full hour when God proclaims its birth,
30 A new and blissful paradise on earth.
    Thrice oer the clime they flapped their dusky wings,
    To lodge rich virtues in its secret springs,
    And ere its gale and mortal banner furled,
    Charm bound its shores, the asylum of the World.
35 Then bade the breezes waft Columbus on,
    To ⟨d⟩crown the triumph which the hero won.
    Columbus comes;—far *land* bedims the sky,
    And rapture kindled in his eagle eye.
    With awe struck soul, the trembling sailor feels
40 What man dishonoured, & what God reveals;
    Found the first Eden's pomp of hills and woods,
    Lost in vast Ocean's watery solitudes.
    Like that rare bird the enamoured Ethiop praised
    Whose peerless beauty all unworshipped blazed,
45 Gift of the Sun, his golden plumage shone,
    In Afric's boundless solitudes,—alone.

Back to the crowded multitudes of men,
Swelled with glad tidings, came the sail again;
Europe's loud welcome bade the wanderers hail,
50 Delighted Wonder listened to their tale.
The eyes of men were fastened on the scene,
Whose distant beauty charmed with light serene.
Adventurous hosts, from Europe's tower-crowned shore,
Claimed boundless realms unvisited before;
55 But 'mid the shouts of rushing nations,—came,
And louder than the trumpet voice of fame,
Prophetic sounds, in solemn murmur heard,
The oracles of Fate breathed out the thrilling word.

—'When dying Europe mourns her lost renown,
60 'Her wasted honour, and her broken crown;
'When Vice and Ruin rend the earth with sin,
'And pour the deluge of destruction in,
'Corruption scorches with his tainted breath,
'And hundred-handed Havoc rides on death;—
65 'Be thou—fair land! their refuge, and their stay,
'The pillared gate to Glory's narrow way.
The sound had ceased, the unearthly host retired
Dark in the North,—and men, with awe, admired.

Time rolls away, but Nature stands the same;
70 Her starry host, her mountain wrapped in flame,
Earth, air, and heaven, which smiled benignant then
On those far travellers from the haunts of men,
With equal lustre now look calmly on
This youthful band,—this goal which they have won;
75 Perhaps bear with them, in their counsels high,
The *near* fulfilment of old prophecy;
And *we*, perchance, may claim with joy to be
The Ministers of Fate, the priests of Destiny.

Here, in the halls of Fate, we proudly stand,
80 Youth's holy fires by Hope's broad pinion fanned;
And while we wait what Destiny betides,
Gaze on the forms which fairy Fancy guides;
Bright apparitions floating on the air,
Which soft approaching claim a guardian care.

85   Shall I see *FORTUNE* wave her silken robe,
      Or strong *AMBITION* comprehend the globe?
      Shall warbling *MUSES* steal the soul away
      To the rich stores of legendary lay?
      Shall *HONOUR* trace the heraldry of Fame,
90   Or *BEAUTY* come, as Cleopatra came?—
      —Not to dull sense shall forms like these appear,
      But conscious feeling finds them hovering near.
      These are the living principles, which weave
      Lifes treacherous web, to flatter and decieve;
95   Through every age, they lead the lot of life,
      And grasp the Urn with human fortunes rife
      The early minstrel, when his kindling eye
      Marked the bright stars illuminate the sky,
      Saw these wild phantoms, in those planets, roll
100   The tides of fortune to their fearful goal.
      There, robed in light, the Genii of the stars
      Launch, in refulgent space, their ⟨shining⟩ ↑ diamond ↓ cars;
      Or, in pavilions of celestial pride,
      Serene above all influence beside,
105   Vent the bold joy, which swells the glorious soul,
      Rich with the rapture of secure controul.
      They read the silent mysteries of fate,
      The slow revealings of the future state;
      Trace the colossal shades of coming time,
110   Pregnant with unknown prodigies of crime,
      While passing on, to ill-omened birth,
      Low in the hapless atmosphere of earth.
      —These were proud visions, and though part were feigned,
      Enough of Truth's sweet union remained.

115   *We* may not stoop dull folly's round to creep,
      And we must climb *Ambitions* rugged steep;
      What though the toil should vex the soul with pain,—
      Beyond its woes, there is a crown to gain.
      We look for days of joy, and groves of peace,
120   Where all the turmoils of ambition cease;
      We love that garland, which the scholar wears,
      Who wreaths new blossoms with successive years,
      Crouched in his cot, amid romantic bowers,
      Domestic visions wing the happy hours,

125   When mellow eve shall paint the saffron sky,
       And light the star of Hesperus on high,
       Hush the wild warble of the lonely grove,
       And charm the hamlet with the tales of love,
       Then, the glad sire shall gather round his door,
130   His ruddy boys, to list his fairy lore;
       By every soothing spell to Nature known
       She courts him willing to her sylvan throne;
       While, oer his sense, her bright enchantment steals,
       Enamoured Memory all her stores reveals;
135   The star oft seen in youth's rejoicing prime
       Rolls back his soul along the tides of time;
       Recalls the spring-time of his health and pride,
       His gay companions bounding at his side;
       The reckless shout which shook the college hall,—
140   The classic lesson potent to appal,—
       The gorgeous dreams which ardent fancy wove
       To gild the blushing morning of his love;—
       All these shall rise for Memory's brilliant theme,
       And float in beauty, like an angel's dream.
145   The old man's fearless gaze salutes the sky,
       Ere savage death hath shut his glazing eye.
       When the grave closed oer Athens' laurelled son,
       The fair-haired Muses wept in Helicon;
       Be our's that tear,—fair Nature's holiest gem,
150   That song, for aye, shall be our requiem.

       But let not eager fancy roam so far,
       Whose tale should now remind us what we are.
       In this bright age, with seeds of glory sown,
       The hand of fate hath placed us,—not our own.
155   When the old world is crumbling with decay,
       And empires unregarded, pass away,
       When the world's days of infancy are told,
       And Nature's crowded destinies unfold,
       Perhaps tis our's—when strength and grandeur fail,
160   And pride and power confess that man is frail,
       When vanquished Virtue's reign is fully past,
       And stern Corruption climbs the throne at last,
       And men kneel down beneath that wasting sway,—
       Perhaps tis our's to rend the veil away;

165   To bid men see their honour, and their bliss,
        The proud connection of that world and this;
        To shew the triumphs of a loftier scene,
        Than on this humble ball hath ever been,
        Ourselves, heavens honoured instruments prepared,
170   Whose little band even savage Death has spared.

        Let not the censure of presumption blot
        The venial boldness of aspiring thought;
        For proudest deeds, the lowliest means are made,
        Where the dark schemes of Providence are laid,
175   So when, of old, to strike a lawless sway,
        The arm of Nemesis was shrined in clay,
        When the black host of earthborn giants strove
        To rend Olympus from the might of Jove,
        When Terror reddened on the Almighty's cheek,
180   And even Jove's thunders whispered they were weak,
        Then was the might, which blessed high heaven with peace,
        Found in the arm of youthful Hercules;
        So heaven may bid this young unhonoured land
        Lead the long changes which mankind demand.

185   I seek no pardon if my wayward lays
        Flow too profusely with my country's praise;
        Shall a vain taunt proscribe my love of home,
        Bid the heart sicken, sacred feeling roam?
        Shall paltry ridicule assail the name,
190   Which twines its honours with Columbia's fame?
        The man whose soul, with patriot ardor thrills
        To scorn the proud world from his native hills?

        But what be these but idle dreams of hope
        Which soon shall fade, and leave the blind to grope?
195   Ah! what be these, amid the night of life,
        The certain, near, inevitable strife?
        We stand on slippery paths; the Ocean's roar
        Is loud around us,—and the world, before;—
        Thousands have crossed the gulf,—but few can tell

200   Of all that countless multitude—how well.
        No glorious lustre gathers round their name,
        Or gives their virtues to the trump of Fame.
        As if men bless them with a brief renown,
        Oh think how sadly purchased was that crown,
205   How malice blights the name it would destroy,
        —Think on *Columbus chained*,—canst *thou* be crowned with joy?

        When mighty thoughts come crowding on the soul,
        And Fancy's dreams in sparkling lustre roll,
        Let not the dreamer heed her baneful charms,
210   Perfidious smiles and Folly's winning arms;
        Fancy and Hope in chill Despair shall end,
        He clasps a viper whom he thought a *friend*,
        And when he finds the rapture of renown,
        —That crown of glory is a thorny crown.

225   We meet to part; then haste, no more delay
        To bid farewell, and stretch our sail away;
        And if a kindred sympathy shall rise
        Here in the hearts, and friendships, which we prize,
        Our heartfelt wish shall gratefully respond,
220   And God will sanction this fraternal bond.
        And we shall cherish long this parting day,
        When *Beauty* smiled to cheer us on our way.
        Think not that heart, and feeling's vital glow
        Part from the little pageant which we show,—
225   No; brightly shrined in Memory's hallowed cell,
        All that we leave, and weep to leave, shall dwell.
        One debt of gratitude remains unpaid
        To those who led us through Minerva's shade;
        The thanks we offer, not by words expressed,
230   Let future years of grateful toil attest;
        Be this our pride and boast to offer here
        A freewill ⟨off⟩homage, grateful & sincere.

        There is no joy to tear ourselves away
        From scenes endeared by life's young holiday.

235 When many days have dimmed the eye with tears,
And darkening round, the sky of life appears,
How will our hearts rejoice to look behind
On these old halls, and call the past to mind.
Spots, where while studies, friends, & pleasures bless,
240 We dreamed the dreams of youthful happiness;
Or learned to venerate the guardian care
Enthroned in Learning's consecrated Chair;
Where ancient Science, with a frown severe,
Appalled the trifler, as he ventured near;
245 Here where we learned to wield the *gun* and *quill*,
Recite in sections, and in sections drill:
Here where we learned, still studious to excel
In arts and arms, to cheer, and to *rebel*;
Recall the pleasant faces which we knew,
250 Which oft put on a sombre colouring too;
The strange vicissitudes of life, which speak
In anxious paleness, on the sufferer's cheek,
Who, while cold terror shakes his frame throughout,
Asks, with a ghastly smile, 'Are the *parts* out?'

255   And many a one, whose sorrow, & whose fears,
Like Arethusa, melt himself to⟨o⟩ tears,
Short youth; disaster trembles in his eye,
An inch too *short* to join "the Company."
In whom both art & nature joined to strive
260 To reach the lofty limit,—"five feet, five';
Perchance, in Commons Hall too sparely fed,
His hopes, alas! proved higher than his head.

    Enough;—Affection may not linger here,
Repeating fond farewells, and vows sincere;
265 Impatient Time doth knit his sullen brow,
Gird up your loins for fates dread mandate now!
May Glory wait you on your proudest ways,
The wise applaud you, while the world obeys,
May Joy attend the journey which we fear,
270 And may God speed our perilous career!

Cambridge July 1821

Notes: Certain portions of this poem are related to fragmentary rough drafts published in the first volume of the *JMN*. Following are given the line numbers of the poem, the page(s) in *JMN*, vol. 1, on which the draft will be found, and, in parentheses, the date of the draft as nearly as can be determined: 1–2: 218 (1820); 45–46: 230 (1820); 101–12: 35–36 (6–12 October 1820); 119–44: 183–84 (8 May 1821); 207: 39 (24 October 1820 [prose]); and 266: 239 (April 1820). *JMN*, 1:353–57, contains a rough draft of ll. 119–20, 123–46, 101–106, 206, 175–80, 171, 147–50, and 79–106, in that order.

Analysis: The phrase "judicial astrology" occurs in a college theme of Emerson's written in October 1819 (*JMN*, 1:171). "Hollis, No. 9.": In his senior year Emerson shared this room with his brother Edward, then a freshman.

Poem: *43* "Phoenix" [Emerson's note]   *96* Cf. *JMN*, 1:320.   *170* "It is a little remarkable that there was not one death in the class during the four years, though the whole number of individuals amounted to eighty" [Emerson's note]   *242* "These lines were a salutation to the President" [Emerson's note]   *248* An allusion to the undergraduate rebellion of 1818, described in the anonymous *Rebelliad* of 1842 (see *Life*, pp. 71–72, and *JMN*, 1:244n95).   *254* I.e., commencement parts or parts in other official exhibitions. It had been Emerson's responsibility as the "President's freshman" to distribute these assignments (see *Memoir*, 1:63).   *256* "Every one acquainted with College knows that admission to the 'Harvard Washington Corps' is a matter of no slight interest" [Emerson's note]. Samuel F. Bachelder, in "'The Student in Arms'—Old Style," *Harvard Graduates' Magazine*, 29 (June 1927): 565, notes that there were "at first about eighty members, only seniors and juniors over five feet five inches in height being eligible. . . . The uniform was an ordinary black hat, blue coat, white waistcoat, white pantaloons, white gaiters, and white belt—a very dressy combination. The officers, all seniors, wore military chapeau, sashes, and sabres."

A CONSERVATIVE TRANSCENDENTALIST:
THE EARLY YEARS (1805–1835) OF FREDERIC HENRY HEDGE

Charles Wesley Grady

ONE MORNING IN JULY 1833, passersby noticed two handwritten slips of paper affixed to the doors of the First Parish Church in the center of the little country village of West Cambridge (later Arlington), some eight miles from Boston. Perhaps only the curious stopped to read them at first, but soon word of the contents attracted a small knot of villagers. Some may have chuckled as they read; others, loyal church members, may have pursed their lips and shook their heads in disapproval. This is what the two notices, virtually identical with one another, said:

> $500 Reward
> Deserted his post & strayed from West Cambridge—the Minister of the Congregational Parish. Whoever will give any account of him, & insure his final removal, and reinstate the Parish in harmony & peace, in numbers & respectability as it was before his settlement, shall receive the above reward from the Parish—West Cambridge   July 1833

The two slips of paper did not long remain on the meetinghouse doors. Someone described as "a friend of the Parish" appeared and removed them. The friend was probably Dr. Timothy Wellington, a leading parishioner, whose son George later presented the notices, along with an explanatory note, to the Arlington Historical Society. His note will serve as well as any narration to introduce the principal actors in a little village drama which was to have a marked effect upon the career of the young minister involved. He wrote:

> Rev. Thaddeus Fiske was ordained to the work of the Gospel ministry in the 2nd Parish in Cambridge afterward being the 1st Parish in West Cambridge

57

April 23d 1788 and resigned his charge May 8th 1828 on account of some ill
feeling between him and his Parish. May 20th 1829 Rev Frederic H Hedge afterward *Dr*. Hedge and a proffessor [*sic*] in Harvard College was ordained as
minister over this first Congregational Parish. Rev Dr Fiske took umbrage at
this and never attended public worship during the time Dr Hedge was the pastor of the Church, which charge he resigned March 9th 1835. The attached notice during a temporary absence of Dr. Hedge, was one morning attached to the
front door of the church by Dr Fiske, but was taken off by a friend of the Parish
and has been preserved by myself ⟨for⟩ after many years

Was the elder minister, retired after forty years of service to the parish,
really the author of what would seem to us today a venomous jab at his young
successor? There is little doubt that he was, for in addition to George Y.
Wellington's testimony, the handwriting on the notices is markedly similar to
known specimens of Dr. Fiske's hand from the same period, also preserved
in the archives of the Arlington Historical Society. How and why the attack
occurred, and the consequences that flowed from the situation it mirrored,
form not only an interesting glimpse into small-town parish life of the period, but also a look at the unique experience of a Boston-area congreation in
painful transition from the faith of the founding Puritan fathers to a liberal,
Unitarian Christianity. More than that, we shall pick up some of the homely
details of the difficult first years of a brilliant young clergyman's ministry—
an experience that undoubtedly altered the course of that ministry, and that
also affected, incalculably, the development of New England Transcendentalism. For as it later turned out, the minister in question was not just another obscure village parson. Frederic Henry Hedge was a friend and confi-
dant of many of the leading Transcendentalists—Ralph Waldo Emerson,
Bronson Alcott, Theodore Parker, George Ripley, Margaret Fuller, and others. He was in on the ground floor, so to speak, when the movement began.
It was Hedge's pen that fashioned the bold and arrogant defense of Coleridge which, appearing in the *Christian Examiner* for March 1833 (just a
few months prior to Dr. Fiske's reward notice), sounded the trumpet call to
battle for the youthful rebels later known as "apostles of the Newness" and
a variety of other, not-so-complimentary names. As Perry Miller put it,
"The article marks the point at which Transcendentalism went over to the
offensive."[1]

Three years later, it was primarily at Hedge's instigation that an informal
band of fellow-spirits began meeting in each other's homes to discuss the
new ideas, and the Transcendental Club was born. Actually, they sometimes
called it "the Hedge Club," for by then he was living in Bangor, off in the
Maine wilderness, and his occasional visits to Boston were the signal for the
group to gather. So long as the group met, he was an important and valued
member, although by 1840 serious differences developed between Hedge

and some of the more radical members—Emerson, Ripley, and Parker. Yet he remained a respected friend of all of them; there was no one in the Club who knew so well the German literature and Idealistic philosophical writings that were a major source of the Transcendentalists' thought—not even Parker.

As an early, influential member of the Transcendentalist circle, Hedge is important in American literary and intellectual history. But he is noteworthy in other ways too. A theological and ecclesiastical conservative, he was an institutionalist, a traditionalist, and very much a churchman. This alone would set him off from most of his fellow-Transcendentalists. During the latter part of his long life (he died in 1890 at the age of eighty-five) he was one of his church's elder statesmen—"the Unitarian doyen of his age."[2] In a stream of articles, sermons, addresses, and books, he espoused a liberal, practicing Christianity that prefigured the social gospel of the early twentieth century. He envisioned a truly catholic, universal Christian Church based only on belief in the leadership of Christ, tolerant of creedal diversity, *federally* united with Jesus as its head. He may have been the first writer to use the term *ecumenical* in its present meaning,[3] and in his eloquent pleading for a Broad Church of all humanity, he was clearly a forerunner of the modern ecumenical movement.

In still a third area he appears to have been a generation or two ahead of his time. He was an historic evolutionist, describing all of history, even Christianity itself, as a progressive unfolding, a process of ontological development. In an early article on "Progress" written in the 1830s he began enunciating his version of early "process" thought, and in other ways applied creative evolution to the idea of God Himself. In a letter of that period addressed to him by Emerson's redoubtable theology-reading aunt, Mary Moody Emerson, she demands "nothing less than your reasons for believing that the Deity is progressive"[4] Hedge's own self-description seems to have been a fair one: ecclesiastically conservative, but intellectually radical.

As a denominational leader he edited the semi-official monthly the *Christian Examiner* from 1857 to 1861, and served in the largely ceremonial yet influential position of president of the American Unitarian Association from 1859 to 1862. After West Cambridge and Bangor, he went to Providence in 1850 to serve the Westminster Congregational Society (Unitarian) there, then in 1856 came to Boston at last, to fill the pulpit once held by his late father-in-law, Dr. John Pierce, in Brookline, until 1872. From the 1850s on, Hedge's contributions to his denomination became considerable: "Hedge's writing, which appeared in prodigious numbers in this later period, (after 1850) were important in providing a rationale for the work of denominational organization that was being led in the post-war period by Henry W. Bellows; and his *Reason In Religion* (1865) was a particularly influential statement of the Broad Church objectives which came to fruition under Bellows' vigorous leadership."[5] Other students of the period seem to agree. One, linking Hedge with Henry Bellows and James Freeman Clarke, feels that the three "established . . . a central tradition in American Unitarianism which is of continuing vitality and relevance."[6]

Hedge's achievements are noteworthy in yet a third field. As a distinguished scholar of German literature, his books, articles, translations, and addresses won him a solid reputation. With his strong (and singable) English version of Martin Luther's great hymn *Ein' feste Burg* (A Mighty Fortress), published in 1853, he touched the lives of most English-speaking churchgoers. As church historian, he seems to have been a successful teacher in his non-residential, part-time post (until 1872) as lecturer in ecclesiastical history at the Divinity School in Cambridge. The School awarded him a D.D. *honoris causa* in 1852; later the College bestowed an honorary LL.D. (1886). From 1872 until 1882 he occupied the chair of German language and literature at Harvard. O. W. Long's assessment may not be too extravagant: "A noted Unitarian clergyman, an inspiring leader among the Transcendentalists, he was also a creative writer, translator, teacher, and lecturer, a cosmopolitan man of learning, possessed of one of the most remarkable minds that this country has produced."[7]

If all this is so, one might well ask why his name and achievements remain so obscure. Today, his fellow Unitarian Universalists have barely heard of him, if at all. Only a few specialists know anything of him, and many seem puzzled at the gap between his qualities and his attainments; in Perry Miller's words: "Hedge was something of a puzzle to his contemporaries, as he remains to us—for with his advantages, intelligence, and talents, he ought to have made more of a mark than he did."[8] According to another recent commentator he became "the most disappointing—and among the most disappointed" of the Transcendentalist circle.[9] And again Perry Miller, on a later occasion, underscored that disappointment: "Frederic Hedge should have made a great name for himself in American intellectual history; his life conveys the impression of an unrealized talent."[10]

Most of these observers recognized that the removal to Bangor, that remote, snowbound "sentry box" as Margaret Fuller called it, had something to do with Hedge's failure to realize his talent: "Hedge was a man of ripe and sound scholarship, and would have played—had he lived nearer to Boston, and had his nature been a little more aggressive—a far more prominent part than he did in the movement. As it is, he must be reckoned one of the earliest and most influential of transcendentalists."[11] Others, no doubt with his later service to liberal Christian churchmanship in mind, felt it was the other way round; Hedge had a greater cause to serve than to lead a vague, misty, literary-philosophical revolt: "It was no doubt fortunate for Frederick [*sic*] Hedge that a call to the Unitarian pastorate in Bangor, Maine, in 1835, made him 'quit the high chair' of fervid, futile Cambridge and Boston talk, and settle down to his professional duties, which were always solidly performed."[12] It may be too much to accuse Hedge of a lack of aggressiveness, for he could be boldly insurrectionary when he felt it was warranted. But he could be icily disdainful in the presence of cant and iconoclastic bombast. The son of a Harvard logician, he inherited a keen critical sense for illogic, a love for balanced argument, and a respect for tradition—traits which kept him plodding along a less mercurial path than did some of his more "inspired" contemporaries. Nevertheless, it seems more than likely that the retreat from West Cambridge to Bangor had a profound effect on Hedge's career, whether we view it as a disaster (as he surely did), or as a "timely removal from the hotbed of religious radicalism."[13]

Yet no historian seems to have inquired much into Hedge's reasons for going to Bangor—a move which he and his friends rightly regarded as banishment from the scene of action. His rustication became a settled fact, in spite of continued attempts to return to the Boston area. For fifteen years, Hedge was prevented not only by distance, but also by embittered feelings and his own conservative bent, from playing the part in Transcendentalist affairs that had seemed his by right.

Born in 1805, Hedge was a child of Cambridge and Harvard Yard. His father was Professor Levi Hedge, author of the famous *Logick*, a treatise that precisely drilled generations of students in systematic thinking. Frederic was a slight, blond child who early revealed an extraordinary aptitude for study—an aptitude most pleasing to his professor father. The boy's talents were rewarded with praise and an intensive program of studies, mostly at home with several tutors, including the young Harvard student George Bancroft, later the well-known historian and politician. At seven, Frederic was well along in Latin, having memorized Virgil's *Eclogues*. At ten he knew large chunks of Homer. By the age of twelve, Frederic was fully ready, academically, to enter Harvard. The professor considered him too young for such early matriculation however, and instead grasped a sudden opportunity that surely changed his son's life. Bancroft, at eighteen, was about to depart for Germany, to study at Göttingen at Harvard's expense. The elder Hedge persuaded Bancroft to take Frederic along, and to oversee his studies in one of the famous German *gymnasia*. The two youngsters sailed from Boston in late June 1818, and Frederic did not return to the parental roof in Cambridge for nearly five years.

Thus Hedge spent his formative, adolescent years away from home, in a different culture, with only letters from home and occasional visits and letters from Bancroft to relieve the strict discipline and the largely classical curriculum of the two schools he attended. He stayed with Bancroft in Göttingen for a few months for preliminary tutoring, then early in 1819 entered the *Gymnasium* at Ilfeld, about thirty miles east of Göttingen. It must have been a lonely, trying experience for the precocious thirteen-year-old, unused to classroom schooling and discipline, singled out as the only foreigner and from savage America at that. Years later he would wryly recall that his classmates initially were amazed that he appeared among them without warpaint and feathers.

More than once he seems to have rebelled, and at first progress in his studies was slow. After a confrontation with a teacher, young Frederic had to be removed from Ilfeld by his mentor, after less than two years there. Fortunately, however, he was now old enough to be enrolled at one of Germany's best schools, Schulpforta. Though his stay was brief, not much over a year, he did much better in this new environment. For one thing, he was allowed to board with a professor rather than live in a school dormitory, as at Ilfeld. By the time his father decided he should return to Cambridge, Bancroft could report that Frederic had gained tremendously in confidence and maturity. The trip back across the Atlantic, in late 1822, was accomplished on his own, Bancroft having gone back to America some months previously. It turned out to be a trip of some privation and danger; one might call it a kind of final examination in strength and fortitude, to cap his overseas education. He had left home a child and came back a young man, poised and learned at seventeen, pronounced fit to enter Harvard College with advanced standing as a junior.[14]

It was at this time that Hedge contracted a most significant and lasting friendship. Thirteen-year-old Margaret Fuller was undergoing the same sort of intensive tutoring he had received. It was unusual, to be sure, in so troubling to educate a female, but it could be excused as a fond father's whim. Even from his seventeen-year-old eminence, Hedge was attracted—not by her physical charms, for they were few, but by her brilliance, her wit, the sparkle of her conversation, her genuine hunger for learning. Evidently she found him fascinating: a college man of seemingly vast erudition, just returned from Germany with first-hand knowledge of the works of such giants as Schiller and Goethe, and the strange new idealistic philosophers. Theirs was a purely intellectual friendship, but a warm one, and it lasted virtually to her death, in 1850.

Entering the College, Hedge soon won honors, was class poet and valedictorian. He was thinking, momentarily, of becoming a poet, and also considered medicine, in the steps of his mother's father, Dr. William Kneeland (in whose comfortable Cambridge home Frederic had grown up). But his father, how forcefully we do not know, pointed his son toward the ministry instead, preferring that he emulate the other grandfather, the Reverend Lemuel Hedge. Accordingly, upon graduation with the Class of 1825, Frederic entered the Divinity School.

It was a three-year course of study. In his final year, at least two notable things occurred: he delivered an original poem, "Modern Poetry," at the anniversary celebration of the Phi Beta Kappa Society, and he became acquainted with a somewhat somber older student from Concord by the name of Ralph Waldo Emerson. Hedge emerged from the Divinity School in the Class of 1828, the faculty having attested him to be prepared to undertake the gospel ministry. He was not yet twenty-three.

To family and friends, Frederic Henry Hedge now stood on the threshold of a career in which the life of the mind was preeminent. Many of the Boston ministers and their churches, including the most prominent, were consolidating a long development out of orthodox Congregationalism into a form of rational, liberal Christianity. And like it or not, the liberals were learning to accept the name of Unitarian, hung on them by their orthodox opponents. Hedge had been a schoolboy in Germany while much of this ferment was going on. Led by the great Dr. William Ellery Channing, whose eloquent sermon "Unitarian Christianity" in 1819 had baptized both the new denomination and the ministry of Jared Sparks in Baltimore, the Boston liberals were on the move. The process had been under way for twenty years and more, as church after church, and the College in Cambridge, too, went over to a larger view of man than the Calvinists could stomach. It was "the marriage of New England Puritanism and the Enlightenment—the farthest, perhaps, that the Puritan mind could go to meet the Age of Reason."[15]

As the son of a Harvard professor, with a more than ordinarily rigorous classical education and a heady exposure to the new German Idealism, Frederic was part and parcel of an exciting new dispensation. The freshly fledged young minister was an intellectual in a land where intellectuals were few. But Harvard was nearby, with a library, a faculty, a student body. There was good talk, the play of ideas, the chance to rub against other questing minds. And Boston was nearby, which meant access to the new books from Germany, England, France; publishers, printing presses, periodicals such as the *Christian Examiner*; and pulpits like Channing's Federal Street Church, Brattle Street, First Church, and the Second Church, all supported generously by the great Boston merchants, themselves often learned men.

It was a yeasty, exciting, changing time. Westward expansion was well under way; canals, steam power, railways were fast changing the landscape, pushed by Boston-based capital. Hedge was living in what really was the Hub, if not of the Universe, at least of America—perhaps of the western hemisphere.

To one of Hedge's background and expectations, what could it have meant, to be a Unitarian minister in the neighborhood of Boston and Cambridge? There were the usual pastoral duties, to be sure—baptizing, marrying, burying, visiting the sick—but these would not loom so large here as they might in a far-off rural, isolated parish. Here, the ministry meant time for study and reflection; for reading, authorship, publishing; for scholarship polished by contact with other men of culture and large affairs. It meant access to metropolitan pulpits from which one delivered thoughtful, scholarly sermons, often reported in the newspapers as events of major public interest and later to be collected and published as a book. It meant the possibility of intellectual and moral leadership upon a rather large stage. It could mean, some day, appointment to the Harvard faculty, or even the faculty of the Divinity School.

Just how much young Hedge thought about these things we do not know, of course, but they must have been in his thoughts to some extent. Cambridge, Harvard, and Boston were his milieu. Study, discussion, and scholarly pursuits were the things he loved most, the things he did best. He was not a man of action.[16] Physically, he was small of stature; Carlyle later called him "one of the sturdiest little fellows I have come across for many a day,"[17] but he was often reported in poor health during the Bangor years.

Everything suggests that Hedge looked forward, at the completion of his theological studies, to a quiet life not too far from Cambridge, a life of scholarship, preaching, and teaching. And conveniently, providentially it must have seemed, it happened that the pulpit of the First Parish in West Cambridge—a village only four miles out the Concord-Lexington Pike from Harvard Yard—was open.

I. THE WEST CAMBRIDGE STORY

It was a young church, by New England standards. The farmers around the little village of Menotomy (the Indian name means "swift-running water") found it a chore to get to the Cambridge meetinghouse, especially in wintertime. They were far up in the northwest corner of the Town, not far from the Lexington boundary. They wanted a church of their own, and after several petitions to the Great and General Court, they got their wish in 1732, being set off as the Northwesterly Precinct in Cambridge, with the right to maintain their own minister and meetinghouse. The meetinghouse came first, a small one, in 1734, but it was several more years before a minister could be found who would settle there. At length Samuel Cooke accepted their call, being ordained and settled in 1739. A man of character and real attainments, he served them with distinction for nearly forty-four years. He was an ardent patriot, encouraging his people both with tongue and pen in the Revolutionary years. When battle swirled round his meetinghouse on the Concord-Lexington road on the memorable 19th of April 1775, he was only with difficulty removed, in a chaise, by his son, from the scene of action as the British regulars retreated.

Parson Cooke died in 1783, aged seventy-five. The church floundered for a time. Some disaffected persons calling themselves "Anti-pedobaptists" were beginning an effort to withdraw support from the parish. A meeting of freeholders in the precinct had voted (1774) not to excuse them from paying their church taxes, but they remained obdurate.

It was four years before a successor to Parson Cooke could be found. Thaddeus Fiske was twenty-five years old and two years out of Harvard when he began to preach to the Second Congregational Church and Society in Cambridge, as the Menotomy parish was called. He was ordained the following spring, and his ministry of forty years began. In later years he wrote:

> I hesitated for some time, whether to decline or accept their invitation. The parish was very small and poor, and considerably involved in debt, . . . and were in a broken state, very much reduced in numbers and property. It was generally thought doubtful whether they would be able to support a minister, or pay the small salary they offered me . . . But it was feared by many, and so stated to me, that if I gave a negative answer, the church and society would not make any further effort to obtain a minister, and would be broken up and dissolved.[18]

In such a situation there was little for Fiske to do but buckle down with Yankee determination to transform his charge into a prosperous community. Despite the departure of the Baptists, who sued to obtain their exemption from church taxes and formed their own congregation, he was successful. First, he relinquished a portion of his tiny salary to relieve the pressure on his small flock. He largely supported himself and his family by teaching, boarding some students in his home and preparing others for college. He gave instruction in both religious and secular subjects to the daughters of his parishioners and other young women from neighboring towns. He supported the local singing school, and established a free "social library" which he maintained in his home for twenty years, personally delivering the books to borrowers throughout the town. He was a member of the Board of Overseers at Harvard College, and in 1821 Columbia College in New York awarded him an honorary degree of Doctor of Divinity.

In 1807, the "Northwesterly Precinct in Cambridge" attained status as a separate and independent Town of the Commonwealth, and the Second Parish became the First Parish in West Cambridge. At least partly due to Fiske's efforts, the village was recovering and beginning to prosper. A mechanical genius named Whittemore invented a machine to make "cards" of wool for spinning, and soon his local factory was humming, bringing in unaccustomed cash to Fiske's people. As he described it, "The appearance of the town, and the morals and habits of the people were seen to improve . . . its favorable aspect induced many individuals and families to come and settle in the place, and aid and share in its growing prosperity."[19]

The pastor, however, did not share in the new prosperity. Toward the close of his forty-year ministry, he received for several years the annual salary of $333.333, the third of a cent being carefully noted in the parish records. The figure must have been of Fiske's own devising. The parish, obviously uncomfortable, each year voted an additional $100 for the minister's "comfort and use." High-minded, ascetic, inflexible, he seems to have been a bit fond of his role as suffering servant *cum* spiritual autocrat. About 1820 he found his sway as religious teacher being challenged: some women of the parish wished to establish a Sunday School. Heretofore, religious instruction had been confined to the home, under the pastor's supervision and examination. Fiske was absolutely opposed to the innovation, and refused the use of the meetinghouse for the purpose. But the leaders, Eliza Bradshaw and Eliza Tufts, were equally determined. They gathered the children for Sunday instruction in the vestibule of the church—a purview to which the minister's rule apparently did not extend.

By the mid-1820s, Fiske's hard-won dominion was being challenged on two new theological fronts. The doctrines of universal salvation had been preached in Boston since before the Revolution. Such doctrines had been denounced by Samuel Cooke in 1783, with virtually his dying breath. Now, John Murray's followers were becoming more numerous. Universalist preachers had established congregations in Cambridge and Cambridgeport. There seems to have been a small Universalist Society in West Cambrdige in 1822, meeting to hear occasional preaching in homes or rented halls.[20] People seemed strangely eager to receive the Universalist message of hope, in place of the old doctrines of fear and damnation. Fiske faced dwindling congregations on Sunday mornings, and the Parish Committee struggled with the problem of similarly dwindling revenues.

The other challenge came from within the Standing Order itself. Harvard College and the Divinity School were producing liberal ministers, from whom emanated Arminian and non-Trinitarian views sharply divergent from the received faith of Calvinistic Puritan Congregationalism. Humanity were not depraved worms, fatally injured and condemned to everlasting punishment by the sin of Adam, but were free moral agents, able to live lives of virtue with the help of God's scripture, and capable of progressively building the Kingdom of God on earth. From his Federal Street pulpit, Channing was proclaiming a Unitarian Christianity, highlighted by the divine potentialities of the human spirit—man's "likeness to God."

In town after town all over eastern Massachusetts, Unitarian sentiments had captured the established churches. With increasing prosperity came better education and a more sophisticated view of the world, and man's place in it. As the older ministers passed away, the Harvard men who took their places brought the new ideas with them. A local example was Convers Francis, born and raised in West Cambridge and Medford, elder brother to the later famed Lydia Child. Graduated from Harvard College in 1815, he was now settled as minister in Watertown nearby, and was a persuasive exponent of the new Liberal Christianity. Among the Old Guard, few remained, notable among them Fiske of West Cambridge and Abiel Holmes, father of Oliver Wendell Holmes, at Cambridge's First Parish. Both were to feel the weight of the forces of change at about the same time.[21]

The children who had received instruction and admonition over the years from Fiske were now grown up and in the places of power in town and parish. A pastor and organizer, he had never been a powerful preacher like Samuel Cooke. Now, as he reached the age of sixty-five, his people grew increasingly restive. Finally Fiske decided to confront them with a choice. A circular letter of support, dated 10 March 1828, was prepared and copied into the Record Book (No. 1, 1732–1837):

> Whereas the Rev. Dr. Fiske has been led to conclude, by the falling off of numbers from his Church & Congregation, that his services, on account of his advanced life, dislike to his preaching, or some other cause, are no longer acceptable, and has informed the Parish Committee of his willingness to retire from his labors, on the twenty-third of April next, at the expiration of forty years of his ministry, to relinquish his Sallary and give place to a younger Pastor, who shall be more active, useful and acceptable he has expressed a wish to know, who are friendly to him, satisfied with his services, and are desirous to have him still continue and be there Minister—Therefore, we put our names to this paper, expressive of our approbation of him, our friendly regard for him as our Pastor, who has spent the vigor and strength of his better days in our service, and of our desire that he may withdraw his proposal and remain with us, as our spiritual guide and Father in the Gospel Ministry.

The letter was circulated mong the Parish, and in a few days Dr. Fiske knew the bitter truth. On 20 April he wrote the Parish Committee:

> Gentlemen—
> I received last week, the names of subscribers, who have expressed a desire to have me continue my ministerial labours. I did not expect to find any of those, whome I had considered among my most substantial friends and who professed to be so, to decline to give their unequivocal assent. As the parish is much reduced, and is small, tis important, that what remains from those, who have already signed off should be united, and tis evident that their union and numbers will be less, by my continuance any longer in the ministry. Nor can I consent, that a few friends should bear all the burden of my support, when others would join them in the choice and maintenance of another Minister . . . It is not in haste that I have come to this conclusion. It has been a subject of much anxiety, as well as of deliberate consideration. Be assured, it has not arisen from any disaffection to the people of my charge, but from this falling off from me, which I have witnessed with deep sorrow and regret . . . I am desireous that the evening of my days may be more free from toil, which I am less able to bear, and

especially that I may enjoy more peace and tranquility, than I have for twelve years past—Considering all circumstances, it has become expedient, for my health and comfort, as well as for the union, peace, and welfare of my Parish, for me to resign my pastoral office—

On May 8 the Parish Committee recommended to the Parish that the resignation be acccepted, but proposed several resolutions:

> . . . that we entertain feelings of respect and reverence, to the charactor of the Rev. Dr. Fiske for his long and laborious services in the ministry among us, and that we shall at all times cherish an affectionate remembrance of his devotedness to the great and glorious cause of his and our Lord and Master.
> Resolved. That we should deplore a dissolution of this interesting connection under any circumstances, which should interrupt the harmony and good feelings generally subsisting between us.
> Resolve, That our best wishes do accompany him in his retirement, and it is our desire to smothe the pillow of his declining years by all those marks of respect and attention which a life spent in the service of his God so richly meret.

Shortly afterwards, the parish directed the Parish Committee to settle Fiske's remaining salary, the treasurer being authorized to give him the parish's note for the amount, or to borrow the necessary sum. A committee of seven was chosen to "supply the Desk"—that is, provide for preaching, with the cost to be met by subscription. And finally, "On Motion, Voted that the Parish Committee invite Dr. Fiske and family to set in the Parish pew so long as he is a parishoner, not to exclude an other Minister when settled."[22]

The departing pastor had much to say to his people by way of farewell. A long and elaborate sermon was "prepared but never preached,"[23] entitled *The Life and Character of St. Paul A Model For Christian Ministers. A Sermon Delivered at West Cambridge, April 13, 1828, by Thaddeus Fiske, D.D., at the Close of His Ministry,* and not published until 1843, fifteen years after the event. It concludes with a firm apologia of his stewardship, a denunciation of the new doctrines, and a moving farewell to his people. Fiske lived on for another twenty–seven years following the composition of this sorrowful valedictory, dying in 1855 at ninety-three—the oldest clergyman in the Commonwealth of Massachusetts.

In the months following Fiske's resignation, several candidates undoubtedly were invited to display their sermonic wares in the West Cambridge pulpit. Evidently the parish felt that what was needed was a young, up-to-date man, for on 9 March 1829 they voted to invite Frederic Henry Hedge to settle with them as their Gospel Minister. The votes were: "yeas 46, nays 1." And, "On motion, voted to give Mr. F. H. Hedge eight $800 hundred dollars per annum as a stated salary."[24] The sum must have stirred strange feelings in the breast of the self-sacrificing Fiske, whose salary never exceeded $433 per year. The change would add considerably to the parish taxes, and should the new minister fail to bring together the three parties which were now forming, the new salary would surely widen their differences. At any rate, on 18 March the Church, the smaller and more conservative body within the larger Parish, voted to "concur with the Parish" in the choice of Hedge as West Cambridge's new pastor.

We do not know how much Hedge himself knew about the ticklish local situation, but parish leaders were aware of the problems and tried to foresee some of them. When the Parish met in April to plan the ordination and installation, they adjourned after appointing a committee "to confer with Rev. Mr. Hedge and stipulate with him." A few days later the committee reported back to the reassembled session, not special terms of settlement, as expected, but that an unwritten understanding had been reached:

> After the most mature deliberations, and after consulting persons whose opinion ought to have weight on this subject, your Committee are well satisfied that no condition can be well entered into, between this Society and the Rev. Mr. Hedge, as it regards a dissolution of the connection between them, which will not have a tendency to produce greater evils, then they are calculated to prevent; your Committee are further of opinion, that there should be a distinct understanding between the parties, that if circumstances should occur, which would render this connection no longer desirable or advisable, that it ought then to be dissolved; your Committee have conferred with the Rev. Mr. Hedge on this subject, and such an understanding does exist; they therefore consider, that it is inexpedient and unnecessary to act any further on this subject.[25]

Now the way was clear for the installation, set for Wednesday, 20 May. Preparations were elaborate, a committee with a marshal and several constables having been appointed. A council of ministers from the neighboring towns met at the local hotel, as was the custom, to examine the minister-elect and certify him fit for the sacred office. Then young Hedge and the council members were escorted ceremonially, in procession, to the meeting-house nearby, a brass band leading the way. Anthems were sung: "Now elevate the sign of Judah" and "Praise God, from whom all blessings flow." There would have been a considerable delegation of friends and relatives from Cambridge and Harvard, headed by a proud Levi Hedge. Hedge's older friend, Convers Francis from Watertown, returned to his native village to deliver the sermon on a text from Luke: "The kingdom of God cometh not from observation. Neither shall they say, Lo here, Lo there, for behold: the kingdom of God is within you."[26] Here, certainly, was a text with a Transcendentalist ring to it.

A special hymn had been written for the occasion by an unknown author, likely by one of Hedge's classmates or colleagues. It might even have been written by Hedge himself; in this year he had written (or was to write) another hymn text for a friend's ordination which has proven more durable than most such poetry. "Sovereign and Transforming Grace" still holds a place in Unitarian Universalist, and other, hymnals.[27] On this occasion, however, the congregation sang, in part:

> Lo! another offering
>   To thy courts this day we bring;
> And another laborer here,
>   To thy vineyard's service cheer;
> Welcome, fellow-laborer, thou!
>   Lord, accept thy servant's vow!
>
> In thy service he would live—
>   Life and strength to thee doth give;
> Nourish'd with immortal truth,
>   May the vigor of his youth,
> Pour'd upon thine altar, be
>   Grateful incense, Lord, to thee.
>
> Without guile and without fear,
>   May he guard thy kingdom here;
> Erring souls from error free,
>   Lead the ransom'd heart to thee;
> Quell unhallowed passion's strife,
>   Quicken languor into life.
>
> Bless *him* who this day doth give—
>   Bless *them* who this day receive;
> Guardian who dost never sleep,
>   Guard the shepherd and the sheep;
> Days of earthly pasture past—
>   Take them to thy fold at last.[28]

The Reverend Austin delivered the opening prayer, and Dr. Gray gave the prayer of ordination. For the Charge to the Minister, a particularly important person arose—Dr. John Pierce of Brookline. His daughter Lucy undoubtedly was present in one of the pews that day, for in little more than a year she and Frederic would be married. Just when the young couple met, and when they became engaged, is not certain, but family tradition has it that they may have met through Margaret Fuller.

Another probable attender was Ralph Waldo Emerson, himself but newly installed as junior minister at Second Church in Boston. Though he did not participate in the service (nor did Hedge at Emerson's installation), "Mr. Emerson's, Boston," was listed among those churches which sent representatives to the Ministerial Council and the service. Their friendship just then was in the process of ripening from casual acquaintance at the Divinity School into a close, warm relationship that, in spite of occasional coolnesses and disappointments, would last until the older man's death. Later, Hedge would be instrumental in bringing Emerson and Margaret Fuller into contact. He had already tried to get Emerson interested in studying German so as to be able to read the new lore in the original. But Emerson smilingly declined to learn the language, Hedge would later recall, saying that "as he was entirely ignorant of the subject, he should assume that it was not worth knowing."[29]

A "Mr. Ripley" spoke and extended the "Right Hand of Fellowship"; likely it was George Ripley, another special friend of Hedge's, now settled in Boston's Purchase Street Church, and still years away from the founding of Brook Farm. Charles Briggs of Lexington, later secretary to the American Unitarian Association, gave an Address to the People; and another particular friend, Caleb Stetson from Medford, just across the Mystic River, spoke the concluding prayer. Two more bursts of song, "He Shall Feed His Flock" and "Hallelujah," closed the celebration, the new minister providing the Benediction.

In this thoroughly conventional manner was Hedge's career launched. Hedge, along with Lucy Pierce and their families and friends, must surely have forecast a long, tranquil ministry at the foot of the rocky hills above Spy Pond. There would be children to brighten the pastoral hearthside, of course, and there would be scholarly interchange with the professors just down the road. He would talk long into the night with brother ministers about Coleridge and Carlyle, about Schelling, Fichte, Hegel, about Cousin, Comte, Fourier, Constant. New worlds would be discovered as the conversation flowed. Articles and books would be written and published; critical reviews would set the public straight on matters transcendental; there might well be a professorship at last. One could happily pass his life in this useful, challenging, rewarding way.

II. MINISTRY AND CONFLICT

Things certainly went well at first. On the very next Sunday, 24 May, Hedge preached his first sermon as the settled minister. For his text he took First Corinthians, 4:1—"Let a man so account of us, as of the ministers of Christ, and stewards of the mysteries of God." Though slight of stature, he made a fine impression in the pulpit, with a rich voice and the beginnings of a grand style. The villagers must have felt proud of their new pastor. With his erudite background and youthful energy, they would be as well supplied with learned and godly discourses as any fashionable Boston church. The falling off of attendance and income recently noticed under Fiske would be halted now, they could safely hope, and the parish united and strengthened.

With a more liberal preacher in the pulpit, less interested in Calvinist hellfire, surely those with Universalist leanings would come back to the fold. As for the followers still faithful to Fiske's teachings, they were few. Though devoted to the old doctrines, they would eventually come around, or die off. After all, First Parish was *First* Parish, part of the Standing Order of Congregational Churches, and really the only church in town unless you counted the Baptists, and few indeed would be inclined that way.

Yet, church finances may have seemed a bit tight when the annual Parish Meeting rolled around the next spring. Every householder in the village, unless he could show legal membership in another church, was expected to pay his assessed church tax. In special cases abatements were granted, sometimes ten per cent, sometimes five. At this Parish Meeting of March 1830, abatements were held to only six or three per cent. The treasurer, Miles Gardner, was authorized to borrow money sufficient to meet the church's debts, and a committee was appointed to negotiate with the Selectmen of the Town for the sale of the hearse, the hearsehouse, and grave-digging implements, hitherto the property of the Parish. The Meeting's final act was to abate entirely Fiske's parish tax for the preceding year.

A few months later, on 7 September, Lucy Pierce and Frederic were married. A small, quiet, pretty, blonde girl, she was three years younger than he, and the fourth daughter in her family. The ceremony, probably conducted by her father, was in the Brookline church. The following June was born Frederic Henry, Jr., their first child and only son.

They were a happy, well-matched couple. Lucy "knew the drill" necessary to keep a minister's household running smoothly. Frederic, ever the scholar, liked to spend much of his time in his study, at the College Library, in Boston bookshops, or in conversation with colleagues like Francis, Emerson, Ripley, and Stetson. Lucy filled in beautifully by handling the many social obligations and even by doing much of the calling, leaving her husband a measure of freedom for his books and writing. Even at that, his burden was considerable.

There was much to be done in the Parish. The Sunday School had languished in the face of Fiske's disapproval and had to be revived. In May 1831, Hedge helped his people organize anew the West Cambridge Sabbath School Teachers Association. He was elected to its Standing Committee, and as minister of First Parish was automatically principal of the Sabbath School itself. It was also at about this time that Hedge took the lead in organizing a lyceum program in the town—a form of education and entertainment begun in Massachusetts only a few years earlier.

Boston and its immediate environs in the early 1830s was an exciting place for a young man of words and ideas. A new intellectual, literary, and social ferment was going on; Hedge plunged into it eagerly. The older Unitarians, led by such great men as Channing, Andrews Norton, the Henry Wares (father and son), Nathaniel Frothingham, and others, had made good their escape from the shackles of Calvinist orthodoxy. Some, like Channing, were still receptive to new ideas at least to a degree; but most still clung to the absolute authority of revealed scripture, the authenticity of Christ's miracles, and the bedrock empirical philosophy of Locke and the Scottish "common sense" realists. Committed to rationalist, enlightenment thought from the eighteenth century, holding that all knowledge is acquired through the senses alone, they disliked and distrusted the new romantic, idealistic philosophy. When the young men talked with growing fervor about innate ideas and intuitive knowledge, the first generation Unitarian establishment in Boston and Harvard reacted by calling the new philosophy of the soul to be no more than mystical moonshine and German twaddle, leading to infidelity and atheism. They were especially stung by the gleeful, we-told-you-so outcries of their Calvinist opponents, who had always predicted that Arian, Socinian Unitarianism was a halfway house to perdition.

In 1832, however, much of this fight was still to come. And it fell to twenty-seven-year-old Hedge to strike some of the first blows in behalf of the transcendental philosphy. Toward the end of this year he was maturing in his mind the first of a series of five articles which, appearing in the next two years, would establish him as a major voice of the new movement. Although devoted to various topics, they would express the viewpoint of the nascent group, and prepare the way for the controversial writings of Emerson, Ripley, Orestes Brownson, and Alcott, later in the decade.

While these preparatory articles gestated in Hedge's West Cambridge study, the first signs of future trouble in the parish began to appear. As is so often the case, the problem emerged as one of financial support. Through 1831, the minister's salary had been met with fair punctuality. Suddenly there was great reluctance to pay church assessments. Parish records tell the story quite clearly. At the annual Parish Meeting of 12 March 1832 it was

> *Voted* that the 5th article, to grant money for the salary of Rev. Mr. Hedge, and contingent expenses, be defered to the next meeting . . . Voted that the Parish Assessors appoint someone to collect the taxes remaining unpaid . . . A communication having been presented to the meeting from a Committee appointed by the Universal Society of West Cambridge proposing a union of the two Societies—Voted: That the Parish Committee with the following persons be a committee, viz Saml. O. Mead, Col. Thomas Russell, James Russell Esq, and Amos Locke, to confer with said committee & with the Rev. Mr. Hedge upon the subject, and report upon that or any other matter having a bearing upon said subject. Voted to adjourn this meeting to the last Monday in April next 3 °clk pm

Parish leaders now had almost seven weeks in which to redeem the situation. They would have to pull the church together financially by persuading those in arrears to pay their taxes, and they would have to find some way of accommodating those who had left to join the Universalist Society—not to mention those still in the church who sympathized with them. No record of their negotiations has come to light, and we do not know what position Hedge took. He may have exacerbated the situation with inflexibility; he could be stubborn. He must have felt caught in a crossfire. We do know that in later life he expressed doubts of the soundness of the doctrines of universal salvation; did his doubts stem from this period? He may have felt a scholar's distaste for the Universalist preachers, relatively unschooled in theology and generally not Harvard men. Their simpler, Biblically-based, evangelical warmth may have seemed to him too much like "enthusiasm."

One clue to the outcome came a week after the 12 March meeting, when the new officers of the Parish took their formal oaths of office and for the first time the name "First *Congregational* Parish" was used. It had not seemed necessary to use the term before. They may have wished to use a term that would distinguish themselves from the Universalists. Perhaps another reason was the legal end of the Standing Order in Massachusetts, which would occur in 1834. Parish churches would be no longer part of the governmental structure of the Towns, but become independent religious societies, often with some sort of denominational term in their names.

On 30 April the Parish Meeting resumed. By then it was apparent that a significant number of parishioners leaned toward Universalism and that an even greater number, for whatever reason, were not willing or able to pay their assessments. Turning again to the postponed Article V, the parish

> Voted: that no money be granted, to be assessed for the salary (and contingent expenses) of the Rev. Mr. Hedge, but that a committee be appointed, to solicit subscriptions of members of the Parish and others for the above named purpose . . . The Chairman of the Com^te appointed at the last meeting to confer with a committee appointed by the Universal Society, upon the subject of uniting the two Societies, made a verbal report, that it was inexpedient so to do. Where upon it was *Voted*: to accept said report.

So the matter stood for the remainder of the year, both sides holding firm. No church taxes were levied or collected. Those who wished to do so, contributed to the church's support. It was a lean time in the Hedge household with no salary coming in. Some parishioners may have given the family foodstuffs and firewood, in lieu of salary. In October, Miles Gardner paid the minister $136—the only income he received in cash from the parish during 1832.

How did it happen that so large a segment of the parish had become alienated from the minister after only three years of service? Documentation is lacking; we can only speculate. A few persons still maintained the old faith with Fiske. Some others had withdrawn to form the Universalist Society, though many of them remained nominal—and voting—members of First Parish. As yet there were not enough Universalists to build a meetinghouse or hire a minister of their own. For now, they had to content themselves with hearing a visiting preacher, such as Otis Skinner, in a home or rented hall. They had boldly proposed union of their small Society with the First Parish and had been rejected. We do not know what their expectations or stipulations were. One might have been that Hedge resign in favor of a Universalist—something the Unitarians would have been bound to reject.

We can surmise that these doctrinal splits were not the whole story. Hedge himself may have contributed to his troubles. The congregation of West Cambridge farmers and shopkeepers may at times have felt hard pressed to understand the young man's more abstruse philosophic flights. In the minutes of the Sabbath School Teachers Association, we read that their meetings "had usually been favored by the reading of highly interesting and instructive dissertations on the existence and attributes of the Deity, from Rev. Mr. Hedge . . ." For some, it may have seemed that a minister educated in Germany *and* at Harvard was simply too much of a good thing.

Moreover, Hedge was neither by inclination nor talent a pastor. People in his Bangor flock remembered him as always somewhat severe and withdrawn, thawing only in familiar company. Pastoral chores may have been performed conscientiously but stiffly in those early years, leaving Lucy to provide some of the warmth he lacked. We have one measure of his attitude in this area: at the close of his West Cambridge ministry, this revealing comment was placed in the parish record by the clerk: "Mr. Hedge kept no records during his ministry; but handed over to his successor several papers from which the chasm between the dismission of Dr. Fiske and the installation of the fourth minister (Hedge's successor), has been in part filled." Except for a few scattered notations supplied by the fourth minister, there is indeed a complete gap in the record of baptisms, weddings, and funerals, between 1829 and 1835.

During this difficult time, Hedge kept busy. His first published article, on Coleridge, appeared in the *Christian Examiner* for March 1833. Emerson was delighted with it, and called it "a living leaping Logos."[30] Yet in spite of its bold defense of Coleridge and the German philosophers, and its rather arrogant assertion that those conservative critics who attack the idealists are simply deficient in understanding, the Old Guard seems not to have taken offense. His old friend and mentor at Harvard, Henry Ware, Jr., even wrote the author a note of congratulation and encouragement. To be sure, Hedge had maintained a correct and reasonable tone, presenting what must have seemed a balanced report, including some minor criticism of Coleridge. And, after all, the young man making his first appearance in print was the son of Professor Hedge of Harvard.

About the same time the article appeared, the annual Parish Meeting for

1833 was held, and it proved to be anything but routine. The Universalists turned out in force and surprised the Unitarians by electing their own parish committee of three members and the parish clerk; the vote was thirty-six to thirty-two. Once in control of the meeting, the Universalist group voted to continue to raise the minister's salary by subscription rather than assessment, which would mean, in effect, little or no salary for Hedge. Before adjourning, however, the meeting showed itself willing to pay assessments, so long as the money would not be devoted to the minister's salary, when they passed two motions permitting assessments to be levied for payment of parish debts and contingent expenses, and to repair the meetinghouse cupola.

Dismayed and angered by this turn of events, the Unitarian group saw it as an attempt to take over the parish and drive out the settled minister. They lost little time in moving to regain control. On 2 April a special meeting of the parish was called by petition "of J. Wellington and others" for the purpose of reconsidering the actions of 11 March. Both sides worked hard to get out the vote; an unprecedented turnout of over one hundred and seventy parishioners crowded into the meetinghouse. Amid considerable parliamentary maneuvering, the Unitarians were able to overturn the actions of the March meeting. The subscription method was thrown out and the minister's salary once again was to be raised by assessment. This time the vote was ninety to eighty-one.

Although back in charge, the Unitarian party was still uneasy. Another takeover attempt might come at any time; some protective measures seemed in order. The Sabbath School Teachers met in an extraordinary session, this time at the Hedges' home, on 13 April. The secretary recorded "a very full and punctual attendance of the immediate members" of the Association "in order to transact business of importance." New officers were elected, with Hedge being returned to the Standing Committee, an office he had not held for some time.

> Then came the *"business of importance"*—viz. The alteration and amendment of the Constitution of this Association in such a manner that the Library and other property of the Sunday School should not be at the disposal of the "First parish in West Cambridge," which, in the fluctuation of party, might become the title of any *sect*, having the power and will to assume it, and to secure them to the Unitarian Society, to whom they had always belonged. To do this effectually, it was unanimously
>
> Resolved—that the Sunday School now connected with the "First Parish in West Cambridge" (as implied by the Constitution of this Association) be hereafter considered entirely independent of said Parish.
>
> Resolved—That the said School be hereafter called the "West Cambridge Unitarian Sabbath School." [31]

The group also deleted that part of their Constitution which automatically made the minister of the First Parish the principal of the School.

This accomplished, the unhappy young minister must have turned his thoughts to leaving West Cambridge. It was by now apparent that those circumstances mentioned by the special committee almost four years ago, "which would render this connection no longer desirable or advisable," had occurred. Though his friends were sure to be on the lookout for a place for him, no pulpit in the Boston area seemed to be immediately available, though of course one might open up at any time. Opportunities further afield were more numerous. The Independent Congregational Society in Bangor, Maine, for instance, had long been seeking a replacement for their ailing minister. They seem to have approached Hedge sometime in the spring of 1833, using the Cambridge minister, John Gorham Palfrey, as their intermediary. Hedge's reply to Palfrey, dated 16 June 1833, seems worth quoting here in full:

> Dear Sir, I have attended to the subject of the letter you were so good as to forward me. I feel greatly obliged to you for the favour you have shown me in this matter. But after due consideration of the proposal which that letter contains, I feel that, in the present state of my affairs, I ought not to accept it.
>
> As I shall probably resign my present situation in the autumn, I think it proper not to be absent for any length of time while I stay. Perhaps you will ask why, if it is my intention to leave at all, I do not leave now. I proposed to do so last May, but after consulting with some of our leading men, it was concluded on both sides that the Unitarian party would be endangered by my leaving at present, as the money now assessed and about to be collected, if not appropriated to *my* support, would be likely to go into the hands of the Universalists. Meanwhile circumstances may occur which will make it desirable for me to remain where I am, or point out a better or happier sphere of action. At all events, while connected with this parish, I am unwilling to take so decisive a step as that implied in the communication from Bangor—a step which once being taken, it may be impossible to retrace. I call it a decisive step because it appears to me that the person who should go there ought and would be expected to go with the intention of remaining. Besides all this, I will not conceal from you that the situation proposed is not the sphere in which I think I could be most useful or happy. Perhaps I am mistaken in supposing that I shall ever find that sphere. Time must decide. At my time of life I can better afford to wait a year or two years, than by one rash cast to sacrifice the most cherished hopes of my heart to what I cannot consider the call of duty. On this point I may have an opportunity of explaining myself more fully at some personal interview. Meanwhile I remain yours most respectfully, Frederick H. Hedge[32]

Here we have an excellent first-hand glimpse into the young minister's mind during this painful time, depicting his own perception of the situation.

It makes explicit his feeling that Bangor is a less-than-attractive prospect, and shows he harbored hopes for something better. Since there were apparently no area pulpits available to him, what sort of hopes could they have been? A letter to his close friend Margaret Fuller a few days after the Palfrey letter affords a clue: "perhaps you will be pleased to hear that I have been talked of as successor to my Father. O! that this thing might have come to pass, long before my Father resigned it was a favourite dream – but alas! *Nicht alle Blüthenträume reifen.*"[33] The budding dream indeed did not flower; not until many years later did the dreamed-of Harvard appointment at last materialize.

In the same letter to "Dear Margarett," Hedge mentioned another dream, to be realized a few years later with the establishment of the famed "Hedge Club": an early proposal that they gather with friends for writing and discussion. "I wish such a society might be formed, small, select, and harmonious, each member should contribute to the common fund something—no matter whether it were grave or trifling—but something purely his own."[34]

Hedge's prediction to Palfrey that he would probably be gone from West Cambridge by fall proved premature; it would be nearly two years before he was finally able to leave. Meanwhile, he did not cease to search for another pulpit, preaching elsewhere whenever opportunity offered. It must have been during one of these expeditions that Fiske saw fit to intervene in the troubled affairs of First Parish by composing and posting the "$500 Reward" notices. Had not their doctrinal differences been so marked, Fiske might have been expected to feel a kindly sympathy for the younger man, who was going through an even worse trial than Fiske had faced. But the bitter feeling of being supplanted by one little better than a heretic won out in the old pastor's heart.

While the village gossiped and speculated on what might happen next, Hedge somehow carried on his scholarly pursuits. They must have seemed a welcome relief from parish affairs. In November his second *Examiner* article appeared, a long, thoughtful piece on Swedenborg. The Swedish mystic was then interesting many Unitarians, and Hedge's study was well received. James Freeman Clarke, who had just graduated that year from the Divinity School and gone out to Kentucky, was enthusiastic. Writing from Louisville, Clarke found it "full of ideas which do the heart good . . . so *liberal* in the true sense—a liberality springing from insight—a liberality which casts aside the letter & grasps the spirit." Clarke was especially concerned to assure his friend that his writings were appreciated:

> It is not a pleasant thing to cast bread upon the waters, but I think you may do so in the full persuasion that not many days are now to pass before you will find it again. The dominant philosophy yet shuts the mouths of those who would gladly speak from a full heart the benefit they receive from such writings as

yours. It possesses the press in all its varied operations—the debating club—the school—the college—the professor's chair—all are obliged to submit to its despotism. No tongue is allowed to speak against it—but this will not be long. The wheel of opinion rolls on as surely as that of time, & everywhere I now meet with spiritually minded men. I hope therefore you will continue to publish & in due season you will reap.[35]

Hedge was already taking Clarke's advice; three more articles were published in the *Examiner* in 1834. In March it was "The Progress of Society," which began as a brief review of Edward Everett's Phi Beta Kappa address on that topic, then launched into an exposition of Hedge's own view of progress. The July issue contained his lengthy review of Carlyle's *Life of Schiller*, which again went far beyond a review into Hedge's own in-depth appraisal of the German dramatist-poet. Here his German schooldays stood him in good stead; he was able to include his own translations of passages from some of Schiller's works.

The last of the five early articles appeared in November. Phrenology, an obsolete pseudo-science, was then exciting great interest and controversy. The *Examiner*'s editors wanted a careful critique, and gave Hedge the assignment. An earlier writer had bungled the job, in their view, by giving phrenology a qualified seal of approval. Hedge, on the other hand, after a searching examination, found the new science wanting in several particulars, and dismissed it as a form of materialism. His condemnation had its lighter side; speaking of the sudden popularity in Boston parlors of character-reading through skull-rubbing, he drily observed:

> No sooner had its late distinguished apostle appeared in our city, than a *pentecost* was witnessed, such as philosophy has not known before, since the days of the later Platonists . . . Heads of chalk, inscribed with mystic numbers, disfigured every mantelpiece. Converts multiplied on every side, some proselytes of the covenant, some proselytes of the gate. A general inspection and registry of heads took place. In defiance of the apostolic injunction, hands were laid suddenly on all men, and many by such imposition were ordained teachers.[36]

Also in the November *Examiner* was a review of an occasional sermon Hedge had preached in June before Boston's Ancient and Honorable Artillery Company. It was his first published sermon, dealing with no less a theme than humanity's struggle to supplant its warlike proclivities with the ways of peace. The reviewer of the printed sermon praised it warmly and quoted large sections from it. Such extensive publication surely must have enhanced greatly the young minister's reputation, but by this time he and his friends knew he was about to accept a call to the same Bangor pulpit he had rejected more than a year earlier.

Much had happened that year besides the printing of articles and sermons. At the annual parish meeting in March the Unitarians were back in control. After a year's interval, familiar Unitarian faces were seen on the parish committee and the clerkship. Universalist voting strength may have diminished as more and more withdrew to join the West Cambridge Universalist Society. A decisive action was taken when the meeting reached the seventh warrant article: "On Motion Voted . . . not to employ any Minister or Ministers Called Universalist to Preach in said Congregational Meeting House in West Cambrdige—"[37] And the clerk wrote it out in an especially large, plain, heavy hand, as if to make certain the content would be understood. The matter of the minister's salary, however, continued to cause concern. In response to the near takeover of the preceding spring, collection of church assessments went well; Hedge received most of his salary in bits and pieces—in all, $765. But now, at the start of a new year, the meeting went back to the voluntary method: his salary would be raised, they hoped, through subscription alone. The Universalists appear to have made their point. This discussion preceded by a few days the birth on 21 March 1834 of the Hedges' second child, a girl, who was christened Charlotte Augusta.

Hedge had told Palfrey he hoped to be gone from West Cambridge by the fall of 1833, yet here he still was, preaching to a weakened congregation, working on his articles, talking to friends about establishing a congenial circle for both discussion and publishing, and looking for a new place. His friends were helping in that search, but so far nothing much had turned up—at least not in the immediate area. Then came in mid-July a letter from Emerson, writing from Bangor, that far-off lumber-town in Maine, whence had come overtures more than a year ago.

Emerson had resigned his charge at the Second Church in Boston two years earlier, had gone to Europe, met Carlyle, and was back, preaching here and there to support himself, and writing. Controversy and fame were still a few years away. Relations between the two men had continued to be cordial since their 1829 ordinations/installations. They had exchanged pulpits occasionally,[38] and when Hedge's *Examiner* articles began to appear, Emerson was delighted to make common cause with him. Now he was in a position to do a friend a favor. After a few days in Bangor, where he was to preach for four Sundays in July, Emerson wrote: "they are very anxious to have a minister of ability settled here & have got beyond the period when a violent Unitarian is wanted. They say that if they can find a man who satisfies the people, there will be no difficulty in giving him an ample support. They gave Mr. Huntoon $1000. But if they found the man they seek they could with equal ease give from $1500 to 2000." Bangor was a wonderful place, said Emerson:

> a great town of 7000 inhabitants which may in a year increase to ten thousand, so fast it grows. It subsists by the lumber trade which brings all the timber from

a vast territory through a hundred lakes and small streams down the Penobscot River . . . I am almost persuaded to sit down on the banks of the pleasant stream & if I could only persuade a small number of persons to join my colony we would have a settlement 30 miles up the river, at once.[39]

Thus encouraged, Hedge agreed to go to Bangor, at least to look the situation over. Sometime in the fall he made the journey to the boom town on the Penobscot. The overland trip took several days in a jolting mail coach; reliable packet service by sea was not yet available. It may have been on the way to or from Bangor in this autumn of 1834 that the thoughtful, troubled young minister composed his best-known poem, "Questionings," published some years later in the *Dial*.[40] These epistemological musings expressed some of the basic Transcendentalist concerns, and upon publication in 1841 they were, in Perry Miller's words, "highly prized by all the fellowship."[41]

The Bangor visit went well. It was a prosperous congregation, full of businessmen, lawyers, and other professional persons. There was perhaps more education and sophistication than Hedge had expected, certainly more than West Cambridge could have boasted. The prospective salary—$1,500 per annum—was quite attractive, compared with the uncertain pay at home. (During his final three years at West Cambridge, Hedge actually received an average of $578 per year.)

Bangor was, to be sure, an isolated spot—especially during the long, cold winters. He would be cut off from his friends except for occasional visits to Boston. However a twice-weekly packet boat service would begin soon, cutting the travel time to only twenty-four hours—if the ice were out of the river and the winds favorable. And perhaps hardest of all, he would have to give up his long-cherished plan for starting a Transcendentalist journal. If he had learned anything from his West Cambridge experience, it was that he would have to buckle down and work harder at being a good pastor as well as a stimulating preacher and scholar. No doubt he would lose much by accepting Bangor's call, but what choice was there? Even his warmest supporters in West Cambridge agreed he ought not remain in the divided, weakened parish. And for the time being, no suitable openings existed near Boston.

The Bangor congregation liked what they heard. After a few Sundays of preaching, they were agreed on calling him at once. Hedge, however, asked for time. It may well be that he still had hopes of something turning up at home, as, indeed, something did. With Bangor, then, he struck a bargain: they would wait till next spring to extend a formal call, and he would resign from West Cambridge at about the same time. Nevertheless he obviously considered his options open. By mid-November he was back in West Cambridge and confiding to Margaret Fuller, "I shall not go to Bangor till spring if I go at all."[42]

That dismal winter, with the Bangor move looming ahead, at least one new opportunity presented itself—nothing less than the editorship of the *Examiner*. We learn of the offer and the doubts it occasioned in another letter to Fuller; he is pondering

> whether to settle in Bangor on a competent living or to stay here & take the editorship of the Christian Examiner which has lately been offered me—on terms which together with the profits of occasional preaching would afford me but a doubtful support. I cannot tell you what perplexity & distraction of mind, what anxious doubts & vexatious questionings this subject has cost me . . . My tastes & wishes incline strongly to the editorship coupled as it is with a residence in this vicinity but can I live by this means? 500 $ according to my best calculation—if health & time will permit me to write a hundred pages per year—the Examiner will yield me. My preaching if I can get the permanent supply of some pulpit in this neighborhood may bring 500 more if not perhaps as little as 300 or even less. And then too if I should not succeed in this business & should be forced to abandon it an offer of settlement such as seldom occurs will have gone by & I shall be thrown anew upon the world to struggle with want and care.[43]

A month later he seemed no nearer a decision, still abominating both alternatives, still hoping for a good nearby settlement, and still clinging, unrealistically, to the idea of a brave new journal.

> My decision on the Bangor question is not yet made up, & the expediency of becoming editor of the Examiner is still a moot point with me. In fact it is only a choice between two evils. It would be impossible for me to make the Christ. Ex. what I wish. It is subject to the management of a commmittee whose control would be very unpleasant. And as for going to Bangor it is like cutting oneself off from all hold upon civilization & all chances of happiness. I am heartily sick of the whole business & only wish I had a good parish in this vicinity.

Then, without a break, Hedge turns to happier matters.

> Mr. Geo Ripley & myself are intending to establish a periodical of an entirely different character from any now existing—a journal of spirit, not philosophy, in which we are to enlist all the Germano-philosophico-literary talent in the country. If you can give us anything transcendental either in the way of critique or essay we should be glad of it. This of course is not a scheme of profit but a missionary enterprise of pure benevolence undertaken for the sole purpose of instructing our generation & converting the heathen of this land . . . it is our desire & strong hope to introduce new elements of thought & to give a new impulse to the mental action of our country. Many persons not unknown to you are included in our list of contributors—with some we have already consulted & the rest we have no doubt of interesting. R. W. Emerson, Dr. Follen, C. S. Henry, R. Dana, Pres. Marsh, W. H. Furness, James Clarke, Thos Carlyle &c &c &c. We expect to begin by the 1st January 1836, to publish yearly about half

as much as the Ch-n Exam. at half the price. When our plan is more mature I will give you further information. With the same view I think also of republishing Carlyle's Sartor resartus & that soon.[44]

It all came to naught at last, at least so far as Hedge was concerned. Little wonder that the disappointed editor seemed loth to contribute much when his friends Margaret and Waldo attempted to realize his dream in the *Dial*, a few years later.

By sharing his doubts with Fuller, Hedge may have been helped to make up his mind. Six days after writing her he directed this communication to the First Church and Society in West Cambridge:

> My Christian friends & brethren
>
> The time has arrived when it seems expedient that the Connexion which has hitherto Subsisted between us should be dissolved. I pray therefore that you would release me from the Pastoral charge which I now hold among you. It is not necessary that I should explain the reasons which have induced me to make this request. You will not, I am sure, ascribe it to any failure in my regard for you, but believe me when I say that I am influenced by a regard for your wants and welfare not less than for my own & that wherever I may hereafter be called I should never cease to feel a lively interest in your prosperity.
>
> With many kind wishes & prayers for your well being & advancement in Christian knowledge and excellence, I am
>
> your affectionate Pastor
> & Brother in Christ
> Frederic H. Hedge

The parish committee were prepared to handle the matter smoothly and quickly. The parish met 9 March, appointed the parish committee to consider the resignation and report. The committee promptly reported its recommendation to accept it, and proposed a laudatory resolution. The meeting just as promptly voted to accept their report and adjourned to the following Friday, four days later, at which time they voted to call the Reverend David Damon of Reading as their new minister at a salary of $650 per annum. Well prepared for the call, Damon immediately accepted, and that was that.

It is interesting to note that the meeting which accepted Hedge's resignation also felt it advisable to approve a motion "that Persons wishing to become Members Leave there [*sic*] names with the Parish Clerk Approved of and Signed by the Parish Committee." This sounds very much as if they were concerned over the possibility of a sudden accession of new members (or renewals of membership) who might seek to bring in another candidate.

Here, in part, is the parish committee's report:

your Committee after maturely considering all the Circumstances connected with this subject and particularly the present Situation of the Society recommend that the request of Mr. Hedge be granted and that his connexion with the Parish be dissolved, and they likewise recommend the adoption of the following resolutions

Resolved. that the members of this Society deeply regret that Circumstances beyond their control render it expedient that the Connexion which has existed between them and there [*sic*] Pastor should now end (and that they are to be deprived of those instructions to which they have listened with so much pleasure, and we trust not without some improvement).

Resolved. that the members of this Society fully reciprocate the kind feelings expressed by Mr. Hedge in his Communication to them; and do earnestly pray that in whatever situation he may be called to act, he may meet with all that success to which his Character and distinguished talents so justly entitle him.[45]

Hedge was now free to accept the call from Bangor, which came on 20 March. It was for a period of one year, at a salary of $1,500. This may well have been Hedge's stipulation rather than Bangor's, leaving him free to go elsewhere if things did not work out, or if a better opportunity offered. On 25 March he accepted the call "for the space of one year . . . I trust you will have patience with my imperfections."[46] In an accompanying letter to Amos Patten, the Bangor committee chairman, he asked that he be granted a two-month vacation period each year, during which he would not be responsible for the supply of the pulpit. Also he suggested that no installation service be held, since the call was to be for one year only.

Little remained to be done to wind up his West Cambridge ministry. To Damon he turned over what few scraps of memoranda he had, regarding baptisms, weddings, and funerals of the past six years. His successor would have quite a time trying to fill the gaps in the once carefully-kept parish records. Hedge's failure to keep such records is hard to explain. From what we know of his mature habits, it seems more likely to have been youthful ignorance, rather than deliberate neglect. He may have felt it was the duty of the Parish Clerk to keep the Parish records.

On 12 April Hedge preached his last sermon as the pastor of the West Cambridge Unitarians, on a text from Second Corinthians: "Finally, brethren, farewell."[47] It was not really a final sermon, as he returned several times over the years as a guest in their pulpit.

On the same day, his friend Waldo wrote him from Concord, "I grieve very much that you should leave our neighborhood."[48]

We cannot know, of course, what might have happened to Hedge—and to the Transcendentalists—if he had stayed in Boston to edit the *Examiner* until a Harvard appointment or a congenial pulpit opened up. Such speculation may be enjoyable but is certainly pointless. What we do know is that he and Lucy served out their fifteen years of Siberian exile in Bangor, relieved by visits home whenever possible, and raising a family that ultimately included a son and three daughters. He wrote and published but little until 1848, when his first book, *Prose Writers of Germany*, finally appeared. His first visit to Europe since his schooldays began in June 1847, and that summer he at last met Carlyle. There was a reunion in Rome with a much-changed Margaret Fuller. What he learned there of her unconventional private life he seems never to have mentioned, at least in public.

During the first few Bangor years Hedge weathered several storms, offering to resign at least twice, and his efforts to move elsewhere were almost continuous. Although he eventually won the respect and even the love of his Bangor parishioners, he was glad to go to Providence in 1850. The change from youthful radicalism to middle-aged respectability, while never complete, was largely accomplished. Ahead lay the Brookline pastorate, co-editorship of the *Examiner* (1857–61), presidency of the American Unitarian Association (1859–62), and the long-coveted places on the faculties of the Divinity School and Harvard College. By the time of his death in 1890 at the age of nearly eighty-five, he was, beyond a doubt, one of Unitarianism's grand old men.

NOTES

1. *The Transcendentalists: An Anthology*, ed. Perry Miller (Cambridge: Harvard University Press, 1950), p. 67.

2. The characterization is in H. M. Stokes, "Henry W. Bellows' Vision of the Christian Church," *Proceedings of the Unitarian Historical Society*, 15, part 2 (1965): 1.

3. George H. Williams, *Rethinking the Unitarian Relationship with Protestantism: An Examination of the Thought of Frederic Henry Hedge (1805–1890)* (Boston: Beacon, 1949), p. 3.

4. Mary Moody Emerson to Hedge, 10 April 1834, MH. This and other letters are quoted with the permission of the Houghton Library of Harvard University.

5. William R. Hutchison, *The Transcendentalist Ministers: Church Reform in the New England Renaissance* (New Haven: Yale University Press, 1959).

6. Frank Walker, "Ecumenicity and Liberty," *Proceedings of the Unitarian Historical Society*, 13, part 2 (1961): 2.

7. O. W. Long, *Frederic Henry Hedge: A Cosmopolitan Scholar* (Portland, Maine: Southworth-Anthoensen Press, 1940), p. 1.

8. *The Transcendentalists*, ed. Miller, p. 67.

9. Joel Myerson, "Frederic Henry Hedge and the Failure of Transcendentalism," *Harvard Library Bulletin*, 23 (October 1975): 396.

10. *The American Transcendentalists: Their Poetry and Prose*, ed. Perry Miller (Garden City, N.Y.: Doubleday, 1957), p. 270.

11. Harold Clarke Goddard, *Studies in New England Transcendentalism* (New York: Columbia University Press, 1908); rpt. in *American Transcendentalism: An Anthology of Criticism*, ed. Brian M. Barbour (Notre Dame: University of Notre Dame Press, 1973), p. 171.

12. Bliss Perry, "Frederick [*sic*] Henry Hedge," in Edward Waldo Emerson, *The Early Years of the Saturday Club 1855–1870* (Boston: Houghton Mifflin, 1918), p. 278.

13. Hutchison, *The Transcendentalist Ministers*, p. 47.

14. For the foregoing brief account of Hedge's life and the schooling period in Germany, I have drawn on Long, *Hedge*, and on two unpublished works: Martha Ilona Tuomi, "Dr. Frederic Henry Hedge: His Life and Works to the End of His Bangor Pastorate" (M.A. thesis, University of Maine, 1935), and Peter King Carley, "The Early Life and Thought of Frederic Henry Hedge, 1805–1850" (Ph.D. diss., Syracuse University, 1973).

15. Stephen E. Whicher, *Freedom and Fate: An Inner Life of Ralph Waldo Emerson* (Philadelphia: University of Pennsylvania Press, 1953), p. 7.

16. "Hedge is a philosopher and ill-fitted for action," wrote Henry W. Bellows to a friend on 28 February 1865 (quoted in Walker, "Ecumenicity and Liberty," 8; original in the Bellows Collection, MHi.)

17. Carlyle to Emerson, 31 August 1847, *The Correspondence of Emerson and Carlyle*, ed. Joseph Slater (New York: Columbia University Press, 1964), p. 428.

18. From an "Account of His Ministry" appended to Fiske's *The Life and Character of St. Paul A Model for Christian Ministers. A Sermon Delivered at West Cambridge, April 13, 1828, by Thaddeus Fiske, D.D., at the Close of His Ministry* (Boston: Charles C. Little and James Brown, 1843).

19. Fiske, *St. Paul*, appendix in "Account of His Ministry."

20. Robert F. Needham, *The Arlington Universalists and Their Church* (Arlington, Mass.: First Universalist Society, [1941]).

21. A brief account of Holmes' troubles at Cambridge between 1827 and 1829 may be found in Earle Morse Wilbur, *A History of Unitarianism in Transylvania, England, and America* (Cambridge: Harvard University Press, 1952), pp. 447–48.

22. First Parish Records, 23 May 1828, MArFP. Apparently Fiske never occupied the Parish Pew set aside for him. When in 1842 the Orthodox Congregational Society of West Cambridge was organized, Fiske was a founding member.

23. According to a note by George H. Gray, an active layman of the period, inserted in the First Parish's copy of the printed sermon, MArFP.

24. First Parish Records, 9 March 1829, MArFP.

25. First Parish Records, 13, 20 April 1829, MArFP.

26. First Parish Archives, from a manuscript notebook, "Record of Sermons," kept by a "Miss Prentiss," MArFP.

27. *Hymns of the Spirit* (Boston: Beacon, 1937); *Hymns for the Celebration of Life* (Boston: Beacon, 1964).

28. First Parish Archives, "Order of Exercises," MArFP.

29. James Elliot Cabot, *A Memoir of Ralph Waldo Emerson* (Boston: Houghton, Mifflin, 1887), 1:139.

30. Emerson to Edward Bliss Emerson, 22 December 1833, *The Letters of Ralph Waldo Emerson*, ed. Ralph L. Rusk (New York: Columbia University Press, 1939), 1:402.

31. First Parish Archives, 13 April 1833, in the minutes of the Sabbath School Teachers Association, MArFP.

32. Hedge to Palfrey, 16 June 1833, MH.

33. Hedge to Fuller, 24 June 1833, MH–AH, bMS 384/1 (14).

34. Hedge to Fuller, 24 June 1833, MH–AH.

35. James Freeman Clarke to Hedge, 2 October 1834, MeBaHi.

36. "Pretensions of Phrenology Examined," *Christian Examiner*, 17 (November 1834): 267.

37. First Parish Records, meeting of 10 March 1834, MArFP.

38. Emerson, manuscript "Preaching Record," MH.

39. Emerson to Hedge, 12 July 1834, MeBa; printed also in fragmentary form in *Letters*, 1:416.

40. In a letter of 1 February 1877 to Caroline Dall, Hedge recalled 1834 as the date of the poem's composition. George Willis Cooke gives the Bangor mail coach as the setting (*The Poets of Transcendentalism* [Boston: Houghton, Mifflin, 1903], p. 314). Miller reprints the text in both *The Transcendentalists* (p. 383) and *The American Transcendentalists* (p. 270). For the pertinent part of the letter to Dall, see Cooke, *An Historical and Biographical Introduction to Accompany* The Dial (Cleveland: Rowfant Club, 1902), 2:72–74.

41. *The American Transcendentalists*, ed. Miller, p. 270.

42. Hedge to Fuller, 17 November 1834, MH–AH, bMS 384/1 (15).

43. Hedge to Fuller, 17 January 1835, MH–AH, bMS 384/1 (16).

44. Hedge to Fuller, 20 February 1835, MH–AH, bMS 384/1 (17).

45. First Parish Records, MArFP.

46. Hedge to the Independent Congregational Society of Bangor, 25 March 1835, MeBaUC.

47. Prentiss, "Record of Sermons," First Parish Archives, MArFP.

48. Emerson to Hedge, 12 April 1835, *Letters*, 1:443.

LONGFELLOW'S BOWDOIN DIALOGUE

Edward L. Tucker

O N FRIDAY, 17 October 1823, President William Allen of Bowdoin College, who also instructed in English rhetoric, assigned the parts for the December Exhibition (a public performance by students).[1] Henry Wadsworth Longfellow, in his third year as a student at the college, together with James Ware Bradbury, was to prepare a presentation called "English Dialogue Between a North American Savage and an English Emigrant."

Longfellow, reasonably pleased, felt the part "a high one," "a very fine subject both to write and speak upon." Although it was not the assignment he "wished for," he was consoled because it was "much higher" in the ranking in the class than he had expected.[2]

The two students decided to make the dialogue interesting by having a conversation between two names familiar to the student body: the English emigrant would be Miles Standish, and the North American savage, King Philip.[3] The selection was satisfactory because both men lived in the first part of the seventeenth century and were in the same region of the United States. Miles Standish (ca. 1584–1656) sailed with the Pilgrims on the *Mayflower* in 1620 and fought at various times against the Indians. King Philip (d. 1676) was the name which the English settlers gave to the chief of the Wampanoag Indians during King Philip's War (1675–76); Standish was, of course, dead at the time of King Philip's War.[4]

But after giving themselves names from the seventeenth century, the students relied on documents that discussed late eighteenth-century and early nineteenth-century attitudes toward the Indians. Longfellow, in preparing for the part of the savage, found in the Bowdoin Library a book entitled *An Account of the History, Manners, and Customs, of the Indian Nations, Who Once Inhabited Pennsylvania and the Neighboring States* by the Reverend John Gottlieb Ernestus Heckewelder (1743–1823), who, as a missionary, had lived among various Indian tribes.[5] As Longfellow read the book, he became more and more aware that the Indians in the United States had become "reviled and persecuted." Although they were "a race possessing magnanimity, generousity, benevolence, and pure religion without hypocrisy," they had been "barbarously maltreated by the whites, both in word and deed."[6] In the dialogue, he relied heavily on the benevolent attitude of Heckewelder.

But to present the other side of the argument, the two students used topics—the Indians' doubtful ownership of the land, the attempts to civilize them, their corruption by the whites—that a number of people, including President James Monroe, were discussing.[7]

The dialogue was presented on Wednesday evening, 10 December, on a bleak day; there had been "a considerable snow-storm." The performance in the "cold" and "uncomfortable" chapel was well attended, the members of the audience being male with the exception of a "few ladies." Longfellow, believing his own presentation rather "unpoetical," felt slightly "chagrined" at performing an Indian Dialogue with ladies present; but, all in all, he believed "it ranked as high as it should have ranked."[8]

The manuscript of this dialogue, dated 10 December 1823, in Longfellow's handwriting, is in the Alderman Library at the University of Virginia, and is presented here for the first time in its entirety.[9]

ENGLISH DIALOGUE

between an English Emigrant and a North American Savage.

Emigrant	James W. Bradbury
Savage	Henry W. Longfellow

Emigrant. How can you appear amongst us with this confidence, after having so often murdered our countrymen?[10] Do you think we can any longer endure the outrages of your savage clans?

Savage. Talk not to me of murders and outrages! The stains of our blood are yet warm upon your hands, and your lips still breathe forth fearful curses against the scanty remnant of our race! And yours that have perished by our hands, were they not those, who with the smile of friendship upon their lips and a treachery, that wore the mask of love came to plunge the dagger in our bosoms?[11]

Em. You have massacred those, that could not injure you. When we were lulled into security by your pretensions of friendship, you treacherously butchered the mother in her sleep and the infant in its cradle.

Sav. Your mothers were slain because they would nurse their young vipers to sting us! and your children because time would give them strength and with it the inheritance of hate against our race, that their fathers possessed. And even now ye are driving us towards the setting sun, and would exterminate our race.[12]

Em. We do not desire your extermination, but only that we may share with you the bounties of a country, which from the smallness of your numbers, you cannot cultivate.

Sav. But does that justify you in taking it from us? Had you been our friends as you professed to be at your first coming when we took you by the hand and bid you welcome to sit down by our fire and live with us as brothers, the lands you have taken by violence should have been yours without it. But now by your treachery, you have lost all title to them.[13]

Em. We were your friends and ever continued to be, until your perfidy and cruelty provoked us to enmity. And do you think your wanderings from forest to forest give you the possession of the whole country, which you traverse![14] Then do the voyages of the sailor make the ocean exclusively his!

Sav. The Great Spirit alotted to each nation their homes; and yours were given you in distant lands! When your pilgrim fathers first came to this clime we received them with gladness and held the chain of peace between us, that was to last as long as the sun shone in heaven, and the rivers flowed with water! Lo! the sun is still there, but his beams, shine not upon the bright chain of our friendship and gild no memorials of the triumphs of love over hatred. The rivers are not dry, but there is a stain of blood upon the waters.

Em. You received us with gladness! Yes with the joy of the tiger at the sight of his prey. You did your utmost to destroy us. While we were suffering from the inclemencies of the climate, from si[c]kness and from famine, not a day nor a night passed in which our calamities were not increased by the massacre of our friends. Does your prior occupancy of this country give you the right to murder and destroy our people? The earth originally belonged equally to all, to obtain from it sustenance: but if any portion of its inhabitants adopt a mode of living, which deprives the rest, not only of their share of it but also of a comfiture[?] for their wants, justice demands, that they should change their mode of life. Having sought an asylum in this western world, we find you, a few scattered tribes, spread over the whole country and claiming an exclusive right to that soil, which you never have cultivated and never intend to cultivate.

Sav. It is true, that whatever liveth upon the land, whatever groweth out of this earth and all, that is in the waters flowing out of the same, was given alike to all, that each should have his equal share. Your homes were given you across the mighty deep, and your labours were to till the soil and to gather in its fruits, whilst to us were given these pleasant abodes and dominion over all the rest of creation.

Em. Talk as much as you please of our homes beyond the waters! We have come here to improve your condition. This spot, that nothing affords but a miserable subsistence to one, we will make richly supply all the wants of twenty. Besides what if every little nation should claim whole continents, that they might subsist by hunting and fishing! The world would not be large enough for a tenth part of its present inhabitants.[15]

Sav. It was never intended that all should live as we do—!—

Em. No, nor that any should thus make brutes of themselves. By living as you do, you deprive yourselves of all, that makes life desirable. The Great Spirit you believe, has put us here to improve our situation. Why then are you unwilling to receive from us the blessings of civilization, and share with us the favours, which our kind mother, earth, bestows on all her children, who will seek them[?][16]

Sav. The blessings of civilization! Pray tell me whether it was your christianity or your civilization that taught you to give the name of brutes to them, that were always your friends? And what are these blessings of civilization? Why only look at one of your civilized Indians,—one that has said to thee: thy people shall be my people and thy God my God! Degraded beings! they skulk about your villages, buffeted from door to door and shooting for liquor with the same bows that their fathers bore to battle. And would you *really* persuade us, that this is a fine thing[?][17]

Em. Yes! I would advise you to do even this rather than to make use of your tomahawk and bow to murder and scalp your own species. If you will not enjoy the blessings of civilization it is your own fault! And that, we may elevate the standard of humanity, by *you* so much lowered, is one inducement to improve you. But blind to your own interest, you still boast of your mode of life and treat ours with contempt. Mark for a moment the difference. While we have fixed habitations, the Savage wanders about without a place to lay his head. Some solitary cave gives him a dangerous lodging for a single night. He must traverse the forest in uncertainty, and satisfy his hunger with whatever chance may throw in his way. Instead of enjoying the sweets of connubial felicity, he must be forever separated from his family, and can have no conception of the heartfelt enjoyments of a home. Instead of the refined pleasures of the mind, his joys are sensual and momentary. Disengaged from the pursuits of war, he lives a life of stupid insensibility: Look into his habitation if he chance to have one and contrast it with that of the white man. On the one hand you see neatness, regularity, and comfort;—on the other filthiness, disorder, and misery!—more fit to be den for beasts, than the abode of man.

Sav. Alas! Did the book, that your maker gave you because of your transgressions teach you to revile us? Go, lie in your very prayers to him that made you! call him your god when you have no god but gold, and thank him that ye are better than we are! Yet the curse shall be upon your own heads! Look! where the landscape reposes in twilight and the moon beams on the valley! Lo! there the busy hamlet sounds to the dull voice of labour, when but a few moons ago the indian cabin stood peacefully by the lake-side and the deer drank at evening. And then the tapering spire that points to heaven, tells not the tale of peace and friendship, but of calamity and hatred, not of your piety and devotion, but of your outrage and hypocrisy! and stands there the record of your impurity and your idolatry. Think, were ye living in a quiet spot like this, and the Indian should break in upon your society and should tell you, that your maker willed, that you should desert your pleasant homes and come and live as he lived, would you have obeyed him?

Em. If when he besought us to adopt his mode of life, he proved beyond a doubt, that it was in every respect preferable to ours,—while we were ignorant of the higher enjoyments, that long form[?] a cultivated mind,—unacquainted with the refined pleasures of virtue and social intercourse,—making no proficiency in these arts, that are an ornament to man, and employing our whole time in procuring the means of a miserable subsistence,—that he actually possessed all these enjoyments and was willing to share them with us, most certainly should I comply with his requ[est.]

Sav. But you never used persuasion with us, for all was violence. And even now y[ou] are driving us forth to slaughter. But think not we shall perish without a struggle! Away! we will not die in silence! The blood of the Moravians cries aloud for revenge! the blood of our nation, that has so often quenched our council fires cries aloud for revenge! the relatives of the slain, that are amongst us, cry aloud for revenge,—and will have revenge![18]

Em. Is it thus you should spurn all our offers of kindness, and glut your appetite with the blood of our countrymen, with no excuse but the mere pretense of retaliation? Shall the viper sting us and we not bruise his head? shall we not only let your robberies and murders pass unpunished, but give you the possession of our very fire-side, while the only arguments you offer are insolence and slaughter? Know ye, the land is ours untill you will improve it. Go, tell your ungrateful comrades, the world declares the spread of the white people at the expense of the red is the triumph of peace over violence. Tell them to cease their outrages upon the civilized world, or but a few days, and they shall be swept from the earth.

Sav. Alas! the sky is overcast with dark and blustering clouds! The rivers run with blood, but never, never will we suffer the grass to grow upon our war path[.] And now I do remember, that the Initiate prophet in my earlier years told from his dreams, that all our race should fall like withered leaves when Autumn strips the forest![19] Lo! I hear sighing and sobing! 'tis the death song of a mighty nation,—the last requiem over the grave of the fallen.

BOWDOIN COLLEGE.
December 10th 1823

Although this youthful exercise, while charming, can scarcely stand on its own weight, it, nevertheless, has some significance in the overall development of Longfellow as a writer. Bradbury, on the occasion of Longfellow's seventy-fifth birthday, in recalling their efforts at the Junior Exhibition, wondered whether the occurrence "had anything to do in suggesting the subject for one of his admirable poems"; Longfellow, he added, "subsequently made a great deal more of Miles Standish" than he did.[20]

But Bradbury did not go far enough in suggesting the importance of the dialogue. For one thing, it indicates the way that Longfellow was to work. Essentially the erudite scholar in his study, he did not rely on first-hand experiences for many of his poems. Instead, like others, he went to authoritative sources; the information he found, combined with the poet's imagination, produced the final works.

Although Longfellow's acquaintance with Indians was slight because not many were in Maine when he was writing,[21] he came in contact with a few. Some members of the Algonquins still survived in the state. Furthermore, Black Hawk, the Sauk chief, with some followers on a peace mission, toured Boston. Longfellow thought their display on the Boston Common was "grand"; these "bold fellows, all grease and red-paint," were "very formidable" with their "war-clubs, bears-teeth—and buffalo-scalps." And when the Ojibway chief Kah-ge-ga-gah-bowh lectured in Boston on "The Religion, Poetry, and Eloquence of the Indian," Longfellow entertained this "good-looking young man" in his home; the Indian left a copy of his autobiography with the poet.[22]

But essentially Longfellow learned about Indians from written sources. Just as he used Heckewelder for the dialogue, he depended on the same writer and other sources for *The Song of Hiawatha* (1854–55): John Tanner, *A Narrative of the Captivity and Adventures of John Tanner* (1830); Henry Rowe Schoolcraft, *Algic Researches* (1839), *Oneóta, or Characteristics of the Red Race of America* (1844–45), *Historical and Statistical Information Respecting the History, Condition, and Prospects of the Indian Tribes of the United States* (1851–54); and the engravings of George Catlin in *Manners and Customs of the North American Indians* (1841). For the Indian conflicts in *The Courtship of Miles Standish* (1857–58), the sources included William Bradford, *The History of Plymouth Plantation* (1651), and Alexander Young, *Chronicles of the Pilgrim Fathers* (1841). The marriage between a baron and an Indian maiden in "The Baron of St. Castine" (1871) in *Tales of a Wayside Inn* comes from William D. Williamson, *History of the State of Maine* (1832).

Bradbury reported that in the dialogue the two students represented King Philip and Miles Standish. This use of historical figures rather than imaginative creations appears later in Longfellow's works: actual Indians include Sitting Bull in "The Revenge of Rain-in-the-Face" (1876), Tituba in *Giles Corey of the Salem Farms* (1868), and Aspinet, Samoset, Corbitant, Squanto, and Tokamahamon in *The Courtship of Miles Standish*. In the poem "Jeckoyva" (1825), a historical Indian chief, overtaken by night while out hunting, accidentally falls down a cliff and perishes alone; the mountain near the White Hills now bears the name of Mount Jeckoyva. The use of Miles Standish in the dialogue was followed by other figures of New England history, such as Priscilla Mullins and John Alden in *The Courtship of Miles Standish*, John Endicott, Richard Bellingham, John Norton, and Wenlock Christison in *John Endicott* (1856–57), and Giles Corey, Martha Corey, John Hathorne, and Cotton Mather in *Giles Corey of the Salem Farms*.

Longfellow's interest in Indians, which was lifelong, started early.[23] In his first poem, "The Battle of Lovell's Pond" (1820), Captain John Lovewell and the Indians battle for a day at Lovell's Pond, a place familiar to Longfellow in his youth.[24] A second poem on the same topic, "Ode Written for the Commemoration at Fryeburg, Maine, of Lovewell's Fight" (1825), was presented and sung to the tune of "Bruce's Address" at a local celebration. Dramatic situations impressed the youthful poet: in "Lover's Rock" (1825), an Indian maiden, all set to be married, finding out her intended husband is "false-hearted," throws herself off Lover's Rock into the "deep cold wave" of the lake; in "Burial of the Minnisink" (1825), a young warrior is buried, but afterwards his horse is shot so that the Indian will be able to use the steed in the happy hunting grounds.

The dialogue presents an important theme: the doomed and tragic end of the Indian as he is forced to move westward to make way for the white man. The Savage states in his condemnation of the Emigrant: "And even now ye are driving us towards the setting sun and would exterminate our race." And at the end of the dialogue, the Savage laments: "the Initiate prophet in my earlier years told from his dreams, that all our race should fall like withered leaves when Autumn strips the forest! Lo! I hear sighing and sobing! 'tis'the death song of a mighty nation,—the last requiem over the grave of the fallen." In some of Longfellow's early poems this theme appears, even to including the image of the withered leaves in autumn. In "The Battle of Lovell's Pond" the "war-whoop is still, and savages's yell / Has sunk into silence along the wild dell." The red men in "Ode Written for the Commemoration at Fryeburg, Maine, of Lovewell's Fight" have left the place; "the remnant takes / Its sad journey on" "tow'rd the setting sun." And the central figure in "The Indian Hunter" (1825) has "bitter feelings" as he looks over the "populous haunts of man." The time is "autumn" and the trees and ground have "withered leaves"; he turns away "from that scene, / Where the home of his fathers had been."

This theme continues in later poems. The chief of the mighty Omahas in "To the Driving Cloud" (1845) once was "strong and great, a hero" when he lived in the woods. But now in his scarlet blanket he walks the "narrow and populous streets" of the city that bears his name. What has caused this sad state for him and his race? "Far more fatal" than "the Crows and the Foxes" and "the tread of Behemoth" were the "big thunder canoe," "the campfires," and the "caravan, whitening the desert"; the arrival of the "Saxons and Celts" brought an end to the red man's way of life. And in a section of *Hiawatha* entitled "The White Man's Foot," "a hundred warriors" came "in the great canoe with pinions": "Painted white were all their faces / And with hair their chins were covered." Hiawatha in a vision beholds "the westward marches / Of the unknown, crowded nations"; the land becomes "full of people, / Restless, struggling, toiling, striving." Then "a darker, drearier vision" comes to him as he sees the nation "scattered"; the "remnants" of the people are "Sweeping westward, wild and woeful . . . / Like the withered leaves of Autumn!"

The other chief theme in the dialogue—actually just an extension of the first—is the way that whites and Indians react when they confront each other. Sometimes the approach is sympathetic. The Savage in the dialogue states that when the pilgrim fathers first arrived, the reds "received them with gladness and held the chain of peace" between the two. The red men took the whites "by the hand" and bid them "welcome to sit down" by the fire and live as "brothers." This close union appears in other works. Some Indians are kind to the white men such as the guide and interpreter Hobomok in *The Courtship of Miles Standish*, described as "friend of the white man." Hiawatha has the same spirit when he tells the people of his village about the approach of the whites: "Let us welcome, then , the strangers, / Hail them as friends and brothers, / And the heart's right hand of friendship / Give them when they come to see us." In "The Baron of St. Castine" the Indian chief Madocawando welcomes the baron, who has left his home in the Pyrenees and come to what is now Maine; aristocrats in France expect "a painted savage" when the baron returns home with the chief's daughter as his wife, but instead they see "a form of beauty undefined / A loveliness without a name."

According to the dialogue, the whites, wanting to "elevate the standard of humanity," bring "the blessings of civilization," including Christianity. Miles Standish in *The Courtship of Miles Standish* does not carry the savages the weapons that they want, but rather the Bible. And in "Hiawatha's Departure," the missionaries bring the joyful news of the Virgin Mary, her Son and His crucifixion. Before Hiawatha leaves, he advises his people: "Listen to their words of wisdom, / Listen to the truth they tell you, / For the Master of Life has sent them / From the land of light and morning!"

But for the most part the confrontation is hostile. In the dialogue the Savage and the Emigrant bitterly condemn each other. Each side is deceived. The Emigrant says that the whites, "lulled into security" by "pretensions of friendship," were provoked to enmity by the "perfidy and cruelty" of the reds. According to the Savage, the whites had "the smile of friendship upon their lips," but at the same time "a treachery"; wearing "the mask of love," the whites "came to plunge the dagger" into the reds. Miles Standish in *The Courtship of Miles Standish* speaks of the opposite deception when the "cunning and crafty" warriors came to greet him: "Friendship was in their looks, but in the hearts there was hatred."

This confrontation can become destructive. Both Miles Standish and King Philip took part in various Indian wars. Tituba, the Indian and slave in *Giles Corey of the Salem Farms*, "with her Evil Eye and Evil Hand," makes whites weak with pain; she brings death to their cattle, blight to their corn. "The Battle of Lovell's Pond" and "Ode Written for the Commemoration at Fryeburg, Maine, of Lovewell's Fight" honor a battle in which the "war-cry rose" and "our fathers bled." In *The Courtship of Miles Standish*, the captain fights the "red devils" who are "grim and ferocious in aspect." When the "self-vaunting" Pecksuot insults him, the "hot blood" of Standish takes over, and he plunges his knife into the savage.

In several ways, then, this dialogue, written early in life, anticipates Longfellow's later interest in Indians. The dialogue basically asks: Which side is right, and which side is wrong? The whites bring civilization, "neatness, regularity, and comfort," "the refined pleasures of the mind." But to the Savage, who feels he has been cheated out of his birthright, the white man presents not "peace and friendship," not "piety and devotion," but rather "calamity and hatred," "outrage and hypocrisy." In "The Revenge of Rain-in-the-Face," written fifty–three years after the dialogue, Longfellow ponders the same question. Sitting Bull and his three thousand "savage, unmerciful" braves surprise and kill General George A. Custer, the "White Chief with yellow hair," and his entire force of over two hundred men in the Battle of Little Big Horn on 25 June 1876. But which side is right in the conflict? The answer is that much can be said for both. The Sioux have "woes and griefs"; the whites have shown "broken faith." And so, the dialogue, a simple college exercise, foreshadows, most specifically, the question asked in a poem written years later: "Whose was the right and the wrong?"

NOTES

1. President Allen, a Congregational minister, noted for his conservation and inflexibility, had briefly served as head of Dartmouth before going to Bowdoin. Longfellow entered Bowdoin College in the fall of 1821, though he did not live in Brunswick until the following year.

2. Longfellow to Anne Longfellow, 26 October 1823, *The Letters of Henry Wadsworth Longfellow*, ed. Andrew Hilen, 6 vols. (Cambridge: Harvard University Press, 1966–82), 1:55–56.

3. The names Miles Standish and King Philip appear in the reminiscence by Bradbury of the college dialogue (Bradbury to H. W. Bryant, *Proceedings of the Maine Historical Society, February 27, 1882* [Portland: Hoyt, Fogg, and Donham, 1882], p. 128, reprinted in *Letters*, 1:56). Bradbury (1802–1901) was later United States Senator from Maine from 1847 to 1853.

4. Philip was the second son of Massasoit. There are numerous references to contacts between the friendly Massasoit and Miles Standish in John S. C. Abbott, *Miles Standish* (New York: Dodd & Mead, 1872).

5. (Philadelphia: A. Small, 1818). The work is Volume I of the Transactions of the Historical & Literary Committee of the American Philosophical Society. Heckewelder, born in Bedford, England, became a missionary of the Unitas Fratrum or Moravian Church to the Indians in the Ohio Territory. Before the Revolutionary War, when he was a messenger to various Indian settlements in Pennsylvania, he spent many hours learning their languages, traditions, and history. His most important work just before, during, and after the Revolutionary War took place when he lived with the Moravian Christian Indians and accompanied them on various missions from Bethlehem to what is now Detroit. After the establishment of the American government, he held a special position with the United States government relating to Indian matters.

6. Longfellow to Zilpah Longfellow, 9 November 1823, *Letters*, 1:57–58.

7. At the time of the dialogue, James Monroe was president of the United States (1817–25), and the Secretary of War was directly responsible for the interests of the Indians. One year after the dialogue, in 1824, the Bureau of Indian Affairs was created within the United States War Department. In 1849 the Bureau of Indian Affairs was transferred to the United States Department of the Interior.

By 1823 two essays by Washington Irving were also available as possible sources: "Traits of Indian Character," *Analectic Magazine*, 3 (February 1814): 145–56; "Philip of Pokanoket," *Analectic Magazine*, 3 (June 1814): 502–15.

8. Longfellow to Elizabeth Longfellow, 14 December 1823, and to Anne Longfellow, 26 October 1823, *Letters*, 1:64–66, 55.

9. The last two paragraphs, with some editorial changes, were published in an anonymous article, "Longfellow's First Wife and Early Friends," *Every Other Saturday*, 1 (19 January 1884): 20–21; these two paragraphs are reprinted in Lawrance Thompson, *Young Longfellow: 1807–1843* (New York: Macmillan, 1938).

Mrs. D. Bradford Wetherell, Jr., in speaking for the Longfellow heirs, has given me permission to publish the manuscript. I also have the permission of the Alderman Library, University of Virginia, as owner of the manuscript. I am indebted to Professors Charles W. Haney and Thomas J. Adriance for their aid in reading certain words in the manuscript.

The only changes in the manuscript have been made in brackets—to indicate added punctuation marks, to supply letters where the manuscript was torn, to indicate that a few words could not be completely deciphered.

10. Heckewelder, *An Account*, p. 335: "The newspapers were filled with accounts of the cruelties of the Indians."

11. Heckewelder, *An Account*, p. 65: Pachgantschilias, a Delaware chief, stated: "the white men . . . do as they please. They enslave those who are not of their color, although created by the same Great Spirit who created them. . . . There is no faith to be placed in their words. . . . They will say to an Indian, 'my friend! my brother!' They will take him by the hand, and, at the same moment destroy him."

12. Heckewelder, *An Account*, pp. 63–64: "where the council fire was yet burning bright, they put it out, and extinguished it with our own blood! . . . we were compelled to withdraw ourselves beyond the great swamps. . . . The whites will not rest contented until they shall have destroyed the last of us, and made us disappear entirely from the face of the earth!"

13. Heckewelder, *An Account*, p. 59: "It was we . . . who so kindly received them on their first arrival into our country. We took them by the hand, and bid them welcome to sit down by our side, and live with us as brothers, but how did they requite our kindness? They at first asked only for a little land on which to raise bread for themselves and their families, and pasture for their cattle, which we freely gave them. . . . They discovered spots of land which pleased them; that land they also wanted, and because we were loth to part with it, as we saw they had already more than they had need of, they took it from us by force and drove us to a great distance from our ancient homes."

14. "The late Chief Magistrate of the United States, in his oration on the festival of the pilgrims, December 22d, 1802, [said]: 'The Indian right of possession itself stands, with regard to the greatest part of the country, upon a questionable foundation. Their cultivated fields, their constructed habitations, a space of ample sufficiency for their subsistence, and whatever they had annexed to themselves by personal labor, was undoubtedly, by the law of nature, theirs. But what is the right of a huntsman to the forest of a thousand miles, over which he has accidentally ranged in quest of prey?'" (*Gales & Seaton's Register of Debates in Congress*, 19 May 1830, p. 1081. This excellent summary of attitudes toward Indians from 1800 to 1830 will hereafter be cited as *Debates*.)

15. "In his message of December 1817, [President Monroe] continues: 'The hunter state can exist only in the vast uncultivated desert. It yields to the more dense and compact form and greater force of a civilized population; and of right it ought to yield, for the earth was given to mankind to support the greatest number of which it is capable; and no tribe or people have a right to withhold from the wants of others more than is necessary for their own support and comfort'" (*Debates*, p. 1087).

16. "In his inaugural address, at the commencement of his second term, 4th March 1805, [Jefferson] comments on the condition of this people more at length: ' . . . humanity enjoins us to teach them agriculture and the arts—to encourage them to that industry which alone can enable them to maintain their place in existence—and to prepare them in time for that state of society which to bodily comforts adds the improvements of the mind and morals. . . . But the endeavors to enlighten them on the fate which awaits their present course of life, to induce them to exercise their reason, follow its dictates, and change their pursuits with the change of circumstances, have powerful obstacles to encounter; they are combatted by the habits of their bodies, prejudice of their minds, ignorance, pride, and the influence of interested and crafty individuals among them'" (*Debates*, p. 1087).

"President Monroe, in his inaugural address of 1817, says: 'With the Indian tribes, it is our duty to cultivate friendly relations, and to act with kindness and liberality in all our transactions. Equally proper is it to persevere in our efforts to extend to them the advantages of civilization'" (*Debates*, p. 1087).

John C. Calhoun, Secretary of War, to President Monroe, 8 February 1822: "the interesting inquiry remains to be solved whether such an education [in schools for teaching Indians] would lead them to that state of morality, civilization, and happiness, to which it is the desire of the Government to bring them; or whether there is not something in their situation which presents insuperable obstacles to such a state? . . . Unless some system can be devised . . . with the progress of education, to extend over them our laws and authority, it is feared that all efforts to civilize them, whatever flattering appearances they may for a time exhibit, must ultimately fail" (*Papers of John C. Calhoun*, ed. W. Edwin Hemphill, 12 vols. to date [Columbia: University of South Carolina Press, 1959–] 6:680–82).

17. "[According to] the *North American Review*, July 1820, p. 93: 'the Indians have. . . mingled with the whites, and thus been confounded with the mass. . . . Drunkenness and other vices . . . have thinned their numbers . . . '" (*Debates*, p. 1082).

Calhoun to Monroe, 8 February 1822: "[If there are] any remains of a tribe surrounded by a dense white population, [the people remain] independent. They lose the lofty spirit and heroic courage of the savage state, without acquiring the virtues which belong to the civilized. Depressed in spirits and debauched in morals, they dwindle away through a wretched existence, a nuisance to the surrounding country" (*Papers*, 6:682).

Washington Irving, "Traits of Indian Character": "the miserable hordes which infest the frontiers, and hang on the skirts of the settlements . . . are . . . degenerate beings, corrupted and enfeebled by the vices of a society, without being benefited by its civilization. . . . They become drunken, indolent, feeble, thievish and pusillanimous. . . . How different was their state while the undisputed lords of the soil" (*The Sketch Book of Geoffrey Crayon, Gent.*, ed. Haskell Springer [Boston: Twayne, 1978], pp. 226–27).

18. Moravians are members of the Protestant sect formed in Moravia and Bohemia in 1457. In 1734 Bishop Nikolaus Zinzendorf sent the first Moravian missionaries to America. After a brief stay at Savannah, Georgia, they went to Pennsylvania. In 1741, the community which they founded on the banks of the Lehigh River was named Bethlehem.

Heckewelder, *An Account*, p. 328: "The worst that can be said of them is, that the passion of revenge is so strong in their minds that it carries them beyond all bounds. But set this aside, and their character is noble and great."

19. Tenskwatawa (ca. 1768–ca. 1834) was maneuvered by William Henry Harrison, the governor of the Indiana Territory, into the disastrous battle of Tippecanoe in 1811 and was defeated. Called the Shawnee prophet, Tenskwatawa had a vision in which he saw the end of the Indian race. Tecumseh (ca. 1768–1813), considered to have been his twin brother, also voiced a prophetic warning: "Where today are the Pequot? where are the Narragansett, the Mohican, the Pokanoket, and other once powerful tribes of our people? They have vanished before the

avarice and the oppression of the White Man, as snow before a summer sun" (See "Tensk-wautawaw," Thomas L. McKenney and James Hall, *History of the Indian Tribes of North America with Biographical Sketches and Anecdotes of the Principal Chiefs* [Philadelphia: Frederick W. Greenough, 1838], pp. 37–49; *The Way: An Anthology of American Indian Literature*, ed. Shirley Hill Witt and Stan Steiner [New York: Alfred A. Knopf, 1972], p. 6).

20. Bradbury's letter to Bryant, printed in *Letters*, 1:56.

21. Within the states of Maine, Massachusetts, Rhode Island, Connecticut, and Virginia, there were only 2,573 Indians in the 1820s out of a total of 313,130 in the United States (*Debates*, p. 1092).

22. Longfellow to Margaret Potter, 29 October 1837, and to Stephen Longfellow, 29 October 1837, *Letters*, 2:45, 46. For Black Hawk and the display on the Boston Common (in 1837), see *Letters*, 2:45, 46. For references to Kah-ge-ga-gah-bowh, see Longfellow's journal entries for 26 February and 12 and 14 April 1849, *The Works of Henry Wadsworth Longfellow*, ed. Horace E. Scudder and Samuel Longfellow, 14 vols. (Boston: Houghton, Mifflin, 1886–91), 13:145, 148. Also see Ernest J. Moyne, "Longfellow and Kah-ge-ga-gah-bowh," *Henry W. Longfellow Reconsidered: a Symposium*, ed. J. Chesley Mathews (Hartford, Conn.: Transcendental Books, 1970), pp. 48–52. I have used *Works*, 6:455–67, for the dates of composition of the poems.

23. Two projects never written were "A Sketch Book of New England" with some stories based on Indian legend and history, and a proposed group of tales told by emigrants crossing the Rocky Mountains, including "The Indian's Tale."

24. His teacher, Thomas Cogswell Upham, earlier wrote a poem on the same subject.

"THAT SAINTED SPIRIT"—WILLIAM ELLERY CHANNING AND THE UNITARIAN MILTON

Kevin P. Van Anglen

READERS HAVE LONG RECOGNIZED the influence of John Milton on the English Romantic movement. For Keats, Shelley, and the rest, he was the very model of the sublime poet, a representative man who figured forth the organic unity of poet and poem which was the goal of their own artistic endeavor. Similarly, for the generation of the French Revolution Milton stood as the type of the unacknowledged legislator, the defender of liberty in an age very much like their own. In both of these capacities he was, above all, a man who possessed that vision by which universal truth is sought and made available through the creation of great art.[1]

Despite the demonstrated importance of Milton for English Romanticism, however, no comprehensive study of his place in American literature during the same era exists. Aside from a brief article by Phyllis Cole and the final chapter of George F. Sensabaugh's treatment of Milton in Colonial and Federalist America, the scholarly literature is singularly bare.[2] Only incidental references or brief analyses of individual works showing Miltonic influence have been published. The exceptions are William Wynkoop's treatment of Milton and Emerson, and Henry F. Pommer's earlier study of Milton and Melville.[3] Even these books do not provide a comprehensive and thorough survey of the Miltonic tradition in America. Unfortunately, one must agree with Cole "that new and broader work is needed on all aspects of the interpretation of Milton in nineteenth-century America."[4]

As a first step towards this broader understanding, this essay will investigate one writer's response to Milton and the critical tradition that had grown up about him. That investigation will, in turn, suggest the more general attitude towards the poet during the American Renaissance. The writer is William Ellery Channing, whose 1826 review of the *De Doctrina Christiana* is one of the first and most important treatments of Milton in nineteenth-century New England.[5] An examination of Channing's review shows a number of things. First of all, it typifies his personal position on matters ranging from philosophy and theology to literature and politics. At the same time the Milton piece outlines—yet differs from—the stock reactions of Channing's fellow New Englanders to the poet and his writings. It also suggests Channing's singular importance in the transition from Edwards to Emerson, not only because of his leading role in Unitarian thought, but also because of his flirtation with those more radical trends within the denomination which culminated in Transcendentalism a decade later.[6] Finally, the tension in the review between these two poles (Channing's tendency towards radicalism on the one hand, and his equally strong conservatism on the other) points to the true importance of the piece. For it is one of the earliest examples of that genre so popular with Emerson and Thoreau in the coming decades: the Transcendental biography.[7]

Perhaps no event affected Milton's reputation more in the nineteenth century than the publication in 1823 of his long-lost Latin treatise, *De Doctrina Christiana*. Not only did this work confirm suspicions about his theological heterodoxy on matters such as polygamy, Christ's divinity, and creation *ex nihilo*, but it also reinforced a general reinvestigation of his prose writings begun earlier in the century. This reassessment was at the heart of the debate in nineteenth-century England between those following the earlier Tory interpretation of Milton, and those who found in him a spirit sympathetic to their own radicalism.[8]

Channing's review on the other side of the Atlantic is no exception to the British pattern. Written for the *Christian Examiner* (a leading Unitarian periodical), it appeared on the publication of Charles R. Sumner's translation of the *De Doctrina* in 1826. Along with the essays on Fénelon and Napoleon it marks a transition point in his career. Behind Channing were the sermons and theological tracts which had put him at the head of the Unitarian movement in the preceding decade. Ahead of him were the twin challenges of Transcendentalism and Abolitionism which were to vex his last years. The Milton essay and its companion pieces mediate between these two periods. They indicate first of all the general intellectual background from which Channing wrote, and his specific contributions to Unitarian thought. At the same time they provide evidence of his growing intellectual restiveness during these years. The Milton essay does more than this, however, since it also places Channing's changing views in a broader focus: the growth of the Whig tradition of Milton studies in England and America.

This broader field is evident from the start, since Channing clearly had more in mind than a discussion of the theological technicalities of this tract.

He proposed instead to deal with Milton's career as a whole, in order to present both a full portrait of the man, and a general outline of the role of art in human psychology. This wider aim is an appropriate one, moreover, because the *De Doctrina* "derives its chief interest from its author" rather than from any narrow theological virtues of its own. Indeed, the greatness of all of Milton's writings is due to his personal genius, and status as a representative man. For Channing found in him not just a poet, or a theologian, or a political controversialist, but a shining example of the possibilities of the human soul. "Milton had" for Channing "that universality which marks the highest order of intellect." This united him with great minds everywhere, but also made him illustrative of the nature of the mind itself. As such, Milton truly "felt that poetry was as a universal presence," and that "great minds were everywhere his kindred" (pp. 4–5).

In describing Milton's genius as an illustration of the workings of the human mind, Channing gives us a particularly vivid portrait of his own intellectual background and beliefs. For instance, he defines the poet's "genius and greatness of soul" as an ability to identify sympathetically with experience, and unite it all in the consciousness (p. 28). In doing this Channing is typical of Boston Unitarianism, since he and his co-religionists were heirs to the tradition of Locke and the Scottish Common Sense School, in which the rational power of the mind to synthesize experience by association was a commonplace.[9] Milton's "great and far-looking mind, which grasps at once vast fields of thought" (p. 22) marks him therefore as one of the few who have exercised their mental powers to the fullest. More significantly, Milton and other great poets exercise this synthetic power on the fundamental affinities which make up all being: human, natural, and divine. Thus, for Channing a study of Milton's life and works provides a practical definition of the power by which the creative imagination works:

> . . . mind is in its own nature diffusive. Its object is the universe, which is strictly one, or bound together by infinite connexions and correspondences; and accordingly its natural progress is from one to another field of thought; and wherever original power, creative genius exists, the mind, far from being distracted or oppressed by the variety of its acquisitions, will see more and more common bearings and hidden and beautiful analogies in all the objects of knowledge. (p. 6)

It is by virtue of his creative imagination that Milton can search out both the essence of things and "the sacred recesses of the soul." Similarly, it is also by virtue of his imagination that he can give these essences concrete expression. As the passage's tone suggests, not only does this make him a great

artist, but something of a religious leader too. For "it is the glorious prerogative of this art, that it 'makes all things new' for the gratification of a divine
instinct" (p. 8). As such, poetry is "the most transcendent" of God's gifts and
gives its possessor "the conscious dignity of a prophet" (p. 7).

Within the Milton essay, then, Channing is toying with a number of ideas
typical of his general aesthetic and philosophical position. His belief in the
religious role of the poet and the metaphysical function of the creative imagination, for example, demonstrates that he is very much like his fellow Unitarians. Yet at the same time he is different too. As Lawrence Buell put it,
Channing "extended the analogy between art and religion to the farthest
limits Unitarianism could bear, by taking seriously, so to speak, the idea of
poetic inspiration, with which his colleagues only flirted."[10] He joined, in
other words, with his fellow Bostonians in seeing the rational perception of
the cosmic affinities as a sign of the conscious will of the creator. And like his
contemporaries he also defined the imagination in a fundamentally religious
and moralistic way, in both the object and the results of its operation. This
fact alone bespeaks the general tone of American criticism at this time.[11] Yet
as we shall see, the view of the creative imagination outlined here also shows
Channing's fundamental uneasiness with the scheme he inherited from the
Scots and Burke.

To be sure, despite the likely personal influence of Wordsworth and Coleridge,[12] Channing's view of the imagination only superficially resembles the
latter's *esemplastic* power. Rather, the imagination of Kames, Stewart, and
Burke is clearly at work here: with its synthetic, associative tendency; its
organic mode of expression; and its function as a regulating and active faculty.[13] Yet if Channing was not himself a crypto-idealist, influences like the
Cambridge Platonists and the Schlegels impelled him—like Hazlitt in England—to carry the older philosphy into new territory. His thought, in other
words, "constitutes only a groundwork, not an actual beginning of the transcendental poetic." Although he "did not reach the heights he celebrates,"[14]
Channing's *Milton* contains the first hints of that new and broader definition
of the poet for which a new philosophy was needed: that of Emerson's *Nature* a decade later.

Channing's *De Doctrina* review opens therefore with definitions of the
imagination and the role of the poet. These definitions are introduced in order to support the specific claim that Milton is a singular and exemplary genius. Just what is meant by this becomes apparent shortly, since for Channing he made contributions in three different fields, in each of which his
genius shone through. Indeed, these three roles make up the structure of
the piece: Milton the poet (pp. 3–20), Milton as a defender of political freedom (pp. 20–40), and Milton the theologian (pp. 40–68). Milton the poet

shows great moral and intellectual genius, and Milton the political and religious controversialist shows true genius in action.

To understand this three-fold definition of Milton's greatness one must remember that the *De Doctrina* piece has strong affinities with the essays on Fénelon and Napoleon. Thus, while in his study of Milton Channing never explicitly divides the poet's genius into these three categories, just such an explicit statement can be found in his review of Sir Walter Scott's life of Napoleon written only a few years later.[15] "*Moral* greatness, or magnanimity," is due as he says there "to that sublime energy, by which the soul, smitten with the love of virtue, binds itself indissolubly, for life and for death, to truth and duty" (p. 118). In the Milton essay Channing implies as much with regard to his subject, since he possessed this largeness of soul to a degree matched only by Shakespeare, Homer, and Dante. As he says there, Milton's "moral character was as strongly marked as his intellectual, and it may be expressed in one word, *magnanimity*. It was in harmony with his poetry. He had a passionate love of the higher, more commanding, and majestic virtues" (p. 31). Furthermore, "we see Milton's magnanimity in the circumstances under which 'Paradise Lost' was written. It was not in prosperity, in honor, and amidst triumphs, but in disappointment, desertion, and in what the world calls disgrace, that he composed that work. . . . But it is the prerogative of true greatness to glorify itself in adversity, and to meditate and execute vast enterprises in defeat" (p. 36). This moral greatness manifests itself in the poet's *energia* or *virtú*, his strength of character which shines through like a personal presence in all his works.

Most important of all, however, with this description of Milton's *magnanimity* Channing comes as close as he ever did to the inspired bard of Emerson's "The Poet." For both critics, the poet is a fundamentally religious figure in terms of his vocation as well as his spiritual insight.[16] Indeed, Channing's ideal poet has—in keeping with his description of Milton as a prophet —a clearly *vatic* role to play:

> The great and decisive test of genius is, that it calls forth *power* in the souls of others. It not merely gives knowledge, but breathes energy. There are authors, and among these Milton holds the highest rank, in approaching whom we are conscious of an access of intellectual strength. A "virtue goes out" from them. . . . The works which we should chiefly study, are not those which contain the greatest fund of knowledge, but which raise us into sympathy with the intellectual energy of the author, and through which a great mind multiplies itself, as it were, in the reader. (pp. 30–31)

Milton the poet is, therefore, an outstanding example of the man of moral genius. Yet as this last passage implies, he is also exemplary for a second kind of exalted virtue. In the Napoleon essay Channing defines it as

> *intellectual* greatness, or genius in the highest sense of that word; and by this we mean that sublime capacity of thought, through which the soul, smitten with the love of the true and the beautiful, essays to comprehend the universe, soars into the heavens, penetrates the earth, penetrates itself, questions the past, anticipates the future, traces out the general and all-comprehending laws of nature, binds together by innumerable affinities and relations all the objects of its knowledge, rises from the finite and transient to the infinite and the everlasting, frames to itself from its own fulness lovelier and sublimer forms than it beholds, discerns the harmonies between the world within and the world without us, and finds in every region of the universe types and interpreters of its own deep mysteries and glorious inspirations. This is the greatness which belongs to philosophers, and to the master spirits in poetry and the fine arts. (pp 119–20)

This passage obviously has roots deep in the ideology of Boston Unitarianism. It emphasizes the synthetic, unifying capacity of the mind, the mind's affinity with all things in the universe, and the connection between the religious and the moral sense in the experience of sublimity. Similarly, it also suggests the influence on Channing of the Scottish philosophy's "rational intuitionism," the "moral sentiment" concept of Hutcheson and Shaftesbury, the rhetoric of Cambridge Platonism, and the Burkeian sublime. As such, it is reminiscent of the opening of the *De Doctrina* review, in which Channing presents a similar view of the mind as a means of suggesting Milton's almost prophetic mental breadth. As he says there, "never was there a more unconfined mind" than his (p. 6).[17]

During the first third of his Milton essay, Channing attempts to take this definition of the poet's intellectual genius and ally it to his moral genius. For him, this effort to portray Milton as a "master spirit" came almost naturally, since he saw the very act of writing as being akin to moral reasoning or religious discourse. All three were, in the aesthetics of Unitarianism, a recognition of the interconnected affinities binding together the universe. Just as he later did in the Fénelon review or his "Remarks on National Literature," Channing here asserts that literature "in its legitimate and highest efforts . . . has the same tendency and aim with Christianity; that is, to spiritualize our nature" (p. 15).[18] As a learned poet and a magnanimous soul, therefore, Milton was singularly well qualified to fuse aesthetic values and religious purpose in his poetry. Channing argues that this fusion centers on the sheer force of Milton's soul, since the "attribute of power is universally felt to characterize" him. As he goes on to say, this spiritual power calls forth the same energy in others and can be specifically identified with the poet's sublimity. Milton's "sublimity is in every man's mouth." "His name is almost identified with sublimity. He is in truth the sublimest of men. He rises, not by effort or discipline, but by a native tendency and a godlike instinct, to the contemplation of objects of grandeur and awfulness. He always moves with a conscious energy" (p. 12).

The poet's moral and intellectual energy are, in other words, part and parcel of his writings, especially *Paradise Lost*. His sublimity is not due to mere technical virtuosity, but partakes of his breadth of soul. Milton is a master poet because he is a master spirit, and his chief literary characteristic bears an organic relationship to his elevated moral and intellectual nature.

There are many examples of this in Milton's poetry, but for Channing the most striking are predictably in the first two books of *Paradise Lost*. More importantly, in describing this "noblest monument of human genius" he indicates in detail just what he means by "sublimity" and to what degree his sense of organicism is that of Reid and Stewart rather than of Kant and Coleridge. Typical is Channing's contrast between the physical torments of Milton's Hell and the spiritual and psychological state of Satan:

> Hell and hell's king have a terrible harmony, and dilate into new grandeur and awfulness, the longer we contemplate them. From one element, "solid and liquid fire," the poet has framed a world of horror and suffering, such as imagination had never traversed. But fiercer flames than those which encompass Satan, burn in his own soul. Revenge, exasperated pride, consuming wrath, ambition, though fallen, yet unconquered by the thunders of the Omnipotent, and grasping still at the empire of the universe,—these form a picture more sublime and terrible than hell. Hell yields to the spirit which it imprisons. The intensity of its fires reveals the intenser passions and more vehement will of Satan; and the ruined archangel gathers into himself the sublimity of the scene which surrounds him. This forms the tremendous interest of these wonderful books. We see mind triumphant over the most terrible powers of nature. We see unutterable agony subdued by energy of soul. (p. 15)

In some respects the view of sublimity here is that of the late eighteenth century. Milton's Hell is a large tableau-like scene in which physical grandeur and neoclassical heroism have their part. Similarly, embedded here is also a very traditional view of the mind, since Satan is said to take in the sublimity of the scene about him and show it forth again. In that sense, Satan is yet another example of the Scottish Common Sense scheme presented at the start of the *De Doctrina* review. At the same time, however, here Channing also shows the degree to which he sought to break away from his intellectual inheritance. He clearly sees mind and the force of sublime genius as triumphant over the natural sublime, even in Hell itself. He also celebrates the breadth and possibility of soul when faced with the strongest passions, vices, and virtues. In a very real sense, despite the pull of an associationist psychology, Channing sees *both* Satan and Milton as master spirits, whose "energy of soul" reaches out and impels the reader. Satan "is a creation requiring in its author almost the spiritual energy with which he invests the fallen seraph." He is, like the poet himself, active and forceful in molding his experience, and gains thereby a triumph over the obstacles before him.

Milton's Satan bears therefore, a very close relationship to his creator. Both are active intelligences of great force, reaching almost beyond the synthetic limits of Channing's philosophical forebears. Yet Channing could not take the decisive step which Emerson took, and interpret the prerogatives of the great soul as overturning the moral limits prescribed by traditional Christianity. His admiration for Milton as a sublime and creative spirit stops short of full approbation for his defiance—a Faustian stance common enough among the Transcendentalists.

This is not to say, of course, that Channing was not *tempted* into the latest form of infidelity. Indeed, he comes very close at one point to precisely the radical and antinomian views that the Emerson of "Self-Reliance" would announce. The passage cited above continues:

> Some have doubted whether the moral effect of such delineations of the storms and terrible workings of the soul is good; whether the interest felt in a spirit so transcendently evil as Satan, favors our sympathies with virtue. But our interest fastens, in this and like cases, on what is not evil. We gaze on Satan with an awe not unmixed with mysterious pleasure, as on a miraculous manifestation of the *power of mind*. What chains us, as with a resistless spell, in such a character, is spiritual might made visible by the racking pains which it overpowers. There is something kindling and ennobling in the consciousness, however awakened, of the energy which resides in mind; and many a virtuous man has borrowed new strength from the force, constancy, and dauntless courage of evil agents. (p. 16)

Channing is clearly taken with Satan's "burning throne" and "thunder-blasted brow." Yet he just as clearly channels this admiration into a morally-safe course. He takes great pains to reject Satan's defiance and sublime pride for the less subversive "power of mind." The very imagery of the passage makes it clear, however, how difficult this attempt to safeguard the moral sensibilities of his readers is. For Satan has a "mysterious pleasure" which "chains" the reader and puts him under "a resistless spell." There is a real sense in which Channing feels himself bewitched, and drawn into forbidden waters by the very sublimity of this figure. Like Milton himself, Milton's Satan overwhelms Channing for a time, and it is only with difficulty that he can maintain his moral balance.[19]

Indeed, the very way Channing moves back from the brink suggests that at the deepest level Satan does more for him than point a moral and adorn a tale. For in turning abruptly just after this to Adam and Eve, he notes that "from hell we flee to Paradise, a region as lovely as hell is terrible, and which, to those who do not know the universality of true genius, will appear doubly wonderful, when considered as the creation of the same mind, which had painted the infernal world" (p. 18). Even the happiness of our first parents pales in comparison with the "higher happiness than theirs" which is the result of a life lived according to the Christian ethic: "a happiness won through struggle with inward and outward foes, the happiness of power and moral victory, the happiness of disinterested sacrifices and wide-spread love, the happiness of boundless hope, and of 'thoughts which wander through eternity'" (p. 18). Thus Channing flees the temptations presented by the grandeur of Pandemonium and its ruler, not only to primordial bliss, but beyond that to the rewards of conventional morality. In the end his vision of the sublime and the power of mind cannot escape the world of Brattle Street and Harvard College. For Channing Milton ultimately is distinguished as a poet not because he is *as* God, but because as a moral, truth-loving soul he bears a *likeness* to God—an attitude that separates him from the Transcendentalists.

Yet Milton was not just a great poet. He was also a great political and theological writer as well. Channing suggests in the Napoleon essay that greatness of *action* (the third sort of genius) is the dominant force behind political and theological greatness. This is, however, a definitely inferior kind when compared to magnanimity and intellectual distinction. Indeed, it is the only kind Napoleon had, since for Channing his soul was marred by *hubris* and egocentrism. The French emperor as a result had a sphere of greatness limited to the battlefield and the arts of war—mere mastery of the physical realm rather than true spiritual achievement (pp. 120–22). Milton, on the other hand, overcame these normal limitations on greatness of action. For in his defense of political and religious liberty he was once more a master spirit.

Channing's treatment of Milton's political writings (pp. 20–40) rests clearly on his earlier exposition of the nature of the great soul. He opens with an argument *ex concessis* that the charge of partisanship made against them must be admitted, yet forgiven (pp. 21–23). This is because the political writings are the products of "a great and far-looking mind" enraptured of freedom and faced with perilous times. The poet's polemical harshness pales therefore beside the greatness of soul he shows in his conflict with Stuart tyranny:

> Liberty in both worlds has encountered opposition, over which she has triumphed only through her own immortal energies. At such periods, men, gifted with great power of thought and loftiness of sentiment, are especially summoned to the conflict with evil. They hear, as it were, in their own magnanimity and generous aspirations, the voice of a divinity; and thus commissioned, and burning with a passionate devotion to truth and freedom, they must and will

speak with an indignant energy, and they ought not to be measured by the standard of ordinary minds in ordinary times. Men of natural softness and timidity,
of a sincere but effeminate virtue, will be apt to look on these bolder, hardier
spirits, as violent, perturbed, and uncharitable; and the charge will not be
wholly groundless. But that deep feeling of evils, which is necessary to effectual
conflict with them, and which marks God's most powerful messengers to mankind, cannot breathe itself in soft and tender accents. The deeply moved soul
will speak strongly, and ought to speak so as to move and shake nations. (pp.
24–25)

Milton's greatness of action proceeds, therefore, out of his magnanimity
and intellectual genius (here called "great power of thought and loftiness of
sentiment"). Just as in the sublimity of *Paradise Lost* Milton's political zeal
expresses a deeper, more spiritual energy. He is once more devoted to
"truth and freedom" and takes on a prophetic character, since he has "the
voice of a divinity." Similarly, like Milton's Satan, Milton the polemicist is
almost (but not quite) beyond the bounds of conventional morality. Although
the charge of a lack of charity is "not . . . wholly groundless," nonetheless,
he "ought not to be measured by the standard of ordinary minds in ordinary
times." This morally privileged status is almost inevitable, in fact, in those
who are "God's most powerful messengers to mankind." For their actions
bear the mark of the divine truth within their own souls and so, cannot help
but shake thrones and move nations—a significant point especially in view of
Channing's own later abandonment of moral suasion for direct confrontation
over the slavery issue.[20]

In the rest of his discussion of Milton's politics Channing essentially expands this view of the organic relationship between the freedom-loving soul
and the politics of revolution. He very quickly distinguishes Milton from
Napoleon, for instance, by the spiritual nature of his political vision. For the
latter served himself, but the former loved God and man, and lacked all egocentrism in his devotion to liberty:

We have offered these remarks as strongly applicable to Milton. He reverenced
and loved human nature, and attached himself to its great interests with a fervor
of which only such a mind was capable. He lived in one of those solemn periods
which determine the character of ages to come. His spirit was stirred to its very
centre by the presence of danger. He lived in the midst of the battle. That the
ardor of his spirit sometimes passed the bounds of wisdom and charity, and
poured forth unwarrantable invective, we see and lament. But the purity and
loftiness of his mind break forth amidst his bitterest invectives. We see a noble
nature still. We see, that no feigned love of truth and freedom was a covering for
selfishness and malignity. He did indeed love and adore uncorrupted religion,
and intellectual liberty, and let his name be enrolled among their truest champions. (p. 25)

This nobility of nature is especially seen in the *kind* of liberty Milton fought for. The poet's "greatness of mind" manifested itself in "his fervent and constant attachment to liberty." Although "freedom, in all its forms and branches, was dear to him," it was "especially freedom of thought and speech, of conscience and worship, freedom to seek, profess, and propagate truth" that he served. This was very different than "the liberty of ordinary politicians" which concerns itself with outward rights and transient issues; "the tyranny" Milton "hated most was that, which broke the intellectual and moral power of the community." His behavior proceeded therefore naturally from his lofty nature and "threw a hue of poetry over politics, and gave a sublime reference to his service of the commonwealth" (p. 34).

Milton's political engagement with the Great Rebellion betrays the direct link between his status as a master spirit and true genius of action. For him, spiritual acts and political acts were of a piece, and the one took its direction from the other. Furthermore, it is because of his failure to note this connection that the Tory criticism of Samuel Johnson is in error. Indeed, it is a classic example of the difference that qualities of soul can make:

> We doubt whether two other minds, having so little in common as those of which we are now speaking, can be found in the higher walks of literature. Johnson was great in his own sphere, but that sphere was comparatively "of the earth," whilst Milton's was only inferior to that of angels. It was customary, in the day of Johnson's glory, to call him a giant, to class him with a mighty, but still an earth-born race. Milton we should rank among seraphs. Johnson's mind acted chiefly on man's actual condition, on the realities of life, on the springs of human action, on the passions which now agitate society, and he seems hardly to have dreamed of a higher state of the human mind, than was then exhibited. Milton, on the other hand, burned with a deep, yet calm love of moral grandeur and celestial purity. He thought, not so much of what man is, as of what he might become. His own mind was a revelation to him of a higher condition of humanity, and to promote this he thirsted and toiled for freedom, as the element for the growth and improvement of his nature. (pp. 37–38)

Johnson's negative view of Milton was, in other words, not just the result of bigotry or narrowmindedness (as Macaulay and other contemporary Whig critics would maintain). Instead it was a failure of genius, a dwelling on the actual and material rather than the potential and the spiritual. And it is precisely in *this* difference, rather than any partisan distinction between Cavalier and Roundhead, that Milton is the greater of the two.

Finally, in the last third of the review (pp. 40–68) Channing turns to Milton as a theologian. Here too he shows genius of action and all of the other qualities mentioned heretofore. Yet perhaps unexpectedly Channing begins on a somewhat negative note. For he finds this aspect of the poet's career less inspiring than his literary and political activities. The reason, significantly, is that Milton's theology (particularly in the *De Doctrina*) often lacks the personal and distinctive imprint of his individual soul found elsewhere. For once, Milton seems largely in thrall to the language and thought of tradition:

> Milton aims to give us the doctrines of revelation in its own words. We have them in a phraseology long familiar to us, and we are disappointed; for we expected to see them, not in the language of the Bible, but as existing in the mind of Milton, modified by his peculiar intellect and sensibility, combined and embodied with his various knowledge, illustrated by the analogies, brightened by the new lights, and clothed with the associations, with which they were surrounded by this gifted man. We hoped to see these doctrines as they were viewed by Milton in his moments of solemn feeling and deep contemplation, when they pervaded and moved his whole soul. (p. 40)

Despite this general falling off in inspiration, however, "still there are passages in which Milton's mind is laid open to us." Not surprisingly these are the very ones in which he is most heterodox, and closest to Channing's own theological views. Indeed, this final portion of the review allies the previous characterization of the poet as an inspired genius with his role as a Unitarian. To be sure, Channing does disagree with his subject on a number of matters (e.g., Original Sin, clerical compensation, the ordering of churches, etc.). Yet significantly these lapses are generally subsumed under the heading of Milton's excessive traditionalism noted above. They are a failure of genius to overcome the transitory and temporal prejudices of the age (pp. 55–56).

Channing emphasizes instead the liberal and Arian side of the *De Doctrina*. The poet's views on Christ's place in the Godhead receive particular attention, for instance. In this regard Channing and his co-religionists "take Milton, Locke, and Newton, and place them in our front, and want no others to oppose to the whole array of great names on the opposite side. Before these intellectual suns, the stars of self-named Orthodoxy 'hide their diminished heads'" (p. 46). Similarly, Milton's anti-Trinitarian views are compared to his anti-sectarian spirit, in which Channing also finds a parallel with modern Unitarianism:[21]

> He would probably stand first among that class of Christians, more numerous than is supposed, and, we hope, increasing, who are too jealous of the rights of the mind, and too dissatisfied with the clashing systems of the age, to attach themselves closely to any party; . . . who contend earnestly for free inquiry, not because all who inquire will think as they do, but because some at least may be expected to outstrip them, and to be guides to higher truth. With this nameless and spreading class we have strong sympathies. We want new light, and care not whence it comes; we want reformers worthy of the name; and we

should rejoice in such a manifestation of Christianity, as would throw all present systems into obscurity. (p. 48)

Channing's Milton is in the forefront of those who believe in freedom of inquiry and the progressive nature of revelation. Despite his over-reverence for the primitive church and the Old Testament on many points (e.g., polygamy—see pp. 51–55),[22] he is essentially at one with liberal Boston Unitarianism in his basic attitude toward authority.

Yet for all these similarities, this last passage suggests that Channing's Milton is to be valued most of all for his love of freedom. Indeed, as we shall see, it is in his emphasis on Milton's libertarianism that Channing most distinguishes himself from other members of his denomination, who were all too ready to take a narrowly sectarian view of the poet. The *De Doctrina* is, therefore, not valuable primarily as a theological handbook. Rather, it is both "a testimony to Milton's profound reverence for the Christian religion, and an assertion of the freedom and rights of the mind" (p. 64). Although he sometimes "did not draw more from the deep and full fountains of his own soul" (p. 67), nevertheless his very heterodoxy was a sign of his devotion to intellectual and spiritual freedom. Like his political writings, Milton's theological works show that "he taught and exemplified that spirit of intellectual freedom, through which all the great conquests of truth are to be achieved, and by which the human mind is to attain to a new consciousness of its sublime faculties, and to invigorate and expand itself for ever" (p. 68). Thus, his attacks on the bishops, like his attacks on their king, are on a much higher plane than their partisan tone may suggest. These books too give evidence of a great soul, the study of which illustrates the nature and potential of the human spirit. In the end, the *De Doctrina* as much as *Paradise Lost* or the *Areopagitica* expresses the divine mission of its author. For as Channing says in conclusion:

In offering this tribute, we have aimed at something higher than to express and gratify our admiration of an eminent man. We believe, that an enlightened and exalted mind is a brighter manifestation of God than the outward universe; and we have set forth, as we have been able, the praises of an illustrious servant of the Most High, that, through him, glory may redound to the Father of all spirits, the Fountain of all wisdom and magnanimous virtue. And still more; we believe that the sublime intelligence of Milton was imparted, not for his own sake only, but to awaken kindred virtue and greatness in other souls. Far from regarding him as standing alone and unapproachable, we believe that he is an illustration of what all, who are true to their nature, will become in the progress of their being; and we have held him forth, not to excite an ineffectual admiration, but to stir up our own and others' breasts to an exhilarating pursuit of high and ever-growing attainments in intellect and virtue. (p. 68)

Channing's review of the *De Doctrina* is typical, therefore, of his own literary and philosophical views. It is also representative of early nineteenth-century New England's responses to Milton as well. As poet, political figure, and religious controversialist, Milton was held to be one of the great men of his or any other age. Like Channing, other New Englanders emphasized his poetic power, religious zeal, and love of liberty. In this they too were heavily influenced by contemporary English criticism and biography. New England's Milton forms, therefore, part of a much broader pattern linking Boston Unitarians and British Whigs. At the same time, however, the *De Doctrina* review also speaks to the uniqueness of Channing's response to Milton, as to everything else in his intellectual world.

For early nineteenth-century American critics, Milton was first and foremost the very model of the poet, broad in imagination, filled with moral power, and sublime in the vigor of his expression. As in Channing's case, this may in part be due to the increasing influence of the English Romantics (especially Wordsworth), howevermuch most Americans still misinterpreted their philosophical position.[23] Yet one need not go to the Lake poets or the German idealists to find reasons for Milton's influence. As Sensabaugh has shown, during the preceding century he was held in general critical esteem in the New World. Moreover, if his star was falling at the start of the new century, certain poetic traits were still associated with his name: sublimity, elevated diction, learning, rhetorical grandeur, and moral seriousness. These were also the very characteristics emphasized by contemporary English Milton criticism.[24] Closer to home, the rhetorical texts used in American colleges (to which Channing and his generation were exposed) also stressed Milton as the poet of moral sublimity, civic virtue, and intellectual breadth.[25]

Typical of these attitudes was John Quincy Adams, the first Boylston Professor of Rhetoric at Harvard, whose inaugural *Lectures* contain a number of passages recommending Milton as a model.[26] Indeed, the praise of Milton in this work (which was a standard Harvard textbook for many years) is fairly consistent. He notes, for instance, that "the powers of language in all the tongues, with which we are acquainted, recognize only three degrees of comparison; a positive, a comparative, and a superlative. But climax is ever seeking for a fourth; and one of the images, in which it most indulges, is that of finding such fourth degree of comparison. Of this grandeur of imagination, which stretches beyond the bounds of ordinary possibility, the most frequent examples are to be found in the daring and sublime genius of Milton."[27] Similarly, Adams holds that Milton was "the sublimest of poets,"[28] especially in Books I and II of *Paradise Lost*. Channing's own brother, Edward Tyrrel (who as Boylston Professor from 1819 to 1851 taught Emerson, Thoreau, Lowell, Edward Everett Hale, and Charles Eliot Norton), comes to much the same conclusion. For him Milton's poetry is powerful rhetoric effective in moving the reader by its sublime morality.[29]

Writers farther removed from Unitarian Boston also echo these sentiments. Timothy Dwight, for example, not only imitated Milton poetically in *The Conquest of Canaan*,[30] but he also saw him as an example of the active, rational powers of the imagination:

> As genius is the power of making efforts, it is obvious that it will never be exerted, or in other words the efforts will never be made, without energy, that is, without the resolution, activity, and perseverance which are necessary to their existence. This energy can never be summoned into action, but by motives of a suitable nature and sufficient magnitude to move the mind. Nor can it act to any considerable purpose, unless attended with proper advantages. Wherever these causes do not meet, the fire will be smothered. . . . How obviously must the real Milton have been inglorious, if he had been mute; and how obviously would he have been mute, notwithstanding all his powers, if his energy had not prompted him, or if commanding motives had not summoned that energy into action.[31]

This view of Milton as an energetic soul (and of such energy as the basis for genius) is shared by another contemporary, William Cullen Bryant. Like Dwight, he largely worked out of the framework of the Scottish Common Sense philosophy. Like Channing, however, he was also open to broader philosophical and literary influences.[32] His 1825 *Lectures on Poetry* bespeak not only his general intellectual similarity to Channing, but the affinity of their views on Milton as well. He too chooses Milton to illustrate his essentially associationist view of the poetic imagination. For Bryant, "the imagination is the most active and the least susceptible of fatigue of all the faculties of the human mind." At its best this activity is both rational and restrained, although "its more intense exercise is tremendous, and sometimes unsettles the reason." Yet the fact that it "is by no means passive" does not lead to disorder, since "it pursues the path which the poet only points out, and shapes its visions from the scenes and allusions which he gives." This rational view of the imagination is specifically illustrated both by "the strength and cultivation" of *Paradise Lost* in general, and by the same two examples Channing had chosen: the portrait of Satan and the Edenic bliss of Adam and Eve.[33] Indeed, Bryant almost repeats Channing's words when he declares "the great epic of Milton" to be "the noblest poem in our language," adding as well that "his *Paradise Regained*" is not "unworthy to be the last work of so great a man."[34]

As one moves closer to Channing's own intellectual milieu the similarity of critical opinion becomes even more striking. F. W. P. Greenwood, for example, although a conservative Unitarian in other ways, was an early supporter of Wordsworth and the other Lake poets in the *North American Review*.[35] His most extensive characterization of Milton is almost a rephrasing of Channing a year earlier:

For ourselves, we can truly say that we never knew Milton, till we were acquainted with his prose writings. We never knew the man till then; never felt how entirely and supremely he was a poet, or, to use his own words, 'a true poem; that is, a composition and pattern of the best and honorablest things.' We never knew till then, what a noble, highminded being, what a contemner of littleness and baseness, what a fearless asserter of right and denouncer of wrong, how pure, how virtuous, how incorruptible, how unconquerable he was. How truly the modern poet speaks of him, when he says; 'His soul was as a star, and dwelt apart.' When we now compare him with his brother stars, we perceive that he has indeed his own separate heaven, where he shines alone, and not to be approached. If we grant that in the single respect of genius he was second to Shakspeare, and to him alone would we grant him to be second, yet what was Shakspeare's life? . . . We think of Shakspeare's poetry, and not of Shakspeare. His name comes to us as a voice, an abstraction, a beautiful sound. But the name of Milton is inseparably united with the man himself.[36]

For Greenwood Milton the man and Milton the poet were bound up together. This strong personal presence in his writings expresses itself, moreover, by the truth, justice and virtue they contain. Such is Milton's moral strength and breadth of sympathy that as in Channing he is given an exalted rank, like the angels.

These views are also shared by A. H. Everett, who allowed heterodox and new ideas to appear in the *North American Review* during his tenure there in the 1830's. He too places Shakespeare first in the literary pantheon, but significantly, for precisely the same reason that Greenwood and Channing praised Milton: "We are free to confess, that with the highest admiration for the genius and character of Milton, we do not recognise in his poetry a talent of the same order with that of Shakspeare. His touch is free and bold, — that of Shakspeare airy and elastic. The coloring of Milton is rich and true, — that of Shakspeare fresh, bright and dewy. In Milton's creations, we feel the hand of a master; — in those of Shakspeare, we forget it."[37]

Milton's personal presence and his status as a sublime truth-teller are frequently contrasted in this way with the negative capability of Shakespeare. Yet even contemporary critics who *dislike* Milton join with Channing and the rest in attributing these same qualities to his poetry. Thus, an anonymous piece from the *Monthly Anthology* compares the physical sublimity of Milton's Satan unfavorably to that moral sublimity which resides in virtuous conduct. "The *moral sublime* is the most essentially and universally sublime of all the species of sublimity," largely because it is not founded on mere physical or material glory, but "on the distinctions which exist between moral good and moral evil, distinctions, as eternal, immutable and important as the Deity himself." Hence, for that "being who can comprehend heaven and earth at a glance," the mere physical sublimity of Homer's Zeus or Milton's Satan "must appear trifling and puerile." The essayist concludes that "when the might of the hero will be despised or forgotten, the goodness of the faint will find its reward in the love and esteem of the highest orders of the moral creation."[38] Such sentiments, of course, contain the seeds of Channing's own position, for he too saw the moral sublime as the highest sort. His contrast between the martial glory of Napoleon and the real spiritual glory of a Milton illustrates this. Yet at the same time one can also see the distance between Channing and this 1803 essay. Although ultimately he flees back to this sort of moralism, Channing lingers long over a broader view of the moral sublime which would include the characteristics of Milton's Satan, and is deeply drawn to the magnificent spirit amid Pandemonium.

Similarly, John C. Gray contrasts Milton unfavorably with Dante because of a religious viewpoint more conventional than Channing's. He notes that "Dante's description of the prince of hell, as well as his kingdom, short as it is, is far more appropriate than Milton's." But this moral uneasiness about the beginning of *Paradise Lost* calls forth a tribute to the sublimity and power of the archfiend not unlike that of Channing: "such is human nature that we cannot but respect the dignity with which he fills the throne even of hell, the readiness he constantly displays to be foremost to act and suffer for the advantage of his community, the lofty spirit which enables him to feel or to feign a hope in the most desperate circumstances." Even in "his address to the Sun" in Book IV Gray finds that Satan's fairness towards God itself "greatly disarms our indignation against an adversary who could acknowledge them [God's perfections] so fairly." Indeed, for a conventional moralist like Gray this is precisely the problem: Milton seems to be of the devil's party without knowing it, and his fallen archangel elicits our admiration and sympathy far too much for comfort. Satan "preserves every where the same gloomy greatness; he always elicits our pity and commands our respect in the character of an 'Arch Angel ruined.' He may well be compared to the Sun in a partial eclipse, shedding every where around him a light faded and solemn, but by no means terrific or baleful."[39]

Lurking in this mixture of attraction and revulsion is the same response that underlies Channing's praise for the energy and *virtú* shown by Satan and his creator alike. W. S. Shaw praised the poem, for example, by saying that "Milton's character of Satan exhibits wonderful powers of mind" and is "the genius of destruction" who "bears on his front the marks of thunder, [and] does 'not repent or change, though changed in outward lustre.'" Shaw's excitement at Satan's powers of soul is also quickly tempered by a characterization very much like that of Channing, although somewhat more orthodox in tone. For he is a being who "in the last degree of abasement and wretchedness . . . retains the memory of his ancient glory, and meditates on new vengeance.—Some trait of his celestial nature may yet be perceived in his infernal soul."[40] The difference—and it is here Channing advances in the direction Emerson was to follow—is that the orthodox recoil from this sublime figure is stronger in the earlier critics. Channing is more complex in his moral feelings and above all keeps before him the organic presence of the poet in all his creations. If Milton was a great soul devoted to truth and virtue, then they would be found even in his vision of Hell itself, no matter how subversive of the moral order that vision might be. The very similarity of his views with those of his predecessors suggests that Channing did not have to invent a new critical vocabulary for his study of Milton. Rather, he merely transposed the one he already had.

The 1826 review of the *De Doctrina* is both typical and yet crucially different from contemporary New England literary attitudes towards Milton. This is even more true of Channing's analysis of Milton the political figure. In England during the first half of the nineteenth century the poet's political writings and service under the Commonwealth especially interested the major Whig biographers and literary historians.[41] The tone of the British contribution has been well summarized by Nelson:

> But during the early years of the nineteenth century, a pronounced reaction to the Tory biographical and critical approach to Milton occurred, signaled, in part, by Macaulay's famous essay of 1825; and by the third decade, a new and radically different approach to Milton biography was being employed by several writers sympathetic to the ideals of the dissenters, Whigs, liberals, and radicals. The new biographies written by Joseph Ivimey, William Carpenter, Cyrus Edmonds, Edwin Paxton Hood, and others were dedicated to the propagation of Milton's political and religious views and activities, and, of necessity, to the exposition of the prose rather than the poetry. This important new direction in Milton biography was accompanied by clear and concise objections to the previous biographical writings, and succinct statements as to the aims and purposes of the new.
>
> In general, the objections to Tory biography were two. First, the biographies by Dr. Johnson and his contemporaries, members of the English church and Tory party, were biased and unsympathetic to Milton, the republican and dissenter; and, in turn, this bias resulted in unbalanced and ill-proportioned biographies which over-emphasized the poetry and slighted the prose. That is, the eighteenth-century biographer usually found it more congenial to talk about Milton's poetry than to discuss his prose, and Milton the poet was more appealing than Milton the man. Second, the biographies were printed in large, elaborate editions which were too expensive for the poorer classes to buy.[42]

These Whig biographies were extremely popular in America[43] and were imitated here as well. Indeed, in England the reviewers saw Channing's own Milton piece as just such an imitation.[44] Macaulay's famous essay, for example, though much more partisan in tone, bears many close resemblances to Channing's effort a year later. Milton's "public conduct was such as was to be expected from a man of a spirit so high and of an intellect so powerful. He lived at one of the most memorable eras in the history of mankind, at the very crisis of the great conflict between Oromasdes and Arimanes, liberty and despotism, reason and prejudice." It was then in Macaulay's view that "the destinies of the human race were staked on the same cast with the freedom of the English people," and Milton among others "first proclaimed those mighty principles which have since worked their way into the depths of the American forests, which have roused Greece . . . [and] have kindled an unquenchable fire in the hearts of the oppressed, and loosed the knees of the oppressors with an unwonted fear."[45]

Channing, on the other hand, is much more broadly interested in Milton as a great man, a spirit of genius, than is Macaulay, who uses the poet as a stick with which to beat latter-day reactionaries. Similarly, Dr. Johnson is handled much more gently by Channing than many contemporary British writers, in part perhaps because of his continuing literary reputation in New England, and the general conservatism of Federalist Boston.[46] On the issue of Milton's defense of liberty, however, Channing and the English agree. His greatness of soul and devotion to the principles of freedom made him for Channing its "most devoted and eloquent literary champion." He too saw the English Civil War as a central turning point in the history of the world. He excuses Milton's partisanship in part precisely on this ground, since "liberty was in peril. Great evils were struggling for perpetuity, and could only be broken down by great power. Milton felt that interests of infinite moment were at stake; and who will blame him for binding himself to them with the whole energy of his great mind, and for defending them with fervor and vehemence?" (p. 24).

Channing's review was both typical and yet unique among American responses to Milton's politics as well. As Sensabaugh has shown, the American Revolution and the political struggles of the Democrats and the Federalists spawned a vigorous tradition of Miltonic satire. Both sides in these disputes (including Loyalists in the Revolution) regularly invoked Milton as "that grand whig." They similarly used *Paradise Lost* and the prose writings as literary models. During the nineteenth century this tradition continued, the most notable example being Whittier's Miltonic invective in his abolitionist tracts.[47] As a result, even the most conservative Americans of Channing's day had a favorable view of the poet's role in the English Civil War. Indeed, the revolt against King Charles was popularly seen as a forerunner of America's own resistance to alleged royal tyranny. It is difficult, therefore, to find American examples of the Tory criticism about which the English Whigs complained.[48]

On the contrary, American biographers and reviewers are almost unanimous in their praise for Milton, often adding that nationalistic and partisan note found in the British critics, but absent from Channing. Francis Parkman in a review of a book on Roger Williams goes out of his way to note that the founder of Rhode Island was an acquaintance of Milton, and like him loved liberty.[49] Similarly, Greenwood in the *North American Review* article already cited begins by saying:

> As Americans, as lovers of freedom, improvement, and truth, we wish to see these two volumes widely circulated among our countrymen, and deeply read. They are fit manuals for a free people. They are full of those eloquent, soul stirring, holy lessons of liberty, which do something more than simply persuade and convince the mind; which give it purpose, and principle, and firm resolve; which brace up the heart, while they strengthen the understanding; which render timidity or apostacy impossible; which, at the same time that they impart the feeling of discipleship, infuse the spirit of martyrdom; because the truths which they inculcate are of such a nature, that those who receive them must contend, and if needs be, must die for them.[50]

Farther south, Rufus W. Griswold, in the "Biographical Introduction" to his 1845 edition of the prose works, not only calls him "the greatest of all human beings: the noblest and the ennobler of mankind," but also defends his justification of the regicides. In reply to a recent Tory biographer he notes that "in the United States, where the divine right of any man to oppress his fellows is not held, we think differently; and our admiration of MILTON suffers no abatement, but rather is greater."[51]

The first full-length American biography of Milton, that of W. Carlos Martyn in 1866, although written long after the period under consideration here, suggests the longevity of the Whig tradition. Not only is it largely a series of citations from such English biographers as Symmons and Ivimey, but it also strikes the familiar nationalistic note with particular stridency:

> Since, on this side of the Atlantic, the republican ideas and the ecclesiastical truths which Milton so ardently espoused and so ably expounded, have effected a fixed and lasting lodgement, and since it may, in some sense, be said that religious and political America sprang from his brain, it is somewhat singular that no American should have undertaken to present Milton's life to his fellow-countrymen, for the edification and instruction of those who stand so heavily in his debt. It certainly seems that this republic, based largely upon his ideas, and wedded enthusiastically to his religious opinions, owes John Milton at least the tribute and the grateful recognition of a biographical record.[52]

Finally, a different kind of evidence of the transatlantic nature of the Whig tradition lies in two poems by Bryant which are imitations of the sonnet, "On the Late Massacre at Piedmont." One (as J. H. Adler has noted)[53] is

"The Massacre at Scio," commemorating a Turkish atrocity in the Greek War of Independence. The other, hitherto unnoticed, is his "Hymn of the Waldenses," an 1824 composition celebrating that people's struggle for religious freedom. The significance of these poems is that this Miltonic sonnet also enjoyed an extraordinary vogue in England as a model for political poems of all stripes.[34]

The element lacking in all of these Whig treatments of Milton the politician is what Channing saw clearly and emphasized strongly: that Milton's political vision could not be separated from either his character or the rest of his life. However much they might agree that Milton loved liberty, Channing parted company with his contemporaries here. For like his subject he loved liberty as a spiritual concept, something ennobling of the human soul, rather than as a specific political remedy for specific political injustices. As a result, here as in his views on Milton's verse, Channing gives a more unified view of the man and his career, and the ways in which they interrelate.

Much the same may be said for Channing's place among contemporary students of Milton's theology. On the one hand, he is representative of the general liberal Unitarian approval of Milton the theologian. Even more, he shares the common admiration for his love of ecclesiastical freedom. Yet Channing's is a much broader and ultimately more satisfying account of the place of these religious wrtings in their author's life. Sidney Willard, for example, in his own review of the *De Doctrina* had held that "connected as were the affairs of church and state at that period, it was impossible that one who had any strong republican tendency, should bear any good will to episcopacy." This double devotion to liberty manifested itself even in the poet's travels to Italy, "at the very seat, and almost in the presence of the papal power." Like Channing, Willard held that this love of freedom was the result of Milton's personal character, "proceeding from a great mind, a mind distinguished by independence, to a degree remarkable at the period."[55] Samuel Osgood (a liberal Unitarian and member of Hedge's Transcendental Club)[56] struck the same note by asserting the need of every age to "inflame its zeal by fire from the old altars of freedom and faith":

> In our day, England has had cause to learn many a lesson at the tombs of her great champions of liberty. In new forms the priestcraft and kingcraft of the Stuarts have risen up to conspire against civil and religious freedom; and in new forms the shades of the stout Independents, with Cromwell and Milton at their head, have gone out to do battle against them. Our own country, although called pre-eminently the land of liberty, has seen something of the same conflict and needs something of the same defence. Some of our Congressional champions of absolutism might be confounded at once by the most familiar truisms of those sages of the old English Commonwealth, from whom our fathers learned

their ideas of constitutional rights; and not a few of our clergy who are making Oxford or Rome the throne of their faith might with great profit diversify their liturgical studies by the careful perusal of the old champions of religious liberty.[57]

Milton is here cast in the familiar role of the friend of religious and civil liberties. Yet this defence is also drawn (as it often was) into those less edifying sectarian quarrels from which New England had not yet weaned itself. The contrast with Channing on this score is important. While obviously weighted in favor of their mutual Arianism, his version of Milton's theology is not marred by the sort of snide reference to Roman or Anglo-Catholicism one gets here. In fact, he very much stands out from the ill-concealed glee with which his co-religionists greeted the appearance of the *De Doctrina.* Almost as soon as the translation arrived in Boston, for example, the *Christian Examiner* rushed suitably Unitarian excerpts of it into print.[58] In the same volume the editors later turned selected passages from "Of Reformation Touching Church Discipline" towards rather more partisan purposes than the general defense of religious liberty. Thus, one passage is explicitly presented to "answer the ominous cries of the opposers of Unitarians and of some irresolutes among themselves, who, as they see one after another of what we deem the theological errors of the day attempted to be removed, are continually exclaiming—'do not go too far!'—'where will you stop!'—as if in the work of reformation we *could* go too far, or as if we ought to stop *at all*, till every strong delusion, every mere device of the human understanding, or of the human passions, is utterly destroyed, and truth and goodness are all in all!"[59] Similarly, the same journal lauds the Unitarian and democratic principles of a Pennsylvania paper called "The Miltonian," and cites in another number the poet's defence of a reasoned and a reasonable religion.[60]

Channing too had hailed Milton as a forward-looking thinker, a believer in free inquiry, toleration, rational religion, a continuing revelation, and the like.[61] However, he avoided the disquietingly sectarian tone found here— and apologized for it when it occured in Milton himself. He breaks therefore with the lively American tradition of using Milton as a source text in religious disputes. As Sensabaugh has shown, both Deists and Christians had done so at the end of the eighteenth century.[62] Its continued viability into Channing's day can be seen by the fact that his Milton piece was appropriated by both sides of the contemporary battle between Unitarianism and Orthodoxy. It was attacked on the one hand by the Reverend Frederick Beasley of New Jersey in a pamphlet which makes much of those passages in *Paradise Lost* bearing a Trinitarian cast.[63] The Unitarians, on the other, themselves took Channing's *De Doctrina* review and abridged it during the 1840s as part of a general campaign against what one of them called "Puseyism and Popery"—a disreputable episode far from Channing's tolerant views, reflecting perhaps the frustration and dissention within the denomination at this time.[64] This edition of the review by the American Unitarian Association was a truncated version differing in a number of telling ways from the original.[65] Channing's comments on Milton's theology are, in general, abridged in order to increase the emphasis on the poet's liberal stance. Similarly, his more orthodox opinions are much downplayed. Most important, all of Channing's literary and political commentary is excised as irrelevant to the purposes of the propagandistic version. The result, as in contemporary treatments of Milton the politician, is that the context for Channing's specific theological appraisal of the work is missing. With it one also loses Channing's fundamental view of his subject as an inspired soul whose writings bear the mark of his special nature and are in an organic relationship to it—perhaps the most central theme of the review as a whole.

Yet this failure by the reverend gentlemen of the American Unitarian Association lay not just in their inability to see the true liberalism of Channing's theological stance. Rather, they failed to understand the genre in which he was writing as well. For Channing was not interested in a mere literary analysis of his subject; nor did he seek to use Milton's writings as proof texts for a series of modern-day disputes. He was instead trying to give a portrait of one man which would stand for all men and their potential. His review of the *De Doctrina Christiana*, in other words, focused on the individual as a means of delineating the transcendent and spiritual. As such, it is generically and thematically a precursor of the Transcendental biographies and autobiographies of Emerson and Thoreau. He attempts here to give a unified account of the writer and his writings as representative in the broadest sense. For him, therefore, Milton was more than a mere moral exemplar or a great writer. Rather, "that sainted spirit" becomes emblematic of man and his spiritual possibilities. Channing's essay because of this takes the aesthetic of Unitarian New England towards its very limits. And by that act of extension he also reaches for a new and broader understanding of Milton than the Whig tradition could provide. Still typical of his contemporaries' attitudes towards the poet, he was also in many ways less narrow than they in his focus on the literary, political, and religious dimensions of his subject. As a result, his essay both sums up the past and points towards the future, and the Milton of Emerson and Thoreau.

NOTES

1. The comments of the English Romantic poets are anthologized in *The Romantics on Milton: Formal Essays and Critical Asides*, ed. J. A. Wittreich, Jr. (Cleveland: Case Western Reserve University Press, 1970). Critical studies of Milton in the early nineteenth century in-

clude R. D. Havens, *The Influence of Milton on English Poetry* (Cambridge: Harvard University Press, 1922), James G. Nelson, *The Sublime Puritan: Milton and the Victorians* (Madison: University of Wisconsin Press, 1963), and Leslie Brisman, *Milton's Poetry of Choice and Its Romantic Heirs* (Ithaca: Cornell University Press, 1973).

2. Phyllis Cole, "The Purity of Puritanism: Transcendentalist Readings of Milton," *Studies in Romanticism*, 17 (Spring 1978): 129–48, and George F. Sensabaugh, *Milton in Early America* (Princeton: Princeton University Press, 1964). A number of dissertations also discuss this topic, although from an almost wholly descriptive or bibliographical point of view: Ruth W. Gregory, "American Criticism of Milton, 1800–1938" (University of Wisconsin, 1938), James Thorpe, "The Decline of the Miltonic Tradition" (Harvard University, 1941), John A. Weigel, "The Miltonic Tradition in the First Half of the Nineteenth Century" (Western Reserve University, 1939), and Lester F. Zimmerman, "Some Aspects of Milton's American Reputation to 1900" (University of Wisconsin, 1950).

3. William M. Wynkoop, *Three Children of the Universe: Emerson's View of Shakespeare, Bacon, and Milton* (The Hague: Mouton, 1966), and Henry F. Pommer, *Milton and Melville* (Pittsburgh: University of Pittsburgh Press, 1950).

4. Cole, "Transcendentalist Readings of Milton," 131.

5. William Ellery Channing, "Milton" [review of *A Treatise on Christian Doctrine, compiled from the Holy Scriptures*, trans. Charles R. Sumner], *Christian Examiner and Theological Review*, 3 (January–February 1826): 29–77. Citations are from *The Works of William E. Channing, D.D.* (Boston: James Munroe, 1848), 1:3–68.

6. Treatments of Channing's place in the intellectual development of Unitarianism into Transcendentalism are David P. Edgell, *William Ellery Channing: An Intellectual Portrait* (Boston: Beacon, 1955), pp. 113–49; Conrad Wright, "The Rediscovery of Channing," *The Liberal Christians: Essays on American Unitarian History* (Boston: Beacon, 1970), pp. 22–40; Lawrence Buell, *Literary Transcendentalism: Style and Vision in the American Renaissance* (Ithaca: Cornell University Press, 1973), pp. 23–54; William R. Hutchison, *The Transcendentalist Ministers: Church Reform in the New England Renaissance* (New Haven: Yale University Press, 1959); and Andrew Delbanco, *William Ellery Channing: An Essay on the Liberal Spirit in America* (Cambridge: Harvard University Press, 1981). Zimmerman, "Milton's American Reputation to 1900," pp. 142–85, gives a summary of Channing on Milton, but from an uncritical perspective which also seriously misreads the former's philosophical position.

7. Buell, *Literary Transcendentalism*, pp. 263ff.

8. For the rediscovery, publication, and reception of the *De Doctrina Christiana*, see Milton, *Two Books of Investigations into Christian Doctrine Drawn From the Sacred Scriptures Alone*, ed. Maurice Kelley and trans. John Carey, in *Complete Prose Works of John Milton* (New Haven: Yale University Press, 1973), 6:3–42.

9. The most thorough account of the intellectual history of New England Unitarianism is Daniel Walker Howe, *The Unitarian Conscience: Harvard Moral Philosphy, 1805–1861* (Cambridge: Harvard University Press, 1970).

10. Buell, *Literary Transcendentalism*, p. 36. For a different view of Channing and the Transcendentalists, which sees him as a crypto-idealist, see Edgell, *William Ellery Channing*.

11. William Charvat, *The Origins of American Critical Thought (1810–1835)* (Philadelphia: University of Pennsylvania Press, 1936), pp. 7–26.

12. Discussed by Cole, "Transcendentalist Readings of Milton," 129–34. Since the evidence for Channing's relationship with Wordsworth and Coleridge comes from his nephew's memoir (which deliberately overstates his affinity with the Transcendentalists), the connection is somewhat dubious.

13. For the general critical history of the imagination in England and America, see Charvat, *The Origins of American Critical Thought*, pp. 27–58, and James Engell, *The Creative Imagination: Enlightenment to Romanticism* (Cambridge: Harvard University Press, 1981), esp. pp. 184–214.

14. Delbanco, *William Ellery Channing*, p. 110.

15. Channing, *Works*, 1:69–166.

16. "The Poet" and such essays as "Intellect" and "Art" represent Emerson's view of the artist as inspired spontaneously by divine power and moving men with his conscious and willed energy. This is fundamentally Channing's position as well, even given his radically different philosophical presuppositions.

17. The intellectual currents found here are dealt with in Howe, *The Unitarian Conscience*, pp. 27–68, 174–204.

18. "Remarks on National Literature" and "Remarks on the Character and Writings of Fénelon" are in Channing, *Works*, 1:243–80 and 1:167–216, respectively.

19. Also discussed in Cole, "Transcendentalist Readings of Milton," 134–35.

20. Delbanco, *William Ellery Channing*, pp. 116–53, gives perhaps the best exposition of Channing's conversion to abolitionism, and its gradual development out of the approbation of sublime moral action expressed here. Moreover, Howe, *The Unitarian Conscience*, pp. 238–305, shows how this opposition between conscience and everyday politics is a common theme in contemporary Unitarian thought.

21. Buell, *Literary Transcendentalism*, pp. 23–54, discusses the characteristic self-image of the Unitarians as a denomination.

22. Channing, *Works*, 1:48–51, provides evidence that Milton's speculations about creation *ex nihilo* and the like touched a responsive chord in him, perhaps because of his own philosophical uneasiness at this stage of his life. See Delbanco, *William Ellery Channing*, pp. 33–54, and Howe, *The Unitarian Conscience*, pp. 27–68, 174–204, for two slightly different views of Channing and the rise of idealism in America.

23. Charvat, *The Origins of American Critical Thought, passim*, demonstrates the general importance of the English Romantics at this period, and significantly, the relatively easier acceptance of Wordsworth than the others by American critics. Havens, *The Influence of Milton*, pp. 177–200, presents the parallel case of Wordsworth's critical assimilation of Milton.

24. Sensabaugh, *Milton in Early America*, pp. 146ff, brings Milton's place in American letters up to about 1810. Weigel, "The Miltonic Tradition," pp. 177–270, outlines the general attitude towards the poet in England during the first half of the nineteenth century, with occasional references to the American scene.

25. Sensabaugh, *Milton in Early America*, pp. 98–110, treats Milton in the rhetoric books up through the early Federalist period. For evidence of Channing's own familiarity with the texts used at Harvard, see Arthur W. Brown, *Always Young for Liberty: A Biography of William Ellery Channing* (Syracuse: Syracuse University Press, 1956), pp. 14–33, 192.

26. John Quincy Adams, *Lectures on Rhetoric and Oratory, Delivered to the Classes of Senior and Junior Sophisters in Harvard University*, 2 vols. (Cambridge: Hilliard and Metcalf, 1810). This is discussed in Sensabaugh, *Milton in Early America*, pp. 193–95.

27. Adams, *Lectures*, 2:127.

28. Adams, *Lectures*, 1:409.

29. Edward T. Channing, *Lectures Read to the Seniors in Harvard College* (Boston: Ticknor and Fields, 1856), p. 100.

30. Milton's pervasive influence on the epic poems of the Early National period is discussed in Sensabaugh, *Milton in Early America*, pp. 158–83.

31. Timothy Dwight, *Travels in New England and New York*, ed. Barbara M. Solomon and Patricia M. King (Cambridge: Harvard University Press, 1969), 4:220–21.

32. An interesting recent attempt to outline Bryant's intellectual background is Robert A. Ferguson, "William Cullen Bryant: The Creative Context of the Poet," *New England Quarterly*, 53 (December 1980): 431–63.

33. *The Prose Writings of William Cullen Bryant*, ed. Park Godwin (New York: D. Appleton, 1884), 1:6–7.

34. Bryant, *Prose Writings*, 2:363.

35. Charvat, *The Origins of American Critical Thought*, p. 73, discusses Greenwood and Wordsworth.

36. F. W. P. Greenwood, "Milton's English Prose Works" [review of *A Selection from the English Prose Works of John Milton*], *North American Review*, 25 (July 1827): 74–75. All attributions of authorship in this journal are taken from William Cushing, *Index to "The North American Review"* (Cambridge: John Wilson, 1878).

37. A. H. Everett, "Early Literature of Modern Europe" [review of M. J. de Chenier, *Tableau Historique de la Littérature Française*, and F. Bouterwek, *Historia de la Literatura Española*, trans. J. G. de la Cortina and N. Hugalde y Mollenido], *North American Review*, 38 (January 1834): 174–75. For Everett's career and support of the Transcendentalists, see Charvat, *The Origins of American Critical Thought*, pp. 182–85.

38. Anon., "Scraps from a Correspondent," *Monthly Anthology and Boston Review*, 1 (December 1803): 60. All attributions of authorship are from M. A. DeWolfe Howe's introduction to *The Anthology Society: Journal of the Society Which Conducts "The Monthly Anthology and Boston Review," October 3, 1805 to July 2, 1811* (Boston: Boston Athenæum, 1910). It is perhaps of some interest that Channing wrote the piece just after this one in the magazine.

39. John C. Gray, "Dante" [review of *La Divina Commedia di Dante Alighieri* and *The Vision, or Hell, Purgatory and Paradise of Dante Alighieri*, trans. H. F. Carey], *North American Review*, 8 (March 1819): 344–345. The comparison of Milton with other poets of classical antiquity and the Elizabethan period is common during the early nineteenth century; see Weigel, "The Sublime Tradition," pp. 179–248.

40. W. S. Shaw, "Silva, No. 29," *Monthly Anthology*, 4 (July 1807): 370.

41. Nelson, *The Sublime Puritan*, pp. 74–105, and Weigel, "The Miltonic Tradition," pp. 92–176, 271–97.

42. Nelson, *The Sublime Puritan*, pp. 77–78. The Whig tradition begins somewhat earlier than Nelson suggests, however, with the biographies of Mortimer (1805) and Symmons (1806).

43. For examples, see Weigel, "The Miltonic Tradition," pp. 170–76, 295–97.

44. Robert E. Spiller, "A Case for W. E. Channing," *New England Quarterly*, 3 (January 1930): 55–81, summarizes this reaction.

45. Thomas Babington Macaulay, "Milton," *The Works of Lord Macaulay* (London: Longmans, Green, 1898), 7:31.

46. New England's literary conservatism and Johnson's continued status there are illustrated in the selections from the *Monthly Anthology* in *The Federalist Literary Mind*, ed. Lewis P. Simpson (Baton Rouge: Louisiana State University Press, 1962). For the parallel political and social conservatism of Unitarian Boston, see Howe, *The Unitarian Conscience*, pp. 121–48.

47. See Sensabaugh, *Milton in Early America*, pp. 122–83, 239–81, on the use of Milton for political ends in late eighteenth-century America. Zimmerman, "Milton's American Reputation to 1900," pp. 247–80, describes Whittier's use of Milton as a model in his anti-slavery writings.

48. Two examples of this Tory criticism in America are the anonymous "Thoughts on Milton," *United States Literary Gazette*, 4 (1 July 1826): 278–90, and J. S. J. Gardiner (the conservative, neoclassical Anglican rector of Trinity Church, Boston), in the *Monthly Anthology*, 6 (February 1809): 87–88.

49. Francis Parkman, "Knowles's *Memoir of Roger Williams*" [review of James D. Knowles, *Memoir of Roger Williams, the Founder of the State of Rhode Island*], *Christian Examiner*, 16 (March 1834): 86. All attributions of authorship are taken from William Cushing, *Index to "The Christian Examiner"* (Boston: William Cushing, 1879).

50. Greenwood, "Milton's English Prose Works," 73.

51. *The Prose Works of John Milton*, ed. Rufus W. Griswold (Philadelphia: H. Hooker, 1845), 1:ix,xi. Griswold is significantly uninterested in the *De Doctrina*, but sees Milton almost exclusively in his role as a champion of political liberty.

52. W. Carlos Martyn, *Life and Times of John Milton* (New York: American Tract Society, 1866), p. 4. This biography, in addition to the fact that it is largely a compilation of passages from earlier British Whig critics, is also openly popular in its orientation.

53. J. H. Adler, "A Milton-Bryant Parallel," *New England Quarterly*, 24 (September 1951): 377–80.

54. Nelson, *The Sublime Puritan*, pp. 30–38.

55. Sidney Willard, "Milton on Christian Doctrine" [review of *A Treatise on Christian Doctrine, compiled from the Holy Scriptures alone*, trans. Charles R. Sumner], *North American Review*, 22 (April 1826): 365–67.

56. Osgood, although a fellow-traveler of the Transcendentalists, ultimately seems to have held back from some of their more radical views. His attitude towards Theodore Parker is particularly telling in this regard; moreover, late in life he became an Anglican priest (see Hutchison, *The Transcendentalist Ministers*, pp. 39n, 116–17, 137).

57. Samuel Osgood, "Milton in Our Day" [review of *The Poetical Works of John Milton*, ed. C. D. Cleveland, and *The Prose Works of John Milton*], *Christian Examiner*, 57 (November 1854): 323–24.

58. *Christian Examiner*, 2 (November–December 1825): 423–29.

59. *Christian Examiner*, 3 (March–April 1826): 121.

60. *Christian Examiner*, 4 (March–April 1827): 196; 3 (May–June 1826): 186–87.

61. For a survey of Anglo-American reactions to the *De Doctrina*, see Weigel, "The Miltonic Tradition," pp. 298–328.

62. Sensabaugh, *Milton in Early America*, pp. 217–38.

63. Frederick Beasley, *A Vindication of the Fundamental Principles of Truth and Order, in the Church of Christ, From the Allegations of the Rev. William E. Channing D.D.* (Trenton, N.J.: Justice, 1830).

64. A particularly fine instance of this sectarian use of Milton is found in the *Christian Examiner*, 35 (January 1844): 301. Hutchison, *The Transcendentalist Ministers*, pp. 1–21, discusses the pressures under which the denomination operated, and Elizabeth R. McKinsey, *The Western Experiment: New England Transcendentalists in the Ohio Valley* (Cambridge: Harvard University Press, 1973), gives an excellent account of the frustrations and rivalries which hampered Unitarianism's attempt to break out of its Boston enclave.

65. Channing, *The Character and Writings of John Milton*, "Memorable Sermons, No. 17" (Boston: American Unitarian Association, n.d.).

CHRISTOPHER PEARSE CRANCH'S "JOURNAL. 1839."

Francis B. Dedmond

CHRISTOPHER PEARSE CRANCH (1813–92) was born into a prominent New England family. His father, William, was a Harvard classmate
of his friend and cousin, John Quincy Adams. On 6 April 1795, William
Cranch married Nancy Greenleaf, a sister of Mrs. Noah Webster; and in
1801, the thirty-two-year-old jurist was appointed by President John Adams
as an assistant judge of the newly constituted Circuit Court of the District of
Columbia. Four years later, President Jefferson made Judge Cranch the chief
justice of the court, a position he held for forty years.

Nancy Cranch bore the Judge thirteen children in twenty-three years.
Pearse, as he was affectionately called by members of his family, was born on
8 March 1813 in Alexandria, Virginia, then in the District of Columbia. By
the time Pearse reached adulthood, only six of his brothers and sisters were
still alive—William Greenleaf (1796–1872), the first born; Elizabeth
(1805–60), who married Rufus Dawes, a romancer and poet who catered to
the annual and gift-book trade; John (1807–91), a portrait painter; Edward
(1809–92), a member of the Cincinnati law firm of Cranch and Vaughan;
Abby (1817–1908), who married her first cousin, William Greenleaf Eliot,
Jr.; and Margaret (1819–95), the baby of the family.[1]

In 1829, the year that Harvard conferred on his father an honorary LL.D.,
the sixteen-year-old Pearse entered Columbian College, now George Washington University, from which he was graduated in 1832. If Edward could
secure a teaching position for him in a private school, Cranch intended to
join the brother he virtually idolized in Cincinnati; but on 15 May 1832, Edward wrote Cranch that his efforts had been in vain. Sensing, however, that
some consolation and brotherly advice was in order, he added: "You will succeed in this world, *I know*, if you do not step wrong at first. Consult your
talents . . . ; but be bold, withal, and decide quickly—and after you have
decided, ask no advice. . . . You are talented and virtuous already—be
bold, and you will be great."[2] The emphasis upon being bold was an obvious

129

reference to the diffidence that was to plague Cranch throughout his life. This time, however, Cranch took a bold step; by September, he was duly enrolled in the Divinity School at Cambridge. But even while there, he continued to receive Edward's counsel. In a letter from Cincinnati written early in 1834, Edward declared that "worse than the devil, that self-diffidence, your curse and bane, . . . prevents you from striking, killing, murdering, and devouring everything that comes your way." Edward was sure that Pearse's lack of firmness and decision would keep his "faculties and natural beauty" from being appreciated.[3]

Cranch graduated from the Divinity School in 1835 and began his preaching career by supplying the Unitarian pulpit in Providence. In late summer, he preached a few weeks in Dover, New Hampshire; but by January 1836, he had moved to Andover, Maine. Six weeks later, plagued by a feeling of inadequacy, he wrote his former Divinity School roommate, John Sullivan Dwight, from Portland, where he had stopped on his way back to Washington, that "I would to heaven that I understood more clearly the great laws of that invisible world within the mind. I would that my faith could support itself more trustingly upon the knowledge of my mental operations—their laws and relations and connections with the world without, . . . my conceptions of the ideal True, which I feel to be something more than vain and empty imaginings, are crushed in the bud."[4]

While in Washington, Cranch wrote his brother Edward a letter in which he mentioned their cousin William Greenleaf Eliot, Jr., who had fixed his fortunes in the West and was preaching in St. Louis.[5] On 15 June from Richmond, where the itinerant preacher was preaching in a tiny frame church, Cranch wrote to Dwight, telling him of two letters he had received that day—one from his brother Edward and one from Eliot.[6] Nine days later, Cranch wrote Edward that Eliot was urging him to come West in September.[7] The twenty-three-year-old roaming missionary determined to go; he would supply Eliot's pulpit for him while Eliot traveled during the winter. Eliot, according to Frothingham, was one of those—along with James Freeman Clarke and Willian Henry Channing—who, before leaving the Divinity School, was caught up in the great interest being felt at the time by "the messengers of the new faith in the West. The cry was about the spiritual wants of that region, and young men, with fresh enthusiasm, were convinced that Unitarianism, the broadest version of Christianity, the purest, freest, most ideal system of religion, would come to full proportions only in the wide reaches of the younger States. The new creed, it was urged, required for its development a new expanse."[8]

On 6 December 1836, not long after his arrival in St. Louis, Cranch wrote to Edward that he was beset by "fears, and anxieties, and bodings and tremblings, and the whole phantasmagoria of ugly spirits that the stomach or the conscience or the imagination, or all combined, send like puppets across the stage before us, to darken and discolor the fair scenery of life which lies in the unknown & void future." Cranch, however, observed that "the best remedy for the blues is *action*, mental and bodily," and that he was determined to take hold in St. Louis with vigor. "It is a great work," he wrote. "I hope, I pray that I may be able to do something towards enlightening and regenerating my fellow creatures in the Western Valley."[9]

Cranch himself found enlightenment in two books he read during those days of adjustment. One was his cousin William Henry Furness' *Remarks on the Four Gospels*, which he described in a letter to Edward as a book containing "fine and original views of the character of the Saviour. . . . It opens a new world of thought. . . . The Philosophy that makes *everything* to depend on the immediate supernatural agency of God—which looks on *all things* as miracles—pulls away those everlasting impediments in the way of Faith and the true Science—the *laws* of nature—and sees the *Supernatural* every where *in* the *Natural*. . . . —this is the only Philosophy that comprehends Religion and Revelation in its paternal embrace along with all Natural Science— . . . and looks up to a Faith of overflowing Love presiding over all—and mingling with all—from Eternity to Eternity."[10] The other book was Emerson's *Nature*, which had been published in early September. The little book made a lasting impression on Cranch; it dealt, in a basic way, with the very questions that Cranch, in his letter to Dwight earlier in the year, had indicated were disturbing him. Years later Cranch wrote Emerson that he remembered "the days, when for the first time I read the first thing I ever saw of yours—'Nature'—and the extreme delight with which I re- and re-read it, and the pleasure of finding others who knew [of] it, and of inducing them to read it."[11] The two books, however, were not sufficient to keep Cranch from having recurring seasons of doubt and spiritual depression.

When Eliot returned to his work in St. Louis in the latter part of March 1837, Cranch moved on to Peoria; but when Eliot went back to Washington in the summer to marry Cranch's sister Abby, Cranch abandoned his little missionary church and went along. On 18 July from Washington, Cranch wrote to James Freeman Clarke, editor of the *Western Messenger* and Unitarian minister in Louisville, suggesting that he be ordained and that Clarke, as he put it, "preach me into the goodly fellowship of the ordained prophets."[12] Clarke ignored the request of the wandering Cranch. Clarke, unlike Cranch, had had no doubts about where he wished to be settled after graduation from the Divinity School in 1833. In his autobiography, Clarke noted that "when the last year of my study in the Divinity School at Harvard was approaching its end, I began to think seriously of my future course. I could either remain in New England, and endeavor to be settled as minister of some existing society, or I could go out to the West and try to build up a society there. . . . I was afraid if I were settled in an old-fashioned Unitarian society I should gradually subside into routine; while in the West there would be no routine, but I should be free to originate such methods as might seem necessary and useful. Then I wished to test my own power and the value of what I had to say."[13]

Cranch was greatly impressed by the resourceful Clarke—impressed with man, message, and the journal he edited. On his original journey to St. Louis back in September 1836, Cranch had stopped off in Louisville for a brief visit with Clarke, had obtained a copy of the latest *Western Messenger* and a bundle of back numbers, and had left, no doubt, some of his own poetry, for three of Cranch's poems appeared in the *Messenger* for January 1837. Eight other of Cranch's poems and prose pieces were published in the monthly issues between February and September. Thus, in September 1837, Cranch was no stranger to the journal that Clarke invited him to edit while Clarke went back East for his annual visit. From Louisville on 14 October, Cranch wrote his sister Margaret as he was putting together the November number: "I have contributed several articles. . . . I would stuff it with more poetry but I am ashamed that so many pieces should go forth with 'C.P.C.' dangling at the end. . . . This child, being left by its father, the Reverend James Freeman Clarke, crieth continually for food. . . . Clarke just let his offspring go to the dickens."[14]

Clarke returned to nurture his child shortly after Cranch wrote Margaret, but not before Cranch began to discover himself socially. The Louisvillians he was finding to be "good pleasant folk . . . and a few musical ones"; George Keats, the brother of John Keats, the English poet, he found to be "very intelligent and gentlemanly" and with several attractive daughters;[15] but, alas, Cranch discovered that "the cares of editorial life" would not permit him to accept as much of the proffered hospitality as he would have liked. He complained: "I can't make visits fast enough. By the time I get acquainted here, as it has always been elsewhere, I am obliged to go."[16] With Clarke back, Cranch felt obliged or, at least, "a little impatient to be back among my little scattered flock at Peoria," although he was reluctant to leave Clark. "It does me good to be with him," he informed Margaret: "He possesses in a marked degree that which I am perpetually conscious that I am most deficient in—that is, boldness. . . . I think I am acquiring of it slowly. The West is a grand school for me in this respect. Still, the lack of it palsies me continually. . . . I am not free enough; I am not bold enough for a minister of the Word of Life. Over and over again do I chide my timidity, my reserve, my sensitiveness. . . . And I think the West is the school where the want is to be supplied."[17]

Cranch did leave Louisville, stopping off in St. Louis for ten days on his way to Peoria; but his stay in Peoria was to be a short one, perhaps hastened by an affair of the heart that went awry. Cranch had fallen in love with Sarah Bigelow, a judge's daughter, before he left Peoria for Washington in May, and the two became secretly engaged. But upon his return to Peoria, he found that Sarah had had a change of heart about her long-absent suitor; she announced that the match was off;[18] and by early spring 1838, Cranch was back in St. Louis. On his way from there to Washington, he wrote an unusual note to an unknown correspondent which was published in the June *Messenger*. In the "Letter on Travelling," Cranch said, "Well, here I am—again a wanderer—another, and still another parting have I endured. For nearly three years it has been my lot to rove from place to place, North, South, East, West—making friends and parting from them—verily, I am growing aweary of such itinerant ways of living."[19] From Washington, Cranch went down to Richmond, from there to White Sulphur Springs, then down the Kanawha River to the Ohio, and up the Ohio to Cincinnati. By July, Cranch was again preaching in Cincinnati. On 23 September, he preached "A Sermon on the Eclipse of the Sun," which he later published in the *Messenger* for January 1839.[20]

Cranch was still in Cincinnati when he received the second annual invitation from Clarke to come down the Ohio and once again tend the *Messenger* while Clarke went about his Eastern travels. Cranch was eager to come. "I will certainly come," he wrote Clarke on 10 October 1838, "and supply for you during your absence, as long as you wish, and will start as soon as Channing arrives."[21] William Henry Channing—Divinity School classmate of Eliot and Clarke—had for some time been looking to the West. On 20 December 1835, he wrote Clarke from Rome: "Most sincerely do I echo your wish that somehow and somewhere we may be fellow-workers."[22] Dr. William Ellery Channing had urged his favorite nephew to "give a little time to the West,"[23] and in September 1838 he accepted an invitation to preach six months in Cincinnati. But Channing did not arrive until December; and by that time, Cranch had been two months in Louisville.

Cranch arrived in Louisville on Sunday, 28 October 1838. That evening he wrote his brother Edward, informing him that Clarke had the November *Messenger* at the printers before he left for the East. "The next no. will be out in a few days," Cranch wrote. Cranch, therefore, set about at once soliciting material for the December number. In a postscript, he asked Edward to "Tell Vaughan to send down his article for the Messenger, as the said Messenger's Devil like his namesake is going about seeking whom he may devour, in the way of 'copy.'"[24] On 21 November, Cranch wrote Clarke: "We received the remainder of your article with a few lines of letter at the bottom, today. . . . There will not be room for the whole of the article in the

December number. . . . Only think of the editor being excluded from his own pages! The December number is full. . . . I have put in a good deal of my own."²⁵ Cranch asked Clarke to send anything he might have for the January *Messenger*. On 16 December, Cranch wrote Miss Julia Myers, a Richmond friend, that "The next 'Messenger' cometh on by steps. Nearly all my fingers are in the pie. Mr. Clarke is expected back soon, probably this week."²⁶ Thus, it is safe to say that Cranch was the sole editor of the December *Messenger* and likely sole editor of the January issue as well.

Apparently in late December, Edward wrote Cranch, urging him to return to Cincinnati. On 1 January 1839, Cranch replied that his being with Clarke was doing him much good and that the next day "we have the Messenger to direct." Cranch informed his brother that Clarke had accepted "with joy" Edward's suggestion that the *Messenger* be transferred to Cincinnati and that Clarke had written Channing about it.²⁷ But Edward had no doubt also made another suggestion and that was that Cranch should hurry to Cincinnati and begin his new work as minister-at-large to the poor, a project that Channing was much interested in.²⁸ But Cranch dreaded the prospects. He wrote Edward concerning Channing and the work:

> It will be a great privilege to me to be in any way associated with him. I shall need much his counsel, encouragement, sympathy and the influence of his mind & character, in the arduous work I am about to engage in. Great and glorious as that sphere of duty is, I feel that I must be another man before I can enter into it as I ought. At times I feel zealous, resolute & full of faith—but I am usually, while looking at it, in prospect, a perfect coward—the slave of self, the sport of habits, temperament, and a wavering faith and purpose. But I hope. Things may go better than I imagine them—when I once get started. It is now all one vague, too often gloomy looking-forward, which presses itself upon me. However, the anticipation, in such cases, is more apt to be gigantic & gloomy than the reality. A very small thing, such as a cloudy, gloomy day, an anticipated disagreeable journey, an unpleasant duty postponed, will generally overcast everything else in my mind, with its dark hues.²⁹

Shortly, Cranch received another insistent letter from Edward. Cranch replied on 7 January 1839, the day before his first entry in his journal, that he had determined to stay "either till the river opens, or till I can travel the roads. It is as much as one's neck is worth, to travel by land." "Would you," Cranch asked, "have me wade knee deep in a mud bank, and stick all night in a chuck-hole . . . —or be ending up a cripple in some vile chinky country-inn—when there is a chance of getting to you by steamboat before a great while?" Cranch explained that he was not fully and completely idle and unprofitable, as Edward might think. He was "gathering material—helping brother James a little, and receiving much from him in return." "If I do not commence the ministry at large, till February," Cranch pointed out, "I dont think much will be lost." Cranch was enjoying himself among the Louisville people and acquiring "a reputation for drollness, comicality—as if all the clergy were not so." And then too there was the February number of the *Messenger*: "Our next number of the Messenger comes on copiously. Two beautiful pieces of poetry by Mr Emerson are to be in it, almost the first poems of his ever published. They are complete efflorescences of Emerson: beautiful in his own spirit."[30]

But Cranch knew that the days he could linger on in socially-appealing Louisville away from the Cincinnati poor, the days he could sit supinely at Clarke's feet, and the days he could continue at the delightful, but spent editorial tasks of the past two months were numbered, if not already exhausted. He must face the reality of his vocation. It is evident, from the title page on, that Carlyle's strictures in *Sartor Resartus* against idleness, diffidence, and murmuring about one's lot in life were in Cranch's mind as he folded and stitched the sheets of his "Journal. 1839." For instance, Teufelsdröckh was told that "*The end of Man is an Action*, and *not a Thought*, though it was the noblest."[31] In the chapter on "The Everlasting Yea," the author declared that, as a God-given mandate, "*Work thou in Welldoing*, lies mysteriously written, in Promethean Prophetic Characters, in our hearts; and leaves us no rest, night and day, till it be deciphered and obeyed."[32] Man had been put on earth to produce a product to the best of his ability. "'Tis the utmost thou hast in thee: out with it, then. Up, up! Whatsoever thy hand findeth to do, do it with thy whole might. Work while it is called To-day; for the Night cometh, wherein no man can work."[33] Cranch weighed himself against Carlyle's dicta and found himself wanting.

Cranch's "Journal. 1839." consisted originally of sixteen sheets (21 1/2 x 28 cm.) folded quarto fashion, the whole being neatly bound with a gray cover of heavier stock, stitched at the fold, and bearing within a border outlined in black ink the inscription "JOURNAL./1839."[34] The first page—the "title" page—is unnumbered, and the back of that page is blank. The pages, however, on which the journal entries are found are numbered; and these page numbers appear in square brackets in the printed text. Unfortunately, some of the sheets, as noted in brackets in the text, are partially cut, cut out altogether, or torn out. It is not known who mutilated the journal or when or why.

JOURNAL.

1839.

"Mein Vermächtniss, wie herrlich weit und breit!

Die Zeit is mein Vermächtniss, mein Acker ist

die Zeit."[35]

ΕΡΓΑ ΚΑΙ ΗΜΕΡΑΙ[36]

"Work while it is day. The night cometh,

Wherein no man can work."[37]

PLATE ONE
The first page in C. P. Cranch's "Journal. 1839."
Courtesy Francis B. Dedmond

[1]   *Journal.*
January. 1839 —
Louisville – Ky – Jan. 8th. –

I begin this day a journal. I think I shall find it highly useful. I do not think it necessary to record herein every day, of my life – but simply to record such events, and
note down such thoughts, feelings and experiences as have a more intimate connection with my mind & character. A journal should be a reflection of the True Life —
the interior being, experience & growth — a mirror of myself, to some extent. I intend to journalize more systematically & philosophically than I have done. This
book, now blank, shall be my friend, my companion, my teacher & monitor, as well
as my record.

I need something of this sort. I need to retire back on myself — take an observation of my longitude & latitude in the boundless ocean of Eternity on which I am
sailing. I must look back. I must look forward — square my accounts. [2] And post
them, clerk-like. I must ask myself, as I enter on this newyear, & this journalbook —
how I stand, with myself, & before God. Thus far I have voyaged, by His all preserv-
ing & continually upholding grace — Nearly twenty six years have I been borne
along the stream of time — a checkered Past! — various experiences! Has this Past
been a *Teacher* to me? God grant it may have been, in some degree. Let not the
years pass by me like the wind, viewless, silent, forgotten! I have many defects, errors, weaknesses to confess, O God, before Thee! Do thou grant strength & light for
the future! Give me a more tender conscience — give me a firmer faith — inspire
me with that spiritual Mind which comes only from Thee!—

And now, I am *Here*. The mystery of life has borne me to this point. And I must
begin afresh, & with that resolution whose absence I continually mourn, yet too
vainly, I must turn a new leaf. — What I want — is *Action*. I must begin to *Live*
more in earnest, than I have done. [3] It seems to me as if those lines of Wordsworth's
applied pointedly to *me*. What a beautiful meaning is in them!

> "My whole life I have lived in pleasant thought,
> As if life's business were a summer mood;
> As if all needful things wd come unsought
> To genial faith, still rich in genial good;
> But how can He expect that others should
> Build for him, sow for him, & at his call
> Love him, who for himself, will take no heed at all?"³⁸

All things must become more *real* to me. I must "see into the life of things."³⁹ I
must *realize*. The great end of life is to *realize*. At present I only *dream*. Half of my
existence seems to be *dreaming*. A deadly *Indifference* hangs over me — like a leth-
argy. It is partly temperament — & partly a habit of mind – I think. I must break this
egg shell—out of this prison I must forth. I must *realize*, & the way to realize, is to
give up dreaming and go to *acting* & *working*. And as to needed knowledge, will it
not "come round" as Emerson says, to him who works and truly lives?⁴⁰ — I find my
[4] self perpetually repining that I am not familiar with books — that I am so ignorant

of things which every man almost knows. But if I may learn *things* instead of books, shall I not be more truly wise than if [I] "had all knowledge."[41] And will not this learning of *things* from the actual collision of Life, be the very best preparation for book knowledge?

As it is now, I *cannot* keep up a thirst for truth. I am wholly indifferent to knowledge — except now & then, when excited. I am not fond of reading, except when a book happens to suit my tastes in most respects. I enjoy *writing* I think more than reading. Nor do I *remember* what I read. Now were I more *alive* — awake — shaken up — by a more active out of door life — much of this might be remedied. I might see in *books* but the *reflection* of what I experienced & saw in *life*. Because I should be ever catching revealings of truths [5] and realities at first hand, I should be best prepared to appreciate them where seen at second hand. I shd remember better and thirst for more habitually, the scattered truths in books.

Then, I want Faith in myself. Unbelief in ourselves, says Carlyle, is the worst skepticism.[42] I want faith in my former impressions & convictions, and aspirings. I want Faith that I am a *Spirit*: and that the hidden energies of a Spirit are wrapped up in me. I must be a more independent *thinker*. I must not be afraid of my thought. I must love it, if it is an earnest & true one, to myself. I must be an independent *feeler* — not grieving if I do not think I feel deeply enough—but trying to be *natural*. I am not now natural enough. I am afraid of those around me. They'll think me affected, strange, undignified or lax in principle. Must not mind them. Do what is right and natural. Obey my higher instincts. [6] In a word — I must begin to *Live*. Then I shall begin to *Realize* — then to think, feel, act, grow.

This ministry to the Poor, may be a great thing for me. A stern discipline, but a salutary.

God grant me faith and patience, and the spirit of self sacrifice!

I have been in Louisville since the 28th of October — about 10 weeks. — Since the 22d December — Clarke has been here. It is delightful & profitable to me, to be with him. The river being closed, but a prospect of its opening, I shall remain here till boats run. The roads are too bad to attempt to go by land.

Jan 9th. It is a blessing to know a mind a character like that of Jas. F. Clarke's. I feel that it does me good to be with him. While I feel my own weaknesses and defects in his society — I feel that it is useful for me to be thus with a superior spirit. I may be gathering material for thought & action which will [7] carry me on with far surer progress than if I had not one near me like him, to whom I may *look up*. It is bad to live always with inferiors or equals. We need sometimes to compare ourselves with those of a larger stature, that we may realize our littleness.

I may learn from him several things. I may learn, first, & chiefly, *Independence*. Independence of mind and of conduct—to be *myself* — and not another. — to be *natural* and *free*.

I may learn 2ᵈ self denial and devotion to Truth & Duty, instead of self seeking. I may learn, 3ᵈ how to realize things — take interest in every thing — and get good out of everything.

Today I wrote to mother — and last evening to Lizzy Appleton[43] — quite a *Sartorish* letter — put in some drawings — "an Intellectual All in All" — and some other comic illustrations of Wordsworth.[44] I have a notion that I will illustrate these pages of my journal by some such things, now & then. Illustrations which have a sense — a *Carlylean* graphic-ness — and truth. There can be a touch of comicality in them too — to give them a relish.

---

[8] Sunday Ev. Jan. 13ᵗʰ——
Last night Clarke & I amused ourselves making illustrations of Emerson's writings.[45] See p. 10 & 11. — We had real fun — instructive also. — This morning I preached — to a large congregation — my "Rain & River" sermon — an old affair — for want of a better. Clarke thought he wd preach in the afternoon. He preached grandly. Text — "The Lord is my shepherd." He has preached it before, but it is still fresh. The Louisvillians do not know what a treasure they have in that man. For my part, take him simply as a *preacher* — I do not know that I have ever listened to preaching so good as his. Such freshness, boldness, earnestness of style, thought, delivery. It is delightful to listen to him. — Such a fine union of deep, original thought with practical illustrations, and of a poetic imagination with the tenderest feeling. His *Independence* in everything he does is truly refreshing. He is no formula-man. He "swallows all formulas," as Carlyle [9] phrases it — thinks, feels, talks & acts *himself*, and not another. I bask in the light of such a man. I think this sojourn with him, has done me good. It ought to. He is a rare genius: a noble spirit.

He spoke in his sermon of the spiritual advantages of *travelling*. 1. The *dangers* of travelling lead us to *reliance* on God. 2. The contemplation of *Nature* in travelling expands the mind & heart. 3. Contemp. of works of *Art*, railroads over mountains & tunnels *through* mountains, for instance — show us the care of God for us. 4. We may see the *Impartiality* of God (in travelling) in the *compensation* made in various lands — a barren rocky land e.g. producing industry — & a rich land indolence &c. 5. Parting from friends a lesson & trial to the spirit. 6. This leads to the parting of *death* — which separates the good only for a time.

Clarke has in him great versatility. He has a face to meet you in, for all moods of mind. This is why, though he is so superior to myself, I can yet
See p. 11
[*Page 10 contains the transparent eyeball caricature (see the frontispiece to this volume). The expanding corn and melons caricature (see Plate Two) is on the top half of page 11.*]
[11] sympathise so freely with him, and open to him my mind & heart. I can laugh with him, pun with him, draw pictures with him, poetize with him, sermonize with him, and be grave or gay as he is so.

[12] Cincinnati. O. Jan. 22ᵈ 1839.

PLATE TWO
Caricature based on a line from Emerson's *Nature* in C. P. Cranch's "Journal. 1839."
Courtesy Francis B. Dedmond

I left Louisville nearly a week ago — the River having broken up. Pleasant trip up — rather hard to leave Clarke.

I am now here — taking meals with Edw. at Mrs Woods, & sleeping in the office.[46] Have not found a room yet.

Before I left, — (Monday Jan 14[)] — we had a juvenile concert in our church in Louisville — fine. Went with Miss G. Keats.[47] Tuesday Ev. Conversation club — next morng. Wednesday — Mr Cooper came in to breakfast — smoked with him.

Last night, Jan. 21. Semicolon, at Mrs Stetsons.[48] Sent in piece on Dreams[49] One of the most delightful parties I ever was in. Have talked with Channing, & Vaughan about Ministry at Large. Nothing definite done yet.

Forgot to mention last Thursday Ev. Jan 17. Conversation meeting at the vestry room — talk about Non-resistance — very good — well attended.

[13] Channing is doing a noble work here. Just the man to send a new life into our stagnating body of Unitarians.

Have made acquaintance with Miss Harding — fine girl — Oliver Prescott — fine man. Perkins I am getting to know — clear, deep man — with fine humor — that *cement* wh. every mind needs to bind strongly & smoothly together every part.

Went up today a little while with Prescott to court. Trial of Butler for murder — they were examining a bad woman — poor creature. She seemed made for better things.

I shall begin to visit soon, I hope, among the poor & degraded.

Jan. 23ᵈ. This afternoon attended sewing circle of ladies at Greens[50] with Channing — a sort of Bible class. Rather interesting talk — but too much to Ch. & myself.

Took tea with Ch. at Greens'. After tea interesting talk on religious & metaphysical subjects. Ch. reminds me of Dwight. He is a noble spirit. So is Greene. I like to talk with such.

[14] Sunday, Jan. 27ᵗʰ —

Thursday Ev. we met in vestryroom & talked about Looking at Consequences in matters of duty.

Friday ev. went to Mr. Fisher's & to Judge Estes'. Saturday Ev. to Debating club. Yesterday afternoon attended Mr Mackay's funeral. Channing officiated in his usual impressive manner. Coming home talked with Perkins about the Ministry at Large. If I do not take it, *he intends to engage in it himself* — and to devote his life to it. We are to talk about it this evening at Channing's room. I shall leave the task to him. He is just the man for it.[51] I was surprised & rejoiced to hear it. What a noble spirit he is! He is *all* spirit, as Edward says. He will make the most efficient minister to the poor, that could be found in the country. He is already fitted for it. I am not. The time that *I* shd spend in learning, he would spend in acting — and acting on the broadest foundation, & with the most earnest & devoted spirit. It will release *me* from my position — a position I have been standing in less from my own will, [15] than from the urgency of my friends. I feel that though this ministry wd be a glorious discipline to myself, yet I am unfitted for it by taste and habits; while with Perkins, it seems to be the very sphere for which everything in him predestines him.

Still some such discipline I must have. But where shall I *now* go? The West is all before me. Shall I remain this side of the Mountains, or not? I must decide quickly.

---

*Jan. 30*th. Perkins will engage in the ministry to the poor. God grant him happiness & success in it. How I wish I could express to him my feelings about it — that I could thank him & praise him with anything like the warmth which my heart feels. I could almost kneel to him. I have felt the tears almost starting when I saw him thus resolved on commencing & going himself to the work. But my manner is all unchanged. No one knows how warmly the stream of feeling & enthusiasm runs [16] beneath the cold icebound exterior of manner, through which it *cannot* break.

And now I am free. I have been making up my mind to go Eastward, to settle. I think I shall do so. I think I shall be happier & more useful at the East than in the West. I shall probably start next week, for Washington, which I shall make my point of lookout, till I can get a parish which suits me.[52]

February.
1st. Young Soeffies — Party at Millers.
2^d. Cold day. No prospect of river opening or rising. Think it likely I shall be obliged to go home by land. Dont like the idea. Doing nothing here — & not supporting myself.

Went to Debating Soc. in evening with Bertha & Kate Wood.[53]
Sunday — 3^d. Went to New Jersualem ch. with Prescott.[54] Good high heads — dull preacher — curious exposition of the miracle of the loaves & fishes. In the eveng heard Channing — most [17] powerful sermon I ever heard.
Text — 1 John. IV. 20. "If any one love not his brother whom he hath seen, how can he love God whom he hath not seen." — He who *loves* not, is an *atheist*. The bigot, the worldling, the sneerer, all who see not the divine in man are atheists. We can only love & see God, through the affections of our heart, with wh. we love one another. There is no other possible way of knowing & loving Him, but by experiencing & developing the common affections of love & smpathy wh. we extend toward man.

The whole discourse was most condensed, original, eloquent & touching. He is a glorious preacher.

Feb 17th. Sunday afternoon —
How time flies! Here tis the middle of February. Doing nothing here.[55] Shall leave for home this week. It is hard to leave Cincinnati — but I must. This loafer life will never do.

Heard Channing preach this morning a noble discourse on Prayer. Worship in spirit & in truth. Spoke of the objections & doubts generally held about prayer. [18] Feb. 21. Shall not leave till next week. River low — ice running. Feeling unsettled — and uncomfortable. Wish I was at home or somewhere, at work. Last Monday Ev. Semicolon at Mrs Stetsons. Tuesday at Vaughan's.

Oh this dreadful *indifference* wh. hangs upon me — ! It is a "nightmare life in death."[56] I am dissatisfied with myself, and almost everything about me. Action — a habitual daily fixed routine of duty can alone "deliver me from the body of this death."[57] I feel now as if I were letting my powers run to waste. It must not be.

———————

March. 14th. 1839. Washington City.
I have been here about a week. Came on with Mr Lynch, Mrs Lucas, &c.
Rather pleasant journey — cold.[58] Find all well here. Have had several talks with Rufus about the New Church. He presents it to me in a more interesting & less sectarian light than I have ever viewed [19] it. Not *sectarian* — that is not the word — but he opens to me a far broader & more elevated view of the New Church truths than what I have been accustomed to see.[59] I am reading Swedenborg's arcana[60] — which is interesting — also Kinmonts Lectures on the Natural History of man.[61] This latter is a very profound and original book — and exceedingly interesting & instructive.

Preached last Sunday for Mr Bulfinch.[62] Have called as yet on scarcely any one.

———————

Ap. 2[d]. — My journal lags too much. One must be *alone* to journalize much. My time has been passing delightfully here. There is no place like home. I have not written much — but have read somewhat — finished Kinmont. I read Swedenborg by fits. Am now reading Cousin[63] — but I never shall be a great reader. Wrote a poem on "Correspondences" which Rufus thinks the best thing he has seen of mine.[64] Last week wrote a Sermon on the text — "Can any good thing come out of Nazareth — come & see." Think it one of my best. Occasionally draw, & india-[20]ink — and flute with Bro. William or Major Hitchcock, or amuse myself with the piano forte. Had one musical evening with Fleischmann.[65] My passion for music is such that I sometimes wonder tis not all-absorbing. No enjoyment of my existence is greater. When I sit down at twilight to the piano forte, and roam over the soul like chords of that glorious instrument, I can feel what *perfect beauty* is. What *God* is. I can feel what the language of the angels must be. That language *must* be music. What else can it be? ——

Next week I shall probably start for the North — shall stop on the way — a good deal — & probably shall go to Northampton — Mass.[66]

I must learn to renounce, more than I do, many of my talents & tastes, in music & drawing, for instance, & give myself more to my profession. I am behind bad in this. I am too desultory — too indolent, too *unclerical.*[67]
[21] Philadelphia — Apr. 18th 1839.
Left home on Saturday last, Ap 13th — in the afternoon cars. Home, dear home —

thou art once more shut out from my eyes — but my heart is still with thee. How many blessings — how many delightful hours were mine during that one month's stay. O may God make me thankful for such a home — for such a father, such a mother, such sisters & brothers, as mine are — ! O, the pleasant hours in that old library, with Rufus! The good times with dear Margy — they are past. I am once more *bemistered*. [*Half of page 21 is cut away.*]

[22] Wednesday morning left Baltimore, & arrived here[68] in the afternoon. Am at Margy Eliots — (Mrs James T. Furness) delightful place — and people — everything as pleasant as possible. Walked about this morning with William Furness[69] — saw houses, public buildings, pictures & people. I am going to stay here two Sundays, while he goes North with his wife.

———————

Ap. 23[d]. — Mr Furness is still here on account of Judy Barnes' sickness [*Rest of page 22 is cut away, as are all of pages 23 through 28.*]

[29] June 24th — I am reading Jouffroy on Philosophy, in Ripley's Spec. of foreign literature.[70] He is a most clear, profound & spiritual writer. It is satisfactory to get hold of such a writer. He seems to do something to fill a *void* in my nature. I need to be *based* firmly upon eternal truths. I want a sound philosophy to prop up my too wavering faith. [*Two-thirds of page 29 has been cut away.*]

[30] Show us any good?" — Commenced with speaking of the freshness, joy, & faith of childhood — then of the enthusiasm &c of mankind — then of the wants of the soul which the world cannot satisfy — and of *virtue* as the only good — the only means of happiness. &c. His delivery is very fine — almost too much gesture. [*Two-thirds of page 30 has been cut away.*]

[*Pages 31 through 60 have been torn out. The last sheet—pages 61 and 62—was cut. Cranch continued the journal on pages 31 through 35, but it likely ended there. There is no indication that there were entries on pages 36 through 62.*]

NOTES

1. For more detailed information about the family, see Leonora Cranch Scott, *The Life and Letters of Christopher Pearse Cranch* (Boston: Houghton Mifflin, 1917); F. DeWolfe Miller, *Christopher Pearse Cranch and His Caricatures of New England Transcendentalism* (Cambridge: Harvard University Press, 1951); and Miller, "Christopher Pearse Cranch: New England Transcendentalist" (Ph.D. diss., University of Virginia, 1942). The works mentioned above will be designated in subsequent references as Scott, *Cranch*; Miller, *Cranch*; and Miller, "Cranch."

2. Edward P. Cranch [Cincinnati] to CPC, 15 May 1832, Cranch Papers, MHi. Manuscripts, typescripts, and journals in the Cranch Papers are quoted with permission of the Massachusetts Historical Society.

3. Edward P. Cranch [Cincinnati] to CPC, 18 January 1834, Cranch Papers, MHi.

4. CPC [Portland, Me.] to John Sullivan Dwight, 19 March 1836, TS copy, Cranch Papers, MHi. Typescripts in the Cranch papers were no doubt prepared by or for Mrs. Scott for possible

use in her *The Life and Letters of Christopher Pearse Cranch.* Across the top of many of the typescripts was written in blue pencil the word *Omit.*

5. Miller, "Cranch," p. 45.

6. Scott, *Cranch,* p. 24.

7. CPC [Richmond] to Edward P. Cranch, 24 June 1836, TS copy, Cranch Papers, MHi.

8. Octavius Brooks Frothingham, *Memoir of William Henry Channing* (Boston: Houghton, Mifflin, 1886), p. 88.

9. Miller, "Cranch," pp. 64–65.

10. Miller, "Cranch," pp. 53–54.

11. CPC [Paris] to Ralph Waldo Emerson, 20 March 1855, TS copy, Cranch papers, MHi.

12. Scott, *Cranch,* p. 35.

13. Clarke, *Autobiography, Diary, and Correspondence,* ed. Edward Everett Hale (Boston: Houghton, Mifflin, 1891), p. 50.

14. Scott, *Cranch,* pp. 37–38.

15. Scott, *Cranch,* p. 38; see J. F. C[larke]., "George Keats," *Dial,* 3 (April 1843): 495–500.

16. Scott, *Cranch,* p. 39.

17. Scott, *Cranch,* pp. 39–40.

18. See Miller, "Cranch," pp. 75–76, for a fuller account of the love affair.

19. *Western Messenger,* 5 (June 1838): 183.

20. *Western Messenger,* 6 (January 1839): 166–73.

21. CPC [Cincinnati] to James Freeman Clarke, 10 October 1838, TS copy, Cranch Papers, MHi.

22. Frothingham, *Channing,* p. 115.

23. Frothingham, *Channing,* p. 141.

24. CPC [Louisville] to Edward P. Cranch, 28 October 1838, Cranch Collection, WyU. Letters in the Cranch Collection at the University of Wyoming at Laramie are quoted with permission. J. C. Vaughan, prominent Unitarian layman, was Edward Cranch's law partner. No article by Vaughan appeared in the December 1838 or January 1839 numbers.

25. CPC [Louisville] to James Freeman Clarke, 21 November 1838, TS copy, Cranch Papers, MHi. Clarke's article was entitled "The Unitarian Reform." The first part had already appeared in the November issue; parts two and three were published in the December 1838 and January 1839 *Messengers.* Cranch contributed four poems and four prose pieces to the December number.

26. CPC [Louisville] to Julia Myers, 16 December 1838, TS copy, Cranch papers, MHi. Clarke returned on 22 December. Cranch's "fingers were in the pie" in the January 1839 number to the extent of four articles and four poems.

27. Ephraim Peabody, who had been assisted in his editorial tasks by James Handasyd Perkins, announced "To Our Subscribers" (*Western Messenger,* 1 [May 1836]: 731) that the *Messenger* had been transferred to Louisville from Cincinnati and that "it will henceforth be under the editorial care of the Rev. James F. Clarke." Clarke continued to edit the *Messenger* in Louisville through the April 1839 number. Although the journal had been moved to Cincinnati, Clarke continued to serve as one of the editors, along with William Henry Channing and James Handasyd Perkins, until the *Messenger* was temporarily suspended after the October 1839 issue. When publication was resumed in May 1840, William Henry Channing was listed as sole editor.

28. Frothingham, in *Channing,* pp. 129–30, says that "Mr. Channing was from the first interested in the organization of charity, the application of religion to the condition of the poor." In Europe, he studied "the beneficent operations of the Catholic Church; [and] in Paris he gave much attention to the working of the Baron de Gerando's plans. On his return he had long conversations with Joseph Tuckerman of Boston, the philanthropist, who suggested his undertaking the ministry among the poor in New York, then projected under the auspices of the Uni-

tarians. . . . The two societies in New York were full of zeal, rich and generous. . . . Dr. [William Ellery] Channing, with all his caution, was convinced that the people would respond to the glad tidings of the soul's capacity and destiny, and advised his nephew to make the attempt. . . . On 27th of December, 1836, he was at work, but the project was less brilliant than had been anticipated." By the middle of August 1837, Channing had decided that he was not fitted for the work; and, like Cranch later, he felt that he was at fault because of his lack of devotion to God's service. In Channing's view, however, the need for the work was, even so, apparently as great as ever, despite his personal failure.

29. CPC [Louisville] to Edward P. Cranch, 1 January 1839, Cranch Collection, WyU.

30. CPC [Louisville] to Edward P. Cranch, 7 January 1839, Cranch Collection, WyU. Cranch misdated the letter "1838". The two Emerson poems were "Each and All" (6 [February 1839]: 229–30) and "To the Humble Bee" (6 [February 1839]: 239–41).

31. Thomas Carlyle, *Sartor Resartus: The Life and Opinion of Herr Teufelsdröckh* (Philadelphia: Henry Altemus, 1894), p. 168.

32. Carlyle, *Sartor Resartus*, p. 194.

33. Carlyle, *Sartor Resartus*, p. 208; see Ecclesiastes 9:10 and John 9:4.

34. The manuscript journal is in the F. B. Dedmond Collection.

35. Cranch borrowed the couplet from the title page of the first American edition of *Sartor Resartus*, edited by R. W. Emerson (Boston: James Munroe, 1836). The couplet, which may be translated as "My legacy, how gloriously far and wide! / Time is my legacy, my acre is time," was omitted from later editions.

36. The Greek expression means "work" as product "and time" in terms of days. In *Sartor Resartus*, Carlyle had underscored the necessity that man produce a product during his allotted days.

37. See John 9:4, "I must work the works of him that sent me while it is day: the night cometh, when no man can work." Carlyle ended "The Everlasting Yea" chapter of *Sartor Resartus* with "Work while it is called To-day; for the Night cometh, wherein no man can work."

38. "Resolution and Independence," 11. 36–42.

39. Carlyle's two-volume work entitled *Miscellanies* was mentioned in the "Critical Notices" in the Cranch-edited December 1838 number of the *Western Messenger*. The critical notice was signed "C", which could have been Clarke, but was likely Cranch. The reviewer wrote: "We know of no life-reviewer equal to Carlyle. He has an eye to see into the soul of man as well as into 'the life of things.' The Real and the Unreal — the True and the False part off and stand asunder beneath his keen philosophic glance, as distinct as Day from Night" (5:138).

40. Emerson said in his lecture "The American Scholar" that many young men are hindered from action by their disgust with the principles by which business is managed. In answer to his own question as to what is the remedy, Emerson replied "that if the single man plant himself indomitably on his instincts, and there abide, the huge world will come round to him. Patience,—patience" (*The Collected Works of Ralph Waldo Emerson*, ed. Alfred R. Ferguson et al., 2 vols. to date [Cambridge: Harvard University Press, 1971–], vol. 2, *Nature, Addresses, and Lectures*, ed. Ferguson (1971), p. 69).

41. See I Corinthians 13:2.

42. I have been unable to locate this statement by Carlyle. Since it is not in quotation marks, it is likely a paraphrase.

43. Likely a cousin. Cranch's Appleton cousins lived in Baltimore.

44. I have been unable to locate the Wordsworth "comic illustrations."

45. The caricatures in the journal were only the first. Cranch and Clarke continued well after that January night to amuse themselves and subsequently a host of others with what Cranch chose to call the Emersonian scraps. On 16 February 1839, Cranch wrote Clarke from Cincinnati that his sister Margaret had written him about Clarke's letter to William Henry Furness "with the Emersons in it" (Scott, *Cranch*, p. 45); and on 11 March, Clarke wrote Emerson that

"Cranch and I were so profane as to illustrate some of your sayings by sketches not of the gravest character. I should like to show them to you, for I think you would like them. . . . C. P. Cranch has quite a talent at drawing diablerie & such like" (*The Letters of Ralph Waldo Emerson*, ed. Ralph L. Rusk [New York: Columbia University Press, 1939], 2:190). Then on 20 May, Cranch wrote Clarke from Philadelphia: "By the way, I lent him [William Henry Furness] my Emersonian scraps to take with him, and it seems by sundry external signs upon them since they were returned to me, that they have been considerably thumbed and pocketed. Great men have looked upon them. . . . Our fame, friend, groweth. It hath been budding with the spring. We are linked in celebrity, and thus will descend to posterity as the immortal illustrators of the great Transcendentalist!" (TS copy, Cranch Papers, MHi). "The originals of C. P. Cranch's caricatures of Emerson's Nature & other things" were in Clarke's possession (Caroline Healey Dall [Worcester] to Mrs. J. F. Clarke, 30 September 1889, MHi). Clarke's collection, entitled "Illustrations of the New Philosophy, 1835," was published in facsimile in Miller, *Cranch*. The date 1835 is no doubt an error since Emerson's *Nature* was not published until 1836.

46. The *Cincinnati Daily Gazette*, 11 June 1838, p. 1, listed the Cincinnati law firms. The office of E. P. Cranch and J. C. Vaughan was located on Main Street above Third Street, over Morgan and Sons Bookstore.

47. Georgiana Emily Keats (1819–55) was the oldest of eight children born to George Keats (1797–1841), brother of John Keats, and Georgiana Augusta Wylie Keats (1801/2–79). George and Georgiana Keats had migrated to America in the summer of 1818.

48. The Stetsons were prominent Unitarians. The Semicolon was a social club primarily attended by Unitarians.

49. Cranch's article on "Dreams" appeared in the *Western Messenger*, 6 (June 1839): 98–100.

50. Miss Harding is unidentified. Oliver Prescott was probably a lawyer, but he too cannot be positively identified. William Greene lived on the corner of Vine and Third Streets. He was associated with Perkins in social reform work.

51. James Handasyd Perkins (1810–48), after two years in the Boston counting-house of his uncle, Colonel Thomas H. Perkins, came to Cincinnati in February 1832, studied law, and was admitted to the bar three years later. Perkins never practiced law; instead he became editor of the *Cincinnati Evening Chronicle*, purchased the paper in the winter of 1835, and united it with the *Cincinnati Mirror*, all the while aiding Ephraim Peabody in editing the *Western Messenger*. Perkins was, by 1838, active in promoting prison reform. Warm was his private sympathy for all who suffered, were tempted, and debased. He felt that the individual was getting lost in the mass. In a letter written to a friend, written shortly after he became minister-at-large, he said: "The mantle of Minister at Large has fallen upon me, and in this vocation I hope somewhat to realize that usefulness to which you allude as the crowning gift of man. The field is wide and undug; my spade is dull and weak. . . . Pauperism, Poverty, Infidelity, Vice, Crime, — these are five well-armed and most determined demons to war with, — true children of the world, the flesh, and the Devil, which, jockey-like, cross and recross their breeds for ever" (*Memoirs and Writings of James Handasyd Perkins*, ed. William Henry Channing [Cincinnati: Trueman & Spofford, 1851], 1:114–15). In his first *Report of the Charitable Intelligence Office*, he declared his chief objectives to have been "to form such connections with the poor as will enable us, in some degree at least, to withdraw them and their children from evil associations, and to combine immediate physical relief with continued moral relief; and second, to find those in need employment" (1:118–19).

52. Despite his plans, Cranch did not leave Cincinnati until probably 2 March.

53. The Cranch brothers took their meals with Mrs. Wood. Bertha and Kate were her daughters. Edward Cranch later married Bertha.

54. Cranch acquired a developing interest in Swedenborg and the New Jerusalem Church. A year later—23 May 1840—he wrote Clarke that he was "getting to be somewhat of a Sweden-

borgian. . . . I do not think we study him enough. . . . For my part, I could be a New Church man, were it not for the doctrine of the identity of Jesus and God" (Cranch Papers, MHi).

55. See Cranch's letter to Clarke, 16 February 1839, in Scott, *Cranch*, pp. 44–46.

56. See Coleridge's "Rime of the Ancient Mariner," 1. 193.

57. See Romans 7:24, "O wretched man that I am! who shall deliver me from the body of this death?"

58. Cranch arrived in Washington on 6 March after a boat trip up the Ohio to Wheeling, by stagecoach to Frederick, Maryland, and by train to Washington. Cranch left Mrs. Lynch and Lucas in Frederick.

59. On 8 March, Cranch wrote Edward from Washington: "Rufus [Dawes] is sitting with me in the old library, reading Carlyle. We had a long talk this morning about the New Church. He talks grandly about it, and almost makes me in love with the system of Swedenborg. He thinks most of the Unitarians today will all come round to the New Church before long" (Cranch Collection, WyU).

60. Emanuel Swedenborg, *Arcana Coelestia: or, Heavenly Mysteries Contained in the Sacred Scriptures, or Word of the Lord, Manifested and Laid Open; Beginning with the Book of Genesis. Interspersed with Relations of Wonderful Things Seen in the World of Spirits and the Heaven of Angels*, 12 vols. (London: J. Hodson, 1789–1806).

61. Alexander Kinmont, *Twelve Lectures on the History of Man, and the Rise and Progress of Philosophy* (Cincinnati: N. P. James, 1839).

62. Possibly S. Greenleaf Bulfinch. Cranch wrote to Edward on 8 March: "I have not yet seen Greenleaf Bulfinch. He is busy moving" (Cranch Collection, WyU). The February 1838 *Western Messenger* published a "discourse" by S. G. Bulfinch, then pastor of the Unitarian Church in Pittsburgh.

63. Cranch was probably reading Cousin's *Elements of Psychology: Included in a Critical Examination of Locke's Essay on the Human Understanding* (New York: Gould & Newman, 1838). Three months later Cranch wrote Edward from Philadelphia: "I am also continuing to read Cousin. He does much to strengthen my faith" (21 June 1839, TS copy, Cranch Papers, MHi).

64. "Correspondences" was published in the *Dial*, 1 (January 1841): 381.

65. I have been unable to identify Major Hitchcock and Fleischman.

66. On 14 April, Cranch wrote Edward from Baltimore: "I shall be in Balt. a few days — they want me to stay over another Sunday, but I shall not have time. Next Sunday I intend to preach in Phila[,] spend a few days in New York, & be in Boston the last week in April. Where I shall then go, I know not yet. Perhaps to Northampton. Mr. Briggs said he would try to arrange it. There are many vacant parishes in N.E." (Cranch Collection, WyU).

67. Over thirty years later, Cranch commented on his problem: "It is my misfortune (as regards worldly & pecuniary success) to have too many sides — to have been born (and educated) with a diversity of talents. . . . I have wooed too many mistresses; and the world punishes me for not shutting my eyes to all charmers but one" ("The Book of Thoughts," unpublished commonplace book, 1872–79, pp. 191–93, Cranch Papers, MHi).

68. Philadelphia.

69. From 1825 to 1875, William Henry Furness (1802–96) was pastor of the First Unitarian Church in Philadelphia.

70. *Philosophical Miscellanies, Translated from the French of Cousin, Jouffroy, and Benjamin Constant* by George Ripley, in his *Specimens of Foreign Standard Literature* series, vols. 1–2 (Boston: Hilliard, Gray, 1838). Cranch could well have been introduced to Jouffroy by William Henry Channing, who was no doubt translating *Introduction to Ethics, Including a Critical Survey of Moral Systems* in two volumes for the *Specimens of Foreign Standard Literature* series (Boston: Hilliard, Gray, 1840–41) before Cranch left Cincinnati in 1839.

A NEW CHECKLIST OF THE BOOKS IN HENRY DAVID THOREAU'S LIBRARY

Walter Harding

A QUARTER OF A CENTURY AGO I compiled a catalogue of the library of Henry David Thoreau (*Thoreau's Library* [Charlottesville: University of Virginia Press, 1957]) based primarily on Thoreau's own catalogues (in the Henry E. Huntington Library) plus any additional volumes I was able to track down that belonged to him or his immediate family before his death in 1862. In the intervening years a number of new volumes from his library have come to light, old volumes have migrated to new locations, and I have been able to correct some of the errors of the earlier list and to make some more specific identifications of some of the more vaguely described items. Thus this updated checklist which I hope may prove of some use to Thoreau scholars.

As in the earlier catalogue, books are listed alphabetically according to their Library of Congress "main entry" classifications. Author, title, place of publication, publisher, and publication date are derived, where possible, from either Thoreau's actual copy of the book or from his catalogue descriptions. (All books which Thoreau listed in his own catalogues are indicated in this list by an asterisk [*] at the beginning of the entry.) When I have derived any of the bibliographical information from any less certain source, I have so indicated it by placing it in square brackets.

In certain cases there has been other pertinent information available and this I have entered in each case in a subsidiary entry. These include such information as how the book is inscribed and/or annotated; from whom or why Thoreau obtained the copy; to whom he gave it; and its present location, where known. In the latter case, if the volume is now in a library, university, or museum, its location is indicated by the symbols employed by the National Union Catalog; if it is owned by a private individual, his name and city of address is given. One private collector, while most cooperative in giving me access to the volumes in her collection, feels that she does not have the facilities to make these volumes available to the general scholar, and so at her request I have omitted her name and address.

The 1957 edition of the catalogue contained a lengthy introduction classifying the books according to topic, source, and provenance. It also included elaborate cross-indexes. Since little of this information has changed over the years, I have not repeated that information here, but simply indicate here its availability.

One of the great pleasures of Thoreau scholarship is working with others in the field. I have never failed to find my fellow workers most helpful. To the names of those whose help I have already acknowledged in the 1957 catalogue, I would like to add those of Raymond R. Borst, Robert Buckeye, Robert Burton, Herbert Cahoon, William Cummings, Grace Davenport, James Edgar, Mary Fenn, A. L. Fiske, Robert Galvin, George Goodspeed, Mitchell Greene, Donald Griffin, John Hirsh, Kathy Hughes, Harold Kittleson, William Lane, Robert Lucas, Rose Marie Mitten, Marcia Moss, Howard Mott, Joel Myerson, Russell Rady, Robert Sattelmeyer, Samuel Wellman, and Elizabeth Witherell.

THOREAU'S LIBRARY

*Abercrombie, [John. Inquiries concerning the] intellectual powers, [and the investigation of truth. New York, Harper] Family Library, [1832.]

Academies. Calcutta. Asiatic Society of Bengal. Bibliotheca Indica. A collection of Oriental Works, published under the patronage of the hon. court of directors of the East India Company, and the superintendence of the Asiatic Society of Bengal. Vol. 15, nos. 41, 50. Calcutta, 1853.

Inscription: "R. W. Emerson from Henry Thoreau. Henry D. Thoreau from Thomas Cholmondeley." Contains the Taittariya Artareya, Soetasvataia, Kena, Isa Katha, Prasna, Mundaka and Mandukya Upinshads, translated from the original Sanskrit by E. Roer. MCoA.

*Adams, [Alexander. The rudiments of] Latin [and English] grammar. New York. [Duyckinck & Long, 1820.]

*[———. Adam's] Latin grammar. [Edited by Benjamin A.] Gould. [Boston: Hilliard, Gray, Little, & Wilkins & Richardson & Lord, 1829.]

*Aesthetic papers. [Boston: E. P. Peabody, 1849.]

Contains the first printing of Thoreau's "Resistance to Civil Government." Given to Elizabeth Weir.

*Agassiz, [Louis] and [A. A.] Gould. Principles of Geology [i.e., zoology. Boston, Gould, Kendall & Lincoln, 1848.]

Thoreau's is almost certainly an erroneous entry of "geology" for "zoology."

*Aikin, [John, ed. Select works of the] British Poets. Philadelphia, [Wardle, 1840.]

*Ainsworth, [Robert.] An abridgement of Ainsworth's dictionary, [English and] Latin, [by Thomas Morell.] Philadelphia, [Carey, 1829.]

*Alcott, Amos Bronson. Conversations [with children] on the gospels. Boston, [James Munroe, 1836–1837.] 2 vols.

Inscription: "Henry D. Thoreau from his friend A. Bronson Alcott." MHarF.

*Allingham, [William.] The music master, [a love story. London: Routledge, 1855.]

F. B. Sanborn suggests this was given to Thoreau by Emerson.

*American almanack [and repository of useful knowledge. Boston: Gray & Bowen,] 1849.

*Andrews, [Ethan Allen. A copious and critical] Latin-English lexicon. [New York: Harper, 1850.]

*Ariosto, [Lodovico. Orlando Furioso translated into English verse by John] Hoole. London, [1783.]

Given to F. H. Bigelow.

*[Arnim, Bettina (Brentano) von.] Gunderode, translated by [Margaret Fuller. Boston: E. P. Peabody, 1842.]

*Atkinson, [James.] Epitome of the art of navigation. London, 1758.

Sanborn suggests that this might have belonged originally to Thoreau's grand-father John Thoreau.

Atlantic Monthlies.

Issues unidentified. Given to Elizabeth Weir.

*Audubon, John James and John Bachman. The quadrupeds of N[orth] America. [New York: Audubon, 1851.]

Inscription: autograph of Thoreau. Given to Walton Ricketson in 1866. MCoA.

*Bachi, Pietro. A comparative view of the Italian and Spanish languages or an easy method of learning the Spanish tongue. Boston, 1832.

Inscription: "D. H. Thoreau." Is this "Spanish Grammar. By Bachi. Boston. 1 v." listed in Thoreau's catalogue? NN (Berg).

*————. A grammar [of the] Italian [language.] Boston, [Hilliard, Gray, Little & Wilkins, 1829.]

*————. Scelta di prose Italiane, tratte da' piu celebri scrittori antichi et moderni. Cambridge, 1828.

Inscription: "Autograph of Thoreau torn out and note by Sanborn, 'Here stood the autograph of H. D. Thoreau. This was his Italian text book in Harvard College; the penciling on p. 15 et seq. are in Thoreau's handwriting.'" NN (Berg).

*————. Teatro scelto Italiano. Cambrigia, 1829.

Inscription: Thoreau's autograph signature. Described in *The Stephen H. Wakeman Collection* . . . (New York: American Art Association, 1924).

*Bacon, Francis. Essays. Boston.

*Bailey, [Ebenezer. First lessons in] algebra. [Boston: Carter, Hendee, 1833.]

*Bailey, [Nathan. A new universal etymological English] dictionary. [London: Osborne & Shipton, 1755.]

Bailey compiled numerous dictionaries, but this seems the most likely to have been in Thoreau's library.

Baird, Spencer Fullerton. Directions for making collections in natural history. Washington: Smithsonian Institution, 1853.

Thoreau acknowledges receipt of this pamphlet in his letter to Baird of 19 December 1853 (NNPM).

*Bartlett, [John Russell.] Dictionary of Americanisms. [New York, Bartlett & Welford, 1848.]

Given to Bronson Alcott (see his entry for 6 April 1873, *The Journals of Bronson Alcott*, ed. Odell Shepard [Boston: Little, Brown, 1938], p. 431).

*Bechstein, [Johann Matthaus.] Cage [and chamber]-birds [. . . incorporating the whole of] Sweet's [British] warblers. [London: Bohn, 1853.]

*Beeson, John. A Plea for the Indians. [New York: Beeson, 1857.]

*Belknap, [Jeremy.] American biography. [New York: Harper, 1844.] 2d vol. 1 v.

*Bell, Thomas. A history of British Quadrupeds. London: Van Voorst, 1837.

Inscription: "Gift of Sophia E. Thoreau" and a few penciled notes. MCo.

*Beltrami, G. C. La deucouverte des sources du Mississipi. Nouvelle Orleans: Levy, 1824.

Inscription: "Gift of Sophia E. Thoreau" and a few penciled notes. Thoreau's autograph has apparently been clipped out. MCo.

*Bible, Holy. Old Testament, New Testament and Apocrypha. Philadelphia, 1788.

Inscription: "1790 Thoreau" "Thoreau Bible 1790." Originally the property of Jennie Burns, Thoreau's grandmother. MCoA.

————. Edinburgh: Mark & Charles Kerr, 1793.

Originally the property of Mary Dunbar. MCoA.

————. Boston: Ewer & Bedlington, 1825.

Originally the property of Thoreau's aunt, Sophia Dunbar. MCoA.

*————. New York: White for the American Bible Society, 1829.

Now in a private library in Maine.

————. Boston, 1834.

Originally the property of Thoreau's sister Helen. MCoA.

*————. [?]

Inscription: "Charles" "Bangor Aug. 30, 1836" "Boston, Sept. 13, 1837." Since the title page is missing, further identification is impossible. It apparently belonged to Thoreau's uncle, Charles Dunbar. MCoA.

*[————. New] Testament. Greek.

Sanborn suggests that this is the Worcester edition. If so, it is probably *Novum testamentum. Juxta exemplar Joannis Millii accuratissime impressum* (Worcester: Thomas, 1800).

Blair, Hugh. An abridgement of lectures on rhetoric. Exeter, N.H.: Williams, 1822.

Inscription: autographed by Helen Thoreau. MCoA.

*————. Sermons. Boston: Thomas & Andrews 1799. 2 vols.

Inscription: "Henry D. Thoreau from Maria Thoreau. Henry D. from Maria Thoreau. Presented to Wm. Allen by Miss Sophia E. Thoreau, June 13, 1872." RPB.

————. Sermons, Philadelphia, 1794.

Inscription: "John Thoreau 1798." This is vol. 3 with the title page of vol. 4, inscribed as above, laid in. MHarF.

*Blake, J[ohn Lauris. A] biographical dictionary[: comprising a summary account of the lives of the most distinguished persons of all ages, nations, and professions. Philadelphia: Cowperthwait, 1856.]

Given to Elizabeth Weir.

*Blanchard, [Samuel] Laman. Sketches [from life. London: Colburn, 1846.] 2 vols.

*Boyer, Abel. French dictionary. Boston: Bedlington & Bradford & Peaslee, 1827.

Inscription: "Gift of Sophia E. Thoreau" and a few penciled notes. MCo.

*[Brewster, David. The] life of [Sir Isaac] Newton. New York: Harper, [1831.]

*British drama, the: a collection of the most esteemed tragedies, comedies, operas, and farces, in the English language. Philadelphia, 1832. 2 vols.

Inscription on front endpapers of each volume: "Henry D. Thoreau." Given to Alcott. MH.

*Broderip, William J. Leaves from the note-book of a naturalist. Boston, Littell, 1852.

Given to MCo by Sophia Thoreau; copy now missing.

Brown, Thomas. Philosophy of the human mind. Hallowell, 1833. 2 vols.

Inscribed on each title-page: "D. Thoreau." MH.

*Brownson, [Orestes.] New view[s of Christianity, society, and the church. Boston: Charles C. Little and James Brown, 1836.]

*Bryson's Canadian Farmer's Almanac, for the Year of our Lord 1852. Montreal: Campbell Bryson, [1851.]

Laid in vol. 1 of Thoreau's Extracts on Canada. NNPM.

*Buchanan, [James.] Sketches [of the history, manners, and customs of the North American Indians. New York: Borradaile, 1824.]

Bunsen, Christianus Carlus Josias. Christanity and mankind, their beginning and prospects. (Vols. 1–2: Hippolytus and his age. Vols. 3–4: Outlines of the philosophy of the universal history, applied to language and religion. Vols. 5–7: Analecta ante-Nicaena.) London, 1854. 7 vols.

The complete set of seven volumes was given to Thoreau by Thomas Cholmondeley. Thoreau has annotated the Chapman list (see *Thoreau's Library*, p. 15) to the effect that the two volumes of the *Outlines of the philosophy of universal history* should be given to Ripley. Sanborn states that he was given seven volumes of Bunsen. I assume then these were volumes 1, 2, 5, 6, and 7 of this set and the two volumes of *Egypt's place in Universal history* listed below. Volumes 1 and 2 are now missing. Volumes 3 and 4 are autographed "Henry D. Thoreau" and in vol. 3 Thoreau has added "from Thomas Cholmondeley." These volumes are now owned by John C. Hirsch of Georgetown University. Volumes 5, 6, and 7 each contain Thoreau's autograph and a note by Sanborn stating he was given these volumes by Mrs. Thoreau after Thoreau's death. They are now owned by Walter Harding, Geneseo, N.Y.

————. Egypt's place in universal history. London, 1848. 2 vols.

Inscription: "Henry D. Thoreau from Thomas Cholmendeley," vol. 1 only. VtMiM. These were given to Thoreau by Thomas Cholmondeley. See note to above volumes.

*Bunyan, John. The pilgrim's progress. New York: Tiebout, 1811.

Now in a private library in Maine.

*Burns, Robert. The poetical works of Robert Burns. London: Jones, 1829 (1833). 2 vols.

Now in a private library in Maine.

*Business man's assistant. [Boston: Butts, 1852.]

*Butler, [Joseph. The] analogy of religion, [natural and revealed, to the constitution and course of nature.] Cambridge.

*Buttman, Philip. Greek grammar for the use of schools. Translated by Edward Everett and edited by George Bancroft and George H. Bode. Boston: Cummings, Hilliard, 1826.

Inscription: "D. H. Thoreau Cambridge, Mass. 1833." MCo.

*Byron, George Gordon, Lord. Works, in verse and prose, including his letters, journal, etc., with a sketch of his life. Edited by Halleck. New York: Dearborn, 1835.

Inscription: Thoreau's autograph. NNPM.

*Cadalso, Jose. Cartas Marruecas y poesias selectas. Boston, 1827.

Inscription: Autograph torn from flyleaf. Note by Sanborn included stating that the autograph was given away, and that the manuscript notes on pp. 38–39 are in Thoreau's hand. RPB.

*Caesar, [C. Julius.] Commentarii. Lipsiae, [1805.]

Given to F. H. Bigelow.

*Canadian guide book, The. [Montreal: Armour & Ramsay, 1849.]

This is apparently one of the two guide books Thoreau records in *A Yankee in Canada* as purchasing on his excursion there. What the other was, or what the map he speaks of there was, I have no idea.

*Carlyle, Thomas. Critical and miscellaneous essays. Boston: James Munroe, 1838–39. 4 vols.

Now in a private library in Maine.

*———. The French Revolution, a history. Boston: Charles C. Little and James Brown, 1838. 2 vols.

Now in a private library in Maine.

*———. The life of [Frederick] Schiller. New York, [Dearborn, 1837.]

*———. Past and present. [Boston: Charles C. Little and James Brown, 1843.]

Inscription on front endpaper: "Henry D. Thoreau from RWE." Given to Sarah Richardson. Now in Carlyle House, London, England.

*[Carpenter, William.] Scripture natural history; [or a descriptive account of the zoology, botany, & geology of the Bible, with improvements by Rev. Gorham D. Abbott. [Boston: Lincoln, Edmands, 1841.]

Carter, James G. A map of New Hampshire, for families & schools. Portsmouth, N.H., Nathaniel March, [183?].

Inscription: autograph of Thoreau. NN (Berg).

*Carver, [Jonathan. Three years] travels [through the interior parts of North-America. Philadelphia: Crukshank, 1789.]

Cellarius, Christophorus. Geographia antiqua; being a complete set of antient geography. London, 1747.

VtMiM.

*[Channing, Walter.] New and old. [Boston, 1851.]

Given to Elizabeth Weir.

*Channing, William Ellery. Discourses, reviews, and miscellanies. Boston: Carter & Hendee, 1830.

Inscription: "D. H. Thoreau, Cambridge, June – 37." Now owned by A. L. Fiske, Spencer, Mass.

*C[hanning], W[illiam] E[llery (the Younger).] Near home; [a poem. Boston: James Munroe, 1858.]

*————. Poems. Boston: Charles C. Little and James Brown, 1843.

Now in a private library in Maine.

*————. Poems; second series. Boston: James Munroe, 1846 (1847).

Now in a private library in Maine.

*————. The Woodman and other poems. [Boston: James Munroe, 1849.]

*Chapin, Loring Dudley. Hand book of plants & fruits or the vegetable kingdom. New York, 1843. 2 vols. in 1.

Inscription: "Henry D. Thoreau." Sold by Parke-Bernet at the Lorimer Sale, 15 January 1963.

*Chesterfield, Philip Dormer Stanhope. The beauties of Chesterfield. Boston: Ewer, 1828.

NNPM.

*Cholmondeley, Thomas. Ultima thule. London: Chapman, 1854.

Inscription: "Henry D. Thoreau from Thomas Cholmondeley." MCo.

*Church, [Benjamin.] The history of King Philip's war. [Boston: Howe & Norton, 1825.]

*Churchman, John. An account [of the gospel labours, and Christian experiences of a faithful minister of Christ. Philadelphia: Crukshank, 1779.]

*Cicero, Marcus Tullius. Orationes. Bostoniae, 1831.

    Inscription: "D. H. Thoreau." VtMiM.

*Clarkson, Rev. David. A discourse [of the saving grace of God.] London, [Parkhurst,] 1688.

Coffin, G. W. A plan of the public lands in the State of Maine. Boston, 1835.

    Now lacking date, scale, and cartographer. MCo.

*Colburn, [Warren. An introduction to] algebra [upon the inductive method of instruction. Boston: Hilliard, Gray, Little & Wilkins, 1826.]

Colebrooke, H. T. Miscellaneous essays. London, Allen, 1837. 2 vols.

    Inscription: "R. W. Emerson from Henry D. Thoreau. Henry D. Thoreau from Thomas Cholmondeley." MCoA.

*Coleman, W[illiam] S[tephen.] British butterflies. [London: Routledge, 1860.]

*————. Our woodlands, [heaths & hedges. London: Routledge, 1859.]

*Coleridge, Samuel T., Percy B. Shelley, and John Keats. The poetical works of Coleridge, Shelley, and Keats. Philadelphia: Howe, 1832.

    Now in a private library in Maine.

Colton's railroad & township map of [the state of] Maine [with portions of New Hampshire, New Brunswick & Canada. New York: J. H. Colton, 1855.]

    Thoreau mentions in *The Maine Woods* carrying this map with him.

Complete railway map . . . to accompany the American Railway Guide. New York: Dinsmore, [n.d.].

    On verso, Map of New-York City. RPB.

Concord, Mass. Reports of the selectmen and other officers of the town of Concord, from March 5, 1860, to March 4, 1861. Concord: Benjamin Tolman, 1861.

    Inscription: "Henry D. Thoreau" in pencil on front cover. Annotations and corrections on p. 50. NN (Berg).

*Copway. G. Traditional history and characteristic sketches of the Ojibway nation. Boston: Sanborn, Carter, Bazin, [n.d.].

    Inscription: "H. D. Thoreau." Thoreau lists this twice in his catalogue, perhaps indicating a duplicate copy, or possibly an inadvertant error. MCo.

Cowper, William. Poems of William Cowper, Esq. with a new memoir compiled from Johnson, Southey and other sources. New York: Leavitt & Allen, [n.d.].

    Inscription: "1858." Now in a private library in Maine.

*————. Task.

Sanborn suggests that this might have been given to Thoreau by Daniel Ricketson.

*[Croly, George.] Life [and times of his late majesty] George IV. New York, [Harper, 1831.]

Cummings & Hilliard. Untitled small engraved map of the eastern Mediterranean, Greece, and Asia Minor. Boston, [n.d.].

This map was probably extracted from a school geography. This, the *Complete railway map* . . . , and the map from Willey's *Incidents in White Mountain history*, were enclosed in a folder of marbled boards, with a cloth back, with a paper label in Thoreau's hand, "Map of Middlesex, Norfolk, & Worcester Counties, &c. & of the White Mountains." They are the "three maps used by Thoreau" listed in the Cohn Sale (New York, Parke-Bernet, 19 October 1955). RPB. In his original catalogue, Thoreau also listed "Sixty Maps" but later erased the listing. I imagine he thus indicated how many maps he owned and not the title of a specific volume of maps, so I have omitted his listing from this catalogue.

*Curtius Rufus, Quintus. Historia Alexandri Magni. Lipsiae, [Tauchnitti, 1829.]

Given to F. H. Bigelow.

*Curzon, [Robert. A visit to the] monasteries [of the Levant. New York: Putnam, 1849.]

*Dana, Richard Henry, Jr. The seaman's friend: containing a treatise on practical seamanship, with plates; a dictionary of sea terms; customs and usages of the merchant service: laws relating to the practical duties of master and mariners. Ninth edition. Revised and corrected. Boston, 1857.

Inscription: "Henry D. Thoreau" "Elizabeth J. Weir." RPB.

*Dante [Alighieri. La divina commedia di Dante Alighieri.] Avignone, [Seguin Aine, 1816.] 3 vols.

Inscription: "D. H. Thoreau Dec. 9, 1836." MCoA. Given to F. H. Bigelow.

*————. Divine comedy: the Inferno. New York: Harper, 1849. Trans. by John Carlyle.

Now in a private library in Maine.

*Davies, Charles. Elements of surveying & navigation. Revised edition. New York: Barnes, 1847.

Inscription: "Henry D. Thoreau." MCo.

*————. Grammar of arithmetic. [New York: Barnes, 1850.]

*De la Borde, Sieur. Relation des *Caraibes*. Amsterdam, 1711.

See *Cape Cod* (Boston: Ticknor and Fields, 1865), p. 143.

*Dial, The. Boston, 1840–44. 4 vols.

> Inscription: Many annotations, the autograph of Thoreau in each volume, and in vol. 2 "To F. B. Sanborn by the hands of Sophia E. Thoreau." ICarbS. Thoreau's copy of the July 1842 issue was sold at the Stockhausen Sale (Sotheby Parke-Bernet) on 20 November 1974.

*D'Israeli, [Isaac.] Curiosities of literature. New York, [Leavitt, 1851.]

> Given to Elizabeth J. Weir.

*Documentary history of the state of New York. Arranged by E. B. O'Callaghan. Albany: Van Benthuysen, 1850–51. 4 vols.

> Inscription: "Henry D. Thoreau" (in each volume). These were apparently given to Thoreau by H. S. Randall (see the *Wakeman Collection*, item 211). MCo.

*Emerson, [Benjamin Dudley.] First class reader. Boston, [Russell, Odiorne & Metcalf, 1833.]

*Emerson, [Frederick.] Key to the [North American] arithmetic, part second and part third. [Philadelphia: Hogan & Thompson, 1845.]

*———. [The North American] arithmetic. [Boston: Lincoln & Edmands, 1832.] 3d printing.

*Emerson, George B. A report on the trees and shrubs growing naturally in the forests of Massachusetts. Boston: Dutton and Wentworth, 1846.

> Inscription: Thoreau's autograph and penciled notes. RPB.

*Emerson, Ralph Waldo. An address delivered before the senior class in Divinity College, Cambridge. Boston: James Munroe, 1838.

> Inscription: "Henry D. Thoreau. With the regards of R.W.E." MH.

*———. The conduct of life. Boston: Ticknor and Fields, 1860.

> Inscription: "Henry D. Thoreau from the Author. Nov. 6, 1860." CtY.

———. English traits. Boston: Phillips, Sampson, 1856.

> Inscription: "Henry D. Thoreau: From the Author." CtY.

*———. Essays. Boston: James Munroe, 1841.

> Inscription: "Henry D. Thoreau, from his friend, R.W.E. 19 March 1841." CtY.

*———. Essays, second series, Third edition. Boston: Phillips, Sampson, 1858.

> Inscription: "Henry D. Thoreau." CtY.

———. The method of nature. An oration delivered before the society of the Adelphi in Waterville College in Maine, August 11, 1841. Boston: Samuel G. Simpkins, 1841.

Inscription by Thoreau on title page states it was the gift of Ralph Waldo Emerson. Now owned by George Goodspeed, Concord, Mass.

*————. Nature. Boston: James Munroe, 1836.

Inscription: "D. H. Thoreau." MH.

————. Nature.

Thoreau lists this volume twice and Sanborn suggests that he may have owned a reprint as well as the first edition.

*————. Nature; addresses, and lectures. Boston: James Munroe, 1849.

Inscription: "Henry D. Thoreau from R.W.E. 7 September, 1849." CtY. Pages 229–37 have been torn out.

*————. Poems. Boston: James Munroe, 1847.

Inscription: "Henry D. Thoreau from R.W.E. 25 December, 1846." CtY.

*————. Representative men. Boston: Phillips, Sampson, 1850.

Inscription: "Henry D. Thoreau, from R. W. Emerson, 30th December, 1849. F. B. Sanborn, from Sophia Thoreau. 1876." Described in the *Wakeman Collection*.

*Euler, Leonhard. An introduction to the elements of algebra. Boston: Hilliard, Gray, Little & Wilkins, 1828.

Inscription: "H. Thoreau, Concord, Mass. A college text book of H. D. Thoreau. F. B. S." The initials are Sanborn's. RPB.

*Euripides. Tragoediae. Lipsiae, Tauchnitii, 1828. 4 vols. in 2.

Given to F. H. Bigelow. Vols. 3–4 described in Robert F. Lucas, *Henry David Thoreau* (Blandford, Mass.: Robert F. Lucas, 1981).

*Farmer, J. and J. B. Moore, eds. Collections, historical, miscellaneous and monthly literary journal. Concord, N.H.: J. B. Moore, 1824. Vol. 3.

Inscription: "D. H. Thoreau." MCo.

Farmer, John. Map of the states of Michigan and Wisconsin, embracing a great part of Iowa and Illinois and the whole mineral region with a chart of the lakes. Detroit: J. Farmer, 1854.

This is supposedly the map on which Thoreau planned the itinerary of his 1861 journey to the West. MCoA.

*Farrar, John. An elementary treatise on astronomy. Cambridge: Hilliard & Metcalf, 1827.

Inscription: "Henry D. Thoreau." VtMiM.

*————. An elementary treatise on mechanics. Cambridge: Hilliard & Metcalf, 1825.

Inscription: "Henry D. Thoreau." MCo.

*————. Elements of electricity, magnetism, and electro-magnetism. Cambridge: Hilliard & Metcalf, 1826.

Inscription: "Henry D. Thoreau." MCo.

*————. An experimental treatise on optics. Cambridge: Hilliard & Metcalf, 1826.

Inscription: "D. H. Thoreau, Cambridge." MCo.

*Farrar, Timothy. Report of the case of the trustees of Dartmouth College against William H. Woodward. Portsmouth, N.H.: Foster, 1819.

MCo.

*Felch, [Walton.] A comprehensive grammar. Boston, [Otis, Broaders, 1837.]

*Fenelon, Francois de Salignac de La Mothe. Les adventures de Telemaque, fils d'Ulysse. Bensancon, 1823.

Inscription: "D. H. Thoreau, Concord, Mass. 1834. Sophia E. Thoreau." Described in the *Wakeman Collection.*

*Finley, Anthony. A new general atlas of the globe. Philadelphia: Finley, 1824.

Inscription: autographs of Charles C. Emerson and H. D. Thoreau. MCoA.

*Fitch, Asa. First and second report on the noxious, beneficial and other insects of the State of New York. Albany: Van Benthuysen, 1856.

Inscription: Thoreau's autograph. RPB.

*Flint, Charles L. Culture of the grasses. An extract from the fourth annual report of Charles L. Flint, secretary of the state board of agriculture. Boston: White, 1860.

This is apparently the volume "Grasses and Sedges" which was given to Edward Hoar.

*Florian, Jean Pierre Claris de. Gonzalve de Cordove. Paris, 1828. 3 vols. in 1.

Given to MCo by Sophia Thoreau; withdrawn in 1918.

*Follen, [Charles T. C.] A German reader. Boston, [James Munroe, 1858.]

*————. [A practical] grammar of the German [language.] Boston, [Hilliard, Gray, Little & Wilkins, 1828.]

Fordyce, James. Addresses to young men. Second American Edition. Boston, 1795. 2 vols. in 1.

Inscription: autograph of Thoreau's father, John Thoreau. VtMiM.

*Foster, [John.] Essays [in a series of letters, on the following subjects . . .] on decision of character. Boston, [Loring, 1833.]

*Fox, Charles J. History of the old township of Dunstable, including, Nashua, Nashville, Hollis, Hudson, Litchfield, and Merrimac, N.H.; Dunstable and Tyngsborough, Mass. Nashua, 1846.

> Inscription: "Henry Thoreau, Concord Mass. Henry Thoreau." Sold by Parke-Bernet on 6 December 1955.

*Franchere, Gabriel. Narrative of a voyage to the North West Coast of America in the years 1811, 1812, 1813, 1814. New York: Redfield, 1854.

> NN (Berg).

*Franklin, [Benjamin.] The life of [Dr. Benjamin] Franklin. Salem, [Cushing & Carlton, 1796.]

*[Freemasons. Concord, Mass.] Corinthian Lodge. [By-Laws of Corinthian lodge of ancient, free, and accepted masons of Concord, Mass.] Concord, [Tolman, 1859.]

*Froissart, [Jean. Chronicles of England, France, Spain and the adjoining countries.] London, Bohn, [1855.] 2 vols.

> Given to Ellery Channing.

Gerando, Joseph Marie de. Self-education, or the means and art of moral progress. Boston: Carter & Hendee, 1830.

> Inscription: "Thoreau." MCo.

*Giraud, Jacob P., Jr. The birds of Long Island. New York: Wiley & Putnam, 1844.

> MCo.

*Goethe, Johann Wolfgang von. Torquato Tasso.

> This volume has been rebound without the titlepage, so that it is impossible to identify it further. MCo.

*————. Wilhelm Meister's apprenticeship. Translated by Thomas Carlyle. Boston: Wells & Lilly, 1828. 3 vols.

> Inscription: "R. W. Emerson to Henry D. Thoreau." There is also a note by Parker Pillsbury stating that it had been given to him by Sophia Thoreau on 17 June 1862. NNPM.

*Goldsbury, [John.] A sequel to a common school grammar. [Boston: James Munroe, 1842.]

*Goldsmith, Oliver. The miscellaneous works of Oliver Goldsmith. Philadelphia: Crissy, 1834.

> Now in a private library in Maine.

Gotama, called Akshapada. Aphorisms of the Nyaya philosophy, with illustrative extracts from the commentary by Wiswanathan. In Sanscrit and English. Allahabad: Printed for the use of Benare College by order of Govt. N. W. P., 1850.

Inscription: "R. W. Emerson by the bequest of Henry D. Thoreau. Henry D. Thoreau from Thomas Cholmondeley." MCoA.

*Gould, Augustus A. Report on the invertebrata of Massachusetts. Cambridge: Folsom, Wells & Thurston, 1841.

Given to MCo by Sophia Thoreau; copy now missing.

*Graglia, [C.] Italian [pocket] dictionary. Boston, [Hilliard, Gray, 1835.]

*Gray, Asa. The botanical text-book. New York: Putnam, 1853.

Inscription: autographed on the flyleaf. Sold by Anderson Galleries, New York, 10 November 1924.

*————. A manual of the botany of the northern United States. Boston: James Munroe, 1848.

Inscription: "Henry D. Thoreau Concord Mass." VtMiM.

*————. Manual of the botany of the northern United States. New York: Putnam, 1856.

Inscription: autographed on the flyleaf. NN (Berg).

*Grund, [Frances J. Elements of] chemistry. Boston, [Jenks & Palmer, n.d.]

*————. Geometry. [Boston: Jenks & Palmer.]

Since Grund published both a plane geometry and a solid geometry, it is impossible to distinguish to which volume Thoreau is referring.

*Guizot, [Frances Pierre Guillaume.] Essay on [the character and influence of] Washington [in the revolution of the United States of America. Boston: James Munroe, 1840.]

*Guthrie, William. A new geographical, historical, and commercial grammar; and present state of the several kingdoms of the world. London: Charles Dilly, 1787.

Inscription on front endpaper: "Henry D. Thoreau." A few penciled notes on front endpaper. Given to Alcott. MH.

Hardy, Robert Spence. Eastern Monachism: an account of the origin, laws, discipline, sacred writings, mysterious rites, religious ceremonies, and present circumstances, of the order of mendicants founded by Gotama Budha. London: Partridge & Oakey, 1850.

Inscription on title page: "A. Bronson Alcott from H. D. Thoreau." A few page references on back endpaper. Given to Thoreau by Thomas Cholmondeley. MH.

————. A manual of Budhism, in its modern development. London: Partridge & Oakey, 1853.

Given to Alcott (see Alcott's *Journals*, p. 349). From the Cholmondeley collection.

*Harlan, Richard. Fauna Americana: being a description of the mammiferous animals inhabiting North America. Philadelphia: A. Finley, 1825.

Inscription: Thoreau's autograph on the inside front cover. NN (Berg).

*Harris, Thaddeus William. A treatise on some of the insects of New England which are injurious to vegetation. Boston: White & Potter, 1852. Second edition.

Inscription on front endpaper: "Henry D. Thoreau." Given to Alcott. MH.

Harvardiana. 1834–1837. 2 vols.

Given to F. H. Bigelow. This may have been a copy of the undergraduate magazine at Harvard in Thoreau's day as a student. But Bigelow describes it as "Harvardiana—Catalogues—Pamphlets &c," which might mean that it was a collection of pamphlets about Harvard. Or, since this is the last item on Bigelow's list, the catalogues and pamphlets may have no relation to the Harvardiana.

*Hawes, [Joel.] Lectures [addressed to the young men of Hartford and New Haven.] Hartford, [Cooke, 1828.]

*[Hawthorne, Nathaniel.] Scarlet letter. [Boston: Ticknor, Reed, & Fields, 1850.]

Sanborn notes that this was canceled in Thoreau's catalogue and suggests that perhaps Thoreau gave the volume away.

*Hayley, William. The life and posthumous writings of William Cowper. Boston: W. Pelham, Manning & Loring, & E. Lincoln, 1803. 2 vols.

Inscription: signatures of John and Henry Thoreau. NN (Berg).

*Hayward, John. New England gazetteer. Concord, N.H.: Boyd & White, 1839.

Inscription: "Gift of Sophia E. Thoreau." MCo.

Hemans, Mrs. Felecia. The poetical works of Mrs. Hemans. Philadelphia: Ash, 1832. 2 vols.

Now in a private library in Maine.

*[Hennebert, L'abbe J. B. Fr. and G. G. de Beaurieu.] Cours d'histoire naturelle, [ou tableau de la nature consideree dans l'homme, les quadrupeds, les oiseaux, les poisson. Paris: Lacombe, 1770.]

I have been unable to find any one-volume editions of the work listed. It is also quite possible that Thoreau was referring to some edition of one of Georges-Louis de Buffon's works, since the phrase "Histoire naturelle" is used in the title of many of his books, and Thoreau refers frequently to Buffon. However, the closest to this specific title that I have been able to discover in his works is *Cours elementaire d'histoire naturelle* (Paris, 1859).

*Herndon, Lieut. William. Exploration of the valley of Amazon, made under direction of the Navy Department, by Wm. Lewis Herndon and Larnder Gibbon, Lieutenants United States Navy. Washington, 1853. Part 1.

Inscription: "Henry D. Thoreau from Horace Mann." RPB. In his letter of 30 October 1854 to Charles Sumner, Thoreau acknowledges receipt of the second volume of Herndon (*The Correspondence of Henry David Thoreau*, ed. Walter Harding and Carl Bode [New York: New York University Press, 1958], p. 347).

Hindu laws. A code of Gentoo laws, or ordination of the Pundits. Translated by N. B. Halhed. London, 1776.

Inscriptions: "Henry D. Thoreau from Thomas Cholmondeley." "E. R. Hoar, from Henry D. Thoreau, May 1862." "Presented to Concord Free Public Library by E. R. Hoar, Jan. 19th, 1895." MCo.

*[Holt, S.] Adventures with animals. Zoological notes and anecdotes. London, Dean & Son, 1852.

Inscription: "Henry D. Thoreau" twice on front endpapers. Given to Alcott. MH.

Homerus. Iliad. Translated by Alexander Pope. Baltimore: Nicklin, Lucas & Jefferts, 1812. 2 vols.

Thoreau notes in his catalogue and in *Walden* that vol. 1 was stolen from his Walden cabin. In the early 1960s it was owned by Mr. Louis Moreau of Concord, Mass., great grand-nephew of Alex Therien, the French Canadian woodchopper. It has however since disappeared again. Vol. 2 is now in a private library in Maine.

*————. Iliad. [From the text of Wolf with English notes, and Flaxman's designs.] Edited by C. C. Felton. Boston, [Hilliard, Gray, 1834.]

————. The Odyssey of Homer. Georgetown, D.C., and Philadelphia: Richards & Mallory, & Nicklin, 1814. 2 vols.

Now in a private library in Maine.

*Horatius [Flaccus, Quintus. Quinti Horatii Flacci opera omnia] ex editione J. C. Zeunii. Londini, [Valpy, 1825.]

Given to F. H. Bigelow.

*————. Quinti Horatii Flacci: opera. By B. A. Gould. Boston: Sumptibus, Hilliard, Gray et Soc., 1833.

Inscription: "Henry D. Thoreau. Mary Wheeler from Miss Thoreau. June 9th, 1874." MCo.

*Houghton, Jacob Jr. Reports of Wm. A. Burt and Bela Hubbard on the geography, topography, and geology of the U. S. surveys of the mineral region of the south shore of Lake Superior, for 1845. Detroit, 1846.

Sold by Parke-Bernet Galleries, New York, 25 January 1940. Inscription: "Henry D. Thoreau from E. P. Dorr Sat. 16th 1857." This volume is listed twice in Thoreau's own catalogue.

*Hubbard, William. A narrative of the Indian wars in New England. Worcester: Daniel Greenleaf, 1801.

Inscription: "Henry D. Thoreau." Pencil brackets marking off certain paragraphs. VtMiM.

*[Hughes, William.] An atlas of classical [geography. Edited by George] Long. [Philadelphia: Blanchard & Lea, 1856.]

*Hunter, John D. Manners & Customs of several Indian tribes. Philadelphia: Maxwell, 1823.

Inscription: "Henry D. Thoreau" and annotations. MCo.

*Indian narratives: containing a correct and interesting history of the Indian wars, from the landing of our pilgrim fathers, 1620, to Gen. Wayne's victory, 1794. Claremont, N.H., 1854.

Inscription: "Henry D. Thoreau." Described in the *Wakeman Collection*.

*Iriarte y Oropesa, Tomas de. Fabulas literarias moratin. Boston: Burdett, 1833.

Inscription: "D. H. Thoreau. Hollis 23. Cambridge, Mass." Hollis is a dormitory at Harvard where Thoreau lived. He did not reverse his initials until after leaving Harvard. The book also contains about 250 words in Thoreau's handwriting, an interlinear translation of part of the text. Offered for sale in the In Our Time (Cambridge, Mass.) catalogue 100 in 1979.

Isvara Krishna. The Sankhya Karika, or memorial verses on the Sankhya philosophy by Iswara Krishna. Translated by Henry Thomas Colebrooke . . . also the Byashya or commentary of Gaurapada. Translated and illustrated by an original comment by Horace Hayman Wilson. Oxford: Oriental Translation Fund, 1837.

A part of the Cholmondeley collection. Emerson records in his journal receiving it from the estate of Thoreau.

*Jackson, [Robert Montgomery Smith.] The mountain. [Philadelphia: Lippincott,] 1860.

*Jaeger, Benedict and H. C. Preston. Life of North American insects. Providence: The Author, 1854.

Originally given to Adams Tolman by Sophia Thoreau. Offered for sale in the Current Co. (Bristol, R.I.), "Henry David Thoreau" catalogue, in 1977.

*[————.] The life of North American insects. [New York,] Harpers, [1859.]

Jaimini. Aphorisms of the Mimansa philosophy with extracts from the commentaries. In Sanskrit and English. Allahabad: Printed for the use of the Benares Colleges, by order of Gov't., N.W.P., 1851.

> Inscription: "R. W. Emerson. Henry D. Thoreau from Thomas Cholmondeley." MCoA.

*[James, George P. R. The history of] Charlemagne. New York, [Harper, 1833.]

*[Jennings, C.] The eggs of British birds. [Bath, 1853.]

Jimutavahana. Two treatises on the Hindu law of inheritance. Translated by H. T. Colebrooke. Calcutta: A. H. Hubbard, 1810.

> Inscription: "R. W. Emerson. The bequest of Henry D. Thoreau." This is a volume from the Cholmondeley collection. MCoA.

*Johnson, [Samuel] and [John] Walker. Johnson's [English] dictionary . . . with Walker's [pronouncing dictionary.] Boston, [Ewer & Carter, 1828.]

*Josse, M. Augustin Louis. A grammar of the Spanish language. Revised by Francis Sales. Boston: Munroe & Frances, 1836.

> Inscription: "D. H. Thoreau." MCo.

*Juvenalis, Decimus Junius and Aulus Persius Flaccus. D. Junlii Juvenalis et A. Persii Flacci satirae in usum serenissimi delphini. Philadelphia: Carey, 1814.

> Inscription: Signatures of Clifford Belcher, Farmington, 1835, and Thoreau. Brief notes by Belcher and Thoreau. This volume was given to MCo by Sophia Thoreau. It disappeared from its shelves sometime prior to 1930. Later owned by the late Warren Colson, Proctor, Vermont.

Kalidassa. Sacontala, or the lost ring. Translated by Monier Williams. Hartford: Austin, 1855.

> According to Thoreau's annotation on the Chapman list this volume was to be given to Elizabeth Hoar. There is now a copy of this edition in Emerson's library in MCoA, but it does not have the usual Thoreau autograph.

Kennedy, Grace. Dunallan, or know what you judge. Exeter, N.H., 1828. 2 vols.

> Inscription: "Helen L. Thoreau's from her brother John." MCoA.

*Kirby, William and William Spence. An introduction to Entomology. London: Longman, Brown, Green, and Longmans, 1856.

> Inscription in an unknown hand: "This book belonged to Henry D. Thoreau Left with other books to A. Bronson Alcott Concord Mass See Alcott diaries for list of books." MH.

*Kirkham, [Samuel. A compendium of English] grammar. Baltimore, [1823.]

*Knapp, John Leonard. Journal of a naturalist. Philadelphia, 1831.

Given to MCo. by Sophia Thoreau; withdrawn in 1920.

Knox, Vicesimus. Elegant extracts; or useful and entertaining passages in prose. Dublin: Byrne, 1793.

Inscription: with autograph of Jane Thoreau on the flyleaf and laid in is a note as to its ownership by Thoreau, by William Allen, to whom the book was given by Sophia E. Thoreau on 13 June 1872. NNPM.

*Kraitsir, [Charles V.] Significance of the alphabet. [Boston: E. P. Peabody, 1846.]

*La Fontaine, Jean de. Fables.

Given to F. H. Bigelow.

Lardner, Dionysius. Popular lectures on science and art. New York: Law, 1856. 2 vols.

Gift of Sophia E. Thoreau. MCo.

*Legendre, A. M. Elements of geometry. Translated by John Farrar. Boston: Hilliard, Gray, Little & Wilkins, 1831.

Inscription: "John Thoreau Jr." MCo.

*Lempriere, [John.] A classical dictionary. New York, [1809.]

Inscription: "D. H. Thoreau." Given to Calvin Greene by Thoreau's mother and sister Sophia (see *Some Unpublished Letters of Henry D. and Sophia E. Thoreau*, ed. Samuel Arthur Jones [Jamaica, N.Y.: Marion Press, 1899], p. xi).

Leonard, Levi W. The Literary and scientific class book. Keene, N.H.: Prentiss, 1826.

Inscription: "Helen L. Thoreau Concord Academy." MCo.

*Lesley, J. Peter. Manual of coal and its topography. Philadelphia: Lippincott, 1856.

Inscription: "Benj. Smith Lyman. Huntingdon, Pa. 1 Sept. 1856. Mr. Henry Thoreau with the regards of B. S. L. Concord. 10 April, 1859." MCo.

*Lewis, [Meriwether] and [William] Clarke. [History of the expedition under the command of Captains Lewis and Clarke, to the sources of the Missouri, thence across the] Rocky Mountains [and down the river Columbia to the Pacific Ocean. Philadelphia: Bradford & Inskeep, 1814. 2 vols.]

Liberty and anti-slavery song book. Boston: King, 1842.

Inscription: autograph by Thoreau. MCoA.

Lincoln, Jairus. Anti-slavery melodies. Hingham: Gill, 1843.

MCoA.

*Lindsay, [William L.] Popular history of British lichens. [London: Reeve, 1856.]

*Locke, [John. An essay concerning] human understanding. Philadelphia: [Troutman & Hays, 1853.]

*(7. Logarithms. Boston. 1 v.)

This is too generalized a title to identify further, although Thoreau may possibly be referring to John Farrar, *An elementary treatise on the application of trigonometry to orthographic and stereographic projection . . . together with logarithmic tables* (Cambridge: Hilliard & Metcalf, 1822), since this was apparently a textbook at Harvard. A volume listed as "Log. Tables" was given to F. H. Bigelow.

*Loudon, John Claudius. Arboretum et fruticetum britannicum. London: Loudon, 1838. 8 vols.

Inscription: "Henry D. Thoreau" in volumes 2, 3, and 4, the only ones located. RPB.

*————. Encyclopaedia of plants. London: Longman, Brown, Green & Longmans, 1855. New edition.

Inscriptions: vol. 1, "Henry D. Thoreau."; vol. 2 "Charles Foster from S. E. Thoreau." VtMiM.

*Lovell, [Robert. Sive enchiridion botanicum, or a] complete herball.

*[Ludewig, Hermann Ernst.] The literature of American local history. [New York: Craighead, 1846.]

*Lyon, G. F. The private journal of Captain G. F. Lyon of H. M. S. Helca, during the recent voyage of discovery under Captain Parry. Boston: Wells & Lilly, 1824.

Inscription: autograph torn from flyleaf. Inscription by F. B. Sanborn that notes on blank flyleaf at end are by Thoreau. RPB.

*Lytton, Edward George Earle Bulwer-Lytton. Athens, its rise and fall. New York: Harper, 1837. 2 vols.

Inscription: "H. D. Thoreau." VtMiM.

*McCulloh, James Haines. Researches on America. Baltimore, 1817. 2d ed.

Given to MCo by Sophia Thoreau; withdrawn in 1915.

*MacDonnel, D. E. A dictionary of select and popular quotations. Philadelphia: Finley, 1810.

Inscription: "Eliza Thoreau. D. Thoreau's." MCo.

*Macgillivray, William. Description of the rapacious birds. Edinburgh: Maclachlan & Stewart, 1836.

Inscription: "Henry D. Thoreau." MCo.

*M'Kenney, Thomas L. Memoirs, official and personal with sketches of travels among the Northern and Southern Indians. New York: Paine & Burgess, 1846.

Inscription: "From the author, as a token of his high respect, & friendly regards, to Miss Fuller. July 3/46. Henry D. Thoreau from W. E. Channing. Apr. 1857." Ellery Channing was Margaret Fuller's brother-in-law. MCo.

*McLellan, Henry B. Jr. Journal of residence in Scotland. Boston: Allen & Ticknor, 1834.

Inscription: "To D. H. Thoreau from his Aunt Elizabeth." MCo.

*MacPherson, [James.] Poems of Ossian.

Mahabharata. Bhagavadgita. The Bhagavad-gita; or, a discourse between Krishna and Arjuna on divine matters. A Sanskrit philosophical poem, translated by J. Cockburn Thomson. Hartford: Austin, 1855.

Inscription: autographed by Thoreau and Bronson Alcott. A part of the Cholmondeley collection. MCoA.

————. The Bhagavad-gita; or the sacred lay: a colloquy between Krishna and Arjuna on divine matters . . . a new edition of the Sanskrit text, with a vocabulary. Hartford: Austin, 1855.

Inscription: autographed by Thoreau and Bronson Alcott. A part of the Cholmondeley collection. Stolen from MCoA in 1941.

Mahabharata. Nalopakhyanam. Nala and Damayanti and other poems. Translated from the Sanscrit into English by Rev. Henry Hart Milman, with mythological and critical notes. Oxford: Talboys, 1835.

Inscription: "R. W. Emerson, May 1863. Henry D. Thoreau from Thomas Cholmondeley." MCoA.

*[Maine. Geological Survey. Charles T.] Jackson. Second [annual] report on the [geology of the] public lands, [belonging to the two states] of Maine and Massachusetts. [Boston: Dutton & Wentworth, 1838.]

*[————. Geological Survey. Charles T.] Jackson. Second report on geology of Maine. [Boston: Dutton & Wentworth, 1838.]

*[————. Geological Survey. Charles T.] Jackson. Third report on geology of Maine. [Augusta, Me.: Smith & Robinson, 1839.]

Manu. Institutes of Hindu law: or, the ordinances of Menu, according to the gloss of Culluca, comprising the Indian system of duties, religious and civil. Verbally translated from the original by Graves Chamney Haughton, with a preface by Sir William Jones. A new edition, collated with the Sanscrit text, and elucidated with notes. London: Revingtons & Cochran, 1825.

Inscription: "R. W. Emerson. A bequest of Henry D. Thoreau." MCoA.

Marcet, Mrs. Jane (Haldimand). Conversations on chemistry: in which the elements of that science are familiarly explained, and illustrated by experiments . . . To which are now added, explanations of the text . . . by J. L. Comstock. Hartford: O. D. Cooke, 1824.

> MCo.

*Martineau, [Harriet.] How to observe. [Philadelphia: Lea & Blanchard, 1838.]

*Massachusetts. Agricultural Societies. Transactions of Agricultural Societies of Massachusetts for 1847. [Boston, 1847.]

*[Massachusetts. General Court.] Documents relating to the n[orth] e[astern] boundary [of the state of Maine. Boston: Dutton & Wentworth, 1828.]

*————. General Court. Report of the joint special committee upon the subject of the flowage of meadows on Concord & Sudbury Rivers. Jan. 28, 1860.

> Inscription: "D. H. Thoreau, Esq. with regards of J. S. K." MCo.

*[————. Geological Survey. Edward] Hitchcock. [Report on the] geology, [mineralogy, botany, and zoology] of Massachusetts. [Amherst: Adams, 1833.]

*————. Zoological and Botanical Survey. Chester Dewey and Ebenezer Emmons. Report on herbaceous plants & quadrupeds of Massachusetts. Cambridge: Folsom, Wells & Thurston, 1840.

> Inscription: "Henry D. Thoreau." MCo.

*————. Zoological and Botanical Survey. D. H. Storer and W. B. O. Peabody. Report on fishes, reptiles, and birds of Massachusetts. Boston: Dutton & Wentworth, 1839.

> Inscription: "Gift of Sophia E. Thoreau." MCo.

*Massillon, [Jean Baptiste.] Sermons, Brooklyn. Tr. by Dickson. 2 vols.

> "Massillon Six Sermons" was given to Elizabeth J. Weir.

Memoir of the Rev. Edward Payson, D.D., The. Portland: Ann L. Payson. 1830.

> Inscription: "Jane Thoreau's. April 4, 1830." Now owned by Walter Harding, Geneseo, N.Y.

Mill, James. The history of British India. London: Madden, 1848. 9 vols.

> Inscriptions: vol. 1: "Henry D. Thoreau from Thomas Cholmondeley." The other volumes contain Thoreau's signature. MCo.

Milton, John. Paradise lost. Philadelphia: Johnson & Werner, 1808.

> Inscription: "Elizabeth Thoreau Sept. 5, 1810." MCoA.

*————. Poetical works. 3 vols.

Sanborn suggests that this is a Boston edition, but I have been unable to discover any three-volume edition published there.

*————. A selection from the English prose works of John Milton. Boston: Bowles & Dearborn, 1826. 2 vols.

Now in a private library in Maine.

*Mirick, B[enjamin] L. The history of Haverhill, [Massachusetts.] Haverhill, [Thayer, 1832.]

More, Hannah. Practical piety. Boston: Munroe & Francis, 1811. Vol. 2.

Inscription: "Jane Thoreau 1811." MCo.

*Morse, [Jedidiah.] The American gazetteer. [Boston: Gaine & Ten Eyck, 1797.]

In his *Journal* (Boston: Houghton Mifflin, 1906), 14:43, Thoreau identifies his edition as that of 1797.

*————. Geography made easy. Boston: Thomas & Andrews, 1807. 11th edition.

Inscription: "Henry D. Thoreau." Also a note on front flyleaf on studying geography and its importance. VtMiM.

Moysant, Francois. Bibliotheque portative des meilleurs ecrivains Francais. Boston, 1810.

Gift of Sophia Thoreau. MCo.

*Murray, [Lindley.] English grammar. Hallowell, [Maine, Goodale, Glazier, 1823.] 2 copies. 1 vol.

*Neuman, Henry and G. M. A. Baretti. Dictionary of the Spanish & English languages. Boston: Hilliard, Gray, Little & Wilkins, 1831.

Inscription: "D. H. Thoreau." MCo.

*[New English-German and] German[-English] dictionary, A. Philadelphia, [Mentz, 1835.]

New map of Massachusetts . . . carefully revised and additions made in 1848. Boston: Dearborn, 1848.

NN (Berg).

*New York (State). Museum, Albany. Third annual report of the regents of the university on the condition of the state cabinet of natural history. Albany: Weed, Parsons & Co., 1850.

Inscription: "Henry D. Thoreau from Wm. E. Channing." The spine title has been blacked out and "Morgan . . . Indians" written in with white ink. Pages 63–95 include Lewis H. Morgan's report on the Indian collection. RPB.

*Olney, J. A history of the United States, on a new plan. New Haven, 1836.

Inscription: "Henry D. Thoreau." Also includes stamped signature of Henry Ward Beecher. Described in Bodley Book Shop (New York City), catalogue 61 in 1972.

*Orpheus. Orphei argonautica et de lapidibus accednust Henrici Stephani in omnia & Josephi Scaligeri in hymnos notae. Trajacti ad Rhenum. Apud Guilelmum van de Water. 1696.

Given to F. H. Bigelow. Sanborn suggests that Thoreau obtained this from the Greaves library at Fruitlands, and I have used the identification from its catalogue.

Ossoli, Margaret Fuller. Woman in the nineteenth century and kindred papers. Boston: John P. Jewett, 1855.

Inscription: "To Henry D. Thoreau's Mother, with the kind regards of their friend, Daniel Ricketson, Concord, June 19, 1856." Now owned by Joel Myerson, Columbia, S.C.

*Oswald, John. An etymological dictionary of the English language, on a plan entirely new. Revised and improved. Philadelphia, 1844.

Inscription: autograph of Thoreau. Given to MCo by Sophia Thoreau, withdrawn in 1906. Now owned by Russell Ready, Berwick, Ont.

Otheman, Edward. Memoir and writings of Mrs. Hannah Maynard Pickard. Boston: D. H. Ela, 1845.

Inscription: "Ellen D. Osgood. With the love of her friend, S. E. Thoreau." VtMiM.

*Ovidius [Naso, Publius. Publii Ovidii Nasonis metamorphoseon libri xv. in usum serenissimi] delphini. Philadelphia, [Long & DeSilver, 1823.]

Given to F. H. Bigelow.

*Paley, [William.] Works. Philadelphia, [Woodward, 1836.]

*————. The principles of moral and political philosophy. Eighth edition, corrected. Vol. 1 (only). London: Faulder, 1791.

Inscription on bookplate: "No. 44 Property of the Social Club." "Henry D. Thoreau." Given to Alcott. MH.

Panoplist and missionary herald, The. Boston: Lincoln, 1807. Vol. 2.

Inscription: "John Thoreau." MCo.

*Peabody, Elizabeth. Record of a school. Second edition. Boston: Shattuck, 1836.

Inscription: "Henry D. Thoreau, from his friend, A. Bronson Alcott." Apparently later given to Ellen Sewall Osgood by Sophia Thoreau. Now owned by Grace Davenport, Los Angeles, Calif.

*(Penmanship, Book on.)

Given to Elizabeth Weir. The description is too vague to identify further.

*Percy, [Bishop Thomas.] Reliques [of ancient poetry.]

Given to Theo Brown.

*Perry, [Matthew Calbraith. Narrative of the expedition of an American squadron to the China seas and] Japan, [performed in the years, 1852, 1853 and 1854. Compiled from the original notes and journals of Com. Perry by Rev. Francis Hawks. New York, 1857.]

Phelps & Squire's Travellers' guide and map of the United States. New York, 1838.

Inscription: Thoreau's signature and six pages of penciled notes in Thoreau's hand, listing titles of books, mainly by English and French authors. NN (Berg).

*[Phillips, Sir Richard.] The univeral preceptor. Greenfield.

*Pickering, John. Greek and English lexicon adapted to the authors read in the colleges and schools of the United States and to other Greek classics. Boston: Hilliard, Gray, Little & Wilkins, 1829. Second edition.

Inscriptions: "Henry D. Thoreau" and brief annotations on pages 37 and 200. Given MCo by Sophia Thoreau; withdrawn in 1906. Now owned by W. Stephen Thomas, Rochester, N.Y.

*Pierpont, [John.] Airs of Palestine, [and other poems. Boston: James Munroe, 1840.]

*[————.] The American first class book. [Boston: Bowen, 1836.]

*————. Introduction to the national reader. Boston, [Richardson & Lord, 1828.]

*Pike, Zebulon Montgomery. An account of expeditions to the sources of the Mississippi. Philadelphia: Conrad, 1810.

Given to MCo by Sophia Thoreau; withdrawn in 1915. The library listed it as Pike, *Journal of a Voyage to Sources of Mississippi*. Kenneth Walter Cameron has pointed out to me that it may thus be a paraphrase of Pike's journal by Nicholas King, entitled *An account of a voyage up the Mississippi River, from St. Louis to its source; made under the orders of the War department, by Lieut. Pike . . . in the years 1805 and 1806* (Washington, 1807?).

*Pindarus. Alcoei, Sapphus, Stesichori, Anacreontis, Simonidis, Alcoonis, etc. Graece et Latine. Heidelberge, 1597.

Given to F. H. Bigelow. Sanborn suggests that Thoreau obtained this from the Greaves Library at Fruitlands and I have taken the identification from its catalogue.

*————. Olympia, Phythia, Nemea, Isthmia, Greek and Latin. 1598.

Inscription: "Henry D. Thoreau from his friend A. Bronson Alcott. Concord, October, 1848." These two Pindarus volumes are bound in one. MCoA.

*Plinius, Secundus. C. Historiae mundi. Apud Jacobum Stoer, 1593. 3 vols.

Inscription: "H. D. Thoreau. 1859. Presented to H. G. O. Blake by Sophia Thoreau in behalf of her brother H. D. T. January 24th, 1863." Names of two earlier owners also appear: "E. C. Parkmanni, 1700" and "J. W. Davis, 1793 and 1795." ICarbS.

*Plutarchus. Lives, [translated from the original Greek by John Langhorne and William Langhorne.] New York.

Sanborn suggests this is the Langhorne translation.

*Pope, Alexander. Poetical works. Baltimore: Neal, Wills & Cole, 1814. Vol. 1. (Pope's Works (2nd stolen). 5 v.).

For other volumes in this set, see Homerus. Now in a private library in Maine.

Puranas. Bhagavatapurana. Le Bhagavata Purana ou histoire poetique de Krichna. Translated by Eugene Burnouf. Paris: Burnouf, 1840, 1844, 1847. 3 vols.

Inscription: "Henry D. Thoreau from Thomas Cholmondeley. R. W. Emerson from Henry D. Thoreau." MCoA.

————. Vishnupurana. The Vishnu Purana: a system of Hindu mythology. London: Murray, 1840.

Inscription: "R. W. Emerson. The bequest of Henry D. Thoreau." MCoA.

Putnam's monthly magazine. March 1853 to June 1854. Numbers 3, 13, 14, 17, 18.

Inscription: Each signed on the front wrapper. Sold by Parke-Bernet at the Stokes Sale, 15 January 1963.

————. December 1853.

Inscription: "Henry D. Thoreau." VtMiM.

————. March 1854.

Inscription: "Henry D. Thoreau." Now owned by Walter Harding, Geneseo, N.Y.

Quarles, Francis. Emblems, Divine and Moral. Chiswick: C. & C. Whittingham, 1825.

Presented by Bronson Alcott to Thoreau. NN (Arents).

*Redpath, James. Echoes of Harper's Ferry. Boston: Thayer & Eldridge, 1860.

Inscription: "Henry D. Thoreau." Brief notes on pp. 39, 442. Broadside announcement of Concord services for John Brown on 2 December 1859 tipped in. NNPM.

*————. The public life of John Brown with an autobiography of his childhood and youth. Boston: Thayer & Eldridge, 1860.

Inscription: "To Henry D. Thoreau from Jas. Redpath." Sold by Anderson Galleries (New York), 10 November 1924.

*[Rennie, James.] Insect architecture. [London: Knight, 1830.]

> Given to Elizabeth Weir.

*[————.] Insect miscellanies. [London: Knight, 1831.] 2 vols.

> Given to Elizabeth Weir.

*[————.] Insect transformations. [London, 1830.]

*[Reynolds, Joseph.] Peter Gott, [the Cape Ann fisherman. Boston: John P. Jewett, 1856.]

*[Ribero y Ustariz, Mariano Eduardo de.] Peruvian antiquities. [New York, 1853.]

*[Richardson, John.] Arctic searching expedition[: journal of a boat voyage in search of ships under command of Sir John Franklin. New York: 1852.]

*[Ricketson, Daniel.] History of New Bedford, [Bristol County, Mass. New Bedford: The Author, 1858.]

Ripley, Ezra. The obligations of parents to give their children a virtuous education. . . . Cambridge: Hilliard and Metcalf, 1820.

> Inscription: "H. D. Thoreau." Now owned by George Goodspeed, Concord, Mass.

*Roberts, [Mary.] A popular history of the mollusca. London: Reeve & Benham, 1851.

*Roget, [Peter Mark.] Thesaurus [of English words and phrases. London: Longman, Brown, Green & Longmans, 1852.]

*Rollin, [Charles. The ancient history of the Egyptians, Carthaginians, Assyrians, Babylonians, Medes & Persians. Macedonians, and Grecians. New York: Long, 1837.] 4 vols.

*[Rouquette, Adrien-Emmanuel.] La Thebaide en Amerique [ou apologie de la vie solitaire et contemplative. New Orleans, 1847.]

> Gift of the author, see below.

————. Les savanes, poesies americaines. Nouvelle-Orleans: Moret, 1841.

> In his *Journal* for 11 November 1854, Thoreau records the receipt of three "ouvrages" from the Abbe Rouquette (7:71). He acknowledges receipt of these three specific titles in his letter to Rouquette of 13 November 1854 (*Correspondence*, p. 349).

*————. Wild flowers. New Orleans, 1848. (Wild Flowers, Rouquette. 1 v.).

> Gift of the author, see above.

Rowbotham, John. Practical grammar of the French language. Boston: Hilliard, Gray, 1832.

> Inscription: "H. D. Thoreau." VtMiM.

*[Russell, Michael.] Life of [Oliver] Cromwell. New York, [Harper, 1833.]

Sadananda Yogindra. A lecture on the Vedanta, embracing the text of the Vedanta-sara, by Jr. R. Ballantyne. Allahabad: Printed for the use of the Benares College, by order of Govt., N. W. P., 1850.

> Inscription: "R. W. Emerson. Henry D. Thoreau from Thomas Cholmondeley." MCoA.

Saddharmapundrika. Le lotus de la bonne loi, translated from the Sanscrit by E. Burnouf, with a commentary and 21 memories. l'Imprimerie Nationale, 1852.

> Inscription: "Henry D. Thoreau from Thomas Cholmondeley. R. W. Emerson. The gift of Henry D. Thoreau." MCoA.

*Sanford, Henry S. The different systems of penal codes in Europe; also, a report on the administrative changes in France, since the revolution of 1848. Washington, 1854.

> Inscription: "H. D. Thoreau." Described in the *Wakeman Collection.*

*Say, J. B. A treatise on political economy; or the production, distribution & consumptions of wealth. Translated by C. R. Prinsep. Sixth American edition, containing a translation of the introduction, & additional notes by Clement C. Biddle. Philadelphia: Griggs & Elliot, 1834.

> Inscription: "D. H. Thoreau H[ollis] 23" with a few pencilled notes by Thoreau. Now owned by Samuel T. Wellman, Gates Mills, Ohio.

*Schiller, [Johann C. F. von. Geschichte des] Dreyssigjariger Krieg. Leipzig, [1812.] 2 vols.

> Given to F. H. Bigelow.

―――. Maria Stuart. Stuttgart and Tubingen, 1801. (2. Maria Stuart. Stuttgart und Tubingen ed. 1 v.)

> Given to F. H. Bigelow.

*[Schoolcraft, Henry Rowe.] Oneota, [or the red race. New York: Wiley & Putnam, 1845.]

> Originally issued in eight numbers.

*[Scott, Sir Walter.] Marmion. Baltimore, [Cushing, 1812.]

Scott, William. Lessons in elocution. Boston: Lincoln & Edmands, 1820.

> Inscription: "[John?] Thoreau." VtMiM.

*Seneca, Lucius Annaeus. Medea. Edited by Charles Beck. Cambridge: James Munroe, 1834.

> Inscription: "H. D. Thoreau." MCo.

*Sewel, Willem. The history of the rise, increase and progress, of the Christian people called Quakers. Third edition. Burlington, N.J.: Collins, 1774.

MCoA.

Sewell, J. S. and C. W. Iddings. Sectional map of the surveyed portion of Minnesota and the northwestern part of Wisconsin. St. Paul: J. S. Sewell & R. C. W. Iddings, 1857.

This is probably the map which Thoreau records purchasing in *The First and Last Journeys of Thoreau*, ed. Franklin Benjamin Sanborn (Boston: Bibliophile Society, 1905), 2:119. NN (Berg).

*Shakespeare, [William. The dramatic works.] Hartford, [Andrus & Judd, 1833. 2 vols.] Edited by George Stevens.

*Shattuck, Lemuel. A history of the town of Concord. Boston: Russell, Odiorne & Stacy, 1835.

Now in a private library in Maine.

*Smeaton, A. C. The builder's pocket companion; containing the elements of building, surveying, and architecture. Philadelphia: Henry Carey Baird, 1850.

Inscription on front endpaper: "Henry D. Thoreau Concord, Mass." Apparently given to Alcott. MH.

*Smellie, [William.] The philosophy [of natural history. Philadelphia: Campbell, 1791.]

*Smithsonian Institution. Annual reports of the regents. Washington, 1851, 1852, 1854, 1855, and 1856.

Inscription in 1855 volume: "Henry D. Thoreau." With a fragment of manuscript from *Cape Cod* laid in. MCo. Inscription in 1856 volume: "Henry D. Thoreau from Horace Mann." MCo.

*Smyth, [William. Elementary] algebra. Portland, Maine, [Sanborn & Carter, 1851.]

*Sophocles. Sophoclis tragoediae [septem.] Lipsiae, [Tauchnitz, 1828.]

Given to F. H. Bigelow.

Southey, Robert. The poetical works. New York: Appleton, 1839.

Now in a private library in Maine.

*Sowerby, [George Brettingham.] Popular British conchology. [London, 1854.]

Given to Edith Emerson.

*Sowerby, Henry. Popular mineralogy, comprising a familiar account of minerals and their uses. London: Reeve & Benham, 1850.

Inscription: Thoreau's autograph on flyleaf. Given to Ellen Emerson. Now owned by Raymond Adams, Chapel Hill, N.C.

*Sowerby, [John E.] The ferns of Great Britain. [London: Sowerby, 1855.]

This seems the most likely of several possible volumes on the subject.

*Spectator. Philadelphia, 1832. 2 vols. in 1.

Inscription: "J. Thoreau." Described in *Some Unpublished Letters of Henry D. and Sophia E. Thoreau*, ed. Jones, p. xii.

*(Spiritual Science, 1 v.)

I have been unable to identify this volume further.

*Stark, [Robert MacKenzie.] A popular history of British mosses. [London: Reeve, 1854.]

*[Sterne, Laurence.] The beauties of Sterne. [Boston: Andrews & Cummings, 1807.]

*————. Sentimental journey.

*Stewart, Dugald. Elements of the philosophy of the human mind. Cambridge: James Munroe, 1833. 2 vols.

Inscription on front endpaper of each volume: "H. D. Thoreau." Given to Alcott. MH.

*Story, Joseph. Commentaries on the constitution of the United States. Boston: Hilliard, Gray, 1833.

Inscription: "Henry D. Thoreau." MCo.

Stowe, Harriet Beecher. Sunny memories of foreign lands. Boston: Phillips, Sampson, 1854. 2 vols.

Inscription in both volumes: "Thos Cholmondeley for Mrs. C. D. Thoreau 1854." Now owned by Raymond R. Borst, Auburn, N.Y.

Sumner, Charles. The barbarism of slavery. Washington: Hyatt, 1860.

Thoreau acknowledges the receipt of this volume in a letter to Sumner of 16 July 1860 (*Correspondence*, p. 585).

————. Position and duties of the merchant; address before the Mercantile Lib. Assoc., Nov. 13, 1854. Boston, 1855.

Thoreau acknowledges the receipt of Sumner's "Address before the Merc. Lib. Association" in a letter to Sumner of 12 March 1855 (*Correspondence*, p. 374).

————. Usurpation of the Senate: two speeches of Hon. Charles Sumner, on the imprisonment of Thaddeus Hyatt. Washington: Buell & Blanchard, 1860.

Thoreau acknowledges the receipt of "Two speeches on the Hyatt Case" in a letter to Sumner of 16 July 1860 (*Correspondence*, p. 585).

*Surault, [Francois Marie Joseph. An easy] grammar of the French [language.] Boston, [Richardson, Lord & Holbrook, 1831.]

Tanner, Henry S. New Hampshire & Vermont. Philadelphia, 1833.

Inscription: "J. Thoreau." NN (Berg).

*Tasso, [Torquato.] La Gerusalemme liberata. Firenze, [Ciardetti, 1823.] 2 vols.

Given to F. H. Bigelow.

*Tatler. London, 1723.

*Tennyson, [Alfred Lord.] In memoriam. [Boston: Ticknor, Reed & Fields, 1850.]

*Tschudi, [Johann Jakob von.] Travels in Peru. [New York: Wiley & Putnam, 1847.]

*Tytler, Alexander Fraser. (Lord Woodhouselee) Elements of general history; ancient & modern with a continuation terminating at the demise of George 3rd, by Edward Nares. Concord, N.H.: Hill, 1824.

Inscription: "Henry D. Thoreau." MCo.

Tytler, Patrick F. Historical view of the progress of discovery on the more northern coasts of America. New York: Harper, 1835.

Inscription: Thoreau's autograph in two places. NhD.

*[United States. Army. Corps of Topographical Engineers. Notes of a military reconnoissance from Fort Leavenworth in Missouri, to San Diego, in California, by W. H.] Emory. [Washington: Wendell & Van Benthuysen, 1848.] (New Mexico and California).

Thoreau's is the spine title.

*[United States. Census Office.] Compendium of the United States Census [of 1850. Washington, 1854.]

Thoreau acknowledges the receipt of this volume in a letter to Charles Sumner of 12 March 1855 (*Correspondence*, p. 374).

*[United States.] Coast and Geodetic Survey. Reports on the coast survey. Washington, 1850, 1851, 1852, 1853, 1854, 1855, 1856, 1857, 1858.

Sanborn states that these volumes were given to Thoreau by Eben J. Loomis, who worked in the Nautical Almanac Office in Washington. But in Thoreau's letter of 30 October 1854 to Charles Sumner, he acknowledges gift of the Coast Survey Report for 1852 (*Correspondence*, p. 347). There seems to be some discrepancy in Thoreau's recording of the number of volumes.
Sanborn also states that these volumes were given to MCo. According to Sarah Bartlett, former librarian, a large number of government publications were withdrawn from circulation in the library in 1906 and returned to Washington. Probably some of the Thoreau volumes were accidentally included in this shipment. At any rate, these volumes are not at MCo. This may also account for the disappearance of several other government publications from Thoreau's library.

*———. Sketches accompanying the coast survey report for 1851. [Washington, 1851.]

A gift from Eben J. Loomis.

*United States. Congress. 32nd Congress. Senate. Report on the trade and commerce of the British North American colonies and upon the trade of the great lakes and rivers, by Israel D. Andrews. Senate Ex. Docs. No. 112. Washington, 1852. Two copies of maps separate.

One volume of maps only. Inscription: "Henry D. Thoreau." MCo.

*[———. 33rd Congress 1st Session. Senate. Report of the select committee of the Senate of the United States on the] sickness [and mortality on board] emigrant ships. [Report Com. No. 386. Washington, 1854.]

Thoreau acknowledges receipt of this book in a letter to Charles Sumner of 5 December 1854 (*Correspondence*, p. 353).

*[———. 33rd Congress. 1st Session. Senate. Report of an] expedition down the Zuni and Colorado Rivers, by [L.] Sitgreaves. [Ex. Doc. Washington: Tucker, 1853.]

Thoreau acknowledges receipt of this book in a letter to Charles Sumner of 5 December 1854 (*Correspondence*, p. 353). He apparently lists this volume a second time in his catalogue as "Colorado Exploring Expedition."

*———. 36th Congress. 1st Session. Senate. Report of the select committee of the Senate . . . on the late invasion and seizure of public property at Harper's Ferry. Report No. 278. Washington, 1860.

Inscription: autograph of Thoreau. MCo.

*[United States. General Land Office.] Report [on the geology and topography of . . . the Lake Superior land district, by John Wells] Foster and [J. D.] Whitney. Washington, 1850.

This was issued in two volumes but Thoreau owned only one—apparently from the spine title he quotes, he had only vol. 1.

*United States. Nautical Almanac Office. American ephemeris and nautical almanac. Washington, 1855–

Given to MCo by Sophia Thoreau; withdrawn in 1906. This was issued annually from 1855 on, so it is impossible to distinguish which volume Thoreau owned, although it was probably the first. Sanborn states that it was the gift of Eben J. Loomis.

*United States. Patent Office. Patent office reports. Washington, 1851, 1853, 1854, 1855, 1856, 1857, 1858, 1859.

Although his wording is a little ambiguous, apparently Thoreau owned the Agriculture reports for 1851, and 1853–59 inclusive, as well as the Mechanics reports for 1858. He probably received most or all of these from Charles Sumner. He acknowledges the receipt of one in a letter to Sumner of 5 December 1854 and of two more in a letter of 16 July 1860 (*Correspondence*, pp. 353, 585).

*[United States. War Department.] Exploration of Red River of Louisiana, by [Randolph B.] Marcy. [Washington: Nicholson, 1854.]

United States Magazine and Democratic Review. December 1840, December 1843, and October 1845.

Inscription on each: "Henry D. Thoreau." VtMiM.

———. May 1844.

Now owned by Raymond Adams, Chapel Hill, N.C.

———. December 1845.

Inscription: "Henry D. Thoreau." Now owned by Mrs. Edmund Fenn, Concord, Mass.

———. December 1844 and October 1845.

VtMiM.

Upham, Charles Wentworth. Life, explorations and public services of John Charles Fremont. Boston: Ticknor & Fields, 1856.

Now in a private library in Maine.

Vedas. Rigveda. Rig-Veda-Sanhita, the oldest authority for the religious and social institutions of the Hindus. Translated from the original Sanscrit by H. H. Wilson. London: Allen, 1854. 2 vols.

Inscription: "Henry D. Thoreau from Thomas Cholmondeley." MCoA.

*Vergilius Maro, Publius. Opera. Interpreatione et notis illustravit Carolus Ruaeus, Soc. Jesu. Jussu Christianissimi regis, ad usum serenissimi delphini. Juxta editionem novissimam Londiniensem. Huic editioni accessit index accuratissimus, ante editis longe locupletior. Philadelphia: A. Small, 1817.

Inscription: "D. H. Thoreau's Hollis 20 Sept. 4th. Elizabeth Jordan Weir from Sophia E. Thoreau." Many pencilled notations. MnM. Thoreau also lists "2 cops. Virgilii Delphini. 1 v." Sanborn suggests these may have belonged to his sister Helen.

*———. [Opera.] London, [Davidson,] 1822.

Given to F. H. Bigelow.

*———. [The works of] Virgil: [containing his pastorals, georgics and Aeneis.] Translated into English verse by [John] Dryden. Philadelphia.

*Verplanck, Gulian C. Discourses & addresses. New York, Harper, 1833.

Inscription: "Mr. John Thoreau. Henry D. Thoreau." MCo.

Visvanatha Nyayapancanana Bhattacharya Tarkalanrara. Bhasha Parichcheda, and its commentary, the Siddhanta Mukta Vali, an exposition of the Nyaya philosophy . . . with an English version. Calcutta: Encyclopaedia Press, 1851.

Inscription: "R. W. Emerson. Henry D. Thoreau from Thomas Cholmondeley." MCoA.

*Voltaire, Francois Marie Arouet de. Histoire de Charles XII. New York: Collins, 1831.

Inscription: "H. L. Thoreau." MCo.

*————. Histoire de l'empire de Russie. Paris: Didot, 1815.

Inscription: "H. D. Thoreau." MCo.

Walker, John. A critical pronouncing dictionary, and expositor of the English language . . . to which are prefixed, principles of English pronunciation . . . The whole interspersed with observations, etymological, critical, and grammatical. New York, 1823.

Given to MCo by Sophia Thoreau; withdrawn in 1906.

*Ware, [Henry.] Formation of the Christian character. Boston, [James Munroe, 1831.]

*Webster, [Noah. An American] dictionary [of the English language. Springfield, Mass.: Merriam, 1848.]

West, Mrs. Letters addressed to a young man, on his first entrance into life. Charlestown, Samuel Etheridge, 1803. 2 vols. in 1.

Inscription: "John Thoreau, Jr. 1834." Now owned by William Cummings, San Jose, Calif.

*Whately, [Richard. Elements of] logic. Cambridge, [James Munroe, 1848.]

Given to Elizabeth Weir.

*————. [Elements of] rhetoric. Cambridge, [Brown, Shattuck, 1832.]

Given to Elizabeth Weir.

*White, [Gilbert. The natural history of] Selborne. [edited by Edward Jesse.] London: Bohn, [1851.]

*Whitman, Walt. Leaves of Grass. Brooklyn, 1855.

Inscription: Thoreau's signature pasted in front. Sold by A. S. W. Rosenbach to R. W. Martin in 1924.

*————. Leaves of grass. Brooklyn, 1856.

Inscription: "H. D. Thoreau from Walt Whitman." DLC.

*Willey, [Benjamin Glazier.] Incidents in White Mountain history. [Boston: Noyes, 1856.]

A map of the White Mountains was extracted from this volume by Thoreau. RPB.

*[Williams, Wellington.] Appleton's railroad and steamboat companion. [New York: Appleton, 1848.]

*Wilson, Alexander. American ornithology. New York: Samuels, 1852.

   Inscription: autographs of Thoreau and Daniel Ricketson. Given to Ricketson. MCoA.

 Wilson, Horace Hayman. Select specimens of the theatre of the Hindus. London: Parbury, Allen, 1835. 2 vols.

   Inscription: "Henry D. Thoreau." A part of the Cholmondeley collection. Thoreau noted on the Chapman list that he intended this volume be given to Emerson. MCoA.

*[Winterton, Ralph. Fragments quaedam accedunt etiam observationes Radulphi Wintertoni in Hesiodum, Cantabrigiae, ex officina Joan Hayes, celeberrimae academicae typographi, 1766.] Poetae Minores Graeci.

   Given to F. H. Bigelow. Sanborn states that Thoreau obtained this from the Greaves library at Fruitlands.

*Winthrop, John. A journal of the transactions and occurrences in the settlement of Massachusetts. Hartford: Elisha Babcock, 1790.

   Inscription: "D. H. Thoreau, Cambridge, Mass." Given to Alcott. MH.

*Wordsworth, William. Complete poetical works. Philadelphia: Kay, 1837 (1839).

   Now in a private library in Maine.

*————. The prelude, or growth of a poet's mind. [London: Moxon, 1850.]

*Wright, Thomas. Dictionary of obsolete and provincial English. London: Bohn, 1857.

   Given to Alcott (see his *Journals* for 6 April 1873 [p. 431]). MH.

*Xenophon. Xenophontis [de cyri institutione libri octo.] Edited by [Thomas] Hutchinson. Philadelphia, [Watts, 1806.]

*Zimmerman, [Johann Georg.] Solitude. Albany, [Barber & Southwick, 1796.]

ROMANTIC EPISTEMOLOGY AND ROMANTIC STYLE: EMERSON'S DEVELOPMENT FROM *NATURE* TO THE *ESSAYS*

H. Meili Steele

THOUGH THE IMPORTANCE of the Kantian epistemological revolution to the definition of Romanticism is now widely recognized, there is still much work to be done on establishing a relationship between this theory of knowledge and the style and structure of the works of the Romantic writers.[1] It is as a case study of this link that Emerson is our subject here, for his extraordinary stylistic and philosphical development between the publication of *Nature* in 1836 and the publication of his two volumes of *Essays* in 1841 and 1844 can be attributed to his shift from an Enlightenment to a Romantic epistemology.[2] In *Nature*, though it is in many ways a Romantic work, Emerson had not completely rejected the Enlightenment epistemological assumption that sensory input is identical with semiotic response, or, to use the terms of the time, that the structure of the mind is identical to the structure of the world. In the later *Essays*, he abandoned the Enlightenment for the Kantian position that the subject is forever separated from the object and can know the object only on the basis of its own limited, mutable categories. With the rejection of the Enlightenment epistemology came the collapse of the whole system that made society part of the natural order and that defined the individual by his role in society.[3] He became alienated from himself and from his audience, both of which were still under the control of Christian and Enlightenment thinking.

When Emerson's attachment to his social role dissolved and his source of value shifted to the self, he was able to assume the rights of the Romantic artist. Along with these rights, of course, came a radically different sensibility and the need to maintain the integrity of this sensibility in style. Emerson's new stand on the nature of consciousness and on the foundation of value gave him a justification for the loosely structured, aphoristic style that made the *Essays* so different from his attempt at systematization in *Nature*. However, it also made style itself take on more importance. For the Romantic Emerson who rejected system-building, the value of experience was no longer determined by its congruence with an existing metaphysical scheme but by its uniqueness. In order to isolate the Enlightenment and Romantic elements of his thinking in *Nature* and the *Essays*, it is necessary to examine the premises of the Enlightenment system and Emerson's struggle with the "mind-matter" problem before 1836.

According to the Enlightenment conception of the world, God endowed the universe with order and value, and man's task was to discover this order, that is, natural law, and adapt himself to it. Society was a natural product, and man derived his identity from his role within this order. Since man and nature were part of the same predetermined machine, the structure of the mind was identical with the structure of the world. This structure was discoverable, perfect adaptation possible, for all that kept man from utopia was ignorance, not original sin.

This explanation collapsed under the pressure of the conflicting data from the social and natural worlds, as well as from its own internal contradictions. The primary blow, of course, was the French Revolution, which for the English Romantics whom Emerson read—Wordsworth, Coleridge, and Carlyle—shattered the rational conception of man, the notion of unity between culture and nature, and the belief in the inherent progress of society. Within the system, the most salient epistemological difficulty was its use of ignorance as an explanation for contradictory perceptions among individuals, while never coming to grips with how ignorance crept into God's perfectly ordered machine. Morally, the predicament was that if every decision was part of the natural order, if "whatever is, is right," how can any choice be invalidated. Even the scepticism of the late Enlightenment was difficult to sustain, since scepticism itself was a judgment of the subject. It is against this backdrop that we need to examine Emerson's concern with the mind-matter problem in his journals.

One of the most important facets of the journals is the structure of the entries. Most of them are short sketches of ideas or quotes rather than systematic arguments, as Emerson himself freely acknowledged: "I dot evermore in my endless journal, a line on every unknowable in nature; but the arrangement loiters longer, & I get a brick-kiln instead of a house."[4] This preference for the *aperçu* rather than a sustained methodical development helped him escape the existing explanations of his culture because he did not force his momentary, random impressions to justify themselves before the accepted principles of meaning. These terse, free-standing statements were to become the foundation of his later style, though at the time he did not have a justification of haphazardly experimenting with ideas. No, these explorations of the 1820s were held together by two articles of faith that he quite consciously asserted and that slowed his Romantic emergence. One was his certainty regarding moral reality: "There is one distinction amidst these fading phenomena—one decided distinction which is real & external and which will survive nature—I mean the distinction between Right and Wrong. Your opinions upon all other topics . . . change."[5]

The second assertion was his belief in a neo-Platonic idealism which he held up against the onslaughts of the phenomenal world.[6] The duality of mind and matter and the moral implications of this idea were the central coordinates of Emerson's thinking during the 1820s: "They did not err widely who proclaimed the existence of two warring principles, the incorruptible mind and the mass of malignant matter" (10 June 1822; *JMN*, 1:140).

When Emerson read Coleridge and Carlyle, he began to transcend materialism instead of just denying it. Though the study of their influence is beyond the scope of this paper, it will be helpful to look at Emerson's exposure to two important areas of Romanticism: epistemology and the relationship of the artist to society. Such an analysis will bring out the missed possibilities of *Nature*, as well as providing a background for our discussion of the Romantic character of the *Essays*.

The most important epistemological ideas that Emerson got from these authors were Kant's distinctions between the Reason and the Understanding, his idea that the categories of the mind are independent of the world—which Emerson did not accept until the *Essays*—and the use of the organic metaphor to replace the machine metaphor as the central explanation of the world.[7] With the Reason-Understanding distinction, the chaotic phenomenal world no longer posed a threat to the spiritual ideas that Emerson wished to preserve, for the external world was the data for the lower mental function, the Understanding; the higher mental function, the Reason, formed its ideas independently of sensory experience, and hence did not have to reconcile its ideas with the lower level of the mind or with the data of experience: "Heaven is the name we give to the True State, the World of Reason not of the Understanding, of the Real, not the Apparent" (4 June 1835; *JMN*, 5:48). He used this distinction, which he maintained in *Nature*, to validate both empirical observations and transcendental assertions, though he could not resolve the problem of how one decides which empirical observations are Reason's truths and which are the transient perceptions of the Understanding. Ultimately, as we will see, he had to abandon the distinction as a means of determining truth and to use it only as a tool for discriminating among different kinds of cognition. The following quote is typical of his perception of the tension between these two faculties: "My Reason is well enough convinced of its immortality. It knows itself immortal. But it cannot persuade its down-looking brother the Understanding of the same" (20 December 1834; *JMN*, 4:365).

It was also through Coleridge and Carlyle that Emerson was exposed to his most successful vehicle for working out the relations of man and nature, the organic metaphor. This metaphor permitted him to account for errors and contradictions in the individual's perceptions of the world without resorting to ignorance, the Enlightenment explanation. If nature is organized like a plant and not like a machine, its manifestations are not predetermined and uniform but open-ended and dynamic: "The Universe is a more amazing puzzle than ever as you glance along this bewildering series of animated forms . . . the upheaving principle of life everywhere incipient in the very rock aping organized forms" (13 July 1833; *JMN*, 4:199). Similarly, the knowledge we derive from the world also advances organically, not mechanically: "all our knowledge is a perpetually living capital, whose use cannot be exhausted, as it revives with every new fact" (17 May 1832; *JMN*, 4:19).

Thus, by redefining man, nature, and God organically, Emerson was able to preserve these categories, that is, reify them as the ultimate explanatory terms in his philosophical explorations. The organic definition could embrace any occurence without threatening the existence of the term, for without knowledge of the whole, which, of course, is inaccessible, how can one judge the part: "The Idea according to which the Universe is made wholly wanting to us; is it not? Yet it may or will be found to be constructed on as harmonious & perfect a thought, self explaining as a problem in geometry." Thus, "all our classifications are introductory & very convenient but must be looked on as temporary" (3 May 1834; *JMN*, 4:287–88). It was not until he tried to systematize his thinking in *Nature* that he discovered that the organic metaphor could serve an Enlightenment theory of knowledge as easily as a Romantic one.

The second important influence from Coleridge and Carlyle was their new conception of the relationship of the artist to society. As the machine metaphor was the principal vehicle for the Englightenment epistemology in philosophy, so the mirror was its most common instrument in literary criticism. The writer's task was, as Johnson said, "to instruct by pleasing," by mirroring the world—within the limits of decorum—that is, by exemplifying the truths of philosophy. Because the mechanical order of the universe was assumed to be immanent, the problem of representation could be reduced to the mirror. The writers differed in matters of taste, style, and their capacities to represent, but what they represented was not questioned. The doctrine of uniformity insisted that despite accidental differences all mirrors, all writers, were alike. In addition, because society was a natural product, the effect of the author's work on society was its ultimate justification. Thus, the social role exhausts identity.

When the Enlightenment explanation collapsed, so did its definition of the role of the writer. The Romantic's identity did not come from his role in society, for society was still operating under the old belief system, but from his own individuality, his unique expressive capacity, the self. Further, the new epistemology which made the mind independent of the world gave him a justification for abandoning the existing modes of approaching and ordering reality in his works.

During the 1830s Emerson began to employ these ideas in his letters, lectures, and journals. The Romantic strategy of separating the self from the role in order to escape the limits of existing institutions was crucial in his decision to reject the ministry for a career as a writer in 1832: "it is often the best part of the man, I sometimes think, that revolts against being the minister. His good revolts from official goodness. If he never spoke or acted but with consent of his understanding, if the whole man acted always, how powerful would be every act & every word. . . . The difficulty is that we do not make a world of our own, but fall into institutions already made & have to accomodate ourselves to them to be useful at all. & this accomodation is, I say, a loss of so much integrity & of course, of so much power" (10 January 1832; *JMN*, 3:318–19). For Emerson culture and role must be emergent, not static: "The profession [the ministry] is antiquated. In altered age, we worship in the dead forms of our forefathers. Were not Socratic paganism better than an effete superannuated Christianity?" (2 June 1832; *JMN*, 4:27).

He also began to develop a theory of rhetoric founded on this new freedom in the relations between man and the world. Man becomes a unique channel for God who courses through him: "My heart lies open to the Universe / I read only what is writ. . . . I am an organ in the mouth of God / My prophecy the music of his lips" (17 September 1833; *JMN*, 4:90). Thus, "God" becomes a justification for innovation: "Every man has his own voice, manner, eloquence. . . . Let him scorn to imitate any being, let him scorn to be a secondary man, let him fully trust his own share of God's goodness" (27 September 1830; *JMN*, 3:198–99).[8] However, such tentative experiments with Romantic strategies did not lead immediately to a Romantic epistemology, for in *Nature* he was still trying to straddle the Enlightenment and Romantic worlds.

The "Introduction" illustrates Emerson's conflation of these two philosophies. The essay concerns the Romantic problem of man's need for a new "relation to the universe," and the analytical terms are Emerson's version of Kant's subject-object distinction: "Philosophically considered, the universe is composed of Nature and the Soul. Strictly speaking therefore, all that is separate from us, all which Philosophy distinguishes as the *Not Me*, that is both nature and nature and art, all other men and my own body, must be ranked under this name, *Nature*" (*CW*, 1:8). However, he vitiates these Romantic tools with his Enlightenment assumption that the mind can perceive the order of the universe: "Undoubtedly we have no questions to ask which are unanswerable: We must trust the perfection of the creation so far as to believe that whatever curiosity the order of things has awakened in our minds, the order of things can satisfy" (*CW*, 1:7).

Emerson then considers "the final cause of the world," using four hierarchical categories of "Uses" which are strung along a material-spiritual continuum. Under the lowest "Use," "Commodity," are ranked "all those advantages which our senses owe to nature." "Discipline," the highest use of nature, is moral: "Every globe in the remotest heaven, every chemical change from the rudest crystal up to the laws of life, every change of vegetation from the first principle of growth in the eye of a leaf . . . shall hint or thunder to man the laws of right or wrong, and echo the Ten Commandments." He concludes: "it has already been illustrated, that every natural process is a version of moral sentence. The moral law lies at the centre of nature and radiates to the circumference" (*CW*, 1:25–26).

In using this taxonomy, Emerson assumes that hierarchy is a characteristic of truth rather than a characteristic of explanation, the assumption that grounds constitutive system building. Hence, it is not surprising that Emerson perceives morality, like natural order, as immanent in the structure of the world, and not as an invention of the subject.

To reinforce his "external" hierarchy in nature, Emerson uses Kant's cognitive, "internal" hierarchy of the Reason and the Understanding. Just as there is natural law behind the chaos of the phenomenal world, so there are the permanent truths of the Reason behind the transient perceptions of the Understanding: "The understanding adds, divides, combines, measures, and finds the nutriment and room for its activity in this worthy scene. Meantime, Reason transfers all these lessons into its own world of thought, by perceiving the analogy that marries Matter and Mind" (*CW*, 1:23). However, despite the use of the Romantic analogical method, this idea does not resolve how one discriminates the perceptions of the Reason from those of the Understanding, and Emerson is not ready to cast all of our experience into epistemological doubt. No, he wants permanent empirical truths, and to get them he carries these remnants of the Enlightenment theory of knowledge into his theory of language and signs.

In the "Language" section he tries to set up another hierarchy for establishing the relations between visual and verbal signs: "1. Words are signs of natural facts. 2. Particular natural facts are symbols of particular spiritual facts. 3. Nature is the symbol of spirit" (*CW*, 1:17). These assertions assume the answers to the questions to be explored: the character of the relationship of mind and language to the world. With these propositions Emerson locks language and the world perfectly together, from the simplest phenomena to the most abstract explanation: "The laws or moral nature answer to those of matter as in face to face in a glass" (_CW_, 1:21). The justifying examples make no distinction between fact and explanation: "A rolling stone gathers no moss" (_CW_, 1:22). Hence, according to his theory, the organization of facts does not reflect the interest and the organizing capacities of the subject; language is isomorphic with the world. In behavioral terms this means that all men use language in the same way. However, if this were the case, there could be no innovation and metaphor, precisely what Emerson calls for throughout the book.

When he confronts the full consequences of the split of subject and object, he defensively rejects them: "The frivolous make themselves merry with the Ideal theory, as if its consequences were burlesque; as if it affected the stability of nature. It surely does not. God never jests with us, and will not compromise the end of nature by permitting any inconsequence in its procession. . . . Any distrust of the permanence of laws would paralyze the faculties of man" (_CW_, 1:29–30). This compromise makes the laws of nature inaccessible and a question of faith; hence, dissonant phenomena need not answer to them. However, if phenomena are linked to natural law by an unfathomable connection, how can "the laws of moral nature answer to those of matter as face to face in glass?" (_CW_, 1:21).

The style and structure of _Nature_ reflect Emerson's attempt to construct a philosophical system founded on ultimate truth. We have already noted the hierarchical categories that control the structure of the essay as a whole. Each section moves to a higher level of abstraction (truth) that subsumes or "includes the preceding uses, as parts of itself" (_CW_, 1:23). However, the structure of the sections themselves is also designed taxonomically in order to separate and expose parallel ideas and to isolate subordinate material. "Beauty" and "Language" are both divided into three hierarchical parts, "Discipline" into two, while "Idealism" has six subdivisions. In addition, there are an abundance of connectives to keep the relations of the paragraphs and sentences clear. Before examining one of the complex sections cited above, it will be useful to look at several paragraphs from the simplest "Use," "Commodity."

After defining this classification as "those advantages which our senses owe to nature" and discussing nature's material benefits, Emerson opens a new paragraph: "Nature, in its ministry to man, is not only the material, but also the process and the result. All the parts incessantly work in each other's hands for the profit of man. The wind sows the seed; the sun evaporates the sea; the wind blows vapor to the field; the ice, on the other side of the planet, condenses rain on this; the rain feeds the plant; the plant feeds the animal; and thus the endless circulations of the divine charity nourish man" (_CW_, 1:11). The first sentence repeats the key word from the preceding paragraph ("material") and introduces two parallel ideas. Emerson uses these two ideas to conrol the development: an example and a restatement of the thesis introduced with a conclusive "thus."

The next paragraph also advances with traditional connectives. The opening sentence is established as a topic sentence that controls the development of the paragraph, while referring back to the preceding discussion of purely natural benefits: "The useful arts are reproductions or new combinations by the wit of man, of the same benefactors." As in the preceding paragraph, the sentences that follow the first sentence are clearly exemplifications of the abstract thesis: "He no longer waits for favoring gales, but by means of steam, he realizes the fable of Aeolus's bag. . . . To diminish friction, he paves the road with iron bars. . . . The private man has cities, ships, canals, bridges built for him. He goes to the post office, and the human race run on his errands" (*CW*, 1:11–12).

"Beauty," the next section is more complex. After considering the pleasurable and spiritual elements of beauty, Emerson addresses beauty "as it becomes the object of intellect." In the rest of the paragraph we can observe the operation of his style when he is forced to undertake a more difficult exposition than the simple proposition-example pattern:

> Beside the relation of things to virtue [the spiritual element], they have a relation to thought. The intellect searches out the absolute order of things as they stand in the mind of God, and without the colors of affection. The intellectual and the active powers seem to succeed each other, and the exclusive activity of the one generates the exclusive activity of the other. There is something unfriendly in each to the other, but they are like alternate periods of feeding and working in animals; each prepares and will be followed by the other. Therefore does beauty, which in relation to actions, as we have seen, comes unsought, and comes because it is unsought, remain for the apprehension and pursuit of the intellect; and then again, in its turn, of the active power. (*CW*, 1:16)

In the first sentence he harks back to the previous section ("beside the relation of things to virtue") before stating the nature of this category. In the next two sentences he again makes reference to the foregoing analysis in order to distinguish his new concept. From this exposition, he announces his conclusion ("therefore does beauty"). Certainly, such meticulous concern for coherence is common in philosophical discourse, regardless of the epistemological premises of the writer. Thus, this essay does not maintain that Enlightenment epistemology necessarily causes Emerson to write in this style, nor that such a style forces him to have an Enlightenment epistemology. No, what is important is to explore why Emerson abandons both his attempt to build a system and the rhetoric that such an attempt requires and expands his lyrical voice in the *Essays*, while using his new epistemology to restructure his experience and to justify his stylistic developments.

In these *Essays*, Emerson sets forth his Romantic theory of knowledge, investigates consequences in various areas of culture and experience, and makes the style of the essays an emblem of the revolution and not a traditional vehicle of meaning. In this theory he no longer maintains that the structure of the phenomenal world is accessible to man; rather, the mind projects itself onto the world, it interposes a screen which both conceals and reveals the "real" world: "We have learned that we do not see directly, but mediately, that we have no means of correcting these colored lenses which we are, or of computing the amount of their errors. Perhaps these subject-lenses have a creative power; perhaps there are no objects" (*W*, 3:75–76). The individual's perceptions cannot be explained solely by reference to associative experience, for the categories of the mind are not just determined by experience but also by *a priori* categories. Thus, the "intellect is the simple power anterior to all action or construction" (*CW*, 2:193). The structure of the external world—for he still asserts that the world has one—is not accessible, for it is "conceived of as a system of concentric circles, and we now and then detect in nature slight dislocations which apprise us that this surface on which we stand is not fixed, but sliding" (*CW*, 2:186). Our separation from nature is not due to ignorance, but is endemic to our conditon: "Nature does not like to be observed and likes that we should be her fools and playmates" (*W*, 3:49).

Because of this impenetrability, Emerson qualifies his propositions based on observable data, leaving his unqualified assertions as a matter of faith. Typical of his instrumentalism is the concluding sentence to the discussion of concentric circles cited above: "Yet is that statement approximate also and not final" (*CW*, 2:186). With this epistemology, even morality must admit the possibility of transcendence: "There is no virtue which is final; all are initial" (*CW*, 2:187).

However, for Emerson, as for other Romantics, the split is not just between mind and world, but within the mind. Rational consciousness, as he says in "The Over-Soul," does not control thought, but observes the passage of the unconscious; "When I watch that flowing river, which, out of regions I see not, pours for a season its streams into me, I see that I am a pensioner; not a cause but a surprised spectator of this ethereal water" (*CW*, 2:159–60). The unconscious, like his faith in the unobservable order behind the phenomenal, enables him to preserve man's unity with God and nature without validating all of man's perceptions: "We see the world piece by piece as the sun, the moon, the animal, the tree; but the whole of which these are the shining parts, is the soul" (*CW*, 2:160). The soul is also behind our fractured

experience of ourselves: "We live in succession, division, in parts, in particles. Meantime within man is the soul of the whole . . . the eternal One"
(*CW*, 2:160).

Though to the modern reader this appears to be a sophistic evasion of the
old problem of reconciling human limitation and recalcitrant nature with a
good, just, divine order, it permits Emerson to abandon an Enlightenment
epistemology without having to abandon his ultimate terms. Nonetheless,
his use of such ultimates was not without its effects. As Stephen Whicher
states, Emerson's belief in the unity of God and man deprives him of a tragic
sense: "My point is that his serenity was not a unconscious *answer* to his
experience of life, rather than an inference from it (even when presented as
such). It was an act of faith, forced on him by what he once called 'the ghastly
reality of things.'"[9]

With this new epistemology comes a new relationship for the individual
and his culture, the ideas that he uses to organize his experience. For the
Enlightenment, the same teleology that informs nature, informs culture.
Thus, over time culture is conceived of as a linear progression in which we
gradually overcome ignorance and become perfectly adapted to the environment. For Emerson, culture is a tool that we use to interpret the world and
control our behavior. If man's understanding is limited to the mutable categories of his flickering consciousness, the coherence of his experience of
himself and the world becomes a matter of the interpretation imposed on
experience, not an immanent coherence in the data of experience. Advances
for the individual and the society are made by transcendence of former
ideas, by breaking down our way of thinking so that we can arrive at a new
conception that will subsume the old one: "Every ultimate fact is only the
first of a new series. Every general law only a particular fact of some more
general law presently to disclose itself" (*CW*, 2:181).

Thus, in "Self-Reliance" he urges us to open ourselves to the randomness
and discontinuity of our perceptions so that we do not look to gratify our
present interpretations by lumping experience under them. The "terror that
scares us from self-trust is our consistency" (*CW*, 2:33). Only if we resist the
pressures of synthetic thinking can we hope to transcend ourselves. By defining selfhood as one's uniqueness, the ways in which one's identity is not
exhausted by culture, Emerson invents a term for giving value to existence
which validates innovation. Hence, it is not surprising that he no longer sees
himself as the regenerator of old truths, as the reconciler of "the laws of
moral nature and those of matter" as he does in *Nature*, but as an experimenter who randomizes his behavior: "No facts are to me sacred; none are
profane; I simply experiment, an endless seeker with no Past at my back"
(*CW*, 2:188).

Though in such moments of expansion he burns with the endless possibilities of his new epistemology, in other moods such as in "Experience," he searchingly delineates some of the difficulties of his new stance:

> There are moods in which we court suffering, in the hope that here at least we shall find reality, sharp peaks and edges of truth. But it turns out to be scene-painting. . . . Nothing is left us now but death. We look to that with grim satisfaction, saying, There at least is reality that will not dodge us.
> I take this evanescence and lubricity of all objects, which lets them slip through our fingers then when we clutch the hardest, to be the most unhandsome part of our condition. (W, 3:48–49)

In this state of mind he is not afraid to explore the morally ambiguous ethic of survival, of lapsing from tough-minded analysis and suppressing our alienation from experience: "To fill the hour and leave no crevice for a repentance or an approval. We live amid surfaces, and the true art of life is to skate well on them" (W, 3:59). His style is founded on this new epistemology, in which the individual is thrust into flux and contigency and where value must be continually renewed.

The structure of both series of *Essays* is not governed by the hierarchy of deduction as is *Nature*, but by the integrity of the sentence. Each sentence, which is often an aphorism, is an assertion of individuality that must be renewed each moment, that does not seek coherence with what has been written or will be written. Emerson's goal is not to build a new philosophical system but to explore new possibilities and to dismantle the shibboleths of his culture. The foundation of value lies more in the exposure of oneself to the random incoherence of thought, in pressing thought into the unthinkable, than in the conclusion at which one arrives: "Damn consistency! What matters is not any thought, but the thinking. In the immortal energy of mind lies the compensation for the mortality of truth."[10] To attempt to organize one's thoughts with subordinating and coordinating connectives or by a predetermined pattern of organization such as a hierarchy or a taxonomy would tend to channel them along conventional lines. Hence, Emerson suppresses transitional words, so that the relationship among the sentences is often reduced to their contiguity or to the tenuous connections of his farfetched analogies or to theme and variation.[11] If the reader is to follow the essay, he must leap from sentence to sentence without the comforting links of traditional discourse, much as he would in a lyric poem. An examination of the structure of "Circles" will illustrate the consequences of Romantic epistemology for the style and development of Emerson's *Essays*.

In the first paragraph he announces his method and subject: "We are all our lifetime reading the copious sense of this first of forms. One moral we have already deduced in considering the circular or compensatory character of every action ["Compensation"]. Another analogy we shall now trace, that every action admits of being outdone. Our life is an apprenticeship to the truth that around every circle another can be drawn" (*CW*, 2:179).

Emerson opens the next paragraph by leaping without transition into the mutability theme: "There are no fixtures in nature. The universe is fluid and volatile." Rather than trying to narrow the scope of his proposition by applying it to one or two areas of culture, as he often does in *Nature*, he develops it with a series of examples and related ideas that suggest many of these possible directions, though he does not follow them up:

> Our culture is the predominance of an idea which draws after it this train of cities and institutions. Let us rise into another idea; they will disappear. The Greek sculpture is all melted away, as if it had been ice. . . . The new continents are built out of the ruins of the old. The new races fed out of the decomposition of the foregoing. New arts destroy the old. See the investment of capital in aqueducts, made useless by hydraulics; fortifications by gunpowder. . . .
>
> You admire this tower of granite, weathering the hurts of so many ages. Yet a little waving hand built this huge wall, and that which builds is better than that which is built. . . . Everything looks permanent until its secret is known. A rich estate appears to women a firm and lasting fact; to a merchant, one easily created out of any materials, and easily lost. . . . Nature looks provokingly stable and secular, but it has a cause like all the rest; and when once I comprehend that, will these fields stretch so immovably wide, these leaves hang so individually considerable? Permanence is a word of degrees. Every thing is medial. Moons are no more bounds to spiritual power than bat-balls. (*CW*, 2:179–80)

Emerson is deliberately overloading his opening proposition with examples and parallel ideas, exploring related meanings without trying to come up with a new synthesis or even confining himself to the loose strictures of the circle analogy, which does not appear in this passage. As opposed to the paragraphs in *Nature*, there is no firm topic sentence that controls the development of the paragraph nor many words which establish coordinate or subordinate relations among the sentences. Emerson further insists on this loose structure when he concludes his paragraph with a simple restatement of the opening proposition ("Permanence is a word of degrees"), without trying to come up with an idea that could subsume or qualify his opening statement so that he could advance the exposition. On the contrary, we seem to waft through the polysemy of flux only to encounter the same platitude. The intervening material changes the meaning of the idea for us, but we are left to make this new synthesis for ourselves. It could be called a theme and variation pattern, though the "pattern" is not predetermined or consistent, and the division between a variation and a new theme is never clearly marked. We can observe Emerson's continued resistance to the hierarchical, synthetic method of *Nature* and the dynamics of his new method in the succeding paragraphs.

After closing the preceding paragraph with an abstract statement on the strength of the spirit, he bounds in another direction, again without offering us connectives: "The key to every man is his thought." Only as the paragraph develops does he bring this statement into touch with the circle analogy and his mutability theme: "Sturdy and defying though he [man] look, he has a helm which he obeys, which is the idea after which all facts are classified. He can only be reformed by showing him a new idea which commands his own. The life of man is a revolving circle, which, from a ring imperceptibly small, rushes outward" (*CW*, 2:180).

His next paragraph hurtles us forward with another epigram that is related to the preceding development, though there is a shift in perspective from the individual to the society: "Every ultimate fact is only the first of a new series." One paragraph later as he concludes his discussion of this idea—for the moment—Emerson employs one of his most frequent rhetorical variations, the shift to the second person in order to exhort the reader: "Fear not the new generalization. Does the fact look crass and material, threatening to degrade thy theory of spirit? Resist it not; it goes to refine and raise thy theory of matter just as much" (*CW*, 2:181–82).

From the tensions that new ideas create for society and the individual, Emerson plunges into consciousness itself in his new paragraph with an unfettered epigram: "There are no fixtures to men, if we appeal to consciousness." Though this sentence parallels his first sentence in the third paragraph ("There are no fixtures in nature"), the intervening and subsequent developments do not treat the circle analogy systematically. Indeed, Emerson passes over a conventional duality that these two sentences suggest: flux in nature and flux in the individual, the Me-Not Me pair that he employs in *Nature*. In the next sentence he postpones a discussion of the transient character of consciousness and pushes his development slightly "askew" by taking up the individual's inexplicability: "Every man supposes himself not to be fully understood; and if there is any truth in him, if he rests at last on the divine soul, I see not how it can be otherwise. The last chamber, the last closet, he must feel was never opened" (*CW*, 2:182).

What permits this desultory development is Emerson's use of abstract, aphoristic statements that suggest a variety of directions for his next thought; thus, he resists the linear advance of exposition by proposition, example, and qualification and its attending devices for channeling thought into coherence, and is free to veer toward a distant echo of meaning at any moment.

In the beginning of the next paragraph, one sentence later, he picks up the problem of consciousness again, using a sentence which "should" have followed the first sentence of the preceding paragraph: "Our moods do not believe in each other." This time he employs yet another mode of development by shifting to the first person and a more concrete, lyrical language: "Today I am full of thoughts and can write what I please. I see no reason why I should not have the same thought tomorrow. What I write, whilst I write it, seems the most natural thing in the world; but yesterday I saw dreary vacuity in this direction. . . . Alas for this infirm faith, this will not strenous, this vast ebb of a vast flow: I am God in nature; I am a weed by the wall" (*CW*, 2:182).

The succeeding paragraphs exhibit this same tendency to leap, as they pass from self-transcendence ("the continual effort to raise himself above himself"), to the threat that the thinker poses to society ("beware when the great God lets loose a thinker"), and then back to the individual ("valor consists in the power of self-recovery"). After touching on a bewildering variety of topics both new and old, the essay ends very appropriately by trickling off into yet another direction without any attempt at synthesis. Thus, it is clear that the essay lacks a logical organizational pattern and that its insouciant, exploratory character is quite conscious, as Emerson asserts in the most important paragraph: "I am careful not to justify myself. . . . But lest I should mislead any when I have my own head and obey my whims, let me remind the reader that I am only an experimenter. Do not set the least value on what I do, or the least discredit by what I do not, as if I pretended to settle anything as true or false. I unsettle all things" (*CW*, 2:188).

This method, which is similar to his method throughout the *Essays*, is a representation of Romantic thinking as well as a discussion of Romantic ideas. Once Emerson accepted the irresolvable tension between mind and world and shifted his source of value from the social role to the self, he revolutionized his style and his philosophy. Meaning was something to be invented not discovered. Language, our primary creative tool, was not anchored to an accessible order in the world or in experience but free to explore and even play. As a Romantic, Emerson discovered the importance of random and ludic experimentation that does not have to answer to the demands of logical coherence and linear development. In the contingent Romantic world, meaning and value cannot be identified with timeless truths such as he tried to demonstrate in *Nature*, but only by continuous reengagement of the self with the world, by plunging himself and his reader into time and chaos in order to seek new possibilites: "Valor consists in the power of self-recovery, so that a man cannot have his flank turned, cannot be outgeneralled, but put him where you will, he stands. This can only be his preferring truth to his past apprehension of truth, and his alert acceptance of it from whatever quarter; the intrepid conviction that his laws, his relations to society, his Christianity, his world, may at any time be superseded and decease" (*CW*, 2:183).

Thus, the dangers of channelling thought to conform to the conventions of coherence are too great, for only randomization can lead to self-transcendence. Certainly, he could have experimented in his journals and then organized his ideas in his essays. But this would have been a translation. He needed not only to explain his identity but to symbolize its dynamism and its uncertainty.

NOTES

1. Among the general Romantic theorists who emphasize epistemology, three of the best are M. H. Abrams, Morse Peckham, and Earl Wasserman: see Abrams, *The Mirror and the Lamp* (New York: W. W. Norton, 1958), and his *Natural Supernaturalism* (New York: W. W. Norton, 1971); Peckham, *Beyond the Tragic Vision* (New York: George Braziller, 1961), *The Triumph of Romanticism* (Columbia: University of South Carolina Press, 1970), and *Romanticism and Behavior* (Columbia: University of South Carolina Press, 1976); Wasserman, *The Subtler Language* (Baltimore: Johns Hopkins University Press, 1959), and "The English Romantics: The Grounds of Knowledge," *Studies in Romanticism*, 4 (Autumn 1964): 17–34. For a discussion of Romantic epistemology in American literature, which is neglected in the works cited above, see R. P. Adams, "American Renaissance: An Epistemological problem," *Emerson Society Quarterly*, 35 (2d Quarter 1964): 2–7, and his "Permutations of the American Renaissance," *Studies in Romanticism*, 9 (Fall 1970): 249–68, as well as Lawrence Buell's *Literary Transcendentalism: Style and Vision in the American Renaissance* (Ithaca: Cornell University Press, 1973).

2. All references to Emerson's works, which will be cited in the text, are to *The Collected Works of Ralph Waldo Emerson*, ed. Alfred R. Ferguson, Joseph Slater, et al., 2 vols. to date (Cambridge: Harvard University Press, 1971–), vol. 1, *Nature, Addresses, and Lectures* (1971), and vol. 2, *Essays: First Series* (1979), and to *The Complete Works of Ralph Waldo Emerson*, ed. Edward Waldo Emerson, 12 vols. (Boston: Houghton, Miflin, 1903–1904), to be cited as *CW* and *W*, respectively.

3. For this use of the self-role distinction as a hallmark of Romanticism, I am indebted to Peckham's *Beyond the Tragic Vision*.

4. *The Correspondence of Emerson and Carlyle*, ed. Joseph Slater (New York: Columbia University Press, 1964), p. 278.

5. *The Journals and Miscellaneous Notebooks of Ralph Waldo Emerson*, ed. William H. Gilman et al., 16 vols. (Cambridge: Harvard University Press, 1960–82), 11 January 1823; 2:82. All references to Emerson's journals, which will be cited in the text as *JMN*, are from this edition.

6. Coleridge's discussion of Hartley's theories in *Biographia Literaria* was probably the most devastating exposure of the materialistic explanation with which Emerson was familiar. According to Hartley, the individual mind does not have a part in creation; rather, "the whole universe co-operates to produce the minutest stroke of every letter. . . . The inventor of the watch, if this doctrine be true, did not in reality invent it; he only looked on, while the blind causes, the only true artists, were unfolding themselves" (*Biographia Literaria*, ed. J. Shawcross [London: Oxford University Press, 1907], 1:82).

7. A discussion of Kant's use of the terms "Reason" and "Understanding" is beyond the scope of this paper. Our concern is only with Emerson's use of this distinction, which he got from his reading of Coleridge and Carlyle rather than directly from Kant.

8. See Sheldon W. Liebman, "The Development of Emerson's Theory of Rhetoric," *American Literature*, 41 (May 1969): 178–206.

9. Stephen E. Whicher, "Emerson's Tragic Sense," *American Scholar*, 22 (Summer 1953): 290.

10. Quoted in Stephen E. Whicher, *Freedom and Fate: An Inner Life of Ralph Waldo Emerson* (Philadelphia: University of Pennsylvania Press, 1953), p. 96.

11. This is not deny that the presence of unifying patterns of imagery or analogy or that Emerson had persuasive as well as expository motives for writing. However, the concern of this paper is the presence or absence of a logical structure.

"CLASSIC ART": EMERSON'S PRAGMATIC CRITICISM

Charles W. Mignon

> The supreme value of poetry is to
> educate us to a height beyond itself,
> or which it rarely reaches; — the
> subduing mankind to order and virtue.
> "Poetry and Imagination"
> (W, 8:65–66)

THE IDEA OF an Equilibrist Perspective, "a spirit of compromise or me-diation" in early nineteenth-century American Romanticism, suggests revisionist criticism of the major figures of that age.[1] Emerson is central. For a critic like R. A. Yoder, Emerson as poet represents "the surrender of self-reliant imagination to the Mundane Shell"—to earthly laws (p. 710). Can the same be said of Emerson the literary critic? There is an example of this disillusionment and compromise in Emerson's literary friendship with Al-cott: Emerson began by praising Alcott's power of awakening the apprehen-sion of the Absolute while pointing to the failures of his rhetoric (1836), and ended by delighting in Alcott's octogenarian sonnets (1882). Even so, be-tween the two responses there is much evidence of Emerson's abiding moral interest in the theory and practice of poetry, disillusionment or not. In his theory of art he retained what Yoder asserts he lost, "a high Romantic sense of visionary renewal" by holding the principle of organic fusion: the uni-verse, the artist, the work of art, and the audience formed in his mind a seamless, interrelated, and continuous unity. He found various aspects at-tractive at different times, but from the larger framework of this unity he never wavered.

His early emphasis on the universe and artist, if taken for the whole the-ory, can be misleading. Richard H. Fogle, for example, asserts that "the organicism of Emerson is overbalanced toward Nature, inspiration, immediate insight."[2] Following Vivian C. Hopkins' view that Emerson's theory of the imagination is a theory of perception,[3] Fogle points to Emerson's full grasp of the organic principle of All in Each and to his less satisfactory handling of "the process by which variety becomes unity" (p. 87). Fogle emphasizes this universe-artist relation when he generalizes: "All Romantic organicism places more importance in Nature than in Art, emphasizes the life more than the form"; Coleridge's version can be distinguished from "the gospel of Nature according to Emerson, in which Art is merely the expression of Nature and the Oversoul within and above it, while the artist is a passive instrument" (p. 89). This characterization of Emerson's theory from only one feature of it points to automism and obscures the moral unity in his organic fusion of universe, artist, work, and audience.

Over against the idea that Art is simply the expression of Nature and Oversoul, and that its themes are often its own inspiration and insight, consider the moral aim of Emerson's art. His early interest in Nature, insight, and imagination are well known, but there is a pragmatic purpose even there. After all, the poet's function is to satisfy man's need for truth by his power to inspire, thereby drawing men to Spirit: "it is dislocation and detachment from the life of God that makes things ugly . . . the poet . . . re-attaches things to nature and to the Whole . . . by a deeper insight" (W, 3:18–19). The poet thus satisfies the needs and legitimate demands of the audience to whom the art is addressed; these needs and demands are the norms of poetic art in the pragmatic theory.[4] In Emerson's view the precise nature of these needs can be summed up in one word, regeneration. Man needs to recover the state of truth he has lost, and the universe encourages that recovery. Nature has "a higher end, in the production of new individuals, than security, namely *ascension*, or the passage of the soul into higher forms" (W, 3:24). The poet can attempt this end because imagination is active in all men: just as it intoxicates the poet to receive and impart the truth, so the successful expression of the fleeting "metamorphosis" "excites in the beholder an emotion of joy. . . . Poets are thus liberating gods" (W, 3:30). Reconciliation to the spiritual life of the universe is possible; the poet can express the immortality of man's essence.

My purpose is to suggest that there is no contradiction between the view of Emerson as an Equilibrist and that of Emerson as a moral critic. Emerson as a moral Equilibrist has a theory of literature which is organic and deeply moral in its elements and his practice of literary criticism is a sympathetic and judicial (though sometimes ambivalent) expression of this theory. Disillusioned or not, Emerson held to the high hope of visionary renewal in his idea of the moral aim of art. The organic unity of this aim can be discussed in mimetic, expressive, pragmatic, and even formal terms, but the final cause of his theory and practice can best be framed in pragmatic terms.

When one turns to Emerson's practical criticism of individual authors, whether classic or contemporary, one can see a range of critical response keyed to this organic and moral theory of literature. The range I propose to explore includes Emerson's criticism of Jones Very, Ellery Channing, Bronson Alcott, Milton, Shakespeare, Goethe, and A. D. Woodbridge. No matter who Emerson considers in his criticism, a central source of his judgment is always the thought that "the soul's communication of truth is the highest event in nature." These announcements of the soul, these revelations are accompanied by the emotion of the sublime because the communication itself is "an influx of the Divine mind into our mind" (*CW*, 2:166). So, behind Emerson's literary judgments there is religious background. The fact that Channing and Alcott, for example, had experienced the soul's communication of truth and that Woodbridge had not was important to him and lay behind his criticism of their work; that Shakespeare saw larger truths but seemed to write without moral purpose colored Emerson's judgment; that Milton's gifts were subordinated to his individual moral sentiments troubled him; and that Goethe was too much a creature of the Understanding certainly set the moral tone for his reaction. In each case the touchstone is genius, and genius has two gifts—the thought and the publication.

If a writer shows the signs of revelation (of that gradual unfolding of human powers which the influx of the Divine mind into our mind causes), then that writer has "thought" and is on the right track. The gradual unfolding of these powers begins with the joyful perception of soul, proceeds with obedience to the soul's communication of truth, and leads to insight into the higher laws of this truth. For publication (the second gift of genius) there must be a fusion of this insight (thought) and affection (moral sentiment) in order to generate the energy of will necessary for the power of expression. Emerson's conception of genius thus involves the power to receive and to impart the truths of higher laws. When he brought this conception to bear in making critical judgments, Emerson could see only *partial* signs of genius: Channing and Alcott both had insight but no fully developed power of communication; Milton, though morally insightful and eloquent, was too much himself the final cause of his poetry—not continuous with or obedient to the higher cause; Shakespeare, with the greatest powers of expression, had no allegiance to higher laws; Goethe, the king of scholars, lacked moral sentiment; and Woodbridge (one of Emerson's contemporaries who sent him poetry), a talent, entirely lacking in insight. In this way we can see how Emerson's practical criticism implies an organic unity of universe, artist, work, and audience in the pragmatic demand for revelation—the unfolding of human powers in the artist and in the audience.

Both Alcott and Emerson described Jones Very's mechanical approach to inspiration. Observed Alcott, Very "professed to be taught by the Spirit and to write under its inspiration."[5] When Emerson was asked to read Very's poems and found spelling errors, he was told that this also was by the dictation of the Spirit. His reply was "cannot the Spirit parse & spell?" (*L*, 2:331). Very could not, in Emerson's opinion, escape the charge of automatism. Emerson solved this problem for himself in "Intellect" by distinguishing the universal principle of intellect (the power behind the laws of human thought) from the human faculties of intellect, both receptive and constructive. By the law of undulation the intellect receptive alternates with the intellect constructive; in the artist both powers are needed. Thinking is a pious reception of truths; the truth rendered in the unfolding of the intuition is itself a power the mind has for illuminating nature:

> Each truth that a writer acquires is a lantern which he turns full on what facts and thoughts already in his mind, and behold, all the mats and rubbish which had littered his garret become precious. . . . Men say, Where did he get this? and think there was something divine in his life. But no; they have myriads of facts just as good, would they only get a lamp to ransack their attics withal. (*CW*, 2:197)

The passive and active powers have their appropriate images: the receptor and the projector, the mirror and the lamp, intellect constructive marries thought to nature: from the store of natural images in memory "the active power seizes instantly the fit image, as the word of its momentary thought" (*CW*, 2:198). And genius has both the gift of thought and of publication. In this way he avoided the charge of automism which he felt Very could not.

Very disclaims the action of human will in expression, extending to the powers of communication his obedience to the soul's communications of truth. Emerson thinks otherwise, relying on the principles of spontaneity *and* of choice: "The thought of genius is spontaneous; but the power of picture or expression in the most enriched and flowing nature, implies a mixture of will, a certain control over the spontaneous states, without which no production is possible. It is a conversion of all nature into the rhetoric of thought, under the eye of judgment, with a strenuous exercise of choice" (*W*, 3:336). The power of expression involves the *use* of nature by the imagination: the poet "unfixes the land and the sea, makes them revolve around the axis of his primary thought, and disposes them anew" (*CW*, 1:31).

When he comes to consider William Ellery Channing's poetry, Emerson confirms his view of the poet's active powers by leaning heavily on the idea of unfinished inspiration: "Yet are the failures of genius better than the victories of talent." While conceding that such verses, not being written for publication, lack "that finish which the conventions of literature require of authors," Emerson almost forms a doctrine of the decorum of imperfection in his apology for those worshippers of ideal Beauty like Channing: "Their face is forward, and their heart is in this heaven. By so much are they disqualified for a perfect success in any particular performance to which they can give only a divided affection."[6] His praise of Channing forced Emerson closer to moral preference than to literary judgment. In a letter to Channing, he wrote:

> I have seen no verses written in America that have such inward music, or that seem to me such authentic inspiration. Certainly I prize finished verses, which yours are not, and like best, poetry which satisfies eye, ear, heart & mind. Yet I prize at such a dear rate the poetic soul, that where that is present, I can easily forgive the licence & negligence the absence of which makes the merit of mediocre verses; Nay, I do not know but I prefer the first draught and to be present at the secret of creation before the vamping & rhetoric are used. (*L,* 2:252–53)

But he was to regret his enthusiasm, for he received the verses back again from Channing soon after, still unfinished. He confided to Elizabeth Hoar:

> All my conjectural emendations of our wonderful Manuscript Poet [Channing] came back to me dishonoured. Raphael [S. G. Ward] & Margaret [Fuller] combined against me. I think the poet has given them philtres that they . . . do face me down with his bad grammar & his nonsense as all consecrated by his true *afflatus.* Is the poetic inspiration amber to embalm & enhance flies & spiders? As it fell in the case of Jones Very, cannot the spirit parse & spell? (*L,* 2:331)

Emerson did not believe that nonsense is automatically consecrated by authentic inspiration; quite the contrary—he had learned that his "Manuscript Poet" was quite happy ignoring the demands of rhetoric. Emerson had failed to be firm with Channing and it had its revenge.

Emerson even went so far as to rationalize his failure to improve Channing's rhetoric by elevating the idea of unfinished inspiration into a generic category—portfolio verse. Lyric poetry, in the romantic re-ranking of the poetic kinds, was of course prominent; even more radical was Emerson's preference for *pre-literary forms* of expression. This illustrates the high value he put on *character* over performance:

> Is there not room then for a new department in poetry, namely, *Verses of the Portfolio?* We have fancied that we drew greater pleasure from some manuscript verses than from printed ones of equal talent. For there was herein the charm of character; they were confessions; and the faults, the imperfect parts, the fragmentary verses, the halting rhymes, had a worth beyond that of high finish; for they testified . . . that the thought was too sweet and sacred to him, than that he should suffer his ears to hear or his eyes to see a superficial defect in the expression.[7]

Emerson had, in the fever of his loyalty for Channing, gone too far in favoring the genius' gift of thought at the expense of the gift of publication, but in so doing he illustrated his requirement of revelation. Channing had the soul's communication of truth and insight into the higher laws of this truth, but he did not have that fusion of insight and affection that would generate the will necessary to communicate these truths fully to an audience.

What he failed to accomplish in Channing's case, Emerson made up for in Alcott's: generous in his praise, but more precise and forceful in his criticism. "Psyche" passed his test for revelation: "I think the book original, and vital in all its parts; manifestly, the production of a man in earnest, & written to convince. I think it possesses, in certain passages, the rare power to awaken the highest faculties, to awaken the apprehension of the Absolute" (*L*, 2:4). But the literary aspects did not come in for unqualified praise and Emerson went on in detail to indicate why Alcott's power of expression was not complete:

> Let me now tell you what, with some diffidence, I deem its defects. Its fault arises out of the subtlety & extent of its subject. I think it grapples with an Idea which it does not subdue & present in just method before us. It seems to me too much of a book *of one idea*, somewhat deficient in variety of thought & illustration, and even sometimes pedantic from the wilfulness . . . with which every thing is forced into the author's favorite aspects & forms of expression. The book has a strong mannerism. . . . But its capital fault I think, is the want of compression; a fault almost unavoidable in treating such a subject, which not being easily apprehensible by the human faculties, we are tempted to linger around the Idea, in the hope, that what cannot be sharply stated in a few words, may yet chance to be suggested by many. (*L*, 2:4–5)

On the basis of this diagnosis Emerson prescribed the science of omitting: "it would please me still better, if you would do for it ["Psyche"] what I am now doing with some papers of my own; that is, to go through the work . . . and take the *things* out, leaving the rest. That extract will be precious as the Sybils remaining scrolls" (*L*, 2:5).

When, two years later, Alcott again sent "Psyche" to Emerson for his judgment, Emerson made no mistake about the revelatory nature of the work and of the artist: "The general design of the book as an affirmation of the spiritual nature to an unbelieving age, is good; the topics good; the form excellent. . . . The ideas out of which the book originates are commanding; the book holy. . . . It is the work of a man who has a more simple & steadfast belief in the soul, than any other man; and so it tends to inspire faith" (*L*, 2:139). Even so, he was puzzled by what he found to be a lack of design, and this he thought was due to Alcott's failure to visualize an audience for his work: "Is it a Gospel—a book of exhortation, & popular devotion? Or, is it a book of thought addressed to cultivated men? Which of these two?" (*L*, 2:139).

Choosing "cultivated men" as the proper audience, Emerson set three requirements for successful communication with that audience: compression, omission, and revision, and attached eight manuscript pages of suggested changes.[8] With such emphasis on rhetorical effects on an audience, it is hard to see how one could think that the expressive critical approach would, by itself, account for Emerson's theory or practice.

To indicate the pragmatic side of his theory it will be wise to consider briefly "Art and Criticism" which concerns the training a poet must have in order to achieve the effects desired in an audience. The elements of rhetoric for Emerson are the poet's principal weapons: the low style, compression, and metonomy. He conceives of writing as something made in order to effect the appropriate responses in its readers, an audience which in his time with the advance of democracy had expanded considerably.

Both the low style and compression are arts derived from everyday life, whereas the art of metonomy engages the imagination, the use which Reason makes of the physical world. Emerson recommends the low style, "a conversation above grossness and below refinement where prosperity resides, and where Shakspeare seems to have gathered his comic dialogue" (*W*, 12:284). The principle is "Speak with the vulgar, think with the wise" (*W*, 12:286). Compression is the science of omitting: "what the poet omits exalts every syllable that he writes" (*W*, 12:290). But for Emerson the test of quality is metonomy, for in it he incorporates his vision of the poet as the seer of the laws of the universe, as the perceiver of the Informing Soul in each natural fact: "Idealism regards the world as symbolic, and all these symbols or forms as fugitive and convertible expressions. The power of the poet is in controlling these symbols; in using every fact in Nature, however great and stable, as a fluent symbol, and in measuring his strength by the facility with which he makes the mood of mind give its color to things" (*W*, 12:300). It is significant and appropriate that Emerson would value the art of metonomy so highly, for of the three rhetorical elements, its success assures the possibilities of revelation.

The effect of revelation on the artist himself leads us not to what Emerson deplored in modern literature—the cult of personality, but to the assertion of the universally organic. When Emerson describes this revelatory effect there is present an element of moral communion with a high necessity. Writing, properly centered in the powers of the soul, is a disclosure of the Informing Soul:

> The art of writing is the highest of those permitted to man as drawing directly from the soul, and the means or material it uses are also of the soul. It brings

man into alliance with what is great and eternal. It discloses to him the variety and splendor of his resources. And there is much in literature that draws us with a sublime charm—the superincumbent necessity by which each writer, an infirm, capricious, fragmentary soul, is made to utter his part in the chorus of humanity, is enriched by thoughts which flow from all past minds; so that, whilst the world is made of youthful, helpless children of a day, literature resounds with the music of united vast ideas of affirmation and of moral truth. (W, 12:303)

Such writing draws an audience with sublime charm just as the writer, partaking of soul, draws directly from it for his work. Both writer and audience, by partaking of soul, are subdued to the order and virtue of higher laws. This kind of writing, out of "the superincumbent necessity," has an effect both on the writer and the reader. These kinds of moral effects are best treated in terms of pragmatic criticism, not expressive.

This becomes even more clear when in "Art and Criticism" Emerson turns to the question "What is the Classic?" His answer shows his willingness to rely on the organic analogy, but with a difference. Whereas Coleridge, claiming that organic form was innate, nevertheless attributed the cause to genius which acts creatively under the laws of its own origination, Emerson, also claiming that organic form was innate, gives the cause to the laws of the universe, the laws of the mind, and the laws of artistic effect—all of which form a continuous unity. "Classic art," he writes, "is the art of necessity; organic; modern or romantic bears the stamp of caprice or chance. One is the product of inclination, of caprice, or haphazard; the other carries its law and necessity within itself" (W, 12:303–304). The self would have no power without the virtue of higher law.

In another part of his answer he uses a political analogy to extend the contrast between his "classic" and the modern "romantic": "The politics of monarchy, when all hangs on the accidents of life and temper of a single person, may be called romantic politics. The democratic, when the power proceeds organically from the people and is responsible to them, are classic politics. The classic unfolds, the romantic adds. The classic *should*, the modern *would*. The classic is healthy, the romantic is sick" (W, 12:304). If romantic writing is like romantic politics, then romantic writing leaves us to the accidents and temper of the artist, at best to "the splendid labyrinth" of that artist's perceptions. If classic writing resembles classic politics, then classic writing gathers its power organically from what is universally accessible to all people. Democratic writing, like democratic politics, is not accidental; it is the art of necessity.

In concluding his thoughts on criticism, Emerson makes it clear that the critic must also, as well as the artist and the audience, attempt to partake of the artist's mind and understand that art cannot be created by rules.

A man of genius or a work of love or beauty will not come to order, can't be compounded by the best rules, but is always a new and incalculable result, like health. Don't rattle your rules in our ears; we must behave as we can. Criticism is an art when it does not stop at the words of the poet, but looks at the order of his thoughts and the essential quality of his mind. Then the critic is poet. 'T is a question not of talents but of tone; and not particular merits, but the mood of mind into which one and another can bring us. (W, 12:305)

So, transcendental, or "classic" art, requires revelation not only in the artist and in the reader, but also in the critic. It would therefore I think be difficult and probably mistaken to view Emerson as a "romantic" in the sense that he believes that "the artist himself becomes the major element generating both the artistic product and the criteria by which it is to be judged."[9] The expressive approach does not fully account for Emerson's theory; Emerson criticism must incorporate the pragmatic dimensions of his art.

As he did in Channing's case, Emerson shows perhaps more moral preference than literary judgment when he considers Milton. His thinking about Milton is paradoxical: preferring Milton's love of moral perfection, he nevertheless sees an undesirable presence of the personal in Milton's work. Once again (as in Channing's case) Emerson is strongly drawn to moral nature— only this time the flaw is the presence of personality, not simply the lack of power to express.

The date of the article on Milton (published in the *North American Review* for July 1838) is significant because the essay takes on some of the character of the Divinity School Address. But as early as 1833 we have the famous passage where Emerson not only defines "morals" as "the science of the laws of human action as respects right and wrong" and "right" as "conformity to the laws of nature as far as they are known to the human mind," but also mentions Milton: "Milton describes himself in his letter to Diodati as enamoured of moral perfection. He did not love it more than I" (J, 3:207–208). Early in his essay Emerson compares Milton to Shakespeare: "As a poet, Shakspeare undoubtedly transcends, and far surpasses him in popularity with foreign nations; but Shakspeare is a voice merely; who and what he was that sang, that sings, we know not. Milton stands erect, commanding, still visible as a man among men, and reads the laws of the moral sentiment to the new-born race" (W, 12:253–54). This moral power was Milton's claim to the highest reputation: "Better than any other he has discharged the office of every great man, namely, to raise the idea of Man in the minds of his contemporaries and of posterity—to draw after Nature a life of man, exhibiting such a composition of grace, of strength and of virtue, as poet had not described nor hero lived" (W, 12:254).

And this moral power extended to literary matters, for Emerson was attracted to the idea that poetry would not be possible unless the poet "have in himself the experience and the practice of all that which is praiseworthy" (W, 12:256). Emerson agrees with Milton's doctrine that "'he who would aspire to write well hereafter in laudable things, ought himself to be a true poem'" (W, 12:256). In the continuous and organic line from the First Cause of Soul through the intermediate means of the inspired earthly poet to the fallen audience, we can see the central place of the necessary and moral foundations of poetry in the character of the poet's communications with that Soul. So, when Emerson speaks of the powers necessary for the delineation of this heroic image of man, he connects Milton's mastery of language to its source—clear conceptions and a devoted heart.

When Emerson puts him to the test—"The supreme value of poetry is to educate us to a height beyond itself . . . the subduing mankind to order and virtue"—he finds Milton the man dominating the poet: "Milton's sublimest song, bursting into heaven with its peals of melodious thunder, is the voice of Milton still. Indeed, throughout his poems, one may see, under a thin veil, the opinions, the feelings, even the incidents of the poet's life, still reappearing" (W, 12:274–75). Emerson sees that the presence of the personal "may be thought to abridge his [Milton's] praise as a poet," and he concedes that "it is true of Homer and Shakspeare that they do not appear in their poems" (W, 12:275), but he does not seem to be able to condemn Milton for this flaw. In fact, when it comes to a final contrast of Shakespeare and Milton, Emerson clearly reveals his preference for moral teaching and the pragmatics this assumes, over the delight in beauty and the expressive approach appropriate to it:

> The creations of Shakspeare are cast into the world of thought to no further end than to delight. Their intrinsic beauty is their excuse for being. Milton, fired 'with dearest charity to infuse the knowledge of good things into others,' tasked his giant imagination and exhausted the stores of his intellect for an end beyond, namely, to teach. His own conviction it is which gives such authority to his strain. Its reality is its force. If out of the heart it came, to the heart it must go. (W, 12:277)

Emerson is just as anxious to defend Milton's poetry as a version of his own life as he is to expose Shakespeare for his lack of moral purpose, but the pragmatic dimension of the artist-reader moral connection must not be overlooked: out of the artist's heart comes the truths of higher laws and to the hearts of his readers these truths must travel. Milton's moral health stands out amidst the figures of Emerson's own day: "He is rightly dear to mankind, because in him, among so many perverse and partial men of genius,—in him humanity rights itself; the old eternal goodness finds a home in his breast, and for once shows itself beautiful. His gifts are subordinated to his moral sentiments" (*W*, 12:262). But the moral sentiments were distinctly Milton's, and it is this flaw of the "personal" which Emerson was to develop more fully in his essay "Thoughts on Modern Literature."

In characterizing the literature of his own age, Emerson finds two principles at work: subjectiveness and aspiration, the Feeling of the infinite. When it comes to modern "personality" we see Emerson in a distinctly classical mood: "But, in all ages, and now more, the narrowminded have no interest in anything but in its relation to their personality. . . . Every form under the whole heaven they behold in this most partial light or darkness of intense selfishness, until we hate their being. And this habit of intellectual selfishness has acquired in our day the fine name of subjectiveness" (*W*, 12:313–14). Personality is an obstacle to moral health; true subjectiveness, on the other hand, is a quality of genius: "It is the new consciousness of the one mind, which predominates in criticism. It is the uprise of the soul, and not the decline. It is founded on that insatiable demand for unity, the need to recognize one nature in all the variety of objects, which always characterizes a genius of the first order" (*W*, 12:313). To further distinguish subjectiveness from personality Emerson relies on the test of tendency, namely, what is the tendency of the poet's composition? Does it lead us "to Nature, or to the person of the writer"? "The great," he insists, "always introduce us to facts; small men introduce us always to themselves" (*W*, 12:314). Great men have a purpose in their communications beyond that of personality—to draw men to Nature, and "to an universal experience."

> The more they draw us to them, the farther from them or more independent of them we are, because they have brought us to the knowledge of somewhat deeper than both them and us. . . . The great lead us to Nature, and in our age to metaphysical Nature, to the invisible awful facts, to moral abstractions, which are not less Nature than is a river, or a coal-mine,—nay, they are far more Nature,—but its essence and soul. (*W*, 12:315)

Subjectiveness is thus the tendency of the age to surpass personality; subjectiveness allows the Poet and the audience to see the informing soul, to see that "the soul is superior to its knowledge, wiser than any of its works" (*W*, 12:321). In Milton's song Emerson hears the voice of Milton still. If his song raises us to a higher platform, if he brings us knowledge somewhat deeper than ourselves, we still see that knowledge inextricably bound to Milton himself. He does not bring us knowledge deeper than himself. Thus his moral strength is also his limitation: character dominates his gifts. Emerson simply prefers character; the lack of it in Shakespeare troubled him.

Emerson's touchstone for *Representative Men* is found in the preface, "The Uses of Great Men"—"great men exist that there may be greater men" (*W*, 4:35). As Shakespeare represents the poet in *Representative Men*, he will be judged by Emerson's highest standards. A review of what these standards are, as delineated in "Poetry and Imagination," will not only help to explain Emerson's judgment of Shakespeare, but will also illustrate his conception of the moral aim of art and the appropriateness of the pragmatic approach to that conception as he shows it in his criticism.

In "Poetry and Imagination" Emerson describes the powers needed by the poet and the needs of the audience from which the norms of art and the canons of critical appraisal should be derived.[10] The chief powers the poet must have are revelation, veracity to that revelation, and the powers of inspiration and expression; the chief need of the audience is moral health.

Emerson's first step in explaining these ideas is to treat "Imagination," an activity he finds in all men. When the poet's inspiration is adequate, the reader's imagination rises to meet and grasp it. Adequacy is measured by the test of comprehension; otherwise the moral aim of art could not be realized. The power necessary to achieve this adequacy is the poet's power to unite his first and second sight in the use of metonymy: second sight uses objects seen by first sight as types or words for the thoughts they signify. The aim of this union of first and second sight is delight and, ultimately, moral use.

Since both the poet and the audience have imagination in common, we can anticipate Emerson's claim that "The very design of imagination is to domesticate us in another, in a celestial nature" (W, 8:20); of course the prerequisite to inspiration is the poet's power to see the truth that soul generates matter: "A poet comes who lifts the veil; gives them [mortal men] glimpses of the laws of the universe; shows them the circumstance as illusion; shows that Nature is only a language to express the laws, which are grand and beautiful;—and lets them, by his songs, into some of the realities" (W, 8:38). Privy to the power of the universe through his perception, the poet then reports as exactly as he can the essential law to mortal men.

The section "Morals" in this essay leaves no doubt that Emerson considers the moral needs of the audience: "None of your parlor or piano verse, none of your carpet poets, who are content to amuse, will satisfy us. Power, new power, is the good which the soul seeks. The poetic gift we want, as the health and supremacy of man,—not rhymes and sonneteering (W, 8:63–64). The poet must have "an adequate message to convey" (W, 8:65) and it is here that Emerson states the touchstone by which literature is to be judged: "The supreme value of poetry is to educate us to a height beyond itself, or which it merely rarely reaches;—the subduing mankind to order and virtue" (W, 8:65–66). Educating the audience involves the imagination common to every man: "The poet should rejoice if he has taught us to despise his song; if he has so moved us to lift us,—to open the eye of the intellect to see farther and better" (W, 8:68).

Man has the power for moral recovery latent in sleeping Reason; his powers are presently blocked by the despotism of the senses and the tyranny of the unrenewed Understanding. More than anyone else, the Poet has the latent and sometimes patent power to act on men through his poetry just as the spirit acts throughout nature, spiritually. Inspiration is, to the poet, a form of regeneration; the same is true for the audience: it may be inspired to a height beyond itself. Inspiration is the opening step to the dance of God, the regeneration of man.

Since we know that nature has a higher end than security, namely ascension, or the passage of the soul into higher forms (W, 3:24), we may not be surprised to see this idea given musical form: "In a cotillon some persons dance and others await their turn when the music and the figure come to them. In the dance of God there is not one of the chorus but can and will begin to spin, monumental as he now looks, whenever the music and figure reach his place and duty" (W, 8:70). The music of inspiration may be heard by any man; it is the power which may move and liberate fallen man in his monumental moral inertia. Emerson symbolizes this power of music to move men in the god Bacchus: "O celestial Bacchus! drive them mad,—this multitude of vagabonds, hungry for eloquence, hungry for poetry, starving for symbols, perishing for want of electricity to vitalize this too much pasture, and in the long delay indemnifying themselves with the false wine of alcohol, of politics or of money" (W, 8:70).

Bacchus' music satisfies the demands of the Spirit (in liberating the soul from the confines of the physical universe). Poets, by means of their art, are indeed liberating gods, for "Every man may be, and at some time a man is, lifted to a platform whence he looks beyond sense to moral and spiritual truth, and in that mood deals sovereignly with matter, and strings worlds like beads upon his thought" (W, 8:70). So the audience will end in seeing what the poet sees. With such emphasis on moral effects, how could we fail to appreciate the possibilities of pragmatic criticism?

It is this moral aim of art which Emerson finds lacking in Shakespeare. So, even if he thinks that Shakespeare unfolds the book of life with unique creative power ("He was the farthest reach of subtlety compatible with an individual self. . . . With this wisdom of life is the equal endowment of imaginative and of lyric power" [W, 4:212]), even if these powers coming together seems to add a new problem to metaphysics, a hint of his final judgment appears in his observation that beauty was Shakespeare's aim: "He loves virtue, not for its obligation but for its grace: he delights in the world, in man, in woman, for the lovely light that sparkles from them. Beauty, the spirit of joy and hilarity, he sheds over the universe." The austere lessons of solitude had taught him that Shakespeare shared "the halfness and imperfection of humanity" (W, 4:215–16)—he had failed to take the deepest view:

> Shakspeare, Homer, Dante, Chaucer, saw the splendor of meaning that plays over the visible world; knew that a tree had another use than for apples, and

corn another than for meal, and the ball of the earth, than for tillage and roads: that these things bore a second and finer harvest to the mind, being emblems of its thoughts, and conveying in all their natural history a certain mute commentary on human life. Shakspeare employed them as colors to compose his picture. He rested in their beauty; and never took the step which seemed inevitable to such genius, namely to explore the virtue which resides in these symbols and imparts this power:—what is that which they themselves say? He converted the elements which waited on his command, into entertainments. He was master of the revels to mankind. (W, 4:216–17)

Shakespeare failed because he lacked the moral view which Emerson had come to expect of the Poet. There is a note of sadness in his final characterization of Shakespeare: "but that this man of men, he who gave to the science of mind a new and larger subject than had ever existed, and planted the standard of humanity some furlongs forward into Chaos,—that he should not be wise for himself;—it must even go into the world's history that the best poet led an obscure and profane life, using his genius for the public amusement" (W, 4:218). And yet, for those who *did* see through objects to what they contained, beauty vanished in what they read: commandments, "all-excluding mountainous duty; an obligation, a sadness, as of piled mountains, fell on them, and life became ghastly, joyless, a pilgrim's progress, a probation" (W, 4:219). Emerson wanted neither a Swedenborg nor a Shakespeare, but someone who could balance the two powers of *prodesse* and *delectare*: "The world still wants its poet priest, a reconciler, who shall not trifle, with Shakspeare the player, nor shall grope in graves, with Swedenborg the mourner; but who shall see, speak, and act, with equal inspiration. For knowledge will brighten the sunshine; right is more beautiful than private affection; and love is compatible with universal wisdom" (W, 4:219). Emerson understands that those like Swedenborg who *do* see causes and spirits through the objects of nature, who do explore the virtue residing in the symbols of nature, deliver us to a doom wherein the heart of the seer and the heart of the listener sink. He sees the error of a narrowness like Swedenborg's (he calls it a "theologic cramp"); this flaw was a result of Swedenborg's having gone *too far* in fastening "each natural object to a theologic notion" (W, 4:121). But Emerson cannot see his own narrowness, the narrowness of framing Shakespeare and Swedenborg together in the same thought. His view of the two indicates his own tendency to find symbolic presentations of ideal nature the most promising way of exploring moral meaning. Finally what we need is the poet priest.

In his later essay on "Art" Emerson stated that art has a necessary existence in Nature as one of the possible forms of the Divine Mind:

All departments of life at the present day—Trade, Politics, Letters, Science, or Religion—seem to feel, and to labor to express, the identity of their law. They are rays of one sun; they translate each into a new language the sense of the other. They are sublime when seen as emanations of a Necessity contra-distinguished from the vulgar Fate by being instant and alive, and dissolving man as well as his works in its flowing beneficence. This influence is conspicuously visible in the principles and history of Art. (*W*, 7:37)

One of the tests of the effectiveness of a work acting upon its audience is the extent to which it is "strictly subordinated to the laws of Nature, so as to become a sort of continuation and in no wise a contradiction of Nature": it must be the production of the universal soul. For it to be so, the poet must resign himself to the public power of the life of the universe and eschew his private power: "The artist who is to produce a work which is to be admired, not by his friends or his townspeople or his contemporaries, but by all men . . . must disindividualize himself, and be a man . . . through whom the soul of all men circulates as the common air through his lungs"; "he is to be an organ through which the universal mind acts" (*W*, 7:48–49). In so far as he is successful, the delight which the audience experiences in his work "seems to arise from our recognizing in it the mind that formed Nature, again in active operation" (*W*, 7:51). It is precisely this quality in the work and power as an artist that Goethe lacks.

While conceding Goethe's incorporation of the materials of his age ("He has owed to Commerce and to the victories of the Understanding, all their spoils" [*W*, 12:322]), Emerson distinguishes him from Homer and Shakespeare: the difference lies in "'the Me, the *Ille ego*, everywhere glimmers through, although without any boasting and with an infinite fineness.' This subtle element of egotism in Goethe certainly does not seem to deform his compositions, but to lower the moral influence of the man. . . . He did himself, and worked always to astonish, which is egotism, and therefore little" (*W*, 12:326). Goethe is the king of scholars, fully a creature of the Understanding. The absence of Reason distresses Emerson: "And what shall we think of that absence of the moral sentiment, that singular equivalence to him of good and evil in action, which discredit his compositions to the pure?" (*W*, 12:328).

Not satisfied with Goethe's defence that there are enough poets of the Ideal, yet not denying the existence of the Actual, Emerson asserts that the Idea is *truer* than the Actual—the Actual is ephemeral, the ideal changes not. Goethe's powers command the Actual. In *Wilhelm Meister*, Emerson writes, "The vicious conventions, which hem us in like prison walls and which the poet should explode at his touch, stand for all they are worth in the newspaper. We are never lifted above ourselves, we are not transported out of the dominion of the senses, or cheered with an infinite tenderness, or armed with a grand trust" (*W*, 12:330–31). Goethe simply lacks the moral power of the poet.

Emerson's main criticism of Goethe then was that he did not have "a moral perception proportionate to his other powers" and this fact was not "merely a circumstance . . . but it is the cardinal fact of health or disease" (*W*, 12:331–32). The amount of moral perception a man has is the index to his moral health. Goethe has refused the opportunity allowed only to genius, to be a Redeemer of the human mind: "Humanity must wait for its physician still at the side of the road. . . . We feel that a man gifted like him [Goethe] should not leave the world as he found it. . . . Shall not a poet redeem us from these idolatries, and pale their legendary lustre before the fires of the Divine Wisdom which burn in his heart?" (*W*, 7:332–33). Unfortunately, Goethe introduces us to himself, not to Nature and Soul. The tendency of his work is to the service of the senses in popular nineteenth-century life. Goethe is the soul of personality and lacks even the benefits of moral character which Milton enjoys.

In his letter to A. D. Woodbridge about her poetry Emerson distinguishes genius and talent. Genius, he wrote in "The Method of Nature," "looks to the cause and life: it proceeds from within outward, whilst Talent goes from without inward. Talent finds its models, methods, and ends, in society, exists for exhibition. . . . Genius is its own end, and draws its means and the style of its architecture from within" (*CW*, 1:134). Trying to prepare Woodbridge for his criticism, Emerson generalizes: "I believe I am very hard to please in the matter of poetry, but my quarrel with most of the verses I read, is this namely, that it is conventional; that it is a certain manner of writing agreed on in society . . . but is not that new, constitutional, unimitated and inimitable voice of the individual which poetry ought always to be" (*L*, 2:415). In conforming to the conventional usages of that "certain manner of writing agreed on in society," Woodbridge has unwittingly acquiesced in the conspiracy against the voice of her own womanhood. Actually, "all poetry should be original & necessary." In concluding his judgment he demeans her talent and asks for what is impossible: "The verses you sent me are uncommonly smooth & elegant, and happily express a pleasing sentiment; but I suppose I should prize more highly much ruder specimens from your portfolio . . . which recorded in a way you could not repeat, some profound experience of happiness or pain" (*L*, 2:415). The absence of genius does not seem to interest him and certainly the presence of talent does not impress him.

The theme of this survey of Emerson's practical criticism is that "idea and execution are not often intrusted to the same head. There is some incompatibility of good speculation and practice, for example, the failure of monasteries and Brook Farms" (*W*, 12:48). To this list he might have added the writers discussed here, for none of them completely satisfied his desire for the genius that would repair the decay of things. Still, he knows that criticism should be commensurate with the activity of genius: "All criticism should be poetic; unpredictable; superceding, as every new thought does, all foregone thoughts, and making a new light on the whole world. . . . It has all things to say, and no less than all the world for its final audience." The Transcendentalists meant to have an effect on their audience, and Emerson most clearly states, in the first number of the *Dial*, the exact nature of this intended effect:

> Our plan embraces much more than criticism; were it not so, our criticism would be naught. Everything noble is directed on life, and this is. We do not wish to say pretty or curious things, or to reiterate a few propositions in varied forms, but, if we can, to give expression to that spirit which lifts men to a higher platform, restores to them the religious sentiment, brings them worthy aims and pure pleasures, purges the inward eye, makes life less desultory, and, though raising men to the level of nature, takes away its melancholy from the landscape, and reconciles the practical with the speculative powers.[11]

A clearer statement of the aims of transcendental art cannot be found: the moral aim of art is romantic and expressive in its means but classic and pragmatic in its ends.

The chief powers of the poet are revelation, veracity to that revelation, inspiration, and expression. The influx of the Divine Mind into the mind of men acts to unfold human powers gradually, and this acts in the artist, in the work, and in the audience. In *both* the artist and the audience this unfolding begins with the joyful perception of Soul, proceeds with obedience to the Soul's communication of truth, and leads to insight into the higher laws of this truth. In the artist this unfolding of power extends to expression, for which there must be a fusion of insight and affection to generate the will to express. In the work of art the unfolding, drawn directly from the Soul, uses the means or material also of the Soul. (Thought must be married to nature; imagination is the use which Reason makes of the material world.) This unfolding in the work brings the audience "into alliance with what is great and eternal. It discloses to him the variety and splendor of his resources" (W, 12:303). The final test of the whole process of unfolding is "the mood of mind into which one and another can bring us" (W, 12:305). Emerson thus illustrates the line of influence from Mind through Artist and work to the audience.

Pragmatic criticism, ordered toward the audience, "looks at the work of art chiefly as a means to an end, an instrument for getting something done, and tends to judge its value according to its success in achieving that aim."[12] In Emerson's practical criticism of writers the theme is the *absence* of the "true Orpheus who writes his ode, not with syllables, but men" (W, 8:66). When he saw the failure of poetry in his own day to subdue mankind to order and virtue, this did not stop him from projecting the spiritual needs of the audience. His regard for the audience is prominent because of his moral concern and his transcendental idealism. The *full* genius of the poet could bring spiritual health to mankind:

> And this is the insatiable craving which alternately saddens and gladdens men at this day. The Doctrine of the Life of Man established after he truth through all his faculties;—this is the thought which the literature of this hour meditates and labors to say. . . . Man is not so far lost but that he suffers ever the great Discontent which is the elegy of his loss and the prediction of his recovery. . . . What, then, shall hinder the Genius of the time from speaking its thought?. . . . It will describe the new heroic life of man, the now unbelieved possibility of simple living and clean and noble relations with men. Religion will bind again these that were sometime frivolous, customary, enemies, skeptics, self-seekers, into a joyful reverence for the circumambient Whole, and that which was ecstasy shall become daily bread. (W, 12:333–36)

Moral norms for moral art; for "Every man may be, and at some time a man is, lifted to a platform whence he looks beyond sense to moral and spiritual truth, and in that mood deals sovereignly with matter, and strings worlds like beads upon his thought" (W, 8:70).[13]

NOTES

1. R. A. Yoder, "The Equilibrist Perspective: Toward a Theory of American Romanticism," *Studies in Romanticism*, 12 (Fall 1973): 705–40; cited in this paragraph by page number.

The following abbreviations are used in this article: *CW* = *The Collected Works of Ralph Waldo Emerson*, ed. Alfred R. Ferguson, Joseph Slater, et al., 2 vols. to date (Cambridge: Harvard University Press, 1971–); *J* = *Journals of Ralph Waldo Emerson*, ed. Edward Waldo Emerson and Waldo Emerson Forbes, 10 vols. (Boston: Houghton Mifflin, 1909–14); *L* = *The Letters of Ralph Waldo Emerson*, ed. Ralph L. Rusk (New York: Columbia University Press, 1939); and *W* = *The Complete Works of Ralph Waldo Emerson*, ed. Edward Waldo Emerson, 12 vols. (Boston: Houghton, Mifflin, 1903–1904).

This essay was originally accepted for publication in *Emerson Centenary Essays*, ed. Joel Myerson (Carbondale: Southern Illinois University Press, 1982), but omitted from that publication for reasons of space.

2. Richard H. Fogle, "Organic Form in American Criticism: 1840–1870," in *The Development of American Literary Criticism*, ed Floyd Stovall (Chapel Hill: University of North Carolina Press, 1955), p. 87; cited in this paragraph by page number.

3. Vivian C. Hopkins, *Spires of Form: A Study of Emerson's Aesthetic Theory* (Cambridge: Harvard University Press, 1951), pp. 23ff.

4. M. H. Abrams, *The Mirror and the Lamp: Romantic Theory and the Critical Tradition* (New York: Oxford University Press, 1953), p. 15.

5. *The Journals of Bronson Alcott*, ed. Odell Shepard (Boston: Little, Brown, 1938), p. 517.

6. Emerson, "New Poetry," *Dial*, 1 (October 1840): 221–22. Thoreau characterized Channing's literary style as "sublimo-slipshod" (*The Journal of Henry D. Thoreau*, ed. Bradford Torrey and Francis H. Allen [Boston: Houghton Mifflin, 1906], 3:118).

7. Emerson, "New Poetry," 221.

8. For Emerson's lengthy comments on compression ("I demand your propositions; your definitions; . . . your facts observed in nature; as in solid blocks"), omission ("all passages conveying this prophetic pretension . . . modifying all passages that are too obvious personal allusions, until they speak to the condition of all . . . The author's Ego must be the human Ego, & not that of his name & town"), and revision ("The dropping of the Scriptural termination, as in do*eth* . . . and the earnest adoption of the language you speak in your own house"), see *L*, 2:138–41.

9. Abrams, *The Mirror and the Lamp*, p. 22.

10. The language of this sentence and the pragmatic perspective itself both originate in Abrams, *The Mirror and the Lamp*, p. 15.

11. Emerson, "The Editors to the Reader," *Dial*, 1 (July 1840): 3–4.

12. Abrams, *The Mirror and the Lamp*, p. 15.

13. I wish to acknowledge in this work the intellectual stimulation and comradeship of Bernice Slote, Mel Lyon, and George Wolf.

THE AMERICAN EPISODE OF *MARTIN CHUZZLEWIT*: THE CULMINATION OF DICKENS' QUARREL WITH THE AMERICAN PRESS

Sidney P. Moss

> The violence of his diatribe—both in the . . . *American Notes* . . . and in the notorious "American chapters" of *Martin Chuzzlewit* . . . is so sustained and supercilious . . . [that it] goes . . . much beyond almost everything else that had been written against the New World, from de Pauw onward. . . . These two books . . . contain a barely revised but powerfully enriched compendium of almost all the slanders ever hurled at the American continent . . . [and] Dickens concentrates them all on the United States . . . —Antonello Gerbi, *The Dispute of the New World: The History of a Polemic, 1750–1900* (Pittsburgh: University of Pittsburgh Press, 1973), pp. 497–99.

TO TRACE THE QUARREL between Dickens and the American press of the 1840s, one can probably do no better than to disclose the real motives that Dickens had in interpolating the American chapters into *Martin Chuzzlewit* and to indicate the reaction of the Americans to those chapters. To accomplish this, it is necessary first to touch upon the events that led to that quarrel.

Nearly thirty years of age and already one of the most popular novelists of his time, Dickens decided to take a breather from his heavy writing schedules, which required him to produce monthly and sometimes weekly installments of novels. This breather was to be a first-time visit to the United States, where he could leisurely collect materials for a travel book that was to be called *American Notes*.

When he arrived in America in January 1842, he was celebrated as perhaps no person in this country, native or foreign, had ever been celebrated before, including George Washington and General Lafayette. William Cullen

Bryant in his *New York Evening Post* of 18 February 1842 said that the ovations to Dickens "may have been carried too far"; nevertheless, he rejoiced that "a young man, without birth, wealth, title, or a sword, whose only claims to distinction are his intellect and heart, is received with a feeling that was formerly rendered only to emperors and kings." Dickens himself, with the excess of euphoria, wrote to a friend on 31 January 1842: "There never was a King or Emperor upon the Earth, so cheered, and followed by crowds, and entertained in Public at splendid balls and dinners, and waited on by public bodies and deputations of all kinds."[1] Yet, within a month's time, Boz, the favorite author of Americans, the man they revered as the friend of the poor and the opposer of social evils, was stigmatized by American newspapers as (to use Dickens' own words) a "mere mercenary scoundrel."[2] It was no wonder that Dickens generalized his misery in writing to an English friend: "I tremble for a radical coming here, unless he is a radical on principle, by reason and reflection, and from the sense of right"; otherwise, "I fear . . . he would return home a tory" because "the heaviest blow ever dealt at liberty will be dealt by this country, in the failure of its example to the earth."[3] To another English friend he wrote with similar disappointment: "This is not the Republic I came to see. This is not the Republic of my imagination. I infinitely prefer a liberal Monarchy . . . to such a Government as this . . . And . . . even England, bad and faulty as the old land is, and miserable as millions of her people are, rises in the comparison."[4]

Two reasons explain this sudden turnabout. Dickens, who considered himself, and indeed was, "the greatest loser by the existing [American copyright] Law, alive," had pleaded at once for an Anglo-American copyright treaty, a pleading that American reprint publishers perceived as promoting Dickens', not to say British, interests at the expense of their own. Secondly, in voicing these pleas for Anglo-American copyright at magnificent dinners held in his honor in Boston, Hartford, and New York, Dickens was seen as violating the propriety of nearly state occasions. As the *Morning Courier and New-York Enquirer* of 12 February 1842 editorialized prior to the New York dinner:

> Mr. Dickens has been honored with two public dinners since his arrival in the United States; and on both occasions he has made an appeal to his hosts in behalf of a law to secure him a certain amount in *dollars and cents* for his writings. We are . . . mortified and grieved that he should have been guilty of such great indelicacy and gross impropriety. . . . The entire Press of the Union were predisposed to be his eulogist . . . ; but had it been otherwise—had the whole Press united to decry and disparage him—they could not have accomplished what he himself has effected . . . by urging upon those assembled to do honor to his *genius*, to look after his *purse* also!

And when Dickens actually carried a petition for Anglo-American copyright to Congress, the last remaining doubts were dissolved. He was perceived as a meddlesome foreigner, content not with the laurels that Americans were bestowing on him, but greedy for their money.

Only a month after his arrival in the States, Dickens wrote to the mayor of Boston to express his shock and disgust at the way the American newspaper press had turned upon him:

> I have never in my life been so shocked and disgusted, or made so sick and sore at heart, as I have been by the treatment I have received here . . . in reference to the International Copyright question. I,—the greatest loser by the existing Law, alive,—say in perfect good humour and disinterestedness . . . that I hope the day will come when Writers will be justly treated; and straightway there fall upon me scores of your newspapers; imputing motives to me, the very suggestion of which turns my blood to gall; and attacking me in such terms of vagabond scurrility as they would denounce no murderer with. I vow to Heaven that the scorn and indignation I have felt under this unmanly and ungenerous treatment has been to me an amount of agony such as I never experienced since my birth.[5]

When Dickens returned to England at the end of June 1842, he proceeded to write his travel book, the last two chapters of which constituted a nearly wholesale indictment of the United States. If that were not enough, he seems to have gone underground with his friend and biographer-to-be, John Forster, to write a series of anonymous anti-American articles for the London *Foreign Quarterly Review*.[6] And if that were still not enough, he arranged to have a circular letter widely published which roundly damned those engaged in the "piracy and plunder" of "popular English works."[7] To make matters even worse, Walt Whitman, in the *New York Evening Tattler* he was editing, published a letter forged in Dickens' name, designed to defame Dickens still further.[8] Needless to say, the journalistic reactions to these outbursts—outbursts either written by Dickens, or attributed to Dickens, or forged in Dickens' name—descended into pure scurrility. *The New York Herald* of 24 October 1842 said that Dickens' comments on America consist of "falsehood, fury, misrepresentation, misquotation, violence, vulgarity, heartlessness, coarseness, and all that low species of tact which distinguishes the literary works of Dickens already before the public," and on 8 November he called him, among other fine things, "a literary bagman," "a cockney," a "penny-a-liner-loafer," and the most contemptible of all travelers who had come to America.

Despite the animosity aroused by *American Notes*, the American reprints of that book returned great profits to their publishers—namely, Harper &

Brothers; Lea & Blanchard; Wilson & Company, which had printed the work both as a *Brother Jonathan* Extra Number and as a book; Jonas Winchester and Park Benjamin, who had printed it as a Double Extra Number of their *New World*; not to mention James Gordon Bennett, who had published "principal portions" of the book in his *New York Herald*. Indeed, *American Notes* had record sales in the United States, a record broken only by *Uncle Tom's Cabin* published a decade later. Naturally, the reprinters, the selfsame ones, as it turned out, were also delighted to publish Dickens' next serial, *Martin Chuzzlewit*, which they proceeded to do as fast as they could receive the monthly numbers and rush them to their print shops. The competition for sales in New York among *Brother Jonathan*, the *New World*, the Harpers, and Lea & Blanchard was so intense that newsboys were sent into the streets to hawk the installments.

If before his trip to America, Dickens had been vexed at receiving no more than £350 from the thousands upon thousands of copies of his books sold in the United States[9] (for all his work had been appropriated by what he called the "dirty hands" of "American Robbers"[10]), he was, upon discovering the vastness of his American market, thoroughly outraged at the wholesale piracy by which he found himself "the greatest loser . . . alive." Thus, as part of his anti-American campaign, begun with his circular letter decrying American book pirates and continued with *American Notes* and the series of articles in the *Foreign Quarterly Review*, Dickens introduced into the seventh installment of *Martin Chuzzlewit* an American episode. The first installment of that episode "exploded," to use John Forster's word, upon the Americans in July 1843. It shows young Martin and Mark Tapley, latter-day versions of Don Quixote and Sancho Panza or even of Lemuel Gulliver, arriving in New York. Before they even disembark in the "Land of Liberty," the first "good-humoured little outbursts" they hear are the screams caused by friends of a defeated alderman who "found it necessary to assert the great principles of Purity and Election and Freedom of Opinion by breaking a few legs and arms," and who, dauntless, pursue "one obnoxious gentleman through the streets with the design of slitting his nose." The second outbursts the newcomers hear are the sounds of a legion of newsboys barking out the filthy contents of New York newspapers, not only "upon the wharves and among the shipping, but on the deck and down in the cabins":

"Here's this morning's New York Sewer! [the newsboys yell]. . . . Here's this morning's New York Stabber! Here's the New York Family Spy! Here's the New York Private Listener! Here's the New York Peeper! Here's the New York Plunderer! Here's the New York Keyhole Reporter! Here's the New York Rowdy Journal! Here's all the New York papers!. . . . Here's full particulars of the patriotic locofoco movement yesterday, in which the whigs was so chawed up; and the last Alabama gouging case; and the interesting Arkansas dooel with Bowie knives . . . [Here's] a full account of the Ball at Mrs[.] White's last night, where all the beauty and fashion of New York was assembled; with the Sewer's own particulars of the private lives of all the ladies that was there! . . . Here's the Sewer's exposure of the Wall Street Gang, and the Sewer's exposure of the Washington Gang, and the Sewer's exclusive account of a flagrant act of dishonesty committed by the Secretary of State when he was eight years old; now communicated, at a great expense, by his own nurse. Here's the Sewer! Here's the New York Sewer, with a whole column of New Yorkers to be shown up, and all their names printed!"

The first installment of the American episode exploded not only upon Americans; it also exploded upon Messrs. Chapman and Hall, Dickens' publishers, for neither gentleman had the least forewarning of Dickens' intention. Indeed, on 22 March 1843 Dickens had cautioned Thomas Mitton, his friend, solicitor, and financial adviser: "If you see either of the firm, say nothing to them of what I am about in the writing way. I am bent on its coming (if it come at all) a surprise."[11] The firm in all its advertisements had described the forthcoming serial only as a "Tale of English Life and Manners"; nothing was said about American life and manners. Judging from the reviews, letters, diary entries, and reported conversations concerning *American Notes*, the British, not to say the Americans, had had quite enough of *that* from Boz.

Though the American episode of *Martin Chuzzlewit* figured in Dickens' anti-American campaign, it was not preconceived nor even well conceived. Occurring to him abruptly, it seemed to be a spontaneous and indiscriminate eruption of hatred against everything American that had been seething in him for some time. Forster, who said that nothing was written by Dickens after 1837 which he "did not see before the world did, either in manuscript or proofs," categorically stated that "Martin's ominous announcement, at the end of the fourth number, that he'd *go to America*" was a "resolve, which Dickens adopted as suddenly as his hero."[12] The London *Athenæum* pointed out the obvious, that "the American episode" is "an excrescence" with "bad temper and prejudice pervading every line of it."[13] The *North British Review*, in also finding the American "chapters . . . an unaccountable excrescence," added that they "form a new and more pungent edition of the American Notes, but with only the harshest censures distilled over [again] and concentrated."[14] Nevertheless, prompted by hatred and loosing his satire upon everything American, Dickens proceeded to exaggerate the worst aspects of the United States and to ignore any of its good ones, excepting, of course, the minor character Bevan, whose good services in rescuing the young Englishmen from that malarial swampland that the real estate jobbers named Eden were required by the plot.

Apart from showing the eating habits of American men to be piggish and the tobacco juice they voided in everyone's vicinity inexhaustible, Dickens satirized American newspapers; American politics; Americans' unremitting brag of liberty and independence; American slavery, all the worse in a land that bragged of liberty and independence; American anglophobia continually blustering about war with England; American commercialism; American repudiation of State debts; and American impoverishment in manners, conversation, and the arts, as representative specimens show:

> [Martin to Colonel Diver, editor of the *New York Rowdy Journal*]: " . . . May I venture to ask, with reference to a case I observe in this paper of yours, whether the Popular Instructor [the American newspaper] often deals in—I am at a loss to express it without giving you offence—in forgery? In forged letters, for instance . . . ?"
> "Well, sir!" replied the colonel. "It does, now and then."
> "And the popular instructed; what do they do?" asked Martin.
> "Buy 'em:" said the colonel. . . . "Buy 'em by hundreds of thousands. . . . We are a smart people here, and can appreciate smartness."
> "Is smartness American for forgery?" asked Martin. . . .

> "We are independent here, sir," said Mr. Jefferson Brick. "We do as we like."

> Mr. [Hannibal] Chollop [the sometime owner of newspapers] . . . always introduced himself to strangers as a worshipper of Freedom; was the consistent advocate of Lynch law, and slavery; and invariably recommended, both in print and speech, the "tarring and feathering" of any unpopular person who differed from himself. He called this "planting the standard of civilisation in the wilder gardens of My country."

> "A slave!" cried Martin, in a whisper.
> "Ah!" said Mark . . . "Nothing else. A slave. Why, when that there man was young . . . he was shot in the leg; gashed in the arm; scored in his live limbs, like crimped fish; beaten out of shape; had his neck galled with an iron collar and wore iron rings upon his wrists and ankles. . . . And now he's a-saving up to treat himself, afore he dies, to one small purchase; it's nothing to speak of; only his own daughter; that's all! . . . Liberty for ever! Hurrah! Hail, Columbia!"

> It was hastily resolved that a piece of plate should be presented to a certain constitutional Judge, who had laid down from the Bench the noble principle, that it was lawful for any white mob to murder any black man: and that another piece of plate, of similar value, should be presented to a certain Patriot, who had declared from his high place in the Legislature, that he and his friends would hang, without trial, any Abolitionist who might pay them a visit.

> Once or twice . . . Martin asked . . . questions . . . about the national poets, the theatre, literature, and the arts . . .

"We are a busy people, sir," said one of the captains . . . "and have no time for reading mere notions. We don't mind 'em if they come to us in newspapers along with almighty strong stuff of another sort, but darn your books."

The greater part [of the explanation for the barren conversation of Americans] . . . may be summed up in one word. Dollars. All their cares, hopes, joys, affections, virtues, and associations, seemed to be melted down into dollars. Whatever the chance contributions that fell into the slow cauldron of their talk, they made the gruel thick and slab with dollars. Men were weighed by their dollars . . . ; life was auctioneered, appraised, put up, and knocked down for its dollars. The next respectable thing to dollars was any venture having their attainment for its end. The more of that worthless ballast, honour and fair-dealing, which any man cast overboard from the ship of his Good Name and Good Intent, the more ample stowage-room he had for dollars. Make commerce one huge lie and mighty theft. Deface the banner of the nation . . . ; pollute it star by star; and cut out stripe by stripe . . . Do anything for dollars! What is a flag to *them*!

"What is the Pogram Defiance?" asked Martin, thinking, perhaps it was the sign of a pub.

"An o-ration, sir" [answered an American] . . . "It defied the world, sir. . . . Defied the world to com-pete with our country upon any hook; and developed our internal resources for making war upon the universal earth."

"May the British Lion [said General Cyrus Choke] have his talons eradicated by the noble bill of the American Eagle, and be taught to play upon the Irish Harp and the Scotch Fiddle that music which is breathed in every empty shell that lies upon the shores of green Co-lumbia."

In commercial affairs he was a bold speculator. In plainer words he had a most distinguished genius for swindling.

"Lord love you, sir [said Mark Tapley] . . . , they're so fond of Liberty in this part of the globe, that they buy her and sell her and carry her to market with 'em. They've such a passion for Liberty, that they can't help taking liberties with her."

Steel and iron are of infinitely greater account, in this commonwealth, than flesh and blood. . . . Look at that engine! It shall cost a man more dollars in the way of penalty and fine, and satisfaction of the outraged law, to deface in wantonness that senseless mass of metal, than to take the lives of twenty human creatures! Thus the stars wink upon the bloody stripes; and Liberty pulls down her cap upon her eyes, and owns Oppression in its vilest aspect, for her sister.

"If ever the defaulting part of this here country pays its debts [said Mark Tapley] . . . they'll take such a shine out of it, and make such bragging speeches, that a man might suppose no borrowed money had ever been paid afore, since the world was first begun."

Wherever half a dozen people were collected together, there, in their looks, dress, morals, manners, habits, intellect, and conversation, were Mr. Jefferson Brick, Colonel Diver, Major Pawkins, General Choke, and Mr. La Fayette Kettle, over, and over, and over again. They did the same things; said the same things; judged all subjects by, and reduced all subjects to, the same standard.

Knowing that his satire sounded more vindictive than amusing and that he would be cried down for it, Dickens had Bevan explain in the opening chapter of the American episode: "I believe no satirist could breathe this air. If another Juvenal or Swift could rise up among us to-morrow, he would be hunted down. If you . . . can give me the name of any man, American born and bred, who has anatomised our follies as a people, . . . and who has escaped the foulest and most brutal slander, the most inveterate hatred and intolerant pursuit; it will be a strange name in my ears, believe me." But even this statement, which by its message and placement seemed intended to disarm readers, resonated with condemnation and became merely consistent with Dickens' other passages on America, further indicating that, where Americans were concerned, Dickens did not care to control his disgust.

In his *Life of Dickens*, Forster said one reason for the introduction of the American episode was that Dickens was moved to reopen in *Chuzzlewit* the disputes that had arisen out of *American Notes*—disputes, he said, that had stretched over most of the year—for none of the counterstatements, said Forster, had dislodged Dickens a square inch from his position regarding the United States. In fact, it may be said, as Forster does not, that the challenges that came with "every mail . . . from unsparing assailants" across the Atlantic "to make good his *Notes*"[15] only settled Dickens all the more in his view of the "Land of Liberty" and its sham "Freedom of Opinion." For, obviously, *Chuzzlewit* does not make good the *Notes*. If that was really Dickens' intention, the novelist was out to lunch. The palpable fact is that *Chuzzlewit* makes worse the *Notes* by the grotesque distortion of Dickens' satire and caricature and outright abuse. This fact was lost on no one. The radical *Westminster Review* did not find it strange that a "vast continent like America . . . should . . . contain . . . slanderers and swindlers . . . considering how many have been sent from our own shores," but it did find it "strange . . . and new and unaccountable that such an observer as Mr. Dickens, travelling from Dan to Beersheba, should find all barren of goodness, and discover no other facts worth signalizing in a country, the rapid growth of which is without a parallel, than the knaveries of land-jobbers, and the abuses of a press conducted often by English editors."[16] The Tory *Monthly Review* sensed how "thoroughly disgusted" Dickens must have been "with his experience of that land of enlightened liberty—America!"—so disgusted that he "could not suffer this opportunity [the writing of *Chuzzlewit*] to pass without showering his heavy sarcasm at their hollow pretensions and professions." [17]

Another reason that Forster offered for Dickens' introducing the American episode had to do with the sales of the monthly numbers of *Chuzzlewit*, though Forster said this reason was of less importance to Boz than the first. Where *Pickwick* and *Nickleby* had sold their forty and fifty thousand copies of each monthly number, and *Master Humphrey's Clock* (Dickens' magazine containing the serialized *Old Curiosity Shop* followed by the serialized *Barnaby Rudge*) had sold a record sixty and seventy thousand *weekly* copies, *Chuzzlewit* was selling only twenty thousand *monthly* copies. The rationale for interpolating the American episode, though in Forster's judgment the novel "lost as a story," was to increase sales, something it achieved, however, by only a few thousand additional purchasers at best. This was a discouraging turn of events for Dickens, especially as *Chuzzlewit* was his most ambitious undertaking to date. But Dickens in introducing the American episode only compounded the mistake of *American Notes*, the mistake, if sales were among his concerns, of further dispelling readers' illusions about himself; and this miscalculation seriously affected even the sales of his next book, *A Christmas Carol*, though in the long run it proved his most popular.

Prior to the publication of *American Notes*, Boz had become, even to his odd *nom de plume*, one of his own fictional characters as it were, part and parcel of the very world he was creating—or so it seemed to a great many of his readers. But with the *Notes* he stepped out of that world, no longer the spellbinder but the breaker of spells, not the man of generous sympathy but the ungrateful critic of the American Republic whose spleen seemed roused by frustrated self-interest in the copyright question. While the mistake of *American Notes* would have been forgiven him in time, the second and ranker one willfully committed in *Martin Chuzzlewit* could not. That mistake, which George Orwell called "the only grossly unfair piece of satire in Dickens' works," as it was the only time "he attacked a race or community as a whole," [18] endeared him to very few Americans or Englishmen.

Forster's observations aside, the plain truth seems to be that Dickens felt compelled to rid himself of his feeling of outrage by outraging those who had incensed him, a process that converted his sense of violation into creative energy. Much as at times he found it difficult to write the American episode—he said it took him "at least twice as long, every line of it, as the ordinary curent [of the English episode]" [19]—he acknowledged: "I have nearly killed myself with laughing at what I have done of the American No." (Chapters 21 and 22 featuring the Watertoast Association and Martin's lionization). [20] Indeed, the evident pleasure he took in laying on the lash can be matched nowhere in his work. Had Dickens been let alone, his feeling of outrage might have subsided, for he said, some months before visiting America, that he had no desire to press the Americans into his service. "In my next fiction," he wrote, "and in all others I hope, I shall stand staunchly by [John] Bull," though he conceded that he might "write an account of my trip," something he considered "another matter."[21] But even when he was comfortably back in London, his "unsparing assailants" from across the ocean, as Forster called them, followed him into his home in the form of newspaper clippings and letters, whether in anger over his circular, or the letter forged in his name, or *American Notes*, or the articles attributed to him in the *Foreign Quarterly Review*. In one day alone Dickens was obliged to thank John Jay, Lewis Gaylord Clark, and Cornelius Felton for their letters *and* their clippings about only one such item, the forged letter.[22] Clark in his *Knickerbocker Magazine* even had to urge correspondents to stop sending him "newspapers addressed to our care for 'Mr. Charles Dickens, London,' wherein, we may assume, his 'Notes' were 'essentially used up.'" Besides, he added, Dickens had informed him that the "innumerable newspapers" sent to him across the Atlantic go back to the post office if there is anything to pay, or unopened into the fire.[23]

But there was violation of a more serious kind, a kind that, as Dickens said in another context, gave him the "vague desire to take somebody by the throat."

William Charles Macready, who, with the death of Edmund Kean in 1833, had become the greatest actor of his age, was Dickens' dearest friend. From the time they met in 1837 until Dickens' death in 1870, they had the deepest concern and tenderest consideration for each other. Dickens could fly into a rage at Forster for "his usual want of tact" and order him out of the house,[24] and Macready could quarrel with just about everyone, he was so irritable and morbid; but for each other they showed unfailing and unconditional regard. When Dickens, about to embark for America, came to take leave of his friend, he said "there was no one whom he felt such pain in saying good-bye to."[25] Macready for his part said, "My heart was quite full; it is much to me to lose the presence of a friend who really loves me."[26] When Dickens became disillusioned with America, he wrote letters to Macready, the intent of which was to rid the actor of the idea of settling in America, for Macready had developed an attachment for the States ever since he had made a successful theatrical tour there in 1826–27. "You live here, Macready . . . !" Dickens incredulously exclaimed in one such letter from America. "Loving you with all my heart and soul, and knowing what your disposition really is, I would not condemn you [even] to a year's residence on this side of the Atlantic, for any money."[27] And when Dickens returned at last to

London and had "expended" himself, as he said, upon his children, he flew off to Macready's house. Macready, in recording the reunion, said, "I was lying on the sofa when a person entered abruptly. . . . Who was it but dear Dickens holding me in his arms in a transport of joy. God bless him!"[28]

In March 1843 Edmund Simpson, owner of the Park Theatre in New York, where Dickens had been feted only a year earlier, was in London and persuaded Macready to do another tour of the United States. As the time for departure arrived, Dickens made plans with Forster and Daniel Maclise to go "aboard the Cunard Steamer at Liverpool, to bid Macready good bye, and bring his wife away."[29] But no sooner had Dickens made these plans than he began to have "great doubts" about accompanying Macready "on board the Steamer" at all, for, as he told the actor, it "will be crowded with Americans at this season of the year" and their being seen together, especially "after the last Chuzzlewit [number]," will be FATAL to your success, and certain to bring down upon you every species of insult and outrage."[30]

Dickens had grounds for his apprehensions. He had only recently received a letter from an American which convinced him that *Martin Chuzzlewit* "has made them all stark staring raving mad across the water."[31] James Gordon Bennett, in one of his travel letters from London, dated 1 September 1843 and published in the *Herald* on the twenty-third, also reflected the American reaction, though he confessed to deriving a perverse satisfaction from "another number of Chuzzlewit" for its "cutting up and satirizing, under feigned names, all those fools, both male and female, who crowded . . . [Dickens'] *levées* during his . . . visit to New York. I have enjoyed it very much—nor do I care how much he cuts and carves up the fools who paid court to him as they did. I hope this number will be published extensively [in the States]." Moreover, on the very morning that Dickens had qualms about boarding the steamer with Macready, he received a letter from Captain Marryat imploring him "not even to go to Liverpool," let alone board the steamer. This plea Dickens conveyed to Macready, adding, since he knew his friend considered him morbid on the subject of America, "when a man who knows the . . . [United States] confirms me in my fears, I am as morally certain of their foundation in Truth and freedom from exaggeration, as I am that I live."[32] In the letter in which he conveyed this intelligence, Dickens urged Macready to champion him in no way while abroad; abjured him, indeed, to address not so much as an envelope to him, but to enclose letters to him in those addressed to mutual London friends; and he ended by saying that he wished to heaven he could "un-dedicate Nickleby" until his friend came home again. Dickens wanted no linkage made between Macready and himself "lest," as he told his best American friend, Professor Cornelius Felton of Harvard, the Americans "injure him; for I know how many head of vermin would eat into his heart if they could, that they might void their hatred even second-hand, upon a man I prized." (The slip into the past tense of *prize* indicates how vivid was Dickens' imagination, as if Macready had already suffered death at the hands of Americans.) For the same reason Dickens told Felton he would not consent to write a single letter of introduction for Macready, not even to Felton himself.[33]

Dickens had good reason to want to keep his association with Macready from becoming common knowledge, for, as the London *Monthly Review* "guessed," the American chapters of *Chuzzlewit* will make the Americans "'rile up pretty considerably smart;' and many a 'dander' is at this time 'riz' never to be cooled, till a complete vengeance on the 'Britishers' has been obtained."[34] Macready himself remarked in his diary: "Read the number of Chuzzlewit's landing in America, *which I do not like*. It will not do Dickens good, and I grieve over it."[35] And only three days before he left Liverpool for the United States, the actor noted: "Read the number of *Chuzzlewit*, . . . as bitter as it is powerful, and against whom is this directed? 'Against the Americans,' is the answer. Against how many of them? How many answer to his description? I am grieved to read the book."[36] Nonetheless, despite Dickens' injunction, Macready on the eve of his debut at the Park Theatre in therole of Macbeth, "defended and explained as I best could [Dickens'] . . . morbid feeling about the States" to a man who had observed that "Dickens . . . must have been ungrateful [for his American reception] and therefore a bad man."[37] Too, in a burlesque called *The Macbeth Travestie*, which opened in New York's Olympia Theatre while Macready was still playing the Park, and in which William Mitchell "performed . . . in imitation of Macready," a *Chuzzlewit* number was cast into the witches' cauldron, to the great delight of the audience.[38]

There is no question that Americans found the American episode obscene and shocking from beginning to end. Thurlow Weed, a New York boss of the Whig Party, had agreed to write travel letters for the *New York Tribune* while abroad. Arriving in London, he naturally wanted to meet Dickens and made arrangements to do so; but when he read the first American number of *Chuzzlewit*, just out, he "indefinitely postponed" his visit. As he reported from London in a letter datelined 12 July and featured on the front page of the *Tribune*:

> I was about to call on "Boz" the day after my arrival in London, with a friend who is well acquainted with him, but delayed the call at the suggestion of Bishop HUGHES, who . . . advise[d] me to read the last number of "Martin Chuzzlewit" before I made my call. Having read that number, it is scarcely necessary to say that the call was indefinitely postponed. Was ever such malice or ribaldry perpetrated? Dickens has actually out-Trolloped [Isaac] Fidler [*Observations on Professions, Literature, Manners, and Emigration in the United*

States, Made During a Residence There in 1833] and [Basil] Hall [*Travels in North America in the Years 1827 and 1828*]. . . . And all this tirade, the grossness of which is only equaled by its stupidity, blurted forth because the American Congress did not think proper to pass an inter-national law of copy-right for an Author who, with idiotic arrogance, made the mercenary object of his visit the principal topic of a speech delivered at Boston immediately after his arrival.[39]

By the eve of Macready's departure to New York, Dickens had become all the more convinced he had done the right thing in deciding not to escort his friend to the steamer. He rehearsed the situation for Angela Burdett Coutts, his heiress friend, whom he would choose as the dedicatee of *Martin Chuzzlewit*:

All of a sudden it occurred to me the other day that if I went to Liverpool with Macready they would bowstring his throat in New York; so tightly that not a word should come out of it upon the stage—and drive him out of the country, straightway. While I was deliberating whether this was probable . . . the Postman brought me a note from Marryatt [*sic*], adjuring me not to go, or Macready was "done for." As he knows the virtuous Americans pretty well and as I think I do too, I immediately abandoned my intention. And so it came to pass that I sat down to Chuzzlewit quietly, and am now in the heart of it.[40]

It would be aesthetically satisfying, but suspiciously symmetrical with Macready's departure to the States, to suppose that Dickens was "in the heart" of Chapter 23, in which his English travelers are "en route to Eden," that region near Cairo, Illinois, where Martin almost meets his death. But far more likely Dickens was at the time in the heart of Chapters 24–26, parts of the English episode. Nevertheless, Dickens had been anxious for months because of his friend's plan to play the States. In his letter to Macready of 1 September, he had written that Marryat "gives expression . . . to every misgiving that has haunted me for months past." Fearful for the actor, he seems to have had dark previsions of Macready's being en route to Eden, and, by no very complicated trick of imagination, to have projected his nightmarish vision upon his characters Martin and Mark. Indeed, Macready's resolution to tour the States and Dickens' growing apprehensions for his friend seem to have precipitated the American episode in the first place. Macready first began "to think seriously" of touring America on 15 January 1843, and by 19 March had resolved once and for all to go.[41] The announcement that Martin would go to America was made in Chapter 12, at the close of the May number, which Dickens had probably begun by 22 March. Martin and Mark actually proceed to America in Chapter 15, a chapter which Dickens finished by the end of April.[42]

If Dickens' forebodings precipitated the American episode, his anxiety for

Macready while the actor was abroad seems to have induced him to terminate the American episode entirely. Anticipating that further American numbers might jeopardize his friend still more, especially if the fact of their friendship became common knowledge, he abandoned Martin and Mark in Eden at the end of Chapter 23 and did not return to them until Chapter 33, the last chapter having anything to do with America, since they were back in England at the outset of Chapter 34.

Did Dickens, not to say Marryat, have exaggerated fears that his friendship might prove dangerous to Macready? Not if an item in the London *Theatrical Journal* of 11 November 1843 written by someone calling himself "An Eye-Witness" can be believed. For "Eye-Witness" had written: "When it became known in New York that Macready was about to make his appearance, a certain lot of critics, indeed the greater portion of them, worked might and main to prejudice the play-going public against him . . . ; indeed, one paper recommended, that as Macready was a friend of Dickens, they should give him a reception accordingly."

Dickens' apprehensions for Macready, however, were precognitive: they were not wrong; they were only premature. For as it turned out, every foreboding Dickens had expressed to Miss Coutts came to pass when Macready made his third theatrical tour of America in 1848–49. Macready *was* identified then as "one of the Dickens' clique"; his throat *was* bowstrung in New York so that not a word he said on stage was heard; and he *was* driven "out of the country, straightway." For two riots, whose sole purpose was the mobbing of Macready, occurred while the actor was playing the Astor Place Theatre in May 1849.[43]

The need to vent the outrage caused by his experience with Americans and exacerbated by premonitory visions of Macready in the States was not Dickens' only motivation for sending Martin and Mark to America. He had another, rather diabolical one: to foil the American book pirates. Dickens knew for a certainty that, despite the bad press of *American Notes*, *Chuzzlewit* would be reprinted in America: every one of his books had been. As he wrote to Longfellow: "I have been blazing away at my new book, whereof the first Number will probably be published under the black flag [of the American pirates] almost as soon as you receive this."[44] Naturally, the news promptly reached Dickens that the same publishers who had reprinted the *Notes* were at it again, hotly competing in selling their *Chuzzlewits*, the one "by Harpers [going] at 3 cents p[e]r No.," as Longfellow informed Forster on 28 February.[45] It seems to have occurred to Dickens that there was yet a way to strike back at the book pirates, even if he had grown hopeless about protecting his literary property in America. That way was to take them by surprise: to interpolate suddenly episodes so offensive to Americans—publishers, booksellers, and readers alike—that one or another of the installments would force the "Robbers" to halt their piracy in mid-career and prevent their republication of the serial, upon its completion, as a book. The idea of getting his own back, if only for the hoax of the forged letter, had its appeal. And if the hoax did not halt the piracies of *Chuzzlewit*, so much the worse for Americans, as he would ridicule and denounce them all the more —to the point, indeed, where, abandoning his role as narrator, he would declaim:

> In their every word [a large class of Americans] avow themselves to be . . . senseless to the high principles on which America sprang, a nation, into life. . . . Who are no more capable of feeling, or of caring if they did feel, that by reducing their own country to the ebb of honest men's contempt, they put in hazard the rights of nations yet unborn, and very progress of the human race, than are the swine who wallow in their streets. Who think that crying out to other nations, old in their iniquity, "We are no worse than you!" (No worse!) is high defence and 'vantage-ground enough for that Republic, but yesterday let loose upon her noble course, and but to-day so maimed and lame, so full of sores and ulcers, foul to the eye and almost hopeless to the sense, that her best friends turn from the loathsome creature with disgust.

But that was yet to come. The *New World*, which began reprinting the *Chuzzlewit* numbers at once, announced on 6 May that the novel was "unquestionably, so far as it has gone, the very best of this admirable novelist's productions." *Brother Jonathan*, in launching its publication of *Chuzzlewit* on 18 February, dubbed Dickens "the prince of serials" and added: "The reception of Martin Chuzzlewit has abundantly shown how difficult it is to throw down a man of genius from his pedestal—even where he himself conspires for the downfall. The newspapers of this country have united against Dickens in an un-opposed crusade, and he himself, by a hasty and supercilious book of travels, has struck the severest blow at his own renown, but his new book finds his popularity as it was, and the belief in his genius and its resources undiminished." Other American responses to the early *Chuzzlewit* numbers were of a similar nature—pleasure that Boz, the most appealing of novelists, had displaced Dickens, the harshest of America's critics, and that he was once again creating a charmed world. Thus, when the steamship *Caledonia* docked at its wharf in East Boston on the evening of 17 July, bringing with it the first American number depicting Martin and Mark disembarking in New York, Boston editors realized they had sensational news on their hands and attempted to scoop each other even before they had a chance to read the installment. Relying on Willmer and Smith's *European News*, issued in Liverpool and sent regularly to subscribing editors, the

Boston Daily Evening Transcript and *Boston Daily Advertiser* carried substantially the same releases on 18 July. Amalgamated, their notices read: "A new number of 'Martin Chuzzlewit' [has arrived], . . . which a Liverpool paper says 'may excite anger, (we hope not), though it can hardly fail to provoke laughter in America. The author has quizzed the editors, the boarding houses, the abolitionists,—the colonels, majors, and captains of the militia,—the manners, characteristics and feelings of certain coteries—in his bitterest vein.'" In New York the next day, Greeley's *Tribune*, also drawing on Willmer and Smith's *European News*, reported that the "new number of *Chuzzlewit* is very abusive and savage in its ridicule of things American. It cannot fail, however, to provoke amusement."

Despite Willmer and Smith's early warning that Dickens had not put America altogether out of mind, nor had reverted entirely to his usual novelistic manner and matter, the bookaneers continued to reprint the *Chuzzlewit* numbers. In doing so, the editors of the piratical weeklies were forced, sooner or later, to do just what Dickens had falsely accused them of in his circular letter—of "coarsely and insolently attacking the author of that very book" they were serializing "and heaping scurrility and slander upon his head." At first, John Neal in his *Brother Jonathan* sought to turn "Boz's view of America" to commercial advantage. Thus, in reprinting the initial chapter of the first American number on 22 July, he said: "Boz's view of America, as exhibited in the present number . . . will be read with great interest. He has broken new ground, and made it his own. Although written in a vein of ridicule, it is really so broad that no one can take offence at the caricature, and it cannot fail to provoke a great deal of amusement." But on 29 July, in reprinting the second chapter of the American number, Neal was no longer amused. He attributed Dickens' "infuriate malice" to his failure to secure a copyright agreement, the "most promising scheme for scraping [dollars] . . . together, ever presented to [Boz's] . . . imagination." As editor of *Brother Jonathan*, however, Neal could ill afford to turn off readers, and he added that he would continue to reprint the serial to satisfy the "raging fever of curiosity" concerning "Martin's adventures among us": "In the mean time there is no occasion to work ourselves into a passion with Chuzzlewit and its author, as we are sorry to see many editors of the daily press have thought it necessary and proper to do for their individual selves, and on the part of their readers." Neal, unwilling to give up reprinting the American numbers but having to save face, returned to the subject on 14 October under the head "MORE CHUZZLEWIT":

Really now, if Mr. Charles Dickens . . . doesn't mend his manners . . . and give us . . . a better pennyworth for our trouble in reading him, than [is found] in . . . these last few chapters—would they were his last! we say . . . if he doesn't change . . . there's an end of Charles Dickens . . . and the sooner he hangs up his fiddle, and himself with it, or jumps into the New River, the better it will be . . .

What! after coming three thousand miles to judge for himself; after being feasted, and fed, and painted, and sculptured—and scalped—and mobbed— . . . after such a tremendous flourish of trumpets over land and sea—to put into the mouths of *American* Editors, of *American* Politicans, of *American* speculators, and of *American* backwoodsmen, the very language he had before appropriated to *English* Editors, *English* Politicans, *English* speculators, and *English* humorists!

. . . . We think he is unpardonable. If he has no shame, no remorse, no "compunctious visitings" on his own account—surely he might have some on account of his American worshippers. Why doesn't he manage to die decently— to keep up appearances a while longer, though he burst!

During the course of writing this diatribe, Neal began to see Dickens' "joke": "But perhaps—and now, we think of it, we wonder it never entered our heads before—perhaps the gentleman is only playing a trick with us, and avenging himself upon our American publishers . . . for their filching propensities. If so—we have nothing more to say. If he hasn't made them ashamed of themselves—and of him—we give up."

That Dickens had introduced the American chapters in order to trick the book pirates was a revelation that also occurred to Henry Chorley. Chorley had the advantage of Neal in that he was reviewing, not monthly *Chuzzlewits* in wrappers, but the entire *Chuzzlewit* in covers; moreover, he was privy to London literary gossip concerning the novel. In the London *Athenæum* he said: "We imagine, indeed, that we can see a special reason, in the piratical reprint of the work [in America], both for the introduction [of the American episode] and for the time when and where introduced." The point Dickens had gained by this maneuver, however, was, he added, "temporary, the injury [to the novel] permanent."[46]

Given the unexpected turn in Martin's adventures, Park Benjamin also altered his view of Dickens whom, a few months earlier, he had called an admirable novelist. In his *New World* of 5 August he wrote:

Mr. Dickens, whatever may be his merits as a writer, is, as will readily be admitted by those who have been most in his society, a low-bred vulgar man. If any one entertain doubts upon this subject, they will be entirely removed by reading the last chapter of his work now in course of publication. There is an in[n]ate vulgarity in his mind and manners—in his very nature—an odor of the Minories and Bow Bells, which a residence of fifty years west of Temple Bar will never deprive him of. He is as unlike a polished, well-bred English gentleman, as a Pawnee Indian.

Becoming as embarrassed as his editorial brethren at reprinting the *Chuzzlewit* numbers, Benjamin on 16 January 1844 blasted Dickens in three full pages of his oversized *New World*. In the course of his denunciation, he reached the same conclusion as had Neal and Chorley, though he expressed it with less explicitness, perhaps because he did not wish to give Dickens full marks for outwitting him. He said that if Boz did not want Americans to read his works, inasmuch as they were not copyrightable in the United States and could yield him no profits, he should "proceed as he is now doing . . . simply by making them—as, in the case of 'Martin Chuzzlewit'—*not worth reading!*"

Dickens obviously succeeded in discomfiting the reprinters, and the *New World* in its advertisements in 1844 began to offer free *Chuzzlewits* to "subscribers and purchasers" of its spin-off, the monthly *Repository of English Romance*, under such heads as "CHUZZLEWIT GIVEN AWAY!!!" and "AH HA! AH HA! DICKENS FOR NOTHING." For Dickens' satire, as it was not without truth, had the cut of a lash. Indeed, from time to time newspaper items seemed to out-*Chuzzlewit Chuzzlewit* in grotesqueness, as in an item featured in the New Orleans *Daily Picayune* on 13 February 1844:

> They have little towns "Out West" . . . overlooked by Dickens. . . . In one day they recently had two street fights, hung a man, rode three out of town on a rail, got up a quarter race, a turkey shooting, a gander pulling, a match dog fight, had preaching by a Methodist circuit rider, who afterwards ran a foot-race for drinks "all round;" and if this was not enough, the judge of the court, after losing a year's salary at single-handed poker and whipping a person who said he didn't know the game, went out and helped Lynch a man for hog-stealing.

Yet, however discombobulated the pirates became at being Dickens' unwilling accomplices in purveying his bitter pictures of American life, they did not, the economic motive being so compelling, discontinue publication of the serial, though they self-righteously turned on Dickens, less for writing the American numbers than for putting them in the humiliating position of having their mercenary motives conspicuously exposed.

Dickens, who must have assumed that the pirates would discontinue publication of the *Chuzzlewit* numbers, began to be somewhat alarmed at the fierce reactions he was arousing and asked Forster: "Don't you think the time has come when I ought to state that such public entertainments as I received in the States were either accepted before I went out, or in the first week after my arrival there; and that as soon as I began to have any acquaintance with the country, I set my face against any public recognition whatever but that which was forced upon me to the destruction of my peace and comfort—and made no secret of my real sentiments."[47] But Forster did not agree with Dickens' proposal "and the notion was abandoned,"[48] perhaps because it was a suitable explanation for the spirit of *American Notes* but not for the animus of *Martin Chuzzlewit*, an animus that impelled Dickens to exhibit

Americans as Yahoos and that, reinforced by the ferocity of their reactions, not to say his own need for narrative consistency, compelled him to continue exhibiting them as Yahoos. At all events, given his vanity, he was not be faced down. Judging from Elizabeth Barrett's remarks to Mary Russell Mitford, the explanation would not have served anyway. "No—" Miss Barrett said in protesting her friend's charge: "I do not think with you about . . . Dickens—nor did I ever hear of anything unbecoming or undignified in his manner of receiving last year the American vows of allegiance and admiration. . . . As to his conduct in America, how would you blame it? How could he help being worshipped, if people chose to worship him . . . ? But it is his conduct *since*, which has used all this honor to dishonor himself—he is an ungrateful, an ungrateful man!"[49]

If it was Dickens' intention to humiliate the American reprinters of *Chuzzlewit* by exposing their greed—a greed that led them to purvey his Swiftian vignettes of Americans—he was successful, though few recognized his success. If, too, it was Dickens' intention to make the charge in his circular letter come true—that American newspaper editors slander authors whose works they reprint—he was also successful. But if, in addition, it was his intention to force the pirates to cease reprinting *Chuzzlewit*, he failed. For Harpers and *Brother Jonathan* and the *New World* and Lea & Blanchard, not to mention such newspapers as the *Pennsylvania Inquirer and National Gazette*, continued to run the serial. *Brother Jonathan*, to be sure, discontinued publishing *Chuzzlewit*, but only because, bought up by the *New World*, it ceased publication altogether with the 23 December 1843 number.

If Dickens assumed that his satire of America, growing wilder with every addition to the American episode, would become too unpopular to reprint, he was mistaken. *Chuzzlewit* was indeed unpopular in the United States—to the point, in fact, of being considered a libel on a people and a nation; but, profits being involved, the notoriety of the work had no palpable effect upon any of its publishers. In fact, it was *Chuzzlewit*'s very notoriety that made the work in serial and book form so very saleable in the United States. Yet, though Dickens failed to stop the pirates from reprinting *Chuzzlewit*, he had, no doubt, the satisfaction, if mixed with some alarm, of hearing them squirm at becoming the unhappy purveyors of his pictures of ugly Americans—Americans who had graveled him with their "democratic" manners, who had libeled him for exercising freedom of speech in *American Notes*, who had forged a letter in his name, who had savaged him for the articles in the *Foreign Quarterly Review*, and who, to top it off, had made the simple act of saying good-bye to his friend Macready seem as charged with doom as the gesture of an executioner.[50]

NOTES

1. *The Letters of Charles Dickens*, ed. Madeline House et al. (Oxford: Clarendon Press, 1965–   ), 3:43; hereafter cited as the Pilgrim Edition.

2. Pilgrim Edition, 3:83.

3. Pilgrim Edition, 3:90.

4. Pilgrim Edition, 3:156.

5. Pilgrim Edition, 3:76–77.

6. Among these were "The Newspaper Literature of America," 30 (October 1842): 197–222; "The Answer of the American Press," 31 (April 1843): 250–81; and "American Poetry," 32 (January 1844): 291–324.

7. This circular letter is reproduced in facsimile in Peter Bracher's "Harper & Brothers: Publishers of Dickens," *Bulletin of the New York Public Library*, 79 (Spring 1976): 316–17, and is printed in Pilgrim Edition, 3:256–59.

8. The forged letter, together with what is presumed to be Whitman's introduction, appears in Pilgrim Edition, 3:625–27.

9. Arthur Waugh, *A Hundred Years of Publishing: Being the Story of Chapman & Hall, Ltd.* (London: Chapman & Hall, 1930), p. 57. Robert Patten put the £350 figure somewhat lower, at £330, in his report published in the *Dickens Studies Newsletter*, 8 (March 1977): 3.

10. Pilgrim Edition, 3:405, 274, respectively.

11. Pilgrim Edition, 3:466.

12. *The Life of Charles Dickens*, ed. A. J. Hoppé (London: J. M. Dent & Sons, 1966), 1:285.

13. *Athenæum*, no. 873 (20 July 1844): 665.

14. *North British Review*, 3 (May 1845): 74.

15. Forster, *Life of Dickens*, 2:50–51, 64.

16. *Westminster Review*, 40 (December 1843): 458.

17. *Monthly Review*, 3 (September 1844): 146.

18. *New York Times Book Review*, 15 May 1949, p. 1.

19. Pilgrim Edition, 3:501.

20. Pilgrim Edition, 3:540.

21. Pilgrim Edition, 2:405.

22. Pilgrim Edition, 3:314–15.

23. *Knickerbocker*, 21 (June 1843): 592. Dickens' letter to Clark appears in the Pilgrim Edition, 3:450–51.

24. *The Diaries of William Charles Macready, 1833–1851*, ed. William Toynbee (London: Chapman & Hall, 1912), 2:74.

25. Quoted by Macready, *Diaries*, 2:153.

26. Macready, *Diaries*, 2:153.

27. Pilgrim Edition, 3:156–57.

28. Macready, *Diaries*, 2:178.

29. Pilgrim Edition, 3:548.

30. Pilgrim Edition, 3:551.

31. Pilgrim Edition, 3:541.

32. Pilgrim Edition, 3:552.

33. Pilgrim Edition, 3:549.

34. *Monthly Review*, 3 (September 1844): 146.

35. Macready, *Diaries*, 2:215.

36. Macready, *Diaries*, 2:218–19.

37. Macready, *Diaries*, 2:224.

38. Nathaniel P. Willis reported the imitation of Macready in the *New Mirror*, 2 (28 October 1843): 63. George C. D. Odell, in *Annals of the New York Stage* (New York: Columbia University Press, 1928–45), noted that the travesty ran for nine successive nights (5:45, 47). The story concerning *Chuzzlewit*, if indeed it was *Chuzzlewit* and not *American Notes*, seems to have been first told by Frederic G. Kitton, *The Novels of Charles Dickens: A Bibliography and Sketch* (London E. Stock, 1897), p. 90; however, I have found no contemporary reference to this event.

39. "Letters from Mr. Weed . . . No. IX," *New York Daily Tribune*, 16 August 1843, [p. 1].

40. Pilgrim Edition, 3:553–54.

41. Macready, *Diaries*, 2:192, 198.

42. Pilgrim Edition, 3:466n5.

43. See Macready, *Diaries*, 2:406, 412, 422–29, and Richard Moody, *The Astor Place Riot* (Bloomington: Indiana University Press, 1958).

44. Pilgrim Edition, 3:407.

45. *The Letters of Henry Wadsworth Longfellow*, ed. Andrew Hilen, 6 vols. (Cambridge: Belknap Press of Harvard University Press, 1966–82), 2:509.

46. *Athenæum*, no. 873 (20 July 1844): 665.

47. Pilgrim Edition, 3:542.

48. Forster, *Life of Dickens*, 1:293.

49. *Elizabeth Barrett to Miss Mitford*, ed. Betty Miller (New Haven: Yale University Press, 1954), p. 198.

50. Anticipating Macready's return from America, Dickens wrote to the actor: "Damn them [the Americans], I can't damage you by coming with open arms to Liverpool (for you won't be going back again in a hurry . . .)" (Pilgrim Edition, 4:12).

This article is from the forthcoming *Charles Dickens' Quarrel with America* (Whitston).

Univ. of Virginia Press

EDGAR ALLAN POE AND JOHN G. CHAPMAN: THEIR TREATMENT
OF THE DISMAL SWAMP AND THE WISSAHICKON

Burton R. Pollin

IN TWO OF THE CREATIVE WORKS OF POE there is a link with the art work of John Gadsby Chapman which justifies a fuller presentation of the material and its significance than has yet been accorded. The earlier piece, "The Philosophy of Furniture," raises interesting questions about Poe's sense of decoration and art and evokes possibilities of information and association going back to his childhood and to an important early poem, "The Lake." The second work—a charming riverscape set in Philadelphia— involves a search for the source of his inspiration, the meaning of details and of terms in his text, and the importance of the connection between the story and its illustration by Chapman in the gift book which printed it.

Very reasonably considered by the late T. O. Mabbott as a kind of narrative, "The Philosophy of Furniture" appeared first in the May 1840 *Burton's Gentleman's Magazine* and next, revised, as "House Furniture" in the 3 May 1845 *Broadway Journal*.[1] It provides insight into Poe's curiously opulent and *dilletantesque* (to use his own coinage) views of house decoration—views which help to explain his choice of a Chapman picture. In "The Philosophy of Furniture," Poe first disparages the "philosophy" or taste of Americans in the decoration of their homes, chiefly because of the confusion between cost and quality or "magnificence" and "beauty," springing from the absence of a tasteful aristocracy. For our lack of harmony in decorating, he instances our misuse of either straight or curved lines and our ill-matched curtains, carpets, mirrors, lamps, and furniture. An ideal "small" drawing-room (thirty by twenty-five feet) would have two windows of crimson glass, silver curtains of a light tissue cloth, heavy crimson drapes, rosewood couches with crimson, gold-figured silk, a red carpet with a raised goldcord motif, and wallpaper of silver gray with small deep red Arabesque designs on which pictures are to be placed thus: "Many paintings relieve the expanse of the paper. These are chiefly landscapes of an imaginative cast, such as the fairy grottoes of Stanfield, or the Lake of the Dismal Swamp of our own Chapman. The tone of each is warm but dark—there are no brilliant effects. Not one of the pictures is of small size. Diminutive paintings give that *spotty* look to a room which is the blemish of so many a fine work of art overtouched" (6:245). In the *Broadway Journal* (1845) this passage is changed to the following: "Many paintings . . . cast—such as the fairy grottoes of Stanfield, or the lake of the Dismal Swamp, of Chapman. There are, nevertheless, three or four female heads, of an ethereal beauty—portraits in the manner of Sully. The tone of each picture is warm, but dark. There are no 'brilliant effects.' *Repose* speaks in all. Not one is of small size. Diminutive . . . Art overtouched."[2] Poe has obviously carefully worked over the passage, although it is not clear how the "tone . . . warm but dark" is to be assimilated to the newly added "portraits in the manner of Sully." Clearly in the first version both the landscapes of Stanfield and of Chapman are "imaginative" or nonrealistic, but of vastly different atmosphere—one being happy and charming, the other mournful and grotesque, as we shall see. Note also the loss of the possessive pronoun in "our Chapman," which differentiates him from the British artist, perhaps because the increasing fame of Chapman in the intervening five years made such identification less necessary.

There is little to be said on the subject of the "fairy grottoes" of Stanfield in view of the fact that Clarkson Stanfield (1798–1867) was a well known marine and landscape painter of England; his training came via his painting theatrical scenery, and later Ruskin called him "the leader of the English realists" and "incomparably the noblest master of cloud-form"—no small praise from Turner's friend and advocate.[3] Of the many titles of his works listed there is nothing suggesting "fairy grottoes" unless it be a picture seen in one of the many annuals to which Stanfield contributed. Mabbott, in glossing Poe's reference, mentions that "his illustration of *Comus* in the Summer House at Buckingham Palace was famous."[4] Equally puzzling is Poe's reference to Stanfield in the first version of "The Landscape Garden" in October 1842, and subsequently removed from the *Broadway Journal* reprinting of 20 September 1845; he writes of him thus: "No such combinations of scenery exist in Nature as the painter of genius has in his power to produce. No such Paradises are to be found in reality as have glowed upon the canvass of Claude, or Poussin or Stanfield" (*Tales*, p. 707). Of the three names only Claude's remained later. Surely Ruskin's tribute and the list of his works make exceptional in Stanfield's work the "Paradisial" landscapes that Poe must have seen some place, in reproduction. But it is surely the contrast of the magical and charming versus the grim and melancholy that Poe is seeking in his two scenes for the walls of his drawing-room.

Even in 1839 the reputation of John Gadsby Chapman was distinguished enough for Poe to "use" one of his many exhibited paintings for the wall of his model room; but why was it this particular picture? With no clue from Poe himself we must surmise a complex of motivational factors. Mabbott, following Robert Morrison, assumes that Poe had personally visited the "Lake" involved, that is Drummond's Pond or Lake Drummond, located in the midst of the Virginia portion of the Great Dismal Swamp, which extends into North Carolina. The evidence is said to be the similarity of details in Poe's poem, "The Lake," in its early form as included in *Tamerlane* (1827) and *Al Aaraaf* (1829) and incorporated, much altered, in the 1831 version of "Tamerlane" (see *Poems*, pp. 47–48, 83–85). I find the autobiographical aspect a bit questionable, since we know of no visits by the Allans while Poe lived with them to such an unlikely "vacation place," over one hundred miles from Richmond while the "facts" proving Poe's personal acquaintance with the area need considerable rationalization to accord with the argument. Poe speaks of a lonely "wild lake, with black rock bound, / And the tall trees that tower'd around." He says: "Death was in that wave" and later refers to "that dim lake."[5] Now Mabbott grants that "that strange body of water is not really rockbound, but the driftwood on its shores, when wet, looks like black rock, and the water was believed to be poisonous. . . . No other lake Poe is likely to have known, so closely fitting his description, has been discovered by commentators" (*Poems*, p. 83). Morrison certainly visited the lake itself and thought he found the proof in the appearance of the lake in reality and in the poem. The line, "Death was in that poison'd wave," he says, proves that Poe knew the legend; this was also exploited by Thomas Moore in his celebrated poem, "A Ballad. The Lake of the Dismal Swamp. Written at Norfolk, in Virginia," in 1803. It was this ballad, incidentally, which gave a literary life to the Dismal Swamp, one historian of the region has said.[6] But does Moore's poem really prove the legend about the poisoned water, as Morrison claims? The "Ballad" has this summarizing headnote:

They tell of a young man, who lost his mind upon the death of a girl he loved, and, suddenly disappearing . . . was never afterwards heard of. As he had frequently said, in his ravings, that the girl was not dead, but gone to the Dismal Swamp, it is supposed he had wandered into that dreary wilderness, and had died of hunger, or been lost in some of its dreadful morasses. (*Anon.*):

Away to the Dismal Swamp he speeds—
. . . .
And, when on the earth he sunk to sleep,
. . . .
He lay, where the deadly vine doth weep
Its venomous tear and nightly steep
The flesh with blistering dew![7]

He also speaks of "the dusky Lake" and of "the dim shore." But this is a very slender prop for the contention that Moore speaks of the "poisonous" water; the plant blisters the young lover, and that is all. And we know that there are no "black rocks" on the shore, nor does Moore, who was certainly there, speak of any illusion of black driftwood resembling rocks. I conclude therefore that on the basis of general ambiance and the rather commonplace "dim lake" phrase, Poe may have had the "Ballad" in mind, but not the actual lake itself. Hence there was no autobiographical motive in his alluding to Chapman's picture.

As a Virginian Poe certainly knew about the Great Dismal Swamp as well as about Chapman's celebrated picture of Lake Drummond. The lake and the swamp had been widely discussed for a long time because of the planned transformation of an almost inaccessible wilderness into a major shipping route and timber source, chiefly through the projected Dismal Swamp Canal. This may also account for Chapman's initial interest in exploiting the scene for his painting, as will be shown. (See Plate Three for a map of the area.) There is a very considerable literature on the Great Dismal Swamp of Virginia and North Carolina, in part because of the extensive picturesque area covered with its unique wild life and in part because of its importance to lumbering and to transportation through the canal system between Norfolk, Virginia, and Albemarle Sound, North Carolina. Its canal system managed to avoid a much longer coastal route of stormy and unsafe waters. It is noteworthy that it is not properly a swamp at all, for six good-sized rivers drain out of the lake, providing water which is pure and clear rather than "poisonous."[8] It was first described in 1728 by William Byrd, who saw its commercial potentialities. In the 1760s George Washington organized a company to construct the first canal and take out some of the timber, but the main waterway, begun only in 1793, required many more years for completion, in part because of the War of 1812. The full canal system was opened in 1829, with the federal government as part owner. From 1830 to the inception of the shorter Albemarle-Chesapeake Canal in 1859, a stream of barges, sloops, shingle boats, and steamboats carried cargoes and people through the canal system to the various ports in Virginia and North Carolina. Very early in its history, the travelers were served by the infamous Half Way House depicted by Thomas Williamson in a print that appeared on authorized currencies of several states from the 1830s to the 1840s. This popular 128-foot "House" was sited exactly on the boundary, near Lake Drummond, available for duels, elopements, and assignations (see Plate Four).[9]

The appearance of Lake Drummond was oddly altered through the construction of the canals and the feeder ditch; the water level was lowered about six feet so that the large cypresses had their bottle-like bases or gnarled knees exposed for several feet (see Plate Five).[10] This weird look must have

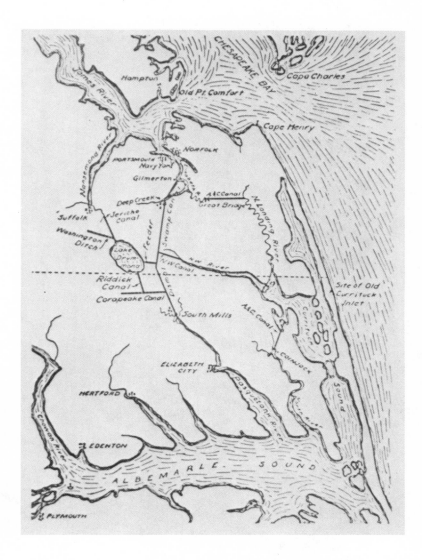

PLATE THREE
Map of the region served by the Dismal Swamp Canal, in Alexander Brown, *The Dismal Swamp Canal* (Chesapeake, Va.: Norfolk County Historical Society, 1970). *Courtesy Burton R. Pollin*

PLATE FOUR

Thomas Williamson's print of the "Half Way House" prepared for the 22 November 1830 *Norfolk Herald*, in J. F. Pugh, *The Hotel in the Great Dismal Swamp* (Old Trap, N.C.: J. F. Pugh, 1964), opposite p. 21.

Courtesy Burton R. Pollin

PLATE FIVE
Cypress trees in Lake Drummond, in Frederick Stansburg, *The Lake of the Dismal Swamp* (New York: Boni, 1925), p. 22.
Courtesy Burton R. Pollin

attracted the attention of Chapman, among other visitors, during the 1830s. The change may even have added a visual confirmation to the myths and superstitions which had always flourished in the region of the Swamp, as Moore's "Ballad" demonstrated. Certainly, Chapman's dripping Spanish moss, dead cypress stumps, rotting "drift" wood, arabesque, clutching branches, and carrion buzzard all provide a gripping Gothic ruin of a landscape (see Plate Six). One of the experts on the Swamp, after surveying the results of lumbering, draining, and canalizing, concluded that, despite all these threats and inroads, it is likely to remain basically unchanged, "as a foil . . . to material progress" and as a symbol of "romance and remoteness," just as it was to Chapman and to Poe in his "well-furnished" room.[11]

Poe's choice of a "painting" by John Gadsby Chapman bore witness to the artist's great popularity and contemporary fame, even though he has lapsed almost into oblivion among art students today. Chapman (1809–89) was born in Alexandria, Virginia, and dedicated himself to art from his earliest years. In 1827 he attended the Pennsylvania Academy of Fine Arts and then studied in Italy, devoted especially to the genre of historical scenes. Returning from abroad, in August 1831, he worked vigorously, exhibited his pictures at the major academies and held shows in Richmond and Washington, where he campaigned intensively for a commission to participate in decorating the Rotunda of the Capitol; he gained this objective late in the decade. Meanwhile, he traveled through Virginia, doing portraits, historical sites, and figures for a large portfolio which he bore to New York City in the fall of 1834. Here he found the publishers of books, periodicals, religious tracts, and literary annuals or gift books eager for his skill in illustration; by 1839 he had become the favorite artist for the subjects of etchings and engravings, some of which he himself executed for every variety of printed material, including commercially sold prints. He received numerous honors and became a mainstay of art circles. Inevitably, the Harper brothers' firm chose him for the *Illuminated and Pictorial Bible*, for which he executed early in the 1840s designs for over 1,400 wood engravings (published in 1845).[12] Between 1837 and 1840 he had done the enormous mural in the Capitol Rotunda, "The Baptism of Pocohontas," a Virginian theme, and yet, in New York City, he tirelessly worked on his sketches, easel paintings and portraits. His considerable skill, especially in illustration, led him to compose (1843–47) a manual *The American Drawing-Book*, richly illustrated, later expanded, revised, abridged, and repeatedly reprinted. In 1848 he left New York for a long sojourn in Rome, returning years later only to demonstrate his adherence to the Confederate cause. During his first fourteen years in New York City he became expert in depicting the scenes of the area, especially the harbor and the varied shores up the Hudson River. Chapman was indefatigable, prolific, versatile, and well patronized. Yet most of his larger original works seem to have disappeared, uncollected by museums and galleries. With our increasing interest in the Hudson River School and other contemporary Americans, we may eventually discover his paintings, including the original painting (probably an ink wash) of "The Lake of the Dismal Swamp."[13]

One wonders where Poe might have seen the original painting which he places on the wall of his ideal room, especially since he was not in New York City in 1836 for the exhibition at the National Academy of Design. It is likely that he saw only the engraving which was made by the highly skilled and well known artist James Smillie for the firm of Bancroft and Holley of New York. He may also have seen it in the *Magnolia of 1837* (probably issued at the end of 1836), an annual published by the same firm. Here it appears as the "plate" for a poem entitled "The War-Eagle of the Dismal Swamp, By the Author of 'Atlantis' and 'The Yemassee,'" that is, William Gilmore Simms. Apparently, the readers are supposed to convert the buzzard into an eagle in their imagination. From the *Magnolia* caption in the preliminary "List of Embellishments" Poe could have learned about the "original painting by J. G. Chapman, N. A."[14] But he probably derived it from the leading monthly of New York, the *Knickerbocker*, which he ready assiduously. Chapman's picture, engraved, appears as the frontispiece in the May 1839 issue (13:367; see Plate Six), with a pointed recommendation in the "Editor's Table" as follows:

> *The Engraving*, executed on steel, which accompanies the present number, will not escape the attention, nor fail, as we think, to elicit the admiration of the reader. The artists, to whose skill must be awarded the praise due to its production, are too well known to require praise at our hands. Although we do not promise, yet we have great pleasure in giving, such specimens of art to our readers; even while we rely upon excellence in other and more important respects, to maintain and enhance the reputation of the *Knickerbocker*. (13:466)

Poe may also have seen another instance of the "imaginative" and the "Gothic ruinous" style in the March 1839 issue, which uses Chapman's "Ruins of James Town" (opposite p. 179), engraved by J. A. Rolph (see Plate Seven), about which Joseph V. Ridgely says: "The sight of the ruined church tower at Jamestown was good for . . . columns of sentimental posturing."[15] In the "Editor's Table" this is underscored by an anonymous poem on "Jamestown" (pp. 274–76). Here Chapman has managed to turn the scene into a close imitation of a Hugo Robert classical landscape of desolation, perhaps also meriting Poe's term of "imaginative"—one of the undesignated pictures on the wall.

The rather decadent and faintly menacing atmosphere of the Chapman view of Lake Drummond accords entirely with Poe's general attitude toward

PLATE SIX
Engraving of J. G. Chapman's "The Lake of the Dismal Swamp" in the May 1839
Knickerbocker Magazine.
Courtesy Burton R. Pollin

PLATE SEVEN

Engraving of J. G. Chapman's "Ruins of James Town" in the March 1839 *Knicker-bocker Magazine.*
Courtesy Burton R. Pollin

lake scenery in his creative work, and this I have previously traced.[16] Very simply, the sea and the lake (including the "tarn") are sources and symbols of disaster to man, with the former usually described as rough, stormy, and dangerous, and the latter as sinister and dark. By contrast, the flowing rivers, or "living waters" in the French phrase, whether large or small, signify the life of man at its most felicitous, busy, changing, illuminated, and forward-looking, as in the sketch of the Wissahiccon (see below). The poem "The Lake" of 1827 is his earliest representation of this orientation ("The terror of the lone lake / . . . Springing from a darken'd mind")—strikingly consistent throughout Poe's entire career.[17] In "Hans Pfaall" (*Southern Literary Messenger*, June 1835) there occurs a noteworthy instance of this; the aeronaut, approaching his satellite goal, finds that his

> fancy revelled in the wild and dreamy regions of the moon . . . where it was all one dim and vague lake, with a boundary-line of clouds. And out of this melancholy water arose a forest of tall eastern trees. . . . The shadows . . . which fell upon the lake . . . sunk slowly and steadily down, and commingled with the waves, while from the trunks of the trees other shadows were continually coming out, and taking the place of their brothers thus entombed . . . the very reason why the waters of this lake grow blacker with age, and more melancholy as the hours run on. (1:575)

And this very passage, largely removed from the later printings of "Hans Pfaall," becomes the germ out of which the tale "The Island of the Fay" (*Graham's Magazine*, June 1841) evolves, even though Poe pretends that the accompanying plate or scene by Sartain "out of John Martin" is the inspiration (see Plate Eight).[18] Here too the descriptive elements are extremely close to the major feature of "The Lake of the Dismal Swamp": "The eastern end of the isle was whelmed in the blackest shade. . . . The trees were . . . wreathing themselves into sad, solemn, and spectral shapes, that conveyed ideas of mortal sorrow and untimely death. . . . The shade of the trees fell heavily upon the water . . . impregnating the depths of the element with darkness. . . . Each shadow . . . became absorbed by the stream; while other shadows issued . . . taking the place of their predecessors thus entombed. . . . Darkness fell over all things . . . " (*Tales*, pp. 603–605). Even "The Fall of the House of Usher" *Burton's Gentleman's Magazine*, September 1839) had shown this strong scenic association of Poe's, in its effective initial setting of the "black and lurid tarn that lay in unruffled lustre by the dwelling" with "the gray sedge, and the ghastly tree-stems" earlier specified as "white" and "decayed" (*Tales*, pp. 397–98), whence comes "a pestilent and mystic vapor, dull, sluggish, faintly discernible, and leaden-hued" (p. 400)—all of it a suitable prelude to the tale of the decay of a family, of morality, and of sanity, a tale of hinted murder, sadism, and incest, which ends when "the deep and dark tarn" engulfs the fragments of the "*House of*

PLATE EIGHT
John Sartain's engraving of "The Island of the Fay" in the June 1841 *Graham's Magazine.*
Courtesy Burton R. Pollin

Usher" (p. 417). Surely it is "the delightful terror of the lone lake" which has made Poe introduce Chapman's scene into that luxurious drawing-room.

By contrast and quite in accord with his general attitude, Poe expresses his pleasure in the scenery of a small creek or brook called The Wissahiccon (later spelled Wissahickon), just outside Fairmont Park in the city of Philadelphia. Arthur Hobson Quinn postulates many an agreeable ramble or outing, sometimes with Virginia and his friends, such as George Lippard and Henry Hirst, along this narrow stream, which empties into the Skuylkill River.[19] There are several unresolved elements for students of Poe in this pastoral sketch, first called "Morning on the Wissahiccon," which was illustrated by John Gadsby Chapman for the gift annual, *The Opal: A Pure Gift for the Holy Days*, of 1844 (issued late in 1843). We are uncertain, for example, about the immediate source of the tale: was it simply Poe's riparian experiences during the spring of 1843; was it the stipulation of writing a prose accompaniment for a specific plate by Chapman in the annual; or was it a parallel prose sketch about the creek, published originally in the December 1835 *Southern Literary Messenger*? This was the same number that included the first of the scenes from *Politian*, "MS. Found in a Bottle," and numerous reviews by Poe. The ambiguity extends even to the second title, "The Elk," that Poe later assigned to the essay-sketch by virtue of the unexpected appearance of the animal at the end.[20] Mabbott's considerable authority has been lent to the theory that Poe intended to offer a prose statement of the subject of Chapman's piece in *The Opal*,[21] this being a procedure that was then extremely common in the periodicals and the keepsakes of the day. It was also an editor's device that Poe himself deplored, despite his resorting to it himself as editor and contributor for both Burton's and Graham's magazines.[22] There is no epistolary evidence that this was true for Poe's piece in *The Opal*, edited by his friend Nathaniel P. Willis in New York City. There are nine illustrations in the volume, including a large vignette for the title page—all by Chapman. Four of them have a religious theme, appropriate for a Christmas gift-book. We would have to assume that independent of Poe's tale, Chapman submitted this picture to Willis to mail to Poe for him to "create" an appropriate tale. This would have been feasible if the writer resided near the publication office, as was true for Poe's half dozen plate articles in Philadelphia magazines. Here such a procedure was impossible.

The likely alternative is that he derived the impetus for the article from the sketch, "The Wissahiccon," anonymously published in December 1835, and was also motivated by his own experiences in that pleasure-ground and his notions about progress or the contrast of the past and present. Mabbott also grants the influence of this earlier essay in saying: "He must have seen an unsigned article . . . which said the deer were gone" (*Tales*, p. 860). It is clear that Poe drew much more than this from the article, which was ascribed to Benjamin Matthias of Philadelphia when it was reprinted in *The*

Philadelphia Book; or Specimens of Metropolitan Literature (1836).[23] Whether or not Poe knew of this authorship he certainly knew Matthias as editor of the Philadelphia *Saturday Chronicle* (1836–42), which published Poe's tale "The Devil in the Belfry" in its 18 May 1839 issue. Reciprocally, Matthias contributed to *Burton's Gentleman's Magazine* of June 1840, Poe being the editor, a two-page piece entitled "The Musical Doctor: or, The Chromatic Prescription. Translated from the French by Benjamin Matthias, Esq., Editor of the Saturday Chronicle." Moreover, in "A Chapter on Autography" in the December 1841 *Graham's* Poe mentioned his "editorial conduct" of the *Chronicle* "to which he has furnished much entertaining and instructive matter."[24] Having become state senator of Pennsylvania, he added a parliamentary manual to his guidebooks, the latter indicating the interest which motivated his *Messenger* contribution.[25]

My brief summary of this 1835 piece will try to underscore the verbal elements which, I believe, Poe used in his own sketch of the brook. Matthias provides thirteen paragraphs about the creek (as does Poe): (1): All Philadelphians have heard of the "beautiful and romantic stream that falls into the . . . Schuylkill, about five miles above the city," but few visit it through undervaluing the "gifts . . . placed within our reach," rather than hundreds of miles away. Otherwise, they would enjoy the "placid waters, its sluggish, meandering course, its richly covered banks, and its imposing precipices," with "picturesque views"; (2): But it is visited by the few "who enjoy Nature in her majesty—free, uncontrolled, undespoiled of her beauty by the effacing efforts of human skill." The stream reaches "the Chesnut ridge . . . progresses, at times indolently, through a narrow valley, hedged in on either side by high hills, steep and craggy cliffs and precipitous mountains," especially within six or eight miles "of its mouth" where "it exhibits . . . the imposing and majestic ledge of rock work through which it passes." "Here," says Matthias, "seated on an eminence," he has watched the heart-warming scene; (3): "I love to clamber among rocks and under precipices . . . to explore the dense forests . . . where the foot of man has never trod, where the sound of civilization has never been heard"; (4): "The scenery . . . is of a wild, romantic and imposing character. . . . High hills . . . covered with a dense and beautifully-variegated foliage" (eight trees are briefly described) with "imposing banks, and hills . . . on either shore; and but for the unpoetic noise of a laboring mill and the span of a rude bridge . . . there would be nothing to betray the presence of man, or to mark the continuity of human enterprise . . . the desolating depredations and officious interference of the outward march of civilization"; (5): The carriage road . . . crosses the stream on a covered bridge . . . and passes over to the ridge. "A foot path . . . reaches a . . . lawn, a . . . little parlor . . . the resort of occasional pic-nic parties." "Here, several clefts and caverns in the granite rocks may be found"; (6): Near the "flax mill" the "foot-path

crosses" with "occasional openings in the dense foliage" to "afford highly picturesque and enchanting views of the surrounding hills"; (7): Matthias describes a great rock over the stream opposite Rittenhouse's mill (probably
Lover's Leap) and alludes to the belief that the mystic Johann Kelpius and
his scholarly friends in the seventeenth century dwelt here.[26] "It was here,
perhaps, on the summit . . . that the original owners of the soil convened
for the war dance" or to "smoke the calumet"; (8): The untutored savage no
longer strolls. . . . The active deer no longer bounds over the hills and
dales." But "these placid waters are still beautiful." Paragraphs 9 and 10 describe a "monastery" of the eighteenth century, and 11 and 12 give other
legends. Paragraph 13 concludes the piece with a reference to the delight
that the "crystal waters" still afford the "pedestrian" who "may ramble
through its attractive forests."

In the development, Poe's "Morning on the Wissahiccon" adheres fairly
closely to Matthias' plan save for the little episode that he devises for the
end: (1) Poe speaks of the unjust contrast often made between the natural
scenery of America and Europe; (2): The British tourists have ignored our
Western scenery (aside from the prairies and the Mississippi) including "the
valley of the Louisiana" with "crystallic streams" as well as our nearby quiet,
obscure "nooks"; (5): The viewer of "the finest landscapes" in America must
go on foot and "risk his neck among precipices," unlike the traveler in Europe; (7): Since "river scenery" is "the favourite theme of the poet," he proposes to describe the Wissahiccon brook which empties into the Schuylkill
"about six miles westward of Philadelphia." This "humble . . . rivulet" has
"picturesque interest"; (9): Fanny Kemble, in her *Journal*,[27] confirmed "adventurous pedestrians" in their view of the "rare loveliness" of the stream,
especially beyond the point where the carriage-road stops, beyond the sixth
milestone along the lane, for the part best explored in a skiff or "by clamber-
ing along" the banks; (10): The "brook is narrow," with "precipitous" banks
and magnificent forest trees, but the shores "are of granite." The stream has
many "windings," and the "gorge" is so narrow as to produce "gloominess,"
especially because of "the density of the foliage"; (11): Recently, on a hot day,
while in a skiff, he revelled in "visions of the Wissahiccon of ancient days—of
the 'good old days' when the Demon of the Engine was not, when pic-nics
were undreamed of . . . and when the red man trod alone, with the elk,
upon the ridges." On a "steep rocky cliff" appeared one of those "elks" of his
vision; (12): But his dream was dispelled by the approach of a black man with
a handful of salt, who subdued the elk and put on his "halter"; (13): "Thus
ended my romance of the elk. It was a *pet*" of an English family in a nearby
villa.

In this brief summary, largely in Poe's words, can be seen the obvious parallels in ideas and general plan and the many coincidences of phrasing that
indicate clearly Matthias' essay as the point of departure for Poe's idyll,

which forms one of a series of river pieces representing the happiest environment for man. Here it is Nature that plays the landscape-artist, while in the others ("The Landscape Garden," "The Domain of Arnheim," and "Landor's Cottage") the affluent dilettante plays that role. There is an implication that social man, in various groups or in industrial operations, is likely to spoil the native beauty of the little valley (as he says in "The Colloquy of Monos and Una": "Green leaves shrank before the hot breath of furnaces" [*Tales*, p. 610]).[28] Poe's allusion to a detested "pic-nic" finds graphic representation in one of the issues of *Graham's*, that of October 1844, after his severance from the journal, when William Croome created a frontispiece to illustrate a positively inane tale by Charles J. Peterson, entitled "The Pic-Nic. A Story of the Wissahickon" (see Plate Nine).[29] The arrangement of the figures, the simpering expressions and contrived postures, and the overdressed characters all pointedly vindicate Poe's general dislike of "plate articles" and of large picnic groups.

How must he have felt about the picture illustrating his own tale in *The Opal*? The question amusingly raises elements of natural history, onomastics, and artistic as well as linguistic license for both Poe and Chapman. The artist, although from Virginia, was clearly devoted to the New York scene and very well knew the environing countryside up the Hudson, as hunter and fisherman.[30] Accordingly, when he was given Poe's prose sketch by the editor Willis as the basis of one of the nine plates that were to become his customary artistic contribution to this annual,[31] he naturally used the Hudson as his "model stream." It is even possible that in his large output of scenes, he had one already in his portfolio that would serve for an illustration, since he entitled the picture accompanying the prose sketch simply "Morning" with no naming of the Philadelphia creek (see Plate Ten). By contrast here is an artist's sketch of the Wissahickon gorge, even including a figure surveying the whole, perched high to the left, as a parallel to the deer. The well-known Granville Perkins depicts the gloom of the narrow gorge and thick underwood only thirty-five years later (see Plate Eleven).[32] Poe was surely specific in his references to the smallness of the creek: "large rivers" in contrast with "more interesting streams" (paragraph 7); "a brook" and a "rivulet" (paragraph 8); "a stream . . . at their own doors" and "mouth of the rivulet" (paragraph 9); "The brook is narrow" and "the narrowness of the gorge" (paragraph 10); "the lazy brook" (paragraph 11) etc. A few photographed scenes of the Wissahickon will show Poe's accuracy (Plates Twelve and Fourteen).[33] Chapman's view is clearly that of a broad river projected beyond the flat cliff of the deer's stance. Moreover, there are similarities to other pictures by Chapman: "The Palisades" (1838) and "The First Ship" (1837). He seemed to be fond of this composition, as we can see in one of his Pocohontas pictures, showing the Indian watching the approaching English (Plates Fifteen and Sixteen).[34]

PLATE NINE
Engraving of W. Croome's "A Pic-Nic on the Wissahickon" in the October 1844
Graham's Magazine.
Courtesy Burton R. Pollin.

PLATE ELEVEN
Engraving of Granville Perkins' "Wissahickon, near Paper-Mill Bridge" in *Pictur-esque America*, ed. William Cullen Bryant (New York: D. Appleton, 1874), 2:43.
Courtesy Burton R. Pollin

PLATE TWELVE
View of the upper Wissahickon in Francis Burke Brandt, *The Wissahickon Valley within the City of Philadelphia* (Philadelphia: Corn Exchange Bank, 1927), p. 41.
Courtesy Burton R. Pollin

PLATE THIRTEEN
Winter on the upper Wissahickon in Francis Burke Brandt, *The Wissahickon Valley within the City of Philadelphia* (Philadelphia: Corn Exchange Bank, 1927), p. 48.
Courtesy Burton R. Pollin

PLATE FOURTEEN

View of the Wissahickon in Francis Burke Brandt, *The Wissahickon Valley within the City of Philadelphia* (Philadelphia: Corn Exchange Bank, 1927), p. 112.

Courtesy Burton R. Pollin

PLATE FIFTEEN
"View of the Hudson River: The Palisades" in Georgia Stamm Chamberlain, *Studies on John Gadsby Chapman* (Annandale, Va.: Turnpike Press, 1963), p. 26.
Courtesy Burton R. Pollin

PLATE SIXTEEN
"The First Ship" in Georgia Stamm Chamberlain, *Studies on John Gadsby Chapman* (Annandale, Va.: Turnpike Press, 1963), p. 27.
Courtesy Burton R. Pollin

Another ambiguity in the picture and story concerns the exact nature of the animal designated at the end of the sketch and in the picture. Poe is definite about its species, calling it an "elk" four times, and a fifth when he names the tale "The Elk" in a letter. But did Poe really mentally picture an elk, or for that matter, could an elk be a "pet" of "very domestic habits" (paragraph 13) in a villa built on the Wissahickon? It is not easy to answer either of the questions, which are interrelated. We know that the literary source of Poe's article, the Matthias sketch, speaks only of the Indian and his hunting of the "deer." Poe probably changed the parallel animal in his own sketch to "elk" both to introduce a difference in language and also to make the animal of his denouement more impressive and more memorable. Mabbott asserts that there was "a real elk resident in the vicinity" which "belonged to the proprietor of a sanatorium at a villa called Spring Bank who kept a number of pet animals for the pleasure of his patients" (*Tales*, p. 867n9). His authority for this is Quinn, whose evidence needs examination, since it has often been cited by students writing on Poe's landscapes and views of animals. He declared: "Poe really saw an elk, and the 'villa' still stands. . . . 'Spring Bank' was in 1838 a sanitarium conducted by Samuel Mason, who kept a number of pets for the amusement of his patients . . . [and] was sold in May, 1838, to George Wilson, a farmer [who] . . . sold it in 1840 to Dr. Edward Lowber, who also had a sanitarium and probably inherited the elk with the property." Quinn ascribes his "facts" to J. Somers Smith, who "still owns" the "place" and to Cornelius Weygandt, the well known historian of Philadelphia. But in reality the source of the "fact" concerning the elk is Poe himself, for nothing is transmitted save a reference to "pets."[35] Would a mature "elk" be a "pet" in a sanitarium for the elderly and the infirm in 1838 or later?

It is not at all likely. The American elk is actually one of two different beasts: either the very large animal called by the Indians (Shawnee) the "wapiti" and driven from eastern Pennsylvania long before Poe's time, or it is the even larger animal called the "moose" from the Ojibway name. Perhaps the confusion exists, in part, between names given by systematizing naturalists and commonsense New World settlers to various animals of the large, antlered species. The latter called the "wapiti" the elk, so that when they saw a true member of the elk family later they had to use the Indian name of "moose." In addition, they gave the name "deer," borrowed from the English red deer, to the very different "white tail and mule deer." One can scarcely wonder therefore at Poe's extension of the word "elk" to an obviously different animal—probably merely a large deer, although we are still obliged to estimate what animal he was designating. Obviously it could not be the moose, which weighs close to one thousand pounds, may extend from eight to ten feet in body length, and stand five to seven feet high at the shoulder. This would be no animal for a sanitarium, no matter how tame. Moreover, the flat or plate-like antlers are distinctly different from the prong-like antlers of the deer and of the wapiti; since Poe expressed no dissatisfaction with the illustration of Chapman, it might be assumed that he did not have the moose in mind. As for the wapiti—it is doubtful that this, being an upland animal, ever was to be found in a wooded area of Philadelphia or could easily have been brought there from the Allegheny Mountains where primitively it was to be found.[36] It could have been imported as a fawn, to be sure, but far more likely, the "Spring Bank" or "pet" of the "villa" was simply a large deer that had become domesticated.[37] We shall assume that Poe, without benefit of big game manuals and dictionaries of wild life in the eastern regions, was simply using the name "elk" rather honorifically—to impress the reader with the majestic appearance of an antlered deer seen on a high bank from the level of the water below. Probably Chapman interpreted his wishes correctly, even though in such small matters as failing to show the "ears erect" (paragraph 11) he erred, as he did in showing the Hudson for the Wissahickon.

The fame and popularity of Chapman made it inevitable that there would be further connections between the artist and Poe, a New York journalist interested in so many phases of the New York art world. None of these connections involved Poe's creative work, but they add a small coda of some art interest. In 1845 Poe gradually found himself in a position to be a commentator on some aspects of Chapman's work. Initially Poe was simply a reviewer and contributing essayist on literary subjects for the *Broadway Journal* (4 January 1845–3 January 1846), but as the year advanced he contrived to encompass more of the functions of the weekly and more of the editorial control. Originally it was headed by Charles F. Briggs, but the 15 March issue added the names of Poe and of H. C. Watson (for music) to the masthead. The second volume (issued 12 July) began without the name of Briggs, and from 25 October on, Poe was named "editor and proprietor." Since the *Journal* had very creditably included art criticism and news in each of the sixteen-page, double-column issues and Poe maintained the policy, Chapman's name came in for mention, indicating his activities and position in the art world of New York. Even before Poe took over, he surely read and absorbed the comments on Chapman by Briggs, which, by and large, are quite hostile compared with Poe's friendly comments. On 18 January, Briggs praised Chapman's two pictures in the February *Columbian Magazine* as rivaling the best imported English engravings in workmanship, but not in pictorial material (1:45). In the next week's number, Briggs comments again on these two designs as "smooth inanities" (1:61). In the 8 February issue, Briggs lengthily attacks Chapman for his cover design, initial letters, ornamental borders, and 437 engravings in the much heralded Harpers' *Illuminated and New Pictorial Bible*.[38] He grants to the drawings by Chapman only "a good deal of truth and sweetness," but repeatedly complains about the lack of variety in having so many illustrations by only one artist. Far more favorable to Chapman as a painter is a 8 March paragraph praising a biblical scene exhibited at the Art Union and very profitably sold—a good omen for other artists, Briggs says (1:156).

In the 22 March issue, a contributor commends the eminent artists, including Chapman, who are individually presenting one of their pictures to the New York Gallery of Fine Arts (1:187). In the 17 May issue, Briggs, in a review of the National Academy exhibition, cites Chapman's work as his best figure painting, which is nonetheless unrelated to the biblical scene supposedly illustrated. Briggs again reviews the *Pictorial Bible* (no. 27) in the 31 May issue as a fitting companion to the weak earlier numbers, but some illustrations he grants to be "neat and spirited" (1:346). Again, in the 21 June issue Briggs returns to the attack on Chapman's bible pictures, which were wearisomely the same (1:396–97).

The first reference to Chapman in the second volume, now devoid of the presence of the adverse Briggs, is in the 6 September issue—a brief paragraph which highly praises the wood engravings of no. 38 of the *Pictorial Bible* as an "honor to the house" of the Harpers. The 29 November issue carried a paragraph of high praise for no. 43 of the *Bible*, with the added dictum that "no English edition approaches this"—obviously referring to the reprint of the John Martin illustrated Bible which Briggs had consistently praised as superior (2:322). In the 27 December issue of the *Broadway Journal* (2:388) Poe declares that the present number of the Harpers' Bible "maintains the high character" of its predecessors. Finally, in the last issue, that of 3 January (2:404), Poe speaks of no. 46 of "this really standard and elegant work." (The advertising revenue for his dying magazine may have somewhat influenced his remarks.[39]) This closes all his comments on the works of this artist, which began with his allusion to the painting of "The Lake of the Dismal Swamp" in 1840. It would seem that he found in these 1845 wood engravings no evidence of the "imaginative" which had caused him originally to single out Chapman's work, nor had Chapman infused any of the "magic" which some have found in Poe's "Morning on the Wissahiccon" into his illustration of the tame "elk." Yet the twofold relationship with Poe casts some illumination on his aims and methods.

NOTES

1. *Burton's Gentleman's Magazine*, 6:243–45; *Broadway Journal*, 1:273–75. For the most convenient edition of this and all Poe texts cited, see *Collected Works of Edgar Allan Poe*, ed. Thomas Ollive Mabbott, 3 vols. (Cambridge: Harvard University Press, 1969–78), vol. 1,

Poems (1969), vols. 2–3, *Tales and Sketches* (1978), 1:495–503. Hereafter these will be cited as *Poems* or *Tales*.

2. Cleanth Brooks, in one of the surprisingly few statements about Poe's sense of interior decoration, relates his "Gothic" qualities in the tales to the furnishings and the "operatic settings," and concludes them to be "bizarreries" ("Edgar Allan Poe as Interior Decorator," *Ventures*, 7 [1968]: 41–46).

3. *Dictionary of National Biography*, 18:885–87.

4. *Tales*, 1:504n12. However, the single illustration by Stanfield on one of the twelve lunettes, each painted by a different artist, seems to date from the 1840s, judging from the title page of the handsome large volume, with fifteen plates, called *The Decorations of the Garden-Pavilion in the Grounds of Buckingham Palace*, "Engraved under the Superintendance of Ludwig Gruner, with an introduction by Mrs. Jameson" (London: Bradbury and Evans, 1845; J. Murray, 1846). Stanfield's picture shows the spirit Comus, a "rabble rout" in nocturnal revels, "a weeping cherub," and an exulting "friend," but no "fairy grottoes."

5. These lines are in the 1827 version and remain unchanged through the last version of 1845 in this poem, often revised by Poe.

6. Robert Morrison, "Poe's *The Lake: To——*," *Explicator*, 7 (December 1948): item 22. For the influence of "A Ballad," see C. F. Stansbury, *The Lake of the Great Dismal Swamp* (New York: Boni, 1925), pp. 3–11, and also Paul W. Kirk, Jr., *The Great Dismal Swamp* (Charlottesville: University Press of Virginia, 1979), pp. 67–71.

7. Thomas Moore, *The Poetical Works* (New York: D. Appleton, 1853), 2:223–25, in "Poems Relating to America."

8. For these and other facts concerning the Swamp here and below, I have relied upon Kirk, *The Great Dismal Swamp*, Stansbury, *The Lake of the Great Dismal Swamp*, H. J. Davis, *The Great Dismal Swamp* (Richmond, Va.: Cavalier Press, 1962), J. F. Pugh, *The Hotel in the Great Dismal Swamp* (Old Trap, N.C.: J. F. Pugh, 1964), Gerald F. Levy, *The Great Dismal Swamp* (Norfolk, Va.: Old Dominion University, 1976) (very graciously sent me by the author), and numerous other materials, many of them made personally available to me in April 1979 in the special collection of the Historical Society and the Public Library of Norfolk, a central repository for books, clippings, pamphlets, etc., on the Swamp.

9. See Kirk, *The Great Dismal Swamp*, p. 66. The illustration, from *The Hotel in the Great Dismal Swamp*, opposite p. 21, is a print of the lithograph made for the *Norfolk Herald* of 22 November 1830 from Thomas Williamson's design.

10. Davis, *The Great Dismal Swamp*, p. 65.

11. Kirk, *The Great Dismal Swamp*, p. 70. The size and density of the Swamp led to Henry Wadsworth Longfellow's "The Slave" (1842) and Harriet Beecher Stowe's *Dred; A Tale of the Great Dismal Swamp* (1856).

12. See the 20 May 1843 *Brother Jonathan*, under "Literary," for a paragraph headed "Magnificent Enterprise" devoted to the "splendid new edition" planned by the Harpers, the eminent Chapman, and the well-known engraver J. A. Adams, the work to appear in fifty numbers (p. 88).

13. Aside from the standard tools for art history, the best sources for information about Chapman—all used for the above sketch—are these: William P. Campbell's exhibition catalogue, *John Gadsby Chapman* (Washington: National Gallery of Art, 1962), pp. 7–22; Georgia Stamm Chamberlain, *Studies on John Gadsby Chapman* (Annandale, Va.: Turnpike Press, 1963); and John S. Wise, "John Gadsby Chapman," *Virginia State Library Bulletin*, 12, nos. 3–4 (July–October 1919): 77–104.

14. I am indebted for the *Magnolia* printing to the assiduity and kindness of Elizabeth Roth, Curator of Prints of the New York Public Library, who referred me to a list of Smillie's engravings donated to the library by his heirs.

15. *Nineteenth-Century Southern Literature* (Lexington: University Press of Kentucky, 1980), p. 32.

16. *Discoveries in Poe* (Notre Dame: University of Notre Dame Press, 1970), pp. 144–65.

17. *Poems*, pp. 48, 85.

18. For the account, see my paper in *The Mystery and Detection Annual* (Beverly Hills, Cal.: Donald Adams, 1972), pp. 33–45.

19. See Quinn, *Edgar Allan Poe* (New York: D. Appleton-Century, 1941), for a reprint of Hirst's obituary of Poe, telling of seeing him more than once daily for two years (p. 654), and for Lippard's being his neighbor and friend (p. 385). See *The Wissahickon*, ed. T. A. Daly (Philadelphia: The Garden Club, 1922), for Lippard's wandering on the creek at the time and later marriage on a cliff there (p. 37). Also see Lippard's *Rose of Wissahickon* (Philadelphia: G. B. Zieber, 1847), Prologue, pp. 3–9.

20. Letter of 28 May 1844 to James Russell Lowell, listing his recent writings, *The Letters of Edgar Allan Poe*, ed. John Ward Ostrom (Cambridge: Harvard University Press, 1948), 1:253.

21. *Tales*, p. xx: "On a few occasions the inspirations came from pictures; 'Morning on the Wissahiccon' was written to accompany an illustration"; and p. 860: "The tale was a plate article, or letter-press, to accompany one of Chapman's pictures . . . showing an elk in romantic scenery."

22. For Poe's objections to the plates of *Graham's Magazine*, see Quinn, *Poe*, p. 341, and for a good analysis of the poor quality then prevalent, see Stuart Levine, *Edgar Poe: Seer and Craftsman* (Deland, Fla.: Everett/Edwards, 1972), pp. 106–14.

23. I indicated this authorship in *Discoveries in Poe*, p. 275n27, with an attribution to Cornelius Weygandt's *The Wissahickon Hills*. The addition of the author's name is the only change in the 1836 reprint (pp. 325–36).

24. This, the last issue that Poe edited, was distinctive in having contributions from the editors of eight journals beside Burton's; hence the appended identification. For the "Autography" entry, see *The Complete Works of Edgar Allan Poe*, ed. James A. Harrison (New York: Thomas Y. Crowell, 1902), 15:212. For a one-paragraph sketch of Matthias, see Dwight R. Thomas, "Poe in Philadelphia, 1838–1844: A Documentary Record" (Ph.D. dissertation, University of Pennsylvania, 1978), p. 850.

25. His books were *Hand-book for travelers . . . between Philadelphia and Baltimore* (1843), *The Traveler's Guide from New York to Philadelphia* (1843), and *Rules of Order* (1848).

26 My identification is based on the excellent maps and text in Daly, *The Wissahickon*, pp. 49–55, while Quinn identifies Poe's "cliff" as "Mom Rinker's Rock," with less certainty, since his directions are brief and less specific than are Matthias' (*Poe*, p. 397).

27. Her *Journal* was reviewed (but not by Poe) in the *Southern Literary Messenger*, 1 (May 1835): 524–31, and, again through summaries or comments, in August (1:716), December 1835 (2:61), this being Poe's summary, and February 1836 (2:158–59); her book is cited by Poe in Harrison, *Collected Works*, 8:50, 9:203–204, 15:116.

28. Poe's fears about "progress" were well-founded. For forty years (1832–73) about sixty mills of varied types in the valley drew their power from the creek, but were all eliminated by 1884 through an Act of the Assembly (1868) to restore the valley as an unspoiled park (see Daly, *The Wissahickon*, p. 39, and *3 Hikes Through the Wissahickon* [Federal Writers' Project] [Philadelphia: Newspaper Guild of Philadelphia, 1936], penultimate [unnumbered] page).

29. *Graham's Magazine*, 25:184–87. Peterson has another masterpiece of puerility, called "The Wissahickon Pic-Nic," in the Sepember 1839 *Casket* (20:103–109), discussed in my paper on "Poe as Probable Author of 'Harper's Ferry,'" *American Literature*, 40 (May 1968): 164–78.

30. Chamberlain, *Studies on Chapman*, p. 27. H. T. Tuckerman eulogizes Chapman and describes his "artist-like" studio thus: "There is a deerskin and antlers, to waken thoughts of woodland freedom, and blue lakes" (*Book of the Artists* [New York: G. P. Putnam, 1867], pp. 216–22).

31. The annual, which varied its subtitle each year, employed Chapman through the volume for 1847, just before his departure for Italy. For 1845, he prepared eight pictures for editor Sarah Josepha Hale; for 1846 and 1847, nine pictures for each volume for editor John Keese. In

1840, as editor of *Colman's Poets of American* (vol. 1), Keese had used Chapman's illustrative drawings.

32. Mary E. Phillips, *Edgar Allan Poe—The Man* (Philadelphia: John C. Winston, 1926), prints this picture (2:849), taken from William Cullen Bryant's *Picturesque America* (New York: D. Appleton, 1874), 2:43, and changes the title "Wissahickon near Paper-Mill Bridge" to that of Poe's tale.

33. The three illustrations of "The Wissahickon" come from Francis Burke Brandt, *The Wissahickon Valley within the City of Philadelphia* (Philadelphia: Corn Exchange Bank, 1927), pp. 41, 48, 112.

34. These two prints come from Chamberlain, *Studies on Chapman*, pp. 26, 27; the first was engraved by Osborne for the *New York Mirror* of 18 December 1838; the second is part of his Pocohontas series, exhibited in the National Academy of Design in 1837 and engraved for *The Token* of 1842.

35. Quinn, *Poe*, p. 397. His sole authority in writing for the elk is H. D. Eberlein, *Portrait of a Colonial City* (Philadelphia: J. B. Lippincott, 1939), pp. 200–203, whose evidence is Poe's tale.

36. See H. H. Collins, *Complete Field Guide to American Wildlife* (New York: Harper and Row, 1959), p. 336, and Jack O'Connor, *The Big Game Animals of North America* (New York: E. P. Dutton, 1961), pp. 128–29, 136.

37. That the elk is a dangerous animal is indicated by Olaus J. Murie, *The Elk of North America* (Harrisburg, Pa.: Wildlife Management Institute, 1951), pp. 69, 263–64, 308.

38. *Broadway Journal*, 1:83–85; a review of nos. 1–17 of the *Bible*, planned for fifty numbers.

39. Significantly, the Harpers did not advertise in vol. 1 of the *Broadway Journal*, while every issue of volume 2, save that of 6 December, had the equivalent of a full column of material.

Feb. 26

Lawrence

This effusion is obviously one of the numerous poems derived from the very popular "Lady Clara Vere de Vere" in Tennyson's *Poems* of 1833 (issued 1832), in which the proud "daughter of a thousand earls" smiles at the youth "of a country heart." He predicts: "You pine among your halls and towers; / The languid light of your proud eyes / Is wearied of the rolling hours" and will be "sickening of a vague disease" (stanza 7). Poe had already treated the theme tangentially in the early "Paean" in his unnoticed *Poems* of 1831, in that a proud maiden has married into great wealth, has sickened and has died amid hostile heirs or false friends (Mabbott, *Works*, 1:204-207). He knew Osgood's later presentation of the theme via

POE, MRS. OSGOOD, AND "ANNABEL LEE"

Buford Jones and Kent Ljungquist

IN POE'S CONTACTS with literary ladies of his time, no relationship stimulated more controversy than that with the poet, Frances Sargent Osgood. For the literary biographer, suspicions of adultery and charges of moral impropriety had to be balanced against Virginia Poe's apparent fondness for Mrs. Osgood. Citing the many innocuous but fashionable literary flirtations of the era, Arthur Hobson Quinn delicately dubbed the relationship "a literary courtship" in which Poe found a convenient outlet for his amatory poems.[1] Expressing doubt that Poe was ever seriously infatuated, Sidney P. Moss has claimed that Mrs. Osgood clearly took the initiative in the flirtation.[2] Adopting a more speculative stance, John Evangelist Walsh has put forth the theory that Poe was the father of Mrs. Osgood's child, Fanny Fay.[3] It is more likely that Poe's relationship to Mrs. Osgood was an injudicious but innocent involvement, but as Edward Wagenknecht has noted, the Poe-Osgood relationship does not lend itself to clear distinctions between fact and fiction: "Nowhere in Poe's story is it more difficult to disentangle truth from falsehood than there."[4] In spite of Thomas Ollive Mabbott's careful annotations of Poe's poems dedicated to Mrs. Osgood,[5] biographical speculation has exceeded the study of literary indebtedness that may have existed.[6] Of particular interest are Mrs. Osgood's comments on "Annabel Lee," in which she stridently claimed that Virginia Poe, "the only woman Poe ever loved," was the sole possible subject of the poem. Mabbott, calling her comments "ingenious and poetic," added: "her motives were certainly complicated. She wanted to minimize the importance of all the women in Poe's life save Virginia Poe and herself."[7] Mrs. Osgood clearly showed special knowledge of "Annabel Lee"; she explained the problematical reference to "high-born kinsmen" as "*kindred* angels" of God who took away the speaker's lost love.[8] Her gloss has generally been accepted by early and later commentators on Poe.[9] Mrs. Osgood's insights transcended self-concern as well as defensiveness about Virginia's reputation. Her remarks were further complicated by her authorship of a poem, entitled "The Life-Voyage," which probably served as a model for "Annabel Lee."

The sources of "Annabel Lee" have received fairly rigorous attention. Perhaps more in the realm of legend than fact is a newspaper obituary mentioning an infant named Annabel Lee.[10] A possible literary source, "The Mourner," displays many similarities to "Annabel Lee," but the date of its appearance in the Charleston, South Carolina, *Courier* (1807) makes Poe's knowledge of it doubtful.[11] Another literary lady, Sarah Helen Whitman, provided a possible model with her "Stanzas for Music," printed in the *American Metropolitan Magazine* of February 1849. Poe claimed to have written "Annabel Lee" in May 1849; thus the publication date of "Stanzas for Music" and Poe's relationship to Mrs. Whitman make likely his exposure to her poem.[12] Other literary ladies vied for favor in the "Annabel Lee" contest. Elmira Shelton[13] and Annie Richmond[14] have both been mentioned as candidates, but a more notable claimant was Stella Lewis. Mrs. Lewis' claim, reported at third or fourth hand,[15] triggered Mrs. Osgood's outburst, which should be quoted at length:

> I believe that she [Virginia] was the only woman he ever loved; and this is evidenced by the exquisite pathos of the little poem, lately written, called Annabel Lee, of which she was the subject, and which is by far the most natural, simple, tender and touchingly beautiful of all his songs. I have heard that it was intended to illustrate a late love affair of the author; but they who believe this, have in their dullness, evidently misunderstood or missed the beautiful meaning latent in the most lovely of all its verses—where he says,
>
>> "A wind blew out of a cloud, chilling
>> My beautiful Annabel Lee,
>> So that her *high-born kinsmen* came,
>> And bore her away from me."
>
> There seems a strange and almost profane disregard of the sacred purity and spiritual tenderness of this delicious ballad, in thus overlooking the allusion to the *kindred angels* of the Heavenly *Father* of the lost and loved and unforgotton wife.[16]

In large measure because of Mrs. Osgood's comments, Virginia's role as a source of inspiration for "Annabel Lee" has received more serious attention than other rival claims.

But Mrs. Osgood's involvement with "Annabel Lee" goes further than her explicit comments indicate. Poe reviewed at length her *Poems* (1846),[17] which contains the following ballad, from which we quote the first two stanzas:

"The Life-Voyage"

Once in the olden time there dwelt
  Beside the sounding sea,
A little maid—her garb was coarse,
  Her spirit pure and free.

Her parents were an humble twain,
  And poor as poor could be;
Yet gaily sang the guileless child,
  Beside the sounding sea.[18]

The most outstanding phrase that this poem shares with "Annabel Lee" is in the second stanza. There Osgood uses the alliterative "sounding sea," an epithet that appeared in the first version of "Annabel Lee."[19] It has generally been agreed that Poe's final phrasing ("In her tomb by the side of the sea") was a mistake to achieve metrical regularity. This change from "In her tomb by the sounding sea," according to one authority, was unfortunate, "since it marred the concluding line, widely regarded as one of the great lines of English verse."[20] In any case, "The Life-Voyage" is the probable source for Poe's phrase "sounding sea."

Other parallels exist between the two poems. Both "The Life-Voyage" and "Annabel Lee" are ballads that begin in fairy tale fashion beside the sea. Osgood's "Once in the olden time" is far more conventional than Poe's roughly anapestic "many and many a year ago." Both poems present a fair maiden of "bright eyes" who is envied by the angels in heaven. In "The Life-Voyage," the angels come down from heaven to win her prized pearl. Roughly conforming to Osgood's published remarks on "Annabel Lee," these angels eventually usher her safely to heaven; they act almost as kinsmen of God or the Heavenly Father. In "Annabel Lee," "the angels, not half so happy in Heaven, / Went envying her and me." It is noteworthy, that, in both poems, these angels are later transformed into demons that threaten the figure of female beauty. The transformation from angels to demons is occasioned by the announcement of death. In Osgood's poem, "A stillness of death" is attended by "dark wind-demons," which attack the pearl maiden. In "Annabel Lee," after wind brings death to his beloved, the speaker is locked in a never-ending conflict between "the angels in Heaven above" and "the demons down under the sea." This theme of angelic-demonic ambivalence appealed to Poe, not only in "Annabel Lee," but also in "The Raven" where the student initially believes that the raven is sent by the angels of the lost Lenore.[21] While Poe is infinitely more successful in approximating the sound of the ocean's ebb and flow, both poets attempt onomatopoetic effects associated with oceanic rhythms. While the theme of adolescent love is absent from "The Life-Voyage," it contains a theme that appealed to Poe as well as other American Romantics. This is the "Voyage of Life" theme, which attempted to "telescope" the human cycle from infancy to death in a single work of literature. The Hudson River painter Thomas Cole employed this theme in his pictorial series "The Voyage of Life." And Poe, in "The Domain of Arnheim," projected the theme of life-voyage in his narrator's trip down a winding stream. Thus, because of Poe's predilection for this theme, Osgood's treatment in her poem would have been congenial to him.[22]

Poe's review of Osgood's 1846 volume makes his exposure to "The Life-Voyage" clear. Subsequent reviews and printings of the poem suggest that his memory may have been refreshed at a time close to his claimed date of composition for "Annabel Lee."[23] Furthermore, the possiblity of mutual or reciprocal influence between "Annabel Lee" and "The Life-Voyage" should not be discounted. Mrs. Osgood's comments on "Annabel Lee" reflect a knowledge of the poem that exceeded any of her contemporaries. Rather uncharacteristically of Poe, he circulated a manuscript of "Annabel Lee" more widely than any of his other poems, sending a copy to Rufus Griswold, Mrs. Osgood's literary executor, in June 1849. By the same token, Poe may have seen a draft of "The Life-Voyage" independently of its publication. Such interchange is not unlikely in view of the Poe–esque titles among Osgood's poems: "Ermengarde's Awakening," "Lenore,"[24] and "Leonor." Another poem on a theme similar to that of "The Life-Voyage" is "The Spirit's Voyage," an elegy on the death of a child which echoes Poe's most famous refrain:

> No more!—ah! never, never more!
> Her precious feet will tead,
> Like light, our dwelling's coral floor,
> By young affection led.[25]

As if in reciprocation for these poetic efforts that bring to mind his characters, themes, and vocabulary, Poe wrote a series of poems to Mrs. Osgood. He also lauded her poetry in his reviews, showing particular fondness for a dramatic poem *Elfrida* in which the hero is a king named Edgar.[26] The literary relationship reached its conclusion with her elegiac tribute to Poe, "The Hand That Swept the Sounding Lyre."[27] In all this give-and-take, the connection between "The Life-Voyage" and "Annabel Lee" may have had the most fruitful and significant literary consequences.

In any case, examination of internal parallels alone would seem to make "The Life-Voyage" a probable model for Poe's final poem. In view of Mrs.

Osgood's personal and literary relationship extending from 1845 to 1849, "The Life-Voyage" merits inclusion in any survey of the provenance of "Annabel Lee."

NOTES

1. Arthur Hobson Quinn, *Edgar Allan Poe: A Critical Biography* (New York: D. Appleton–Century, 1941), p. 478.

2. Sidney P. Moss, *Poe's Literary Battles: The Critic in the Context of His Literary Milieu* (Durham: Duke University Press, 1963), p. 208.

3. John Evangelist Walsh, *Plumes in the Dust: The Love Affair of Edgar Allan Poe and Fanny Osgood* (Chicago: Nelson-Hall, 1980). The scholarly character of Walsh's volume is belied by his desire to turn the Poe-Osgood "affair" into a romantic thriller. For a careful refutation of his findings, see Moss' review-essay, "Did Poe Father Fanny Fay?" *Poe Studies*, 13 (December 1980): 40–41.

4. Edward Wagenknecht, *Edgar Allan Poe: The Man Behind the Legend* (New York: Oxford University Press, 1963), p. 194.

5. The titles listed in the Poe–Osgood relationship are "To Frances S. Osgood," "To Frances," "Impromptu—To Kate Carol," "To [Violet Vane]," "The Divine Right of Kings," "Stanza," and "A Valentine," in *The Collected Works of Edgar Allan Poe*, ed. Mabbott, 3 vols. (Cambridge: Harvard University Press, 1969–78), Vol. 1, *Poems* (1969), pp. 233–37, 379–91. John E. Reilly discusses Mrs. Osgood's role in this series of poetic exchanges in "Mrs. Osgood and *The Broadway Journal*," *Duquesne Review*, 12 (Fall 1967): 131–46.

6. See Walsh's strained speculation that the "dread burden" in "Ulalume" is the corpse of Fanny Fay Osgood (*Plumes in the Dust*, pp. 146–48).

7. *Poems*, p. 474.

8. The comments first appeared in the *Boston International Magazine* of 1 October 1850, before appearing in Rufus Griswold's "Memoir of the Author," *The Works of Edgar Allan Poe* (New York: W. J. Widdleton, 1861), 1:liii.

9. See *Poems*, p. 474; John Henry Ingram, *Edgar Allan Poe: His Life, Letters, and Opinions* (London: W. H. Allen, 1888), pp. 176–77; *Poems of Edgar Allan Poe*, ed. Killis Campbell (New York: Ginn, 1917), p. 295; and *Poe*, ed. Richard Wilbur (New York: Dell, 1958), p. 151.

10. See Mabbott's comments on the story, *Poems*, pp. 470–71.

11. This possible source was first cited by Robert Adger Law, "A Source for 'Annabel Lee,'" *Journal of English and Germanic Philology*, 21 (April 1922): 341–46.

12. *Poems*, pp. 472–73. For qualifying remarks on this poem as a source, see Ingram, *Poe*, pp. 398–99. John Carl Miller's edition of the correspondence of Ingram and Mrs. Whitman reflects the latter's certitude that her poem inspired "Annabel Lee"; see *Poe's Helen Remembers* (Charlottesville: University Press of Virginia, 1979), pp. 33, 36, 144.

13. Bradford Booth, "The Identity of Annabel Lee," *College English*, 8 (October 1945): 17–19.

14. See Mabbott's comments, *Poems*, p. 475.

15. For hearsay information that may lack reliability, see Caroline Ticknor, *Poe's Helen* (New York: Scribners, 1916), pp. 132–33.

16. Quoted from Griswold, "Memoir," 1:liii.

17. The earliest notice appeared in the 1 March 1846 *Broadway Journal*. Longer reviews

appeared in the 13 December 1845 *Broadway Journal* and in the March 1846 *Godey's Lady's Book* (see *The Complete Works of Edgar Allan Poe*, ed. James A. Harrison, 17 vols. [New York: Thomas Y. Crowell, 1902] 13:17–26, 105–25; hereafter cited by volume and page number).

18. The first two stanzas of "The Life-Voyage" are here reprinted from Frances Sargent Osgood, *Poems* (New York: Clark and Austin, 1846), pp. 212–18. Poe undoubtedly read the poem upon its earlier appearance in *Graham's Magazine*, 21 (November 1842): 265–66, during a period when he was providing editorial expertise.

19. *Poems*, p. 478.

20. Mabbott notes that the phrase "sounding seas" is found in Milton's "Lycidas" (*Poems*, p. 481).

21. Kent Ljungquist, "Poe's Raven and Bryant's *Mythology*," *American Transcendental Quarterly*, no. 19 (Winter 1976): 28–30.

22. The relationship of "The Domain of Arnheim" to the "Voyage of Life" theme is discussed in Jeffrey Hess, "The Sources and Aesthetics of Poe's Landscape Fiction," *American Quarterly*, 22 (Spring 1970): 177–89, and Edward Halsey Foster, *Civilized Nature: Backgrounds to American Romantic Literature, 1817–1860* (New York: Free Press, 1975), pp. 82–83.

23. For a later printing of "The Life-Voyage," see *The American Female Poets With Biographical and Critical Notices*, ed. Caroline May (Philadelphia: Lindsay and Blakiston, 1848), pp. 385–89; see also Poe's 1846 and 1849 reviews of Osgood (*Works*, 18:176–88; 15:94–105).

24. Reilly, indicating that "Lenore" may have been written prior to Mrs. Osgood's meeting Poe, is tentative in claiming this poem as part of the literary courtship ("Mrs. Osgood and *The Broadway Journal*," 138–39). Despite the problematical composition dates of these poems that are part of the literary courtship, Poe and Mrs. Osgood clearly inferred amorous or promotional implications from poems that may have been composed prior to their initial meeting in March 1845.

25. Three of these poems appeared in the 1846 volume by Mrs. Osgood (pp. 136, 60–64, 151–53); "Ermengarde's Awakening" appeared in the later collected *Poems* (Philadelphia: Carey and Hart, 1850), pp. 22–27.

26. In his *Godey's* review of Mrs. Osgood's *Poems*, Poe quotes from *Elfrida*, as Walsh indicates (*Plumes in the Dust*, p. 131).

27. Osgood, *Poems* (1850), pp. 465–66.

CONTEXTS OF BRAVERY:
THOREAU'S REVISIONS OF "THE SERVICE" FOR
A WEEK

Linck C. Johnson

ROM THE TIME IT WAS PUBLISHED IN 1849, critics have recognized that *A Week on the Concord and Merrimack Rivers* contains a good deal of material Thoreau wrote during the period of his literary apprenticeship in the early 1840s.[1] "The leaves of his portfolio and river-journal seem to have been shuffled together with a trustful dependence on some overruling printer-providence," James Russell Lowell objected in an otherwise laudatory review: "We trace the lines of successive deposits as plainly as on the sides of a deep cut."[2] These "successive deposits" included "Homer. Ossian. Chaucer," translations of Anacreon, and "Aulus Persius Flaccus," all of which Thoreau had published in the *Dial*. He also revised portions of early unpublished essays, including "Sir Walter Raleigh" and "The Service," an essay on bravery written in 1840. But the few scattered sentences from "The Service" in the digression on music at the end of the "Monday" chapter merely hint at his sustained efforts to salvage portions of the essay as he revised and expanded *A Week* during 1846–48. Surviving manuscripts, however, indicate that Thoreau copied out three pages of extracts from "The Service," probably when he began to expand the first draft of *A Week* in 1846. During the next two years, he revised and expanded these extracts at least three times. Although he finally omitted the bulk of this material from *A Week*, Thoreau's revisions of "The Service" illustrate his increasing literary craft and artistic maturity. More significantly, they reveal the conflict between his youthful notions about bravery, exemplified in "The Service" by chivalric soldiers marching off to battle, and his later opposition to the Mexican War, which prompted the savage critique of military life in "Resistance to Civil Government," published the same month as *A Week* in May 1849.

"The Service" was the culmination of Thoreau's early interest in the subject of bravery.[3] In December 1839, three months after members of the Transcendental Club decided to establish the *Dial*, Thoreau copied into his Journal passages "From A Chapter on Bravery," most of which he later revised for "The Service."[4] In a passage that would not find its way into the essay, he observed that "when war too, like commerce and husbandry, gets to be a routine, and men go about it as indented apprentices, the hero degenerates into a marine, and the standing army into a standing jest" (*J*, 1:94). But in the following paragraphs he used a figure of ancient heroism, "the brave soldier" marching to the sound of a drum, as a paradigm of the brave man, "the sole patron of music" (*J*, 1:94–95). Those twin figures were still on his mind early in 1840, when he included "The Brave man" in a list of projected lectures and essays, most of them probably intended for the *Dial*.[5] After completing "Aulus Persius Flaccus," which Emerson pressured Margaret Fuller to accept for the first issue of the *Dial*, Thoreau began to draft "The Service," which he sent off to Fuller in July 1840.

In the essay, Thoreau sought to define a kind of heroic individualism. "The Service" was divided into three parts: "Qualities of the Recruit," "What Music Shall We Have?" and "Not How Many But Where the Enemy Are," a series of titles that suggests the military imagery of the essay. In the rather abstract and vaporous opening section, he sharply distinguished between the coward and the brave man, whose "eye is the focus in which all the rays, from whatever side, are collected" (*RP*, p. 4). In an effort to suggest a concrete type of this "spherical" man, Thoreau in the second section illustrated the brave man's harmony with the universe by citing the example of the soldier. "When Bravery first grew afraid and went to war, it took music along with it," he remarked in the first paragraph: "Especially the soldier insists on agreement and harmony always. . . . If the soldier marches to the sack of a town, he must be preceded by drum and trumpet, which shall identify his cause with the accordant universe" (*RP*, p. 9). Thus, although he began the essay by observing that "bravery deals not so much in resolute action, as healthy and assured rest" (*RP*, p. 3), Thoreau's imagery was drawn from active and heroic pursuits. Consequently, despite his half-hearted efforts to distinguish between the soldier and the brave man, the imagery of "The Service" increasingly identified its author with the heroic combatant. "I see Falsehood sneaking from the full blaze of truth, and with good relish could do execution on their rearward ranks with the first brand that came to hand," he exuberantly proclaimed in the third and concluding section:

> We too are such puny creatures as to be put to flight by the sun, and suffer our
> ardor to grow cool in proportion as his increases; our own short lived chivalry
> sounds a retreat with the fumes and vapors of the night, and we turn to meet

mankind with its meek face preaching peace, and such nonresistance as the chaff that rides before the whirlwind. Let not our Peace be proclaimed by the rust on our swords, or our inability to draw them from their scabbards, but let her at least have so much work on her hands, as to keep those swords bright and sharp. (*RP*, p. 13)

As this passage illustrates, "The Service" was partly a response to contemporary events. "Its form was perhaps suggested by the discourses on Peace and Non–Resistance which in 1840 were so numerous in New England," F. B. Sanborn remarked, "while the native pugnacity of Thoreau provoked him to take up the cause of war and persist in the apostolic symbolism on the soldier of the Lord, and the Middle-Age crusader."[6] Later critics have denied Sanborn's contention, including Sherman Paul, who rightly insisted that "Thoreau did not demand war where the peace societies demanded peace; he demanded the moral equivalent of war, that spiritual crusading for truth . . . that would galvanize the feebler virtues of his age."[7] But the militant tone and military imagery of "The Service" suggest that Thoreau was reacting against the spirit, if not the letter, of the peace movement, which gained impetus during the crisis following the establishment of the Texas Republic in 1836. As early as 1836, William Lloyd Garrison committed himself to Henry C. Wright's program of the inviolability of life and announced in the *Liberator* that the Quaker doctrine of nonresistance erred only in not going far enough.[8] In the Declaration of Principle of the New England Non-Resistance Society, formed in 1838, Garrison thus proclaimed a doctrine at the furthest extreme from "The Service." Whereas Thoreau sketched an idealized portrait of the soldier of the Lord, Garrison cited the example of Christ, the "Prince of Peace," as the basis for the doctrine of nonresistance:

We register our testimony, not only against all wars, whether offensive or defensive, but all preparations for war; against every naval ship, every arsenal, every fortification; against the militia system and a standing army; against all military chieftains and soldiers; against all monuments commemorative of victory over a fallen foe, all trophies won in battle, all celebrations in honor of military or naval exploits; against all appropriations for the defense of a nation by force and arms, on the part of any legislative body; against every edict of government requiring of its subjects military service. Hence we deem it unlawful to bear arms or to hold a military office.[9]

Thoreau had ample exposure to these doctrines. In the Declaration of Principle, Garrison continued: "We expect to prevail through the foolishness of preaching—striving to commend ourselves unto every man's conscience, in the sight of God. From the press we shall promulgate our sentiments as widely as practicable."[10] Such sermons were delivered in the *Liberator* and the *Non-Resistant*, both of which probably found their way into the Thoreau household, dominated by members of the Women's Anti-Slavery Society. Garrison's eloquent pleas for abolition and nonresistance later had a marked impact on him, but Thoreau initially remained aloof from these causes. Thus, on 27 January 1841, six months after he submitted "The Service" to Margaret Fuller, Thoreau participated in a discussion at the Concord Lyceum of the question "Is it ever proper to offer forcible resistance?" As his early treatment of bravery would lead us to expect, Thoreau argued in the affirmative.[11]

"The Service" found little favor with its earliest readers. Fuller held on to the manuscript until December 1840, when she rejected it in a celebrated letter to Thoreau. "The essay is rich in thoughts," she observed: "But then the thoughts seem to me so out of their natural order, that I cannot read it through without *pain*. I never once feel myself in a stream of thought, but seem to hear the grating of tools on the mosaic."[12] Despite her perceptive evaluation of its structural weaknesses, Fuller invited Thoreau to revise and resubmit the essay to her, but he apparently did not do so. In fact, F. B. Sanborn suggested that the manuscript of "The Service" was not returned to Thoreau at all, but was sent instead to Emerson, who retained possession until after Thoreau's death.[13] If so, Emerson must have shared some of Fuller's objections, since he made no effort to publish "The Service" after succeeding her as editor of the *Dial*.

But other evidence indicates that Thoreau retained possession of the manuscript of "The Service" and remained preoccupied by the subject of the essay. He included "Bravery" in a new list of writing projects drawn up in the fall of 1841, a probable indication that he planned to rework "The Service" for inclusion in a book along the lines of Emerson's *Essays*.[14] The subject also played an important role in "Sir Walter Raleigh," written in 1843. "He was a proper knight, a born cavalier, and in the intervals of war betook himself still to the most vigorous arts of peace, though as if diverted from his proper aim," Thoreau admiringly observed: "He makes us doubt if there is not some worthier apology for war than has been discovered . . . In whatever he is engaged we seem to see a plume waving over his head, and a sword dangling at his side."[15] Thoreau's chivalric idéalism survived even the controversy over the Annexation of Texas, which gave added impetus to the nonresistance movement, for he later took three pages of extracts from "The Service" for addition to the first draft of *A Week*, written in 1845.

In his extracts, Thoreau revised and rearranged scattered sentences and paragraphs from "What Music Shall We Have?," the second section of "The Service."[16] For example, in the essay the section begins: "The brave man is the sole patron of music; he recognizes it for his mother tongue; a more mellifluous and articulate language than words, in comparison with which, speech is recent and temporary. It is his voice. His language must have the same majestic movement and cadence, that philosophy assigns to the heavenly bodies. The steady flux of his thought constitutes time in music" (*RP*, p. 9). Thoreau sharply compressed such prolix passages. "The brave man is the sole patron of music and recognizes it as his mother tongue," he jotted down in the extracts: "The steady flux of his thought constitutes time in music" (MH, 4, D). By repressing the labored and distracting analogy between music and speech, and by omitting the pedantic allusion to the music of the spheres, he more effectively suggested the brave man's harmony with the universe.

Similarly, Thoreau began the extracts with a revised and compressed version of the third paragraph in "What Music Shall We Have?": "A bugle heard in the stillness of the night sends forth its voice to the farthest stars and marshals them in new order and harmony. The notes seem to flash out in the horizon like heat lightening, quickening the pulse of creation" (MH, 4, D; cf. *RP*, pp. 10–11). In this redaction of the original paragraph, Thoreau omitted four sentences, including the facile concluding comment, "The heavens say, Now this is my own earth" (*RP*, p. 11). Rather than forcing his meaning upon the reader, he increasingly relied on his imagery to suggest the harmonious relation between heaven and earth, between the sound of the bugle and the responsive stars. Like his other extracts from "The Service," the revised paragraph reveals the artistic strides Thoreau made between 1840, when he was just beginning his literary career, and 1846, when he probably began to expand the first draft of *A Week*.

There is ample evidence that Thoreau took the extracts from "The Service" for addition to the first draft of *A Week*.[17] First, he wrote the extracts on two leaves of the same paper he had used for the bulk of the first draft. Second, the paper and handwriting of the extracts also match other additions to the first draft, including a passage from "Sir Walter Raleigh" (MH, 19). Finally, the extracts from "The Service" are followed by a paragraph copied from a longer entry in the Journal of January 1843 beginning, "I hardly know of any subject on which so little has been said to the purpose as music" (MH, 4, D; cf. *J*, 1:446–47). Added to his selection of extracts from "The Service," all of which concern music, the paragraph from the Journal indicates that Thoreau gathered material for addition to a brief digression on music at the end of "Monday" in the first draft of *A Week*.

The extracts from "The Service" smoothly fit their new context in *A Week*. In a remark that occasioned the digression on music, Thoreau observed in the first draft: "Far into the night we heard some tyro beating a drum incessantly in preparation for a country muster . . . and thought of the line 'When the drum beat at dead of night'" (FD; cf. *J*, 1:132). That remark, first jotted down in the Journal of June 1840, when Thoreau was drafting

"The Service," shared the martial spirit of the essay on bravery. It also offered an appropriate setting for the extracts from "The Service," which began, "A bugle heard in the stillness of the night sends forth its voice to the farthest stars" (MH, 4, D). Moreover, by adding the extracts from "The Service," Thoreau began to construct a plausible chain of associations: drum—martial music—heroism—harmony—natural laws. In fact, the extracts from "The Service" were less effective in the original essay, where Thoreau dealt with bravery as an abstraction, than in *A Week*, where he depicted the brothers' voyage as a heroic endeavor to attain harmony with nature and with the laws of the universe.

As he worked on a second draft of *A Week* during late 1846 and 1847, Thoreau continued to revise and rearrange the extracts from "The Service." Two leaves among the surviving manuscripts of *A Week* contain successive versions of the material: the first, paged "195–196," was probably a part of the manuscript sent off to Evert Duyckinck of Wiley & Putnam in May 1847 (MH, 15, 0); the second, paged "210–211," was written later in 1847, possibly when Thoreau revised and expanded the manuscript before submitting it to various publishers that summer. Following the lines, "Therefore a current of sadness deep / Through the strain of thy triumph is heard to sweep" (see *AW*, p. 175), Thoreau in the second of these versions continued:

> As polishing expresses the vein in marble and the grain in wood, so music brings out what of heroic lurks anywhere. The brave man is the sole patron of music, and recognizes it as his mother tongue. The steady flux of his thought consitutes its time. According to the ancients Harmony was begotten of Mars and Venus. The soldier especially always insists on agreement & harmony. If he marches to the sack of a town even he must be preceded by drums and trumpets, which will identify his cause with the concordant universe. It is the friendship there is in war that makes it chivalrous & heroic. It was the dim sentiment of a noble friendship for the purest soul in history that gave to Europe a crusading era. The coward blows a shrill & feeble blast, and hears no concordant note in the universe, but is a consciously outcast & deserted man; but the brave man compels concord everywhere by the universality and tunefulness of his soul. A man's life should be a steady march to an inaudible but sweet and all pervading music; and when he seems to halt, he will still be marching on his post. His heart will sharpen and attune his ear, and he will never take a false step, even in the most arduous circumstances, for then the music will swell into corresponding sweetness and volume, and rule the movement it inspired. I believe it is Plutarch who says that "Plato thinks the gods never gave men music, the science of melody & harmony for mere delectation or to tickle the ear; but that the discordant parts of the circulations & beauteous fabric of the soul, and that of it that roves about the body, and many times for want of tune and air breaks forth into many extravagances and excesses, might be sweetly recalled and artfully wound up to their former consent and agreement." (MH, 15, 0, paged "210–211")

Although he managed to fuse the scattered paragraphs from "The Service" into a single coherent paragraph in the second draft of *A Week*, Thoreau obviously made little effort to reconsider his earlier notions about soldiers, heroism, and war in the light of contemporary events. As noted above, he probably took the extracts from "The Service" in early 1846, after the controversy over the Annexation of Texas but before the outbreak of the Mexican War. Following the declaration of war and his own arrest for failure to pay the poll tax, he wrote in the Journal of July 1846: "There probably never were worse crimes committed since time began than in the present Mexican war . . . the vilainy is in the readiness with which men, doing outrage to their proper natures—lend themselves to perform the office of inferior & brutal ones."[18] As the Journal entry makes clear, Thoreau was thinking of army recruits, so it is all the more surprising that he continued to treat the soldier as a paradigm of the brave man in the second draft of *A Week*, written during the following year. It was one thing casually to refer to soldiers marching to the sack of a town in 1840, before America had awakened to its "manifest destiny"; it was quite another to refer to it in 1847, while American soldiers were laying siege to Vera Cruz in March and to Mexico City in August, when the manuscript of *A Week* was making the rounds of publishers. No doubt the references to the Crusades, plus the addition of an allusion to Venus and Mars, were intended to suggest a heroism both ancient and virtuous. But, however much Thoreau may have idealized the soldier of Christ in "The Service," by 1847 he no longer believed that war was "chivalric & heroic"; he surely also understood that "friendship," and especially "friendship for the purest soul in history," had nothing to do with events south of the Rio Grande.

Thoreau was apparently aware of some of the contradictions between the idealized notions of "The Service" and the realities of the Mexican War. Following the statement that "Harmony was begotten of Mars and Venus" in the manuscript of *A Week*, which failed to find a publisher in 1847, he later interlined: "That harmony which exists naturally between the heroes' moods & the universe, the soldier would fain imitate with drum & trumpet" (MH, 15, 0, paged "211"). Apparently the sound of that "tyro beating a drum," which had prompted the digression on music in the first draft of *A Week*, and the notes of "a bugle heard in the stillness of the night," the first line in the 1846 extracts from "The Service," had begun to take on more sinister implications in 1847. In a revised and expanded version of the passage probably written in 1848, Thoreau later used the interlined sentence to introduce the digression of harmony and heroism, which began:

> That harmony which exists naturally between the heroes' moods and the universe—the soldier would fain imitate with drum & trumpet. The soldier especially insists on agreement and harmony always. Indeed it is the friendship

there is in war that makes it chivalrous & heroic ever. It was the dim sentiment of a noble friendship for the purest soul in history that gave to Europe a crusading era. If the soldier marches to the sack of a town even he must be preceeded by drums and trumpets which will as it were identify his cause with the accordant universe. The rollcall musters for him all the forces of nature. He is no longer insulated but infinitely related thus, and the hostile territory is as it were preoccupied for him.

When we are in health, all sounds pipe and drum for us—   As polishing expresses the vein in marble and the grain in wood, so music brings out what of heroic lurks anywhere.

Marching is when the pulse of the hero beats in unison with the pulse of nature, and he steps to the measure of the universe. When the body marches thus to the measure of the soul, then is there true courage and invincible strength.

The coward substitutes for this thrilling sphere music a universal wail, for this melodious chant a nasal cant, and but whistles to keep his courage up. He blows a feeble blast of slender melody and can compel his neighborhood only into a partial concord with himself, because nature has but little sympathy with such a soul; hence he hears no accordant note in the universe, and is a coward or consciously outcast and deserted man. But the brave man without drum or trumpet compels concord everywhere by the universality and tunefulness of his soul.

I have heard a strain of music issuing from a soldier's camp in the dawn which sounded like the morning hymn of creation. The birches rustling in the breeze, and the slumberous breathing of the crickets seemed to hush their murmuring to attend to it. (MH, 2, [1r–1v])

Thoreau obviously had a good deal of difficulty reconciling the martial imagery of "The Service" with his own growing hostility to the military. The opening remark that the soldier merely imitates the brave man's harmony with the universe seems to contradict the assertion from "The Service" that the soldier "insists on agreement and harmony always." Furthermore, in contrast to the two versions drafted in 1847, in which he had used only a small portion of the opening paragraph of "What Music Shall We Have?," Thoreau in 1848 incorporated two additional sentences from the paragraph: "The rollcall . . . preoccupied for him" (cf. *RP*, p. 9, and MH, 4, D). Thus, not only does the soldier continue cheerfully to march to the sack of a town, but his rollcall now once again musters "the forces of nature," through which he becomes "infinitely related," insuring his victory over hostile forces.

In the second and following paragraphs of the 1848 version, Thoreau sought to shift attention from the soldier to the heroic individual, who marches to a different drummer. But here, as in "The Service," the contrast between the brave man's "thrilling sphere music" and the coward's "universal wail" also implicitly elevates the soldier, who at least marches to drum and trumpet. Following the depiction of the stirring notes from the soldier's camp, suggested by yet another paragraph in "The Service" (*RP*, pp. 10–11), Thoreau added a revised version of an entry "From a Chapter on Bravery" in the 1839 Journal which he had not used in "The Service." A comparison of the original Journal entry and Thoreau's 1848 revision illustrates his changing attitude toward soldiers:

Journal

No pains are spared to do honor to the brave soldier. All guilds and corporations are taxed to provide him with fit harness and equipment—   His coat must be red as the sunet—or blue as the heavens. Gold or silver—pinchback or copper—solid or superficial—mark him for fortune's favorite. The skill of a city enhances and tempers his sword blade—the Tyrian dye confounds him with emperors and kings. Wherever he goes, music precedes and prepares the way for him. His life is a holiday and the contagion of his example unhinges the universe. The world puts by work and comes out to stare. He is the one only man. He recognizes no time honored casts and conventions—no fixtures but transfixtures—no governments at length settled on a permanent basis. One tap of the drum sets the political and moral harmonies all ajar. His ethics may well bear comparison with the priest's. He may rally, charge, retreat in an orderly manner—but never flee nor flinch. (*J*, 1:94)

1848 Revision

The soldier is the degenerate hero, as the priest is the degenerate saint, and soldier and priest are still as closely related as hero and saint. Their virtue has but one name originally in all languages. The ones discipline will well bear comparison with the others. Mankind still pays to the soldier the honors due only to the hero, as to the priest those due only to the saint. All guilds and corporations are taxed to furnish him with fit harness and equipment—to adorn him with silver and gold, and the colors of the rainbow. Music is for him especially and his life is a holiday. (MH, 2, [2r])[19]

Thoreau completely altered the tone and imagery of the original Journal entry. In the preceding entry in the Journal, he had noted that, when war becomes a routine, "the hero degenerates into a marine, and the standing army into a standing jest" (*J*, 1:94). But in 1839 he clearly distinguished between such "indented apprentices" and the "brave soldier" honored for his heroism. But by 1848 even that "brave soldier" had become "the degenerate hero," comparable to the priest, "the degenerate saint." In a further effort to disassociate the soldier from the hero, Thoreau in the 1848 version interlined, "But true virtue is a bravery beside which that of the soldier & the priest are cowardice" (MH, 2, [2r]). That depiction is a far cry from the idealized soldier of "A Chapter on Bravery," whose rejection of all "time honored casts and conventions" mirrored Thoreau's own radical individualism. The "brave soldier" of the Journal is independent of governments; implicitly, the soldiers of the revised version are servants of the state, just as priests are servants of the church, institutions Thoreau attacks elsewhere in *A Week* (AW, pp. 63ff, 129ff). Observing that the soldier "is the one only man," Thoreau in 1839 celebrated the soldier's unflinching bravery in the face of the enemy; in 1848, after the ignoble conclusion of the Mexican War, Thoreau emphasized that such bravery was no virtue, especially if the soldier's cause was unjust.

Despite his attempt to distinguish between the soldier and the hero, Thoreau's imagery tended to link the two. In the 1839 Journal entry, the soldier is arrayed in "fit harness and equipment," which Thoreau described in elaborate and glowing detail. He apparently sought to transfer those appurtenances to the hero, but because of the ambiguous "he" and "him" at the end of the paragraph in the 1848 version the soldier and the hero tend to merge into a single compound figure, adorned "with silver and gold, and the colors of the rainbow," whose "life is a holiday." In the concluding paragraphs of the 1848 version, however, Thoreau depicted such a life in contemplative rather than active terms:

> Bravery does not exhibit itself in deeds, but in a life. It does not consist so much in resolute action as in healthy and assured rest. One moment of serene and confident life is more glorious than a whole campaign of daring. It sleeps securely within its camp not even dreaming of a foe. The stars are its silent sentries by night, and the sun its pioneer by day. From its abundant cheerfulness spring flowers and the rainbow, and its infinite humor and wontonness produce corn & vines.
>
> Man should have an accompaniment of music through nature. It relieves the scenery, which is seen through it as a subtler element, like a very clear morning air in Autumn.
>
> One music seems to differ from another chiefly by its more perfect time, to use this word in a true sense. In the steadiness and equanimity of music lies its divinity. It is the only assured tone. When men attain to speak with as settled a faith, and as firm assurance, their voices will sing and their feet march as do the soldier's.
>
> These melodious cadences plainly proceed out of a very deep meaning and a sustained soul—   They are perhaps the expression of the perfect knowledge to which the saints attain.
>
> I feel a sad cheer when I har these lofty strains because there must be something in me as lofty that hears—   But ah! I hear them not always!
>
> There are in music such strains as far surpass any faith which man ever had in the loftiness of his destiny.
>
> Things are to be learned which it will be sweet to learn. This cannot be all rumor.

The clear morning notes seem to come through a veil of sadness to me—for possibly they are only the echo which my life makes "Therefore a current of sadness deep / Through the strains of thy triumph is heard to sweep." (MH, 2, [2r–2v])

These paragraphs reveal a pronounced shift in emphasis. In the 1846 extracts, the two drafts written in 1847, and the opening of the 1848 version, Thoreau had exclusively drawn upon the second section of "The Service," "What Music Shall We Have?," especially the paragraphs on soldiers and war. But these concluding paragraphs of the 1848 version were suggested by the opening section of "The Service," "Qualities of the Recruit," from which Thoreau lifted the sentence, "It does not consist so much in resolute action as in healthy and assured rest" (cf. *RP*, p. 3, and *J*, 1:91). That conception of bravery was far more appropriate to Thoreau's evolving view of life in *A Week*. Probably for that reason, he later revised "Bravery," with its strong connotations of physical valor, to "courage," from the Latin *cor*, heart, which implies a quality of mind or spirit. He also interlined: "How much virtue there is in simply seeing. We may almost say that the hero has striven in vain for preeminence if the student oversees him. The woman who sits in the house & sees is a match for a stirring captain" (MH, 2, [2r]).

But after those confident assertions of the ascendency of the contemplative life, Thoreau fell back upon a military analogy. Describing such a healthy, harmonious life, he observed: "When men attain to speak with as settled a faith, and as firm assurance, their voices will sing and their feet march as do the soldier's." Although he clearly did not intend it, the analogy implied that the heroic individual somehow aspires to the condition of the soldier rather than to that "perfect knowledge" of the saint or to that lofty destiny adumbrated in the brief final paragraphs of the 1848 version. Indeed, such military imagery, so integral to "The Service," proved to have a life of its own, which resisted Thoreau's determined efforts to adapt it to sharply different purposes in *A Week*.

Thoreau finally abandoned his effort to transfer the martial imagery of "The Service" to *A Week*. With the exception of brief passages, he omitted the entire 1848 version from the digression on music in "Monday," which contains only a few sentences from "The Service," including the one beginning "As polishing expresses the vein in marble . . . " (*AW*, p. 175; *RP*, p. 10), the quotation from Plutarch (*AW*, p. 175; *RP*, p. 10), and a favorite sentence about the "clarion sound and clang of corselet and buckler," which he used in "The Service," in drafts of "Sir Walter Raleigh," and finally in *A Week* (*AW*, p. 177; *RP*, p. 17). In his only remaining reference to soldiers in the digression on music, Thoreau briefly dismisses their claim to heroism. Anticipating the "different drummer" passage in *Walden*, he observes: "The hero is the sole patron of music. That harmony which exists naturally between the hero's moods and the universe the soldier would fain imitate with drum and trumpet. . . . Marching is when the pulse of the hero beats in unison with the pulse of Nature, and he steps to the measure of the universe; then there is true courage and invincible strength" (*AW*, p. 175).

In a final ironic commentary on soldiers in *A Week*, Thoreau in "Thursday" describes a brief meeting with an absurdly comic figure "going to muster in full regimentals" (*AW*, p. 313).[20] Whereas in "Monday" the sound of a drum, "in preparation for a country muster" (*AW*, p. 173), prompts the lofty meditation on music and heroism, the ungainly youth in "Thursday" inspires laughter and derision. Like young Thoreau in "The Service," the youth has "thoughts of war and glory," but his appearance, shivering "like a reed in his thin military pants" and skulking past the brothers "as if he were driving his father's sheep under a sword-proof helmet," reveals the gap between those illusory thoughts and the realities of military life: "It was too much for him to carry any extra armor then, who could not easily dispose of his natural arms. And for his legs, they were like heavy artillery in boggy places; better to cut the traces and forsake them. His greaves chafed and wrestled one with another for want of other foes" (*AW*, pp. 313–14). The youth's awkward bearing and clumsy outfit, to which the addition of "any extra armor" would be an absurdity, mocks those chivalric figures who had marched through Thoreau's youthful imagination into the pages of "The Service." "But he did get by and get off with all his munitions, and lived to fight another day," Thoreau disingenuously concludes; "and I do not record this as casting any suspicion on his honor and real bravery in the field" (*AW*, p. 314). The word "bravery," closely linked to the soldiers of "The Service," clearly had no meaning when applied to the representative "soldier lad" of *A Week*.

Thoreau, however, reserved his harshest treatment of soldiers for his essay on civil disobedience, delivered as lectures in January and February 1848, when he was revising *A Week*, and published as "Resistance to Civil Government" the same month as *A Week* in May 1849. On 23 February 1848, Thoreau wrote to Emerson: "I read [a lecture] last week to the Lyceum on The Rights & Duties of the Individual in relation to Government—much to Mr. Alcott's satisfaction" (*C*, p. 208). Alcott, who had seven years earlier debated Thoreau on the question "Is it ever proper to offer forcible resistance?," no doubt took satisfaction in Thoreau's adoption of the Garrisonian position on peace and nonresistance. That change in attitude informs Thoreau's depiction of soldiers in "Resistance to Civil Government," where he observes:

> A common and natural result of an undue respect for law is, that you may see a file of soldiers, colonel, captain, corporal, privates, powder-monkeys and all, marching in admirable order over hill and dale to the wars, against their wills, aye, against their common sense and consciences, which makes it very steep marching indeed, and produces a palpitation of the heart. They have no doubt

that it is a damnable business in which they are concerned; they are all peaceably inclined. Now, what are they? Men at all? or small moveable forts and magazines, at the service of some unscrupulous man in power? (*RP*, p. 65)

This savage depiction of the soldier contrasts sharply to those in Thoreau's earlier writings on Bravery. In "The Service," he celebrated the Crusader, marching to the accompaniment of music under the banner of Christ; in "Resistance to Civil Government," he describes "a file of soldiers, colonel, captain, corporal, privates, powder-monkeys and all," in other words the soldiers who actually marched off to the Mexican War. Instead of serving God, they have forsaken their own consciences, the God-like part of man. Their marching "produces a palpitation of the heart," an intuitive sense that they are violating those higher laws of human decency and divine love, because war is truly "a damnable business." Indeed, Thoreau's emphasis on conscience recalls Garrison's appeal "unto every man's conscience" a decade earlier. In contrast to the gorgeously bedecked soldier of 1839 in "A Chapter on Bravery," whose "life is a holiday" (*J*, 1:94), the soldier of "Resistance to Civil Government" is not a man but a machine, "a mere shadow and reminiscence of humanity, a man laid out alive and standing, and already, as one may say, buried alive under arms with funeral accompaniments" (*RP*, pp. 65–66). The idealized soldier of Thoreau's youthful dreams of glory had thus been superseded by a grotesque, nightmarish figure conjured up by the injustices of the Mexican War.

Thoreau's futile efforts to revise portions of "The Service" for *A Week* and his implied disavowal of "The Service" in "Resistance to Civil Government" reveal his dramatic growth between 1839 and 1849. On one level, that growth is evidenced in his increasing craft, illustrated by his selection, compression, and rearrangement of material from "The Service," and by his careful revisions of that material in various drafts of *A Week*. He not only learned that imagery might speak for itself, without the heavy-handed impositions of "The Service," but that the martial imagery of "The Service" retained its stridency despite his best efforts to modulate it. Thoreau therefore omitted all but a few sentences of "The Service" from *A Week*. But that decision was moral as well as artistic, a result of his changing attitudes during the 1840s. "The Service," full of youthful bravado, was a response to those like Garrison, who preached peace and nonresistance. But under the impact of the Mexican War, Thoreau moved closer and closer to Garrison's position, so it was difficult for him to sustain the chivalric ideals of "The Service." *A Week* depicts a radically different kind of heroism from the abstract virtue adumbrated in "The Service," while "Resistance to Civil Government," with its sinewy prose and cogent argument, charts Thoreau's movement away from the vaporous abstractions and naive idealism of "The Service."

But the attitudes assumed in *A Week* and the views expressed in "Resistance to Civil Government" were not fixed. In *Walden*, which he had hoped to publish soon after *A Week*, Thoreau once again dismissed "their heroism who stood up for half an hour in the front line at Buena Vista," one of the battles in the Mexican War that contributed to his sense of "some sort of itching and disease in the horizon" as he worked in "The Bean Field."[21] By the time *Walden* was published in 1854, however, events, and especially the passage of the Fugitive Slave Act, were driving Thoreau and other abolitionists from nonresistance toward increasingly violent and militant positions. "Slavery in Massachusetts," delivered on 4 July 1854 and swiftly published in Garrison's *Liberator*, reveals that shift. Whereas in *Walden*, as in "Resistance to Civil Government," he rejected forcible resistance, wittily observing, "I preferred that society should run 'amok' against me, it being the desperate party" (*W*, p. 171), in "Slavery in Massachusetts" Thoreau celebrated the "heroic attack on the Boston Court-House" (*RP*, p. 105), an ill-fated attempt to free Anthony Burns, a fugitive slave, from a Boston jail. "My thoughts are murder to the State," he savagely proclaimed, "and involuntarily go plotting against her" (*RP*, p. 108).

Thoreau's conviction that forcible resistance had become necessary anticipated his eloquent apologies for John Brown, addresses delivered in 1859–60 that blended the martial spirit of "The Service," the disgust for military life evident in "Resistance to Civil Government," *A Week*, and *Walden*, and the violent revulsion against the state announced in "Slavery in Massachusetts." Making his earlier distinction between bravery and courage, Thoreau in "A Plea for Captain John Brown" compared him to the heroes of the American Revolution: "They could bravely face their country's foes, but he had the courage to face his country herself, when she was in the wrong" (*RP*, p. 113). Consequently, unlike the "momentary charge at Balaclava, in obedience to a blundering command, proving what a perfect machine the soldier is," Brown had led a steady charge "against the legions of Slavery, in obedience to an infinitely higher command" (*RP*, p. 119). Although Brown, a soldier in citizen's dress, lacks the colorful outward accouterments of the soldiers of "The Service," he, too, is a soldier of the Lord, one whose "armor" was a righteous cause (*RP*, p. 117). Indeed, as Thoreau affirmed in "The Last Days of John Brown," in death the hero and martyr had laid down his Sharps' rifle to take up "the sword of the spirit—the sword with which he has really won his greatest and most memorable victories" (*RP*, p. 152). Thus, the chivalric crusaders of "The Service," driven from *A Week* by the Mexican War, reemerged two decades after the essay was written in portraits of a modern day crusader, final exemplar of Thoreau's own militant idealism and radical individualism.

NOTES

1. For an account of its writing, reception, and later reputation, see my Historical Introduction to *A Week on the Concord and Merrimack Rivers*, ed. Carl Hovde et al. (1980), in *The Writings of Henry D. Thoreau*, ed. Walter Harding et al., 7 vols. to date (Princeton: Princeton University Press, 1971–). Hereafter cited as *AW*, by page number.

2. *Massachusetts Quarterly Review*, 3 (December 1849): 40–51.

3. For a brief discussion of the writing of the essay, see the Textual Introduction to "The Service" in *The Writings of Henry D. Thoreau, Reform Papers*, ed. Wendell Glick (1973), pp. 261–64. Hereafter cited as *RP*, by page number. Thoreau's interest in the subject of bravery during 1839–40 was probably spurred by Emerson, then revising a lecture on "Heroism" for *Essays*, published in March 1841.

4. *The Writings of Henry D. Thoreau, Journal, Volume 1: 1837–1844*, ed. John C. Broderick et al. (1981), pp. 91–98. Hereafter cited as *J*, by volume and page numbers.

5. The complete list, which also contains Thoreau's preliminary title for an account of the 1839 trip on the Concord and Merrimack, which he began to reconstruct in June 1840 (*J*, 1:124ff), is printed in *AW*, p. 437.

6. *The Service*, ed. F. B. Sanborn (Boston: Charles E. Goodspeed, 1902), pp. vii–viii.

7. Quoted in Kenneth E. Harris, "Thoreau's 'The Service'—A Review of the Scholarship," *American Transcendental Quarterly*, no. 11 (Summer 1971): 60–63, which contains a useful survey of critical comments on the essay.

8. Helpful accounts of the growth of the nonresistance movement in America include Alice Felt Tyler, *Freedom's Ferment* (Minneapolis: University of Minnesota Press, 1944), pp. 411–17, and Louis Filler, *The Crusade Against Slavery* (New York: Harpers, 1960), passim.

9. *William Lloyd Garrison on Non-Resistance*, ed. F. G. Villard (1924); rpt. in *The Peace Movement in America* (New York: Jerome S. Ozer, 1972), p. 25.

10. *Non-Resistance*, p. 27.

11. The surviving records of the Concord Lyceum, which offer an illuminating glimpse of the major reform issues during the period, are printed in *The Massachusetts Lyceum During the American Renaissance*, ed. Kenneth Walter Cameron (Hartford, Conn.: Transcendental Books, 1969), pp. 101–90. The other participants in the discussion were Thoreau's brother John, who argued with him in the affirmative, and Bronson Alcott, who took the opposing position. The involvement of other members of the Thoreau household in reform movements is sketched in Walter Harding, *The Days of Henry Thoreau* (New York: Alfred A. Knopf, 1965).

12. *The Correspondence of Henry David Thoreau*, ed. Walter Harding and Carl Bode (New York: New York University Press, 1958), pp. 41–42. Hereafter cited as *C*, by page number.

13. *The Service*, ed. Sanborn, p. x. Wendell Glick notes that it "seems reasonable to trust Sanborn's account of the provenience of the manuscript," which came into Sanborn's possession after Emerson's death in 1882 (see *RP*, p. 262).

14. The complete list is printed in *AW*, p. 440. For a discussion of Thoreau's plans at this time to write a book of essays, see Thomas Blanding, "Apollo Serving King Admetus: Thoreau Bargains for a Farm and a Book in 1841," an unpublished lecture on deposit at the Thoreau Lyceum, Concord, Massachusetts.

15. *The Writings of Henry D. Thoreau, Early Essays and Miscellanies*, ed. Joseph J. Moldenhauer (1975), p. 181.

16. The two leaves of extracts, incorporating revisions made in the manuscript of "The Service," are at MH, bMS Am 278.5, folder 4, D. Quotations from manuscripts in the Houghton Library are by folder number within bMS Am 278.5, and are by permission of the Harvard College Library.

17. Wendell Glick, who used the revised versions of two paragraphs in the extracts as copy-

text for those portions of "The Service," does not date the leaves or refer to *A Week* (*RP*, pp. 262–63). William L. Howarth, however, has correctly identified the two leaves of extracts as part of the surviving manuscripts of *A Week* (see *The Literary Manuscripts of Henry David Thoreau* [Columbus: Ohio State University Press, 1974], p. 195, entry D5m). For a detailed description and an edited text of the first draft, see Linck C. Johnson, "A Complex Weave: The Writing of Thoreau's *A Week on the Concord and Merrimack Rivers*, with the Text of the First Draft" (forthcoming), hereafter cited as FD.

18. *The Writings of Henry D. Thoreau, Journal, Volume 2: 1842–1848*, ed. Robert Sattel-meyer (1983), p. 263.

19. Thoreau initially interlined this revision in pencil in the Journal: see *The Journal of Henry David Thoreau*, ed. Bradford Torrey [and Francis H. Allen], 14 vols. (Boston: Houghton Mifflin, 1906), I:101–102n.

20. The account of this meeting, probably an imaginary one, was apparently a late addition to *A Week*. Thoreau made no allusion to it in his excursion notes, in the early Journal or in Journal transcripts for *A Week*, in the first draft, or in any of the surviving manuscripts from 1846–47. He probably added the account in 1848, when he wrote Horace Greeley, "My book is swelling again under my hands" (*C*, p. 225).

21. *The Writings of Henry D. Thoreau, Walden*, ed. J. Lyndon Shanley (1971), p. 118. Here-after cited as *W*, by page number.

THE BIBLE IN *WALDEN*: FURTHER ADDITIONS

Edward C. Jacobs

THOREAU'S USE OF THE BIBLE is now beginning to receive the attention it merits. Larry R. Long's recent "The Bible and the Composition of *Walden*" in STUDIES IN THE AMERICAN RENAISSANCE 1979 (pp. 309–53) and past dissertations by Long and others (listed along with other similar studies by Long on p. 326) categorically prove Thoreau's deliberate use of the Bible and explore the influence of biblical thought, imagery, and style upon Thoreau's writings. Appendices to Long's article offer "a complete list [to date] of the biblical uses found in the *Walden* materials" (p. 326). A list of some sixteen other heretofore unnoted "biblical uses" found in *Walden* which I cite below supplement Long's list. Using J. Lyndon Shanley's edition of *Walden* (1971) in *The Writings of Henry D. Thoreau*, ed. Walter Harding et al., 6 vols. to date (Princeton: Princeton University Press, 1971–), I cite Thoreau's text by chapter title and page and line number, and then quote the relevant text, concluding with a parenthetical reference to the location of this text in Walter Harding's edition of *The Variorum Walden* (New York: Washington Square Press, 1963). Beneath Thoreau's text I identify and quote from the King James translation the relevant biblical text(s) and offer, at times, textual or interpretative comments of my own.

"Economy" (Shanley, 8:30–31): "Old deeds for old people, and new deeds for new." (Harding, 5:26–27.)

> Matthew 9:17: "Neither do men put new wine into old bottles . . . they put new wine into new bottles . . ." (cf. Mark 2:22; Luke 5:37–39). Thoreau, again, refers to this passage, as Long notes, in "Economy" (Shanley, 24.2–3; Harding, 16.32) and in the "Conclusion" (Shanley, 331.4–8; Harding, 250.17–20).

"Where I Lived, and What I Lived For" (Shanley, 83.35–84.1): " . . . I had had my seeds ready. Many think that seeds improve with age. I have no doubt that time discriminates between the good and the bad." (Harding, 62.16–18.)

> Matthew 13:24–30, 36–43: Long's appendices cite five references in *Walden* to Matt. 13. In the passage I cite above Thoreau has subtly approximated the biblical imagery and thought found in the parable of the wheat and tares (vs. 24–30, 36–43). In this parable Christ makes clear that "time" or "age" will eventually "discriminate" between the good and bad seeds that have been sown in the farmer's field. Compare this "seed" imagery with that already noted by Long: "The soil, it appears, is suited to the seed, for it has sent its radicle downward . . ." (Shanley, 15:28–29; Harding, 10:28–30).

"Where I Lived, and What I Lived For" (Shanley, 91.5–11): " . . . to drive life into a corner . . . and be able to give a true account of it in my next excursion." (Harding, 67.31–36.)

> Romans 14:12: "So then every one of us shall give account of himself to God" (cf. also Job 33:13; Ps. 144:3; Matt. 12:36; Luke 16:2. Relevant, too, is Milton's "When I consider . . . ," 11. 5–6, which are based in part upon Romans 14:12).

"The Bean-Field" (Shanley, 166.31–36): "The true husbandman will cease from anxiety, as the squirrels manifest no concern whether the woods will bear chestnuts this year or not, and finish his labor with every day, relinquishing all claim to the produce of his fields, and sacrificing in his mind not only his first but his last fruits also." (Harding, 126.2–5.)

> Matthew 6:25–34: Although the biblical allusion in the last lines regarding sacrifice has been noted, the other sustained allusion upon which Thoreau has modeled this passage has been overlooked: that is Christ's admonition to his disciples in Matt. 6:25–34 (and Luke 12:22–31) for their anxiety over what "tomorrow will bring." Be like "the fowls of the air," Christ urges (like "the squirrels," Thoreau advises), "for they sow not, neither do they reap, nor gather into barns," or like "the lilies of the field. . . . Take therefore no thought for the morrow." So likewise advises Thoreau: "The true husbandman will cease from anxiety . . . and finish his labor with every day." Thus Thoreau's passage implicitly asserts something of the same idea with which Christ concludes this passage: "for the morrow shall take thought for the things of itself."

"The Ponds" (Shanley, 188.7–11): "Not a fish can leap or an insect fall on the pond but it is thus reported in . . . the heaving of its breast." (Harding, 143.11–14.)

> Matthew 10:29–30: "Are not two sparrows sold for a farthing? and one of them shall not fall on the ground without your Father. But the very hairs of your head are numbered." Walden Pond, like God, knows and encompasses all within its waters of perfection, its "sky water," "so fair, so pure."

"House-Warming" (Shanley, 251.13–17): "Mechanics and tradesmen . . . even pay a high price for the privilege of gleaning after the wood-chopper." (Harding, 190.34–37.)

> Deuteronomy 24:21: "When thou gatherest the grapes of thy vineyard, thou shall not glean *it* afterward: it shall be for the stranger, for the fatherless, and for the widow" (cf. Leviticus 19:9–10; 23:22). The Book of Ruth, not heretofore noted as a possible source for Thoreau, employs this "privilege of gleaning" as a major structural and thematic device in the narrative of Boas and Ruth's courtship. Moreover the metaphor of gleaning is a familiar one in the prophets: Isaiah 17:6; Jeremiah 6:9, 49:9; and Micah 7:1. Thoreau's allusion ironically contrasts with the biblical law and subtly stresses—as does the rest of this paragraph in *Walden*—the growing commercialism of Concord. In Thoreau's town it is not the stranger, or fatherless, or widow who gleans for the much needed wood. Rather it is the tradesmen who glean, after paying "a high price" for a privilege that biblical law stressed should be free to the needy.

"Former Inhabitants; and Winter Visitors" (Shanley, 258.10–13): "With him dwelt Fenda, his hospitable wife, who told fortunes . . . large, round, and black, blacker than any of the children of night . . ." (Harding, 195.35–38.)

> 1 Thessalonians 5:4–5: "But ye, brethren, are not in darkness. . . . Ye are all the children of light, and the children of the day . . . not of the night." Consciously and playfully Thoreau is up to his old tricks: inverting a familiar biblical phrase and upsetting, thus, the scheme of values that such phrasing connotes to a settled mind (cf. "Economy," Shanley, 71.1–3; Harding, 52.1–3).

"Former Inhabitants; and Winter Visitors" (Shanley, 266.18–19): " . . . endeavoring to realize me, vague object or mote that interrupted his visions." (Harding, 201.37–38.)

> Matthew 7:3–5: "And why beholdest thou the mote that is in thy brother's eye. . . . Let me pull out the mote of thine eye. . . ." then shalt thou see clearly to cast out the mote. . . ." The image of the mote

greatly impressed Thoreau, for, as Long's essay has noted, Thoreau employs this image in two other passages; see Shanley, 51.26 and 159.14 (Harding, 37.26–27 and 120.15–56).

"Former Inhabitants; and Winter Visitors" (Shanley, 266.28–30): " . . . he ["a barred owl"] found a new perch, where he might in peace await the dawning of his day." (Harding, 202.5–6.)

> Job 3:9: "Let the stars of the twilight thereof be dark . . . neither let it see the dawning of the day." Job 7:4: "And I am full of tossings to and fro unto the dawning of the day" (cf. also Judges 19:26). Pertinent also is 2 Peter 1:19 wherein the speaker urges the Church to heed prophecy. It is "a light that shineth in a dark place, until the day dawn. . . ."

"Former Inhabitants; and Winter Visitors" (Shanley, 268.3–4): "Who can predict his [a poet's] comings and goings?" (Harding, 203.3.)

> Ezeckiel 43:11: " . . . show them . . . the goings out . . . and the comings in . . ." (cf. Acts 9:28). Isaiah 37:28: "But I know . . . thy going out, and thy coming in . . ." (cf. 2 Kings 19:27 and 2 Samuel 3:25). Pertinent also for phrasing and/or idea are Job 34:21, Psalms 68:24, Proverbs 5:21 and 20:24.

"The Pond in Winter" (Shanley, 293.33–294.6): "While yet it is cold January, and snow and ice are thick and solid, the prudent landlord comes from the village to get ice to cool his summer drink; impressively, even pathetically wise, to foresee the heat and thirst of July now in January,—wearing a thick coat and mittens! *when so many things are not provided for*. It may be that he lays up no treasures in this world which will cool his summer drink in the next." (Italics mine. Harding, 222.5–11.)

> Long's essay has noted the biblical allusion to Matthew 6:20 present in the second of these two sentences, but the longer preceding sentence, and in particular its final subordinate clause which I have italicized, clearly recalls Matthew 6:25–33 (or Luke 12:22–31) wherein Christ rebukes his disciples for their anxiety over what they "shall drink" in the future ("in July," Thoreau phrases it) as well as what they will eat and wear. Christ assures them that "your heavenly Father knoweth that ye have need of all these things . . . and [that] all these things shall be added unto you" (or in Thoreau's words "provided for" you). Through this allusion then, Thoreau provides his biblically-reared nineteenth-century reader with a sharp contrast between a right and a wrong way of action concerning material wealth in time-future. Moreover, Thoreau's choice of the verb phrase "are not provided for" echoes and recalls other familiar passages from the King James translation that contain

similar advice from Christ. In particular are Luke 12:16–21 and 32–33. These verses frame Luke 12:22–31 which contains the same text as that in Matthew 6:25–33, cited above. Luke 12:16–20 narrates "the parable of the rich fool" who tears down his smaller barns in order to build greater ones to hold his wealth. God rebukes this man for his avaricious prudence: "*Thou* fool, this night thy soul shall be required of thee: then whose shall those things be, which thou hast provided?" (cf. Thoreau's "when so many things are not provided for"). Again the use of the verb "provide" in Christ's advice in verse thirty-three calls to mind Thoreau's phrasing and contrasts sharply with the actions of Thoreau's "prudent landlord." Christ says: "Sell that ye have, and give alms; provide your- selves bags which wax not old"; and the last half of this verse (as well as Matthew 6:20) contains the obvious thought which Thoreau alludes to in his second sentence of the passage quoted above. Christ concludes: "a treasure in the heavens that faileth not, where no thief approacheth, neither moth corrupteth."

"Spring" (Shanley, 308.30–31): "It convinces me that Earth is still in her swaddling clothes. . . ." (Harding, 233.13–14.)

Luke 2:7: "and wrapped him in swaddling clothes. . . ."
Luke 2:12: "Ye shall find the babe wrapped in swaddling clothes. . . ." These are the only two instances of the phrase "swaddling clothes" in the Bible.

"Spring" (Shanley, 318.24): " . . . that sometimes it [Nature] has rained flesh and blood!" (Harding, 240.20.)

Psalms 78:27: "He rained flesh also upon them as dust . . ." (cf. Exodus 16:4, Psalms 78:24, and Luke 17:29). The phrase "flesh and blood" is also a popular biblical one: see, e.g., Matthew 16:17, I Corinthians 15:50, and Ephesians 6:12.

"Conclusion" (Shanley, 324.13–16): "As if Nature . . . could not sustain . . . flying as well as creeping things. . . ." (Harding, 145.18–21.)

Leviticus 11:21–23: "Yet these may ye eat of every flying creeping thing. . . . But all *other* flying creeping things . . . *shall be* abomina- tion unto you." The phrase "creeping thing(s)" is a familiar Old Testa- ment one: e.g., Genesis 1:26, 7:14, and Leviticus 5:2.

"Conclusion" (Shanley, 326.3–5): "Let every one mind his own business, and endeavor to be what he was made." (Harding, 246.30–31.)

I Thessalonians 4:10–11: " . . . we beseech you, brethren . . . that ye study to be quiet, and to do your own business, and to work with your own hands. . . ."

"Conclusion" (Shanley, 333.32–33): "Only that day dawns to which we are awake. There is more day to dawn. The sun is but a morning star." (Harding, 252.18–19.)

Long's essay cites only Revelation 2:28 and 22:16 as sources for the sun as morning star but 2 Peter 1:19 is likewise important for the entire final paragraph: see Edward and Karen Jacobs, "*Walden's* End and 2 Peter 1:19," *Thoreau Journal Quarterly*, 10, no. 2 (April 1978): 30–31.

NEW EVIDENCE FOR MELVILLE'S USE OF JOHN HARRIS IN *MOBY-DICK*

John M. J. Gretchko

IT IS OLD NEWS, of course, to report that the *Navigantium atque Itiner-antium Bibliotheca; or, a Compleat Collection of Voyages and Travels* by John Harris (1667?–1719) is a source of some importance in *Moby-Dick*. However, it is news to demonstrate several other important Melville uses of the two folio volumes of John Harris and to establish his use of the 1705 edition, published in London.

All written material which Melville borrowed and paraphrased from Harris came from volume one of the first edition, with possibly one exception. Howard P. Vincent, in *The Trying-Out of Moby-Dick*, calls attention to the Heidelburgh Tun which Harris illustrates and describes in volume two.[1] Melville may have seen the Tun there since his unusual spelling of Heidelburgh corresponds to the spelling in the travel article by Maximilian Mission. Other spellings of the German city occurring in Harris are variant ones. However, if Melville saw Mission he certainly did not paraphrase him as is Melville's habit. It is always possible that Melville's Heidelburgh spelling is a peculiar quirk since he intended to spell the city in that fashion in his 1856–57 *Journal*.[2]

The so-called Harris second edition of 1744–48, reprinted 1764, all London published, was edited by John Campbell (1708–75), whose name does not appear on the title page nor in the volumes themselves. Except for a few items taken from the first edition, Campbell's edition bears little resemblance to the first. It should properly bear a different title and author. The editions vary in much the same way as a popular reference work would if it were reissued long after an author's death, considerably revised, and now incorporating new matter. Although the same material on the Heidelburgh Tun appears in the second edition, there is no substantial evidence that Melville ever saw that edition. If he had, he most probably would have borrowed from the article "Captain Cowley's Voyage round the Globe." But the

34th extract of *Moby-Dick* having that title comes from a part of William Dampier's *A Collection of Voyages*, not the second edition of Harris where the wording of "Cowley's Voyage" is greatly different.[3]

Melville's initial debts to Harris are evident in extracts 27 through 30. However, only two of the four, the 28th and the 30th, does Melville attribute to him. To date, neither of these has been located in Harris, although the Mansfield-Vincent edition of *Moby-Dick* identifies the 29th. While the 27th extract is attributed to "*Thomas Edge's Ten Voyages to Spitzbergen, in Purchass*," Melville evidently forgets his source, for it appears almost verbatim in Harris (1:574, col. 2). Melville's spelling of Purchass is a clue to his source since Harris similarly attributes one too many *s*'s to his name. The 28th extract, "*Sir Thomas Herbert's Voyages into Asia and Africa*," appears practically verbatim in Harris (1:406, col. 1). The 29th extract, "*Schouten's Sixth Circumnavigation*," is similar to Harris (1:38, col. 1).[4] The 30th extract, which is really five separate quotations, "*A Voyage to Greenland, A.D. 1671*," is straight out of sections in Harris by Friederich Marten (1:617, col. 1; 632, col. 1; 631, col. 1; 630, col. 2; 629, col. 2).[5] Some of these quotations are verbatim. The last quotation of the five is the most important of the group because Melville takes it from a page in Harris which supplies him with copious whaling material for Chapter 75, "The Right Whale's Head—Contrasted View." Opposite this page is the plate of the odd-looking whales which Melville reports in Chapter 55 (see Plate Eighteen).

The head of the Right or Greenland Whale in Chapter 75 reminds Melville of a "gigantic galliot-toed shoe. Two hundred years ago an old Dutch voyager likened its shape to that of a shoemaker's last." That old Dutch voyager is Friederich Marten who is presented by Harris. Marten says of the Right Whale: "In short the whole Fish resembles in shape a Shoe-maker's Laste, if you look upon it from beneath" (1:629, col. 2). Melville, then, continues: "But as you come nearer to this great head it begins to assume different aspects, according to your point of view. If you stand on its summit and look at these two *f*-shaped spout-holes, you would take the whole head for an enormous bass-viol." Similarly, Marten says: "On his Head he has a Bump or Knob before the Eyes and Fins: On the top of it is on each side a Spout-hole, directly opposite to one another, bended like an S." The S of Marten is just that and not the old typeface *S*, or Gothic long *S*, which Melville takes it for.[6]

Next Melville strolls his readers into the Right Whale's mouth: "while these ribbed, arched, hairy sides, present us with those wondrous, half vertical, scimetar-shaped slats of whalebone, say three hundred on a side." The germ of this dependent clause is again Marten: "The *Whale-bone* within the *Mouth* is all hairy. . . . In some Whales the *Whale-bone* is bended like a

PLATE SEVENTEEN
Whaling scenes from John Harris, *Navagantium atque Itinerantium Bibliotheca* . . .
(1705), opposite 1:617.
Courtesy TxU

PLATE EIGHTEEN
Whales with perpendicular flukes in John Harris, *Navagantium atque Itinerantium
Bibliotheca* . . . (1705), opposite 1:629.
Courtesy TxU

Cimetar. . . . On each side are 250 Pieces, which makes 500 in all" (1:629, col. 2). Melville's chapter continues with borrowings from other whaling sources including *The Penny Cyclopaedia*[7] and concludes with a discussion of the whale's tongue. Melville writes: "It is very fat and tender, and apt to tear in pieces in hoisting it on deck. This particular tongue now before us; at a passing glance I should say it was a six-barreler; that is, it will yield you about that amount of oil." This passage also appears to be lifted from Marten who speaks of the tongue: "It is very large, and ty'd close to the undermost Chap. Its substance is a soft spongy Fat, which being very soft, and consequently very difficult to cut, is commonly thrown away, tho' otherwise it would afford six or seven Barrels of Train Oil" (1:629, col. 2).

In Chapter 92 Melville discusses the smelliness of whales and mentions the old Dutch village, Schmerenburgh or Smeerenberg, on the coast of Greenland where the Dutch whalemen tried-out their blubber. The first spelling *Schmerenburgh* comes from Marten in Harris (1:619, col. 1); the second is from William Scoresby.[8] But the paragraph in *Moby-Dick* which precedes the introduction of Schmerenburgh has similarities to the paragraph preceding the same village in Marten. Melville speaks of the whaling ships which would bring cut blubber back to London and the god-awful smell upon unloading it from the ship's hold: "The consequence is, that upon breaking into the hold, and unloading one of these whale cemeteries, in the Greenland dock, a savor is given forth somewhat similar to that arising from excavating an old city grave-yard, for the foundations of a Lying-in Hospital." With the same macabre sense, Marten describes the coast of Greenland: "Just in the middle of this Harbour lies an Isle marked with No (16) called the *Dead-man's Isle*, because here they bury their dead Men in Coffins, and afterwards lay great heaps of Stones upon them, nothwithstanding which, the white Bears will sometimes dig them up; for it is observable, that dead Carcasses will remain entire here, without the least signs of Putrefaction, for ten years and longer." Where Melville excavates a city grave-yard, here white bears do the deed.

Do Harris' extracts from Marten have any influence upon Chapter 95, "The Cassock"? Marten says: "The Yard of the Whale is a strong Sinew, of six, seven, or eight Foot long, according to the bigness of the Animal" (1:630, col. 1). Melville writes that it is "longer than a Kentuckian is tall." Scoresby, however, could just as easily be Melville's source here.

In Chapter 55 of *Moby-Dick*, Melville describes some pictures of whales which he has seen in Harris: "In old Harris's collection of voyages there are some plates of whales extracted from a Dutch book of voyages, A.D. 1671, entitled 'A Whaling Voyage to Spitzbergen in the ship Jonas in the Whale, Peter Peterson of Friesland, master.' In one of those plates the whales, like rafts of logs, are represented lying among ice-isles, with white bears running over their living backs. In another plate, the prodigious blunder is made of representing the whale with perpendicular flukes." (See Plates Seventeen and Eighteen for the illustrations from Marten in Harris.) Melville fuses together both the title of the article by Friederich Marten and its first sentence (1:617, col. 1). The title reads: "*The first Part of the Voyage to* Spitzbergen *and* Greenland . . . *from* April *the 15th*, to August *the 21st*, 1671." And the abstract's first sentence, which Melville also used for his extracts, reads: "We set sail from the *Elbe*, wind N. E. in the Ṡhip call'd the *Jonas in the Whale, Peter Peterson of Frieseland* Master." The second picture from the top in the plate opposite that page shows one and only one whale, like a log in an icy scene with a bear running over its back. The next plate, facing page 629, a page which served as the source of a few words used by Melville, shows three whales with perpendicular flukes.

Melville may also make further use of Harris' selections from Thomas Edge, whom he quotes in the extracts. Edge says: "When it is boiled enough, the small pieces of Blubber, called *Fritters*, will look brown as if they were fried" (1:574, col. 2). Melville writes in Chapter 65: "Among the Dutch whalemen these scraps are called 'fritters.'" Melville could have found these fritters in either Edge or J. Ross Browne, who also refers to them. Melville likens their smell to "dough-nuts or oly-cooks." The similar spelling of *Oyl* subsequently follows in the next Edge sentence. Further down the column Edge calls the Sperma Ceti whale Trumpa, a name to be found in Melville's cetology chapter. Across from that in column one, Edge compares the whale's eyes to those of an Ox. Perhaps this additional short-lettered, capitalized *O*-word caught Melville's attention, since three sentences after *oly*, he compares the whale to an ox. The same analogy to an ox appears in Scoresby. In fact, Scoresby paraphrases Edge.[9] He even speaks of Edge's having been published in Purchas.[10] This is why Melville connects Edge to Purchas, through Scoresby.

Commenting on the splendor of whiteness in Chapter 42, Melville writes: "even the barbaric, grand old kings of Pegu placing the title 'Lord of the White Elephants' above all their other magniloquent ascriptions of dominion." Two travels in Harris, which Melville had the opportunity to use, similary delineate the royal elephant. Under the page heading "Description of Pegu," Harris reads: "Such is the esteem that this monarch has for an Elephant of this Colour, that he brings this in amongst the rest of his Titles; To be King of the White Elephants is a big and lofty a one with him as any other that he assumes" (1:210, col. 2). Another abstract renders this: "The King of *Pegu*, among his other Titles, is call'd the King of the white Elephants" (1:227, col. 2). Neither of these travels seem to furnish any other matter pertinent to *Moby-Dick*.

Melville removes a large chunk of material from the travels of John Leo in Harris and adds it to Chapter 104. Vincent suggests in a footnote to his discussion of this quotation that it may derive from the 1705 edition of Harris.[11] Indeed, that is its origin, "A Description of *Africa*, and all its Provinces. Taken from John Leo and *Marmol*: With Discoveries in most Parts thereof, etc" (1:318, col. 1:)

> "Not far from the Sea-side, they have a Temple, the Rafters and Beams of which are made of Whale-Bones; for Whales of a monstrous size are oftentimes cast up dead upon that shore. The Common People imagine, that by a secret Power bestowed by God upon the Temple, no Whale can pass it without immediate death. But the truth of the Matter is, that on either side of the Temple, there are Rocks that shoot two Miles into the Sea, and wound the Whales when they light upon 'em. They keep a Whale's Rib of an incredible length for a Miracle, which lying upon the Ground with its convex part uppermost, makes an Arch, the Head of which cannot be reached by a Man upon a Camel's Back. This Rib (says John Leo)[12] is said to have layn there a hundred Years before I saw it. Their Historians affirm, that a Prophet who prophesy'd of Mahomet, came from this Temple, and some do not stand to assert, that the Prophet Jonas was cast forth by the Whale at the Base of the Temple."

With few exceptions, Melville's paragraph quoting Harris is verbatim: the last six words from Melville differ from the last five in Harris, which reads "upon the Shoar of Messa"; Melville capitalizes the *C* in "Common," whereas the Harris text does not; Harris capitalizes "Shore," "Death," and "Truth," while Melville does not; Harris makes a contraction, "reach'd," while Melville does not; Melville hyphenates "Whale-Bones," a familiar spelling, for example, in Marten; and Melville fails to italicize the names of John Leo, Mahomet, and Jonas. The common link between the John Leo quotation and the four other Harris authors in the extracts—Edge, Herbert, Schouten, and Marten—is the word "Whale" in the index of volume one. Perusing the index, Melville would quickly be led to his whaling sources. If he had any antipathy to volume two, it might be because that volume's index lacked the entry "Whale."[13]

Elements in Chapter 102, which appears just before the above quotation, point to Harris' John Leo as a source as well. Just as the people in John Leo have a whale-skeleton temple near the sea, so does the kingdom of Tranque in this chapter possess such an edifice, also near the sea. Melville writes: "but have a care how you seize the privilege of Jonah alone; the privilege of discoursing upon the joists and beams; the rafters, ridge-poles, sleepers, and under-pinnings, making up the frame-work of leviathan." Common to Melville and John Leo are the words "beams" and "rafters," and "Jonah" or "Jonas."

Melville, indeed, refers to Harris by name at the conclusion of Chapter 83: "And some three centuries ago, an English traveller in old Harris's Voyages, speaks of a Turkish Mosque built in honor of Jonah, in which mosque was a miraculous lamp that burnt without any oil," but as Vincent demonstrates Melville confuses his sources, attributing to Harris material he paraphrases from Pierre Bayle.[14] What is unique to the Harris data is the word "Jonah" or "Jonas," which occurs in the John Leo quotation, the extract from Marten, the reference to Marten's pictures, and the Chapter 83 misattribution.

Melville may have become familiar with Harris' *Navigantium* during the composition of *Mardi*, for a fragment of the endless, page-long subtitle of the former almost certainly appears in Melville's book. Chapter 75 begins: "In the Oriental Pilgrimage of the pious old Purchas, and in the fine old folio Voyages of Hakluyt, Thevenot, Ramusio, and De Bry." This is almost the same sequence of authors in the subtitle of Harris' folios: "Consisting of about Four Hundred of the most Authentick Writers; Beginning with *Hackluit, Purchass*, etc. in *English*; *Ramusio* in *Italian*; *Thevenot*, etc. in *French*; *De Bry*, . . . in *Latin*." The second edition has the same sequence of authors but interspersed with four others. It is possible that here Melville uses the second edition. The same paragraph in *Mardi* also refers to Marco Polo whose travels appear only in the second Harris edition. Of course, Melville need not have seen Harris to write of Marco Polo. However, considering Melville's strong use of the first edition in *Moby-Dick* and considering that the second edition's subtitle contains other authors not mentioned by Melville in *Mardi*, it should not stretch things to infer that Melville also employs the first Harris edition in *Mardi*.

A later citation of Harris can be found in the reconstruction of Melville's South Sea's lecture of 1858–59 by Merton M. Sealts, Jr. Here Melville mentions "Harris' old voyages" as one source for the expression, "South Seas," in contrast to the modern usage, "Pacific."[15]

Future scholars will undoubtedly uncover further uses of Harris by Melville. It could very well prove that Melville owned a copy of at least the first volume of the 1705 folio.[16]

NOTES

1. (Boston: Houghton Mifflin, 1949), p. 263. Vincent's findings are also used in *Moby-Dick*, ed. Luther S. Mansfield and Vincent (New York: Hendricks House, 1952).

2. *Journal of a Visit to Europe and the Levant October 11, 1856–May 6, 1857*, ed. Howard C. Horsford (Princeton: Princeton University Press, 1955), p. 252. Melville writes "Heidleburgh" instead of "Heidelburgh."

3. (London, 1729), 4:6. Melville probably discovered the quotation by turning to the index under "whale" in volume four.

4. The 1744 edition follows closely here the 1705 edition, changing but one word while dropping another.

5. Melville refers to Marten in Chapter 32 where his name appears in a long list of whaling authorities. This part of the list Melville takes from Thomas Beale. Harris, too, spells his name Marten; various spellings are Friederich or Frederick Marten or Martens.

6. Vincent (in *Trying-Out*, p. 255), cites *An Account of the Arctic Regions* by Scoresby as Melville's source for this information. But Scoresby himself must have borrowed from Harris, and Melville in fact may have acquired some of this from both sources, although his reference to the Dutch voyager of two hundred years ago would favor Marten in Harris. Marten's "Bump or Knob," translated into a "crown" by Scoresby, becomes in *Moby-Dick* the crown or bonnet of the Right Whale. Again Melville may use both Marten and Scoresby when he says, "Look at that hanging lower lip! what a huge sulk and pout is there!" Marten observes, "Nay, on the under Lip is a certain Concavity" (1:629, col. 1). Melville continues, "a sulk and a pout that will yield you some 500 gallons of oil and more." Vincent states that Melville twists a sentence of Scoresby here in order to have the whale yield 500 gallons instead of the two ton in Scoresby.

7. Kendra H. Gaines, "A Consideration of an Additional Source for Melville's *Moby-Dick*," *Extracts*, no. 29 (January 1977): 10.

8. *An Account of the Arctic Regions*, 2 vols. (Edinburgh, 1820), 1:147; 2:52, 140, 143, 144, 145.

9. Scoresby, *An Account*, says of the whale's eyes, "They are remarkably small . . . being little larger than those of an ox" (1:456). Edge says, "his Eyes not much bigger than those of an Ox." Marten has almost the same wording (1:629, col. 2). In turn, *The Penny Magazine*, 2, no. 74 (31 May 1833): 202, might paraphrase Scoresby: "They are singularly disproportionate . . . being scarcely larger than those of an ox." *The Penny Cyclopaedia* (London, 1843), 27:296, could paraphrase Edge or even Marten: "The eyes, not much larger than those of an ox." Comparing the right whale to an ox was apparently a favored metaphor. The *American Magazine of Useful and Entertaining Knowledge*, 2, no. 1 (September 1835): 5, likens the right whale's feeding habits to those of an ox.

10. Scoresby, *An Account*, 1:453.

11. Vincent, *Trying-Out*, p. 358n.

12. The Mansfield-Vincent edition does not set quotation marks before and after the parenthetical phrase, (says John Leo), as does the Norton edition, ed. Harrison Hayford and Hershel Parker (New York: W. W. Norton, 1967).

13. Before quoting so liberally from John Leo in Harris, twice in Chapter 104, "The Fossil Whale," Melville employs an unusual word, "pre-adamite." A nineteenth-century John Harris wrote *The Pre-Adamite Earth: Contributions to Theological Science* (London, 1847; rev. and enl. ed., Boston, 1850) to reconcile theology with the geological thought of the day. Strangely, the use of "pre-adamite" comes two paragraphs before the Harris-John Leo and once again four paragraphs after it, which is in the following chapter. Two of the "pre-adamite" words stand as sentinels around the quotation from John Leo. The three uses of "pre-adamite" within these two chapters are the only occurrences of this word in *Moby-Dick*.

14. Vincent, *Trying-Out*, p. 285. This account appears greatly altered in Harris, but in the spurned second volume. See also the Mansfield-Vincent edition, p. 782.

15. *Melville As Lecturer* (Cambridge: Harvard University Press, 1957), p. 157.

16. The 1705 folio of *Navigantium* was published in London by T. Bennet. I am grateful to the Humanities Research Center of the University of Texas at Austin for permission to reproduce pages from its copy of this work and to the John G. White Collection of the Cleveland Public Library for extensive use of the Harris volumes.

MARY RUSSELL MITFORD:
CHAMPION OF AMERICAN LITERATURE

John L. Idol, Jr.

MARY RUSSELL MITFORD overcame an early distaste for American literature and worked tirelessly to support the careers of many American writers. Prompted by her disappointment with American authors, she anticipated in 1818 Sidney Smith's notorious charge against the state of the arts in America. Writing to one of her many correspondents, Mitford asserted that Americans "are a second-hand, pawnbrokers'-shop kind of nation—a nation without literature, without art, and totally unconscious of the beautiful nature by which they are surrounded."[1] But she was to change her mind when she later read more works by American authors, began to meet them and their publishers, and started to exchange letters with them. She could even proudly claim before her death, and with considerable justice, that few English writers had done as much as she to promote American literature in England. Her advocacy of American writers appeared in numerous letters and in *Recollections of a Literary Life* (1852), an autobiographical and critical work containing selections from her favorite writers. The story of Mitford's conversion from abhorrence to energetic endorsement of many American writers now regarded as among our best deserves a place in the history of the literary relationship of England and America, a story told much too briefly and only partially by Marjorie Astin over fifty years ago.[2]

Widely read both at home and in America at the time of her death and for a good half-century afterwards, Mitford has now been largely forgotten except for her incomparably fine vignettes of rural English scenes and characters entitled *Our Village*, published in five volumes between 1824 and 1832 and often reprinted since then. Her early poems,[3] tragedies (the most successful of which was *Rienzi*), tales, and letters have long been out of print. And for the past six decades, only a half-dozen critical pieces on her work have appeared. Her nineteenth-century admirers found her a worthy successor to Jane Austen and superior to Maria Edgeworth, regarded her description of English rural life a prose equivalent of George Crabbe's poetic sketches, and praised her letters as being as lively and interesting as those of Thomas Gray and William Cowper, but none of these estimates has served to keep her from sinking to near obscurity in the present day.[4] The neglect is undeserved, if for no other reason than she became an eager champion of American literature.

This unlikely advocate of American letters was the only child of Mary Russell, daughter of a clergyman, and George Mitford, a physician who never practiced but rather spent his time gambling, talking, and squandering—first, a prize of £20,000 that his daughter won in a lottery and then the earnings she had from her plays, tales, and anthologies. Besides consuming his wife's and then his daughter's fortune and income, Dr. Mitford required a great deal of nursing, given lovingly for years by his daughter while at the same time she was writing to earn enough to support the Mitford household. During the time her father's need was greatest, she cared for him all day and far into the evening, and then, taking laudanum, she pushed on with her writing until the early morning hours. She was able, however, to give up the drug once her father's death freed her of nursing duties.[5]

In spite of her extraordinarily heavy duties at home, she enjoyed a wide range of literary friendships, built mostly on pilgrimages to her home, first at Three Mile Cross near Reading, and then at Swallowfield, also near Reading, or on letters to scores of writers and lovers of literature. Among her visitors and correspondents were John Greenleaf Whittier, Catharine Sedgwick, James T. Fields, William D. Ticknor, Bayard Taylor, Nathaniel Willis, Daniel Webster, Oliver Wendell Holmes, Henry Wadsworth Longfellow, Nathaniel Hawthorne, to name the Americans first, and in her own country Elizabeth Barrett Browning, William Harness, Charles Kingsley, Harriet Martineau, William Bennett, Charles Boner, Sir William Elford, Benjamin Haydon, Douglass Jerrold, and John Ruskin. And she kept abreast of literary activities in France, England, and the United States by voracious reading. What she liked—or disliked—as she read, what news she gleaned about literary doings, what bits and pieces of gossip she picked up, she wrote about in hundreds of letters, many of which remain unpublished.

It is through these letters that most of her opinions about American literature and literary figures can be traced, but the firmest evidence of her shifting attitude toward American writing appears first in a series of anthologies of American writings she edited. The first venture began possibly at the suggestion of her publisher, who knew, as Mitford modestly confided to one of her friends, that the name of the now famous author of *Our Village* as the editor of an anthology would assure good sales.[6] Pressed as she was for income, Mitford embraced the offer in 1828 or 1829 and began reading American annuals and giftbooks to gather tales, stories, sketches, and essays by American writers. Entitled *Stories of American Life, By American Writers*, this collection was published by Henry Colburn and Richard Bentley in 1830 in three volumes and contained twenty-seven pieces. Mitford included works by James Kirke Paulding, Willis, James Hall, Sedgwick, Gulian Crommelin Verplanck, William Cullen Bryant, Richard Henry Dana, and lesser known writers. Intended as a collection for young English readers, these volumes provided glimpses of American life.

As she culled material for this collection, Mitford found stories suitable for small children and quickly put together another anthology, this one called *American Stories of Little Boys and Girls* and published in three volumes by Whittaker, Treacher and Company in 1831. Once again the stories were pulled from annuals and giftbooks and featured the morally instructive work of such authors as Lydia Sigourney and Lydia Maria Child.

The success of the first two collections prompted her to edit yet another anthology of pieces by American authors, this one aimed at children above ten years of age and entitled *American Stories for Young People*, likewise published by Whittaker, Treacher and Company (1832). The opening sentence of the preface revealed that Mitford was ready to admit that America had both a literature and a sense of the beautiful: "In turning over a large mass of the lighter literature of America, the little books intended for children appeared to me to possess peculiar excellence. They are almost universally distinguished not only by the acute observation and cheerful common sense to be expected from the country of Franklin, but by a strong religious feeling, and an unaffected love of the beautiful and true" (p. iii).

For this gathering she once more was indebted to Sedgwick, whom she called a friend, and to other writers of children's tales. But she chose to share some poems, those of Lucretia Mason Davidson, and a memoir of Alexander Wilson, a noted early nineteenth-century American ornithologist.

She decided also to retain most of the peculiarly American expressions. "With regard to the Americanisms, I have generally left them as I found them. Children, like all inexperienced persons, are fastidious and bigoted adherents to their own narrow range of language and manners, and it seems to me no mean part of an enlarged and liberal education to shew them that the standard of gentility differs in different countries, and that intelligent and cultivated people may, without the slightest tincture of vulgarity, use words and idioms of which these little exclusives never heard before" (pp. iv–v). This generous acceptance of Americanisms is a far cry from the snobbish insularity she expressed in the quotation at the beginning of this essay. Now she would not replace *store* with *shop* or *fall* with *autumn*, for example, because Americanisms reflected America and its people.

Aware by this time (May 1832) both of the marketability of anthologies of

American writing and the value of the work she was trying to place before a wider British audience, Mitford once more compiled an anthology. Called *Lights and Shadows of American Life*, it was brought out by Henry Colburn and Richard Bentley in 1832 and contained stories and sketches by Paulding, W. J. Snelling, Henry C. Sturges, Sedgwick, Verplanck, J. M. Barker, W. C. Leggett, and Timothy Flint. Flint's sketch of "The Young Backwoodsman" was singled out for special comment in the preface: "It is a homely, graphic story, full of deep religious feeling, and almost equal to Defoe in the minute fidelity and perfect verisimilitude of narration. In reading it we never think of the author; but we know exactly how the family of Masons got through the first difficulties of the settlement, how they cleaned their field, and planted their corn. And this seems to me no mean praise" (pp. iii–iv).

She now began to be more concerned about who the authors she had been drawing upon were. She was happy to identify Flint, Paulding, Barker, and Sedgwick as authors represented in this new collection and sorry that the practice of anonymous authorship prevented her from naming the writers of the other pieces.

Her work as an anthologist had taught her something about the state of American letters in the 1820s and early 1830s. What she had once scorned she now was recommending to her countrymen, what she had once considered as an uncouth nation now appeared to have traits worthy of imitating, and what she had written off as second-hand now sometimes seemed good enough to compare to some of the best writing Englishmen had done. In addition, she had learned that Americans were capable of being admirers and customers of her work, for her writing was selling steadily and well in America.[7]

The work building a wide readership for her on both sides of the Atlantic was *Our Village*, a book indebted to Washington Irving. Upon launching her most celebrated venture, she told her friend Sir William Elford that the book would have "essays and characters and stories, chiefly of country life, in the manner of the *Sketch Book.*"[8]

It was *Our Village* and her play *Rienzi* that brought to her home at Three Mile Cross an admiring letter from Sedgwick just at the time (1830) that Mitford was publishing the first of her anthologies of American literature and Sedgwick's novel *Hope Leslie* was appearing in England. Sedgwick's letter contained praise of Mitford's writing and questions about Mitford's home and village. Mitford's answer revealed her recent concern with American letters. Of *Hope Leslie* she wrote: "I rejoice to find your book not merely reprinted but published in England, and will contribute, together with the splendid novels of Mr. Cooper, to make the literature and manners of a country so nearly connected with us in language and ways of thinking, known and valued here." Cooper, she reported, stood next to Scott as the most read novelist, and Irving and William Ellery Channing had a strong following in England. She added, speaking of her first collection of American stories: "I have contributed, or rather, am about to contribute, my mite to this most desirable interchange of mind with mind."[9]

This exchange of letters led to many years of cordial correspondence and a visit to Three Mile Cross by Sedgwick in 1839, an account of which by the American novelist brought a rare outburst of anger from Mitford. Describing her arrival at the Mitford cottage, Sedgwick wrote, "Miss M is truly 'a little body,' and dressed a little quaintly, and unlike as possible to the faces we have seen of her in the magazines, which all have a broad humour bordering on coarseness. . . . Her voice has a sweet, low tone, and her manner a naturalness, frankness, and affectionateness that we have been so long familiar with in their other modes of manifestation, that it would have been indeed a disappointment not to have found them."[10] These words together with the remainder of the account of Sedgwick's visit appeared in 1841 in *Letters From Abroad To Kindred At Home*, published first in New York. An editor at the firm of Moxon and a friend of Mitford, John Kenyon, deleted the offending words about Mitford's personal appearance but not before a few review copies had left the Moxon office. One of the reviews, the *Literary Gazette*, printed the full account. Mitford seethed when she read the original text:

> Our coachman (who, after telling him we were Americans, had complimented us on our speaking English, 'and very good English, too') professed an acquaintance of some twenty years standing with Miss M., and assured us that she was one of the 'cleverest women in England,' and 'the Doctor' (her father) 'an 'earty old boy.' And when he reined his horses up to her door, and she appeared to receive us, he said, 'Now you would not take that little body there for the great author, would you?' and certainly we should have taken her for nothing but a kindly gentlewoman, who had never gone beyond the narrow sphere of the most refined social life.[11]

Mitford, who had some time before entertained two of Sedgwick's kinsmen, felt betrayed. She wrote, obviously annoyed, to a friend: "If you have a mind to see a specimen of the very coarsest Americanism ever put forth, read the *Literary Gazette*. . . . When you remember that [Sedgwick's] brother and nephew spent twice ten days at our poor cottage—that she was received as their kinswoman, and therefore as a friend, you may judge how unexpected this coarse detail has been. . . . Of course its chief annoyance to me is finding the aunt of a dear friend so grossly vulgar."[12] Extremely shy about personal publicity at all times, Mitford recoiled from these details and from the person who wrote them as if she had met the mother or sister of Henrietta

Stackpole, Henry James' journalist who sought out intimate details of English life. In time, the wound healed and the exchange of letters resumed, but a reserve replaced the former intimacy.

The visit by the Sedgwicks was apparently the second call by admiring American visitors, the first having been made by Nathaniel P. Willis, who later exchanged letters with Mitford. Later visitors were Daniel Webster, George Ticknor, William D. Ticknor, Bayard Taylor, and James T. Fields. These visitors brought her news of the state of writing in American, they sent her books, autographs, and portraits, and they clipped notices of her books in the American press. They were in short, part of her bridge to America, the most important pylon of which was Fields, who met her in 1847 and kept a correspondence going with her until she was too feeble to write. And he and Ticknor published Mitford's last work, *Atherton*, in 1854.

Long before these visitors began coming to her home, Mitford had started to build her own bridge to America. Not surprisingly, the first span was Irving's *Sketch Book*. To her friend Mrs. Hofland, she wrote (1 June 1820) that Irving's book was "the only American work that I ever read that possessed any talent," but she qualified her praise by adding, "the author really writes like an Englishman"[13] When she made her way into the second volume of the *Sketch Book* she excitedly wrote to Sir William Elford that it was "incredibly good. . . . It is a little sentimental — too sentimental, certainly— but the comic part is excellent. . . . I should think the Americans must crow over Mr. Washington Irving"[14] To the same correspondent, she later recommended Irving's *A History of New York*, calling it a clever work.[15] More than three decades later, after having tasted and digested many other American writers, Mitford complained of *Bracebridge Hall* to Charles Boner that it was "a little unreal and a little long. Being himself a copy, Washington Irving is a bad model."[16]

If Irving turned out to be, as she thought, better material for the British section of her bridge, she was sure she had found in Cooper a more distinctly American writer. Coming upon Cooper's *The Pilot* and *The Spy* in 1824, Mitford could scarcely contain her excitement. She asked Sir William Elford if he had read them, saying, "In my mind they are as good as anything Sir Walter Scott ever wrote." She much preferred Cooper's sea novels to Smollett's, which she found too coarse. She urged Sir William to read them. "Imagine the author's boldness in taking Paul Jones for a hero, and making one care for him! I envy the Americans their Mr. Cooper."[17] Her ringing endorsement of *The Last of The Mohicans* found her putting Cooper ahead of Sir Walter Scott except for the latter's first three novels and *Heart of Midlothian*. Cooper presented a true and new picture of a new and great people. "How wonderfully," she exclaimed in 1826 to the painter Benjamin Haydon,

"America is rising in the scale of intellect!" So much had she forgotten her earlier denigration of America that she now foresaw coming greatness in literature, especially in the novel. "Depend on it that America will succeed us as Rome did Athens."[18] The excitement created in the 1820s did not die out, for in 1849[19] and again in 1852[20] she was recommending Cooper's novels to her friends, even though by 1849 she had developed a distaste for the personality of Cooper, describing him as a "sad coxcomb."[21]

If Cooper the man sank in her esteem the more she came to know him, she had just the opposite opinion of Daniel Webster, of whom she began to speak after a visit to her home by George Ticknor in 1835. Hard upon the heels of Sedgwick's visit in 1839 came that of Webster, whom Mitford characterized to her friend Mrs. Anderdon as "the man who more completely realizes my idea of a truly great man than any one whom I have ever seen."[22] She considered him noble in person and manner and would later compare him physically to Hawthorne. And she thought so highly of his oratory that she put Webster among the literary men she included in her *Recollections of a Literary Life*, reprinting beside her appreciation of him Webster's speech at the trial of John Knapp in Essex, Massachusetts. She fully expected him to become president, approved of his stand against fanatic American abolitionists, and mourned his death.[23]

Following her discoveries of the mid 1820s and early 1830s, Mitford came away from this first phase of building her bridge with only one writer she had ranked alongside England's best, and that was Cooper. As we have seen, she had read many others and, through her four collections, saw to it that her countrymen, adults and children, had access to American writing. Although she continued to explore American works throughout the 1840s,[24] she was not deeply or eagerly involved until after the visits of James T. Fields. Meeting him showed her that new building supplies for her bridge were pouring forth from American writers. She returned to her task with renewed interest, examining essayists, poets, and novelists as she read, but except for Bayard Taylor and Richard Henry Stoddard, not venturing far beyond the Boston-Concord group of writers. For my purpose, it is best to trace her opinions of the essayists before turning to the poets and novelists.

She liked the essays and articles of E. P. Whipple and James Russell Lowell,[25] but she found the work of Margaret Fuller and Ralph Waldo Emerson unsatisfying. Of the former she wrote, "Margaret Fuller was always writing, and never produced anything of the least merit. They say she was about to write a great book—a book of the highest power—but then not a page was written, so it is a mere matter of faith."[26] Even though she objected to Fuller's writing, she found the woman herself fascinating and passed along tidbits of gossip about her to her literary friends, as in this passage to Mrs.

Hoare. Margaret Fuller "was, they say, insupportable at Boston, but became better at New York, where she was treated only as a lion; better still at Paris, where she knew little French; still softer in England, where she was talked over by Carlyle; and really good and interesting in Italy, where the woman took completely the place of the sybil."[27] Mitford had heard of Margaret Fuller through her correspondence with Elizabeth Barrett Browning[28] and later read a biography of Fuller. Her final regret about Fuller was that, like other women of genius, she chose a husband unwisely.[29]

Just as Fuller had failed to realize her potential so had Emerson, in Mitford's opinion, fallen short of his. She told Charles Boner that Emerson "would have been a great writer and thinker, if Carlyle had not fallen in his way. Now he appears a mere copyist of the Scotchman."[30] Since she objected to Carlyle's style, she also faulted Emerson for the same reason. "I am . . . so fidgety respecting style, that I have the bad habit of expecting a book which pretends to be written in our language to be English, therefore I cannot read . . . Thomas Carlyle, or Emerson."[31]

As the author of several books of poems herself, she gave far more attention to poets than to essayists. She followed with keen interest the careers of Edgar Allan Poe, Whittier, Fitz-Greene Halleck, Longfellow, T. W. Parsons, Bayard Taylor, Stoddard, Lowell, and Holmes.

Apparently, she had not noticed Poe until Fields began talking about his work and escapades. Poe's life Mitford deemed "painful and disgusting," but she strongly recommended Poe's tales and poems to her friends, writing, for example, to still another of the literary correspondents she had, a Mrs. Jennings, "I have been reading Edgar Poe's Tales and Poems—very remarkable."[32] For Fields she chose to be more specific, confessing that she liked "The Bells" better than "The Raven."[33] The collection that now (1852) came into her hands convinced her that she would have to add Poe's work if she lived to publish another volume of *Recollections of a Literary Life*.[34]

Whittier had already won a place in that book, his place being earned both on the basis of his friendship and the merit of his poems. When the English editor Henry Chorley coaxed her into writing an article for the *Lady's Journal*, she took up the task with the thought that "one pleasure will be doing what justice I can to certain American poets, Mr. Whittier, for instance, whose 'Massachusetts to Virginia' is amongst the finest things ever written."[35] This poem and "Cassandra Southcote" went into her *Recollections* as works expressive of America's "most intensely national" poet.[36] Whittier exchanged letters with her, passing along literary news of Boston and Concord, one item mentioning the publication of Julia Ward Howe's *Passion Flowers* and another Holmes' lecture on the English poets. He told her: "We have recently had a delightful visit from Ralph Waldo Emerson. I wish thou wouldst meet him. He is not admired, but loved."[37] Whittier not only wrote letters but also sent her "an illustrated edition of his works, bound in scarlet morocco, with a vast quantity of gilding and a portrait." Mitford finally decided that she liked Whittier's *Songs of Labor* best.[38]

Though she found Halleck "a poet of different stamp, with less of earnestness and fire, but more of grace and melody," she chose a sampling of his verse, including "On the Death of Joseph Rodman Drake," to make up part of the twenty-sixth chapter of her *Recollections*.

Halleck's voice was small but worthy of hearing, thought Mitford. She had no doubt, however, that Longfellow's was a major voice. She had watched Longfellow's rise to fame in England with pleasure, convinced that he deserved his popularity,[39] which she thought was based more on the love of his short poems than on *The Spanish Student* or *Evangeline*.[40] His poems soon became as widely known as Alfred Tennyson's, a fact bringing joy to Mitford since it confirmed her notion that American authors were being read for their "pith and substance.[41]" She spelled out her reasons for agreeing with her countrymen that Longfellow's fame was just: "the terseness of diction and force of thought delight the old; the grace and melody enchant the young, the unaffected and all-pervading piety satisfy the serious; and a certain slight touch of mysticism carries the imaginative reader fairly off his feet."[42]

She took a special delight in Longfellow's *The Golden Legend*, finding it "full of salt and savour—rich, racy, graphic,—breathing the air of the middle ages, of Gothic architecture, grand cathedrals, quaint German towns."[43] She eagerly recommended the book to her friend Mrs. Jennings. She wrote Fields that she hoped to be "only one among the multitude who think that this is the greatest and best thing he has done."[44]

Her preference for this volume led her to place "Nuremberg" as the first poem among the half dozen chosen to represent Longfellow in the sixth chapter of her *Recollections*. The others were "The Open Window," "The Old Clock on the Stairs," "Twilight," "Resignation," and a section of "Address to a Child."[45] This extremely favorable notice of his work by Mitford prompted Longfellow to ask Fields to pass along his "kindest acknowledgments" when Fields next wrote her.[46]

As much as she praised Longfellow's verse, she could see his faults, as shown by her remarks to critic and playwright Digby Starkey. Longfellow "owes his success here quite as much to his faults, his obscurity, his mysticism, and his little dash of cant, as to his merits." And about his prose, she was blunt: "His prose is trash." She confided, finally, "For my own part, I greatly prefer the healthy and cheerful masculine verse of Dr. Holmes."[47]

Mitford owed to Fields the opportunity of discovering the poems of

Holmes, whose *Astrea* arrived in the same package as *The Scarlet Letter* and Whittier's *Songs of Labor* early in 1851. By 8 February of that year Mitford was promoting Holmes to her circle of friends, the first notice being given to a Mrs. Ouvry.[48] To Charles Boner she wrote: "We have had nothing like it for years. It is a combination of Goldsmith, Pope and Dryden, but thoroughly native and original, full of strength and beauty, of pathos and power, with a graphic force of diction, a harmony of versification, and a general finish that we look for in vain on this side of the water. What a model for our young poets!"[49]

Holmes was too good, she thought, to be kept within her circle of friends. She therefore quickly moved to do an article on Holmes for the *Lady's Companion*, where she recounted something of his life as she had heard it from Fields and included some extracts from his poems. Fields obviously told Holmes of Mitford's admiring recommendation, for Holmes immediately sent a copy of his collected poems to her with the following words on the fly-leaf: "For Miss Mitford, with Dr. Holmes' best respects."[50]

When friends asked her where Holmes' poems could be bought in London, she wrote to give addresses of booksellers and the cost of the book. And she hastened to include a generous amount of his verse in her *Recollections*, giving over chapter thirty-one to Holmes. Here she repeated her belief that Holmes belonged in the tradition of Dryden and Pope while, at the same time, proving his right to be called an original American poet. To represent him, she chose the opening of *Astrea* and then a couple of items from Holmes' collected poems, including "On Lending a Punch-Bowl."[51]

Of course Holmes was pleased with such favorable notice. He wrote Fields to tell Mitford that a letter full of his gratitude would soon be on its way to her.[52] Holmes' debt to her was indeed considerable, for, through Mitford's strong praise and active promotion of his work, Holmes' poems were reprinted in England.[53] For the remainder of her life, Mitford championed the poetry of Holmes, considering it a kind of touchstone[54] and expressing the desire that such English poets as Elizabeth Barrett Browning would learn something about polish by studying Holmes.[55]

Although Holmes was her favorite American poet,[56] Mitford stood ready to welcome new voices as they began to appear in America, among them the voices of Bayard Taylor, Stoddard, Lowell, and T. W. Parsons.

Mitford evidently asked Fields to see that the work of Taylor be sent to her, a request passed along to Taylor, who, in answer (10 May 1850) to Fields, replied: "I hope to be supplied on Monday or Tuesday, and then remember all my friends, Miss Mitford included. This time I am really going to send her all my three works in one lump,—enough to terrify the poor old lady."[57] Approving of what she found in Taylor's poems, she later told Fields that Taylor as well as his friend Stoddard were in Fields' words "fame-sure" and would be given a place in her *Recollections* if a new series ever appeared.[58] Perhaps encouraged by Fields to do so, Taylor visited Mitford when he went to England in the fall of 1852, reporting back to Fields that he and Mitford had a "merry afternoon."[59] Mitford described the visit to Miss Jephson, yet another of her friends devoted to literature, and shared her impression of him: "He is a person of no common learning, an excellent classical scholar, and speaking French, German, Italian, Spanish, and Arabic as well as his native tongue. . . . A very clever person, and a very remarkable one . . . as good as he is clever—but yet I did not fancy him. . . . He is shy and gawky, long rather than tall . . . , and with a total absence of that strange, delightful thing called charm."[60] She nonetheless sent him off with her good wishes as he left for further travels, and she hastened to share with Miss Jephson news about Stoddard and to quote for her a couple of stanzas of Stoddard's verse by way of illustrating what this low-born, working class poet could do.[61] She also advised her friend Mrs. Jennings to read Taylor and Stoddard and repeated her intention to give specimens of their work if another volume of *Recollections* ever saw print.[62]

As was her usual practice once she had read or met a writer, she followed the careers of Taylor and Stoddard. She wrote to thank Taylor for his books on his travels in the East, accurately divining that "wandering is your destiny, dear friend, and your power of writing and of speech make it a destiny profitable to your country and to ours."[63] Taylor's response to this letter (15 September 1854) expressed his thanks for her praise and recalled his visit to her nearly two years earlier: "Your kindness to a rough stranger like myself made me at once your friend, and I shall never think of you otherwise . . . than with the sincerest friendship and esteem. Stoddard and I speak of you often and involuntarily as an old and tried friend, so near and familiar the thought of you has become."[64] He reported that he and Stoddard continued to work together, that he was aware that poetical fame came slowly, and that he had seen nearly all the leading American authors that summer: Irving, Lowell, Holmes, Longfellow, and Willis, all "idling at present."[65]

For his part, Stoddard sent her an autographed copy of his newest project, *Poets of America*. Defying her doctor's caution against letter writing, Mitford sent a note thanking him for his gift and telling him of her impatience to see the latest books by Taylor and Parsons.[66] When Taylor's books came, she was much pleased, describing his work as exquisite to W. C. Bennett, a minor English poet and one of her many correspondents. But as she said in the same letter (30 September 1854) while commenting on a letter from Stoddard and on some verses of Stoddard's she had recently shared with Bennett, "Return Mr. Stoddard's letter . . . you see his verses are bad,— and you also see his great over-estimate of his own doings."[67]

In addition to Taylor and Stoddard, Mitford began to value Parsons' poetry enough early in 1853 to decide to give him the supportive push of being included in her next series of *Recollections*. This dentist-turned-translator of Dante's *Divine Comedy* and poet in his own right had won Mitford's attention by his poems on Dante and Webster: "In my mind no poems ever crossed the Atlantic which approached his stanzas on Dante and on the death of Webster, and yet you have great poets too."[68]

Parsons sent her an inscribed copy of *Poems* (1854), wrote letters to her, and received notes from her by way of Fields. Mitford was beginning to think of him as one of America's greatest poets, a ranking present-day readers find surprising, but Parsons' place seemed both high and secure to his contemporaries.[69]

Another of the Athenians, as she also termed the Boston group of writers she knew and boosted, was Lowell. While she was preparing copy for *Recollections*, she asked W. C. Bennett to find a copy of Lowell's verse in a London bookshop. By the time the volume came to her, her work was too far advanced to put anything by Lowell in. If and when a new series came out, Lowell would have a chapter to himself, she told Bennett.[70] Her letters are silent both on her reasons for liking Lowell and on what poems she would have selected to represent him. She had some good things to draw from: *The Biglow Papers, First Series, A Fable for Critics*, and *The Vision of Sir Launfal*. Mitford's interest in American poets never seemed to wane. She admired Bryant's "To a Yellow Violet" early and stayed to celebrate the latest efforts of Taylor and Lowell. Unlike poetry, American fiction seemed not to hold her attention nearly so long. She came back to Cooper time and again and spoke favorably of Robert Montgomery Bird and William Ware, but she put Harriet Beecher Stowe's *Uncle Tom's Cabin* down in disgust and never took it up again. She gave her reasons for doing so, the first of which was its onesidedness and exaggeration. In the face of its great popularity in England, she held firm in her stand that the "de-merits of the book have more to do with its popularity than any sort of excellence; the cant about slavery being a good cry."[71] Although Mitford supposed she should press on to finish the book, she found too many objections to reading it. To her, Stowe seemed, like Fuller, one of the "strong-minded women," a phrase roughly equivalent to *feminist*. And she recoiled from Stowe, too, because Stowe had undertaken a defense of Lady Byron. Stowe's attack of Lord Byron, *Lady Byron Vindicated*, displeased her in part because it grieved one of Byron's closest friends, William Harness, a dear friend of Mitford as well.[72] Mitford therefore was happy to learn that William Ticknor had not been able to go beyond page forty. She held out for sixty more, but cast it aside and refused to encourage anyone to read it.[73]

She never had the same problem with the work of Hawthorne, although she did find unevenness in his writing. From her discovery of *The Scarlet*

Letter in 1851 until her death in 1855, Hawthorne's work and career left her with no doubt that America had produced a great, if sometimes flawed, writer of fiction. Whenever she could, she boosted his writing, lending her copies of Hawthorne's novels to friends and reviewers. She eagerly awaited a visit by Hawthorne to her home and she exchanged letters with him. But most significantly she gave Hawthorne's fiction an enthusiastic endorsement in her *Recollections*. She became, in short, an ardent champion.

She seems to have missed the pirated edition (1849) of *Twice-Told Tales*, "The Celestial Railroad" (pirated in 1844), and *Mosses from an Old Manse*, first printed in England in 1846. Her introduction to Hawthorne came early in 1851 when Fields sent her a copy of *The Scarlet Letter* along with works by Whittier and Holmes. Her first remark was brief; she described the novel as "a wild romantic tale of the elder days of Boston."[74] Two weeks or so after this first notice (11 February 1851), she had spent time with the novel and was lamenting the fact that it was not available in England. (A pirated edition appeared two-and-a-half months later.) She told Charles Boner that the novel was "very striking and poetical."[75] She was already looking forward to the publication of his next work, which she had learned from Mrs. Jared Sparks, Hawthorne's first beloved, was finer than anything yet printed.[76] The work she looked forward to was *The House of The Seven Gables*, a copy of which she received from Fields. By July, Mitford was ready to agree that it surpassed the earlier novel in some ways: "The legendary part dim, shadowy, and impressive, and the living characters exquisitely true, vivid, and healthful. The heroine, Phoebe, is almost a Shakespearian creation, as fresh and charming as the Rigolette of Eugene Sue."[77] On the same day (20 July 1851) that she was writing the preceding evaluation to Charles Boner, she was sending much the same thing to Fields. She turned to Fields for information about Hawthorne, wanting to know his age and profession. Whatever she learned of him, she was already sure that Hawthorne was "one of the glories of your most glorious part of great America."[78] Fields was to answer her questions some months later when he visited her home. Meanwhile, Fields quoted her praise of the novel to Hawthorne in a letter dated 14 August 1851.[79] Hawthorne graciously returned the compliment, writing (18 August 1851) that he was "glad . . . that the Seven Gables have pleased Miss Mitford, whose sketches [*Our Village*], long ago as I read them, are as sweet in my memory as the scent of new hay."[80]

Mitford, at this time (27 September 1851) busy preparing her *Recollections*, was happy to receive from Fields a copy of the newly published two-volume edition of *Twice-Told Tales*, which she declared "inferior" to the novels.[81] A few weeks later (mid-October) Fields arrived, bringing a copy of *A Wonder Book for Girls and Boys* and much news about its author. Mitford wasted no time spreading word of Hawthorne the man to her friends. She told W. C. Bennett (17 October 1851) that Fields had reported that Hawthorne "blushes like a girl when praised—is still young—and a magnificent specimen of manhood almost a giant (I thought he was tall and large)—Mr. Fields says he would cut out into four of Dr. Holmes who is a compact little man. Hawthorne is upon the model of Webster. . . . [Hawthorne] thinks himself the most overrated man in all America."[82]

Fields, obviously in an expansive mood, told her a good deal more about Hawthorne, including the story of his own role in publishing *The Scarlet Letter*. Mitford seized upon the story and hastened to share it, telling a number of correspondents how Fields had found Hawthorne in "extreme penury" in Salem, how Fields upon hearing of Hawthorne's poverty had gone to him and declared his confidence in Hawthorne's power, promising to print 2,500 copies of any work that Hawthorne would give him and allowing a twenty-five per cent royalty. What Hawthorne had reluctantly put into his hands was a part of *The Scarlet Letter*, the greatness of which Fields saw and the success of which he was sure if only Hawthorne would complete the work.[83]

She soon took up the *Wonder Book*, telling Francis Bennoch, who later was to become Hawthorne's closest English friend, that she felt "charmed" by the book. "I always love children's books, but this is fit for any age. I am not sure (with the exception of George Sand) that Mr. Hawthorne is not the best living writer of prose fiction."[84]

Firmly committed to promoting Hawthorne, she told Fields early in 1852 that she had had "the honor of poking him into the den of the Times, the only civilized place in England where they were barbarous enough not to be acquainted with 'The Scarlet Letter.' I wonder what they'll think of it. It will make them stare."[85]

What Mitford had been thinking and saying privately she was now ready to express publicly, for, after much work, her *Recollections* now came from the press, affording her the opportunity to place Hawthorne's novels among the works of other American novelists. Good as were Cooper's novels, especially *The Pioneers*, William Ware's *Zenobia*, Robert Montgomery Bird's *Nick of the Woods*, and as fine as were the stories of Irving, no one excelled Hawthorne, the "new star . . . lately sprung into light in the Western horizon . . . [who] will hardly fail to be a bright illumination over both Europe and America."[86] Mitford then undertook to blend a critical estimate of *The Scarlet Letter* and *The House of the Seven Gables* with a synopsis of each before reprinting more than ten pages as a sample. She was especially taken with Hepzibah, confessing that once in the midst of her struggle to support herself she had thought of setting up as a shopkeeper herself. "Ah, I have a strong fellow-feeling that poor Hepzibah—a decayed gentlewoman, elderly,

ugly, awkward, near-sighted, cross!"[87] Preferring the realistic to the legendary element, Mitford extracted from the portions of the novel dealing with
Hepzibah and Phoebe. Herself an adept in the use of realistic detail, Mitford
likened Hawthorne's use of realism to Balzac and to Dutch painting, a remark which must have pleased Hawthorne since he admired Dutch painting
above all other. It was this same love of realism that led Mitford to down-
grade *The Blithedale Romance* when she compared it to *The House of the
Seven Gables*. Like Herman Melville, Mitford preferred larger servings of
roast beef (realism) than Hawthorne provided.

While Mitford was doing her utmost to champion the work of a genius,
Hawthorne was settling down to a job he had never done before, writing a
letter of introduction to an English author, in this case a letter to Mitford for
Grace Greenwood (Sarah Jane Clarke). As he accepted the request, he said,
"I suppose it would be no more than courtesy to write, as she has made such
kind mention of me in her book [*Recollections*]; and I shall be glad to requite
her kindness so abundantly as by introducing Grace Greenwood."[88]

Before she left for her fifteen-month sojourn in England and her visit to
Mitford's home, Hawthorne finished his introductory note and asked Greenwood "to read and seal it, before delivering. Tell the good old lady everything that you think will please her, about my gratitude and appreciation of
her good opinion—and it will every word be true."[89] The day following the
writing of the note (3 May 1852), Hawthorne told Fields that he planned to
take the liberty of writing Mitford soon.[90]

Besides her introductory note from Hawthorne, Greenwood probably arrived with a copy of *The Blithedale Romance* in hand when she visited Mitford in early July. Mitford speedily thanked Fields for sending it and frankly
told him what she saw wrong with it: "It seems to me too long, too slow, and
the personages . . . ill chosen." Zenobia she disliked because she linked her
to Fuller or some other unsexed female. Hollingsworth reminded her of a
disgusting English preacher of loathsome memory, and Westervelt and Priscilla were "almost equally disagreeable." She complained of Hawthorne's
"want of reality," convinced that the lack of realism in his early tales delayed
his climb to fame. She was also sure that his practice of allegory, his projection of thought through some "ideal medium," would prevent the extension of his fame "if he do not resolutely throw himself into the truth." The
fine parts of the book, she insisted, were the realistic, the search for Zenobia's body (based on a real drowning in Concord), the "burst of passion in
Eliot's pulpit," and "likeable" and "honest" Silas Foster, "who alone gives
one the notion of a man of flesh and blood." She added that she found the
plot well constructed.[91] Flawed as it was, she was pleased to recommend it to
her friends and to say, "with all its faults [the book] is one that nobody but

Hawthorne could have written."[92] She maintained this view despite having known since June 1852 that E. P. Whipple, "the best American critic, [had] seen Mr. Hawthorne's new work . . . and [said] that it exceeds in power and beauty the 'Scarlet Letter' and 'The House of the Seven Gables.'"[93] Writing to thank Hawthorne for autographing the copy Fields had sent her, Mitford told him that his writing reminded her of Balzac's, "not by imitation, but by resemblance" (6 August 1852). She praised "the passion of the concluding scenes, the subtle analysis of jealousy, and the exquisite finish of style." Her reservations were not so strong that she backed away from her practice of boosting Hawthorne, for she sent the copy she had received from Boston to Willmott of the *Times*, where, she told Fields, it had gotten a "highly eulogistic critique."[94]

More exciting than the appearance of *The Blithedale Romance* was the news in the fall of 1852 that Fields expected to come to England in the spring of 1853 and would bring Hawthorne with him.[95] Infirm as she was at the time, she hoped to rally before they arrived so she could be up "to show Mr. Hawthorne all the holes and corners my own self."[96]

While she waited for them to come, she continued to mention Hawthorne in letters to her friends, telling Mrs. Jennings, for example, that she hoped Hawthorne's newest work would help him recover the reputation he had lost after publishing *The Blithedale Romance*. She boasted that she had also had "the pleasure of sending [Hawthorne] word a month ago [December 1852] about the Russian translation of *The House of the Seven Gables*. She explained to Fields that an appointment to a public office by Franklin Pierce would be good for Hawthorne's art. "It will be as excellent thing for his future books,—the fault of all his writings, in spite of their great beauty, being a want of reality, of the actual, healthy, every-day life which is a necessary element in literature. All the great poets have it,—Homer, Shakespeare, Scott."[97] And she shared a bit of gossip with Bennett, passing along word of Hawthorne's shyness. She had heard, she said, that Hawthorne "will be only a foil to his charming wife, a brilliant companion." Getting Hawthorne to converse would be difficult, but his talk "was good . . . when it did come."[98]

As the time of Hawthorne's arrival in England (23 July 1853) drew near, Mitford could scarcely contain her excitement. But time and again she would be disappointed, first by the fact that Ticknor, not Fields, would be accompanying Hawthorne, and then by the duties in Liverpool that Hawthorne never seemed able to leave behind.[99] Finally, every obstacle overcome, the visit was set for 6 August. She hastened to tell such friends as Charles Kingsley to be there when Bennoch, Ticknor, and Hawthorne arrived, but Hawthorne was once again delayed. Her letter to Hugh Pearson on 8 August shows the depth of her disappointment: "Ah! dearest friend, how we wished for you! Hawthorne did not come." She told him why and then added that Hawthorne would leave Liverpool for London at the end of the month. "*Then* he will certainly come here, and you *must* meet him."[100] But there was never to be a visit from Hawthorne, though Ticknor did call, finding "little of [her] available except the head and the heart. Of course the recent bad weather has not improved my rheumatism—and now I must put off my hopes of amendment to next spring. Then I trust if not before that I shall have the great pleasure of making personal acquaintance with one [Hawthorne] whom I can never think of except as a friend."[101]

A recently arrived book, *The Tanglewood Tales*, sent by Fields, had renewed her longing to meet Hawthorne. She rushed to tell Hawthorne how much she admired the book: "In addition to that wash of prose poetry which is so peculiarly your own, and which reproduces in so exquisite a manner the early history of your country—you have contrived to blend your own fancy with some of those lovely classical fables. . . . How many thousands will think of you as the name of some glorious old legend comes on to them! It is a fine thing to make a holiday book of that which to school boys has too often been a dry lexicon."[102]

The close of 1853 did not mark an end to the hope that Mitford and Hawthorne would meet, a fact borne out by Hawthorne's note to her on 16 January 1854: "The Steamer (just arrived from Boston) has brought the enclosed letter from our friend Fields. . . . I am glad that it gives me an opportunity to say what a pleasure it is to me to be in the same country with you. When Mr. Fields comes over again (which he tells me will be in May) I cherish the hope of seeing you in company with him; but even if that should not happen, I shall still feel like a neighbor—the sense of inaccesibleness being removed."[103]

By May Mitford's health had declined so much that she felt she could see only the dearest of friends. She wrote Fields that she still wanted him to visit, "but any stranger—even Mr. Hawthorne—is quite out of the question."[104] One thing seemed uppermost now, saving her strength to see an edition of her dramatic works and her final pieces of fiction, *Atherton and Other Tales*, through the press. Even in the midst of that push, made propped in bed and with limited use of her right arm, she sought to keep up with literary events in America. Because Fields was slow in getting a volume of Parsons' poems to her, W. C. Bennett asked Hawthorne to help him find a copy for Mitford. Hawthorne happily obliged by writing Fields. He also told Bennett that news of her illness grieved him, "For though I never had the happiness of meeting her, my feelings towards her are those of a warm personal friend."[105] Bennett sent this kind remark on to Mitford and received one every bit as cordial from her: "I return Mr. Hawthorne's charming letter—very charming in every point—some day or other you must tell him (for you will be friends) how much I feel his kindness and lament not having known him." [106]

Two more acts of friendship occurred before her death in the spring of 1855. Hawthorne, not sure of reaching Fields in time, asked Ticknor to send a copy of Parsons' poems before she died. When the book finally appeared in October 1854, she believed that Hawthorne's intercession had been responsible for its arrival. She wrote to Bennoch: "One of my reasons for praying, if it be His will, for a prolongation of life is to know and to thank Mr. Hawthorne." [107] And her final act of friendship was to ask Fields to send Hawthorne a copy of *Atherton*. [108]

Those two acts of friendship do not quite end the story, for about a year following Mitford's death, Hawthorne learned something more about her when Bennoch took him to some government offices on Downing Street to talk with William Harness about a monument for Mitford. Their conversation revealed that the British public seemed cool to the notion of a monument for her. He was also "surprised to hear allusions indicating that Miss Mitford was not the inevitably amiable person that her writings would suggest: but the whole drift of what they said tended, nevertheless, towards the idea that she was an excellent and generous person, loved most by those who knew her best." [109]

In choosing the word *generous*, Hawthorne fixed upon the exact word needed to describe Mitford's attitude toward American writers after she had taught herself that America was not "a second-hand, pawnbrokers'-shop kind of nation." Her generosity tended to push her toward panegyric, leading her to overrate a few writers, Parsons, for example. Her attachment to Fields and the Boston-Concord circle of writers, while enabling her to discover a Holmes or a Hawthorne earlier than she otherwise might have, left her with too little knowledge of American writers to boost careers just as deserving as those she chose to champion, a few examples being Charles Brockden Brown, William Gilmore Simms, and Melville. Her dependence on Fields and the other Athenians provided her with some gossip and prejudiced views that she would have corrected had she known the full or true story, the most obvious instance being Fields' account of how he rescued Hawthorne from poverty. Even as this limitation is mentioned, we must recall that long before Fields made his pilgrimage to her home she had eagerly shared her gleanings from such writers as Sedgwick, Paulding, Verplanck, Hall, Flint, William Joseph Snelling, and Bryant with her countrymen and that she had found in Irving's *Sketch Book* the idea leading to her most celebrated work, *Our Village*. Readings in these earlier authors prepared her to accept Americanisms as proper to literature and taught her what ideas American writers sought to present. She was therefore prepared to recognize the content, forms, and flavor of American literature before coming upon the writings of the writers of the American Renaissance. Having a fairly good knowledge of the work of their forebears, she could more adequately judge the higher achievement of her beloved Athenians. And having visited with Webster, George Ticknor, and Fields, and having read such poems as Whittier's "Massachusetts to Virginia," she was well enough acquainted with America's divided views on slavery to know that Stowe's *Uncle Tom's Cabin* had a liberal sprinkling of cant and exaggeration.

Mitford was neither a literary historian nor a professional critic, as we now define those roles. Instead, she was a champion of literature, be it French, British, or American, to name her three favorite national branches. Her schooling and early friendships opened her eyes to the beauties of English and French literature, but her fame as a writer brought her the chance to learn what American writers could do when a London publisher asked her to edit a collection of American stories. From that experience, she gained respect for American writing. Respect gave way to admiration, and in time, admiration was to underlie the repeated private and public steps she took to call attention to American works. She became a champion, one able to see flaws, as shown by her comments on Hawthorne, one of her particular pets, but one inclined to excessive praise. She capped her promotion of American writing by the generous boost given American writers in her *Recollections*. A year after that work appeared, she proudly claimed to Charles Boner (20 March 1853): "I find the influence of these volumes has been great—Dr. Holmes has been reprinted in consequence. . . . Whittier and Hawthorne both say I have done more for their reputation than all the rest of the critics put together—and that's not only in England but in America. Longfellow, I understand, says the same."[110]

This claim may indeed be an exaggeration but there is no doubt that Mary Russell Mitford was an extremely active and successful builder of the bridge linking British and American literature. That role was one she was happy to play and one she wanted to be remembered for after her six chapters on American authors in *Recollections*. As if recalling her snobbish remark made three decades before publishing her thoughts on American literature, Mitford said in a letter to Fields, "I think you will find more justice done to American authors than in any work of English criticism—as indeed it would not have confessed my own true feelings and opinions if I had not done so."[111]

NOTES

1. *The Letters of Mary Russell Mitford*, ed. R. Brimley Johnson (London: John Lane, 1925), p. 28.

2. *Mary Russell Mitford* (London: Noel Douglas, 1930), pp. 119–29. I am grateful to the British Library, the Berkshire Museum, the Houghton Library of Harvard University, the Huntington Library, Middlebury College, the New York Public Library and the Astor, Lenox, and Tilden Foundations, the Barrett Library of the University of Virginia, and the Young Library of St. Lawrence University for permission to quote from letters in their possession.

3. Whittier was among the first American writers to applaud her verse, writing her in 1813 to express his admiration for her *Narrative Poems on the Female Character* (Astin, *Mitford*, p. 119).

4. Edmund Gosse, Virginia Woolf, and Marjorie Astin have written most favorably of Mitford's achievement.

5. Harriet Martineau, *Biographical Sketches*, 2d ed. (London: Macmillan, 1869), pp. 356–57.

6. Vera Watson, *Mary Russell Mitford* (London: Evans Brothers, 1949), p. 193.

7. Her plays *Julian* and *Rienzi* were well received.

8. As quoted from Watson, *Mitford*, p. 161.

9. W. J. Roberts, *Mary Russell Mitford: The Tragedy of a Blue Stocking* (London: Andrew Melrose, 1913), pp. 301–302.

10. *Letters From Abroad to Kindred at Home* (New York: Harpers, 1841), pp. 46–47.

11. Sedgwick, *Letters*, p. 46.

12. Watson, *Mitford*, p. 238.

13. *The Letters of Mary Russell Mitford*, 2d Series, ed. Henry Chorley (London: Richard Bentley and Son, 1872), 1:94; hereafter cited as *Letters*.

14. *The Life of Mary Russell Mitford Related in a Selection of Letters to Her Friends*, ed. A. G. L'Estrange (London: R. Bentley, 1870), 2:107; hereafter cited as *Selection of Letters*.

15. *Selection of Letters*, 2:122.

16. *Memoirs and Letters of Charles Boner With Letters of Mary Russell Mitford to Him During Ten Years*, ed. R. M. Kettle (London: Richard Bentley, 1870), p. 267; hereafter cited as *Letters to Boner*.

17. *Selection of Letters*, 2:177.

18. *Selection of Letters*, 2:226–27. Upon coming upon *The Pathfinder* and *The Deerslayer* in 1851, Mitford began reading Cooper's early novels about Leather Stocking and was struck by their merit, "more than when I first read them" (letter to W. C. Bennett, 28 June 1851, CSmH).

19. Letter to W. C. Bennett, 3 August 1849, Egerton MS 3774, BL.

20. *Letters*, 2:169.

21. *Letters to Boner*, p. 126.

22. *Letters*, 1:162.

23. James T. Fields, *Yesterdays With Authors* (Boston: James R. Osgood, 1872), p. 315.

24. She was well acquainted with the work of William Ware, Robert Montgomery Bird, Whittier, and Fitz-Green Halleck in the 1840s.

25. Fields, *Yesterdays With Authors*, pp. 284, 343.

26. *Letters*, 2:159.

27. *Selection of Letters*, 3:232.

28. Letter to W. C. Bennett, 9 October 1850, Egerton MS 3774, BL.

29. *Selection of Letters*, 3:236.

30. *Letters to Boner*, p. 181.

31. *Selection of Letters*, 3:230.

32. *Selection of Letters*, 3:234.

33. Fields, *Yesterdays With Authors*, p. 300.

34. Fields, *Yesterdays With Authors*, p. 301.

35. Fields, *Yesterdays With Authors*, p. 285.

36. *Recollections of a Literary Life: Or Books, Places, and People* (New York: Harpers, 1852), p. 334; hereafter cited as *Recollections*.

37. *The Letters of John Greenleaf Whittier*, ed. John B. Pickard (Cambridge: Harvard University Press, 1975), 2:248.

38. *Selection of Letters*, 3:362.

39. Fields, *Yesterdays With Authors*, p. 286.

40. *Recollections*, p. 63.

41. *Recollections*, p. 62.

42. *Recollections*, pp. 62–63.

43. *Selection of Letters*, 3:228.

44. Fields, *Yesterdays With Authors*, p. 293.

45. *Recollections*, pp. 63–69.

46. *The Letters of Henry Wadsworth Longfellow*, ed. Andrew Hilen, 6 vols. (Cambridge: Harvard University Press, 1966–82), 3:338.

47. A. G. L'Estrange, *The Friendships of Mary Russell Mitford* (New York: Harpers, 1882), p. 368; hereafter cited as *Friendships*.

48. *Letters*, 2:119.

49. *Letters to Boner*, p. 199.

50. *Letters to Boner*, p. 207.

51. *Recollections*, pp. 399–410.

52. John T. Morse, Jr., *Life and Letters of Oliver Wendell Holmes* (Boston: Houghton, Mifflin, 1896), 2:278. Evidently, Holmes' letter did not survive.

53. Astin, *Mitford*, p. 128.

54. Fields, *Yesterdays With Authors*, p. 352.

55. Letter to Fields, 10 February 1851, MS Eng. 189.5, MH. Fields omitted the final sentence in this letter in *Yesterdays With Authors*; it reads, "I wish she would polish like Dr. Holmes."

56. Fields, *Yesterdays With Authors*, p. 313.

57. Marie Hansen-Taylor and Horace E. Scudder, *Life and Letters of Bayard Taylor* (Boston: Houghton, Mifflin, 1885), 1:171.

58. Taylor, *Life and Letters*, 1:230.

59. Taylor, *Life and Letters*, 1:241.

60. *Friendships*, p. 399.

61. *Friendships*, p. 405.

62. *Selection of Letters*, 3:283.

63. Taylor, *Life and Letters*, 1:278–79.

64. Taylor, *Life and Letters*, 1:280.

65. Taylor, *Life and Letters*, 1:280.

66. Letter to Richard Henry Stoddard, 28 September 1854, published in *Aldine*, 5 May 1872, p. 108.

67. Letter to W. C. Bennett, 30 September 1854, Egerton MS 3774, BL.

68. Fields, *Yesterdays With Authors*, p. 345.

69. Max J. Herzberg, *The Reader's Encyclopedia of American Literature* (New York: Thomas Y. Crowell, 1962), p. 856.

70. Letter to W. C. Bennett, 25 April 1853, Egerton MS 3774, BL.

71. *Selection of Letters*, 3:245.

72. Roberts, *Mitford*, pp. 370–71.

73. *Letters*, 2:208.

74. *Letters to Boner*, p. 199.

75. *Letters to Boner*, p. 206.

76. *Letters*, 2:38.

77. *Letters to Boner*, pp. 189–90.

78. Fields, *Yesterdays With Authors*, p. 289.

79. Fields to Hawthorne, 14 August 1851, NN.

80. Hawthorne to Fields, 18 August 1851, NCaS.

81. *Letters to Boner*, p. 215.

82. Letter to W. C. Bennett, 17 October 1851, Egerton MS 3774, BL.

83. *Letters to Boner*, p. 217. L. Neal Smith says that "Sophia burned when, in England, she learned that Fields had 'dined out' on this revelation of generosity" (personal letter to the author, 7 May 1980).

84. *Letters*, 2:229.

85. Fields, *Yesterdays With Authors*, p. 295.

86. *Recollections*, p. 517.

87. *Recollections*, p. 520.

88. Hawthorne to Grace Greenwood, 17 April 1852, NN.

89. Hawthorne to Grace Greenwood, 2 May 1852, MPM.

90. Hawthorne to Fields, 3 May 1853, ViU.

91. Fields, *Yesterdays With Authors*, pp. 304–305.

92. *Friendships*, p. 383.

93. *Letters*, 2:170–71.

94. Fields, *Yesterdays With Authors*, p. 313; George P. Lathrop, *A Study of Hawthorne* (Boston: James R. Osgood, 1876), pp. 229–30.

95. *Friendships*, pp. 390.

96. Fields, *Yesterdays With Authors*, p. 309.

97. Fields, *Yesterdays With Authors*, p. 320.

98. Letter to W. C. Bennett, 9 May 1853, Egerton MS 3774, BL.

99. *Letters*, 2:180.

100. *Letters*, 2:207.

101. Letter to Hawthorne, 2 October 1853, NN.

102. Julian Hawthorne, *Nathaniel Hawthorne and His Wife* (Boston: James R. Osgood, 1885), 2:35.

103. Hawthorne to Mitford, 16 January 1854, Collection of C. E. Frazer Clark, Jr.

104. Fields, *Yesterdays With Authors*, p. 344.

105. Hawthorne to W. C. Bennett, 7 September 1854, VtMiM.

106. Letter to W. C. Bennett, 8 September 1854, Egerton MS 3774, BL.

107. *Letters*, 2:257.

108. Fields, *Yesterdays With Authors*; Sophia's account book (MSaE), lists the presentation copy of *Atherton* (personal letter from B. Bernard Cohen to the author, 18 March 1981).

109. *The English Notebooks*, ed. Randall Stewart (New York: Modern Language Association, 1941), pp. 323–24.

110. *Letters to Boner*, p. 250.

111. Letter to Fields, n.d. [late 1852?], MS Eng. 189.5., MH.

ARRANGING THE SIBYLLINE LEAVES: JAMES ELLIOT CABOT'S WORK AS EMERSON'S LITERARY EXECUTOR

Nancy Craig Simmons

JAMES ELLIOT CABOT was a man who chose to be inconspicuous. Reticent and modest, quietly affluent, he led an exemplary but secluded life. Likewise, in his work as Ralph Waldo Emerson's appointed literary executor and biographer, he remained discreetly in the background, performing competently, but noticed by few. The two-volume biography he wrote, *A Memoir of Ralph Waldo Emerson* (1887), was criticized for its lack of color, and the works he selected and edited between 1875 and 1893, for four volumes of the standard Emerson editions, have never seemed completely authentic. In 1979, the editors of the new *Collected Works of Ralph Waldo Emerson* made a decision about the three posthumous volumes compiled by Cabot that clearly sounds the verdict of contemporary scholarship on Cabot's contribution as Emerson's first editor. The new edition will include the contents of nine volumes whose publication was supervised by Emerson between 1841 and 1875—volumes 1–9 of both the Riverside (1883–93) and Centenary (1903–1904) editions—aiming to present the text closest to the author's initial intention. However, from the three posthumous collections will be drawn a single volume of pieces published by Emerson but not collected by him.[1] The other matter in these volumes will be saved for a separate edition of Emerson's later lectures. Except for six or seven Cabot compositions that seem destined to remain in the eighth volume (*Letters and Social Aims*), this action will effectively banish Cabot's editorial efforts from the Emerson canon.

The decision does not, however, alter the significance of Cabot's contribution, both to the shaping of Emerson's modern reputation and to our understanding of his work. Creating "synthetic" essays like "Greatness," "The Sovereignty of Ethics," "Fortune of the Republic," and "Natural History of

Intellect" was only one of the many functions Cabot performed during the twenty years he worked for Emerson. First, in 1875, Cabot responded to the Emersons' plea to help the aging author compile *Letters and Social Aims*. The next year, Emerson's new will named Cabot literary executor with authority to determine what should or should not be printed from his manuscripts. A year later he accepted the responsibility of writing the family-authorized biography. During the last six years of Emerson's life, Cabot served as a sort of literary secretary and editor, searching the lecture manuscripts for material for lectures and essays, and reconstructing these pieces or shaping them into new wholes, creating readings and printed essays for Emerson. At the same time, he was organizing the very confused jumble of manuscript from almost four hundred lectures and beginning to collect information for a biography. Emerson's death in 1882 made Cabot's role as literary executor official. With thoroughness and dedication, he collected and catalogued the correspondence, continued work on other papers (particularly reading and cataloguing over 180 journals and notebooks), and supervised publication of the Riverside Edition of the *Works*. Upon completing the eleven-volume edition with its two posthumous collections in 1884, Cabot returned to the biography, published in 1887. Still his work was not finished: in 1893, publication of the twelfth volume of the *Works*, *Natural History of Intellect and Other Papers* (including a very long title essay compiled by Cabot), brought his obligation to an end.

The Emersons were extremely grateful to Cabot for his help at a very difficult time. Emerson expressed his appreciation in a codicil to his will in 1881: a bequest of a thousand dollars to each of Cabot's children (in fact, seven sons) recognized his "goodness in rendering me a service which no other could render." From the beginning Emerson's daughter Ellen claimed that heaven had sent help just in time. Years later Edward Emerson summarized Cabot's "great task, a labour of years," and judged it "nearly perfectly" done.[2]

Cabot himself was more modest about the value of his work. In the "Autobiographical Sketch" he wrote late in his life, he distinguished between his "aid" to Emerson during his lifetime and his work on the biography, omitting all reference to other services. He found compiling essays for Emerson to print or read an interesting occupation, but hardly deserving of the immense gratitude felt by the Emersons. However, a mixture of shy pride and stern self-criticism tints Cabot's quiet summary of his "diligent work" on the "account" he wrote of Emerson's life. In his concluding remark, "This was my *opus, magnum* or not," Cabot appears to refer only to the *Memoir*.[3]

Though *A Memoir of Ralph Waldo Emerson* was certainly Cabot's most important achievement, it is best understood within the total context of his association with Emerson. This essay will attempt to define that context by focusing on Cabot's role as "literary executor." The relationship between the two men, the situation that led the Emersons to select Cabot, his view of Emerson and his wishes, and the work he performed—all of these contribute to our understanding of Emerson as an immensely popular figure who spoke for the values, attitudes, feelings, and desires of many nineteenth-century Americans. Seeing himself as a trustee, Cabot took on the responsibility to preserve the image Emerson had created for himself and to organize and make available the manuscript materials for future generations, which could better assess their worth and determine their proper disposition. In his work he justified the Emersons' faith in him and served as the most important single link in the chain of transmission between Emerson and the future.

The recent exclusion of Cabot's compositions—probably fifteen of the fifty-four pieces Cabot printed in volumes 10–12 of the *Works*—reflects changes in audience and editorial standards over the past century. Pressured by the Emersons, Cabot created these essays for an audience of Victorian men and women from London to Maine to California, who had been inspired by this lay preacher. In both the *Works* and the *Memoir*, Cabot sought to digest the best of Emerson, to present his thought for a general audience. The modern textual editor faces a different audience. Students and scholars today want the original material to work with, not prose in any package. Thus, *The Journals and Miscellaneous Notebooks* (1960–82) and the *Early Lectures* (1959–72), along with other planned publications from manuscript materials, have superseded Cabot's editorial work. To the modern mind, unrevised, initial thoughts and arrangements seem closer to the "real" Emerson than Cabot's somewhat spurious productions.

Modern standards of textual editing have also contributed to Cabot's dismissal. Whereas Cabot is generally conceded to have been a good editor in the best nineteenth-century tradition of responsible, conservative, family-dominated editing, his goals and methods now seem antiquated. Editors today seek to reproduce not the author's latest, final intentions, but the earliest layer of his thought, and to enable the scholar to trace the subsequent development of these ideas as they grow or diminish by providing tables of alterations, emendations, and variants, now-standard pieces of scholarly apparatus unheard of in Cabot's day. Cabot, on the other hand, sought primarily to do what "Mr. Emerson" wanted him to do, in the way that Emerson would have done it himself—to preserve, that is, the public Emerson carefully created in a half-century of lectures and books. Printed essays, Emerson believed, represented the latest and most polished form of his thought: for the press, "they must have on their Greek jackets," he explained; and he himself did not hesitate to cut a tight jacket when editing pieces by his friend Henry Thoreau.[4] Cabot's goal in compiling lectures and essays for Emerson had been to approximate Emerson's own latest arrangement of his materials. Publishing was a public performance, and Cabot sought to present a product, not a process.

Cabot's methods grew out of his definition of his role. Named "literary executor" in Emerson's 1876 will, with the authority (in cooperation with Emerson's heirs) "to publish or to withhold from publication any of Emerson's published papers," Cabot saw himself as a trustee, an executor, an agent of another man's will.[5] It was his responsibility to invest Emerson's literary estate as prudently as possible. Guided by this sense of responsibility, Cabot sought to understand Emerson's methods and attitudes and to discover his plans for future publications. Cabot's own view was that Emerson had published everything he saw fit to print, and that further publication of second-rate pieces could only diminish his lustre. Those who wanted to see uncollected printed pieces, he believed, could look them up.[6] Pressured by the family to produce an edition of the *Works*, however, Cabot labored to execute the task to the best of his ability, incoparating Emerson's latest revisions as noted in various places, proofreading carefully for mechanics and accuracy, collecting and copying pieces to represent the wide spectrum of Emerson's thought from 1832 to 1882, and working conscientiously to give coherent shape to some of Emerson's scattered thoughts. His study of Emerson's methods of transforming lectures to essays, at least in the late *The Conduct of Life* (1860), suggested that Emerson had largely adopted the sentences and paragraphs of the lecture, "striking out whatever could be spared," and Cabot tried to do the same.[7] Above all, he strove to avoid repetition: he did not wish to make Emerson look foolish by revealing how often he had recycled old ideas. Cabot's own opinion was that the essays he compiled were not truly Emersonian, or literary, or necessary: his help during Emerson's lifetime was an act of friendship, but once Emerson was gone, Cabot would happily have forgotten these productions.

Intelligent, well educated and well read, widely travelled, reserved, and financially independent, Cabot was a man admirably suited to his task. In particular, as Edward Emerson pointed out, Emerson trusted his "taste and judgment."[8] Born into an affluent Boston merchant clan in 1821, the year Emerson graduated from Harvard, Cabot himself attended Harvard from 1836 to 1840, Emerson's most explosive period. However, it was not until he went to Europe for three years of post-collegiate study and travel that Cabot became aware of Emerson, whom he saw (from afar, through his reading of the *Dial* and the first *Essays*) as the "Socrates" of the "Athens of the (Yankee) North."[9] Returning to Boston in the summer of 1843, Cabot made anonymous contact with Emerson the next year by sending him an essay on Kant for the *Dial* (printed in the last number, April 1844). Some additional anonymous contributions prompted Emerson to discover Cabot's identity; and some time between March and May 1845, he went to Divinity Hall, Cambridge, to look up Cabot, then a resident and second-year student at Harvard Law. Soon after meeting Cabot, Emerson described him as a "rare scholar, though a better metaphysician than poet," a juxtaposition that well defines the differences between the two men.[10]

After law school, however, Cabot's zest for the literary life cooled. Repeatedly he disappointed Emerson, who attempted to enlist him in various causes: a new journal, a club, the Civil War, lecturing to private classes. Returning a book in 1856, Emerson called Cabot a "rententive man who only seems to have a right to speak," and wondered when he would "break the long silence of these rare studies."[11] But Cabot did not speak in the way Emerson wished he would. Instead, he pursued a variety of "avocations," as he called them: after practicing law for less than two years, Cabot served one year as Theodore Parker's editorial assistant on the *Massachusetts Quarterly Review*; in 1848 he accompanied Louis Agassiz to Lake Superior and later printed a "Narrative" of that expedition; in 1849 he joined his brother Edward's architecture firm, practicing this profession intermittently for some fifteen years before his retirement, after the Civil War, at the age of forty-four. During this period he had married (in 1857), enjoyed a year-long European honeymoon, started his family, and established himself in his own home in Brookline (in 1859). Dividing his time between this estate and his Beverly Farms summer home, as well as camping and fishing trips from Maine to Minnesota, Cabot devoted the rest of his long life until his death in 1903 to wide reading, philosophical study, and writing (printing almost fifty essays, reviews, and translations), to his expanding family (sons numbers six and seven were born in 1872), and to social, civic, and educational service: work for the Boston Athenæum, Boston Museum of Fine Arts, Brookline School Committee, Harvard Board of Overseers, and the board of the new Technological Institute (MIT). At Emerson's urging he joined the Town and Country Club (1849), attended the famous founding dinner for the *Atlantic Monthly* (1857), became a member of the Saturday Club (1860), and lectured at Harvard (1870). However, only his work for Emerson seemed to Cabot to redeem the dilettantish life he had led.

The first product of Cabot's working relationship with Emerson was *Letters and Social Aims*, published in 1875. A collection of eleven essays on disparate subjects, the book reflected the range of Emerson's most popular lectures over the past fifteen years. First came a long essay, "Poetry and Imagination," a conflation of several lectures from as far back as 1854 on the subjects of poetry and criticism. Next were "Social Aims," "Eloquence," and "Resources," titles of lectures read on well over a hundred separate occasions between 1864 and 1872. Four previously printed pieces provided a sort of nucleus: "The Comic" (*Dial*, October 1843), "Quotation and Originality" (*North American Review*, April 1868), "The Progress of Culture" (the 1868 Phi Beta Kappa Address, first printed as "Aspects of Culture," *Atlantic Monthly*, January 1868), and "Persian Poetry" (*Atlantic Monthly*, April 1858). The volume closed on a loftier note with more refurbished lectures: "Inspiration," "Greatness," and "Immortality." What the book did not include was any reference to Cabot's involvement or explanation of the origin of these "new" pieces. Nevertheless an astute New York reviewer thought he detected the covert hand of a "skillful editor or secretary,—a daughter, perhaps, or friend." [12]

By the time that Cabot and Edward Emerson reissued *Letters and Social Aims* in 1883, it seemed prudent to explain the presence of the friend. In his "Preface," Cabot gave what Edward called a "conscientious account of his share in its preparation": he told of Emerson's problems with the long overdue book and his deteriorating mental condition, which led the family to ask him to help. Soon Emerson had relinquished the "business of selection and preparation for the press, almost entirely" to Cabot, a job that was much complicated by the confused state of the manuscripts and by Emerson's compositional practices. In bringing together scattered pieces under particular headings, Cabot insisted he was following Emerson's own method. Though his active participation in the work was very limited, Emerson made some suggestions and generally approved the new selections and arrangements of old material. [13] Once these facts had been revealed, Cabot repeated his story in the *Memoir* and his "Autobiographical Sketch" (privately printed in 1904); Edward Emerson also retold the tale in his filial biography, *Emerson in Concord* (1889), in his prefaces to volumes 1 and 8 of the Centenary Edition (1903–1904), and in his sketch of Cabot in *The Early Years of the Saturday Club* (1918).

The story, as it unfolded in all these and other accounts, had begun long before publication of *Letters and Social Aims*. Cabot first became involved with Emerson's literary affairs in July 1875, when Ellen Emerson took it upon herself to travel to his home at Beverly Farms with a "secret message": worried about her father and the future of his manuscripts, Ellen confided to Mrs. Cabot her wish that Cabot would agree to act as Emerson's literary executor. When Cabot, probably assuming that his task would not begin for several years, assented, Emerson (according to Ellen's recollections) accepted the news with mixed feelings—"alarmed" that Ellen had been so rash as to impose on Mr. Cabot, he was also delighted and relieved. [14]

However, this was the summer of 1875, and Emerson had more immediate worries than the question of who would be responsible for his literary remains after his death. At his back he constantly heard the demands of the London publishers, Chatto and Windus, for a book promised some five years earlier. Incapable of correcting the three-year-old proofs of an essay on poetry and criticism, he had not even determined the remainder of the contents. Ellen had watched her father fretting over this unwanted volume ever since the project first hatched in 1870.

The book had been a mistake from the beginning. Moncure D. Conway, one of Emerson's enthusiastic younger followers, had agreed to write an introduction for an unauthorized collection of previously written essays, to be brought out by the English publisher John C. Hotten. However, when in 1870 Emerson collected some of these pieces himself in *Society and Solitude*, Hotten decided to reprint some old *Dial* pieces instead. Informed of these plans by Conway, Emerson protested a "selection made in the dark by some person necessarily ill-informed, & possibly inserting papers not mine, or only partly mine, & papers that I wish to forget." [15]

Urged by both Conway and Alexander Ireland to "adopt" the book he was powerless to prevent, in the fall of 1870 Emerson reluctantly promised Hotten his next work within a year. In some papers reserved from *Society and Solitude*, he had the beginnings of a book, to be composed "mainly of Criticism." [16] However, his second course of Cambridge lectures, a six-week trip to the west coast, work on *Parnassus* (the collection of Emerson's favorite poems long championed by his younger daughter Edith Emerson Forbes), and his deteriorating mental and physical condition consumed his time, and with "alarm" Emerson discovered that the alotted year had passed. In October 1871 he wrote Conway again, confessing that the Hotten business weighed "heavily" on his soul, but insisting he was hard at work on what he hoped would be some of his "best unpublished matter." Six weeks later, promising not to rest until the book was complete, Emerson admitted to Conway that he was still working on the first piece, now considerably longer than planned. [17] Lectures and other obligations filled another six months, preventing progress on the dreaded project everyone now called the "Hotten book." Then came the final blow. As Ellen explained later to Cabot, "June 24, 1872, the house burned, a week or two later Father was quite sick, on the bed most of the time for some days. The proof-sheets which had always been in his hands for a month perhaps were still always in his hands." [18] Even Emerson could see the piece was flawed, but he was incapable of understanding or correcting the problems. Ellen, who for some time had acted as her father's secretary and travelling companion, then tried to help. She was shocked to discover the repetition of whole sentences and even longer passages and a confusion of order.

By the time Ellen wrote a synopsis of her father's symptoms for Dr. Edward Clarke on 1 September 1872, she had probably acknowledged that Emerson had reached the end of his creative working life. Advancing age struck Emerson in a vulnerable spot, his memory, which he called in an 1857 lecture "a primary and fundamental faculty, without which none other can work; . . . the thread on which the beads of man are strung." At the age of sixty-nine, Emerson was losing what Cabot termed his "mental grasp"—the ability to concentrate and to find the right words to express his ideas.[19] Forgetful, apt to repeat himself or to lose the thread of his conversation, he became increasingly unwilling to talk to strangers or to read to any but private audiences, and then from carefully prepared lectures, drawn from his forty-year-old savings bank of manuscripts.

For at least two years before the fire, Emerson's ability to concentrate had been deteriorating. He had worked in a desultory fashion at his last complete book, *Society and Solitude*, published on 5 March 1870, two months after its scheduled publication. Unlike his three previous volumes, this "poor little book" (as Emerson labeled it in a letter to Cabot) lacked the structure provided by the central idea of *Representative Men*, *English Traits*, or *The Conduct of Life*.[20] While he was reworking the material for *Society and Solitude*, in the fall of 1869, Emerson was also anticipating his course of "philosophical lectures" on the "Natural History of the Intellect," to be offered at Harvard in February and March 1870. According to Cabot, who also taught in this course and who met several times with Emerson during the planning stages, Emerson looked forward to this opportunity to bring together his thoughts on the chief project of his life. But, once undertaken, the obligation to present eighteen connected lectures had proven "oppressive," and the results dissatisfying. At the time, Emerson had consoled himself, as he wrote to Carlyle, with the thought that he had prepared himself for a repetition of the course the next year. He hoped, "partly out of these materials, & partly by large rejection of these, & by large addition to them, to construct a fair report of what I have read & thought on the Subject." Nevertheless, in the spring of 1871, after the second course, Emerson could only call his results a "doleful ordeal."[21]

The exposure and shock that followed the fire in June 1872, then, forced Emerson's family to recognize what was becoming painfully obvious. Friends and admirers from far and near contributed to the fund to rebuild the house and to provide Emerson a vacation designed to restore his failing health. Emerson wrote Hotten, postponing their book, and in October he and Ellen set sail for Egypt. Though apparently they did contact Hotten in London some months later, Emerson effectively forgot the dreaded book, and a year after their return, Hotten was dead. Emerson now considered himself relieved of the business.

Not until the spring of 1875 did the Hotten book return to haunt the Emersons. Chatto and Windus had bought out the publishing firm from

Hotten's widow, including all claims for works in progress, and now they expected something from Emerson. It was at this point that Ellen attempted to piece something together. She began with the three-year-old proofs. The essay was built on a lecture, "Poetry and English Poetry," read in 1854 in Philadelphia and at Cambridge to a small group of students in Conway's room. Henry Wadsworth Longfellow, who was also present, had found the lecture "full of brilliant and odd things; but not very satisfactory," and when revised for publication twenty years later, it was still chaotic.[22]

Transforming lectures—particularly the later ones—into essays, Ellen was discovering, was no matter of simple transcription. As oral presentations, Emerson's lectures had struck many hearers as fragmentary, a series of eloquently stated points on a lofty theme, with a structure that was more emotional than logical; in print, the gaps between these "anecdotes of the spirit" became painfully obvious. The problem was complicated by the state of the manuscripts. Particularly for the later lectures, the bundles of loose leaves—gathered under their last title—were collections of Emerson's thoughts on particular topics: inspiration, country life, American nationality, the transcendency of physics, moral forces. Often introductions and conclusions were lacking; or one bundle might contain two or more introductions used at different times. The renumberings of the manuscript sheets (some leaves contain as many as six different numbers in ink, pencil, and crayon) helped only slightly in ascertaining the original order.[23] The method of repeatedly retooling his materials to new uses had served Emerson well during his long lecture career; for Ellen, however, the shufflings were a nightmare.

Through the summer of 1875, Ellen and her father worked together to meet the publisher's demand for copy. But, by mid-August, Ellen could no longer bravely face the series of difficulties that confronted her. Often in the past three years she had suggested Cabot might help. Soon after the fire in 1872 Emerson had begun to worry about the future and mentioned his trust in Frederic Henry Hedge and Cabot. Repeatedly, Ellen reported to her sister, Emerson would return to Cabot as the man most "fit to have his papers, as *the* valuable and dear companion, as having a real understanding in philosophy." Yet, when she suggested that Cabot might help with the proofs, her father seemed to consider the idea briefly before responding, "No, *nobody* could do it."[24] Though he admired and respected Cabot for his rare combination of philosophical acumen and executive ability, as well as his taste and judgment, Emerson feared to impose on his friend. Using his own work as an excuse, Cabot had always maintained a distance, refusing numerous opportunities to know Emerson better—at the Saturday Club, at the Forbeses' retreat at Naushon where Emerson went each August, even on the journey to Egypt. By the summer of 1874, however, Cabot's resistance had begun to break, and he joined the family at Naushon for more than a week while they were working together on *Parnassus*.[25] Thus, when Ellen became desperate in August 1875, she looked again to Cabot, speaking first to his wife at Beverly. By 25 August all was arranged: Cabot would travel to Concord to help. Ellen reported that her father's "spirits rose" at the prospect: he even suggested informing the *Boston Daily Advertiser* of his new "partnership."[26]

Cabot's work began immediately upon his arrival in Concord on 27 August for the weekend. He understood the problem and set to work doing, as Ellen confessed, what she could not: taking "a broad view at a glance," saying "'needed' and 'not needed.'" By the time he left the following week, the first task (presumably revising the essay on poetry and criticism) was accomplished. A vacation trip to Maine prevented Cabot's return to Concord until 25 September, when he quickly began "collating & copying & never knowing just when I am to have any time to myself." Within five days he had begun to "supply the publisher with copy in a way that will rejoice his heart."[27] When it became evident the job could not be completed immediately, Cabot made plans to return the following week.

Cabot spent much of October on the book. Arriving at the Emerson home on a Thursday and staying through Saturday, he enjoyed getting to know Emerson, his family and friends, and his Concord. As the deadline approached, Ellen was enthusiastic and confident about both Cabot's accomplishments and her own work under the new editor. On 15 October most of the copy was in the hands of James Osgood, their American publisher. Now Cabot assumed the tasks of reading and correcting proofs. By 20 October he was back in Brookline, working over the second essay, "Social Aims." When Ellen saw another of their compilations, "Greatness," in proof in November, she immediately sent for Cabot, who spent two days on the piece.

Final corrections and revisions went smoothly, and on 15 December 1875, the newest volume of Emerson's writings, *Letters and Social Aims*, was published in Boston. Immediately Cabot wrote Emerson to thank him for the "comely volume," but even more to express his gratitude for "a store of pleasant memories which the sight of it will always awaken." According to Edward Emerson, when speaking to Cabot his father always called this volume "your book."[28] To Ellen's profuse thanks, he responded, "I think there is much more danger that my exertions in behalf of the book will be overestimated, rather than the contrary. The only comfort is that any shortcomings in point of revision will probably be attributed to me—a position I am naturally well qualified to sustain."[29]

Although some reviewers found shortcomings in the work, none attributed them to Cabot. A new volume by Emerson was an "event," no matter what the circumstances of its birth, and on the whole readers were kind.

George Parsons Lathrop (Hawthorne's son-in-law), writing for the *Atlantic Monthly Magazine*, was the harshest critic, saying the book seemed the result of a mind that had travelled in a circle. Though he found much to praise in these, as in all of Emerson's essays, Lathrop detected a greater "want of sequence in the arrangement of ideas." After seeing the review, Ellen admitted it was "appalingly true." [30] Other reviewers, however, remarked on the increased coherence of many of the essays, and several found the Emerson-Cabot compilation "Immortality" visible evidence of the "maturing or mellowing" of Emerson's thought and "surprisingly near the sentiments . . . held by all religious men." [31]

Cabot's "frank" confession of his involvement in this volume still leaves many questions concerning his total contribution. According to the 1883 preface, Emerson left practically everything to Cabot, devoting little time or effort to the book. However, both Ellen and Edward gave their father a more active role. Writing to refresh Cabot's memory in 1883, Ellen said, "Father gave us much assistance in Letters & Social Aims, supplied better words, wrote sentences, and corrected proof. I think he wrote entirely new for us the last three or four lines of Greatness." [32] This was not the impression given by Cabot's preface; and in his preface, added to the volume in 1903, Edward sought to right the wrong. Crediting Cabot with the book's "careful arrangement and its finish," he said Cabot had helped his father greatly by locating the weak places so that Emerson could "write the needed sentence, or recast the defective one." [33]

Any comparison of extant manuscripts with the finished volume makes it clear that Cabot did more than point out defective passages in need of repair. The work began with choosing nominal subjects for the selections. In the *Memoir*, Cabot explained that "only one or two" of the essays had been decided on before he took over, and "the rest were added with Mr. Emerson's approval, but without much active cooperation on his part." In the 1883 preface Cabot explained somewhat ambiguously that some old lists made by Emerson suggested contents for future volumes, "but many of the papers had been lying by him for years unpublished, and it is open to any one to say that he never really decided upon publishing them, and that if he had been left to himself, never would have published them." [34]

Cabot seems to have used Emerson's lists only so far as they were convenient. Among his working papers are three groups of titles in Emerson's hand that show what the author had in mind when he offered Hotten a volume "mainly of Criticism." An untitled list contains thirteen items, primarily uncollected printed pieces. Four of these appear in some form in *Letters and Social Aims*. A second list, titled "Critical Essays," contains seventeen different titles, mainly unprinted lectures. Three of these provided the titles for four essays in the volume. A third list of nine items, labeled

"Poetry & Criticism," includes three titles close to those printed. Only "The Progress of Culture," "Greatness," and possibly "Eloquence" do not appear in any of Emerson's plans.[35]

Determining the contents was only the beginning of Cabot's task. Preparing copy for the printer involved several different responsibilities. In the four already-printed pieces, Cabot made a number of minor changes in punctuation, spelling, and paragraphing; and occasionally he eliminated a phrase, sentence, or example from the new version. For "Poetry and Imagination," already in type, he worked with Ellen and Emerson to eliminate the glaring repetitions and to provide better transitions between passages. Extant printer's copy for this essay (121 pages in Emerson's hand) both supports Ellen's statements and reveals the extent of Cabot's revisions. Although copy is lacking for the last thirty pages of the printed essay, the surviving manuscript testifies to Emerson's loss of faculty or interest even while he worked on the piece. Most of the introductory section—eighteen manuscript pages—is a true fair copy, written in a firm hand with a minimum of authorial alterations. This section was printed virtually unchanged: only a few slight repetitions and sentence fragments have been eliminated.

However, after the introduction, the quality of the manuscript begins to deteriorate. Many revisions by Emerson in ink and pencil, along with the combination of different papers, inks, numbering, and handwriting, all signify that the essay has been incompletely compiled from many lectures read at different times. Though the number of variants from manuscript to printed version increases, the final essay continues to follow the manuscript closely through manuscript page 35 (page 17 in the 1903 edition). It is in Emerson's discussion of genius and the act of the imagination that the obvious repetitions begin. In somewhat different form Emerson repeated four times one of his central ideas: "All physical facts are words for spiritual facts, & Imagination by naming them is the interpreter, solving the riddle of the world."[36] The passage seems to have offended so much that it was eliminated entirely from the printed essay, although the idea occurs several times. In another obvious repetition, on manuscript pages 95 and 97, the second instance has been excised. Probably it was Cabot's decision to delete these and other passages, to add a number of passages not found in this manuscript, and to change the order of some paragraphs, as well as to make a number of smaller changes throughout.

The largest chore was compiling the six "new" essays, none of which derived wholly from any single lecture. Working as a team, Cabot and Ellen sought out appropriate passages and fitted them together in a rather haphazard way that obscured the origins of these pieces—even to the compilers. When in 1883 Cabot queried Ellen concerning the sources for "Social Aims," she noted it was a "Lecture like Resources originally & combined with other lectures, Table-Talk, Homes & Hospitality, Home, Manners all of which we worked into this."[37] The second lecture in Emerson's very popular course on "American Life," first offered in 1864, "Social Aims" had undoubtedly undergone much change already in more than seventy readings from Boston to Milwaukee. Though the first third of the printed essay closely follows the outline provided by an 1864 account in the Boston *Commonwealth*, the remainder incorporates large chunks of material on conversation (largely from "Table-Talk," another "American Life" lecture) and public action, suggesting how Cabot worked the additional material into the framework of the old lecture.[38] "Resources" had been the third lecture in the "American Life" course: the 1864 version, as reported in the *Commonwealth*, contained discussions of both material and intellectual resources. Eventually this lecture was divided (probably when Emerson was preparing his Harvard series in 1869–70), the latter half becoming a separate lecture, "Inspiration."[39] Read again in 1871 and 1872, a version of "Inspiration" was also printed in *Letters and Social Aims*.

The other essays have equally mixed origins. "Greatness" underwent much transformation between its lecture and essay stages. Though Cabot recalled that this late lecture was "not much worked over," the printed essay does not closely follow either of the two extant 1868 manuscript versions. Edward Emerson's notes in the Centenary Edition seem closer to the truth: he claims the piece was "drawn largely from the concluding lecture" of an 1868 Boston course, but adds that "the essays on The Scholar, The Man of Letters, Aristocracy and Manners very probably have matter drawn from the lectures on Greatness, and that here given is only a portion of the lecture as delivered."[40] Like most of Cabot's work, "Greatness" is a composite, rearranged from several sources. "Eloquence" was another lecture that was "not much worked over," according to Cabot. This "Eloquence" (not to be confused with an earlier lecture of the same title printed in *Society and Solitude*), was first delivered in Chicago on 4 March 1867. It was read at least nine more times before being retired a year later.[41]

The last of Cabot's compilations was "Immortality," read initially to the Parker Fraternity in Boston on 29 December 1861; William Charvat, who lists seventeen known readings, explains that Emerson used this as a free Sunday "sermon" in towns where he had spoken the previous night, so frequently that he probably read it to rags.[42] Though Cabot says the piece was "much worked over," the compilers probably worked from a fairly continuous manuscript, which Edward Emerson says his father gave away. (According to a comment by Ellen, the recipient was Charles Eliot Norton, in December 1875, because "Father" was unwilling to copy the piece, and the family already had more than enough lectures.[43])

Though the amount of editorial tinkering varied with each piece, the basic method did not. Cabot and Ellen worked from manuscripts which, as Cabot explained, consisted of "loose sheets, laid together in parcels, each marked on the cover with the title under which it was last read as a lecture, but often without any completely recoverable order or fixed limits." He was even more blunt in the *Memoir*: there was "no danger of disturbing the original order, for this was already gone beyond recovery."[44] In using the material, Cabot tried to follow Emerson's own habit of reworking it for new occasions. Everything, Cabot maintained, was written by Emerson even if the sentences and paragraphs were combined in new ways and the results unlike anything Emerson chose to publish.

Cabot's work on *Letters and Social Aims* initiated a relationship that continued for the next seven years. His position became official when Emerson's new will, signed on 15 April 1876, named him "literary executor." However, Cabot did not begin to exercise his authority immediately. Though Ellen was eager to produce two more collaborative books right away, Cabot felt no need to publish. At this time he acted more as an adviser than an agent, for about a year after publication of "his" book, remaining largely uninvolved in the Emersons' literary affairs. At the same time, frequent visits back and forth between the two families strengthened their new friendship.

As soon as *Letters and Social Aims* was finished, the family turned to a new project, the Little Classic Edition of Emerson's works, published between April and October 1876. Only the poems, however, for which the family sought a selection from the two earlier volumes, involved much new work. Cabot, who was generally unfamiliar with the poetry, preferred to let Ellen and Edward exercise their talent and judgment on these matters. Still, he made a few suggestions and mediated some disputes; he entertained Ellen's questions when she visited him in Brookline in March; and after he and four sons spent nine days at Naushon with the Emerson clan in August, Ellen gushed about how wonderful Cabot had been on "the poem question."[45]

Cabot seems to have had little to do with the address that Emerson read at the University of Virginia in June 1876. Though in his notes to "The Scholar," as the Virginia address was titled in volume 10 of the *Works*, Edward Emerson acknowledges Cabot's "kind and ready help" in arranging sheets from earlier college addresses, the printed essay is essentially the 1845 Middlebury Address, for which the complete manuscript survives, edited slightly by Ellen, who began working on it early in May.[46] As editor, Ellen may have consulted with Cabot on the selection and revision of this piece.

However, soon Cabot took over from Ellen the job of preparing an occasional lecture for Emerson to read. He also created some essays for the press and began sorting and arranging the manuscripts, playing the unusual role of literary executor to a man who was still living. In the "Note" to *Lectures and Biographical Sketches* (volume 10 of the *Complete Works*), where most of these essays and lectures were eventually printed, Cabot explained his role simply: the previously unpublished pieces "I got ready for [Emerson's] use in readings to his friends or to a limited public," using the method described in the preface to *Letters and Social Aims*.[47] Once again, the "confession" conceals as much as it reveals. It is unclear exactly how many "readings" Cabot prepared, how much Ellen Emerson contributed, how faithfully they followed a single manuscript, or how closely a later printed version reflects the lecture as it was read on a particular occasion. The answers to these questions also vary with the individual pieces.

For some insight into the matter, we can look at a single extreme example, Ellen's explanation of the "Fortune of the Republic," read in Boston by Emerson at least twice in 1878: at the Old South Church on 25 February and at Cyrus Bartol's on 30 March. The family was especially fond of this piece, which Cabot called a "summing-up of the position of the country after the war, and its spiritual needs and prospects for the new generation."[48] Disappointed by the *Atlantic's* decision not to print the lecture, the collaborators were now reworking it for separate publication. Concerned that this collection of miscellaneous remarks, clustered around a lecture of the same title read frequently by Emerson in 1864, might appear "ante-diluvian," Ellen sought her brother-in-law Will Forbes' "political enlightenment . . . because probably it is greater than Mr. Cabot's." Instead, she received a severe reprimand from her sister Edith, incensed that the collaborators had tampered with the "original order" of the piece. Ellen's long response explained that the "original order" had always been "Mr. Cabot's and mine. We have never changed [Father's] order I think where it could be ascertained. This is a collection of every general remark on the country from many lectures of many dates."

If Edith had in mind the lecture as Emerson had read it to the family at Thanksgiving, Ellen wished to set her straight. The first time Edith had heard it,

> most of it [was] from the lecture named F. of R. which Mr. C. had already sifted but there was then no order at all. As read at the Old South it had copious additions from Moral Forces and some other lectures, one on N. England particularly. As read at Dr. Bartol's it had been helped by all we could collect from American Nationality. So don't think this last is any more my version than all the rest for from the beginning I have done as much in arrangement as Mr. Cabot. . . . Father never had these things combined, so *he* never had any order for them. I thought and so did Mr. C. that the final arrangement was truer and easier for the mind, but maybe it isn't so . . .

> The corrections are largely Father's . . . where he could understand what
> was wanted. [When he didn't] Mr. Cabot had to make it and he always does it in
> the modest manner of scratching out a word or altering a tense, or something
> that will leave it still Father's words if possible.[49]

As Ellen's comments indicate, the origins of this address were particularly
cloudy, prompting Cabot to question several years later, "Put together by us;
out of what materials?"[50]

Fortunately for Cabot, all of his work during this period was not so complex. In the period before Emerson's death, he was responsible for printing
eight pieces: "Demonology" (*North American Review*, March 1877), "Perpetual Forces" (*North American Review*, September 1877), "The Sovereignty of Ethics" (*North American Review*, May-June 1878), *Fortune of
the Republic* (1878), the "General Introduction" to *The Hundred Greatest
Men* (1879), "The Preacher" (*Unitarian Review*, January 1880, and separately), "Impressions of Thomas Carlyle in 1848" (*Scribner's Magazine*, May
1881, and, as "Tribute to Carlyle," *Proceedings of the Massachusetts Historical Society*, 1880–81), and "The Superlative" (*Century Magazine*, February
1882). Many of these derived, at least in part, from the "readings" Cabot put
together for Emerson during these years: "Fortune of the Republic" (Old
South and elsewhere, 1878); "The Superlative" (Amherst, 19 March 1879);
"The Preacher" (Divinity School, Cambridge, 5 May 1879); and "Carlyle"
(Massachusetts Historical Society, Boston, 10 February 1881). Others of
Cabot's compilations that Emerson read were printed posthumously:
"Boston" (Concord Lyceum, 14 February 1877; Boston, 16 April 1877; Con-
cord[?], 4 May 1877); "Education" (Concord Lyceum, 8 February 1878;
"Sophy's" [?], 12 March 1878; Exeter, N.H., before 17 June 1878); "Mem-
ory" (Concord Lyceum, 5 March 1879; Boston, [24?] May 1879; Concord
School of Philosophy, 2 August 1879); "Historic Notes of Life and Letters in
New England" (Concord Lyceum, 4 February 1880); and "Aristocracy" (Con-
cord School of Philosophy, 13 August 1880).[51]

A few of these titles had appeared on Emerson's lists, especially one gathering of thirteen items from Journal ST (which Cabot dated 1870–75?) titled
"Available Lectures." Here we find "Doctrine of Leasts" (in a pencil notation
by Cabot identified as "The Superlative"), "Memory," and "Rule of Life"
(identified as "Sov. of Ethics"). "Carlyle" from the *Dial* (apparently Emerson's review of *Past and Present*, July 1843), appears on five of the lists.
Though the prefatory note to volume 10 suggests Emerson read some version of "The Man of Letters" during Cabot's tenure, no evidence to support
this exists.

As with the pieces in *Letters and Social Aims*, the extent of Cabot's work on these essays and readings varied in each case. Writing to Cabot in 1883, Ellen mentioned that even before Cabot entered the picture, her father had depended on a few old but intact lectures to get him through his speaking engagements. Specifically she cited "Perpetual Forces," "Memory," "Boston," and "The Superlative." This suggests that the last two named lectures, "Boston" (first read in 1861) and "The Superlative" (first read in England in 1847), may have required little revision by Cabot before Emerson reread them. However, the version of "Boston" read before the New England Society in New York City in 1870 differs vastly from both the extant manuscripts and the version later printed in the *Atlantic* and volume 12 of the *Works*.[52] Emerson himself had reworked "Memory," which dated from 1857 and 1858, for both of his Harvard courses in 1870 and 1871; reordering the now-confused material in 1879 probably involved more work for Cabot than either "Boston" or "The Superlative."

In choosing subjects for Emerson's readings, Cabot often sought a continuous manuscript appropriate to the occasion. According to Edward Emerson, "Historic Notes of Life and Letters in New England," a fit subject for Emerson's one-hundredth appearance before the Concord Lyceum, derived from a seldom-read parlor lecture and required little assistance from Cabot. Cabot, however, recalled that he and Ellen had put together this reading. "The Preacher," well suited to the divinity students, made use of a lecture of the same title, read at the Boston home of J. T. Sargent in 1867. Nevertheless, the version that Emerson read seems to differ from both the 1867 lecture and the printed essay. A note made by Ellen on the cover of the latest manuscript of this lecture (not in Emerson's hand) states, "This lecture exactly as delivered May 5, 1879," to which Cabot added, "including sheets from paper at Mr. Sargents Sept. 16, 1867—also from Cause & Effect & Health. These have been returned to their places."[53] "Carlyle" was a combination of Emerson's early and later comments. Of all the readings, only "Education"—on a subject of great interest to both Cabot and Emerson— seems to be a radically new creation, compounded from a wide range of sources, including an 1837 address on the subject, 1838 lectures on "Home" and "School," and the Waterville, Dartmouth, and Middlebury addresses of 1863–64.

Although many of the printed essays derived from Emerson's "readings" during this period, Cabot was first drawn back to the Emerson factory to provide something publishable. In January 1877, Ellen enlisted Cabot's aid after Julius Ward, acting editor of the *North American Review*, requested a piece from Emerson for the March number. Though Cabot initially suggested the "Essay on Education might be launched in that way," the *Review* got "Demonology" instead, an 1839 lecture reworked for the 1871 Harvard course.[54] The later version seems to have served as Cabot's basic text. Beginning in February and continuing into June, Cabot spent many weeks working at the Emersons'. Probably it was then that he began the larger job of organizing the lecture manuscripts: many of the paper covers on which he made notes about each lecture bear the date 1877.

During the summer Cabot and Ellen were at work on another essay, "Perpetual Forces," to be printed in the *North American Review* in September. Though this was one of the lectures that Ellen said required little work for her father to read before Cabot took over, the team spent a great deal of time on an arrangement of material from the 1862 lectures "Moral Forces" and "Perpetual Forces," bolstered by passages from the 1863 notebook "Forces and Forms" and other sources. In August they spent a week at Naushon correcting proofs. Though Emerson improved with the constant company and enjoyed their excursion to Gay Head, Ellen was distressed when he decided to leave before the work was finished. "I am very anxious lest something went wrong in this formidable separation of the three authors," she wrote to Edith. "Let Father ponder his sad lesson well . . . gentle submission to his daughters' arrangements . . . would have saved these disasters and agonies." Meanwhile, though he agreed to obey their "united optimism with thanks & trust," Emerson was unhappy with some of the corrections Cabot had made in his absence.[55]

As the fall progressed, new worries forced the Emersons to turn again to Cabot. On 10 November 1877, an anxious Edward wrote Cabot urging him to accept the task of writing Emerson's life. Though he and his sisters realized this was a "great boon" to ask, Edward felt the circumstances warranted their action. They were particularly anxious because of "strong suspicions we have that one or two persons are already collecting materials for that purpose." Though Edward did not name these persons, one was probably Moncure Conway, who did print a study of Emerson soon after his death. The other may have been F. B. Sanborn or C. E. Norton. Not only were the Emersons concerned, but "two gentlemen, friends of the family" (revealed in a draft of the letter as Henry James, Sr., and William Henry Channing) had separately urged them to resolve the question before it resolved itself, and "not as Father or his family would desire." Edward assured Cabot that "Father has a regard and affection for you such as he has for almost no other man" and, admitting Emerson would not make such a request himelf, said it would be a relief to him to know Cabot was willing to undertake the work.[56]

Honored by the request, Cabot expressed immediate readiness to be "of use." Writing to Edward three days later, he said he felt incompetent to write a life but would be willing to "collect the materials for the right man when he shall appear," and meanwhile, "if the occasion arises," he might make a sketch that "may do for the nonce."[57]

At this point Ellen was still trying to keep the collaboration a secret. Several months after the publication of "Perpetual Forces," however, she was distraught by her father's candor during a visit from Allen Thorndike Rice, editor of the *North American Review*, on 29 January 1878. Rice had come, Ellen reported, believing Emerson had written "Perpetual Forces" "fresh *for* the review." Emerson, however, blithely told him "he never did anything about it, that Mr. Cabot and I compiled these things &c. &c." Inwardly raging, Ellen maintained her outward composure and had to admit it was "all true."[58]

As if on cue, Cabot arrived two days later to continue work on "The Sovereignty of Ethics," scheduled for the May–June number of the *North American Review*. He and Ellen had been composing this "mosaic" for eight months, choosing passages from several lectures: "Morals" (1859), "The Essential Principles of Religion" (1862), "The Rule of Life" (1867), "Natural Religion" (1869), and "possibly others." Some of the "others" noted by Cabot on the manuscript, dated 1877, are "Moral Sense" and "Moral Forces." The finished essay also contained bits from "Religion" (1837), the "Address to the People of East Lexington" (1840), and "Prospects," the concluding lecture of the 1839–40 series on "The Times."[59] After choosing the pieces, the problem was to find a suitable arrangement. These pieces gave Cabot trouble. Despite several reworkings, the essay still lacked continuity, and Ellen was worried. Before long, however, she came to believe that Cabot's efforts had "licked it into shape more than seemed possible when we used to struggle through the piles of homogeneous but disjointed sentences."

In fact, Ellen was pleased with their work on three lectures. In addition to "Sovereignty," they were getting up a "splendid one on Education," she explained to Edith, and trying to make "the Fortune of the Republic, for the Old South, a first-class lecture."[60] "Education," due for a reading at the Concord Lyceum later that week, was actually the greatest problem during this session. On 2 February, the family gathered at Edward's home to hear Emerson rehearse the finished compilation. "It took just an hour which pleased him and he said he understood it better," Ellen reported; "We all liked it." All the town went to hear Emerson read on Friday evening. "He got through it, hoarsely but beautifully," according to Ellen.[61]

This project completed, work resumed on "The Sovereignty of Ethics." Early in April, when Emerson was reading proofs of this collection of thoughts on the moral sentiment, Ellen reported his reaction. "If I had been asked I never should have allowed this thing to be offered to the magazine. Why it's a long sarmint." But, as he continued to read, his admiration grew. "The beginning was bad," he said later, "but where I am now—why, it's very good!" After finishing the piece, he was even more affirmative. "I don't know where you found all this, but it improves upon acquaintance, and the improvement works backward as well as forward, even the beginning turns out at last to be good too."[62] By the next month, the collaborators were back at work on "Fortune of the Republic," Emerson's Old South Address read in February. Published in August 1878, the piece was praised by reviewers grateful that Emerson was still "giving spiritual comfort to his countrymen."[63]

During the fall and winter, Cabot completed the job of sorting and sifting Emerson's manuscripts. Three new projects occupied him during the spring of 1879. In March, Emerson travelled to Amherst to read Cabot's version of "The Superlative." On his return to Concord, Emerson faced a greater problem, furnishing an introduction for *The Hundred Greatest Men*, an elaborate coda to an age that worshipped heroes and great men. Although Ellen had tried to work with her father on this task the preceding November, it was not until March that she called for Cabot's help. Both Cabots travelled to Concord for the week of 6 April.

Since no real precedent for this introduction existed, Cabot was forced to be more resourceful than usual, but by this time it was no problem for him to put together something Emersonian by casting about in the shuffled manuscripts. Combining passages from widely varied sources—early lectures, the 1866 course called "The Philosophy of the People," the 1870 Harvard course, and a number of journals—Cabot created a three-page "General Introduction," a resounding affirmation of the power of the human mind to idealize the universe. The object is to get "feeling and doing" "before our eyes as thought." If "Fortune of the Republic" was a collection of every remark Emerson had made on the country, this short piece seems a collection of his most striking thoughts on the miracle of the mind, the intellect, the wonder of Being: "Behold what was in me, out of me! Behold the subjective now objective! Behold the spirit embodied." In a few days, Cabot had assembled the needed introduction and set to work on the "lecture on Preaching" for the divinity students in May.[64]

The establishment of the Concord School of Philosophy in 1879—a very late fruit of Emerson's influence—brought a new audience to hear the old seer of Concord. Infirm, scarcely capable of knowing what he was reading, Emerson gave the Concord Philosphers two of Cabot's compilations. For the first session, on 2 August he reread the ironically titled "Memory," his Lyceum lecture from the preceding March. (The August reading may have been a new version.) The following year, Emerson returned to the Concord School on 13 August and, with Ellen at his side to make sure he did not lose his place or shuffle his papers, managed to struggle through "Aristocracy." The subject, whether called heroism, self-reliance, character, or greatness, was one Emerson had returned to repeatedly and, Edward claimed, Cabot "skilfully incorporated the best later fragments with the substance of the English lecture."[65] Between these two summer ventures, on 4 February 1880,

Emerson gave his one-hundredth reading before the Concord Lyceum. The old lecturer received a standing ovation before delivering "Historic Notes of Life and Letters in New England."[66]

Meanwhile, work on the manuscripts continued, though few public statements remained. Carlyle's death in January 1881, however, demanded a response from his oldest American friend. For Emerson's brief reading at the Massachusetts Historical Society in Boston on 10 February, Cabot helped Ellen combine an old lecture with some earlier statements about the Scottish writer. With further revisions by Cabot, the piece was soon printed in the *Proceedings* of the Society as well as in *Scribner's Magazine*. Cabot's last labor for Emerson during his lifetime was to provide an essay for the *Century Magazine*. After Ellen begged for help when the *Century's* editor wrote "importunately again" in December, Cabot had immediately gone to Concord.[67] He touched up "The Superlative," an old lecture variously called "Doctrine of Leasts" and "Leasts and Mosts," read by Emerson at Amherst in 1879. Printed in the *Century* for February 1882, this refurbished essay was Emerson's last public word before his death on 27 April.

The Cabots had planned to go to Concord on Monday, 24 April, when the family telephoned with news of Emerson's illness, asking them to postpone their visit. Soon, however, they sent for Cabot, who arrived in Concord on Thursday afternoon. According to Edward, when Emerson heard that Cabot was coming, he said "joyfully, 'Elliot Cabot? Praise!'" That evening Emerson died, and three days later the Cabots returned for the funeral, at which Cabot served as one of the eight pallbearers. Mrs. Cabot called the five-hour service "a long farewell," and added that it seemed as if "he was very near to us all the time."[68]

Emerson's will named Cabot literary executor and recognized his service in a bequest of a thousand dollars to each of Cabot's children. To his friend and executor, Emerson left a special gift, his three-volume edition of the *Essais de Montaigne*. The gift was well chosen: Emerson saw Montaigne as a worldly figure, a man of balance between the extremes of the "abstractionist and the materialist," a man "sufficiently related to the world . . . and, at the same time, a vigorous and original thinker."[69] This rare combination of intellectual and practical abilities had drawn Emerson to Cabot and had enabled Cabot to serve Mr. Emerson well.

During the years that he worked for Emerson, Cabot's creations of lectures and essays grew out of his continuing work on the manuscripts. He would carry carpet bags of materials to Brookline during the winters, returning each spring with fresh ideas and a better sense of the whole. Before Emerson's death, Cabot had methodically worked his way through almost four hundred lectures. He attempted to identify to what lecture each leaf belonged, collected the leaves under their original headings, and worked to recover the original order. He then repackaged each lecture, writing its title and date and place of delivery, if known, on the paper cover. Often he made other notations: "probably the latest revision"; "Not to be copied"; "This I suppose to be the right paper"; "Made up in part of 'Rule'"; "Some sheets taken from this for Resources." As he worked he was familiarizing himself with everything Emerson had written and reconstructing the lecture career.

It is clear how Cabot defined his role in this partnership. In January 1880, Ellen was impatient with Cabot's thorough, but tediously slow, methods. Though she had envisioned several printed volumes by this time, their labors had produced only a few scattered essays. When Cabot came to Concord, she "attacked" him "on the subject of publishing a new book." Her summary of Cabot's reply anticipates the continuing struggle between the executor's conservative instincts and the daughter's zeal.

Cabot was willing to arrange things but not to print another book. He did not believe any of Emerson's later work was equal to the earlier essays and, he said, "the lustre of his Works is dimmed by each succeeding volume of second-rate ones." He also believed that Emerson had made his final selection from the unpublished material when he compiled *Society and Solitude* in 1870. In effect, Cabot believed, the author had decided not to publish anything else, and they should not reverse his decision. Cabot also saw no point in collecting the synthetic essays printed under Emerson's name during the past four years. Anyone sufficiently interested could locate them.

The indisputable logic of Cabot's position made Ellen defensive. She feared the future, what might happen should their "chaotic work . . . fall into other hands & be most severely judged," a justifiable reaction "if we only derange without rearranging." Less than receptive to Cabot's suggestion, that they "finish and polish" their work and leave the task of rearranging to future generations, Ellen eventually accepted Mrs. Cabot's solution that they write an "apology." They could explain to their successors that Cabot had acted in Emerson's interest, "and perhaps didn't consider enough the needs of the world which might be instructed and pleased with what he proposed to withhold." Pacified, Ellen determined to keep Cabot coming twice a week.[70]

Cabot was also straightforward about his method. In the preface to the reprinted *Letters and Social Aims*, the "Note" to *Lectures and Biographical Sketches*, the *Memoir*, and his "Autobiographical Sketch," Cabot told the same story. After describing the confused state of the lecture manuscripts, he reiterated his belief that Emerson wished him to follow his own practice. Past lecture titles and Emerson's lists provided headings; the job was then "to bring together under the particular heading whatever could be found that seemed in place there, without regard to the connection in which it was found." With the "former lecture serving as a nucleus for the new," Cabot and "Miss Ellen" hunted the manuscripts for related passages. Together they "patched and excerpted," turning occasionally to Emerson for a word or sentence. In this way, as Cabot said of "Immortality," passages written at widely different times were brought together.[71]

The results of these searches, each a more or less "synthetic" lecture or essay, were eventually printed as the "new" essays in the last three volumes of the *Complete Works*, all but one or two of which derived from the pieces compiled during Emerson's lifetime. Everything in these pieces, Cabot maintained, came from an earlier lecture, supplemented occasionally by a passage from the journals, even though individual titles were unreliable as indicators of the original source.[72]

Cabot's apparent candor did little to suppress inevitable questions about the sources and composition of these later essays, questions that were exacerbated by Edward Emerson's notes to the Centenary Edition. Such qualifications as "seems to be almost identical," "it probably also contains some leaves from . . . ," "possibly it may have been read . . . ," along with the younger Emerson's restoration (in the notes) of omitted passages that "belonged here" in the lectures, all lead the modern reader to question the authenticity of these essays. Edward frankly called "The Sovereignty of Ethics" "the best mosaic" that Cabot could make.[73]

Though retracing Cabot's steps is a time-consuming task, comparison of almost any of the "synthetic" essays with their manuscript sources attests to the accuracy of these statements. "Memory," printed in the last volume of the *Works* in 1893, provides a clear example. Emerson's own projected list of "critical essays" suggests he had planned to print this piece; Ellen recalled it was available for readings; and Emerson read some version of it on at least three occasions while Cabot was in command. In 1877, when Cabot was working his way through the manuscript lectures, he collected all the loose sheets that seemed related to this subject, a total of more than two hundred leaves, most of which were written on both sides. Four distinct units, however, were discernible: the original lecture, delivered in 1857 and 1858; two additional groups of leaves, added when the material was used again in both the 1870 and 1871 Harvard courses; and an assortment of anomalous leaves containing stray passages copied from the journal or quotations and examples from a wide range of both literary and colloquial sources.[74]

The collection was further complicated by Emerson's method of composing lectures. Instead of copying from the first lecture to compile something to read at Harvard, Emerson had interleaved the new with portions of the old. His habit of writing a single paragraph per leaf, usually occupying one and a half sides, made it easy to shuffle the individual paragraphs about, and when he needed a transition, he would boldly cover an entire new sheet with a single sentence and file it in its place. One way of reordering the materials is to thread through the maze of numbers that decorate each leaf. A "16" becomes a "37" and then "22½." In 1879 Cabot probably returned to the now-organized material, retrieved what was essentially the 1858 lecture, larded it with passages from the 1870–71 lectures, and packed off Emerson to read "Memory" to his audiences.

In addition to these materials in Emerson's hand, for "Memory" one more level of composition exists. This is a continuous manuscript in several hands, virtually identical with the printed version, from which probably derived the final typed printer's copy. Although this is most likely a later version than the one prepared for Emerson to read in 1879, the twenty-seven pages reveal how the collaborative team worked. Mrs. Cabot has replaced Ellen as chief copyist for this late piece, transcribing many passages marked in Emerson's manuscript with Cabot's blue pencilled arrows. However, Ellen, Edward, and Cabot also copied. Once passages had been selected and copied, Cabot proceeded to arrange them, sometimes cutting and pasting to bring together paragraphs originally widely separated, sometimes crossing out whole paragraphs or, less often, a single sentence, or occasionally inserting a single sentence to gain a smoother transition. The completed essay was a composite that used approximately half of the material that Cabot had identified as belonging to the 1857–58 lecture, supplemented with about twenty additions from the 1870–71 series. Only a few passages appear to have no source in the extant collections of material on memory.

A comparison of the essay with these sources reveals both Cabot's fidelity to Emerson's words and his freedom in creating a new order. Ignoring an anecdote Emerson had used as page 1 in the 1858 version, Cabot took his introduction from a leaf Emerson had first numbered "7," changed to "6," and finally may have decided on for his own introduction at some later time, possibly for one of the Harvard courses. Cabot's version, however, moves a sentence from Emerson's next paragraph into this opening. At the beginning of his second paragraph, Cabot interposed a sentence from the 1870–71 lectures before picking up most of the remainder of the second paragraph on this leaf.

The weaving of the two major sources continues throughout the essay. Cabot's third paragraph follows exactly a single leaf, numbered "5" and then "3," and heavily revised by Emerson. For his next two paragraphs, Cabot used a long paragraph (written on four sides of two continuous leaves) that exists in three separate manuscript versions, originally numbered "19" and "21" in the 1858 lecture. Here Cabot made several changes: he deleted a phrase from the opening sentence, broke the long paragraph after the third sentence, and moved the second half of this matter to a position near the center of the printed essay—ten pages later. Since the first half of the sixth paragraph has no source in the packages now labeled "Memory," it probably derived from some other lecture, to which it was restored. The remainder of this paragraph is a mosaic of sentences that appear together, but in somewhat different order, in the two packets of 1870 and 1871 material. Paragraphs eight, nine, and ten reproduce exactly three leaves, originally numbered "69," "9," and "35," from the 1858 lecture.

Occasionally, however, Cabot was compelled to do more than cut, paste, and rearrange. For paragraphs eleven through thirteen he made a number of slight revisions as he wove together matter from seven separate leaves. He transposed Emerson's "We live late in life by memory . . . " to read "Late in life we live by memory." He made a precise reference to "the artist" more general (necessary in a context that had nothing to do with artists) by changing it to the pronoun "one." For his most complicated revision, Cabot began with a passage that read, "Never was truer fable than of the Sibyl's writing on leaves which the wind scatters. A. asked me, if the thought clothes itself in words? I answer—yes; but they are instantly forgotten." In the printed version this became, "Am I asked whether the thoughts clothe themselves in words? I answer, Yes, always; but they are apt to be instantly forgotten. Never was truer fable than that of the Sibyl's writing on leaves which the wind scatters."[75] Only a few of his revisions, however, show Cabot taking this kind of liberty with Emerson's Sibylline leaves. His work was largely a matter of selection, excision of examples and quotations, and recombination.

As Cabot explained, his method of compiling "essays" was determined by what he understood to be Emerson's own practice, a practice that not only resulted from a long career as a busy and successful lecturer but also created the chaos of the manuscripts Cabot inherited. However, Cabot was also interested in making Emerson intelligible. He saw that Emerson had constructed a lecture by gathering particular thoughts on a general subject and arranging them as logically as possible. As Emerson said to Hedge in 1838, he sought in his lectures "the amplest cloak of a name whose folds will reach unto & cover extreme & fantastic things."[76] However, when he reworked his lectures into essays, Emerson had pruned considerably. Cabot reached the same conclusion when he compared newspaper accounts of the lectures on "The Conduct of Life" with the book of the same name. Emerson had retained sentences and whole paragraphs with very little change, and the "elaboration," Cabot asserted, "consisted in striking out whatever could be spared, especially anecdotes and quotations."[77]

In his work as Emerson's editor, Cabot was also practicing some of his own critical principles, enunciated at various times over the past thirty years. As far back as 1848 he had approved of a French translation that amounted "almost to rewriting Kant, and writing him better." Since he believed the goal of philosophy was to explain, Cabot praised this translator's "useful" work in undertaking "to rearrange the original matter, amplify it in some places, but more often to condense, and reproduce it with a strict regard to the original peculiarities of phraseology and method." Cabot had remained faithful to this principle, praising twenty years later a translation of Fichte that had "here and there condensed the original, but . . . without injury to the sense."[78] Similarly, when reviewing William Wallace's translation of Hegel's *Logic* in 1874, Cabot had found the translator's emphasis on meaning admirable: "The success of this attempt seems remarkably complete, and not at all diminished by the fact that many words and even sentences are to be found in the translation which are not in the original." Wallace, he felt, had succeeded in introducing Hegel's ideas to America by his carefully balanced position "betwixt a literal version and a paraphrase."[79]

However, Emerson's essays were closer to poetry than philosophy; his object was not to explain, but, as Cabot had said in 1864, in a long essay on art, to paint the image of the ideal in the mind of the beholder. Cabot believed Emerson's method was to throw out a series of poetic images, each a part that indicated a whole. The artist must believe, Cabot had gone on to say in his essay, that the "idyl in the landscape is there because he sees it, and will appear in the picture without the help of demonstration."[80] This was a method of composition based not on logic but on faith.

Much has been said about the apparent lack of method that characterizes the typical Emerson essay. James Russell Lowell's description of the lectures as a "chaos full of shooting-stars" fits even more aptly the severely classic essays, and Emerson himself confessed to Carlyle that in his work each sentence seemed an "infinitely repellent particle."[81] Nevertheless, scholars have labored to demonstrate that Emerson was guided by a theory of "organic" form, that his essays do cohere by their own internal logic. In the composiiton of the later essays, at least, this theory seems to have been rather primitive. Faith in correspondence, belief that every particular fact was a means to spiritual truth, led Emerson to trust that a higher unity existed in any collection of particulars. The poem, he said in "The Poet," had an "architecture of its own," a form that would emerge as the natural consequence of "metre-making argument."[82]

In the construction of the essays, however, Emerson began not with single poetic images, but with images he had gathered into thoughts—sentences and paragraphs—the results, as he said, of "perceptions of single relations of the laws of nature."[83] The definition is very close to Cabot's own reiterated belief that knowledge is the perception of relations. These moments of perception provided the building blocks of Emerson's lectures and essays; once chiselled, the blocks retained their shape despite their rearrangement.

The key to Emerson's method lay in his faith in the law of identity between nature and spirit: order in the natural world reflects an ideal, pre-existent unity discoverable by the mind. In his 1836 lecture on "The Humanity of Science," Emerson had said, "The scattered blocks with which [the mind] strives to form a symmetrical structure, fit. The design following after, finds with joy that like design went before. Not only man puts things in a row, but things belong in a row." [84] In his composition of the essay he called "Natural History of Intellect," Cabot abutted this block with another thought, drawn from Emerson's 1858 and 1866 lectures on the mind: "It is certain that however we may conceive of the wonderful little bricks of which the world is builded, we must suppose a similarity and fitting and identity in their frame. It is necessary to suppose that every hose in Nature fits every hydrant; so only is combination, chemistry, vegetation, animation, intellection possible. Without identity at base, chaos must be forever." Both Cabot and Emerson believed it was not necessary to succumb to a materialistic view of nature. As Cabot put it, "the world is not a heap, but an organism." [85] Emerson believed that the scattered thoughts of his lectures and journals would coalesce into a complete whole. Both men were confident that the mind, engaged in the creative act of perception, could resolve all seeming discrepancies, and that truth grows by perpetual inclusion of the contradictory. This shared belief made it possible for Cabot to put together essays to be published under Emerson's name and lectures to be read by Emerson.

With Emerson's death in 1882, Cabot began the second phase of his work as literary executor. He saw himself as a trustee, one legally responsible to hold a property interest, charged with managing the literary estate for the benefit of Emerson's heirs. His cardinal principle was to do this as Emerson would have wished. But Emerson had hesitated to define, to dogmatize, to arrive at a conclusion that might preclude other conclusions. He distrusted analysis, dissection, and doctrine. According to Cabot, Emerson's legacy was an "open vision of things spiritual across the disfigurements and contradictions of the actual." [86] Thus, it was important to Cabot to keep the vision open as Emerson had tried to do.

But Cabot was also a master of philosophy, a metaphysician, methodical in his life and his thought. To Cabot, Emerson had gone too far in his distrust of method: no one could benefit from a mountain of unclassified material. As executor, Cabot believed his most important job was to organize the chaos and then to preserve the material for future use. As early as 1875 Cabot had recognized the importance of Emerson's manuscripts. Learning that Emerson had mentioned burning his sermons, Mrs. Cabot conveyed her husband's views to Ellen Emerson: Cabot hoped they would not comply, "as he considers that your Father is no judge whatever of their value." The Cabots promised the material "house-room" and good care if Emerson should persist in his desire to destroy these early papers.[87] Cabot had begun the organizing with his work on the lecture manuscripts.

The next concern was how to distribute the wealth. Obviously every scrap could not be printed; and not only was the job of patching up essays time-consuming and difficult, but also the results were far from satisfactory. An open vision demanded an open form, and Cabot's idea seems to have been to combine his roles as literary executor and official biographer by printing a collection of Emerson's thoughts carefully selected from the journals, correspondence, sermons, lectures, and fragments of essays, loosely arranged to convey the natural history of Emerson's intellect. By providing an underlying chronological structure and necessary biographical information, Cabot could allow the selections to tell the inner story of Emerson's life, while some brief commentary along the way would reveal relationships and continuities, themes in Emerson's thought. Cabot preferred to refrain from interpreting his composition; this was not Emerson's method, and like Emerson, Cabot wanted to keep the particles in suspension. He wished to serve as mediator, not critic; to act as a translator of Emerson to his public.

Ellen and Edward Emerson, however, had different ideas about the proper disposition of their father's estate. They believed in books: they wanted to add the unpublished manuscripts to a "definitive" edition. To accompany this, they wanted a "Life" that would define Emerson's position. Charged to act "in cooperation with [Emerson's] children," Cabot had the problem of deciding which heirs came first: the family or the "readers and friends" he addressed in the *Memoir*.

Cabot ended by compromising, striking a balance. He defined his aim and method and told the Emersons clearly what he intended to do and why. He began his sorting and arranging. But when the Emersons went ahead and contracted to publish a *Complete Works*, Cabot shelved his own work on the *Memoir* and acted in their interest. For over a year he was involved in editing eleven volumes, including two new collections of early and late pieces. Ten years later he finished his task by bringing the *Works* to an even dozen. If Emerson's heirs had to have an edition, at least it would be respectable.

Immediately after Emerson's death, Cabot returned to his work on the papers entrusted to him, spending his first week as "literary executor" working "constantly" on the papers, especially the correspondence, journals, notebooks, and miscellaneous materials.[88] After some preliminary sorting at Bush (the Emerson home), Cabot moved his workshop first to Brookline and then, as the summer progressed, to Beverly. There he would unpack the carpetbags of materials from Concord, patiently and methodically examining, cataloguing, and making extracts for future use. Sorting the papers and collecting materials for the life he was to write occupied most of Cabot's time from May through September 1882.

Surveying this mine of materials, Cabot continued to feel inadequate to the task. "I am working on in a dreamy way over my papers—& feeling as if I were losing my wits & becoming incapable of any exertion," he wrote early in June to his wife who was travelling in Europe with their son Ted.[89] But, as the summer advanced, Cabot found himself drawn into the work. The months were punctuated by the regular arrival of additional material that he studied in the privacy of his Beverly Farms home, and each new carpetbag produced new treasures: drafts of letters to Carlyle, early notebooks and unfinished poems, some John Sterling and Thoreau letters, "quasi-sermons," Grandfather Emerson's journal, material on Jones Very. At the same time, he was collecting correspondence and reminiscences from Emerson's oldest living friends. As he discovered gaps in his material, Cabot turned to Ellen, who searched the remaining manuscripts at Bush to produce what he sought. In August both Ellen and Edward visited Cabot at his workshop in Beverly.

Although the Emersons had acquiesced to Cabot's desire to work at his own pace, during the summer their relationship was complicated by Cabot's attempt to decline Emerson's bequest to his sons. Believing he deserved no payment for his work, Cabot wrote Edward Emerson and Will Forbes requesting they cancel the legacy. The Emersons refused to yield, and probably Cabot gave in to them in the end.[90]

The preliminary work went on steadily. By the end of July, Cabot reported that his calendar of Emerson letters had reached number 1,650, and on 28 August he sent Ellen a list of all the notebooks he had examined.[91] For at least another year, Cabot continued to work his way through the manuscripts and to amass his materials for the life. Part of his work involved itemizing the manuscripts in a series of cross-referenced calendars, tables, and notebooks. His "calendar of Emerson papers" is a chronological listing of 2,128 items, numbered and entered into six small examination-style blue books. To accompany this list, Cabot drew up nine separate indexes devoted to Mary Moody Emerson, Margaret Fuller, miscellaneous undated letters, Ruth Haskins Emerson and others, other family members and Elizabeth Hoar, Emerson's correspondence (in two blue books, labeled "1807–1847" and "1848–1880 and undated"), another list titled "Letters of R.W.E., not entered upon the Calendar," and a list of letters from Emerson to his brother William, labeled "in possession of Dr. Haven Emerson of New York."

Other blue books contained more lists. Only one of the booklets in which Cabot listed the Journals survives, covering the volumes to which Cabot gave the designations "C–M." In a few other blue books Cabot recorded conversations with the Emersons, Eliza Thayer Clapp, and Elizabeth Palmer Peabody, transcribed some of Ellen's family anecdotes, and began two calendars of the life of Emerson, one beginning with the birth of William Emerson in 1769, and one detailing the period covered by the Fuller correspondence, from 1837 to 1848. He was also collecting information about lectures from newspaper reports and about various persons from the journals and correspondence.[92]

Cabot's work soon outgrew these little examination books, and at some point he began arranging his materials in larger volumes. In a tall ledger with alphabetical index tabs, he began to collect Emerson's ideas under such headings as Alcott, books, Concord, intellect, and poetry. In a second ledger, containing close to four hundred pages of material, Cabot expanded upon many of these topics, bringing together clippings, notes, and extracts from the sermons, journals, conversation, letters, and printed works. He arranged his gleanings alphabetically under such topics as criticism, dates of writing, *Dial*, "George Muller & the Doctrine of Particular Providences," intellect, morals, philosophy, religion, and slavery. An occasional paragraph written into this volume summarizes Cabot's thoughts on a particular topic.

Cabot supplemented these preliminary materials with two large binders crammed with extracts from Emerson's writings, especially the journals and letters. The first folder, almost three inches thick, contains extracts arranged under the headings "Boyhood," "Ordination," "Society," "Divinity Hall," "CCE" (Emerson's brother Charles), and "Lectures." The reports of lectures—from the New York *Times* and *Tribune*, the Boston *Journal*, *Evening Transcript*, and *Daily Advertiser*, and other newspapers—gradually overwhelmed this folder. A second fat binder continued what was begun in the first, under the headings "Personal," "Friends & Contemporaries," "Transcendentalism," "Europe," "Carlyle," and "Publications." In these collections lies the germ of Cabot's method in the *Memoir*, "to furnish materials for an estimate . . . without . . . undertaking any estimate or interposing any comments beyond what seemed necessary."[93]

As Cabot was warming to his task, collecting and organizing his materials, Edward was negotiating for a new edition of Emerson's *Works*, and on 7 September 1882, he signed an agreement with the Houghton, Mifflin publishing firm.[94] Although Cabot remained unconvinced about the wisdom of additional publications, he was soon diverted from preparing the life to editing eleven volumes of old and new writings. By the following January, the general format had been determined, as indicated by a printed announcement designed to solicit subscriptions for the special "Edition de Luxe," limited to five hundred sets. The new edition would include "the prose and poetical writings of Mr. Emerson hitherto published in book form, and in addition, two new volumes of Essays prepared for publication, in accordance with the terms of Mr. Emerson's will, by his literary executor, Mr. J. Elliot Cabot, and by his son, Dr. Edward W. Emerson." [95]

By the time the announcement appeared, the editorial team was already at work on this very large project. Writing to her sister early in December, Ellen called the Cabots' recent visit "a failure in a business point of view." She went on to explain: "Mr. Cabot brought his arrangement of Education [which Emerson had read in 1878] for us to read, and we couldn't. He carried it home again. Absolutely nothing accomplished there. Edward submitted his arrangement for Aristocracy [read in 1880] but Mr. Cabot couldn't look at it. He carried that home." Six months later Edward and Cabot had finally come up with an arrangement of the troublesome "Education" that still failed to please Ellen, who discovered an important page had been lost and began to tinker with the piece herself late in June. [96]

Much of the work was far more humdrum than creating new essays or even searching the manuscripts for "extra passages" for those that seemed a little slim. The family group was involved in every phase of work, from incorporating Emerson's corrections in marked copies, copying previously printed pieces, and locating manuscript for old addresses, to determining the format and binding of the volumes and selecting pictures and mottoes. Cabot acted as general manager and editor-in-chief. Will Forbes attended to most of the legal matters, while Edward busied himself with the proofs in general and the *Poems* in particular. Ellen was kept occupied copying from the *Dial*, *North American Review*, and *Atlantic*.

The variety of the work is suggested by the correspondence that passed between Edward Emerson and Cabot during this year. On the first of April, Edward sent Cabot a marked volume of *Essays: Second Series* to be used as printer's copy; with it he sent two essays, printed in the *North American Review* and slated for use in volume 10. He noted that Ellen was copying some *Dial* essays on the typewriter and working on the "extra passages" for "New England Notes." He reminded Cabot to send the introduction, copy for the first volume, and a complete list of titles so that Houghton, Mifflin could begin stamping the bindings. The next month Edward sent Cabot a marked *English Traits* along with several queries, and a few days later he was trying to answer Cabot's questions about some passages in *The Conduct of Life*. After Edward read the printer's copy for *Representative Men*, he restored some commas Cabot had deleted, in places, he explained, where only "as dull a reader as I am . . . might, without them mistake the sense." [97]

The work continued through the summer and into the fall. In June, Edward sent Cabot preliminary tables of contents for the new volumes; the next month he worried about providing explanatory notes for some of the "new essays" and reported progress in copying additional pieces. Near the end of the month he sent Cabot a large group of essays for volume 10 and some background information for notes; and he enclosed his choices for mottoes (short poetic passages to precede each essay) for this volume, urging Cabot to "alter or shift [them] about as seems best to you." A week later Edward was answering questions about his corrections of "Mary Moody Emerson," to be printed in the *Atlantic* for December. In August, Edward passed along some titles suggested by Ellen, which he found "eminently undesirable." He was "well pleased," however, with Cabot's work on "M. M. E.," as the essay was familiarly called by now.[98] With the fall came additional work on *Poems*, the sketch of Samuel Hoar, and the contents and arrangement of the new volumes.

The general editorial policy was conservative. The group attempted to incorporate Emerson's latest revisions, as indicated in his marked copies, and to make sense of an occasional confusing passage. They altered some punctuation and paragraphing, as collations of essays printed from other sources show. Very rarely a word or sentence was added or deleted. The primary worry concerned repetition. In July 1882, Cabot had asked Norton to suppress a passage from one of Emerson's letters to Carlyle, used in "Fortune of the Republic," "on the ground of first publication," if this would not spoil the letter, and the problem of Emerson's duplications continued to bother these editors.[99] Edward, who was not only the authority on *Poems* but also must have known his father's works almost by heart, repeatedly pointed out to Cabot passages that appeared elsewhere, leaving the final adjudication to the executor. In some cases (as with some repetitions Edward spotted in *English Traits*) one of the offending passages was eliminated; in others (as with three parallels in "War," "The Preacher," and "Education") it seemed all three could be kept "with advantage." In another case, a similar passage that occurred in *The Conduct of Life* and "Character," Edward believed there was "no real repetition & the image was better left in both places."[100]

Although Edward was willing to assume responsibility for reprinting the earlier works, believing it was not right to "impose" on Cabot except for the late volumes, Cabot was very much involved in the entire edition. He conscientiously prepared printer's copy for each volume, making occasional verbal and punctuation changes, and he corrected proofs, pointing out to Edward some mistakes that had gotten past him. He wrote prefaces and the few notes for volumes 1 and 8–11. And to him fell most of the responsibility for the two new volumes, including selecting, arranging, and preparing essays for the printer, and explaining to the public what he had done.

On 15 June Edward sent a "list of contents of Additional Volumes" (which does not survive) to Cabot for his consideration and revision. The plan provided for one volume of occasional pieces that early assumed its final title, *Miscellanies*, and a second volume that everyone thought of as "Essays, Third Series." In a letter to H. O. Houghton, editor F. J. Garrison estimated the *Essays* would approximate the size of the first two series, about three hundred pages. For the *Miscellanies*, however, he foresaw a "scarcity of material," estimating the book might come to 250 pages. Although he had not yet seen the copy, Garrison feared they would have to add more bulk.[101] Edward's first table of contents was repeatedly revised during the summer. As each collaborator championed his favorites, more and more material was brought into the volumes.

On 10 August Cabot sent to Ellen his own tentative tables of contents. For "Essays, 3rd Ser" he listed twenty-seven pieces, fourteen of which appeared in the completed volume of eighteen selections, *Lectures and Biographical Sketches*, as it was published in 1883. In Cabot's original plan, the volume was to begin with two of Emerson's earliest printed essays, "Michael Angelo" and "Milton" (*North American Review*, January 1837, July 1838), followed by nine essays from the *Dial* ("Thoughts on Modern Literature," "W. S. Landor," "Prayers," "The Chardon Street Convention," "Agriculture in Massachusetts," "Europe and European Books," "Past and Present," "A Letter to Contributors," and "The Tragic," all printed between 1841 and 1844) and "War" (printed in Elizabeth Peabody's *Aesthetic Papers* in 1849). Of this group, only "The Chardon Street Convention" made it into the volume.

These were to be followed by "The Waterville Address 1863" (called "The Man of Letters" in the finished volume) and ten "essays" that Cabot labeled "put together by us": "Demonology," "Aristocracy," "Perpetual Forces," "Character" (in fact, not compiled by them), "Education," "The Superlative," "The Sovereignty of Ethics," "The Preacher," "The Virginia Address," and "Historic Notes." The final group, which Cabot said were "in original forms," consisted of the "Introduction" to *Plutarch's Morals* (1871), "Dr. Ripley," "Mary Moody Emerson," and "Samuel Hoar."[102] As correspondence about the last two pieces indicates, they were not as finished as Cabot believed in August. The completed volume was as much "Cabot's book" as *Letters and Social Aims*: nine of its eighteen pieces derived from the synthetic lectures or essays composed during Emerson's lifetime, while at least three others required revision and rearrangement.

Cabot's preliminary table of contents for volume 11, *Miscellanies*, very closely approximated the finished book. He listed twenty of Emerson's statements on public occasions, ranging from the 1832 sermon on the Lord's Supper to the 1878 "Fortune of the Republic," the latter the only piece compiled by Cabot. As printed in 1883, the volume contained twenty-three selections (Edward Emerson added seven more to the Centenary Edition in 1903). *Miscellanies* differed from Cabot's original selection only in omitting the "Letter to the Second Church" and the letters to Henry Ware, Jr. (which Cabot decided to reserve for his "life") and in adding the "Historical Discourse at Concord," "War" (originally assigned to volume 10), "John

Brown—Speech at Salem," "Walter Scott," and the "Speech at the Second Annual Meeting of the Free Religious Association."

In their decisions about these volumes, especially the *Miscellanies*, the editors were respecting Emerson's wishes as far as they could be ascertained. Two of the lists Cabot copied from Emerson's late journals were titled "Proposed Book of Occasional Discourses" (from Journal GL, 1862) and "Miscellanies, Vol II" (from FOR, 1863). Eight or nine of the eighteen "occasional discourses" listed by Emerson appear in volume 11 and one each in 10 ("Carlyle") and 12 ("Walter Savage Landor," originally assigned to 10), six others had already been collected elsewhere, and one or two were added to the *Works* by Edward Emerson in 1903. "Miscellanies, Vol II" lists twelve titles, seven of which duplicate items on the "discourses" list and nine of which were printed in volume 11. (Two more were added by Edward in 1903.) Thus, with the exceptions of the "Sermon on the Lord's Supper," "The Editors' Address for the *Massachusetts Quarterly Review*," "Woman," "Sir Walter Scott," and a few late pieces composed by Emerson after he drew up these lists, all of the reprinted pieces seem to reflect the will of the author. However, the editors had to rely on newspaper accounts for some of the occasional speeches. As a result, as Ellen pointed out to Cabot when he was working on the preface to volume 11, they could not truthfully claim that all of these works were printed "in the form left by Father." They had no reason to suppose that Emerson had given his manuscript to the reporter "in the case of those for which we have only newspaper reports," though Ellen did believe her father had corrected the pieces that were printed in pamphlets or books.[103]

The family team headed by Cabot worked diligently, and a year and a half after Emerson's death, the eleven volumes were ready to begin rolling off the presses at regular intervals ("two volumes a fortnight" before the holiday season). In mid-September, H. O. Houghton reported there had been no charges for extra corrections and added, "which argues that the copy was exceedingly well prepared. It is very rarely that a set of books like these go through the press without any charge for extra corrections."[104]

Only two problems threatened the projected design to have Emerson in the marketplce by the end of 1883. One concerned the contents of volume 10, "Third Essays." In June, when the team was beginning work on this volume, the publisher estimated its contents would make about three hundred pages—slightly more than some of the others. By September, however, when they had all of the copy in hand, the publisher's estimate leaped to 650 pages. It seemed the volume would have to be divided. Edward, who favored a division, saw no easy way to distribute the contents. He puzzled at great length over the problem:

Historic notes would group well with the biographical sketches . . . but what could this book be called? "Historic Notes" without "of Life & Letters in New England" might raise false expectations. Yet the full title would include the M. M. E. Dr. Ripley S. Hoar & Thoreau well enough, but would leave Carlyle out in the cold as no New Englander. The four or even the five biographical sketches, plus Hist. Notes would hardly fill a volume unless the Dial Chapters were added. In that case, would "Historic Notes and Papers from the Dial" do? Pretty long! Or the five biographical papers & those from the Dial might be grouped under the title "Dial Papers and Biographical Sketches," leaving Historic Notes with the Lectures.

Asking Cabot to consider the problem, Edward planned to talk to Houghton about the possibility of printing all 650 pages on thinner paper.[105]

Fortunately for everybody, Edward did not need to come up with new titles. At his meeting with Houghton the next day, he learned that neither suggestion—thin paper or a divided volume—was practical from a business point of view. Thinner paper would mean selling a 650-page book for the price of one half as long, and dividing the volume would mean giving those who had subscribed for the eleven-volume set a free book. Instead, something had to go.[106]

Houghton preferred to retain some of the material for the last volume, and Edward suggested the *Dial* papers and introduction to Plutarch. Instead of the "Dial Papers and Biographical Sketches" Edward had considered, the orphan was finally christened *Lectures and Biographical Sketches*. The removal of nine pieces, however, failed to reduce the volume sufficiently, and by the next week Cabot had agreed to omit three more essays, "Michael Angelo," "Milton," and "War." A few days later, Cabot told the publisher to remove the papers from the *Dial*, with the exception of "The Chardon Street Convention."[107]

Although leaving in "The Chardon Street Convention" required cutting, and patching or resetting five plates, it remained the lone *Dial* paper in volume 10. A ghost of these last-minute changes haunts Cabot's note to this volume, where he explains that some of the pieces had been printed by Emerson, "namely, those from the Dial."[108] More interesting, however, is the sudden reference to the "last" volume. Admittedly, eleven is an odd number for a complete works; yet no mention of a twelfth volume had occurred before this. That Houghton meant volume 12 becomes clear in Edward's decision two weeks later, that since "Milton" and "Michael Angelo" did not belong with the topical pieces in volume 11, they too should wait for volume 12.[109]

The pruning, it turned out, was a bit overzealous. On 19 October the printers discovered volume 10 now came to only 435 pages and could accomodate slightly more material if the editors desired. The introduction to

Plutarch seemed the only one that could be easily restored, so back it went.[110] Despite all of these last-minute revisions, however, the edition came out on schedule.

The second problem, concerning the definition of Cabot's role as literary executor, temporarily threatened the equilibrium of the publishing group. In many respects, Cabot was the ideal mediator for Emerson: his native reticence tempered the Emersons' rage to publish and his high standards assured a dignified treatment of the texts. Nevertheless, he wished to remain transparent and he resented the Emersons' attempts to push him beyond what he saw as the parameters of his job.

As literary executor, Cabot defined his duty strictly in the terms of Emerson's will and his own capabilities: he would make decisions about publishing the manuscripts and he had agreed to "furnish materials" for an "estimate." By January 1883, however, Edward (who had handled all of the negotiations for the new edition in which Cabot had become an unwilling partner) was insisting that Cabot also provide an introduction to the *Complete Works*. Cabot must have balked, prompting another letter in which the son quoted from his father's will and reiterated, "We all feel quite sure that you are the person to write the introduction."[111]

Cabot acquiesced, dispatching immediately an extremely brief introductory note. In four tight little sentences he outlined the contents of the new edition: the first eight volumes, the *Poems*, and the two volumes of posthumously printed pieces. The last sentence simply justified Cabot's use of Emerson's manuscripts "in pursuance of the authority given in his will to me." The whole was almost a legal document. Three days later, as he began his work on *Essays: Second Series*, Edward acknowledged that Cabot's preface "seemed to cover the ground," though he felt the need of "justifying" their alterations in the poems.[112] Throughout this venture, Edward fussed over his *Poems* and beseiged Cabot with his questions and problems. Now he wanted the executor's imprimatur in the preface.

On the first of April, Edward wrote reminding Cabot to send his introduction, along with proofs for the first volume. He also promised Cabot a marked *English Traits* and unbound copies of *The Conduct of Life* and *Society and Solitude*. Three weeks later, after looking over the prefatory note, to which Cabot had obligingly added a sentence justifying Edward's decisions about the poems, Edward had more suggestions. He was particularly bothered that Cabot's statement explaining their rejection of some of Emerson's late revisions failed to account for their alterations in "May-Day": "Our change was in the spirit of Fathers change for Selected Poems; but was not actually authorized." Covering two pages with a rambling discussion of these emendations, Edward finally concluded that the disclosures could be made in the preface to the *Poems*. Expressing his wish that Cabot sign the prefatory note, Edward ended by saying he was happy to let Cabot correct proof alone if he wished.[113]

Cabot was unsuccessful in keeping Edward at a distance, however, and by June, when the executor had worked his way up to *Representative Men*, Edward was still harping on how to handle the poem question in the preface. Now he reversed himself on the question of explaining what they had done, asking whether it was "worth speaking" of the "few verbal alterations & omissions that it has seemed justifiable & desirable to make." He noted that Cabot had ignored his suggestion to change "some" to "one or two" as well as the entire content of his circular discussion of the changes in "May-Day" "to make it closer to the time order of the March of the Spring signs." He also queried the wisdom of presenting "to the person who glances at the preface to see what new treasures he has secured by buying the new edition, the least attractive dish, viz. the Occasional Discourses." By the end of June, Edward had told Garrison to add Cabot's name to the prefatory note, despite Cabot's obvious disinclination to do so.[114]

At the end of July, Cabot was working on *Letters and Social Aims* when Edward wrote again, a long letter about various matters, including more changes in the preface he had insisted Cabot write. He preferred "Ellen's sentence about Father's illness," Edward explained, "because I am prejudiced against the expression 'nervous prostration.'" The reference to Emerson's "loss of memory and of mental grasp" in the preface to the eighth volume seems to represent Ellen's more delicate handling of this subject. Among other suggestions, Edward believed it "desirable" to provide a separate "explanatory preface" for *Letters and Social Aims*, instead of the editorial silence of 1875.[115]

At this point the usually imperturbable Cabot appears finally to have lost his patience. He must have responded immediately, since the following day Edward wrote a conciliatory note expressing his concern "at your dismay." Referring to other matters—the mottoes, changes in "Mary Moody Emerson," his choice and arrangement of other material—Edward bowed to Cabot's authority, saying, "You are the appointed critic and we, having made our representations, gratefully abide your decisions."[116] Noting that Houghton, Mifflin wished to promote the new edition by printing three essays in the *Atlantic Monthly* at the end of the year, Edward suggested "Aristocracy, Virginia, & Historic Notes." Cabot, however, chose to give them "Historic Notes," "Ezra Ripley," and "Mary Moody Emerson."

Ellen, who reviewed the prefaces Cabot wrote at Edward's request, had her own ideas about what the executor should and should not say. Early in August she responded: in the preface to volume 10, she was critical only of

Cabot's claim that he had not helped with the paper on Carlyle, reminding him that he had not only advised and assisted her when she pieced together the 1881 reading but also had revised this compilation extensively before its publication. She still objected to the titles "Miscellanies" or "Essays 3rd Series" for volume 11 and suggested "Occasional Speeches & Letters" as an alternative. And, she was very unhappy with Cabot's statement that the selections in this volume were "in the form left by Father." They simply did not know, she pointed out, how close to Emerson's words were the pieces they were reprinting from newspaper accounts. Concerning the preface to volume 8, Ellen felt that Cabot's statement about Conway had been "softened" too much. Though Edward felt much indebted to Conway, she claimed, the explanation was no longer true to "Father's feelings & course of conduct." But, in particular, she hoped that the story of Cabot's involvement in *Letters and Social Aims* could be told without reference to herself. "It should not go in that I had anything to do with it because it was only a thing of proximity not of taste. My lines lie in a different direction, I never knew my Papa as a literary man, nor had the slightest knowledge of nor interest in his work." Instead of any specific reference to her, she suggested, Cabot could use the phrase "his family."[117]

The prefaces were not the only problem during this difficult summer. Edward's meddling in what Cabot considered his rightful territory—the compilation of the last two volumes—also strained the relationship between the executor and the son. In mid-August, Edward and Ellen travelled to Beverly Farms, where Cabot had retreated to do his job in peace. After their visit Ellen was relieved to report improvements: Houghton, it seems, acted as mediator and their talks "had made it clear that they were of one mind more than [Edward] had feared."[118] Nevertheless, it was an uneasy peace. Cabot's revised preface to the *Poems* incorporated verbatim most of Edward's hobby-horses, including a one-paragraph explanation of the changes in "May-Day" to make the poem more "representative of the march of Spring." But in returning this preface to Edward, Cabot added sardonically that he wished to see any notes Edward might decide on before the book was printed, "that I might swear that I always thought so." Edward complied by sending the final copy for *Poems* to Cabot early in September, suggesting it might require additions to the prefaces or notes and inviting Cabot to override his decisions as he wished.[119]

As the fall progressed, the pace slowed. The business end of the enterprise was auspicious: the firm had successfully placed all of the special large-paper sets. Some problems remained: while Cabot was re-establishing himself at Brookline for the winter, a batch of proof sent to him at Beverly went astray. "Historic Notes" seemed to open abruptly no matter what Cabot started with, and though Edward admitted he had heard Ellen speak of a "missing beginning," he knew nothing of it. A few changes from the *Atlantic* printings of "Mary Moody Emerson" and "Historic Notes" remained to be made as late as October; there were some problems with *Poems* and questions about how to indicate that the new material in volume 10 had never been published before in book form. On 2 November Edward wrote concerning the still-missing prefaces for volumes 10 and 11.[120] And, proofreading and minor revisions continued to occupy the team up to press time.

The reception of the eleven-volume edition of Emerson's *Complete Works* in 1883 and 1884 seemed to support Cabot's belief that further publication was far from necessary. Few periodicals noticed the event. The comments of one of these, the *Nation*, restricted to volumes 5–8, were sandwiched between references to the new "Parchment Shakspere" and the "Classic Series" in an omnibus section called "Notes." The reviewer focused on Cabot's explanation of the "melancholy circumstances" under which *Letters and Social Aims* was prepared. He found the fact that these synthetic essays were "as truly Emersonian as if their author had struck them off in one heat" a "curious illustration" of the way Emerson's mind worked; and he regretted that the volumes failed to make clear the dates of composition, delivery, and first publication of the essays.

Ten days later, Cabot responded to this last point with a letter to the editor of the *Nation*, explaining the impossibility of ascertaining dates of composition and delivery. Admitting it would be possible to state publication dates, he explained his desire to keep the works as "free as possible from editorial comment, and to reserve bibliographical details for a future occasion."[121]

Other reviews, such as those in two English periodicals, provided general estimates of Emerson rather than any specific comment on the new editions of the *Works*. An *Athenæum* reviewer focused on Emerson's role in educating the American people, while Richard Holt Hutton, laboring to categorize Emerson in the *Spectator*, called him an "oracle."[122] A more substantial review appeared in San Francisco's *Overland Monthly*. Yet here too, the writer, Edward Rowland Sill, was more interested in Emerson in general than the works themselves. Sill found Emerson not a seer or a prophet; instead, his importance lay in his application of the "positive spirit" of science to human facts.[123]

Despite occasional tensions and the critical silence, the 1883–84 *Complete Works* marked an important step in shaping Emerson's lengthened shadow. Here was Emerson in formal dress, fitted out for public audiences, his legacy made available for future generations. As the standard edition of Emerson, reprinted with a few additions and Edward Emerson's notes in the Centenary Edition, the *Works* have stood for almost a century.

In November 1893, ten years after publication of the *Complete Works* and six years after the *Memoir* appeared, the last volume in Emerson's *Works*,

Natural History of Intellect and Other Papers, was published in Boston. In addition to the long title essay, the volume contained two of the lectures Cabot had prepared for Emerson to read, "Boston" (1877) and "Memory" (1879). The remaining contents were the pieces that had been excised from volume 10 in 1883: the two early essays "Michael Angelo" and "Milton," printed in the *North American Review*, and eight "Papers from the Dial." The volume also contained an eighty-page general index to the *Complete Works* (prepared by Professor John H. Woods of Jacksonville, Illinois) and an index of quotations. Though the *Critic* called this "a noteworthy event in current literary history" and a writer for *Poet-Lore* found reading the title essay a "source of genuine pleasure," probably more readers would have agreed with the reviewer for the *Athenæum* who found it fortunate that Emerson's fame "does not rest upon the articles now reprinted." [124]

Natural History of Intellect has remained an anomaly. Its questionable status was not improved by Edward Emerson's addition of five more pieces, some of which he composed using Cabot's method, to the volume in 1903. The most interesting questions, however, turn on the essay Cabot called "Natural History of Intellect" (retitled "Powers and Laws of Thought" in 1903). Cabot himself both suggested and denied that the work represented Emerson's philosophical *summa*. And, though Frederic Ives Carpenter called the piece an "extraordinary . . . clarification of ideas which had been vague, although implicit, in Emerson's earlier writing," few scholars have felt compelled to consult the piece to discover the outline of Emerson's thought. [125]

The position of the essay "Natural History of Intellect" in the Emerson canon is only one of the questions surrounding this volume. The book's origins and timing have never been explained. Until the fall of 1883, the *Complete Works* was to be an eleven-volume set. The proliferation of contents for volume 10 resulted in talk of a new volume. Yet, in the large correspondence about the Emerson work in the 1880s, no further reference to another book occurs. In fact, after 1887, communication between Cabot and the Emersons virtually ceased, except for Cabot's opposition to the Emersons' wish that he accept the royalties as his payment for his work on the *Memoir*. Perhaps disturbed by the implication that he had been hired to do what he considered an honor, Cabot adamantly refused the money and hoped that "the light of calm reason" would soon dawn in Concord. To Edward he tried to explain that any businessman would agree that "the essential part of the book is that which belongs to your father's family." Many would have volunteered their time to use this material, and Cabot hoped Edward would take the "rational view." [126]

The volume did not resurface until 1890. In November of that year,

Houghton, Mifflin asked Edward Emerson whether there was "any immediate prospect of having the additional volume so long promised." Earlier that same year, in February, Ellen visited the Cabots and briefly discussed "Nat. Hist. of Int." with Cabot, but neglected to record what was said. Also in 1890, Cabot asked his son Richard, now studying at Harvard Medical School, to read the synthetic essay he had composed on the subject of the natural history of the intellect. Richard frankly saw no reason to publish it. "All that I have read has been said elsewhere by himself or others—," he wrote.[127]

By mid-summer 1891, however, at least a portion of this twelfth volume was in production: Houghton, Mifflin wished to print an essay in the *Atlantic* and suggested "Boston," in proof for the book by October. Horace Scudder, the *Atlantic's* editor, wanted Cabot to write a brief historical note explaining the circumstances and date of composition of the essay. After "Boston" appeared in the January 1892 *Atlantic* (without any explanation), Scudder felt the many "gratifying expressions" assured the success of the forthcoming volume.[128] Still, the expected book did not appear for almost two more years—a very long time considering the eleven-volume edition was produced in a little over a year. Indeed, there seems to be no further correspondence on the matter until October 1893, when the book was back in production. *Natural History of Intellect* was finally published on 15 November.

Several factors probably combined to delay the volume. Two obvious reasons were Cabot's work on the *Memoir* and family anxiety concerning the illness of his second son, Ted. Ted's death from diabetes in 1893 ended ten difficult years for the Cabots, during which they had sought cures, doctors, and companionship for their dying child. Another explanation would seem to be the problem of contents. Ten short pieces would hardly fill a volume, and now that Emerson was no longer alive to sanction his work, Cabot must have been even more reluctant to put together new second-rate pieces. It is reasonable to assume that Cabot was once again pressured into contributing. However, the choice of subject matter was probably his own. As before, he chose to do what he believed Emerson would wish him to do. The project, as well as the method Cabot adopted, did have authorial sanction. From Emerson's "suggestions for future publications," Cabot had copied the following memo from Journal ST, which he dated 1872–75: "Two articles in 'The Dial,' 'Landor,' and 'Carlyle' and my 'Cambridge Lectures on Philosophy,' fourteen, I believe, from which I should rather select the best pages, than attempt to print any entire discourses."[129] Moreover, as he worked on the *Memoir* Cabot had watched Emerson struggling for almost forty years to formulate his "First Philosophy," his philosopher's description of the way the mind grasps reality. Emerson was by nature a poet, and he thought in poetic images, but he envied the scientist's cool, analytical ability to stand aside from his subject matter and study it as object. His doctrine of correspondence suggested the same method might be applied to the study of the mind—the Intellect or Spirit. Giving form to the utterances of a lifetime on a complex and important subject, scattered through at least forty-six lectures and several journals, may have proven as discouraging to Cabot as it had been impossible for Emerson, and possibly the delay resulted from his inability to weld these materials into a whole that satisfied him.

Cabot was not the first person to become interested in these notes toward a scientific poetic. In 1870, Bronson Alcott claimed that Emerson's Harvard lectures would give his "metaphysic at last."[130] When *Letters and Social Aims* was reviewed in *Scribner's* in 1876, the writer was especially disappointed not to find Emerson's "best" lecture since the "Divinity School Address," a lecture on "The Natural Method of Intellectual Philosophy." He had heard this piece twenty years before, he explained, and found it "brilliant beyond even his wont with wit, and insight, and quotation." But even more, the lecture had a "degree of method and continuity which would, if it could be printed, disarm the most Philistine critic."[131] F. B. Sanborn, in "The Homes and Haunts of Emerson" (1879), had referred to the mass of Emerson's unpublished papers, pointing out particularly the wealth that lay in the philosophical lectures read at Harvard, designed to make part of what Emerson called "The Natural History of the Intellect." Then Sanborn went on to explain the grand design of this unwritten *summa*, which he predicted would be printed even if unfinished: "This work . . . was to be the author's most systematic and connected treatise. It was to contain, what could not fail to be of interest to all readers, Mr. Emerson's observations on his own intellectual processes and methods . . . which he has carefully noted down."[132] Emerson himself had fueled such speculation by admitting, at the end of his first Harvard course, that his readings had helped to clarify his own views, which he hoped to state more completely. At the same time he wrote Carlyle that he hoped "to construct [for the next year] a fair report of what I have read & thought on the Subject."[133] And, in 1883, Annie Fields, wife of the publisher James T. Fields and one of the registrants in the Harvard course, printed her impressions of these striking lectures in the *Atlantic*, in the form of letters to a friend.[134]

Even before his work on the *Memoir*, however, Cabot had several opportunities to consider the importance of this topic to Emerson. He had lectured (on Kant) in the same Harvard series in which Emerson had unsuccessfully attempted to gather his "anecdotes of the intellect" into a comprehensive whole, and the two men had talked at length about their plans before the course began. Moreover, despite his argument that Emerson had already selected everything he saw fit to print, Cabot must have noticed, as he sorted the manuscripts, that little had been printed from this considerable body of Emerson's thought. The subject, first presented in lectures on "The Natural History of Intellect" read in England in 1848 and repeated after Emerson's return, had resurfaced as "The Natural Method of Mental Philosophy" in 1858, "The Philosophy of the People" in 1866, and the Harvard lectures in 1870 and 1871. The bundles of manuscripts ranged from complete stitched lectures to collections of fragments, and in both content and form they often differed substantially from Emerson's printed essays. The first 1848 lecture, "Powers and Laws of Thought," for example, exists in three complete manuscript versions, probably as delivered in 1848, 1849, and 1850; and an 1858 lecture, "Self-Possession" (from which Cabot borrowed many passages for his "Natural History of Intellect"), stands as a virtually complete and coherent lecture. Repeatedly, Emerson had returned to the subjects of intellect and thought, attempting to classify and describe the powers, laws, and metres of mind.

However, Cabot may not have recognized the full significance of this material until he began to work it into the *Memoir*. On the one hand, Cabot believed that Emerson distrusted systematic reasoning. Often in the *Memoir* he points out how little concerned Emerson was with "speculative difficulties" and the "process by which his convictions were reached." Emerson was temperamentally unable to arrive at a "comprehensive theory" or reconciliation of his conflicting impressions, unable to take the "polemical tone." All of these ideas come together in Cabot's discussion of the "Natural History of Intellect" lectures of 1870, where he quotes Emerson on his "repugnance to introversion," his "expectant" metaphysics, his "disgust" at the pretensions of metaphysicians. [135]

On the other hand, as early as 1829, Emerson had admired Coleridge's "philosophy," which he felt "compares with others much as astronomy with the other sciences." The keynote of his 1866 course, "The Philosophy of the People," also came from Coleridge: "Philosophy is the doctrine and discipline of ideas." [136] He saw a philosophical method as a means of scientifically ordering chance impressions. When in England in 1833, Emerson had referred to "that species of moral philosophy I call the first philosophy," [137] a subject he returned to frequently in later years. For his earliest lectures (read in 1833 and 1834), Emerson drew his topics from natural science, admitting the advantage the scientist had over the poet in the study of nature, an idea that reappeared in the introduction to "Powers and Laws of Thought" in 1848. Cabot quoted from one of these early lectures, "The Naturalist" (1834), in which Emerson affirmed his belief in the methods of both the poet and the *savant*, "in the poetry and in the dissection. Accuracy, then, that we may really know something; but under the guidance of the pious sentiment of curiosity to know ourselves and the whole." [138] As Cabot pointed out, the central idea of correspondence between the natural world and the operations of the mind, or between science and philosophy, reappeared in *Nature* as well as Emerson's last lectures at Cambridge.[139]

Cabot explored at length Emerson's earliest attempt to expound his "First Philosophy" or the "original laws of the mind, the science of what is, in distinction from what appears," in his journal in 1835. According to Cabot, this contrast of the offices of Reason and Understanding constituted the "fundamentals of Transcendentalism." Despite these philosophical overtones, however, Cabot was not willing to grant Emerson's discussion the status of "systematic metaphysics." Instead, Emerson was laboring to express "religious emotions, [to be] grasped by the imagination in poetic wholes, rather than set down in propositions." Emerson's admiration for science could not outweigh his distrust of systematic reasoning, because science seemed to preclude the further apprehension of truth. Yet Cabot also defended Emerson against the charge that he was "incapable of reasoning." Questions of God's existence, or of the poetic wholes that Emerson perceived, could not be argued.[140]

Emerson's continued interest in these questions can be seen in such essays and lectures as "The Head," "Intellect," "Literary Ethics," and "The Method of Nature." However, the 1848 London lectures represented his most ambitious attempt to formulate his science of mind. His topics were "The Powers and Laws of Thought," "The Relation of Intellect to Natural Science," and "The Tendencies and Duties of Men of Thought." In the *Memoir*, Cabot's discussion of these lectures constituted the single departure from his narrative treatment of the English lecture tour. The first fifty-seven pages of this chapter are a mosaic constructed from Emerson's journals and letters, held together by a scant forty lines of editorial commentary. However, in the last six pages of the chapter, Cabot's commentary balances his lengthy excerpts from the lectures. The problem that interested Emerson, the one he would return to again and again, was stated in the first lecture: "Why cannot the laws and powers of the mind be stated as simply and as attractively as the physical laws are stated by Owen and Faraday? . . . The Natural History of the Intellect would be an enumeration of the laws of the world. . . . In the human brain the universe is reproduced with all its opulence of relations; it is high time that it should be humanly and properly unfolded, that the Decalogue of the Intellect should be written."[141] The lack of response to this new course, Cabot inferred, must have disappointed Emerson, who had "long cherished [the idea] of reading a series of connected discourses on the first principles of philosophy." Moreover, at the time, Emerson had seen these lectures as the nucleus for a "kind of book of metaphysics" and had entertained the idea of teaching Moral Philosophy at Harvard.[142]

These observations established Emerson's interest in this topic as an undeniable "fact," which Cabot subjected to Hegelian scrutiny in his penultimate chapter, covering the years 1864 through 1872. He explained that Emerson welcomed this opportunity to return to the "chief task of his life . . . to write the natural history of reason," and he traced these ideas as they developed in several series of lectures. Never, Cabot asserted, had Emerson gotten beyond a general statement of his principle. His work on the 1870 series represented a "supreme effort [to] bring together what he wished to say."[143]

Cabot then devoted ten pages to an analysis of Emerson's ideas, placing them in relation to "the problem of philosophy, . . . the coming together of thought and thing in our assent to a fact." He went on to define the business of philosophy, "to explain and to justify the connection, and thereby distinguish knowledge from the mere association of ideas."[144] In Hegelian fashion, Cabot's analysis revealed the limitations of Emerson's approach—the limitations of the identity-system that only ignored the problem rather than solving it and ended in tautology rather than doctrine.

In the *Memoir*, Cabot's discussion of the lectures and the reasons for their failure constitutes his single real evaluation of Emerson's accomplishment. Only when Emerson attempted to contend with philosophers did Cabot feel he had erred. He concluded that the "philosophic lectures" were no different from Emerson's usual loose collections of brilliant thoughts. Cabot believed Emerson had failed because of his method, his habit of presenting "metaphysical notions . . . as if they were poetical images, which it would be useless and impertinent to explain." In his discussion of the Harvard lectures, Cabot went on to explore the futility of this approach, which ended by dissolving all reality into a formless unity, a progressive discovery of illusions. Emerson had made the mistake of confusing metaphysics and system with dogmatism, Cabot insisted. In his distrust of dogmatism he had emptied out "the child with the bath."[145]

Cabot also recognized a discrepancy between the statements produced by Emerson's poetic method and what he really wished to say, and as he had done in his many reviews, Cabot modestly restated the true implications of Emerson's efforts, resolving them into a more complete statement of the truth: "What he wished to impress on the young men, if I understand him, was not the identity but the infinity of truth; the residuum of reality in all our facts, beyond what is formulated in our definitions. So that no definition is to be regarded as final, as if it described an ultimate essence whereby the thing is utterly discriminated from all things, but only as the recognition of certain of its relations; to which, of course, no limit can be set."[146]

As a result of his work on the problem, Cabot may have felt that the one project Emerson would wish him to undertake was to collect these thoughts into a coherent whole. Cabot's discussions in the *Memoir* had not allayed speculation concerning the existence of an unfinished system, a key to Emerson's thought, and the public should judge for themselves how well Emerson had accomplished his goal. However, whether Cabot was influenced by the Emersons, how long he worked on the project, and why the work apparently delayed publication of volume 12 for so long—these questions remain unanswered.

In composing this essay, Cabot used the synthetic method of the earlier lectures. Looking at the manuscripts today, one wonders why Cabot did not simply touch up a few of the more continuous lectures to illustrate Emerson's method on this topic rather than creating a composite. But, guided perhaps by Emerson's journal entry, Cabot tried instead to give a synthetic view of this subject, one that would reflect the continuous development of Emerson's thought beyond 1849 or 1858; this meant interpolating later "anecdotes" into the earlier structures, just as Emerson had done in his later use of this material. Moreover, the problem of "prior publication" continued to dominate editorial decisions, and large portions of the later material had already been cannibalized for "Poetry and Imagination," "Inspiration," and "Memory." In the prefatory note to the volume, Cabot briefly recapitulated his findings on this topic before stating that "The lecture which gives its name to the volume . . . was the first of the earliest course [here, in the 1903 edition, Edward Emerson interpolated "at Harvard University," but clearly Cabot meant the 1848 London lectures], and it seems to me to include all that distinctly belongs to the particular subject."[147]

Cabot's evasive explanation concealed a great editorial labor. The statement suggests that the printed lecture derived almost wholly from a single earlier lecture containing the germ of all of Emerson's later thoughts on the subject. Nothing could be further from the truth. Although the first four paragraphs of Cabot's "Natural History of Intellect" reproduce almost exactly the opening paragraphs of the 1849 "Powers and Laws of Thought," in constructing this essay Cabot drew from many of the forty-six packets of lecture material and a number of the late journals and notebooks—among them, EO ("Fate"), IT ("Intellect"), IL ("Intellect" or "Affirmative"), TO ("To Intellect the Guardian"), ML ("Moral Law"), and PH ("Philosophy")—and probably a number of other lectures and journals. The fifth paragraph came from the 1866 "Flux," and most of the seventh was from the 1858 "Identity." Though I have not identified sources for the next two paragraphs, Cabot took his tenth paragraph from the beginning of the first 1870 Harvard lecture, "Praise of Knowledge." After returning to the 1849 lecture for several pages, he began, with his twenty-first paragraph, to weave together passages from "Powers of Mind" (1858), "Praise of Knowledge" (both the 1870 and 1871 versions), and the 1870 "Identity," with excerpts from "Self-Possession" (1858), "Seven

Metres of Intellect" (1866), "Instinct, Perception, Talent" (1866), "Intellect Pure" (1866), and "The Transcendency of Physics" (1870). The forty-seventh paragraph came from an 1836 lecture, "The Humanity of Science."

This analysis covers only a third of Cabot's essay, but it is representative of his method throughout. In the next seven pages, he relied heavily on the 1848–49 "Relation of Intellect to Natural Science," weaving into it passages from the 1858 and 1870 "Identity" lectures and the 1858 "Powers of Mind." As with the synthetic lectures and essays he had prepared for Emerson during his lifetime, for the most part Cabot simply rearranged Emerson's scattered thoughts, usually retaining paragraph-sized blocks of material, but selecting carefully and pruning examples, quotations, and amplifications.

Although the juxtaposition of dislocated passages frequently produces a jarring effect, the pastiche is, as Cabot claimed, a fair sample of what Emerson had to say on this subject. In one instance, however, Cabot may have distorted Emerson's meaning. Early in the essay, Cabot pieced together a discussion of method, taken largely from the introductory lecture for the 1870 course. Here Emerson confesses to a "little distrust" of the metaphysician's attempt to construct a complete system, defines the new metaphysics, and suggests that philosophy will one day be "taught by poets." In "Poetry and Imagination," Emerson had said, "The metaphysician, the poet, only sees each animal form as an inevitable step in the path of the creating mind," clearly suggesting an equality between the two species of thinker.[148] But "Powers and Laws of Thought" stresses the antagonism between these two roles in a way that may reflect Cabot's bias more than Emerson's. From Journal ST Cabot drew a passage that Emerson had labeled "*Objection to Metaphysics*," but which does not seem to have been used in the lectures: "The poet sees wholes and avoids analysis; the metaphysician, dealing as it were with the mathematics of the mind, puts himself out of the way of the inspiration."[149] In the next paragraph Cabot continued the invidious contrast. The first statement, "Philosophy is still rude and elementary. It will one day be taught by poets," appears in both the 1866 "Seven Metres of Intellect" and the 1869–70 Notebook PH. But in both places Emerson made no comparison with the metaphysician. Instead, he elaborated on the office of the poet, calling for a "Homer of our thoughts." For his neat juxtaposition of the offices of poet and philosopher, Cabot had to rely on a quotation that Emerson had copied into PH: "Poets must believe, not like philosophers, [who] have, after some struggle, a preponderance of reasons for believing." But Emerson's own position on this subject seems closer to other statements in this same notebook: "Metaphysics, the true Science of the mind, is reckoned arid. There can be no greater mistake." And again, "Analysis, too, is legitimate to a poetic soul."[150]

The resulting discussion of intellect, as the reviewer for the *Critic* was quick to point out, was "fragmentary in construction, like an aggregation of detached passages from a note-book."[151] The essay begins well, establishing clearly the significance of Emerson's title and its relationship to philosophy, and his aim and method in investigating the laws of intellect. At the end of this lengthy showcase of brilliant passages, Cabot positioned the three heads Emerson had established for his 1848 course. However, about midway through the printed essay, the power of these heads to hold the material in line has been exhausted, and the essay seems to lurch into the third topic six pages before the appearance of Roman numeral III. These pages derive mainly from the 1866 "Laws of Mind," "Seven Metres of Intellect," and "Instinct, Perception, Talent," and the 1858 "Self-Possession," with a bit of the 1871 "Will" thrown in.

Beginning with the third subdivision on page 33 of the 1903 edition, the essay returns to the track for a while, with a long discussion of instinct and inspiration, drawn largely from the 1848 "Tendencies and Duties," 1866 "Instinct, Perception, Talent," and 1870–71 "Instinct. Perception." Following discussions of perception and the conduct of the intellect, the essay takes a desultory turn, glancing at talent, genius, and power. Four pages from the end, Cabot appears to move into the conclusion, announcing two rules, "obey your genius" and "embrace the affirmative." A few paragraphs later, he used a passage from the 1870 "Laws of Mind—Metres of Mind" that asserted "the height of culture . . . consists in the identification of the . . . biographical Ego" with the "grand spiritual Ego." The final paragraph, from the notebook EO, puts an Hegelian bandage on the fragments by asserting, "We wish to sum up the conflicting impressions by saying that all point at last to a unity which inspires all. Our poetry, our religion are its skirts and penumbrae."[152]

Cabot believed that Emerson's effort to systematize his thought represented no advance on his usual poetic method. It was an evolutionary dead-end. "He had always been writing anecdotes of the spirit," according to Cabot, who felt those that ended up in the series on the "Natural History of Intellect" differed little from the usual impressions that Emerson registered and recorded.

Cabot's work for Emerson was his "*opus, magnum* or not." In performing his many roles he remained faithful to one central principle: to do what Emerson would like. Each man writes his own biography, Emerson had said, and the world knows only what he tells of himself. It was Cabot's responsibility to decide what Emerson had chosen to tell his public and to transmit that legacy to his heirs, to shape the lengthening shadow of the man. In his editorial work as well as in the *Memoir*, Cabot presented the evidence: the words and thoughts, public and private, of a man who wished always to remain alive to new impressions and thus hesitated to arrive at a conclusion, yet who felt the need of a complete artist to achieve full expression of his thoughts. This conflict formed the drama of his artistic life. For both Cabot and Emerson, the proper vehicle for these ideas was an open form in which the conflicting impressions could be suspended without reconciliation; both finally believed they could not be stated as propositions but must be realized in a life.

Cabot's work for Emerson put the final stamp on the self-image Emerson had been creating for many years. Cabot reassured the faithful that Emerson had neither abandoned his youthful vision nor attempted to smash idols. He created a broad context in which to understand Emerson's role as a teacher, a man of profound vision, a "committed conscience," as John Jay Chapman called him, in the best tradition of American teachers and preachers. Cabot's synthetic essays and discussions and his genetic approach all contributed to the impression of a "static" Emerson whose thought had undergone little change, and his portrait of a "pure spirit" perpetuated the identification of the writer with the man. The selection made by Cabot from the manuscripts and correspondence remained the only source for these materials until the journals were printed in 1909–14, followed by the letters in 1939; and his *Memoir* served as the source for all the succeeding biographies until Oscar W. Firkins' *Ralph Waldo Emerson* in 1915. Cabot's work ushered Emerson into the twentieth century and shaped our perception of Emerson and our response in subtle but significant ways.

NOTES

1. "Statement of Editorial Principles," *The Collected Works of Ralph Waldo Emerson*, ed. Joseph Slater et al., 2 vols. to date (Cambridge: Harvard University Press, 1971–   ), vol. 2, *Essays: First Series* (1979), ed. Alfred R. Ferguson, p. xxxiv.
The following intials are used for names cited frequently in the notes in this article:

EDC	Elizabeth Dwight Cabot (Mrs. J. Elliot Cabot)
EEF	Edith Emerson Forbes
ETE	Ellen Tucker Emerson
EWE	Edward Waldo Emerson
JEC	James Elliot Cabot
RWE	Ralph Waldo Emerson

2. Ralph L. Rusk, *The Life of Ralph Waldo Emerson* (New York: Scribners, 1949), p. 505 (hereafter cited as *Life*); ETE to EEF, 8 September 1875, MH; EWE, *The Early Years of the Saturday Club 1855–1876* (Boston: Houghton Mifflin, 1918), p. 266.

I wish to thank William H. Bond, Rodney Dennis, and the staff of the Houghton Library for making the materials in the collection of the Ralph Waldo Emerson Memorial Association available to me. All quotations from these manuscripts are by permission of the Ralph Waldo Emerson Memorial Association and the Houghton Library of Harvard University.

I am also grateful to Mrs. Edith Emerson Webster Gregg and Professor Eleanor M. Tilton, who kindly made it possible for me to use manuscript materials and notes in their possession. Quotations from these materials are by permission of Mrs. Gregg and Professor Tilton.

3. Nancy Craig Simmons, "The 'Autobiographical Sketch' of James Elliot Cabot," *Harvard Library Bulletin*, 30 (April 1982): 151.

4. Quoted by EWE, *Complete Works of Ralph Waldo Emerson*, 12 vols. (Boston: Houghton Mifflin, 1903–1904), 4:361; hereafter cited as *CW*; see RWE to Thoreau, Concord, 8 September 1843, "The Emerson-Thoreau Correspondence," *Atlantic Monthly Magazine*, 69 (May 1892): 592–93.

5. RWE will, 14 April 1876 (copy), Hugh Cabot Collection, A-99, MCR-S. I wish to thank the staff of the Schlesinger Library of Radcliffe College for making these materials available to me; all citations from these manuscripts are by permission of the Schlesinger Library.

6. ETE to EEF, 17 January 1880, MH.

7. *A Memoir of Ralph Waldo Emerson*, 2 vols. (Boston: Houghton, Mifflin, 1887), 2:569; hereafter cited as *Memoir*.

8. EWE, "Preface," *CW*, 1:v.

9. JEC to Eliza Follen, Göttingen, 2 January 1843, MCR-S.

10. *The Letters of Ralph Waldo Emerson*, ed. Ralph L. Rusk, 6 vols. (New York: Columbia University Press, 1939), 3:286; hereafter cited as *Letters*.

11. *Letters*, 5:28.

12. [J. B. Holland], "Emerson's *Letters and Social Aims*," *Scribner's Monthly Magazine*, 11 (April 1876): 896.

13. EWE, "Preface," *CW*, 8:vii; JEC, "Preface to the First Edition," *CW*, 8:ix–xiii *passim*.

14. ETE to JEC, Concord, 17 July 1883, Collection of Mrs. Edith Emerson Webster Gregg.

15. *Letters*, 6:134.

16. *Letters*, 6:124.

17. *Letters*, 6:180–81, 185.

18. ETE to JEC, Concord, 17 July 1883, Collection of Mrs. Gregg.

19. See *Life*, pp. 455–56; "Memory," *CW*, 12:90; *Memoir*, 2:655.

20. *Letters*, 6:101.

21. *Memoir*, 2:633; *The Correspondence of Emerson and Carlyle*, ed. Joseph Slater (New York: Columbia University Press, 1964), pp. 570, 578 (hereafter cited as *CEC*).

22. Samuel Longfellow, *The Life of Henry Wadsworth Longfellow, with Extracts from His Journals*, 2 vols. (Boston: Ticknor, 1886), 2:243.

23. Information about the condition and contents of Emerson's lecture manuscripts derives from my examination of these materials in the collection of the Ralph Waldo Emerson Memorial Association, MH.

24. ETE to EEF, Waterford, Maine, 22 August 1872 (notes in possession of Professor Eleanor M. Tilton).

25. EDC to ETE, Brookline, [?] 1872, MCR–S; ETE to EEF, Concord, 30 August 1872, MH; ETE to EWE, Naushon, 11 and 17 August 1874, MH; ETE to Haven Emerson, Concord, 2 September 1874, MH.

26. ETE to EEF, Concord, 16 and 25 August 1875, MH.

27. ETE to EEF, [?] August 1875, MH; JEC to EDC, Concord, 27 and 28 September 1875, MCR–S.

28. JEC to RWE, Brookline, 16 December 1875, MH; EWE, "Preface," *CW*, 8:viii.

29. JEC to ETE, Brookline, 18 December 1875, MH.

30. Lathrop, "Recent Literature," *Atlantic Monthly Magazine*, 38 (August 1876): 240–41; ETE to EDC, Concord, 20 August 1876, MCR–S.

31. Holland, "Emerson's *Letters and Social Aims*," 896; [Review of *Letters and Social Aims*], *International Review*, 3 (March 1876): 250; cf. *American Catholic Quarterly Review*, 2 (January 1877): 175–77, and *Dublin Review*, 27 (July 1876): 253–54.

32. ETE to JEC, Concord, 17 July 1883, Collection of Mrs. Gregg.

33. EWE, "Preface," *CW*, 8:v, vii.

34. *Memoir*, 2:669; JEC, "Preface to the First Edition," *CW*, 8:xiii.

35. Lists in Cabot's working papers, MH. All information about these papers derives from my examination of the materials in the Houghton Library. Because Emerson read two different lectures under the title "Eloquence" (first delivered in 1847 and 1867) and printed the first in *Society and Solitude* in 1870, it is unclear which "Eloquence" is referred to in these lists.

36. "Poetry and Imagination. Copy for Letters and Social Aims (1873–1876)," MH bMS Am 1280.214(3), p. 41; cf. pp. 43 (a cancelled draft), 48, and 68; "Poetry and Imagination," *CW*, 8:3–75.

37. JEC to ETE, with notations by ETE, Beverly Farms, 10 August 1883, MH.

38. *Uncollected Lectures*, ed. Clarence Gohdes (New York: William Edwin Rudge, 1932), pp. 17–22, 31–38.

39. *Uncollected Lectures*, pp. 24–29; EWE, "Notes," *CW*, 8:390.

40. JEC to ETE, Beverly Farms, 10 August 1883, MH; "VI. Greatness. (16 November 1868)," "Greatness—read at Mr. Sargent's house. 28 May 1868," manuscript lectures, MH bMS Am 1280.210(11, 12); EWE, "Notes," *CW*, 8:429, 430.

41. See William Charvat, *Emerson's American Lecture Engagements: A Chronological List* (New York: New York Public Library, 1961), pp. 43–44.

42. Charvat, *Emerson's Lectures*, p. 9.

43. EWE, "Notes," *CW*, 8:434; ETE to EEF, Cambridge, 9 December [1875?] (notes in possession of Professor Tilton).

44. JEC, "Preface to the First Edition," *CW*, 8:xi–xii; *Memoir*, 2:669–70.

45. ETE to Lidian Emerson, Naushon, 8 and 11 August 1876, MH; ETE to EWE, Naushon, 16 August 1876, MH.

46. EWE, "Notes," *CW*, 10:563; "Discourse read before the Philomathesian Society of Middlebury College in Vermont, 22 July, 1845," "Oration addressed to the Senior Class of the University of Virginia, 28 June, 1876," manuscript lectures, MH bMS Am 1280.199(9) and 214(10); ETE to EEF, 8 May and 2 June 1876, Collection of Mrs. Gregg.

47. JEC, "Note," *CW*, 10:v.

48. *Memoir*, 2:677.

49. ETE to EEF, Concord, 16 and 18 May 1878, MH.

50. JEC to ETE, Beverly Farms, 10 August 1883, MH.

51. In compiling this list, I have drawn particularly on Charvat's *Emerson's Lectures* and Emerson family correspondence, supplemented from JEC's bluebook list titled "Lectures 1860–so" (MH) and "Concord School of Philosophy," *Journal of Speculative Philosophy*, 14 (January, April 1880): 138, 253. Where these sources contradict each other, I have chosen the dates and titles suggested by the correspondence. Charvat lists "Boston" as the subject of Emerson's 1876 Concord Lyceum lecture (on 1 March) and "Natural Forces" for 1877 (on 14 February). These titles and dates appear also in the Concord Lyceum lecture schedule printed in *The Massachusetts Lyceum During the American Renaissance*, ed. Kenneth Walter Cameron (Hartford, Conn.: Transcendental Books, 1969), pp. 184–85. However, ETE to Ellen Davidson, 17 February 1877, clearly states that Emerson read "Boston" the previous Wednesday, which would have been 14 February (Collection of Mrs. Gregg). Perhaps Emerson read "Natural Forces" in 1876. Charvat and Cameron also both list "Fortune of the Republic" as Emerson's Concord Lyceum lecture for 1878 (6 February), whereas Ellen's correspondence mentions sev-

eral times the work on "Education," read 8 February 1878. See ETE to EEF, Concord, 4, 6, and 8 February 1878, MH.

52. ETE to JEC, Concord, 7 August 1883, Collection of Mrs. Gregg; "Boston. 15 May 1861," "Boston. (1861–1877)," and "Boston. (Miscellanies)," manuscript lectures, MH bMS Am 1280.206(7–9); RWE, "Oration," *The New England Society Orations*, ed. Cephas Brainerd and Eveline Warner Brainerd, 2 vols. (New York: Century, 1901), 2:373–93; "Boston," *Atlantic Monthly Magazine*, 69 (January 1892): 26–35.

53. EWE, "Notes," *CW*, 10:572–73; Charvat, *Emerson's Lectures*, p. 48; JEC to ETE, Beverly Farms, 10 August 1883, MH; "The Preacher," manuscript lecture, MH bMS Am 1280.214(19).

54. JEC to ETE, Brookline, 8 January 1877, MH.

55. ETE to Miss Dabney, Naushon, 15 August 1877; ETE to Lidian Emerson, Naushon, 16 August 1877; ETE to Haven Emerson, Naushon, 17 August 1877, MH; *Letters*, 6:307.

56. EWE to JEC, Concord, 10 November 1877 (with draft manuscript), MH; ETE to EEF, Waterford, Maine, 22 August 1872, mentions that RWE, worried about the future of his papers, fears Conway and Sanborn (notes in possession of Professor Tilton). In ETE to EEF, Cambridge, 9 December [1875?], Ellen refers to C. E. Norton's "disappointment . . . about Mr. Cabot," suggesting that Norton had hoped to perform the role played by Cabot (notes in possession of Professor Tilton); the family's feelings about Conway are suggested in JEC to ETE, Brookline, 28 May 1887, MH.

57. JEC to EWE, Brookline, 13 November 1877, MH.

58. ETE to EEF, Concord, 30 January 1878, MH; compare, however, Ellen's later recollection that the printed "Perpetual Forces" was nearly in its "original form," not a composite of the same order as "Aristocracy," "Education," or "The Preacher" (ETE to JEC, Concord, 7 August 1883, Collection of Mrs. Gregg).

59. ETE to EEF, Concord, 31 January 1878, MH; "The Sovereignty of Ethics," manuscript lecture, MH bMS Am 1280.214(14); see also *The Early Lectures of Ralph Waldo Emerson*, ed. Stephen E. Whicher, Robert E. Spiller, and Wallace E. Williams, 3 vols. (Cambridge: Harvard University Press, 1959–72), 3:366–67; hereafter cited as *EL*.

60. ETE to EEF, Concord, 1 February and 31 January 1878, MH.

61. ETE to EEF, Concord, 4, 6, and 8 February, 1878, MH.

62. ETE to Elizabeth Hoar, Concord, 6 April 1878, MH.

63. [Review of *Fortune of the Republic*], *Scribner's Monthly Magazine*, 16 (October 1878): 902–903.

64. ETE to EEF, Concord, 28 May, 11 November 1878, MH; see *Letters*, 6:318–19; "General Introduction," *The Hundred Greatest Men* (London: Sampson Low, Marston, Searle, and Rivington, 1879), pp. i–iii; ETE to EEF, 9 and 10 April 1879, MH.

65. EWE, "Notes," *CW*, 10:519–20.

66. Charvat, *Emerson's Lectures*, p. 48.

67. ETE to JEC, Concord, [?] August 1883, Collection of Mrs. Gregg; ETE to EEF, Concord, December 1881, MH.

68. EWE to JEC, Concord, 17 October 1886, MH; EDC to Mrs. Walter C. Cabot, Brookline, 3 May 1882, MCR–S.

69. Kenneth Walter Cameron, *The Transcendentalists and Minerva*, 3 vols. (Hartford, Conn.: Transcendental Books, 1958), 3:862; "Montaigne; or, The Skeptic," *CW*, 4:154–55, 162.

70. ETE to EEF, 17 January 1880, MH.

71. JEC, "Preface to the First Edition," *CW*, 8:xii; "Note," *CW*, 10:v; "Autobiographical Sketch," p. 151; *CW*, 8:xiii.

72. *Memoir*, 2:670.

73. EWE, "Notes," *CW*, 8:373, 357, 434, 366; 10:549.

74. "Memory," manuscript lectures, MH bMS Am 1280.203(8) and 212(5,6); transcription in several hands, MH bMS Am 1280.203(9).

75. "Memory," *CW*, 12:95.

76. *Letters*, 2:121.

77. *Memoir*, 2:569.

78. JEC, [Review of Three Histories of Modern Philosophy], *Massachusetts Quarterly Review*, 1 (June 1848): 378–79; [Review of J. G. Fichte, *The Science of Knowledge*, trans. A. E. Kroeger], *North American Review*, 106 (April 1868): 741.

79. JEC, [Review of *The Logic of Hegel*, trans. William Wallace], *North American Review*, 119 (October 1874): 435.

80. JEC, "On the Relation of Art to Nature," *Atlantic Monthly Magazine*, 13 (March 1864): 327.

81. "Emerson the Lecturer," *The Complete Writings of James Russell Lowell*, 16 vols. (Boston: Houghton, Mifflin, 1904), vol. 2, *My Study Windows*, p. 396; *CEC*, p. 185.

82. "The Poet," *CW*, 3:9–10.

83. "Mental Philosophy III. Powers of the Mind (1858)" and "Introduction: Praise of Knowledge (1870)," manuscript lectures, MH bMS Am 1280.203(6) and 212(1).

84. "The Humanity of Science," *EL*, 2:25.

85. "Powers and Laws of Thought," *CW*, 12:20; JEC, [Review of John Fiske, *Outlines of Cosmic Philosophy, Based on the Doctrine of Evolution, with Criticisms on the Positive Philosophy*], *North American Review*, 120 (January 1875): 201.

86. *Memoir*, 2:627.

87. EDC to ETE, Brookline, 19 October [1875?] (notes in possession of Professor Tilton).

88. EDC to Mrs. Walter C. Cabot, Brookline, 3 May 1882, MCR-S.

89. JEC to EDC, Brookline, 5 June 1882, MCR-S.

90. JEC to EWE, Beverly Farms, 10 July 1882, MH; EEF to JEC [unsigned draft, ca. 1882], MH; JEC to ETE, Beverly Farms, 15 June and 15 July 1882, MH; JEC to EDC, 16 and 23 July, 20 August 1882, MCR-S.

91. JEC to EDC, Beverly Farms, 30 July 1882, MCR-S; JEC to ETE, Beverly Farms, 28 August 1882, MH.

92. JEC to EDC, 10 September 1882, MCR-S; JEC working papers, MH.

93. *Memoir*, 1:iii–iv.

94. Houghton, Mifflin to W. H. Forbes, 7 September 1882, Houghton, Mifflin Letter Books, 27 May–29 December 1882, MH.

95. Specimen page for "Announcement of new 'Edition de Luxe,'" enclosure in F. J. Garrison to EWE, 13 January 1883, MH. The last phrase, the reference to Edward Emerson, is struck through in ink, presumably by Cabot.

96. ETE to EEF, 10 December 1882, 13 and 23 June 1883, MH; ETE to JEC, Concord, 13 and 21 April, and [27?] June 1883, Collection of Mrs. Gregg; ETE to EEF, 22 May 1883, Collection of Mrs. Gregg.

97. EWE to JEC, Concord, 1 April 1883; Lakewood, 22 April 1883; Delaware Water Gap, Penn., 1 and 4 May 1883; Concord, 31 May 1883, MH.

98. EWE to JEC, Concord, 15 June 1883; Richmond, 15, 30, 25, 31 July, and 11 August 1883, MH.

99. JEC to ETE, Beverly Farms, 17 July 1882, MH.

100. EWE to JEC, Delaware Water Gap, Penn., [1] May 1883; Richmond, 8, 14, and 15 July 1883, MH; ETE to JEC, Concord, 12 July 1883, Collection of Mrs. Gregg.

101. EWE to JEC, 15 June 1883, MH; F. J. Garrison to H. O. Houghton, 20 June 1883, Houghton, Mifflin Letter Books, 2 January 1883–3 January 1884, MH.

102. JEC to ETE, Beverly Farms, 10 August 1883, MH.

103. JEC working papers, large binder 2, MH; ETE to JEC, Concord, 7 August 1883, Collection of Mrs. Gregg.

104. Garrison to Houghton, [Boston], 29 May 1883; Houghton to T. Leverett, 14 September 1883, Houghton, Mifflin Letter Books, 2 January 1883–3 January 1884; also enclosed in EWE to JEC, Concord, 19 September 1883, MH.

105. T. L[everett]. to EWE, 18 September 1883; EWE to JEC, Concord, 19 September 1883, MH.

106. EWE to JEC, Concord, 20 September 1883, MH.

107. EWE to JEC, Concord, 20 September 1883, Houghton to EWE, 27 September 1883, Houghton, Mifflin Letter Books; A. D. H. to JEC, 28 September, 1883, MH.

108. A. D. H. to JEC, 28 September 1883, MH; JEC, "Note," *CW*, 10:v.

109. EWE to JEC, Concord, 20 September 1883; Boston, 3 October 1883, MH.

110. Garrison to EWE, 19 October 1883, with note from EWE to JEC, MH.

111. EWE to JEC, Concord, 27 January 1883, MH.

112. See "Prefatory Note," *CW*, 1:v–vi. JEC's original preface can be reconstructed by deleting the interpolations suggested by EWE's subsequent correspondence; EWE to JEC, Concord, 30 January 1883, MH.

113. EWE to JEC, Concord, 1 April 1883; Lakewood, 22 April 1883, MH.

114. EWE to JEC, Concord, 5 and 30 June 1883, MH.

115. EWE to JEC, Richmond, 30 July 1883, MH; JEC, "Preface to the First Edition," *CW*, 8:x.

116. EWE to JEC, Richmond, 31 July 1883, MH.

117. ETE to JEC, Concord, Saturday [August 1883], 7 and 1 August 1883, Collection of Mrs. Gregg.

118. ETE to EEF, 7 and 14 August 1883, MH.

119. JEC, "Prefatory Note," *The Complete Works of Ralph Waldo Emerson*, Riverside Edition, 11 vols. (Boston: Houghton, Mifflin, 1883–84), 9:v-vi; JEC to EWE, Beverly Farms, 23 August 1883; EWE to JEC, Concord, 8 September 1883, MH.

120. Garrison to Houghton, 5 June 1883, Houghton, Mifflin Letter Books, MH; A. D. H. to JEC, Boston, 28 September 1883; EWE to JEC, Concord, 1, 3, 8, 18, and 25 October 1883; Boston, 3 October and 2 November 1883; Garrison to JEC, Boston, 5 October 1883; Leverett to EWE, 1 November 1883, MH.

121. "Notes," *Nation*, 37 (25 October 1883): 352–53; JEC, "The New Edition of Emerson's Works," *Nation*, 37 (8 November 1883): 391.

122. [Review of *The Works of Ralph Waldo Emerson* with an Introduction by John Morley, and *The Works of Ralph Waldo Emerson*, Riverside Edition], *Athenæum*, no. 2941 (8 March 1884): 306–307; Richard Holt Hutton, "Emerson as Oracle," *Spectator*, 2 February 1884; rpt. in *Criticisms on Contemporary Thought and Thinkers, Selected from the Spectator*, 2 vols. (London: Macmillan, 1894), 1:53–58.

123. Edward Rowland Sill, "The Prose and Verse of Emerson," *Overland Monthly*, n.s. 4 (October 1884): 440.

124. "Literature. A New Book by Emerson: *The Natural History of Intellect, and Other Papers*," *Critic* [New York], n.s. 21 (30 December 1893): 421; "Emerson's Last Volume," *Poet-Lore*, 6, no. 2 (1894): 93; "American Literature," *Athenæum*, no. 3519 (6 April 1895): 439.

125. Carpenter, *Emerson Handbook* (New York: Hendricks House, 1953), p. 69.

126. JEC to ETE, Brookline, 18 November 1887; JEC to EWE, Brookline, 18 November 1887, MH.

127. Houghton, Mifflin to EWE, 22 November 1890, Houghton, Mifflin Letter Books, 18 October 1890–8 June 1891, MH fMS Am 1185.3(3); ETE to EEF, Concord, 12 February 1890, MH; Richard Clarke Cabot to JEC, Brookline, [?] 1890, MCR-S.

128. Horace E. Scudder to EWE, Chocana, N.H., 27 July 1891; [Boston], 9 and 14 October

1891, Houghton, Mifflin Letter Books, 8 June 1891–13 February 1892, MH fMS Am 1185.3(4); Scudder to JEC, 15 October 1891, 6 February 1892, Letter Books, 8 June 1891–13 February 1892, MH fMS Am 1185.3(4).

129. JEC working papers, large binder 2, MH.

130. *The Letters of Bronson Alcott*, ed. Richard L. Herrnstadt (Ames: Iowa State University Press, 1969), p. 166.

131. Holland, "Emerson's *Letters and Social Aims*," 896.

132. Sanborn, "The Homes and Haunts of Emerson," *Scribner's Monthly Magazine*, 18 (February 1879): 509.

133. *CEC*, p. 570.

134. Annie Fields, "Mr. Emerson in the Lecture Room," *Atlantic Monthly Magazine*, 51 (June 1883): 818–32.

135. *Memoir*, 1:101, 153; 2:391, 397, 634–35.

136. Quoted in *Memoir*, 1:161; "Philosophy of the People I: Seven Metres of Intellect (1866)," manuscript lecture, MH bMS Am 1280.209(1).

137. *Memoir*, 1:199; cf. *The Journals and Miscellaneous Notebooks of Ralph Waldo Emerson*, ed. William H. Gilman, Ralph H. Orth, et al., 16 vols. (Cambridge: Harvard University Press, 1960–1982), 4:79 (hereafter cited as *JMN*).

138. *Memoir*, 1:227; cf. *EL*, 1:79.

139. *Memoir*, 1:227.

140. *Memoir*, 1:246–50, *passim*; cf. *JMN*, 5:270–76; *Memoir*, 1:336, 339.

141. *Memoir*, 2:558.

142. *Memoir*, 2:557.

143. *Memoir*, 2:633, 634.

144. *Memoir*, 2:640.

145. *Memoir*, 2:560, 637.

146. *Memoir*, 2:642–43.

147. EWE, "Notes," *CW*, 12:421.

148. "Powers and Laws of Thought," *CW*, 12:12, 14; "Poetry and Imagination," *CW*, 8:10.

149. "Powers and Laws of Thought," *CW*, 12:14; cf. *JMN*, 16:210.

150. Notebook PH, MH bMS Am 1280 H (86).

151. "Literature. A New Book by Emerson," 422.

152. "Powers and Laws of Thought," *CW*, 12:64.

BOOKS RECEIVED

Caroline Bokinsky

ALLEN, GAY WILSON. *Waldo Emerson: A Biography.* New York: Viking Press, [1981]. [xxvi], 751 pp.: front., illus.; 23 cm. Appendixes ("Genealogy," "Sources of Illustrations"): pp. 673–675; index. LC 81–65275. ISBN 0–670–74866–8. $25.00.

Allen's biography emphasizes a more personal side of Emerson than previous biographies and includes biographical interpretations of his works as well as an overview of the social and intellectual background of America in the nineteenth century.

BORST, RAYMOND R. *Henry David Thoreau: A Descriptive Bibliography.* [Pittsburgh]: University of Pittsburgh Press, 1982. xvi, 232 pp.: front., illus., facsims.; 24 cm. (Pittsburgh Series in Bibliography.) Appendixes ("Compiler's Notes," "Principal Works About Thoreau"): pp. 217–218; index. LC 81–50638. ISBN 0–8229–3445–0. $30.00.

Each of the five sections describes in chronological order of appearance: "Separate Publications"; "Collected Works" through 1906 published by Houghton, Mifflin, as well as the *Princeton Edition*; "First-Appearance Contributions to Books and Pamphlets"; "First-Appearance Contributions to Magazines and Newspapers"; "all one-volume collections composed of various writings from Thoreau's works." Each section is amply illustrated with facsimiles of title pages, wrappers, and dust-jackets.

BOSWELL, JEANETTA. *Nathaniel Hawthorne and the Critics: A Checklist of Criticism, 1900–1978.* Metuchen, N.J., and London: Scarecrow Press, 1982. x, 273 pp.; 22 cm. (The Scarecrow Author Bibliographies, No. 57.) Indexes. LC 81–9398. ISBN 0–8108–1471–4. $17.50.

An unannotated list of 2,816 articles, books, and essays, in alphabetical order by critic.

BRIDGMAN, RICHARD. *Dark Thoreau.* Lincoln and London: University of Nebraska Press, [1982]. xvi, 306 pp.: front.; 22 cm. LC 81–4788. ISBN 0–8032–1167–8. $17.50.

By analyzing the incoherence, opacity, and confusion in Thoreau's writing—marked by violent imagery and "ambiguous syntax, vague pronoun references, and a shifting subject and tone"—Bridgman argues that these are manifest features of a man under psychological strain who has suppressed anxiety, resentment, pessimism, and hostility.

BRYANT, WILLIAM CULLEN. *The Letters of William Cullen Bryant: Volume III 1849–1857.* Edited by William Cullen Bryant II and Thomas G. Voss. New York: Fordham University Press, 1981. [viii], 564 pp.: front., illus.; 23 cm. (The Letters of William Cullen Bryant.) Appendix ("Abbreviations and Short Titles"): pp. 549–550; indexes. LC 74–27169. ISBN 0–8232–0993–8. $35.00.

Collects 340 letters by Bryant, the majority of which are to his wife and family, and to the *Evening Post*, where they appeared in the editorial columns.

CAMERON, SHARON. *The Corporeal Self: Allegories of the Body in Melville and Hawthorne.* Baltimore and London: Johns Hopkins University Press, [1981]. [x], 166 pp.; 23 cm. LC 81–47602. ISBN 0–8018–2643–8. $12.95.

Cameron argues that "American novels do not tell stories as much as offer paradigms for the problem of relationship—specifically for the relationship between identity and epistemology, between what a self is and what it is able to know." Using this premise, she shows how in *Moby-Dick*, Melville oscillates between the dual tension of self-embodiment as a separate entity and self-disembodiment when fused with the world's body or another character; in his tales, Hawthorne's characters, suffering from a split within the body, seek allegorical correspondences between parts of the body and the external world.

COOPER, JAMES FENIMORE. *Gleanings in Europe: England.* Historical Introduction and Explanatory Notes by Donald A. Ringe and Kenneth W. Staggs. Text Established by James P. Elliott, Kenneth W. Staggs and R. D. Madison. Albany: State University of New York Press, [1982]. xl, 375 pp.: facsims., illus.; 23 cm. (The Writings of James Fenimore Cooper.) Appendixes ("Explanatory Notes," "Appendix A: Bentley's Analytical Table of Contents," "Textual Commentary," "Textual Notes," "Emendations," "Word-Division"): pp. 309–360; index. LC 80–16993. ISBN 0–87395–367–3: cloth, $29.50; ISBN 0–87395–459–9: paper, $9.95.

A CSE-edition of Cooper's fourth book in his travel series. Basis for the copy-text, with the exception of one leaf of manuscript, is the first American edition published in two volumes in 1837.

COOPER, JAMES FENIMORE. *Wyandotté, or the Hutted Knoll. A Tale.* Edited, with an Historical Introduction, by Thomas and Marianne Philbrick. Albany: State University of New York Press, [1982]. [xxxiv], 434 pp.: illus.; 23 cm. (The Writings of James Fenimore Cooper.) Appendixes ("Explanatory Notes," "Textual Commentary," "Note on the Manuscript," "Textual Notes," "Emendations," "Rejected Readings," "Word-Division"): pp. 377–434. LC 81–1132. ISBN 0–87395–414–9: cloth, $29.50; ISBN 0–87395–469–6: paper, $9.95.

A CSE-edition of Cooper's novel, first published in 1843, using Cooper's manuscript as copy-text.

CORSE, LARRY B., and SANDRA CORSE, compilers. *Articles on American and British Literature: An Index to Selected Periodicals, 1950–1977.* Athens: Ohio University Press, Swallow Press, [1981]. xii, 413 pp.; 28 cm. LC 81–4010. ISBN 0–8040–0408–0. $30.00.
An unannotated bibliography indexing 48 periodicals and journals which survey all periods of American and British literature, intended for "undergraduate students and others for whom completeness is not a primary concern."

COWAN, BAINARD. *Exiled Waters: Moby-Dick and the Crisis of Allegory.* Baton Rouge: Louisiana State University Press, [1982]. xii, 194 pp.; 23 cm. Bibliography: pp. 183–191; index. LC 81–19354. ISBN 0–8071–1002–7. $18.50.
The greatest moment of American allegory surfaced at the time of Melville in his fictional allegory, *Moby-Dick*, with the contradiction between the text and its interpretation. "Melville's great epic moves between two focal points of Romantic allegory, the exilic allegory of the city and the quest allegory of nature."

CUMBLER, JOHN TAYLOR. *A Moral Response to Industrialism: The Lectures of Reverend Cook in Lynn, Massachusetts.* Albany: State University of New York Press, [1982]. [viii], 160 pp.; 23 cm. (SUNY Series on American Social History.) Appendix ("Textile Towns"): pp. 146–148; "Selective Bibliography": pp. 153–154; index. LC 81–9338. ISBN 0–87395–558–7: cloth, $30.50; ISBN 0–87395–559–5: paper, $9.95.
Reprints Joseph Cook's Music Hall Lectures in 1871, a conservative call for social reform based on moral issues during the heyday of the industrial revolution in a textile manufacturing town. Because the volatility of the lectures stirred up controversy and instigated public response, letters from factory owners, male and female factory workers, clergymen, and townspeople are also printed.

DARRAH, WILLIAM C. *Cartes de Visite in Nineteenth Century Photography.* Gettysburg, Penna.: W. C. Darrah, Publisher, [1981]. [vi], 221 pp.: photos., facsims.; 28 cm. Bibliography: pp. 201–202; indexes. LC 81–69489. ISBN 0–913116–05–X. $27.00.
A comprehensive survey of cartes de visite, portrait photographs, or "album" photographs, popular between 1857 and 1900. Darrah explains that, noted for their small size, their diversity, and their low cost for reproducing, the cartes de visite democratized photography by allowing more people to be photographed and, later, by making photographs of travel scenes and artwork available to all people.

DIEHL, JOANNE FEIT. *Dickinson and the Romantic Imagination.* Princeton: Princeton University Press, [1981]. [x], 205 pp.; 22 cm. "Selected Bibliography": pp. 187–195; indexes. LC 81–47121. ISBN 0–691–06478–4. $16.50
Dickinson is placed among the Romantics, represented by Wordsworth, Keats,

Shelley, and Emerson, because "her preoccupations—the self's relation to nature, the power of the imagination as it confronts death, a heroic questing that leads to a trial of the limits of poetic power—are the primary concerns of Romanticism as well." She diverges from the tradition, as a self-conscious female heir to a patriarchal hierarchy that relies on a female muse for poetic inspiration, by asserting independence from the poet/muse relationship.

Directory of American Studies Resources in Europe. Brussels: Center for American Studies, 1982. [xii], 85 pp.; 21 cm. Paper, 200 Belgian Francs.
This listing of 200 libraries in Western Europe with holdings in American studies includes information on the nature of the holdings, address, phone numbers, names of contact persons, and opening hours of the institution.

EMERSON, RALPH WALDO. *Emerson in His Journals.* Edited by Joel Porte. Cambridge, Mass. and London: Belknap Press of Harvard University Press, 1982. [xx], 588 pp.: illus., photos., facsims.; 24 cm. Index. LC 81–20255. ISBN 0–674–24861–9. $25.00
Using the Harvard edition of Emerson's *Journals and Miscellaneous Notebooks,* Porte takes selections from the journals that reveal "Emerson personally" and "that cast light on his doubts, dreams, fears, aspirations, quirks, social and intimate relations, and the like."

EMERSON, RALPH WALDO. *The Journals and Miscellaneous Notebooks of Ralph Waldo Emerson: Volume XV, 1860–1866.* Edited by Linda Allardt, David W. Hill. Associate Editor, Ruth H. Bennett. Cambridge and London: Belknap Press of Harvard University Press, 1982. [xxiv], 591 pp.: facsims.; 23 cm. Appendixes ("Appendix I: Journals and Notebooks in the Harvard Edition," "Appendix II: Montreal Herald Report of 'Classes of Men,'" "Textual Notes"): pp. 541–550; index. LC 60–11554. ISBN 0–674–48478–9. $40.00
In these journals of the Civil War period—October 1860 through February 1866—Emerson records his responses to the war and his reading in European military history, his comments on French and German literature and culture, and his reactions to the deaths of friends and relatives—Clough, Thoreau, Hawthorne, and his aunt, Mary Moody Emerson.

ENSLEY, HELEN. *Poe's Rhymes.* Baltimore: Enoch Pratt Free Library, The Edgar Allan Poe Society, Library of the University of Baltimore, 1981. 18 pp.; 23 cm. ISBN 0–910556–17–2. Paper, $2.50.
Defends Poe whose innovative rhyming techniques have been misinterpreted as extravagant or imperfect. Often, his Southern pronunciation determined rhyming words, and this penchant for rhyme was carried to the point of creating absurd images or "dragging in words or twisting constructions for the sake of rhyme."

FAUST, DREW GILPIN, editor. *The Ideology of Slavery: Proslavery Thought in the Antebellum South, 1830–1860.* Baton Rouge and London: Louisiana State University Press, [1981]. [xii], 306 pp.; 23 cm. (Library of Southern Civilization.) "Selected Bibliography of Secondary Works on the Proslavery Argument": pp.

301–306. LC 81–3755. ISBN 0–8071–0855–3: coth, $35.00; ISBN 0–8071–0892–8: paper, $8.95.
Reprints seven representative essays by proslavery thinkers in the South, demonstrating the evolution and eventual rift in the argument and exposing its paradoxes.

FIELDS, RICK. *How the Swans Came to the Lake: A Narrative History of Buddhism in America.* Boulder, Colo.: Shambhala, 1981. [xviii], 433 pp.: photos.; 23 cm. "Sources and Notes": pp. 380–424; index. LC 81–50971. ISBN 0–394–52147–1: cloth, $19.95; ISBN 0–394–74883–2: paper, $12.95.
Traces the history of Buddhism in America, officially introduced into this country in 1893 at the World Parliament of Religions in Chicago. However, Fields, considering this "the culmination of a movement that had begun much earlier," discusses the significance of Emerson's intellectual interest, Thoreau's living "in a Buddhist way," Melville's search for symbols behind the visible world, Whitman's absorption of Hindu poems, and Edwin Arnold's popular book, *The Light of Asia.*

FLUCK, WINFRIED, JÜRGEN PEPER, WILLI PAUL ADAMS, editors. *Forms and Functions of History in American Literature: Essays in Honor of Ursula Brumm.* [Berlin]: Erich Schmidt Verlag, [1981]. xiv, 204 pp.: front.; 23 cm. Appendix ("Publications by Ursula Brumm, 1955–1980"): pp. 197–200; index. ISBN 3–503–01660–0.
Included in the essays are: Sacvan Bercovitch, "The Ideological Context of the American Renaissance," proposes that the ideology of American culture from the Puritans up through the Revolution rests in the rhetoric of the myth of America, a fusing of myth and history, but there has been a widening rift since the Civil War when the American Romantics opted for the mythic spiritual pilgrimage at the expense of social realities; Larzer Ziff, "Questions of Identity: Hawthorne and Emerson Visit England," suggests that Emerson's and Hawthorne's English travels, a quest for self-identity and American-identity, enforced for them the belief in the individual over society; Horst Kruse, "Hawthorne and the Matrix of History: The Andos Matter and 'The Gray Champion,'" says "Hawthorne combines two distinct historical events and by doing so transcends history, as it were, to arrive at a truth surpassing that of the bare facts as transmitted in the annals of the New England historians"; Ursula Brumm, "American Writers and European History: Nathaniel Hawthorne and Mark Twain," discusses how American writers in the nineteenth century had to come to terms with Europe: Hawthorne felt the English heritage was a burden that he could not overcome; Twain considered Europe inferior to America's standards, progress, and democracy.

FOSTER, LAWRENCE. *Religion and Sexuality: Three American Communal Experiments of the Nineteenth Century.* New York and Oxford: Oxford University Press, 1981. [xiv], 363 pp.: tables; 23 cm. "Appendix": pp. 249–255; "Essay on Sources": pp. 341–352; index. LC 80–18104. ISBN 0–19–502794–9. $19.95
Examines how the communal ventures of three millenial religious groups—the Shakers, the Oneida Perfectionists, and the Mormons—following the Biblical interpretations of their prophetic leaders, were aimed at radical changes in the structure of the family and society, and the value of the individual: the celibacy of the Shakers

equalized men and women in church work by "its subordination of individual sexual life to the larger interests of the community"; the "complex marriage" of the Oneidas abolished conventional monogamous marriage to permit freedom of sexual expression and loyalty to all members; and the polygamy of the Mormons allowed the "best" men procreation of the "best" offspring and "would enable the patriarchal leaders of the Mormons to have the largest families, and thereby gain the most status and power, both on earth and in heaven."

FRANKLIN, WAYNE. *The New World of James Fenimore Cooper.* Chicago and London: University of Chicago Press, [1982]. x, 275 pp.; 22 cm. Index. LC 81–16121. ISBN 0–226–26080–1; paper, $17.00.
Rather than seeing Cooper rendering actual images of America, Franklin says that Cooper is most significant for envisioning a "'new country,'" discovering adventure in the wilderness, and creating an imaginative new world in his fiction.

GIANTVALLEY, SCOTT. *Walt Whitman, 1838–1939: A Reference Guide.* Boston: G. K. Hall, [1981]. [xxii], 465 pp.; 28 cm. (A Reference Guide to Literature.) "Appendix": p. 413; index. LC 81–6538. ISBN 0–8161–7856–9. $50.00.
"Assembles in one place . . . the bibliographical information on all significant known commentary on Whitman published in English from the earliest discovered mention of him in the press in 1838 through 1939," in chronological order and with annotations. This is the most comprehensive Whitman bibliography yet published.

GURA, PHILIP F., and JOEL MYERSON, editors. *Critical Essays on American Transcendentalism.* Boston: G. K. Hall, [1982]. [1ii], 638 pp.; 24 cm. (Critical Essays on American Literature.) Index. LC 81–7269. ISBN 0–8161–8466–6. $60.00.
Collects over 50 essays on American Transcendentalism reflecting critical responses in both the nineteenth and twentieth centuries. In the introduction there is an historical overview of Transcendentalism by Gura, showing the transition in interpretation from "theological radicalism," to a "philosophical movement," to its place in the American historical and literary tradition, and a bibliographical essay of the books and articles related to the movement by Myerson.

HALL, DONALD, editor. *The Oxford Book of American Literary Anecdotes.* New York and Oxford: Oxford University Press, 1981. xxiv, 360 pp.; 22 cm. Indexes. LC 80–27436. ISBN 0–19–502938–0. $15.95.
An anthology of stories about authors taken from biographies, letters, and memoirs, with a generous selection of nineteenth-century authors since "the richest moment of the American anecdote is the 19th century."

HAMMOND, J. R. *An Edgar Allan Poe Companion: A Guide to the Short Stories, Romances and Essays.* Totowa, N.J.: Barnes & Noble Books, [1981]. xii, 205 pp.: front., illus.; 22 cm. Appendix ("Film Versions"): pp. 189–192; "Select Bibliography": pp. 196–201; index. LC 81–167695. ISBN 0–389–20172–3. $27.50.
A guide to Poe and his works based on "the conviction that he was a literary crafts-

man of very considerable importance and that his significance to the twentieth century is only now beginning to be appreciated."

HARDING, BRIAN. *American Literature in Contex, II: 1830–1865.* London and New
York: Methuen, [1982]. [viii], 247 pp.; 22 cm. (American Literature in Context.)
Index. LC 81–22302. ISBN 0–416–73900–8: cloth, $19.95; ISBN 0–416–
73910–5: paper, $8.95.
A collection of essays on the representative writers of the period. Each chapter includes an extract from an author's major text followed by a discussion of the exerpt in
relation to the whole work.

HARRIS, LAURIE LANZEN, editor. *Nineteenth-Century Literature Criticism: Excerpts
from Criticism of the Works of Novelists, Poets, Playwrights, Short Story Writers, and other Creative Writers Who Lived between 1800 and 1900, from the
First Published Critical Appraisals to Current Evaluations.* Vols. 1 & 2. Detroit: Gale Research, [1981, 1982]. 588 pp.; 658 pp.; 28 cm. Appendixes: pp.
573–583; pp. 633–645; indexes. LC 81–6943. ISBN 0–8103–5801–8: Vol. 1,
$64.00; ISBN 0–8103–5802–6: Vol. 2, $64.00.
Entries on authors from a variety of genres and countries include a selection from the
criticism, a biographical sketch, and a select bibliography. American authors that
appear are: Bronson Alcott, Cooper, Emerson, Hawthorne, Irving, Longfellow,
Lowell, Poe.

HATHAWAY, RICHARD D. *Sylvester Judd's New England.* University Park and London:
Pennsylvania State University Press, [1981]. [viii], 362 pp.: front., illus.; 21 cm.
Bibliography: pp. 351–355; index. LC 81–17854. ISBN 0–271–00307–3.
$17.95.
A biographical/critical study of Judd, "a microcosm of his times."

HAWTHORNE, NATHANIEL. *Tales and Sketches: Including Twice-Told Tales, Mosses
from an Old Manse, and The Snow Image; A Wonder Book for Girls and Boys;
Tanglewood Tales for Girls and Boys; Being a Second Wonder Book.* Edited by
Roy Harvey Pearce. [New York]: The Library of America, [1982]. [xi], 1493
pp.; 20 cm. Appendixes ("Chronology," "Notes on the Texts," "Notes"): pp.
1471–1493. LC 81–20760. ISBN 0–940450–03–8. $25.00.
Based on the CEAA Centenary Edition of Hawthorne's *Works,* this volume "gathers
together all the tales and sketches collected by the author, as well as those which
remained uncollected during his lifetime, and rearranges them in the order of their
first appearance before the American public."

IHRIG, MARY ALICE. *Emerson's Transcendental Vocabulary: A Concordance.* New
York and London: Garland, 1982. [x], 290 pp.; 22 cm. (Garland Reference Library of the Humanities, vol. 323.) LC 81–47965. ISBN 0–8240–9264–3.
$40.00.

A concordance, keyed to the first seven volumes of the Centenary Edition of Emerson's *Works* (1903–1904), of nine word-clusters: Beauty, Culture, Fate, Genius, Greatness-Heroism, Nature, Prudence, Soul-Spriit, Wealth-Riches.

INGE, M. THOMAS, editor. *Handbook of American Popular Culture.* Volume 3. Westport, Conn.: Greenwood Press, [1981]. x, 558 pp.; 24 cm. Indexes. LC 77–95357. ISBN 0–313–22025–5. $35.00.
Covers 18 areas of popular culture, reflecting tastes and interests of society. Each chapter deals with one area and provides an "Historic Outline," an essay on "Reference Works," "Research Collections," "History and Criticism," and a "Bibliography" of sources used in the chapter.

IRVING, WASHINGTON. *Life of George Washington.* Volumes I–V. Edited by Allen Guttmann and James A. Sappenfield. Boston: Twayne Publishers, 1982. xlvi, 716 pp.: Vols. I and II; [xvi], 342 pp.: Vol. III; [xviii], 552 pp.: Vols. IV and V: fronts., illus.; 24 cm. (The Complete Works of Washington Irving, Vols. 19–21.) Appendixes for Vols. I and II ("Explanatory Notes," "Textual Commentary," "Note on the Manuscript and Author-Corrected Proof," "Discussions of Adopted Readings," "List of Emendations," "List of Rejected Substantives," "List of Compound Words Hyphenated at End of Line"): pp. 578–716; Appendixes for Vol. III ("Explanatory Notes," "Discussions of Adopted Readings," "List of Emendations," "List of Compound Words Hyphenated at End of Line"): pp. 294–342; Appendixes for Vols IV and V ("Explanatory Notes," "Discussions of Adopted Readings," "List of Emendations," "List of Rejected Substantives," "List of Compound Words Hyphenated at End of Line"): pp. 478–552. LC 81–4506. ISBN 0–8057–8511–6 (set). $80.00.
A CEAA-approved edition of the 1855–1859 text crediting Irving as a professional historian, whose indepth research and more stylistically interesting narrative produced a more popular biography of the president than the other historians of Washington at the time who created pleasant portraits by editing true facts.

JACKSON, CARL T. *The Oriental Religions and American Thought.* Westport, Conn., and London: Greenwood Press, [1981]. xii, 302 pp.; 24 cm. (Contributions in American Studies, no. 55.) Bibliography: pp. 269–288; index. LC 80–25478. ISBN 0–313–22491–9. $27.50.
Charts the rise of Oriental religions (restricted to "religions of the eastern half of the Asian continent, mainly to India, China, and Japan") in America, with the discovery and greatest period of exploration being the nineteenth century. "Emerson's Discovery of the East" explains how Emerson wanted a synthesis between Oriental idealism/spiritualism and Western materialism/intellectuality. Thoreau, Alcott, and Parker were significant Transcendentalists who assimilated Eastern ideas with their own.

KANE, JOSEPH NATHAN. *Famous First Facts: A Record of First Happenings, Discoveries, and Inventions in American History.* Fourth Edition Expanded and Revised. New York: H. W. Wilson Company, 1981. [viii], 1350 pp.; 26 cm. Indexes. LC 81–3395. ISBN 0–8242–0661–4. $60.00.

First published in 1933, the revised edition contains 9000 items arranged alphabetically by subject, with four indexes for cross-referencing.

KENNEDY, J. GERALD. *The Astonished Traveler: William Darby, Frontier Geographer and Man of Letters.* Baton Rouge and London: Louisiana State University Press, [1981]. [xiv], 238 pp.: illus.; 23 cm. Bibliography: pp. 231–234; index. LC 81–3711. ISBN 0–8071–0886–3. $22.50.

This biographical/critical study of Darby (1775–1854), noted as a nineteenth-century surveyer and writer of geographical publications, uncovers the concealed identity of the writer of Cooperesque romance tales of the frontier for the Philadelphia *Casket* (forerunner of *Graham's Magazine*) and the *Saturday Evening Post* under the pseudonym, Mark Bancroft. Prints two tales from the *Casket* and excerpts from the geographical writings.

KOSTER, DONALD N. *American Literature and Language: A Guide to Information Sources.* Detroit: Gale Research, [1982]. [xiv], 396 pp.; 22 cm. (American Studies Information Guide Series, vol. 13.) Indexes. LC 82–2917. ISBN 0–8103–1258–1. $40.00.

An annotated bibliography of general background guides, references, histories, and individual author bibliographies for the study of American language and literature. Authors cited in the author bibliographies include most of the major writers of the American Renaissance.

LEASE, BENJAMIN. *Anglo-American Encounters: England and the Rise of American Literature.* Cambridge and New York: Cambridge University Press, [1981]. [xvi], 299 pp.; 22 cm. Index. LC 81–3914. ISBN 0–521–23666–5. $29.95.

Analyzes ten nineteenth-century American writers—Irving, Cooper, John Neal, Poe, Hawthorne, Melville, Stowe, Emerson, Thoreau, and Whitman—whose connections with England helped shape American literature. While writers like Irving, Cooper, and Poe fought against England's literati for literary independence, Emerson, Thoreau, and Whitman were able to produce an American literature by maintaining friendship and correspondence with English writers.

LEE, ROBERT A., editor. *Nathaniel Hawthorne: New Critical Essays.* [Totowa, N. J.]: Barnes and Noble, [London]: Vision Press, [1982]. 254 pp.; 22 cm. Appendix ("Notes on Contributors"): pp. 251–252; index. ISBN 0–389–20281–9. $27.50.

Contains the following essays: Brian Way, "Art and the Spirit of Anarchy: A Reading of Hawthorne's Short Stories," examines several stories in which Hawthorne suppresses deeper truths within an artistic order, but, through the power of anarchic laughter, "releases immense disruptive energies in the world of men, and analogous dramatic energies in the world of art"; Harold Beaver, "Towards Romance: 'The Case of Roger Malvin's Burial,'" focusing on the one story, shows how Hawthorne transforms history into romance with ambiguous symbols and uncertain outcomes—resisting any single interpretation by using subversive rhetoric; A. Robert Lee, "'Like a Dream Behind Me': Hawthorne's 'The Custom-House' and *The Scarlet Letter*," suggests that while "The Custom-House" and the text of *The Scarlet Letter* can stand as independent units, together "The Custom House" acts as a "prolegomena" to the past, defining Romance, and setting up "intimate writerly and readerly terms of reference whereby the ensuing fiction might most profitably be understood"; Mark Kinkead-Weekes, "The Letter, the Picture, and the Mirror: Hawthorne's Framing of *The Scarlet Letter*," explains that because of Hawthorne's "obtrusive artfulness"—a tight structure, a literary voice, and an expository tone—the reader is constantly aware of the artifice before him so that he never plunges into the mysterious symbolism; Richard Gray, "'Hawthorne: A Problem': *The House of the Seven Gables*," argues that the shifting tone, equivocal style, irony, and lack of a resolution at the end of the novel are manifestations of Hawthorne's personal problems: exposing a family legend, lack of self-confidence as a writer, and the fact that he is trying to accomodate his writing to public criticism; Keith Carabine, "'Bitter Honey': Miles Coverdale as Narrator in *The Blithedale Romance*," shifts the view of Coverdale as a distrusted narrator to a sympathetic character because he "allows Hawthorne to dramatize his own troubled, ambivalent perceptions of the artist's role and function"; Graham Clarke, "To Transform and Transfigure: The Aesthetic Play of Hawthorne's *The Marble Faun*," proposes a new "angle of vision" for the novel—its focus is on the nature of aesthetics and the interrelation of art and life; Arnold Goldman, "Hawthorne's Old Home," speculates that in *Our Old Home*, Hawthorne realizes England and America are in the brotherhood of mankind, and for him to come to a peaceful resolution, he must come to terms with "the dust from which we have come and to which we return"; Eric Homberger, "Nathaniel Hawthorne and the Dream of Happiness," concludes that with the choice between isolation and immersion into the community in their search for "the dream of happiness," some characters are able to make a resolution with "secret communities"; Eric Mottram, "Power and Law in Hawthorne's Fictions," sees a "vocabulary of law" permeating the works: there is an antithetical struggle between "the chaos of democratic principles," the American spirit to defy unjust authority, and an obedience to the power of society's laws that enslaves individuals; Richard Brodhead, "Hawthorne, Melville, and the Fiction of Prophecy," proposes that Hawthorne was a literary avatar to Melville—Melville deciphered his mentor's enigma to be an ability to see the Truth of things through fiction.

LILLIEDAHL, ANN. *Emily Dickinson in Europe: Her Literary Reputation in Selected Countries.* [Washington, D.C.]: University Press of America, [1981]. [x], 215 pp.: illus.; 22 cm. "Bibliography": pp. 183–199; indexes. LC 81–40308. ISBN 0–8191–1890–7: cloth, $20.25; ISBN 0–8191–1891–5: paper, $10.25.
Surveys the critical reception of Dickinson from 1900 to 1977 in Sweden, Swedish-speaking Finland, Norway, Denmark, France, French-speaking Switzerland, and Germany.

LINDBERG, GARY. *The Confidence Man in American Literature.* New York and Oxford: Oxford University Press, 1982. [xii], 319 pp.; 23 cm. Index. LC 80–29233. ISBN 0–19–502939–9. $19.95.
The image of the confidence man and the game of identity in American literary history are discussed, with studies of Melville's masquerader in the confidence game,

stripping away masks to reveal deeper levels of meaning; Poe, confidence man as artist; Emerson's self-reliant man who assumes the role of "jack-of-all-trades"; and Thoreau, "master game-player" in the private game in *Walden*.

LUNDE, ERIK S. *Horace Greeley*. Boston: Twayne, [1981]. 138 pp.: front.; 21 cm. (Twayne's United States Authors Series, TUSAS 413.) "Selected Bibliography": pp. 131–134; index. LC 81–1234. ISBN 0–8057–7343–6. $10.95.
A biographical/critical survey of one of the nineteenth century's advocates of American social reform, progress, democratic nationalism, and an independent literature. Among writers Greeley patronized and encouraged were Poe, Whitman, Thoreau, and Fuller.

MADDEN, DAVID, and RICHARD POWERS. *Writers' Revisions: An Annotated Bibliography of Articles and Books about Writers' Revisions and Their Comments on the Creative Process*. Metuchen, N.J., and London: Scarecrow Press, 1981. xiii, 241 pp.; 22 cm. Indexes. LC 80–22942. ISBN 0–8108–1375–0. $13.50.
Lists approximately 500 items of general sources of information on the writing process, secondary material about specific writers' revisions, and books and articles "in which writers talk about writing." Cites sources about Dickinson, Emerson, Hawthorne, Lowell, Melville, Poe, Thoreau, Whitman.

MAILLOUX, STEVEN. *Interpretive Conventions: The Reader in the Study of American Fiction*. Ithaca and London: Cornell University Press, [1982]. 228 pp.: illus.; 22 cm. Appendixes ("Reader-Response Criticism and Teaching Composition", "Bibliographcial Note"): pp. 208–220. LC 81–70712. ISBN 0–8014–1476–8. $18.50.
One chapter presents a reader-response analysis of Hawthorne's "Rappaccini's Daughter" based on reading conventions intended by the author in creating the text—Hawthorne encourages the reader, during the process of reading, to make judgments on the characters' motivation, while at the same time withholding a final moral judgment until the text is synthesized.

MANI, LAKSHMI. *The Apocalyptic Vision in Nineteenth Century American Fiction: A Study of Cooper, Hawthorne, and Melville*. [Washington, D. C.]: University Press of America, [1981]. xii, 334 pp.; 21 cm. Appendixes ("Hindu Eschatology," "Key to Abbreviations and Bibliographical Notes"): pp. 278–323; index. LC 80–69060. ISBN 0–8191–1602–5: cloth, $20.75; ISBN 0–8191–1603–3: paper, $11.75.
Proposes that these three writers take an ironic stance toward millenial vision pervading America in the nineteenth century and "view the ebullient optimism as a form of spiritual myopia in an increasingly materialistic society." Cooper is skeptical about America's utopian democracy because of man's fallibility so that in his works he oscillates between a pastoral wilderness and a "doomsday vision of his country's destiny." Hawthorne censures man because of his impure heart, but "he envisions America evolving as a second paradise through a proper synthesis of morality and

creativity," as expressed in *The Marble Faun*. Melville, the most pessimistic, sees "America tending towards an appalling apocalypse," particularly in the black comedy of *The Confidence-Man*.

MARCELL, DAVID W. *American Studies: A Guide to Information Sources*. Detroit: Gale Research, [1982]. [xx], 207 pp.; 22 cm. (American Studies Information Guide Series, vol. 10.) Indexes. LC 73–17559. ISBN 0–8103–1263–8. $40.00.
An annotated bibliography, arranged by subject, of "the most important works representing interdisciplinary American culture studies" since the beginning of the movement in the 1930s.

MELVILLE, HERMAN. *Israel Potter: His Fifty Years of Exile*. [Edited by Harrison Hayford, Hershel Parker, G. Thomas Tanselle. Historical Note by Walter E. Bezanson.] Evanston and Chicago: Northwestern University Press and The Newberry Library, 1982. x, [401] pp.: facsims., illus.; 24 cm. (The Writings of Herman Melville: The Northwestern-Newberry Edition, Volume 8.) Appendixes ("Historical Note," "Note on the Text," "Discussions of Adopted Readings," "List of Emendations," "Report of Line-End Hyphenation," "List of Substantive Variants," "Melville's Basic Source"): pp. 171–401. LC 82–81178. ISBN 8101–0552–7: cloth, $29.95; ISBN 8101–0553–5: paper, $7.95.
A CEAA-approved text of *Israel Potter* with copy-text based on the serial publication in *Putnam's Monthly*, making it "the first twentieth-century edition to employ as copy-text the earlier magazine text." Also reproduces in facsimile Melville's source, Trumbull's *Life and Remarkable Adventures of Israel R. Potter*.

MELVILLE, HERMAN. *Moby-Dick; or, the Whale*. Berkeley, Los Angeles, London: University of California Press, [1979]. [xvi], 577 pp.: illus.; 26 cm. LC 81–40320. ISBN 0–520–04354–5. $24.95.
A reduced facsimile reproduction of the 1979 limited Arion Press edition designed by Andrew Hoyem and illustrated with wood engravings by Barry Moser, which was based on the Northwestern-Newberry text of *Moby-Dick*.

MELVILLE, HERMAN. *Typee: A Peep at Polynesian Life, Omoo: A Narrative of Adventures in the South Seas, Mardi: and a Voyage Thither*. Edited by G. Thomas Tanselle. [New York]: The Library of America, [1982]. [xi], 1333 pp.; 20 cm. Appendixes ("Chronology," "Note on the Texts," "Notes"): pp. 1317–1333. LC 81–18600. ISBN 0–940450–00–3. $25.00.
The texts of Melville's first three novels are based on the Northwestern-Newberry Edition of Melville's *Writings*.

MESSENGER, CHRISTIAN K. *Sport and the Spirit of Play in American Fiction: Hawthorne to Faulkner*. New York: Columbia University Press, 1981. [xviii], 369 pp.; 23 cm. Index. LC 81–4843. ISBN 0–231–05168–9. $24.00.
An historical survey of the sports hero in American fiction. Discusses Hawthorne, "the first great American writer to firmly sense play as a response to the human need

to move out of the tormented self"; Irving, who uses the play spirit "to assert the fantastical and timeless"; Cooper, whose Natty Bumppo is the ideal mythical hunter; and Thoreau, who in "Higher Laws," "assigns sport a role in a moral education."

MOSELEY, JAMES G. *A Cultural History of Religion in America*. Westport, Conn.: Greenwood Press, [1981]. xviii, 183 pp.; 21 cm. (Contributions to the Study of Religion, No. 2.) "Bibliographic Essay": pp. 167–178; index. LC 80–23609. ISBN 0–313–22479–X. $25.00.
Arguing that religion is an important aspect of America's culture, Moseley examines each generation and how it produced its own form of religion, a variation of America's basic religion—Protestant Christianity. The chapter "Transcendentalism: The Religion of Nature in the Form of Literature" centers around Emerson, and how Thoreau elaborated on Emerson's views, whereas Melville tested them in *Moby-Dick*.

MOSSMAN, JENNIFER, editor. *Pseudonyms and Nicknames Dictionary*. Second Edition. Detroit: Gale Research, [1982]. 995 pp.; 28 cm. "List of Sources Cited": pp. 13–20. LC 80–13274. ISBN 0–8103–0547–X. $135.00.
The second edition, an expansion of the first edition (1980), lists 50,000 pseudonyms used by 40,000 historical and contemporary personalities.

MUSHABAC, JANE. *Melville's Humor: A Critical Study*. [Hamden, Conn.]: Archon Books, 1981. xii, 199 pp.; 22 cm. Bibliography: pp. 181–191; index. LC 81–10981. ISBN 0–208–01910–3. $19.50.
Seeing that "Melville's humor is central to his greatness," Mushabac discusses how Melville follows and builds upon a tradition of "prose humor" that began in the Renaissance. *Billy Budd*, however, is "not a work of humor—nor of irony nor of satire."

MYERSON, JOEL, editor. *Emerson Centenary Essays*. Carbondale and Edwardsville: Southern Illinois University Press, [1982]. [xiv], 218 pp.; 22 cm. Index. LC 81–18516. ISBN 0–8093–1023–6. $19.95.
A collection of the following essays: Evelyn Barish, "The Moonless Night: Emerson's Crisis of Health, 1825–1827," discusses how Emerson's dealing with early health problems and his coming "to terms with death not as fantasy, but as reality" significantly shaped his philosophy and idea of self-reliance; Wesley T. Mott, "'Christ Crucified': Christology, Identity, and Emerson's Sermon No. 5," suggests that Sermon No. 5, first preached on 24 June 1827, formulates Emerson's values in his "groping toward self-definition at the start of his ministry," and "points toward concepts of heroism that Emerson would proclaim for years to come"; Jerome Loving, "Emerson's Foreground," says *Nature* is the bridge between Emerson the minister and Emerson the author, "the catalyst and catharsis that took him from the expository prose of the preacher-lecturer to the freer, more irresponsible speech of the poet"; Glen M. Johnson, "Emerson on 'Making' in Literature: His Problem of Professionalism, 1836–1841," examines how Emerson developed himself as a professional writer, who could meet the demands of producing a product, yet maintain the creative inspiration of art; David Robinson, "*The Method of Nature* and Emerson's Period of Crisis,"

suggests that the oration delivered in 1841, dealing with his ecstasy at finding permanence in nature and the questions raised about that illumination, identifies a time of crisis for Emerson when personal, moral, and religious doubts depressed him; Richard Lee Francis, "The Poet and Experience: *Essays: Second Series*," discovers that *Essays: Second Series* marks a transitional stage in Emerson's life—the initial projection of himself as visionary poetic genius was being redirected to a persona of practical writer of essays; David W. Hill, "Emerson's Eumenides: Textual Evidence and the Interpretation of 'Experience,'" proposes, "The structure of the essay—the seven 'lords of life,' or moods, labeled as if they were ideas—moves through incomplete states of thought and feeling to the image Emerson built from Flaxman's drawing of the *Eumenides* of Aeschylus." The accruing structure implies that Emerson realized that experience is refracted from different voices rather than a resolution of disparate themes into a whole unit; Sanford E. Marovitz, "Emerson's Shakespeare: From Scorn to Apotheosis," traces how Emerson's developing appreciation of Shakespeare, influenced by several people, climaxed in great praise of the representative transcendental poet in whom "truth and beauty, spirit and nature, fused, as seeming contraries merged"; Robert E. Burkholder, "The Contemporary Reception of *English Traits*," finds that, although the work marked a turn in Emerson's public reception, the lectures and notices of the work as it was in progress and its more concrete style attributed to its wide critical reception and acceptance; Ronald A. Sudol, "'The Adirondacs' and Technology" investigates how the poem, reflecting Emerson's vacation in the Adirondacs at the time the transatlantic cable was being laid, indicates the "poet's spiritual renovation" because he proclaims a union of east and west and praises human technological advances; Merton M. Sealts, "Emerson as Teacher," says Emerson was the great teacher because he inspired his students with self-reliance and independence.

MYERSON, JOEL. *Ralph Waldo Emerson: A Descriptive Bibliography*. [Pittsburgh]: University of Pittsburgh Press, 1982. xviii, 802 pp.: front., facsims., photos., illus.; 24 cm. (Pittsburgh Series in Bibliography.) Appendix ("Principal Works About Emerson"): pp. 753–756; index. LC 81–11502. ISBN 0–8229–3452–3. $70.00.

The analytical description of the writings of Emerson includes photographs of books and facsimiles of title pages, copyright pages, wrappers, and dust jackets. Eight sections provide a chronological listing of works under the following categories: separate publications, collected editions, miscellaneous collections, first book and pamphlet appearances, first-appearance contributions to magazines and newspapers, books edited by Emerson, reprinted material, material attributed to Emerson.

MYERSON, JOEL. *Theodore Parker: A Descriptive Bibliography*. New York and London: Garland, 1981. xii, 225 pp.: facsims.; 22 cm. (Garland Reference Library of the Humanities, vol. 307) Index LC 81–43354. ISBN 0–8240–9279–1. $30.00.

Each of the five sections in this, the first full bibliography of Parker's writings, lists in chronological order of appearance "all books, pamphlets, and broadsides wholly by Parker, including all printings of all editions in English through 1980"; "all collected editions"; "all miscellaneous collections of and selections from Parker's writings in

English through 1973, the date of the last located item"; "all books edited by Parker"; "miscellaneous material not by Parker but often attributed to him."

NELSON, RAYMOND. *Van Wyck Brooks: A Writer's Life.* New York: E. P. Dutton, [1981]. xii, 332 pp.: photos.; 24 cm. "List of Works Quoted": pp. 319–322; index. LC 81–2485. ISBN 0–525–03054–9. $21.75.
A biography of Van Wyck Brooks (1886–1963) with analysis of his works that redeem the literary historian from the disesteem he has lapsed into today.

NEMANIC, GERALD, general editor. *A Bibliographical Guide to Midwestern Literature.* Iowa City: Univeristy of Iowa Press, [1981]. xxiv, 380 pp.; 24 cm. Appendixes ("A: 101 Additional Midwestern Wrtiers," "B: 101 Additional Midwestern Fictional Narratives"): pp. 365–380. LC 81–4087. ISBN 0–87745–079–X. $28.50.
"A reference guide to the study of midwestern literature and culture" of material published up to 1976, which includes "nine topical bibliographies on the region's culture, basic bibliographical data on 120 midwestern authors, and appendices covering additional authors and works of fiction."

OTNESS, HAROLD M. *Index to nineteenth century city plans appearing in guidebooks: Baedeker, Murray, Joanne, Black, Appleton, Meyer, plus selected other works to provide coverage of over 1,800 plans to nearly 600 communities, found in 164 guidebooks.* [Santa Cruz, Calif.]: Western Association of Map Libraries, 1980. xxiv, 84 pp.: illus.; 23 cm. (Occasional Paper No. 7.) Bibliography: p. xviii; Appendixes ("List of Books Indexed and Key to Abbreviations," "Key to Location Symbols"): pp. 71–84. LC 80–24483. Paper, $6.00.
An index of cities whose city plans appeared in nineteenth-century guidebooks. Otness explains that the index serves as a record of the popularity of tourism as well as "a record of the technological advances made during the nineteenth century in map printing."

O'TOOLE, JAMES M. *Guide to the Archives of the Archdiocese of Boston.* Inventories prepared by Margaret M. McGuinness. Forward by Humberto Cardinal Medeiros. New York and London: Garland, 1982. xviii, 328 pp.: photos.; 22 cm. (Garland Reference Library of Social Science, vol. 84.) Appendix ("Glossary"); pp. 301–306; index. LC 80–8989. ISBN 0–8240–9359–3. $50.00.
A description of the contents of the archival collection, arranged in two parts: Part I categorizes the records under "Bishops and Archbishops," "Auxiliary Bishops," "Chancery," "Parishes," "Institutions," "Nondiocesan Agencies," "Personal Papers," "Audiovisual Materials"; Part II gives a biographical sketch and full inventory for the papers of the first four bishops of Boston.

PACKER, B. L. *Emerson's Fall: A New Interpretation of the Major Essays.* New York: Continuum, [1982]. xii, 244 pp.; 21 cm. Appendix ("Textual References"): pp. 213–231. LC 82–1439. ISBN 0–8264–0191–0. $14.95.
Probes into the rhetoric of the major essays, from *Nature* to *Representative Men*, to

argue that Emerson's apparent ambiguities, paradoxes, and contradictions are, in fact, part of a unified personal mythology—an ironic acceptance, not a resignation, of the Fall by which "he found himself forced to fabricate his own fables in explanation of the fallenness of the world."

PEARSON, CAROL, and KATHERINE POPE. *The Female Hero in American and British Literature.* New York and London: R. R. Bowker Co., 1981. [x], 314 pp.; 23 cm. Bibliography: pp. 297–305; index. LC 81–10939. ISBN 0–8352–1402–8: cloth, $24.95; ISBN 0–8352–1466–4: paper, $12.95.
The authors suggest that whereas "on the archetypal level the journey to self-discovery is the same for both the male and female hero," the female hero must violate traditional sex roles in order to begin the quest, assume certain male attributes to continue the journey, and assert her humanness to arrive at wholeness and autonomy at the end. Louisa May Alcott, Dickinson, Melville, and Hawthorne mentioned throughout.

PERLMAN, JIM, ED FOLSOM, and DAN CAMPION, editors. *Walt Whitman: The Measure of His Song.* Introduction by Ed Folsom. Minneapolis: Holy Cow! Press, 1981. [1vi], 394 pp.: ports.; 22 cm. Appendixes ("The Poets Respond: A Bibliographic Chronology," "Notes on Contributors"): pp. 359–394. LC 80–85268. ISBN 0–930100–09–3: cloth, $20.00; ISBN 0–930100–08–5: paper, $10.00.
"A collection of poems and essays written to and about Whitman by contemporary poets," organized by year, beginning with 1855.

POCHMANN, HENRY A., compiler. Arthur R. Schultz, editor. *Bibliography of German Culture in America to 1940.* Revised and corrected by Arthur R. Schultz with addenda, errata, and expanded index. Millwood, N.Y., London, and Nendeln, Liechtenstein: Kraus International Publications, 1982. cclxxxvi, 489 pp.; 26 cm. Index. LC 81–17188. ISBN 0–527–80593–9. $86.00.
An unannotated bibliography, listed in alphabetical order by author, that demonstrates reference to, involvement of, or influence by German culture on American history. This revised edition adds 4900 new sources to those in the 1953 edition of this book.

POE, EDGAR ALLEN. *Marginalia.* Introduction by John Carl Miller. Charlottesville: University Press of Virginia, [1981]. [xx], 235 pp.: front., facsim.; 22 cm. Index. LC 80–22585. ISBN 0–8139–0812–4. $11.95.
A complete reprinting of the seventeen magazine installments of *Marginalia*, appearing in the order in which they were published, and incorporating corrections made by Griswold (1856), Stedman and Woodberry (1895), and Harrison (1902).

POLLIN, BURTON R., editor. *Word Index to Poe's Fiction.* New York: Gordian Press, 1982. xviii, 485 pp.; 26 cm. LC 82–2869. ISBN 0–87752–225–1. $25.00.
Computerized concordance to Poe's works, keyed to the Harvard University Press edition of *Tales and Sketches* in *Collected Works* (1978) and the Twayne edition of *Collected Writings: The Imaginary Voyages* (1981).

PORTER, CAROLYN. *Seeing and Being: The Plight of the Participant Observer in Emerson, James, Adams, and Faulkner.* Middletown, Conn.: Wesleyan University Press, [1981]. xxiv, 339 pp.; 23 cm. Index. LC 80–29234. ISBN 0–8195–5054–X. $22.50.

Based on Marxist methodology of relating literary text to social process, Porter discusses four writers who responded to their society and shaped the development of the reified consciousness from the 19th century to the 20th century by trying to compensate for or resist that reification under the constraints imposed by capitalism. Emerson's confrontation of his alienation from the world, in the image of a transparent eyeball making man "a detached observer of his own life," allowed James, Adams, and Faulkner to implicate the observer in the narrative he was watching or telling.

ROBBINS, J. ALBERT, editor. *American Literary Scholarship: An Annual/1980.* Durham: Duke University Press, 1982. [xx], 625 pp.; 22 cm. Indexes. LC 65–19450. ISBN 0–8223–0464–3. $37.75.

Includes reviews of research which appeared in 1980 in the following areas: "Emerson, Thoreau, and Transcendentalism," by Wendell Glick; "Hawthorne," by David B. Kesterson; "Poe," by G. R. Thompson; "Melville," by Hershel Parker; "Whitman and Dickinson," by Jerome Loving; and "19th-Century Literature," by Kermit Vanderbilt.

ROBINSON, DAVID. *Apostle of Culture: Emerson as Preacher and Lecturer.* Philadelphia: University of Pennsylvania Press, 1982. xiv, 205 pp.; 23 cm. Index. LC 81–16228. ISBN 0–8122–7824–0. $16.50.

Finds continuity in Emerson's career as preacher, lecturer, and writer because his early experience as Unitarian minister, and then public orator, shaped his writing by the religious influence on his moral vision and the polemical style of his essays. His proclivity more to writing was marked by a disillusionment in the failure of "communion between the artist and his audience" and the challenge of "creating a vital prose style."

ROOS, ROSALIE. *Travels in America: 1851–1855.* Based on *Resa till Amerika: 1851–1855,* edited by Sigrid Laurell. Translated and edited by Carl L. Anderson. Carbondale and Edwardsville: Southern Illinois University Press, [1982]. [xviii], 152 pp.: front., illus.; 23 cm. LC 81–187. ISBN 0–8093–1018–X. $19.95.

A translation of the Swedish text which recounts Roos's journey in America and settlement in Charleston, S. C., and collects her letters home. Anderson points out in his introduction that the book reveals insight into the institution of slavery and the independence of American women from the vantage point of a foreigner.

ROSE, ANNE C. *Transcendentalism as a Social Movement, 1830–1850.* New Haven and London: Yale University Press, [1981]. xii, 269 pp; 23 cm. Appendixes ("Note to Appendixes A and B," "Appendix A: Establishment and Dissolution of Boston Churches to 1860," "Appendix B: Growth Rates of Boston Churches, 1820–1860," "Appendix C: Members of Brook Farm, September 1841 to April

1845," "Appendix D: A Demographic Profile of Working People Who Joined Brook Farm in 1844," "Appendix E: Kinship at Brook Farm, September 1841 to January 1845," "Abbreviations and Short Forms") pp. 227–244; Bibliography: pp. 245–258; index. LC 81–3340. ISBN 0–300–02587–4. $22.50.

Concentrates on six "leading" Transcendentalists—Orestes Brownson, George Ripley, Elizabeth Peabody, Margaret Fuller, Bronson Alcott, and Ralph Waldo Emerson—who participated in public and private reforms. Rose suggests that beginning with the philosophers of the Unitarian awakning in the 1830s, "the Transcendentalist controversy (1836–40) was the catalyst which transformed revisionists of religious philosophy into radical social reformers." The movement ended at mid-century when it became evident that society was not accepting the Transcendentalists' visions.

SCOTT, DONALD M., and BERNARD WISHY, editors. *America's Families: A Documentary History.* New York: Harper & Row, [1982]. xx, 682 pp.: front., facsims., illus., photos., tables; 24 cm. Selected Bibliographies: pp. 171, 388–389, 673; "General Bibliography": pp. 674–676; index. LC 79–3402. ISBN 0–06–014048–8: cloth, $30.00; ISBN 0–06–090903–X: paper, $12.95.

Analyzes "how the family has at once helped make and responded to social and cultural change" during the last 400 years. Divided into sections of periods in history, "Part Two: Testing the Limits of Life, 1820–1900" has excerpts by Lydia Maria Child, Longfellow, and two articles on Brook Farm.

SEALTS, MERTON M., JR. *Pursuing Melville: 1940–1980.* [Madison]: University of Wisconsin Press, [1982]. [xii], 419 pp.: front.; 23 cm. Appendix ("Additions and Changes in the 'Check-List of Books Owned and Borrowed' (1966)"): pp. 347–354; index. LC 81–70014. ISBN 0–299–08870–7. $27.50.

A collection of fourteen essays and selected letters to Charles Olson and Henry A. Murray about Melville scholarship. "Melville and the Platonic Tradition [1980]," printed here for the first time, argues that "Melville's first-hand acquaintance with the Platonic dialogues antedated his knowledge of Emerson, beginning early in 1848 and constituting a major influence on both *Mardi* and *Moby-Dick.*"

SHURR, WILLIAM H. *Rappaccini's Children: American Writers in a Calvinist World.* [Lexington]: The University Press of Kentucky, [1981]. [viii], 165 pp.; 23 cm. Index. LC 79–57573. ISBN 0–8131–1427–6. $13.00.

Suggests that a Calvinist heritage persisting in American culture in the nineteenth and twentieth centuries has shaped the literature of the period. Evidence of this is exemplified in six nineteenth-century writers—Emerson, Hawthorne, Holmes, Melville, Thoreau, Whitman—who acknowledge the limitations of Calvinism but have achieved liberation from the national religion by rebuking its restraints.

SMITH, DAVID L. *Symbolism and Growth: The Religious Thought of Horace Bushnell.* [Chico, California]: Scholars Press, [1981]. xvi, 190 pp.; 22 cm. (American Academy of Religion Dissertation Series, Number 36.) "Bibliography of Works Cited": pp. 183–190; index. LC 80–14600. ISBN 0–89130–409–6: cloth, $14.00; ISBN 0–89130–410–X: paper, $9.95.

Discusses the way Bushnell "modeled his religious thought on a theory of how human persons shape each other—for better or worse—through their social and linguistic interactions." Smith argues that a "theory of communication" provides the inner structure and unity to Bushnell's thought and is the basis for his belief that God's intercourse with man is through subjective interpreation and transference of the divinity onto man.

SPANN, EDWARD K. *The New Metropolis: New York City, 1840–1857.* New York: Columbia University Press, 1981. [xvi], 546 pp.: illus.; 23 cm. (Columbia History of Urban Life.) Appendix: pp. 429–433; Bibliography: pp. 511–533; index. LC 81–91. ISBN 0–231–05084–4. $19.95.

A study of the development of the port of New York during its formative period of urban, industrial, and economic progress into the complex modern metropolitan center of 1860, which became both "a magnificent expression of human intelligence" and "a disturbing example of human failure."

STERN, FREDERICK C. *F. O. Matthiessen: Christian Socialist as Critic.* Chapel Hill: The University of North Carolina Press, [1981]. xv, 281 pp.: front.; 20 cm. Bibliography: pp. 261–268; index. LC 80–29013. ISBN 0–8078–1478–4. $24.50.

Assesses Matthiessen's achievement as a critic in his ability to synthesize contradictory "form-content" crticial creeds into his own methodology—with the text as an aesthetic work; by the way the writer enhances man's moral, social, and religious conditions; within the American tradition and its relationship to the European tradition; and according to his own subjective response to the work. A detailed examination of Matthiessen's "masterpiece," *American Renaissance*, shows how it deals with the primary material as well as the cultural climate surrounding the writers of the works.

STOKES, ROY, editor. *Esdaile's Manual of Bibliography: Fifth revised edition.* [Metuchen, N.J.]: Scarecrow Press, 1981. x, 397 pp.: facsims., illus., photos.; 22cm. Appendix ("Glossary"): pp. 382–390; index. LC 81–9088. ISBN 0–8108–1462–5. $22.50.

A revised edition of Esdaile's manual, first published in 1931, which was to provide an introduction to bibliography for students, librarians, and book collectors.

STOWE, HARRIET BEECHER. *Uncle Tom's Cabin or, Life Among the Lowly, The Minister's Wooing, Oldtown Folks.* Edited by Kathryn Kish Sklar. [New York]: The Library of America, [1982]. [xi], 1477 pp.: illus.; 20 cm. Appendixes ("Chronology," "Note on the Texts", "Notes"): pp. 1469–1477. LC 81–18629. ISBN 0–940450–01–1. $25.00.

Texts of the three novels in this volume are from the first American book editions of each. Although *Uncle Tom's Cabin* and *The Minister's Wooing* appeared in serials prior to book publication, the editor states that "the book edition represents Stowe's intentions more completely" because of the correction changes she made.

SUTHERLAND, DANIEL E. *Americans and Their Servants: Domestic Service in the United States from 1800 to 1920.* Baton Rouge and London: Louisiana State University Press, [1981]. xv, 229 pp.: ports., facsims., photos.; 23 cm. "Bibliographical Essay": pp. 201–222; index. LC 80–29689. ISBN 0–8071–0860–X. $20.00.

A history of American domestic service which includes the reformers who wanted to increase the number of faithful servants by improving servant/employer relations: William Alcott, Catharine Beecher, Sarah J. Hale, and Catharine Sedgwick.

TAWA, NICHOLAS E. *Sweet Songs for Gentle Americans: The Parlor Song in America, 1790–1860.* Bowling Green, Ohio: Bowling Green University Popular Press, [1980]. 273 pp.: ports., photos., facsims.; 23 cm. Appendixes: 198–268; index. LC 78–71394. ISBN 0–87972–130–8: cloth, $21.95; ISBN 0–87972–157–X: paper, $10.95.

An historical study and re-evaluation of America's popular form of music, enjoyed by the urban middle class, in the nineteenth century.

THOREAU, HENRY D. *Journal, Volume I: 1837–1844.* Edited by Elizabeth Hall Witherell, William L. Howarth, Robert Sattelmeyer, Thomas Blanding. General Editor, John C. Broderick. Princeton: Princeton University Press, 1981. 702 pp.; facsims., photos.; 20 cm. (The Writings of Henry D. Thoreau.) Appendixes ("Indexes of Original Journal Volumes, 1837–1840," "Indexes of MS Volumes I–6; 'Transcripts, 1840–1842'; 9: 1837–1844," "Annotations"): pp. 499–541; index; Editorial Appendixes ("Notes on Illustrations," "Acknowledgments," "Editorial Contributions," "General Introduction," "Historical Introduction," "Textual Introduction," "Textual Notes," "Table of Emendations," "Table of Alterations," "End-of-Line Hyphenation," "Selected Later Revisions"): pp. 573–702. LC 78–70325. ISBN 0–691–06361–3. $25.00.

A CSE-approved text of the first complete edition of Thoreau's journal, based on both the manuscripts and Thoreau's transcriptions from original volumes now lost.

THURIN, ERIK INGVAR. *Emerson as Priest of Pan: A Study in the Metaphysics of Sex.* Lawrence: Regents Press of Kansas, [1981]. xviii, 292 pp.: front.; 22 cm. Bibliography: pp. 269–273; index. LC 81–4818. ISBN 0–7006–0216–X. $19.95.

By examining Emerson's views of metaphysical and physical polarity in relation to his views of sexual polarity, Thurin proposes that Emerson's vision of a bi-polar universe is a dialectic, not a well balanced duality.

TINGLEY, ELIZABETH, and DONALD F. TINGLEY. *Women and Feminism in American History: A Guide to Information Sources.* Detroit: Gale Research, [1981]. [xii], 289 pp.; 22 cm. (American Government and History Information Guide Series, vol. 12.) Indexes. LC 80–19793. ISBN 0–8103–1477–0. $40.00.

An annotated bibliography about women from the standpoint of feminism, defined as "all efforts and sets of beliefs that have proposed bettering the condition of women in any way."

TRACHTENBERG, STANLEY, editor. *American Humorists: 1800–1950*, Volumes 1 (A–L) and 2 (M–Z). Foreword by Steve Allen. Detroit: Gale Research, 1982. [xiv], 305; [x], [307]–706 pp.: ports., facsims., illus.; 29 cm. (Dictionary of Literary Biography, Vol. 11.) Appendixes ("American Humor: A Historical Survey," "Humorous Book Illustration," "Newspaper Syndication of American Humor," "Selected Humorous Magazines (1802–1950)"): pp. 585–682; "Contributors": p. 683; cumulative index. LC 81–20238. ISBN 0–8103–1147–X (set). $140.00.

Critical and biographical articles on 72 American humorists including Irving, Lowell, and Seba Smith.

TRAUBEL, HORACE. *With Walt Whitman in Camden: September 15, 1889–July 6, 1890*, Volume 6. Edited by Gertrude Traubel and William White. Carbondale and Edwardsville: Southern Illinois University Press, [1982]. x, 504 pp.: front., photos., facsim.; 22 cm. (With Walt Whitman in Camden.) Index. LC 8–5603. ISBN 0–8093–1047–3. $35.00.

This is the sixth volume of the publication that began in 1906 of the transcripts of Traubel's conversations with Whitman in his last few years in Camden.

TUSHNET, MARK V. *The American Law of Slavery 1810–1860: Considerations of Humanity and Interest*. Princeton: Princeton University Press, [1981]. [x], 262 pp.; 22 cm. Appendixes ("List of Works Cited," "Table of Cases"): pp. 248–258; index. LC 80–8582. ISBN 0–691–04681–6: cloth, $20.00; ISBN 0–691–10104–3: paper, $9.50.

Tushnet examines the developing problem of the slave law in the south. Because of the "dichotomy between law and sentiment," the problem of legal codification of slaves, and, especially, the contradictions between the static nature of southern slavery in a dynamic bourgeois economy and society, were dilemmas which could only be resolved by breaking the dual tension in the Civil War.

URDANG, LAURENCE, and FREDERICK G. RUFFNER, JR. *Allusions—Cultural, Literary, Biblical, and Historical: A Thematic Dictionary*. Detroit: Gale Research, [1982]. xx, 487 pp.; 23 cm. Bibliography: pp. 397–434; index. LC 82–1088. ISBN 0–8103–1124–0. $48.00.

This dictionary has 7000 references "to all of the divers elements that make up what [the editors] classify under the general rubric of culture," arranged in alphabetical order by thematic category.

VALLIER, JANE E. *Poet On Demand: The Life, Letters and Works of Celia Thaxter*. [Camden, Maine]: Down East Books, [1982]. [xx], 267 pp.: front., illus.; 23 cm. Bibliographies: pp. 254–260; indexes. LC 81–67591. ISBN 0–89272–136–7: cloth, $14.95; ISBN 0–89272–130–8: paper, $9.95.

Prints 53 poems, a story, and includes a critical biography of Thaxter, reassessing the once popular, now unknown, writer as a serious poet and master of poetic technique, and places her in the tradition of nineteenth-century American female poets.

WALLER, ALTINA L. *Reverend Beecher and Mrs. Tilton: Sex and Class in Victorian America*. Amherst: University of Massachusetts Press, [1982]. [xiv], 177 pp.: illus., tables; 24 cm. Bibliography: pp. 169–174; index. LC 81–15982. ISBN 0–87023–356–4. $15.00.

Waller presents the adultery trial of 1875 involving Beecher and Tilton as a symbol of the changing values and culture in America in the nineteenth century.

WEATHERSBY, ROBERT W., II. *J. H. Ingraham*. Boston: Twayne, [1980]. 164 pp.; 21 cm. (Twayne's United States Authors Series: TUSAS 361.) "Selected Bibliography": pp. 147–159; index. LC 80–16555. ISBN 0–8057–7302–9. $13.95.

Biographical/critical overview of a little known now, but prolific writer with a vast audience in the nineteenth century, whose short stories and novels range from didactic melodrama to regional realism to a biblical novel trilogy.

WEIXLMANN, JOE. *American Short-Fiction Criticism and Scholarship, 1959–1977: A Checklist*. Athens, Ohio: Swallow Press, Ohio University Press, [1982]. xii, 625 pp.; 22 cm. Appendix ("List of Serial Publications Indexed"): pp. 618–625. LC 81–11208. ISBN 0–8040–0381–5. $40.00.

This unannotated listing of critical works, interviews, and bibliographies includes material on American Renaissance authors of short stories and novellas.

WHITMAN, WALT. *American Bard: The Original Preface to Leaves of Grass Arranged in Verse by William Everson*. Foreword by James D. Hart. New York: The Viking Press, [1982]. 37 pp.: illus.; 24 cm. LC 81–68382. ISBN 0–670–11706–4. $12.95.

A transmutation of Whitman's prose preface into poetic form. Everson "only redivides lines and repunctuates Whitman's prose, altering neither words nor word order, to let its inherent poetry find full expression."

WHITMAN, WALT. *Complete Poetry and Collected Prose: Leaves of Grass (1855), Leaves of Grass (1891–92), Complete Prose Works (1892), Supplementary Prose*. Edited by Justin Kaplan. [New York]: The Library of America, [1982]. [xi], 1380 pp.; 20 cm. Appendixes ("Chronology," "Note on the Texts," "Notes"): pp. 1347–1359; indexes. LC 81–20768. ISBN 0–940450–02–X. $25.00.

Reprints the first edition and final edition of *Leaves of Grass*, and the prose, with a supplement of Whitman's "fugitive prose pieces."

WHITMAN, WALT. *Leaves of Grass. A Textual Variorum of the Printed Poems*. Volumes 1 (Poems, 1855–1856), 2 (Poems, 1860–1867), 3 (Poems, 1870–1891). Edited by Sculley Bradley, Harold W. Blodgett, Arthur Golden, William White. [New York]: New York University Press, 1980. [lxxx], 272; [xiv], 273–562; [xiv], 563–779 pp.: facsims.; 26 cm. (The Collected Writings of Walt Whitman.) Appendixes in Vol. 3 ("Appendix A: 'Old Age Echoes,'" "Appendix B: A List of Variant Readings within Editions of, and Annexes to, *Leaves of Grass*"): pp. 757–769; index (for Vols. 1–3 in Vol. 3). LC 78–65727. ISBN 0–8147–1014–X:

Vol. 1; ISBN 0–8147–1015–8: Vol. 2; ISBN 0–8147–1016–6: Vol. 3; ISBN 0–8147–1024–7: Set. $125.00 (set).
Includes all variants of the poems from 1855 through 1891. The copy-text is based on the 1891–1892 *Leaves of Grass* as authorized by Whitman.

WILLIAMSON, EDWARD C. *American Political Writers: 1801–1973.* Boston: Twayne, [1981]. 190 pp.; 21 cm. (Twayne's United States Authors Series: TUSAS 394.) "Selected Bibliography": pp. 171–182; index. LC 81–1090. ISBN 0–8057–7327–4. $13.95.
Categorizes the political writers under major topics—Jacksonian democracy, slavery, the rise of the Republican party, Reconstruction, industrialism, Populism, imperialism—and gives a brief overview of the political writers within each period representing the range from the liberal to the conservative views. Writers included are Orestes Brownson, Frederick Douglass, William Ellery Channing, and William Lloyd Garrison.

WOLFE, GERARD R. *The House of Appleton: The history of a publishing house and its relationship to the cultural, social, and political events that helped shape the destiny of New York City.* Metuchen, N.J., and London: The Scarecrow Press, 1981. [xviii], 450 pp.: illus., facsims.; 24 cm. Appendixes ("The Appleton Colophon," "Genealogy of the Appleton Family," "The Appleton Family in America," "Appleton Best Sellers Through the Years and Pulitzer Prize Winners," "Periodicals Published by Appleton's," "Addresses of the House of Appleton"): pp. 405–417; Bibliography: pp. 418–427; index. LC 81–2564. ISBN 0–8108–1432–3. $17.50.
Records the growth of D. Appleton and Company from 1825, through its rise, decline, and rebirth, into its present company, Appleton-Century-Crofts.

YANNELLA, DONALD. *Ralph Waldo Emerson.* Boston: Twayne, [1982]. 147 pp.: front.; 21 cm. (Twayne's United States Authors Series, TUSAS 414.) "Selected Bibliography": pp. 139–141; index. LC 81–20321. ISBN 0–8057–7344–4. $10.95.
A biographical/critical "introduction to Ralph Waldo Emerson not for specialists in the literature of nineteenth-century America but for general readers," concentrating on criticism of the essays and poems.

CONTRIBUTORS

CAROLINE BONKINSKY, a graduate student in English at the University of South Carolina, has been the STUDIES IN THE AMERICAN RENAISSANCE editorial assistant since 1981. Her dissertation is a study of Wallace Stevens.

FRANCIS B. DEDMOND, Professor of English at Catawba College, has published *Sylvester Judd* and numerous articles on Poe, Emerson, Thoreau, Ellery Channing, and Cranch. He is currently editing the letters of Ellery Channing.

CHARLES WESLEY GRADY, Senior Minister of the First Parish Unitarian Universalist Church in Arlington, Massachusetts, is working on a biography of Frederic Henry Hedge, portions of which have appeared in *Kairos* and *Unitarian Universalist Christian*.

JOHN M. J. GRETCHKO has contributed to *Melville Society Extracts* and *Maledicta*. He has recently finished a book on *The Revelation of Herman Melville*.

WALTER HARDING, Distinguished Professor Emeritus at the State University of New York, College at Geneseo, is secretary of the Thoreau Society.

JOHN L. IDOL, JR., Professor of English at Clemson University, has published widely on Hawthorne and Thomas Wolfe.

EDWARD C. JACOBS is Associate Professor of English at Louisiana Technical University.

LINCK C. JOHNSON is Associate Professor of English at Colgate University and an Associate Editor of *The Writings of Henry D. Thoreau*. His *A Complex Weave: The Writing of Thoreau's* A Week on the Concord and Merrimack Rivers, *with the Text of the First Draft* will be published soon.

BUFORD JONES, Professor of English at Duke University, is finishing work on an annotated secondary bibliography of Nathaniel Hawthorne.

KENT LJUNGQUIST, Associate Professor of English at Worcester Polytechnic Institute, has published in *American Literature, American Studies, American Transcendental Quarterly,* and *Poe Studies.* He is co-editor of *Poe Studies Association Newsletter* and of the forthcoming edition of Cooper's *The Deerslayer.*

CHARLES W. MIGNON, Professor of English at the University of Nebraska-Lincoln, has published on Emerson in *American Transcendental Quarterly* and *ESQ: A Journal of the American Renaissance,* and on Edward Taylor in a number of journals. He is presently at work on a two-volume edition of Taylor's "Upon the Types of the Old Testament."

SIDNEY P. MOSS, Professor of English at Southern Illinois University, has written widely on American literature, especially on the work of Poe. His latest book, *Charles Dickens' Quarrel with America,* is forthcoming from Whitston.

BURTON R. POLLIN has published extensively on Poe, most recently *Word Index to Poe's Fiction* and an edition of *The Imaginary Voyages.* He is currently editing *Poe's Brevities,* vol. 2 of *Collected Writings.*

NANCY CRAIG SIMMONS, Assistant Professor of English at the Virginia Polytechnic Institute and State University, did a biography of James Elliot Cabot as her dissertation at Princeton University. She has edited Cabot's autobiography and will be a co-editor of Thoreau's *Journal.*

H. MEILI STEELE is a graduate student in comparative literature at the University of North Carolina whose interests are nineteenth- and twentieth-century American and French literature.

EDWARD L. TUCKER, Associate Professor of English at Virginia Polytechnic Institute and State University, is the author of a number of studies of Southern literature, including *Richard Henry Wilde: His Life and Selected Poems.* His *Longfellow's "John Endicott": Its History, Including Two Early Versions* was recently awarded the emblem of the Center for Scholarly Editions.

KEVIN P. VAN ANGLEN, Assistant Professor of English at the University of Pennsylvania, has published on Thoreau in *ESQ: A Journal of the American Renaissance* and STUDIES IN THE AMERICAN RENAISSANCE. He is the editor of the *Translations* volume published in *The Writings of Henry D. Thoreau.*

ALBERT J. VON FRANK, Assistant Professor of English at Harvard University, published *Whittier: A Comprehensive Annotated Bibliography*. He is co-editor of the forthcoming edition of Emerson's poetry notebooks.

NOTE

A comprehensive list of corrections and additional information for the sixteen volumes of *The Journals and Miscellaneous Notebooks of Ralph Waldo Emerson* (Harvard University Press, 1960–82) is currently in preparation for future publication in STUDIES IN THE AMERICAN RENAISSANCE. Readers who have noted errors in any of the volumes, or who have information on unidentified persons, places, events, quotations, or books referred to, are asked to write to Ralph H. Orth, Chief Editor, *JMN*, English Department, University of Vermont, Burlington, Vermont 05405–0114.